THEOLOGY OF THE BODY

EXPLAINED

THEOLOGY OF THE BODY
EXPLAINED

A Commentary on John Paul II's "Gospel of the Body"

Christopher West

With a Foreword by
George Weigel

BOOKS & MEDIA
Boston

Nihil Obstat: Rev. Msgr. Lorenzo M. Albacete, S.T.D.
Censor Deputatus

Imprimatur: +Most Reverend Charles J. Chaput, O.F.M. Cap.
Archbishop of Denver
February 27, 2003

Library of Congress Cataloging-in-Publication Data
West, Christopher, 1969–
Theology of the body explained : a commentary on John Paul II's
"gospel of the body" / Christopher West.
    p. cm.
Includes bibliographical references.
ISBN 0-8198-7410-8 (pbk.)
    1. John Paul II, Pope, 1920– Theology of the body. 2. Body,
Human—Religious aspects—Catholic Church. 3. Catholic
Church—Doctrines. I. Title.
BT741.2.J643 W47 2003
233',5—dc21
                                        2003004876

Cover design by Helen Rita Lane, FSP

Printed and published in the U.S.A. by Pauline Books & Media, 50 Saint Pauls
Avenue, Boston, MA 02130-3491.

www.pauline.org

Pauline Books & Media is the publishing house of the Daughters of St. Paul, an
international congregation of women religious serving the Church with the com-
munications media.

4 5 6 7 8 9 10 11 12   13 12 11 10 09 08 07 06 05

For my brother,
Nathan Paul Gardner West

CONTENTS

PART I

WHO ARE WE?
ESTABLISHING AN ADEQUATE ANTHROPOLOGY

Cycle 1: *Original Man*

Cycle 2: *Historical Man*

Cycle 3: *Eschatological Man*

PART II

HOW ARE WE TO LIVE?
APPLYING AN ADEQUATE ANTHROPOLOGY

Cycle 4: *Celibacy for the Kingdom*

Cycle 5: *The Sacramentality of Marriage*

Cycle 6: *Love and Fruitfulness*

ACKNOWLEDGMENTS

I am grateful to the following men and women who have helped make this book a reality:

Pope John Paul II, for the tremendous gift of his theology of the body;

Mary Jane Rice, for first introducing me to the Pope's catechesis on the body;

Steve Habisohn, for his steadfast moral support and for helping finance the sabbatical that enabled me to write this book;

all the staff at Pauline Books and Media, especially Sister Marianne Lorraine, FSP, for her dedication to this project and for her expert editing;

Monsignor Lorenzo Albacete, for all the wisdom he has passed on to me, for his affirmation of my work, and for bringing his theological genius to bear in reviewing my manuscript;

George Weigel for writing the foreword;

Archbishop Chaput, for his support and encouragement of my "mission";

Jeanne Monahan and Jay Wonacott, for critiquing early drafts;

Father Richard Hogan, for critiquing the Prologue;

Eric Scheidler, for his extensive help reviewing and restructuring the initial manuscript;

Nathan West and Jessica Wunsch, for their research;

and Wendy West, for proofing the original text, adding feminine insight, and for all her sacrifices during the three years it took me to complete this project.

FOREWORD

Future generations will remember Pope John Paul II for many things: his great personal witness to the truths of Christian faith; his epic role in the collapse of communism; his ecumenical initiatives; his healing the wounds of centuries between Catholics and Jews. The list could go on and on.

In writing *Witness to Hope: The Biography of Pope John Paul II,* I came to the conclusion that John Paul's longest-lasting theological contribution to the Church and the world might well be something that very few people have ever encountered: his innovative "theology of the body," which he laid out in 129 general audience addresses between 1979 and 1984. In my biography of the Pope, I described the "theology of the body" as a bit of a theological time bomb, something that would explode within the Church at some indeterminate point in the future with tremendous effect, reshaping the way Catholics think about our embodiedness as male and female, our sexuality, our relationships with each other, our relationship with God—even God himself. I also wrote that the dense, compact audience addresses that make up the "theology of the body" needed explication for those who weren't specialists in biblical studies, theology, or philosophy.

I am delighted that Christopher West has taken up that challenge in *Theology of the Body Explained.* With intellectual care, with the experience bred of long years of teaching this material in the classroom and the parish, and taking account of his own experiences as a husband and father, he explains each of the Pope's 129 addresses, showing how the meaning of each address fits into a coherent whole. Christopher West also demonstrates how the "theology of the body" is readily applicable to the quotidian realities of marriage and family life. Teachers and students, priests and pastoral workers, couples preparing for marriage, couples looking to deepen their marriages, and couples reflecting back on the meaning of their venerable marriages will all find much here to think about and pray over.

In his great encyclical, *Veritatis Splendor,* John Paul II takes the story of Christ's dialogue with the rich young man (Mt 19:16–22) as the paradigm of the Christian moral life. What good must I do, the young man asks, in order to have eternal life? For that is the purpose of the moral life: to fit us for beatitude, to make us the kind of people who can live with God forever. It takes a special kind of people to do that—in a word, it takes saints. And saints are what we all must become, if we are to realize our baptismal destiny. The "theology of the body" shows us how sexual love within the bonds of faithful and fruitful marriage is a path to sanctity—and thus a path to God and to eternal life.

A sex-saturated culture imagines that the sexual revolution has been liberating. The opposite is the truth: men and women chained to their appetites and passions are not free. What can liberate us from that kind of bondage? The "theology of the body" answers the question: loving truly, loving chastely, loving in ways that are radically life-giving and life-affirming rather than life-avoiding or life-denying. Some will, no doubt, find it odd that the Catholic Church takes human sexuality far more seriously than the editors of *Playboy* and *Cosmopolitan.* But that's the plain truth of the matter. And the "theology of the body" shows why and how that's the case.

Catholics should remember that the "theology of the body" is not *for-Catholics-only.* John Paul II has made a tremendous contribution to human thought, and to the possibility of human happiness, with these groundbreaking audience addresses. So I wish for Christopher West's book the widest possible audience. Catholics should share it with other Catholics, to be sure. But Catholics should also share it with Protestant, Orthodox, Jewish, Muslim, and even agnostic friends. The responses, especially among women, may be surprising—happily surprising.

The great struggle of the twenty-first century, like the twentieth, will be the struggle to defend and promote the dignity of the human person. John Paul II's "theology of the body" is a tremendous resource for all those who fight that good fight. Christopher West has put us in his debt by making the "theology of the body" available to a wide—and, I hope, appreciative—readership.

George Weigel

PREFACE

I remember October 16, 1978 very clearly. I was in the third grade at Sacred Heart School in Lancaster, Pennsylvania. The Bishop had given a holy card of the "smiling Pope" (John Paul I) to all the students in the diocese just two weeks earlier. Now, after the pope's sudden death, we were sitting in class awaiting news of his successor.

The following scene is seared in my memory. Our teacher's aid, Sister Eugene—a quiet, elderly nun who must have had some Slavic blood in her—had been keeping vigil in front of the television across the hall. In a loud flurry, she burst into our classroom with eyes and hands raised to heaven screaming at the top of her lungs, *"He's Polish! He's Polish! He's Poooool-ish!"*

Little did I know then what an impact this Polish Pope would have on my life. Although I would not discover it for another decade and a half, a series of talks that John Paul began within the first year of his pontificate would forever change the way I view the universe and my place within it.

During the same time John Paul II presented his catechesis on God's glorious plan for the body and sexuality, I was being groomed in the sexual lies promoted within our culture. After several years of unchaste living, I returned to my faith with multiple questions about God's plan for man and woman's relationship. Looking for answers, I began a prayerful study of the Scriptural texts on marriage and sexuality. Over the course of about two years of intense study, a grand "nuptial vision" began to emerge. The spousal imagery of the Scriptures brought my faith to life, shedding light on the entire mystery of man and woman's creation, fall, and redemption in Christ. Moreover, this "nuptial vision" was setting me *free* from the lies that had formed me growing up. I was on fire. Expecting an enthusiastic response, I began sharing this vision with others. Instead, Christians I considered more learned than I often responded with blank stares or worse.

In early fall of 1993, a committed Catholic woman who taught at my sister's high school came to dinner, and I hesitantly decided to test some of my "nuptial vision" on her. To my surprise, she immediately replied, "You must have read the Pope's theology of the body." "What's that?" I probed. "Gosh, I thought you'd already read it. What you're saying sounds like the Pope." I pressed her, *"What is this theology of the body? Where can I get it?"* She told me that the Daughters of St. Paul published it in four volumes (since 1997 it has been available in one volume).

I devoured the entire catechesis in a matter of weeks. Not only did I find abundant confirmation of what I had learned in my own study, the Pope's reflections took me to a new level altogether. I intuited that these four little volumes contained a revolution for the Church—the answer to the crisis of our times. I knew then I was going to spend the rest of my life studying the Pope's thought and sharing it with others. When I learned that the Pope had established a theological institute for the specific purpose of exploring the "nuptial mystery," there was no question where I would go for graduate studies.

Today, more and more people are hearing about the theology of the body. Still, for the vast majority of Christians, the actual content of the Pope's catechesis remains an untapped treasure. Why? As papal biographer George Weigel observes, "The density of John Paul's material is one factor; a secondary literature capable of 'translating' John Paul's [theology of the body] into more accessible categories and vocabulary is badly needed."[1] This book attempts just that. However, as you can tell from its size, this is not a *Reader's Digest* version. While smaller-scale efforts are also needed, my goal is to unpack the entire catechesis from start to finish.

After setting the stage in the prologue, I follow the 129 addresses very closely, explaining the Pope's method, his train of thought, his scholarly vocabulary, and his original ideas and concepts. Points of interest and application are set aside in gray boxes to distinguish them from my exposition of the actual catechesis. I also reference the *Catechism of the Catholic Church* extensively to demonstrate the organic relationship of the theology of the body with the whole of Catholic Faith. Furthermore, while I designed this book to stand alone, I encourage those with the aptitude to read it in tandem with the Holy Father's addresses, weighing all that I say against the actual text.

By design, and by necessity of my own limitations, this is not the work of a stellar, academic theologian. Rather, it is the work of a teacher and a catechist trained in theology with an ardent desire to extend the lib-

---

1. *Witness to Hope* (New York, NY: Harper Collins, 1999), p. 343.

erating message of the Pope's catechesis beyond the realms of academia. Some scholars, too, seem to have difficulties understanding John Paul II's project. If this book is of service to them, I will be delighted. But scholars will forgive me, I hope, if I am not always as rigorous as they might be in my exposition of the Pope's thought. At the same time, those not trained in theology will forgive me, I hope, if at any point I fail to bring John Paul's dense teaching down to their level. Popularizing the Pope's theology of the body is virtually uncharted territory. Finding the best language, images, and anecdotes with which to do so remains a process of trial and error.

Readers should also know that, while deeply rooted in the tradition, John Paul's catechesis on the body brings an authentic and sometimes even daring development of thinking. Such developments always afford a creative tension in the Church as scholars, catechists, and laity alike seek to understand them and apply them in Christian life. Differences in interpretation and the debates they engender are a healthy part of this process. I, like every interpreter of the Pope's thought, bring my own personal perspectives, gifts, and shortcomings to the table. As St. Paul says, "test everything; hold fast to what is good" (1 Thess 5:21).

Ultimately, no human words can do justice to the sacred mystery revealed by the human body and by man and woman's communion in "one flesh." As St. Paul says, this is a "great mystery" that refers to Christ and the Church (see Eph 5:31–32). If the human words contained in this book provide only a glimmer into the "great mystery" of that one divine Word, they will have served their purpose. Glimmers are all we get on this side of eternity. But they are enough to light a burning fire of hope within us for the consummation of the "Marriage of the Lamb." *Let it be, Lord, according to your Word.* Amen.

Christopher West

Prologue

The Human Body, Catholicism, and John Paul II

Theological reflection on the human body and sexuality has a checkered past. On the one hand, throughout history Christian thinkers have contributed extensively to an integral understanding of the goodness of the body and valiantly fought heresies to the contrary. On the other hand, one can find unflattering and even contemptuous treatments of the body and sexuality in the writings of numerous churchmen. John Paul II's "theology of the body" builds on the positive foundations of the past and definitively corrects the "suspicion toward the body" that has plagued many sons and daughters of the Church.

The fact that it has taken two thousand years of Christian reflection to arrive at such a winning theology of the human body attests to the difficulty of the task. Only now has history provided the right soil for such a revolutionary theology to take root and blossom. The turbulence of the twentieth century itself marked the beginning of a "new passover" of sorts for the Church and humanity. Passover implies new life, but it also implies death. The century that began with the hope of unlimited progress ended as the bloodiest of all centuries. Its first half produced two world wars and the deadliest totalitarian regimes in history. Its second half spawned fears of global destruction by nuclear war and saw the West jettison the sexual mores that—by upholding marriage and the family—place human society on its only firm foundation. Without doubt, the sexual revolution's subsequent "culture of death" brought far more carnage than the warfare and death camps that reddened the landscape of the bloodiest century.

The "signs of the times" show that we stand at a critical moment in the human drama. The many negative factors of today's world can breed pessimism. But John Paul II insists that "this feeling is unjustified: we have faith in God our Father and Lord and in his mercy.... God is preparing a great springtime for Christianity, and we can already see its first signs."[1] Human-

---

1. *Redemptoris Missio*, n. 86.

ity must now cross the "threshold of hope." We must now "passover" from a culture of death to a culture of life. Only in this context can we understand the full significance of John Paul II's theology of the body.

1. The Gospel of the Body?

We are familiar with the Gospels of Matthew, Mark, Luke, and John. What does it mean to speak of the "Gospel of the body"? It means that in some way the human body is a sign and instrument of the same message of our salvation in Christ. From the first pages of Genesis, human embodiment and the call of man and woman to unite in "one flesh" signifies and foreshadows the mystery of Christ (see Eph 5:31–32).

A. Encounter with the Living, Incarnate Christ

Christ's body, above all, justifies the expression "the Gospel of the body." Christ's body conceived of a virgin, born in a stable in Bethlehem, circumcised on the eighth day, raised by Mary and Joseph, baptized in the Jordan river, transfigured on the mountain, "given up for us" in his passion and death, risen in glory, ascended to the Father and participating eternally in the life of the Trinity—the story of this body and the spiritual mystery it points to *is* the Gospel.[2] And every*body* that comes into the world is destined to share in this Gospel by becoming "one body," one spirit with Christ.

This is the deepest meaning of our creation as sexually embodied persons—we are destined for union with the God who, himself, has taken on a body. For the body is meant for the Lord, and the Lord is meant for the body (see 1 Cor 6:13). As the Second Vatican Council teaches: "The truth is that only in the mystery of the incarnate Word does the mystery of man[3] take on light. For Adam, the first man, was a figure of him who was to come, namely Christ the Lord. Christ, the final Adam, by the revelation of the mystery of the Father and his love, fully reveals man to himself and makes his supreme calling clear."[4] This is John Paul II's anthem. And his theology of the body, one might say, is nothing but an extended commen-

---

2. See *Catechism of the Catholic Church* (CCC), n. 515.

3. For the sake of consistency with the Pope's catechesis and other magisterial documents, "man" is to be understood as inclusive of the entire human family throughout this book unless the context indicates only the male. Understanding "man" in this sense sheds important light on John Paul's biblical exegesis and on the equal dignity he accords the sexes.

4. *Gaudium et Spes,* n. 22.

tary on this fundamental truth: Christ fully reveals man to himself through the revelation—*in his body*—of the mystery of the Father and his love.

"The richest source for knowledge of the body is the Word made flesh."[5] Therefore, from start to finish, John Paul's theology of the body calls us to encounter the living, Incarnate Christ and to ponder how his body reveals the meaning of our bodies. Yet, if we are to do so, we need more than ever to hear the Lord's words, so often repeated by John Paul II —"Be not afraid!"

B. Perfect Love Casts Out Fear

In our fallen world, the naked body has become a symbol of licentiousness and indignity. Guided by Christ's words, John Paul challenges us to realize that "from the beginning it was not so" (Mt 19:8). Before sin, the naked body witnessed to "the glory of God," which, according to St. Irenaeus' familiar expression, "is man fully alive." After sin—having accepted the perennial deception that God is not to be trusted, that God is not love—embodiment and nakedness is now linked to a crippling fear: "I was afraid, because I was naked; and I hid myself" (Gen 3:10).

As St. Francis recognized in his slogan "*Nudus sequi nudum Christum*" ("Naked to follow the naked Christ"), the Gospel calls us to a relationship with the Father liberated from Adam's fear. Naked before the Father in his birth and death, the *New Adam* witnesses to the Father's "perfect love" which "casts out fear" (1 Jn 4:18). The "naked Christ" vanquishes the lie that spawns fear. As St. Cyril of Jerusalem triumphantly proclaims, Christ "was nailed naked to the Cross, and by his very nudity defeated the principalities and powers, dragging them into his triumphal cortege."[6]

Adam's fear marks an utter tragedy: the loss of original holiness, the loss of God's "full life" in man. Yet "Jesus came to restore creation to the purity of its origins."[7] He came so that we might again have life, and have it to the full (see Jn 10:10). This does not mean that Christian men and women are suddenly empowered to be naked without shame. Even after Baptism the effects of sin remain, as the ongoing battle for purity pointedly attests.[8] This inner struggle will not cease until the resurrection. Yet, as the *Catechism* teaches, "The Holy Spirit enables one whom the water of Baptism has regenerated to imitate the purity of Christ."[9] Therefore, "Even

---

5. *Letter to Families,* n. 19.

6. *Mystagogical Catechesis,* 2:2.

7. *CCC,* n. 2336.

8. See *CCC,* nn. 978, 1226, 1426.

9. *CCC,* n. 2345.

now [purity of heart] enables us to see *according to* God...; it lets us perceive the human body—ours and our neighbor's—as a temple of the Holy Spirit, a manifestation of divine beauty."[10]

Helping men and women understand, live, and experience their bodies as "a manifestation of divine beauty" is the goal of John Paul's catechesis. The body not only speaks to the mystery of man. It also speaks to the mystery of God. The body is a *theology*. This is the "good news," the gospel of the body.

2. Defining "Theology of the Body"

Since Pope Pius IX began the custom in the 1870s, the weekly "general audience" has provided one of the main platforms for the pope to address his flock. John Paul II was the first pope, however, to use his Wednesday general audiences to develop a systematic catechesis on a given topic. Based on his extensive pastoral and ecclesial experience, he saw that the most pressing catechetical need was to develop an extended biblical theology of marriage and sexual love. Hence, on September 5, 1979 John Paul began the first and perhaps most important catechetical project of his pontificate. Over five years later, on November 28, 1984, he delivered the 129th and final address[11] in the catechesis he gave the working title "theology of the body."[12]

---

10. *CCC*, n. 2519.

11. Papal travels and the assassination attempt in May 1981 interrupted the series which was also suspended from February 9, 1983 to May 23, 1984 during the Holy Year of the Redemption.

12. These 129 addresses were first published weekly in the Vatican newspaper *L'Osservatore Romano*. The official English translation was subsequently published by the Daughters of St. Paul in four volumes: *Original Unity of Man and Woman* (1981); *Blessed Are the Pure of Heart* (1983); *The Theology of Marriage and Celibacy* (1986); and *Reflections on Humanae Vitae* (1984). These are no longer in print. However, the Daughters of St. Paul later published a one-volume edition under the title *The Theology of the Body: Human Love in the Divine Plan* (1997). This edition was copyedited to address some awkwardness in the Vatican translation. It makes for easier reading overall, but I prefer the "feel" of the original, which retains the Pope's signature use of quotation marks and italics, so in this work I will quote from that version. For ease of reference, quotes will be cited by the date of the audience and by the page numbers of the one-volume work (abbreviated TB). However, readers should be aware that differences exist when referring to the copyedited edition.

One of the Pope's main goals in his catechesis was to provide a biblical defense of the Church's sexual ethic that would resonate with the modern world. Inadequate, legalistic formulations of moral theology coupled with the disparaging treatment of sexual matters by some previous churchmen had led many people to reject the Church's teaching. John Paul thought the entire question needed to be reframed. Instead of asking: "How far can I go before I break the law?" we need to ask, "What does it mean to be human?" "What does it mean to love?" "Why did God make me male or female?" "Why did God create sex in the first place?"

Thus, through an intense reflection on the Scriptures, specifically the words of Christ regarding human embodiment and erotic desire, John Paul set out in the first half of his catechesis to develop an "adequate anthropology"—that is, a thorough understanding of who man is as God created him to be. Embodiment as male and female is the basis of this anthropology which is also theological since man is made in God's image as male and female. The term "theology of the body" does not refer to "part" of a theological anthropology, as if we needed to add to this a "theology of the soul." The novelty of the Pope's project lies in the assertion that an "adequate anthropology" must be a theology *of the body*. As the Pope says, "When we speak of the meaning of the body, we refer in the first place to the full awareness of the human being."[13]

In the second half of his catechesis John Paul specifically applies his theological anthropology to the moral questions of how man is to live the truth of his own embodiment. He examines this first in terms of life-vocation and then provides a new, affirming context for understanding the Christian sexual ethic.

A. The Pope's Thesis

The length of this catechesis and its place as the inaugural teaching project of John Paul II's pontificate points to its fundamental significance. In fact, the theological vision detailed in these addresses informs all his subsequent papal teachings. We have not fully penetrated the teachings of John Paul II if we have not penetrated his theology of the body.

This is a formidable task. These 129 catechetical addresses constitute a dense tome. While this does not mean that only the elite can understand John Paul's teaching, it does mean that those who wish to understand it and those who present it must make a diligent effort if the Pope's words are to become bread broken for all.

---

13. 6/25/80, TB 124.

For starters, many people feel unfamiliar and even uncomfortable with the Pope's emphasis on the human body. They expect religious instruction to emphasize the "spiritual" realm. For John Paul, this is a false dichotomy. Without question, the spirit has an ontological priority. Yet, as the *Catechism* relates, "As a being at once body and spirit, man expresses and perceives spiritual realities through physical signs and symbols. As a social being, man needs signs and symbols to communicate with others. ...The same holds true for his relationship with God."[14]

The human body is the pre-eminent and primordial "sign" of the ultimate spiritual reality. John Paul wants to study the human body from this perspective—not as a biological organism, but as a *theology*, as a sign of the spiritual and divine mystery. In the Christian sense, "mystery" does not indicate a puzzle to be solved. It indicates the hidden reality and plan of God. Although man is forever seeking this mystery, he cannot discover it on his own. The divine mystery is invisible, intangible, incommunicable, ineffable. It is so far "beyond" man that the only way man can possibly encounter it is if the Mystery chooses to reveal himself. This is what Christianity *is*. If man desires to find God, God also desires to reveal his mystery to man.[15] He initiates this revelation from the beginning by creating us as *embodied* persons, as male and female in his own image. Embodiment itself—as the Incarnation will attest—is, therefore, a kind of divine revelation.

The Pope's entire catechesis hinges on this fundamental truth. So it is important from the start to clarify what we mean (and do not mean) by speaking of the human body as a "sign" of the divine mystery. A sign is something that points us to a reality beyond itself and, in some way, makes that transcendent reality present to us. Words themselves are nothing but signs. When the letters a-p-p-l-e are put together, they signify a reality which exceeds and transcends those letters. Yet, in signifying that transcendent reality, those letters "present" that reality to us. We cannot reduce the apple to the letters which signify it. Yet we need the word "apple" in order to speak about the reality this word signifies.

Similarly, the human body is a sign of a spiritual and divine reality which infinitely exceeds and transcends the body itself. Yet, in signifying that transcendent reality, the body in some way "presents" the spiritual and divine reality to us. As John Paul says, "In this sign—and through this sign—God gives himself to man in his transcendent truth and in his love."[16]

---

14. *CCC,* n. 1146.

15. See *CCC,* nn. 35, 50.

16. 7/28/82, TB 306.

We cannot reduce the spiritual and divine mystery to its bodily sign. Nor does the body afford a total clearing of the mystery it signifies. Yet, as human beings, we need the sign of the body in order to speak about the mystery of God's self-revelation.

"The body, in fact, and it alone," John Paul says, "is capable of making visible what is invisible: the spiritual and divine. It was created to transfer into the visible reality of the world, the mystery hidden since time immemorial in God, and thus to be a sign of it."[17] This is the Pope's thesis statement, the brush with which he paints his entire catechesis. This is why he speaks of a theology *of the body*. Through the veil of a sign, the human body makes visible the invisible, makes touchable the intangible, communicates the incommunicable. The human body "speaks" of the ineffable, whispering to us something of the deepest secret hidden in God from all eternity.

What is this secret? It is the mystery of Trinitarian Life and Love—of Trinitarian *Communion*—and the plan "hidden for ages in God" (Eph 3:9) that man is destined in Christ to share in this eternal exchange.[18] This is what the body stammers to proclaim; this is the body's mysterious "language." According to John Paul's catechesis, it is specifically the visible beauty and mystery of sexual difference and the call of man and woman to communion that enables us to understand the human body in this way. "The sacrament, as a visible sign, is constituted with man," the Pope says, "by means of his 'visible' masculinity and femininity." In this context "we understand fully the words that constitute the sacrament of marriage, present in Genesis 2:24 ('A man leaves his father and his mother and cleaves to his wife, and they become one flesh')."[19] From the beginning, the "great mystery" of man and woman's communion in "one flesh" foreshadows the infinitely greater mystery of Christ's communion with the Church (see Eph 5:31–32). Communion with Christ—to which every human being is destined—is a pre-eminently spiritual mystery. Yet this spiritual mystery has literally taken on flesh.

B. Epiphany of the Body

Because of sin, we all have blurred vision when it comes to reading this theological language of the body. We know the body says *something,* something we all have a deep hunger to know, understand and experience.

---

17. 2/20/80, TB 76.

18. See *CCC,* n. 221.

19. 2/20/80, TB 76.

But we need an epiphany to realize that that "something" is the "great mystery" of Christ and his Church.

The following experience brought this home to me. I had always been drawn to a beautiful old chapel at the seminary in the Archdiocese of Denver where I teach. One day I overheard a tour guide explain the rich symbolism of the architecture. The chapel, built in the shape of a cross, has an elaborate chandelier representing Christ as "light of the world," which hangs at the place of Jesus' head on this cross. Twelve pillars in the nave represent the twelve Apostles, and seven arches between these pillars represent the seven sacraments. Every detail has a meaning. The architect had designed this chapel in the lines and curves of its bricks and mortar to proclaim the "great mystery" of Christ and the Church. Although this had drawn me to it, I needed to have someone who understood the chapel's meaning explain it. When he did, it was like putting on a new pair of glasses. When he did—epiphany!

The analogy with the chapel is more pertinent than one might first think. The human body itself is a chapel of sorts—a "temple of the Holy Spirit." The divine Architect designed our male and female bodies in the very lines and curves of our flesh and bones to proclaim the mystery of Christ and his life-giving union with the Church. This, ultimately, whether we realize it or not, is why we are all drawn to the human body—why we are deeply stirred by the mystery of its masculine and feminine beauty and why we all yearn for intimacy and communion. Sin has blurred our vision. We are dyslexic and sometimes even illiterate when it comes to reading this "language." We are even prone at times to desecrate this holy temple because of our blindness. In some sense, each one of us is the blind man in the Gospel who must cry out, "Jesus, son of David, have mercy on me! I want to see!" John Paul's theology of the body is like a pair of reading glasses that brings the Word proclaimed by the body into focus. With these glasses, we are able to see the body for what it is—a proclamation of the "great mystery" of Christ and the Church.

3. The Link Between Theology and Anthropology

John Paul II's theological vision of the body can seem almost too grand. How could something so "earthy" and human be meant to reveal something so heavenly and divine? As the phrase "theology of the body" indicates, John Paul wants to help us embrace the profound link between theology (the study of God) and anthropology (the study of man). John Paul observes in one of his early encyclicals that many currents of thought both in the past and at the present tend to separate theology and anthropology and even set them in opposition. The Church, however, "seeks to link them up in human history in a deep and organic way."[20] In fact, the Holy Father states that a renewed emphasis on this theology-anthropology link is perhaps the most important contribution of the Second Vatican Council. Hence, he insists that "we must act upon this principle with faith, with an open mind and with all our heart."[21]

A. The Sacramentality of the Body

John Paul does precisely this throughout his catechesis on the body. By virtue of the Incarnation, *the human body is the link* between theology and anthropology. As the Holy Father says, Christ's body is "a tabernacle of glory...where the divine and the human meet in an embrace that can never be separated."[22] By pressing into this link "with faith, an open mind, and all his heart," John Paul pushes the Catholic sacramental imagination to new heights. He demonstrates that a courageous biblical reflection on the body not only enables us to penetrate the essence of the human, but also to glimpse the mystery of the divine. By embracing our embodiment, we become poised and ready to receive the eternal and utterly gratuitous gift of divine life. For in Christ "the whole fullness of deity dwells bodily" (Col 2:9). In the Incarnate Christ we see "the human face of God and the divine face of man."[23]

Therefore John Paul II's treatment of the body as a theology should not surprise us. As he puts it: "Through the fact that the Word of God became flesh the body entered theology...through the main door."[24] Elsewhere the Pope writes: "The mystery of the Incarnation lays the foundations for an anthropology which, reaching beyond its own limitations and contradictions, moves toward God himself, indeed toward the goal of 'divinization.'"[25] Because of the Incarnation, St. John can proclaim it is that "which we have heard," that "which we have seen with our eyes," that "which we have touched with our hands" that we proclaim to you concerning the Word of life. And that life was made visible (see 1 Jn 1–3).

This making visible of the invisible is what the Pope means by speaking of the sacrament, or "sacramentality," of the body. This is obvi-

---

20. *Dives in Misericordia*, n. 1.

21. Ibid.

22. *Orientale Lumen*, n. 15.

23. *Ecclesia in America*, n. 67.

24. 4/2/80, TB 89.

25. *Novo Millennio Ineunte*, n. 23.

ously a broader meaning of the word than the sense in which we speak of the seven sacraments (we will clarify this distinction later). The body, in this broader sense, is the "sacrament" of the person because it makes the invisible reality of the person visible. Furthermore, in Christ, his body becomes the "sacrament" of the divine person of the Word.[26] The *Catechism* teaches that "in the body of Jesus 'we see our God made visible and so are caught up in love of the God we cannot see.' The individual characteristics of Christ's body express the divine person of God's Son."[27] "In his soul as in his body, Christ thus expresses humanly the divine ways of the Trinity."[28] God "has made himself visible in the flesh."[29] Therefore, as Christ himself tells us, with the help of the Holy Spirit, those who have seen Christ have seen the Father (see Jn 14:9).

God's Trinitarian mystery revealed in human flesh; theology of the body—this is the very "logic" of Christianity. It is also the particular scandal of Christianity.

B. The Scandal of the Body

The paradox and implications of an enfleshed God never fail to confound the human heart. If God himself took on a body, this would imply not only a blessing of the highest degree upon the whole physical world; it would also imply the *divinization* in some sense of human flesh—which necessarily includes human sexuality. This may seem like *too much* to accept. A phantom deity is much more tenable and, let us be honest, much more becoming than a God with a human body—a male body which was, as the patristic saying goes, "complete in all the parts of a man."

A suspicion toward the physical world and discomfort with all things sexual is by no means a neurosis induced by Christianity. It hangs like a dark shadow over all human experience.[30] Like the rest of humanity, Christians have been and still are affected and even infected by it. Through the centuries the Church has defended the goodness of the physical world and the sacredness of the human body against many heresies.[31] The

---

26. See *CCC*, n. 515.

27. Ibid., n. 477.

28. Ibid., n. 470.

29. Ibid., n. 1159.

30. For an excellent treatment of this, see the chapter entitled "Flight from Sex" in Christopher Derrick's book *Sex & Sacredness* (San Francisco, CA: Ignatius Press, 1982).

31. See *CCC*, n. 299.

Church still struggles today to counter the heretical "spirit good—body bad" dichotomy which many people assume to be orthodox Christian belief.

Christianity does not reject the body! Quite the contrary—Christianity acknowledges that God has raised human flesh to the highest heights of heaven, and Christians believe this to be God's plan for every*body*. Christians are those who face squarely the implications and the scandal of an incarnate God and proclaim: "I believe" *(credo)*. The Catholic Church remains forever immersed in wonder at this paradox, honoring and praising the womb that bore him and the breasts he sucked (see Lk 11:27). In fact, Catholics believe that Jesus' male body and Mary's female body are *already* dwelling in those heavenly heights.[32] In a virtual "ode to the flesh," the *Catechism* proclaims: "'The flesh is the hinge of salvation.'[33] We believe in God who is creator of the flesh; we believe in the Word made flesh in order to redeem the flesh; we believe in the resurrection of the flesh, the fulfillment of both the creation and the redemption of the flesh."[34]

Suspicion toward the body, sexuality, and the material world is not only alien to authentic Catholic belief, but is its very antithesis.[35] Catholics (and members of other sacramental Churches) encounter God not through some super-spiritual reality, but *through their bodies* and the elements of the material world: through bathing the body with water; anointing the body with oil; eating and drinking the body and blood of Christ; confessing with one's own tongue; laying on of hands; and yes, through that reality by which a man and woman join their lives together so intimately as to be "one flesh."[36]

According to John Paul, marriage is not just one of the seven sacraments. Insofar as marriage points us "from the beginning" to the infinitely greater and transcendent mystery of Christ's union with the Church, it is the foundation of the entire sacramental order.[37] Marriage is the prototype, in some sense, of all of the sacraments[38] since each has as its aim to unite us with Christ our Bridegroom in a fruitful and indissoluble union of love. This earthy, nuptial symbolism is imbedded in the Catholic imagination and permeates John Paul's theology of the body.

---

32. See *CCC,* nn. 648, 659, 966.
33. Tertullian, *De res.* 8, 2: PL 2, 852.
34. *CCC,* n. 1015.
35. See 10/29/80, TB 168.
36. See *CCC,* nn. 1084, 1113.
37. See 9/29/82, TB 332–333.
38. See 10/20/82, TB 339.

4. The Nuptial Mystery

Scripture uses many images to describe the mystery of God's relationship with humanity: father and son, king and subjects, bridegroom and bride, shepherd and sheep, vine and branches, head and body. Each has its own valuable place. But only one of these images constitutes a sacrament that efficaciously communicates the mystery it signifies: the nuptial image.[39] The Scriptures use this image more than any other. The greatest mystics also favor it. John Paul, deeply imbued with Carmelite mysticism, shares this nuptial favoritism.

Without intending to undermine other theological traditions in any way (they are all vital to the universality of the Church), the Holy Father says that nuptial imagery "contains in itself a characteristic of the mystery which is not directly emphasized...by any other analogy used in the Bible."[40] Of course, as John Paul also points out, "analogy" always indicates, at the same time, both similarity and substantial dissimilarity.[41] "It is obvious that the analogy of earthly...spousal love cannot provide an adequate and complete understanding of that absolute transcendent Reality which is the divine mystery. ...The mystery remains transcendent in regard to this analogy as in regard to any other analogy, whereby we seek to express it in human language."[42] Hence, all analogies limp in their attempts to communicate the incommunicable. Yet, speaking of marriage and the family, John Paul states, "In this entire world there is not a more perfect, more complete image of God, Unity and Community. There is no other human reality which corresponds more, humanly speaking, to that divine mystery."[43] In other words, if all analogies are inadequate, John Paul believes the spousal analogy is the *least* inadequate because within "the very essence of marriage a particle of the mystery is captured. Otherwise the entire analogy would hang suspended in a void."[44]

Throughout his catechesis, the Pope wants to explore this "particle" of the mystery found in the nuptial relationship. He wants to break it open, penetrate it, and unfold it. Yet even if we focus on the similarity within the spousal analogy, we must carefully maintain the greater dissimilarity be-

---

39. See *CCC,* nn. 757, 772, 796, 808, 823, 867, 1089.

40. 9/29/82, TB 331.

41. See 7/30/80, TB 129.

42. 9/29/82, TB 330.

43. Homily on the Feast of the Holy Family, December 30, 1988.

44. 8/18/82, TB 313.

tween human-spousal communion and divine-Christian communion. Without this recognition, there is a danger of moving too continuously from creaturely life to divine life. This does not mean the analogy is extrinsic. It only means that throughout our analysis of the spousal analogy, we must always respect the mysterious and infinite difference between God and his creatures.[45] We must avoid every tendency to reduce the ultimate divine reality to its bodily sign. In fact, the human-spousal analogy is always a matter ultimately of a divine-Christian "katalogy." This means that the movement upwards ("ana") from the creature to God implies a prior downward ("kata") movement from God to the creature. In other words, theology can be linked with anthropology only because God can (and in the Person of the Word did) humble himself and "come down" to our level. Without this divine-Christian "katalogy," we could not cross the infinite abyss and "go up" to God's level. In such case it would be almost meaningless to apply the human-spousal analogy to divine life.[46]

A. Nuptiality Embraces the Universe

In a word, nuptial love indicates the total gift of self. Penetrating further, the mystery of "nuptiality" rests on three interrelated dynamisms: the complementarity of sexual difference or "otherness"[47]; the call to communion through the self-giving love to which this summons us; and the fecundity to which this communion leads.[48] According to God's original plan, the paradigmatic expression of this nuptiality is found in Genesis 2:24—"the two shall become one flesh." This union, in turn, in some way sheds light on all genuine expressions of love. As the Pontifical Council for the Family expresses, "Every form of love will always bear this masculine and feminine character."[49]

Nuptiality is a permanent dimension of love since all love entails some sort of complementarity ("otherness"), mutual self-giving, and fruitfulness. The eternal prototype is found in the Trinity itself: in the God who

---

45. See *CCC*, nn. 42, 43, 212, 300, 370, 2779.

46. My thanks to Dr. David Schindler for helping me articulate this important point.

47. Since the body reveals the interior mystery of the person, sexual complementarity cannot be reduced to biological complementarity. It refers to the whole mystery of man and woman as incarnate persons.

48. See Angelo Scola, "The Nuptial Mystery at the Heart of the Church," *Communio* (Winter 1998): pp. 631–662.

49. *The Truth & Meaning of Human Sexuality,* n. 10.

is love, in the God who is an eternal life-giving *Communion of Persons.* Of course we cannot speak of *sexual* difference and communion in the infinitely transcendent, Uncreated mystery of God. As the *Catechism* observes, "In no way is God in man's image.... God is pure spirit in which there is no place for the difference between the sexes. But the respective 'perfections' of man and woman reflect something of the infinite perfection of God."[50] We might say that male-female "otherness" and the call to fruitful communion is an "echo" in the created order of the transcendent mystery of "otherness," communion, and generous fruitfulness found in the Trinity. It is in *this* image that we are made as male and female. The divine Love is so generous that it bears fruit in the gift and mystery of our creation.

According to John Paul II, the term "nuptial" manifests in a word "the whole reality of that donation of which the first pages of the Book of Genesis speak."[51] Nuptiality, he says, is inscribed in the mystery of creation and redemption so profoundly that in some way it "embraces the universe."[52] When we glimpse the full implications of this nuptial mark that is stamped upon reality, we realize that we cannot adequately understand the inner "logic" of the Christian mystery without understanding its primordial revelation in the nuptial meaning of our bodies and that biblical vocation to become "one flesh." As John Paul stresses, "The 'great mystery,' which is the Church and humanity in Christ, does not exist apart from the 'great mystery' expressed in the 'one flesh'...reality of marriage and the family."[53]

In short, to ask the question about the meaning of human embodiment and nuptial union begins an exhilarating journey that—if we stay the course—leads us to the heart of the mystery of the cosmos, the mystery of our humanity, and even allows us to glimpse something of the eternal mystery of God. John Paul's theology of the body goes far beyond a catechesis on sex and marriage. According to the Pope, it is a specific, evangelical, Christian education—and the most suitable and fundamental method of education—in the meaning of being a body, in the meaning of being human.[54]

---

50. *CCC,* n. 370.
51. 1/16/80, TB 66.
52. 12/15/82, TB 354.
53. *Letter to Families,* n. 19.
54. See 4/8/81 and 9/8/84, TB 215 and 396.

Therefore, the theology of the body should not be considered merely a minor or peripheral discipline. According to the Holy Father, what we learn in his catechesis on the body and nuptial union "concerns the entire Bible"[55] and plunges us into "the perspective of the whole Gospel, of the whole teaching, in fact, of the whole mission of Christ."[56] John Paul's theological examination of the body, though it focuses primarily on questions of sexuality, affords "the rediscovery of the meaning of the whole of existence, the meaning of life."[57] Papal biographer George Weigel pointed to the scope of the Pope's catechesis when he wrote that "John Paul's portrait of sexual love as an icon of the interior life of God has barely begun to shape the Church's theology, preaching, and religious education. When it does, it will compel a dramatic development of thinking about virtually every major theme in the Creed."[58]

B. Spousal Theology Rooted in the Scriptures

While the Holy Father's catechesis takes the nuptial paradigm to a new level, this kind of "spousal theology" has strong roots in Scripture and the Catholic theological tradition. Both Old and New Testaments reveal God's love for his people as the love of a husband for his bride. The Bible begins and ends with stories of marriage—the marriage of the first Adam and Eve and the marriage of the New Adam and Eve, Christ and the Church.

Spousal theology looks to the nuptial "book ends" of Genesis and Revelation as a key for interpreting what lies between. From this analogical perspective we come to understand that God's mysterious and eternal plan is to espouse us to himself forever (see Hos 2:19)—to "marry" us.[59] As John Paul writes in his *Letter to Families,* "By describing himself as 'bridegroom,' Jesus reveals the essence of God and confirms his immense love for mankind."[60] Respecting our freedom, the Bridegroom proposes

---

55. 1/13/82, TB 249.

56. 12/3/80, TB 175.

57. 10/29/80, TB 168.

58. *Witness to Hope,* p. 853.

59. Of course, the nuptial mystery is not the only lens through which to view the truths of the faith, even if the Pope believes that it is fundamental. As already stated, there are other vital theological traditions and the Holy Father's thought is not intended to undermine them. A comparative study of the theology of the body with these other traditions would be helpful, but is beyond the scope of this project.

60. *Letter to Families,* n. 18.

this marital plan to man and awaits the bride's *fiat*. Furthermore, a theology of the body illuminates that this eternal plan is not "out there" somewhere. It could not be any closer to us. It is *right here,* mysteriously recapitulated in our very being as male and female. The Gospel mystery is inscribed sacramentally in our bodies and in the call of man and woman to become "one flesh" in a life-long, life-giving communion. This mystery was lived by man and woman "in the beginning," was lost through original sin, and is restored in Jesus Christ.

The spousal analogy, then, is not extrinsic. It is not merely a happy coincidence. This is the fundamental manner in which God chose to reveal his own covenant of life and love to the world—by creating us in such a way (as male and female) that we could image this covenant and participate in it. When God establishes his covenants with man, whether it is with Adam (Gen 1:28), Noah (Gen 9:1), Abraham (Gen 17:5–6), Jacob (Gen 35:10–12), or Moses (Lev 26:9), we always see the call of bridegroom and bride to signify this covenant in fruitful nuptial union. And at the beginning of the New Covenant, Mary's *fiat* marks a new *virginal* expression of nuptial love and fruitfulness. In offering her "yes" to God's marriage proposal, she stands as "the archetype of humanity."[61] In turn, this biblical "woman" becomes the guarantor of realism in the life-giving communion of God and man. With her *fiat* she quite literally conceives eternal life within her. She is impregnated with the fulfillment of all God's promises and the realization of man's eternal destiny. As the *Catechism* states, "The spousal character of the human vocation in relation to God is fulfilled perfectly in Mary's virginal motherhood."[62]

■ In due time we will examine the Holy Father's profound insights regarding the meaning of consecrated celibacy. Its esteem in the Christian life lies not in a dualistic separation of "spiritual values" over the values of the body and sex. Although lived out differently, celibacy, too, John Paul insists, is a bodily expression of nuptial love—of total self-giving. As we will see, far from devaluing sexuality, the celibate vocation points to its greatness by revealing the sexual body's ultimate purpose and meaning. We will also learn that before sin there was no opposition between a true unity of persons and virginity. The "loss of virginity" which results from man and woman's union in "one flesh" is a result of the rupture caused within man and between man and woman as a result of original sin.

---

61. See *Mulieris Dignitatem,* n. 4.

62. *CCC,* n. 505.

C. Signs of the Covenants

In order to understand better the fundamental importance of the "nuptial mystery" in revealing the hidden plan of God, all we need do is look to those physical signs which God established in order for man to perceive the spiritual mystery of the Old and the New Covenants. Think for a moment about the promise given to Abraham: "Behold my covenant is with you, and you shall be the father of a multitude of nations. ...I will make you exceedingly fruitful" (Gen 17:4, 6). God then demanded that a sign of this covenant be carved into Abraham's flesh: "You shall be circumcised in the flesh of your foreskins, and it shall be a sign of the covenant between me and you. ...So shall my covenant be in your flesh an everlasting covenant" (Gen 17:11, 13).

Male circumcision is a central element of Old Testament revelation. Despite a common reluctance to do so, we must ponder this oddity: Why would the Heavenly Father demand of his people that the most intimate part of the male genitalia be perpetually relieved of its natural covering? Why did the Lord of the Universe institute *this* to set his chosen people apart and identify them as his followers? How is this physical symbol an effective sign of God's spiritual, covenant love in the world?

While scholars of Scripture and Jewish history can answer these questions more fully, I will offer the following plausible musings. Who would most often see this sign and when? Every time a male descendant of Abraham consummated his marriage, he and his wife would be reminded of God's promise of fruitful nuptial love. Circumcision "speaks" in some way of the mystery of fatherhood, and of the price required of men if they are truly to image God's Fatherhood in the world. By inflicting this wound upon the male, it appears as if the Heavenly Father is saying that men must come to learn something that women already seem to know. Namely, participation in God's generous love involves the shedding of blood and the sacrifice of one's own flesh.

Is this not precisely what Christ the Bridegroom teaches us? Circumcision foreshadows his ultimate sacrifice of flesh and blood.[63] The promise of fruitful nuptial love given to Abraham is definitively consummated in Christ's body "given up for us." The cross, in turn, John Paul tells us, becomes "a fresh manifestation of the eternal fatherhood of God."[64] Here we gain insight into why it was the Heavenly Father's will, as Karol Wojtyla (the future John Paul II) once reflected, for Christ to allow himself to be

---

63. See *CCC,* n. 1150.

64. *Redemptor Hominis,* n. 9.

"stripped naked" in the hour of his passion.[65] What might the spectators have noticed about the man crucified in the middle? He was a son of Abraham, a Jew—a "chosen one." Yet this was not simply any Jew. This was "King of the Jews." This was *the* Chosen One. Those gathered at the foot of the cross—Jews and Gentiles alike—were eyewitnesses to the definitive and most intimate revelation on earth of the mystery of the Father's love unveiled in Christ's (circumcised) flesh.

In the "naked Christ" and his body "given up for us," do we not see how the sign of the Old Covenant—circumcision—is fulfilled in the sign of the New—Eucharist? The Eucharistic sacrifice, in fact, effects the most fruitful "nuptial" communion of the cosmos. John Paul II describes Holy Communion as *"the sacrament of the Bridegroom and the Bride."* Thus, the Eucharist serves in some way "to express the relationship between man and woman, between what is 'feminine' and what is 'masculine.' It is a relationship willed by God in both the mystery of creation and in the mystery of Redemption."[66]

D. This Is a "Great Mystery"

This great nuptial mystery is revealed and confirmed in that marvelous passage of Ephesians where St. Paul links the "one flesh" union of Genesis with the union of Christ and the Church. "'For this reason a man shall leave his father and mother and be joined to his wife, and the two shall become one flesh.' This is a great mystery, and I mean in reference to Christ and the church" (Eph 5:31–32). Christ left his Father in heaven; he left the home of his mother on earth—to give up his body for his Bride, so that we might become "one body" with him.[67] This we do whenever the Eucharistic sacrifice is offered by the Bridegroom and faithfully received by the Bride. This is obviously not a "sexual" encounter, but the consummation of a mystical marriage. It is a physical sign that effects the profound spiritual mystery it symbolizes. And that mystery is the mystery of life-giving communion between God and man and among all men.

The nuptial mystery reveals this beautifully. God himself is a life-giving Communion of Persons and we are destined to share in that Communion as the Bride of Christ. Everything God wants to tell us on earth about who he is, who we are, the meaning of life, the reason he created us, how we are to live, why evil exists, as well as our ultimate destiny can be illumined through the lens of the "great mystery" of nuptial communion.[68]

---

65. See *Sign of Contradiction* (New York: Seabury Press, 1979), p. 192.

66. *Mulieris Dignitatem,* n. 26.

67. See *CCC,* nn. 790, 791, 1396, 1621.

68. See *Letter to Families,* n. 19.

In his theology of the body John Paul takes upon himself the formidable task of unfolding this cosmic drama from origin to eschaton. And what a burning need there is to reunite the modern world with this nuptial mystery! The further man is from this mystery, the less he knows who he is and who he is meant to be. The Pope observes that as "the result of estrangement from the 'great mystery' spoken of by the apostle" in Ephesians 5, "contemporary man remains to a great extent a *being unknown* to himself."[69]

But *why* is it—and *how* is it—that man has become so detached from the truth of his own body and the nuptial mystery it proclaims? The ultimate answers to these questions are found only by returning to "the beginning." For, as Karol Wojtyla tells us, the first pages of Genesis contain "the key to understanding the world of today, both its roots and its extremely radical—and therefore dramatic—affirmations and denials."[70]

5. The Great Divorce

In the beginning, God created everything through his Word—the Word that is love, the Word that is "gift." If all of creation involuntarily echoes this Word, God gave man and woman their own voices with which to recite it freely. As the Second Vatican Council expresses, this "freedom is an exceptional sign of the divine image within man. For God has willed that man remain 'under the control of his own decisions'" (see Sir 15:14).[71] Man is the only creature on earth that God created for "its own sake." However, man is not meant to live for his own sake. He can only find himself "through the sincere gift of himself."[72] This key teaching of the Council is the divine Word inscribed in the nuptial meaning of the human body. In the beginning, at the sight of each other's nakedness, the truth of this Word welled up in the hearts of man and woman as a spontaneous love song, sung in the original harmony of what Genesis calls "one flesh." This is why the Scriptures present them as being naked without shame—because they lived the truth of "the gift," at least initially.

Between the experience of original nakedness and the entrance of the fig leaves, man and woman would have their first encounter with "the

---

69. Ibid.

70. *Sign of Contradiction,* p. 24.

71. *Gaudium et Spes,* n. 17.

72. Ibid., n. 24.

father of lies." His goal was to get them to deny the gift of God's love, to deny the divine Word. Hence, Wojtyla/John Paul II describes Satan as the "anti-Word."[73]

A. Plagiarizing the Primordial Sacrament

Tertullian, an early Christian writer, insightfully observed that Satan seeks to counter God's plan by plagiarizing the sacraments.[74] In the sacraments God accomplishes his plan for man and in them we find the meaning of life and true happiness. By commandeering the sacraments for his purposes, the deceiver markets his counterfeit version of man's path to happiness. In the beginning, there was only one sacrament, what John Paul calls the "primordial sacrament"—the union of Adam and Eve in marriage. This is where Satan attacks. Thus, we can conclude with John Paul that "Sin and death entered man's history, in a way, through the very heart of that unity which, from 'the beginning,' was formed by man and woman, created and called to become 'one flesh.'"[75]

God revealed himself to the first man and woman as the God of love, the God of the covenant. This was the Word inscribed in the sacramentality of their bodies and their call to become "one flesh." Soon thereafter, however, the anti-Word entered the scene purveying his own counterfeit version of reality. In a retreat preached to Pope Paul VI in 1976, the future Pope John Paul II observes that if Satan's ultimate goal is to have man deny God's existence, such a denial was not possible "in the beginning." God's existence was all too obvious to the first man and woman. Hence, the first "lap" in the devil's scheme was to "aim straight at the God of the covenant."[76] In other words, Satan sets out to convince man that God is not to be trusted; that he is not a loving Father, but a tyrant, an enemy, against whom man has to defend himself. The Holy Father later emphasizes in his international best-seller, *Crossing the Threshold of Hope*, that this *"is truly the key for interpreting reality.... Original sin attempts, then, to abolish fatherhood."*[77]

The truth and meaning of this gripping statement will come to light throughout our analysis of the theology of the body. For now, if we are to

---

73. See *Sign of Contradiction,* pp. 29–34 and *Dominum et Vivificantem,* n. 37.

74. *Prescription Against Heretics,* Book 40, cited in Father Gabriele Amorth, *An Exorcist Tells His Story* (San Francisco, CA: Ignatius Press, 1999), p. 182.

75. 3/5/80, TB 77.

76. *Sign of Contradiction,* p. 30.

77. *Crossing the Threshold of Hope* (New York: Alfred A. Knopf, 1994), p. 228.

understand the nature of the weed which John Paul is trying to uproot in his catechesis, it is important to understand the method by which the deceiver constructs this counterfeit world-view. The devil cannot create out of nothing. As a creature himself, all he can do is take what God created to reveal the mystery of his own Fatherhood and twist it, distort it—or, more aptly, tempt us to do so. So if we are looking for that which is most sacred in this world, all we need do is look for that which Satan most often profanes: the gift of the body and sexuality.

B. The Symbolic and the Diabolic

In our culture's violent attack on God's plan for the body and sexuality, we see a great clash between the "symbolic" and the "diabolic." In the Greek, *symballein* means to bring together, gather up, unite. *Diaballein* means to scatter, break apart, rupture. God's eternal plan for man as *symbolized* through the body is union, communion, marriage—this brings life. The deceiver's counter-plan for man as *diabolized* through the body is separation, fracture, divorce—this brings death.

In a word, Satan aims to make the symbolic *diabolic*. God created the body and the mystery of sexuality with a sacramental language that speaks his own Word. The deceiver incessantly commandeers this holy ground in order to scramble the body's language so that it contradicts the divine Word.

Confronted by a culture that so gravely distorts the meaning of the body and sexuality, Christians can be tempted to eschew these divine gifts. Indeed, one of the main threats facing the Church today is a "super-spiritualism" in which people disembody their call to holiness. Yet if we respond to the lies in this way, we have not conquered those lies; we have inadvertently bought into them. The body proclaims the Word. The spirit that denies this "incarnational reality" is none other than that of the anti-Word (see 1 Jn 4:2–3).

How, then, do we conquer these lies and live an integrated life, an embodied spirituality? We must first reclaim what Satan has plagiarized. John Paul's entire catechesis on the body is a clarion call to do just that. The very title—*theology* of the *body*—calls us to the integration of the spiritual and the material. Without this integration we inevitably suffer from a kind of "split personality."

C. "Angelism" and "Animalism"

The spiritual has an ontological priority over the physical. Yet, without blurring the distinction, God united spirit and matter by creating man from the dust of the ground and from the breath of his own life (see Gen 2:7). In this way, man is similar to both angels and animals, but also remarkably different. Angels are spiritual persons, but they do not have bodies and, hence, are not sexually differentiated. Animals have bodies and are sexually differentiated but they are not persons. Human beings, however, are a strange combination of the two. We are "angimals," so to speak; spiritual *and* physical creatures; we are sexually differentiated *body-persons*.[78] This means that man can be neither reduced to the material world, nor divorced from it. Although the "invisible" determines man more than the "visible," the visible expresses the invisible.[79]

This original harmony of body and soul, sexuality and spirituality was sustained by the harmony between God and man and was manifested most pointedly in the original harmony of man and woman. Like nothing else, the primordial sacrament—that indissoluble union of two persons in one flesh—speaks to the original alliance of spirit with flesh. Yet when man accepted the anti-Word, his sin shattered these harmonies introducing a "great divorce" into the order of the cosmos. A fallen world, then, is a world of estranged spouses: estrangement between divinity and humanity; heaven and earth; soul and body; spirituality and sexuality; sacredness and sensuality; masculinity and femininity. According to its own diabolic logic, such alienation leads to death. When such estrangement becomes embedded in the fabric of society, that society can be nothing but a "culture of death."

Those who perpetuate such a culture tend to live that "great divorce" within their spiritual/material nature as if it were completely normal. Lacking the reintegration of spirit and flesh to which we are called in Christ, they inevitably lean toward one side of the divide or the other, toward what we could call "angelism" and "animalism." One manifests a spiritual value deprived of earthiness while the other manifests an earthiness blind to spiritual value.[80] Both contribute equally to the disintegration of man and culture.

Angelism promotes a "spiritual life" divorced from the body. Failing to uphold the body's personal dignity, it tends toward prudishness and puritanism. Because it considers the body and all things sexual inherently tainted and "unspiritual," it leads to repression of sexual feelings and desire. The angelistic moral code is rigorism; it condemns even some of the most natural manifestations of sexuality as impure. Many Christians

---

78. See *CCC*, nn. 327, 362–368.

79. See 10/31/79, TB 42.

80. See Rocco Buttiglione, *Karol Wojtyla: The Thought of the Man Who Became Pope John Paul II* (Grand Rapids, MI: Eerdman's Publishing, 1997), p. 25.

throughout history have fallen prey to this distortion. Even today people make the calamitous mistake of considering this "holiness."

Animalism, on the other hand, springs from a materialistic world view and promotes a "carnal" life divorced from the spirit. Since in this outlook the body and sexual matters are not informed by man's spiritual dignity, animalism tends toward the indecent and the shameless.[81] It encourages men and women to indulge their fallen sexual impulses without restraint and promotes bodily pleasure as man's ultimate fulfillment. The animalistic moral code is permissiveness; it condemns any manifestation of temperance as a hindrance to freedom. All we need to do is turn on the television or walk through the check-out line at a grocery store to see how prevalent this distortion has become.

D. The Crucial Need of Balance

Cultural trends tend to oscillate between these two extremes. The twentieth century, for example (at least in much of the West), began with a widespread prudishness in which the mere sight of a woman's ankle could cause scandal. Yet it ended with a widespread shamelessness that has "normalized" even the most base sexual perversions. In this way we see how angelism and animalism each contain the seeds of the other. There is no "pure" angelist just as there is no "pure" animalist. Each is trying unsuccessfully to suffocate an indomitable aspect of his own nature which, resisting the weight of repression, will eventually explode with a force that propels the person (and the culture) to the other extreme. Pendulum swing is understandable, but John Paul II teaches another way—the path of reintegrating spirit and flesh.

The need for man to discover his true (integrated) self could not be any more pressing. The stakes are incredibly high. Karol Wojtyla knows well that a dualistic anthropology leads to the gas chamber, to the abortion mill, to the culture of death. According to Wojtyla's read on "the signs of the times," it seems the ancient clash between the "nuptial mystery" and the "great divorce," between the "symbolic" and the "diabolic" is coming to a head. In the retreat given to the Roman Curia in 1976, Cardinal Wojtyla boldly stated that we may now be "experiencing the highest level of tension between the Word and the anti-Word in the whole of human history." He even went so far as to suggest that this may be "the last lap along

---

81. Shamelessness is not to be equated with the experience of nakedness *without* shame as in Genesis 2:25. In fact, these two experiences are antithetical (see §16 for a further discussion of this point).

that way of denial which started out from around the tree of the knowledge of good and evil."[82]

The attack on God's Fatherhood—on the truth that "God is love"—was only the first lap in "a very long process that winds its devious way throughout history." The deceiver has worked in stages, patiently awaiting the opportune time to induce man toward the ultimate denial of God's very existence. In "the first stage of human history this temptation was not only not accepted but had not been fully formulated. But the time has now come," Wojtyla tells us; "this aspect of the devil's temptation has found the historical context that suits it." Man is now prepared to deny the very existence of God. This is not the atheism of the skeptics or the despairing that has dotted history. This is a planned, systematic attempt at "liberation from the very idea of God in order to bolster man."[83] This is the idea that to believe in God—especially the Christian God—is inherently dehumanizing. The French Jesuit theologian Henri de Lubac described this as "atheistic humanism."[84] In Karol Wojtyla he would find a voice of agreement that this radical denial of God is at the heart of all the man-made hells of the twentieth century.

6. The Deepest Substratum of Ethics and Culture

John Paul II champions human life, dignity, and freedom precisely because of the crucible of death, degradation, and tyranny in which he was formed. The Nazis invaded his beloved Poland when he was nineteen. Death and degradation surrounded him. The stench of burning bodies from nearby Auschwitz hovered in the air. He would have been sent there, too, or shot on the spot, had his role in the underground resistance or his clandestine seminary studies been discovered. Several brushes with death, and, at times, his inexplicable survival, seem to indicate that providence had special plans for Karol.[85] The Nazis left Poland six years later, but another totalitarian power took control. As a young man Wojtyla mounted a cultural resistance to Communism that would continue throughout his life as priest, bishop, cardinal, and pontiff, ultimately playing an essential role in the collapse of the Iron Curtain.

---

82. *Sign of Contradiction,* pp. 34–35.

83. Ibid., pp. 31, 34.

84. See Henri de Lubac, *The Drama of Atheistic Humanism* (San Francisco: Ignatius Press, 1995). See also *CCC,* n. 2124.

85. See *Witness to Hope,* pp. 69–72.

A. The Root of Evil

While many of his contemporaries concluded that life was absurd, Wojtyla wrestled with God, searching for answers to life's hardest questions. How? Why? What could lead man, who is bestowed with God-like dignity, to drink from the dregs of raw evil? Surface solutions did not interest Wojtyla. He wanted to go to the root of it all and find the first event in the chain reaction that led humanity to embrace the evils that flow from "atheistic humanism." What is that root? Summarizing John Paul's thought, it is our rejection of God's revelation of love that he *inscribed in our bodies by creating us male and female.*

The Holy Father is convinced that the call to nuptial love and communion inscribed in our masculine and feminine bodies is "the fundamental element of human existence in the world,"[86] "the foundation of human life,"[87] and, hence, "the deepest substratum of human ethics and culture."[88] *This* is the root of it all. John Paul's quest for answers to the enigma of human existence has led him to the firm conviction, as he himself states, that the dignity and balance of human life depend always and everywhere on the proper ordering of love between the sexes. Who will woman be for man? Who will man be for woman? The human project stands or falls on the answer to these questions.[89] For if we live according to the true nuptial meaning of our bodies *we fulfill the very meaning of our being and existence.*[90] But if we reject the true meaning of the body, we forfeit the transcendent, spiritual truth of love and separate ourselves from God—and civilization ultimately implodes.

While this dynamic is played out primarily in marriage and family life, it applies to all men and women, whatever their state in life. For every man and woman, the answers to the most basic questions about human life pass by way of human sexuality. "What does it mean to be a man?" is the most important question a man can ask himself. Likewise, "What does it mean to be a woman?" is the most important question a woman can ask herself. These are *inherently sexual* questions because, created as male and female, we are inherently sexual beings. As John Paul affirms, "sexuality...is by no means something purely biological, but concerns the in-

---

86. 1/16/80, TB 66.

87. *Ecclesia in America,* n. 46.

88. 10/22/80, TB163.

89. See 10/8/80, TB159.

90. See 1/16/80, TB 63.

nermost being of the human person as such."[91] Thus, the way men and women answer the above questions determines whether the entire edifice of culture and society rests on solid rock or shifting sands.

B. The Wellspring of Culture

We can appreciate the vital role of the sexual relationship in shaping ethics and culture in the simple truth that the family is the fundamental cell of society. As the family goes, so goes culture.[92] But, pressing further, what is the origin of the family if not the "one flesh" union of spouses? Wojtyla describes the conjugal union of man and woman, then, not only as "the *natural* foundation" but also as "the ontological core of the family."[93] In this sense conjugal union is also the fountainhead of civilization, the wellspring of culture. Open to God's inspiration and ordered toward love and life, it builds families and, in turn, a culture of love and life. Closed to divine inspiration and ordered against love and life, sexual union not only disorients and disintegrates marriage and the family, it ultimately leads to a culture of utility and death. In short, the relationship of the sexes becomes the meeting place of God and man and the origin of a truly human culture, or it becomes man's point of closure to God and the first step in the disintegration of civilization.

Is this not why fruitful nuptial union was so strongly emphasized throughout salvation history, beginning with the Creator's first instruction to man and woman to "Be fruitful and multiply" (Gen 1:28)? This is not merely an injunction to propagate, but in some way holds the key to human flourishing. For it calls us to live in the image in which we are made. It calls us to love as God loves, by first receiving that love and then sharing it in life-giving communion with the "other." This sums up the Gospel and is the key to human happiness. Hence, the "new" commandment Christ gives us to love as he loves (see Jn 15:12) is nothing but an echo and reformulation of the original human vocation outlined in Genesis— and, as we learn in a theology of the body, this vocation is stamped in our flesh. The family relationships founded on the union of the sexes provide the most basic school in which we learn the law of life which is God's self-giving love. The nuptial meaning of the body proclaims the basic truth upheld by the Church's teaching on sexual morality, that man can only find himself through the sincere gift of himself.

---

91. *Familiaris Consortio*, n. 11; See *CCC*, n. 2332.

92. See *CCC*, n. 2207.

93. "Parenthood as a Community of Persons," in *Person & Community: Selected Essays*, trans. Theresa Sandok (New York: Peter Lang, 1993), p. 339.

Hence, confusion about sexual morality, as Karol Wojtyla wrote in his 1960 book *Love & Responsibility*, "involves a danger perhaps greater than is generally realized: the danger of confusing the basic and fundamental human tendencies, the main paths of human existence. Such confusion," he concluded, "must clearly affect the whole spiritual position of man."[94] Because human life itself passes by way of sexual union, the choices and actions of men and women "take on all the weight of human existence in the union of the two."[95]

This is why John Paul II devoted 129 general audiences to developing a theology of the body. If his goal is to show the world the path for building a culture of life, the only adequate starting point is to return to God's original plan for the body and sexuality. As the Holy Father states, it "is an illusion to think we can build a true culture of human life if we do not...accept and experience sexuality and love and the whole of life according to their true meaning and their close inter-connection."[96] Unless we regain an incarnate theological vision of man and woman and their call to communion, we will remain divided at the deepest level of the interaction of body and soul, and the "great divorce" will reign supreme over the "nuptial mystery."

7. Healing the Rift

The first sentence of John Paul II's first encyclical serves as the lodestar for his entire pontificate: "The Redeemer of man, Jesus Christ, is the center of the universe and of history."[97] This radical "Christo-centrism"—a specific rebuttal to modern atheistic ideologies—reveals John Paul II's deepest conviction: Only in the mystery of the Word made flesh does the enigma of the universe, of history and of humanity come to light. "Christ fully reveals man to himself and makes his supreme calling clear" specifically by revealing the love of the Father, poured out to heal the rift in us caused by original sin.

A. *Reintegration in the Word Made Flesh*

The very dynamism of the Incarnation effects this healing. The Word made flesh *is* the reconciliation of the "great divorce" between God and

---

94. *Love & Responsibility*, p. 66.

95. 6/27/84, TB 376.

96. *Evangelium Vitae*, n. 97.

97. *Redemptor Hominis*, n. 1.

man, heaven and earth, soul and body, sacredness and sensuality, spirituality and sexuality, man and woman. All is made one, all is summed up, all
that had been fractured is brought back together in Christ (see Eph 1:10).
Through the "redemption of the body" and the "life in the Spirit" afforded
by Christ's death and resurrection, man is re-created in the unity of flesh
and spirit (see Rom 8).

Of course, talking about this reintegration in Christ is one thing. Experiencing it is another. The effects of original sin and the temptations of
the fallen world weigh on man like the leverage of a crowbar continually
trying to pry flesh and spirit apart. How, then, is one to experience this
healing? Above all, it requires faith.

If original sin leads us to doubt the benevolent love of the Father and
to close our hearts to the free gift of his life, John Paul tells us that *"faith,*
in its deepest essence, is *the openness* of the human heart to the gift: *to
God's self-communication in the Holy Spirit.*"[98] This life is poured out for
us in Christ's self-gift to his Bride on the cross. In essence, Christ's self-
gift says to us: "You don't believe in the Father's love? Let me make it
real for you; let me incarnate it for you so that you can taste and see. You
don't believe that God wants to give you life? I will bleed myself dry so
that my life's blood can vivify you. You thought God was a tyrant, a slave-
driver? You thought he would whip your back if you gave him the chance?
I will take the form of a slave; I will let you whip my back and nail me to a
tree; I will let you lord it over me to show you that the Father has no desire
to lord it over you. I have not come to condemn you, but to save you. I
have not come to enslave you, but to set you free. Turn from your disbe-
lief. *Believe* and *receive* the gift of eternal life I offer you."

This is Christ's "marriage proposal." He entrusts himself as a gift to
our freedom. Faith, then, is the human heart's openness to the gift of divine love. It is man's freely given "yes" to heaven's marriage proposal.[99]
Understood in this way, faith is the *only* path to reconciling the "great
divorce" and to that holiness which gradually heals man's internal split.
John Paul tells us that "holiness is measured according to the 'great mystery' in which the Bride responds with the gift of love to the gift of the
Bridegroom."[100] Holiness, in other words, is Love loved. Each time a human heart receives and reciprocates God's love, the reconciliation of divinity and humanity, body and soul, man and woman takes root. Bringing

---

98. *Dominum et Vivificantem,* n. 51.

99. See *CCC,* nn. 14, 142, 166.

100. *Mulieris Dignitatem,* n. 27 (see also *CCC,* n. 773).

about this reconciliation is the meaning and purpose of the Incarnation and Redemption. As the Holy Father says, the man who opens himself to Christ's gift

> ...finds again the greatness, dignity and value that belong to his own humanity. In the mystery of the redemption, man becomes newly "expressed" and, in a way, is newly created. He is newly created! ...The man who wishes to understand himself thoroughly—and not just in accordance with immediate, partial, often superficial, and even illusory standards and measures of his being—must with his unrest, uncertainty and even his weakness and sinfulness, with his life and death, draw near to Christ. He must, so to speak, enter into him [Christ] with all his own self, he must "appropriate" and assimilate the whole reality of the Incarnation and Redemption in order to find himself. If that profound process takes place within him, he then bears fruit not only of adoration of God but also of deep wonder at himself.[101]

If atheistic humanism claims to be the "religion" that trumpets man's greatness, the Pope insists that "the name for that deep amazement at man's worth and dignity is the Gospel, that is to say: the Good News. It is also called Christianity."[102] Christianity is the religion that upholds man's dignity and calls him to embrace his own greatness. But there is a "catch" of sorts, a rub. To embrace his own greatness, Christianity teaches that man must also embrace his own death. He must follow Christ the whole way to the cross if he is to be re-created (resurrected) in the unity of flesh and spirit.

Coping with the pains of our disintegration (whether we tend toward angelism or animalism) can seem like a fine alternative to being nailed to a tree. Even for those who "take up their crosses and follow," the path to integrating body and soul remains arduous. The deceiver is always at work plagiarizing the Word and lying to us about the meaning of our bodies and our sexuality. Yet the "reason the Son of God appeared was to destroy the works of the devil" (1 Jn 3:8). Christ appeared bodily to restore the body's original symbolic meaning; to enable us once again to read the "language" of the body in truth and to enter into holy communion—within ourselves, with one another, and with God. This theological language of the body, as exemplified in Christ, proclaims that God is "gift," he is love, he is benevolent Father. This is the body, John Paul tells us, "a witness to Love."[103] It is this same divine love which our bodies invite us to participate in as male and female by becoming "one flesh."

---

101. *Redemptor Hominis,* n. 10.

102. Ibid.

103. 1/9/80, TB 62.

B. Need for a Paradigm Shift

To reckon with the mystery of Christ crucified is to recognize the need for a radical reorientation of the basic premises with which most men and women view the universe. Contemplating the "naked Christ" and his body "given up for us" compels a radical paradigm shift both in the way we view God (theology) and in the way we view ourselves (anthropology), especially with regard to our own sexual embodiment. Christ crucified is the divine rebuttal to the deceiver's lies. Here the true Word inscribed in human flesh (self-donation) definitively trumps the anti-Word (self-gratification).

In the beginning the evil one had placed in doubt the truth that God is Love, leaving man with the sense of a master-slave relationship. Ever since, as John Paul says, man has felt "goaded to do battle against God,"[104] even to the point of murdering his incarnate Son. Yet in this moment—when the Son of God allowed us to nail him to a tree—we realize, as the Holy Father states, that *"the paradigm of master-slave is foreign to the Gospel."*[105] It is a paradigm drawn from a world in which God is an absent father, not a loving Father. It is a paradigm drawn from a lie, a paradigm constructed by the "father of lies."

This revelation changes *everything*. We live under friendly skies. We can put our defenses down and open to the heavens without fear. When we do, we find our posture straightening as the weight of a universal deception falls from our shoulders. When we "repent and believe in the good news" (Mk 1:15), we realize, perhaps for the first time, that life is "very good" (Gen 1:31) and that our existence is nothing but a sheer, gratuitous gift. Life, then, becomes thanksgiving offered to God *(eucharistia)* for so great a gift. In turn, we desire to become the same gift to others that life is to us. The real epiphany comes when we realize that these transcendent, spiritual truths—God is love; life is good; "the gift" of life and love is meant to be experienced and shared—have been stamped in our bodies all along. "Be fruitful and multiply." "Therefore a man leaves his father and his mother and cleaves to his wife, and they become one flesh." These texts of Genesis already contain in some way the fundamental truth of who God is and who we are made in his image and likeness. These texts reveal that Love—divine love, the generous Love of the eternal Father, the Love of the life-giving Trinity—is the Word implanted in our souls and inscribed in our flesh. To read this Word in truth and to put it into practice is to discover "the very meaning of our being and existence."

---

104. *Crossing the Threshold of Hope,* p. 228.

105. See ibid., p. 226.

C. Man Cannot Live without Love

The truth that we are made in the image of life-giving love explains why the body and sexuality fascinate us and make us crave intimacy, touch, and union. Yes, in our fallen world this fascination expresses itself in gross distortions which destroy lives. But once we learn with Christ's help to "untwist" all of our confusions and lusts, we discover in the mystery of human sexuality man's basic hunger for the God who is Love. As John Paul so eloquently states: "Man cannot live without love. He remains a being that is incomprehensible for himself, his life is senseless, if love is not revealed to him, if he does not encounter love, if he does not experience it and make it his own, if he does not participate intimately in it. This...is why Christ the Redeemer 'fully reveals man to himself'"[106]—because his body "given up for us" reveals the truth about incarnate love.

We need not be conformed to the lies that assail us. We can be transformed by the renewal of our minds if we, like Christ, offer our bodies as a living sacrifice to God. This *bodily* offering, St. Paul tells us, is our *spiritual* act of worship (see Rom 12:1-2). If we are truly willing to die with Christ, we too can live a new life, an incarnate life, an embodied spirituality. Only then do we feel at home in our own skin. Only then do the deepest desires of our hearts for intimacy and union make sense. Only then do we know who we are, why we exist, how we are to live, why there is evil in the world (and how to overcome it), and what our ultimate destiny is (and how to reach it). Christ does not cancel our humanity; he restores it to its original glory. Christ does not nullify our deepest desires and aspirations; he fulfills them superabundantly.

This is the Church's proposal to the world. Unfortunately, even in traditionally Christian nations, the vast majority of modern men and women have not yet heard the Christian proposal in its full glory. Hence, John Paul II has incessantly spoken about the need for a "new evangelization." The epilogue of this book will seek to show how the theology of the body undergirds this new evangelization. Before we unpack the Pope's catechesis, however, we need to understand how it imbues Karol Wojtyla's life-long philosophical and theological project and how, through this project, he attempts to engage the modern world with the truth about Jesus Christ.

---

106. *Redemptor Hominis,* n. 10.

8. Wojtyla's Philosophical Project

Why does the modern world seem almost programmed to tune out the Church's proposal? Along with revolutions in economics, politics, science and technology, the complex process of change in Western civilization called "modernization" has brought with it a critical shift of consciousness, a new rationalist mind-set that has no place for the "great mystery" of Christ and the Church. While neither of the following can be blamed for modernity's abandonment of Christianity, the lives and work of two great men have come to symbolize in some way the Western world's break with the Church. One is credited by many as the founder of modern experimental science; the other as the father of modern philosophy. Galileo Galilei—or, more aptly, the "Galileo affair"—and Rene Descartes' dictum, "I think, therefore I am," would leave an indelible mark on the way "modern" men and women understand themselves.

A. The Church and the Modern World

Nothing has done more to instill in the modern mind the image of a Church opposed to freedom, human progress, and scientific inquiry than the Galileo affair. Tragically, the churchmen who opposed the Copernican revolution Galileo promoted could not disassociate their faith from an age-old cosmology. Three hundred and fifty years after Galileo's death, the commission which John Paul II established to re-examine the Galileo case finally acknowledged that those who condemned Galileo had been seriously mistaken.[107] Unfortunately, a rift between religion and science had long since been seared into the historical consciousness.

The philosophy of Rene Descartes, one of Galileo's contemporaries, also contributed significantly to this rift. In fact, John Paul II describes his dictum *"Cogito, ergo sum"* as "the motto of modern rationalism."[108] Descartes turned his back on metaphysics and inaugurated the "anthropological turn" in philosophy. Modern philosophy *starts with man*. In other words, rather than starting with the objective realm of "being" and "existence," modern philosophy begins with man's *subjective and conscious experience* of being and existing—"I think, therefore I am." John Paul exclaims: "How different from the approach of St. Thomas, for whom it is not *thought which determines existence, but existence...which determines thought!"*[109]

---

107. See Cardinal Paul Poupard, "Galileo: Report on Papal Commission Findings," *Origins* (November 12, 1992), pp. 374–375.

108. *Crossing the Threshold of Hope,* p. 51.

109. Ibid., p. 38.

A philosophy of being acknowledges that I think because there is an objective reality beyond me—an Uncreated Being that *is* existence—that created me as I am (to think). My subjective thoughts are therefore answerable to this objective reality. A philosophy of pure consciousness, on the other hand, reduces reality to what man can think about it, because only "that which corresponds to human thought makes sense. The objective truth of this thought is not as important as the fact that something exists in human consciousness."[110] Man, then—not God—becomes the measure of the real. We see here the roots of modern rationalism and moral relativism.

Both the Galileo affair and Descartes' "turn to the subject" help us to understand the importance of Karol Wojtyla's philosophical project. Modernity has rejected so much of the Christian view of man, especially in the field of ethics, because traditional explanations of the faith were based on a metaphysics (the Aristotelian-Theistic philosophy of being) which depended on a physics (philosophy of nature) that modern science has shown faulty. In light of the Galileo affair, it seemed that reason had trumped faith. In turn, the blunder of certain churchmen greatly contributed to the mass allegiance shift from religion to science.

Yet truth can never contradict truth.[111] If the Christian faith teaches truth, there must be a way to reconcile it with what science has shown to be true. From Wojtyla's perspective, if the Church was to climb out of its credibility crisis and proclaim Christ convincingly to the modern world, Christian scholars would need to forge a new philosophical path. This new approach would need to reclaim the metaphysical truths St. Thomas taught in a manner that not only freed Christian argumentation of elements opposed to science, but also appealed to the way modern people think.[112] By boldly setting out to engage modern philosophy on its own terms, Wojtyla would seek to demonstrate that objective reality could be affirmed and reclaimed through a careful but nonetheless explicit appeal to subjective human experience.

The "problem," however, is that objective reality calls man to objective morality. Modern man has embraced a notion of freedom that chafes

---

110. Ibid., p. 51.

111. See *CCC*, n. 159.

112. See Rocco Buttiglione, *Karol Wojtyla: The Thought of the Man Who Became Pope John Paul II*, p. 74.

under anything other than a "morality of personal preference." One of the greatest challenges for the Church today is to recover the inherent link between *freedom* and *truth* taught by Christ (see Jn 8:32). Wojtyla seeks to do so by placing the moral life on the foundations of an "adequate anthropology." *The* question of the times, in Karol Wojtyla's mind, is "Who is man?" "What does it mean to be a human person?" Answering these questions is indispensable if men and women are to realize that the Gospel's demands are not against them; they are not an imposition. These demands instead correspond to the deepest longings and desires of the human heart.

But what are the deepest desires of the human heart? And how do the moral demands of the Christian life correspond to them? Such questions demand a penetrating reflection on man's self-experience. Why do I long for "something more" than this life can offer? Why do I suffer? Why do I intuitively realize that I am created for freedom? Why am I taken by beauty? By love? By lust? Why are peace and happiness so illusive?

As alluded to previously, the rich and often pained texture of Karol Wojtyla's life (particularly under Nazi occupation and Communist Poland) made him uniquely suited to press into these questions. Wojtyla has not reflected on the human condition through binoculars or dodged the tough questions. He is a man with calloused hands who has been personally involved in the greatest tragedies and triumphs of the twentieth century. Far from abstract musings, Wojtyla's thought is the fruit of a constant confrontation of doctrine with lived experience.[113] While it is beyond the scope of this book to trace in detail how Wojtyla's thought developed, it is important to sketch an overview.[114]

---

113. See *Love & Responsibility*, p. 15.

114. Many books have been written on the history and development of Wojtyla's anthropology. For the serious student, I would especially recommend Kenneth Schmitz's *At the Center of the Human Drama: The Philosophical Anthropology of Karol Wojtyla/ Pope John Paul II* (Washington, DC: Catholic University of America Press, 1993); Mary Shivanandan's *Crossing the Threshold of Love: A New Vision of Marriage in the Light of John Paul II's Anthropology* (Washington, DC: Catholic University of America Press, 1999); Rocco Buttiglione's *Karol Wojtyla: The Thought of the Man Who Became Pope John Paul II* (Grand Rapids, MI: William B. Eerdmans Publishing Co., 1997); and Jaroslaw Kupczak's *Destined for Liberty* (Washington, D.C.: Catholic University of America Press, 2000).

B. How Wojtyla's Thought Took Shape

Behind his high-profile life as the 263ʳᵈ successor of St. Peter is the life of an orphan (his mother and brother died when he was a boy, and his father when he was twenty), a quarryman, factory worker, athlete, avid outdoorsman, actor, mystic, poet, playwright, patriot, parish priest, confessor, spiritual director, philosopher, theologian, author, university professor, bishop, father of the Second Vatican Council, and cardinal.

He began to express his thoughts, questions, and yearnings in the poetry[115] and plays[116] he wrote as a young man. Already in these earliest works we see Wojtyla reflecting on the themes of human experience that will mark his most developed anthropology. His vision of man subsequently evolved through two doctoral dissertations. In the first, he examined the lived experience of faith according to St. John of the Cross.[117] Faith, he concluded, is not merely an intellectual assent to objective truths. The intellect cannot grasp God, for God is not merely a concept or an object. In the "dark night of the soul" the emotions are purified and the intellect gives way to love. Through this love the believer *experiences* God in the mutual exchange of self-donation. The insights Wojtyla gained in his study of the Spanish mystic—the possibility of authentic purification (redemption) of the inner man, faith as the experience of love, love as self-donation—would permeate the rest of his life's work.

This insight into faith as an *experiential* reality also provided an important foundation for Wojtyla's second dissertation on the thought of German philosopher Max Scheler.[118] Scheler was a disciple of Edmund Husserl (1859–1938), the founder of a modern philosophical method called "phenomenology" which begins with human experience. In an effort to counter Immanuel Kant's ethics of pure duty,[119] Scheler developed a rich

---

115. A complete collection of Karol Wojtyla's poems can be found in *The Place Within: The Poetry of Pope John Paul II* (New York, NY: Random House, 1982).

116. See Karol Wojtyla, *The Collected Plays & Writings on Theater* (Berkeley, CA: University of California Press, 1987).

117. See *Faith According to St. John of the Cross* (San Francisco, CA: Ignatius Press, 1981).

118. Unfortunately, this has not been published in English. The Spanish edition is *Max Scheler y la etica cristiana* (Madrid: Biblioteca de Autores Cristianos, 1982).

119. In Kant's ethics of pure duty, man must detach himself from any subjective or emotionally-felt value. An ethical action is purely a willing of the law. The only relevant "feeling" is that which arises from duty for duty's sake.

ethical system based on the emotional experience of values. However, if Kant ignored the emotional life in favor of duty, according to Wojtyla, Scheler fell prey to the opposite problem. He failed to make clear that the human person not only *feels* value, he also aspires to value. Until a person's internal world of values is entirely purified, duty continues to play an important role in the ethical life. Thus, Wojtyla concluded that Scheler's approach could not be considered a self-sufficient basis for Christian ethics. Nonetheless he recognized that a reformed phenomenological approach could be integrated with the faith and would greatly aid in bringing the much-needed stamp of subjective experience to the normative science of ethics. This is what Wojtyla set out to do.

Wojtyla would further develop the themes of experience and ethics, person and nature, freedom and law, value and duty, subjectivity and objectivity in the lectures and essays he delivered as a professor at the Catholic University of Lublin.[120] During these years (beginning in 1954 and diminishing throughout the sixties and seventies as his ecclesial duties increased) Wojtyla would sharpen his ideas against the minds of other great scholars in the "Lublin School of Philosophy." By engaging in a bold philosophical initiative that sought to link the three great fields of *metaphysics*, *anthropology*, and *ethics*, the Lublin School believed their work—if given proper exposure—could redirect the entire course of modern philosophy. Stefan Swiezawski, one of Wojtyla's colleagues in the School, would later write: "In the work and discussions of our group...we were deeply convinced that our efforts...had crucial significance not just for our university, for Poland, and for Europe, but for the whole world." The exposure they needed came when one of their own was elected pope. Swiezawski comments that their work had "suddenly found a simply unprecedented opportunity to reach all parts of the world and influence the development of the spiritual face of the coming age in every corner of the globe."[121]

Karol Wojtyla wrote his first book, *Love & Responsibility,*[122] in the late 1950's, based on years of intense pastoral work with young people

---

120. See *Person & Community: Selected Essays,* trans. Theresa Sandok (New York: Peter Lang, 1993). Other volumes of his essays are in production.

121. Ibid., pp. xiii, xvi.

122. This was first published in English in 1981 (New York, NY: Farrar, Straus, and Giroux) and reprinted in 1993 (San Francisco, CA: Ignatius Press). Citations in this book from *Love & Responsibility* are taken from the Ignatius Press edition.

and engaged and married couples. This philosophical treatise (we might even call it a "philosophy of the body") scrutinizes the way men and women experience the sexual urge, emotion, sensuality, shame, etc., and shows how these can and must be integrated with an "education in love." Wojtyla argues that failure to accept "responsibility for love" turns people into objects to be used. Furthermore, he convincingly demonstrates that Catholic moral teaching on sex and marriage corresponds perfectly with the dignity of the person and the desires of the heart for betrothed love.

The Second Vatican Council was the next major force to shape Wojtyla's thinking. The young bishop from Krakow would serve as one of the main protagonists at this pre-eminently "pastoral" Council, which sought to engage an ever-changing modern world with the unchanging truth of Jesus Christ. George Weigel reports in his biography of the Pope that Wojtyla had prepared a prescient essay for the Ante-Preparatory Commission of the Council. In it he stressed that the question of a humanism adequate to the aspirations of today's men and women should be the epicenter of the Council's concerns. The Church needed to furnish her twenty centuries-old answer to the human question in a way that would "ring true" in late modernity. With two thousand bishops from around the globe proposing and debating the best way to do so, the Council would become a kind of postdoctoral school of philosophy and theology for Wojtyla.[123] It would also spawn two more books from the Polish bishop before his ideas on implementing the Council would forever shape Church history as papal documents.

Wojtyla wrote *The Acting Person*[124] in his "spare time" following the Council to explore the philosophical foundations of the conciliar documents. This extremely dense work of philosophical anthropology is Wojtyla's most elaborate effort to wed a traditional realist philosophy with the modern turn to the subject—in other words, to wed the visions of "person" found in St. Thomas and Max Scheler. His thesis, as the title indicates, is that the irreducible core of the person is revealed through his *actions*. Experience confirms that, while some things passively happen to us, we are also free to *determine* our own actions. We are not only passive objects, but *acting subjects*. We expe-

---

123. See *Witness to Hope,* pp. 158–160.

124. *The Acting Person* was first published in Polish in 1969. It was published in English in 1979 *(Analecta Husserliana* 10; Dordrecht, Holland: Reidel). For a discussion of the controversy surrounding the English translation, see *Witness to Hope,* pp. 174–175. For an excellent summary of *The Acting Person,* see Gerard Beigel's *Faith and Social Justice in the Teaching of Pope John Paul II* (New York, NY: Peter Lang, 1997), chapter 2.

rience our actions as "our own" and "no one else's." Here "action" is incorporated into subjectivity. In this experience of freedom and subjectivity (what Wojtyla calls "efficacy") man begins to experience his own transcendence as a person. Wojtyla believes there is a law of self-giving that defines the person *objectively*. And in the experience of his own freedom, his own ability to act, man comes to experience this truth of his personhood *subjectively*.

One of the main tasks of the Council was to make the objective truths of faith an experience of life, to bring about their subjective appropriation. If *The Acting Person* seeks to provide a philosophical basis for this task, Wojtyla's book *Sources of Renewal* seeks to facilitate its pastoral implementation. This concerns not so much "how" but "what" is to be implemented. According to Wojtyla, this is the more important question.[125] The sources of the Church's renewal are found in the Holy Spirit's work in the Council and its teachings. Renewal itself, however, comes only when the work of the Spirit is incarnated through a vibrantly lived and personally appropriated faith in Jesus Christ. The "proof of the realization of the Council," Cardinal Wojtyla wrote, will be manifested when "the doctrine of faith and morals" that the Council presented resounds in "the consciousness of Christians." The Council therefore afforded "an enrichment of faith in the objective sense, constituting a new stage in the Church's advance toward 'the fullness of divine truth.'" But what is more hoped for as a fruit of the Council—and what *Sources of Renewal* seeks to facilitate—"is an enrichment [of the faith] in the subjective, human, existential sense."[126]

The next milestone in our brief retracing of the development of Wojtyla's thought was the lenten retreat he preached to Pope Paul VI and the Roman Curia in 1976. The full text of the twenty-two conferences he delivered is published under the title Wojtyla assigned: *Sign of Contradiction*.[127] Based on these words which Simeon addressed to Mary (see Lk 2:34), Cardinal Wojtyla wove a broad tapestry of uplifting, sobering, and even daring reflections on what he considers to be the question of the day: "Who is man and how does Christ fully reveal man to himself?" Through his insightful reading of the "signs of the times," he envisioned "a new Advent for the Church and for humanity. ...A time of great trial but also of great hope." He concluded, "For just such a time as this we have been given the sign: Christ, 'sign of contradiction' (Lk 2:34). And the woman

---

125. See *Sources of Renewal* (San Francisco: Harper & Row, 1979), p. 420.

126. Ibid., pp. 17–18.

127. *Sign of Contradiction* (New York: Seabury Press, 1979).

clothed with the sun: 'A great sign in the heavens' (Rev 12:1)."[128] Here again we see the way signs serve to communicate transcendent, spiritual realities. The signs Wojtyla spoke of are those of a man and a woman—the New Adam and the New Eve.

Nowhere is the Church, following her Bridegroom, more of a "sign of contradiction" than in her teaching on man and woman's relationship. Similarly, nowhere is there more of a disconnection between Church doctrine and the consciousness of Christians than in the Church's sexual ethic. Wojtyla knew that if the renewal the Council envisaged was to take root, a bridge had to be built that would enable Christians to appropriate personally and live vibrantly God's plan for human sexuality. In a 1974 essay on marriage and the family, he emphasized the need for "a special theological synthesis," in this regard, "a special theology of the body, so to speak."[129] Sometime later Cardinal Wojtyla began working on one of the most notable projects of his life—a biblical, theological reflection on the human body and sexuality founded upon and imbued with the philosophy of the human person he had developed throughout his academic and pastoral career. Little did he know, however, that he would complete his "theology of the body" as Pope John Paul II and bring it to the world-stage as his first major papal catechetical project.

■ The Holy Spirit works with the gifts, talents, and experiences of the men he chooses as successors to the Apostle Peter. Thus, a necessary continuity links the work of Karol Wojtyla and of Pope John Paul II. Even so, it is important to recognize and maintain a specific discontinuity. Although general audiences rank lower than other forms of papal teaching, the "theology of the body" falls somewhere under the umbrella of papal and magisterial teaching. This gives it a different "status" than if it had been delivered by the philosopher/theologian Karol Wojtyla. This has advantages and disadvantages. Academic proposals receive helpful academic critiques. John Paul's catechesis on the body might have benefited from this had it been a proposal of Wojtyla's. Nonetheless, the Holy Spirit's choice for pope of a man who was developing a comprehensive, biblical theology of the body based on a life-time of unique experiences and philosophical reflection seems to be a divine endorsement of the project.

---

128. Ibid., p. 206.

129. *Person & Community: Selected Essays,* p. 326.

C. What is Phenomenology?

John Paul's theology of the body echoes and contains in some way the entire history of his thinking about man. It may be his most critical attempt to forge a link between objective reality and subjective human experience, between truth and freedom, ethics and anthropology, God and man. While plunging its roots deep into the theological tradition, the Pope's theology of the body also presents "one of the boldest reconfigurations of Catholic theology in centuries."[130] Its novelty, as well as its genius, lies in the Holy Father's philosophical method and approach. Just as Augustine integrated his synthesis of the faith with the philosophy of Plato, and Aquinas with Aristotle, Karol Wojtyla/John Paul II inaugurates a new era for the Church by integrating his synthesis of the faith with phenomenology.

It is difficult to define "phenomenology." As a philosophical method, it has many variants. Though the word "phenomenology" can sound intimidating, Wojtyla's use of the method is not threatening but is quite refreshing. He uses phenomenology to retrieve the ordinary experiences of everyday life and study these phenomena *as we experience them*. By penetrating such phenomena he seeks to approach the reality of things-as-they-are. With human experience as a point of departure, Wojtyla gains a much needed and traditionally neglected perspective on the interior life of the human *person*. He discovers in the subjectivity of man's inner world a unity with the objectivity of man's outer world. By analyzing this unity he can confirm objective truths while avoiding "objectivizing" abstractions. He demonstrates that the Church's vision of man is not foisted upon him from "the outside," but corresponds to his self-experience as a person on "the inside."

With full knowledge that the Church's message "is in harmony with the most secret desires of the human heart,"[131] Wojtyla does not need and does not attempt to force assent to his proposals. Rather, he invites men and women to reflect honestly on their self-experience to see if it confirms his proposals. In doing so, Wojtyla shows remarkable respect for and trust in the freedom of the person and a bold confidence in the ability of each person's conscience to recognize—and desire—the truth when it presents itself. His presentation of the faith, therefore, is never an imposition, but always and only a proposition—an appeal to each person's freedom.[132]

---

130. *Witness to Hope,* p. 336.

131. *CCC,* n. 2126.

132. As the Council teaches, "The truth cannot impose itself except by virtue of its own truth, as it makes its entrance into the mind at once quietly and with power" *(Dignitatis Humanae,* n. 1).

Wojtyla/John Paul II's vision of man and of the ethical life cannot be understood apart from his passion and respect for human freedom. There is no place for a tyranny of truth in the life of a personal subject created for "his own sake." Truth can only have meaning in a person's life if he freely embraces it. If freedom for Wojtyla is inviolable within just limits, it also entails a particular responsibility to search for the truth and adhere to it once found.[133]

Modern philosophy has focused on subjectivity to the neglect of objectivity, and thus has erred by divorcing freedom from truth. At the same time modern philosophy has challenged men like Wojtyla to recognize that traditional formulations of the faith may well have focused on objectivity to the neglect of subjectivity. In this vein some in the Church have tended toward a presentation of truth which lacked respect for the freedom of peoples and individuals. Hence, Wojtyla believes modern philosophy's desire to begin with the subjective themes of experience, consciousness, and freedom can enrich the faith, even if Catholic thought generally opposes this to a philosophy of being and of objective truth. As a Thomist, Wojtyla would certainly side with the philosophy of being if forced to choose between the two. But he does not see it as an either/or proposition. His philosophical project has been to find the both/and—to give proper recognition to the discoveries of phenomenology without renouncing the philosophy of being; to "make room" for subjectivity within a realist philosophy.

■ Developments in theological reflection invariably meet with some resistance. Karol Wojtyla's project is no exception. Some modern students of St. Thomas, for example, see Wojtyla's acceptance of modern philosophy more as a departure from the Church's heritage than an authentic development. Yet St. Thomas himself encountered similar criticism when he built on Augustine's work and integrated his thought with Aristotelian philosophy. Thomism remains Wojtyla's intellectual foundation, but when the need arises, foundations *must* be built upon.[134] Those who are classically trained may find themselves a bit uncomfortable with Wojtyla's new approach, but there is room to go beyond St. Thomas' understanding of who man is as a person. This Pope can take us there precisely because he is a Thomist who uses all the good aspects of phenomenology.

---

133. See *CCC,* n. 2467.

134. See *Witness to Hope,* p. 87. For a fine summary of the need for John Paul's new synthesis, how this need developed, and how John Paul's new synthesis addresses this need, see Father Richard Hogan's *Dissent from the Creed* (Huntington, IN: Our Sunday Visitor, 2001), chapter 6.

Contrary to some criticisms, Wojtyla/John Paul II's respect for and use of modern philosophy in his presentation of the faith does not by any means imply a yielding of Catholicism to relativism. Rocco Buttiglione assures us that "John Paul II could repeat the words of his predecessor, Pius X, who refused to accept the errors of modern times. But the rejection of the errors of modern times does not mean that we should not correct the one-sidedness of the exposition of sound doctrine, which furnished the occasion for the rise of these errors."[135] How often is the Church's doctrine rejected because it is thought to be hopelessly removed from "real life" experience? How often have children educated in the faith rejected it as adults because their teachers—whether parents, pastors, or others—tended to impose religion upon them without respect for and education in authentic human freedom? The Church's reconciliation with freedom, Buttiglione concludes, is "of central importance in order to understand both Karol Wojtyla's pontificate and Vatican II and the contemporary crisis of the Church."[136] Freedom must be challenged to submit itself to truth, but no one can be forced to accept the truth without doing violence to the dignity of the person. When truth is presented in its full splendor, it does not need to be imposed. It has its own appeal which naturally attracts men and women. When Christians witness joyfully to the "splendor of the truth," others seek it out and embrace it freely.

In coming to embrace truth, Wojtyla distinguishes between "knowledge" and "consciousness." "According to Classical tradition, 'knowledge' is a receptive faculty, and receives the given. 'Consciousness' is rather the faculty which either interiorizes the given or rejects such an interiorization, and by doing these things constitutes the inward world of a person."[137] Knowledge of reality—and a willingness to accept that reality exists independent of me—is, of course, the first step. But this is not enough. If *knowledge* passively accepts objective truth, *consciousness* actively works to give it a subjective context and meaning in one's own life. This is extremely important. For one can know reality, but remain at odds with it by failing to interiorize it. In such case the incongruity eventually becomes too painful and the person will often deny reality in favor of a counterfeit that promises "relief." But such a person lives an illusion in which peace eludes him. For a person to be at peace with himself and the

---

135. *Karol Wojtyla: The Thought of the Man Who Became Pope John Paul II,* p. 372.
136. Ibid.
137. Ibid., p. 354.

world, he must not only know the truth, he must interiorize it, feel it, experience it, and freely embrace it as his own. To do so, he must trust the truth wholeheartedly, have an impassioned love for the objective good and abandon himself to it fearlessly. This is only possible if truth is perfect love, which is only possible if truth itself is a perfect person. Truth is. Truth's name is Jesus Christ.

Here Wojtyla's philosophy opens itself to theology, to divine love. Wojtyla's phenomenology (echoing what he learned from St. John of the Cross) ultimately calls us to an awareness of objective truth through the *experience* of divine love—through an experience of reality as the good, beatifying, gratuitous gift that it is. In *Crossing the Threshold of Hope*, John Paul observes that classical philosophy recognizes that "nothing is in the intellect that was not first in the senses." Nevertheless, he then emphasizes that *"the limits of these 'senses' are not exclusively sensory."* Man can "sense" the transcendent. He has a "religious sense."[138] "It is therefore possible," the Pope affirms, "to speak from a solid foundation about *human experience, moral experience, or religious experience*. And if it is possible to speak about such experiences, it is difficult to deny that, in the realm of human experience, one also finds good and evil, truth and beauty, and God."[139]

This interior *experience* of God is gained not only by intelligent discernment and technical knowledge (although these are important), but also through the engagement of the deepest impulses of one's person—through the meeting of one's freedom with the God who gave us freedom as the capacity to meet him. In short, if the traditional philosophy of being addresses the "God question" by providing rational proofs for his existence, Wojtyla's philosophical project addresses the same question by inviting each person to "taste and see"—engage your freedom in self-donation and *experience* God's love for yourself. In this way "proof" of God's existence is verified not only in the mind but even more so in the heart. People understand a concept with the mind, but people love persons with the heart. Ultimate Reality is much more than a concept. It is a Person. "And we find ourselves by now," John Paul asserts, "very close to St. Thomas, but the path passes not so much through being and existence as through people and their meeting each other, through the 'I' and the 'Thou.'...In the *sphere of the everyday* man's entire life is one of 'coexistence'—'thou' and 'I'—

---

138. For an in-depth study of this idea, see Luigi Giussani, *The Religious Sense* (Montreal: McGill-Queen's University Press, 1997).

139. *Crossing the Threshold of Hope,* pp. 33–34.

and also in the *sphere of the absolute and definitive*: 'I' and 'THOU.'" And so John Paul concludes that our *"faith is profoundly anthropological,* rooted constitutively in coexistence, in the community of God's people, and *in communion with this eternal 'THOU.'"*[140]

■ The following image may help to distinguish between "knowledge" and "consciousness." If it is raining outside, metaphysical knowledge would accept this as a given—as an objective reality outside oneself and not determined by oneself. But if it is raining, our experience can and should confirm this. Not only could we look outside and see it, but we could step outside and *feel* it. Applying the image, if the Church's doctrine on faith and morals is true, our experience can and should confirm this. John Paul's goal is to get us to step into the rain, to *experience* it, get soaked, and to spend our lives joyfully playing in the rain like a child. Taking this image a step further, we can recognize the need of childlikeness if we are to *experience* the objective truth as a liberating good ("unless you turn and become like children"—Mt 18:3). Some might have a (metaphysical) knowledge of the rain, but be at odds with it internally. If such a person fails to become like a child, he will either live in a state of continual resentment toward the rain, or he will deny its existence and create his own illusory world "unhindered" by "undesirous" weather. But herein lies the devil's perennial deception—reality (God) is not a hindrance, it is not undesirous. Submission to reality (God) is ultimate freedom and the fulfillment of every desire. But only a "child" can see this. Only children like to play in the rain.

D. Wedding Objectivity and Subjectivity

By wedding the objective and subjective world views, John Paul II provides a "total vision of man" that avoids the pitfalls of abstraction *and* subjectivism. Here again we encounter the great "nuptial mystery." At the crux of the marriage of objectivity and subjectivity is the union of God and man in the person of Christ. In Christ, our humanity—body and soul—embraces ultimate reality without any incongruity. From Wojtyla's perspective, the moral relativism that has resulted from the modern "turn to the subject" is only the product of an anthropological stagnation in the absence of faith. In other words, man turns to himself and "stays" there, failing to see that his own humanity points him beyond himself. To use the nuptial image, moral relativism results from the Bride (man) looking in a mirror without recognizing the nuptial meaning of her own body which

---

140. Ibid., p. 36.

opens her to union with her Bridegroom (Christ). In the absence of this openness to the "Other"—that is, in the absence of faith (recall John Paul's definition of faith as "openness to the gift of God")—the Bride opts for a sterile, narcissistic self-focus. At this point the "subjective turn" erodes into subjectivism.

But when the Bride recognizes the nuptial meaning of her humanity and opens to Christ, human subjectivity is gradually purified and ultimately becomes completely objective.[141] Human subjectivity becomes informed by Truth himself. In the marriage of subjectivity and objectivity, the subjective "ethic of feeling" (the imbalance of Scheler) and the objective "ethic of duty" (the imbalance of Kant) become integrated in the perfectly subjective and objective "ethos of redemption" (the balance of Wojtyla/John Paul II).

■ As we shall see, prior to sin, the subjective experiences of Adam and Eve completely accorded with objective reality. The harmony of subjective experience with objective reality becomes tenuous only as a result of having lost "purity of heart." Redemption in Christ, however, offers us the possibility of gradually regaining the purity of our origins. The harmony of subjective and objective reality, then, solidifies in our *experience* of the efficacy of redemption—that is, in the real power of redemption to restore "purity of heart." Because of the strong tendency to impurity, people often hold the subjective experiences of the heart in suspicion, fearing they can never come in tune with objective reality. This is understandable. But, as John Paul stresses, "Man cannot stop at putting the 'heart' in a state of continual and irreversible suspicion.... Redemption is a truth, a reality, in the name of which man must feel called, and 'called with efficacy.'"[142]

Therefore, John Paul's Christo-centric theological anthropology saves the modern desire to "start with man" from ending in subjectivism. If it is true, as faith teaches, that man is made in the image of God and is created for eternal union with him, then starting with man—if we stay the course—will ultimately end with God. Starting with the subjective perspective will ultimately lead to objective reality *if* we follow John Paul and *press into that link between theology and anthropology* "with faith, an open mind, and all our heart."[143]

---

141. See Mary Shivanandan, *Crossing the Threshold of Love* (Washington, DC: Catholic University of America Press, 1999), p. 21.

142. 10/29/80, TB 167.

143. *Dives et Misericordia,* n. 1.

If modern rationalism makes man the measure of all things, theological anthropology discovers that *the God-man* is the measure of all things. Jesus Christ "is the center of the universe and of history." The Word made flesh "fully reveals man to himself"—not by tyrannically asserting his divine prerogatives (this would contradict the dignity of a creature made for "its own sake"), but by making the humble and sincere gift of himself to man. Man, in turn, discovers his rightful place in the universe when he freely receives this gift and makes a "sincere gift" of himself back to God and to others.[144] As we shall see more clearly through our study of the Pope's catechesis, these profound truths are stamped in the "great mystery" of masculinity and femininity and in our call to become "one flesh."

Rationalism fails man right here. It "does not accept the mystery of man as male and female, nor is it willing to admit that...*Christ reveals man to himself.* In a certain sense this statement of the Second Vatican Council," John Paul II proclaims, "is the reply, so long awaited, which the Church has given to modern rationalism."[145] The epilogue will revisit this "reply to modern rationalism" in light of all that we learn from the Pope's theology of the body. As an extended commentary on *Gaudium et Spes,* n. 22, the theology of the body is perhaps Wojtyla's most important, provocative, and challenging engagement with modernity because it takes us to the crux of the crisis: the relationship of man and woman and the meaning of their union in "one flesh."

9. The *Humanae Vitae* Crisis

In the first year of his papacy, John Paul II, with his distinctive Christian humanism, had already challenged Marxist ideology in Latin America and Communism in his native Poland. In early September, 1979 he began challenging another modern revolution with the "full truth" of the human person—the sexual revolution. Based on our previous discussion about the roots of ethics and culture, and as history attests, this revolution was

---

144. These passages from *Gaudium et Spes,* n. 22 ("Christ fully reveals man to himself") and n. 24 (man is created for "his own sake" but can only find himself through "the sincere gift of self") summarize the essential theological and philosophical proposals of the Second Vatican Council regarding who man is and how he is to live. They are so pivotal in the work of John Paul II that one would be hard pressed to find any significant catechetical project of his that did not use these texts.

145. *Letter to Families,* n. 19.

bound to bring disaster. But where sin abounds, grace abounds even more. If the Holy Spirit grants the Church what she needs when she needs it, the gift the Holy Spirit has given to the Church in our day is John Paul II's theology of the body.

A. The Point of Contention

Wise men and women throughout history, and certainly not just Christians, have recognized that respect for the procreative function of sexual union is the linchpin of sexual morality.[146] Hence, if the modern brand of sexual "liberation" was to flourish, this linchpin had to be removed. Here lies the main point of contention in the clash between the Church and the modern world—the Church's insistence that God established an inseparable link between sex and procreation, a link that man cannot break. This clash involves two irreconcilable anthropologies— two irreconcilable concepts of the *human body* and of human sexuality.[147] Rationalism sees the body only as a biological reference point while the Church has always taught that the body is an integral part of the human *person.*

These disparate anthropologies collided when Pope Paul VI's encyclical *Humanae Vitae*—which reaffirmed the Church's constant teaching on the immorality of contraception—fell like a bomb on the Church in 1968. If it was understandable that people outside the Church might dismiss the papal pronouncement as antiquated gibberish, the uproar the encyclical caused *within the Church* showed how far the rationalist view of man had seeped into the minds of Catholics. Yet when the *Humanae Vitae* crisis broke, Karol Wojtyla was already well prepared to dialogue with the modern world on this issue. In 1978, after the whirlwind of two conclaves within seven weeks—the second of which ended with the election of this Polish philosopher and theologian—it seemed God was saying that Wojtyla's new ethical synthesis had great import for the universal Church.

---

146. Even Sigmund Freud observed in his *Introductory Lectures in Psychoanalysis* (New York: W. W. Norton and Company, 1966) that the "abandonment of the reproductive function is the common feature of all perversions. We actually describe a sexual activity as perverse," he wrote, "if it has given up the aim of reproduction and pursues the attainment of pleasure as an aim independent of it" (p. 392).

147. See *Familiaris Consortio,* n. 32.

B. The Need for a Personalist Ethic

One thing is certain about the complex ecclesial crisis that followed *Humanae Vitae:* the old-style ethics of the moral manuals—often legalistic, impersonal, and authoritarian—proved woefully inadequate to stem the cultural tide pushing for contraception. John Paul was confident, however, that the philosophical project he and his colleagues from the Lublin school had so carefully nurtured could make a difference. By bringing this project to bear in full force, John Paul courageously believed he could demonstrate that *Humanae Vitae* was not against man but unstintingly *for* him; that *Humanae Vitae* was not opposed to conjugal love and sexual pleasure, but called men and women to the most spiritually intense expression of them. In light of the virtual catechetical failure of Paul VI's encyclical, John Paul knew he had to make a compelling case for *Humanae Vitae.* For the newly elected pope understood well that contraception effectively disorients "the deepest substratum of human ethics and culture." It alters humanity's course at its foundations—away from a culture of love and life and toward a culture of utility and death.[148] The *Humanae Vitae* crisis is anything but peripheral. Just two and a half months before taking the chair of Peter, on the tenth anniversary of *Humanae Vitae*, Karol Wojtyla described the issue of contraception as a "struggle for the value and meaning of humanity itself."[149] As the title of the encyclical indicates, the integral truth *of human life* is at stake—the integral truth of the human person. The discussion had to be framed accordingly.

The cry that the Church "just isn't 'in touch' with real life experience" especially targets her sexual ethic. Prior to the mid-twentieth century, Church pronouncements on sexual matters had focused mainly on the exterior "duties" of spouses, and the objective "ends" of the sexual act—formulated in a strict hierarchy as procreation, the mutual help of spouses, and the remedy for concupiscence. Attention seemed almost fixated on the "primary end" of procreation with little or no attention given to the mean-

---

148. For a detailed discussion of the destructive sequellae of contraception, see Christopher West, *Good News About Sex & Marriage: Answers to Your Honest Questions About Catholic Teaching* (Ann Arbor, MI: Servant Publications, 2000), pp. 118-125. See also Patrick Fagan, "A Culture of Inverted Sexuality," *Catholic World Report,* November 1998, p. 57.

149. Cited in *Crossing the Threshold of Love,* p. 113.

ing and experience of conjugal love.[150] Objectively speaking, the traditional formulation on the ends of marriage is true. But for most people today, focusing merely on the objective reality tends to create a "disconnect" with the interior experience of the persons involved. As John Paul says, "We cannot consider the body an objective reality outside the personal subjectivity of man." Hence, questions of sexual morality are closely bound up "with the content and quality of the subjective experience" of the persons involved.[151]

C. The Personalistic Norm

Personalism treats ethical questions from this "insider's" point of view. In his book *Love & Responsibility*, Wojtyla seems to reproach antiquated explanations of sexual ethics, insisting that the "personal order is the only proper plane for all debate on matters of sexual morality."[152] Accordingly, students of theology will recognize a new focus in the Pope's analysis. For example, John Paul speaks much more about the *interior meaning* of sexual union as self-donation for the sake of the communion of persons than about the *objective end* of sexual union as procreation. However, as the Pope himself asserts, "In this renewed formulation, the traditional teaching on the purposes of marriage (and their hierarchy)" is not done away with, but "is reaffirmed and at the same time deepened from the viewpoint of the interior life of the spouses."[153] John Paul's personalism, therefore, does not separate us from objective truth as some think. Rather, through his explicit appeal to personal experience, the Holy Father provides "subjective resonance" for objective norms.

Applying his philosophical project, the Pope recognizes that as a person, man is conscious of his acts. This means he can *experience* the objective good that fulfills him and the evil that harms him. When he does, the objective norm no longer feels imposed from the outside, but wells up from within. People no longer feel forced to conform to truth. They *want* to conform to truth. John Paul maintains that, despite sin, an "echo" of God's original plan remains deep within every human heart. In his theol-

---

150. Some have tried to find a place for conjugal love among the traditional ends of marriage by equating it with the "mutual help of spouses." Love, however, is not an "end" of marriage at all. It is the governing form of marriage from which the ends flow (see §97).

151. 4/15/81, TB 218.

152. *Love & Responsibility,* p. 18.

153. 10/10/84, TB 407.

ogy of the body, the Pope aims to help people peel away the layers of debris that cover the true desires of their hearts so that this "echo" can resound. The more it does, the more our subjective experience harmonizes with objective reality. The more that echo resounds, the more we can read the "language of the body" and the desires of our hearts "in truth." People who come to understand the Pope's theology of the body cannot help but recognize the inner movements of their own hearts being laid bare. It rings true. "I can identify with this," they respond. "I experience life this way. I desire this."

This "insider's view" of the ethical life crystallizes in what Wojtyla calls the *personalistic norm*. In its negative form, it states that *a person must never be used as a means to an end*. We know from our experience that this violates our dignity. In its positive form, it states that *the only proper response to a person is love*.[154] We know also from experience that the deepest desire of our hearts is to love and be loved. The opposite of loving, then, for Wojtyla, is not hating, but *using*. Such using often masquerades as love. Since the sexual revolution dawned, at least two generations of men and women have now been groomed in the "art" of sexual utility.

But the human heart cannot feign solace in a world of sexual utilitarianism for long. As more and more people *experience* the self-inflicted wounds of a counterfeit sexual liberation, the world is fast becoming a mission field ready to soak up John Paul's message. By relinking the desires of the human heart with the truth, the theology of the body offers true sexual liberation—the freedom for which Christ has set us free, the freedom to love in the image of God as male and female. In fact, the Pope's theology of the body has already sparked an ever-growing "sexual counter-revolution." It resembles the revolution that toppled the iron curtain—starting slowly and quietly in human hearts that welcome the truth that this Polish Pope proclaims about the human person. Then it spreads from heart to heart, gathering a great multitude who glimpse their true dignity and will not rest until the shackles of dehumanizing ideologies (political, sexual, or otherwise) break.

This revolutionary quality of the Pope's catechesis led George Weigel to describe the theology of the body as "a kind of theological time bomb set to go off, with dramatic consequences...perhaps in the twenty-first century." Since Karol Wojtyla has taken modern philosophy's "turn to the subject" so seriously, Weigel believes that when this time bomb explodes, "the *theology of the body* may well be seen as a critical moment

---

154. See *Love & Responsibility*, p. 41.

not only in Catholic theology, but in the history of modern thought."[155] Looking at the subject alone turns us into navel-gazers. In this environment, an idolatrous, self-indulgent cult of the body trumps the "abstractions" of theology. However, a theology *of the body*—which links the modern turn to the subject with objective and ultimate reality—provides the necessary bridge for the modern world to reconnect with Christ.

Christ—the *theological* Word made *flesh*—is the link between the human person and the ultimate reality. Christ himself *is* ultimate reality. In his body "given up for us," we come to see the ultimate meaning of our own bodies revealed. In this way "Christ fully reveals man to himself." John Paul II's theology of the body, then, is nothing but an incarnate meeting with the Incarnate Christ. As such, it is not only a dramatic "time bomb," but also a gentle, whispering affirmation of the truth every person intuits—we are made as male and female for a love that never ends. The "revelation of the body" is that that love is God: Father, Son, and Holy Spirit.

D. Structure of the Catechesis

Modern rationalism presents only partial truths about man and effectively divorces him from the nuptial mystery the body reveals. Paul VI recognized this "disconnect" when he stated that the problem of birth regulation, like every problem regarding human life, must be considered beyond partial perspectives. It must be seen in light of a "total vision of man" and his vocation, not only his natural and earthly, but his supernatural and eternal vocation.[156] Herein lies the main inspiration for John Paul II's catechesis.[157]

Through an in-depth reflection on Christ's "key words" about human embodiment and erotic desire, John Paul provides this "total vision of man," or what he calls an "adequate anthropology." These "key words" refer to Christ's discussion with the Pharisees about God's plan for marriage "in the beginning" (see Mt 19:3–9), his words in the Sermon on the Mount regarding lust and adultery committed "in the heart" (see Mt 5:27–28), and Christ's discussion with the Sadducees regarding the body's resurrected state (see Mt 22:23–33). We call these "key words," John Paul says, "because they open for us, like a key, the individual dimensions of theological anthropology."[158] By constructing this theological anthropol-

---

155. *Witness to Hope,* p. 343.
156. See *Humanae Vitae,* n. 7.
157. See 4/2/80, TB 87.
158. 1/26/83, TB 365.

ogy based on Christ's own words about the body, John Paul not only places the Church's sexual ethic in its proper anthropological context, but he also shows that the teaching of *Humanae Vitae* is rooted in divine Revelation—in the words of Christ himself.

In short, John Paul's catechesis seeks to tackle the *Humanae Vitae* crisis by addressing two questions: "Who is man?" and, based on this, "How is he supposed to live?" These questions frame the two main parts of the catechesis, what we will call "Establishing an Adequate Anthropology" and "Applying an Adequate Anthropology." In turn, each of these two parts of the catechesis contains three "cycles."[159]

The first three cycles are known as the "triptych" of the theology of the body and are based on those three "key words" mentioned above. To understand adequately who man is, we must look at the three "levels" or "stages" of the human drama: Cycle 1, *Original Man*, concerns man's experience of sexual embodiment before sin; Cycle 2, *Historical Man*, concerns man's experience of sexual embodiment affected by sin yet redeemed in Christ; and Cycle 3, *Eschatological Man*, concerns man's experience of sexual embodiment in the resurrection. The order of the cycles is part of the proposed theological methodology for an adequate anthropology.

■ The clear boundaries between these "stages" of human experience (original sin delineates original man from historical man and Christ's second coming delineates historical man from eschatological man) speak of the discontinuity between them. Yet, as we shall see, a profound continuity also marks the human drama. Christ is this continuity, for he—as the eternal One and as the center of the universe and of history—is "present" in all three states as in one moment. We must separate this eternal moment into different stages within time, but they all refer to Christ and in him they are one.

The final three cycles of the Pope's catechesis address how man is to live by applying "the triptych" to the issue of vocation and to "the deepest substratum of ethics and culture." Cycle 4 addresses *Celibacy for the Kingdom*; Cycle 5, *The Sacramentality of Marriage*; and Cycle 6, entitled *Love and Fruitfulness*, re-examines the teaching of *Humanae Vitae* in light

---

159. Some expositions of John Paul's theology of the body are not clear on its basic two-part, six-cycle structure. The fact that the English texts were originally published in four volumes may have caused some confusion. The proper structure is important for understanding the Pope's overall project and approach.

of the entire preceding analysis. The Holy Father even describes all that he has said in his catechesis "as an ample commentary on the doctrine contained in the encyclical *Humanae Vitae*." Questions come from this encyclical, he says, that "permeate the sum total of our reflections." Hence, the contents of the final cycle are also found in the first cycle and throughout the catechesis. "This is important," John Paul says, "from the point of view of method and structure."[160]

With regard to this method and structure, some people find the Pope's talks annoyingly repetitive. He repeats himself not only to recap the previous week's themes, but also because of his circular style of reflection. Linear thinking starts from point A and goes straight to Z. But this is not as conducive for a mystical phenomenologist seeking to penetrate the "great mystery." Rather than a straight line, John Paul's catechesis is more like a spiral that takes us deeper and deeper into its basic themes. Each time he revisits a theme, he brings us another revolution deeper into the spiral, drawing us ever closer to the "heart" of that mystery that reunites God and man in an eternal embrace.

Prologue—In Review

1. Christ's body justifies the expression "the Gospel of the body." The story of Christ's body—from its conception in the womb of a Virgin to its crucifixion, resurrection, and ascension into heaven—*is* the Gospel. And every*body* that comes into the world is destined to share in the Gospel that is Christ's body by becoming "one body" with Christ. We seek to ponder this mystery in our study of John Paul II's theology of the body.

2. Remaining "naked" before the Father, the New Adam presents the specific antidote to Adam's fear: "I was afraid, because I was naked; and I hid myself." Christ reveals the perfect love of the Father which casts out fear. In this way the Incarnate Christ "fully reveals man to himself."

3. Physical signs convey transcendent, spiritual realities. The Pope speaks of a theology *of the body* because the human body is the original "sign" of God's own mystery in the world. The divine mystery certainly cannot be reduced to its sign. Yet the sign is indispensable in the revelation of the mystery. Only the body is capable of making visible what is invisible. In fact, according to the Pope's thesis, the body "was created to transfer into

---

160. 11/28/84, TB 420, 422.

the visible reality of the world, the mystery hidden since time immemorial in God, and thus to be a sign of it."

4. John Paul's catechesis on the body seeks to link theology and anthropology in a deep and organic way. The body reveals as in a "sacrament" the mystery of the person. Christ's body is a sacrament of a divine Person and thus reveals the divine ways of the Trinity. The scandal of this "divinization" of the flesh never fails to confound the human heart.

5. All analogies are inadequate in their attempts to communicate the divine Mystery. Yet the spousal analogy appears as the *least* inadequate because it captures a particle of the Mystery itself. In focusing on this particle, we must always be careful, however, to respect the mysterious and infinite difference that exists between human-spousal communion and divine-Christian communion.

6. The "nuptial mystery" provides a lens through which to view and penetrate the most important theological and anthropological truths of our faith. Hence, John Paul's theology of the body is not merely a catechesis on sex and marriage, but a specific, evangelical, Christian education in the meaning of being human. It concerns God's entire plan for man in creation and redemption.

7. We can see the fundamental importance of the nuptial mystery by looking at the signs of the Old and New Covenants. The sacrifice of Abraham's flesh and blood in the sign of circumcision seems to foreshadow Christ's sacrifice of flesh and blood in the Eucharistic/paschal mystery. Both of these signs indicate in their own respective ways the mystery of fruitful love and communion—the mystery of God's generous Fatherhood.

8. If the primordial sacrament of nuptial communion enabled the first man and woman to participate in God's life and love, the deceiver—intent on divorcing man from God's life and love—mounted his counter-plan by attacking this sacrament. John Paul's theology of the body is a clarion call for Christians to reclaim what Satan has plagiarized.

9. The original temptation attacked God's benevolent love. *"Original sin, then, attempts to abolish fatherhood."* In man and woman's heart, the primordial sign of God's covenant love became, in some way, a counter-sign. In other words, by accepting the devil's lie, the "symbolic" became "diabolic."

10. Man and woman must now contend with the "great divorce" that ruptured the original harmony of body and soul. Without reintegration in Christ, people either lean toward a "spiritual" life cut off from the body

("angelism") or a "carnal" life cut off from the spirit ("animalism"). This body-soul split lies at the root of the "culture of death."

11. The call to nuptial love and communion revealed by our sexual bodies "is the fundamental element of human existence in the world," "the foundation of human life," and, hence, "the deepest substratum of human ethics and culture." Indeed, the human project stands or falls based on the proper ordering of love between the sexes. Thus, it "is an illusion to think we can build a true culture of human life if we do not...accept and experience sexuality and love and the whole of life according to their true meaning and their close inter-connection."

12. Christ heals the "great divorce" and reunites us with the nuptial mystery through the very dynamism of the Incarnation. If man is to find himself, "he must 'appropriate' and assimilate the whole reality of the Incarnation and Redemption." He must be willing to die with Christ in order to be resurrected in the unity of flesh and spirit. Man cannot live without Christ because man cannot live without love. Christ's body—and every body—is a witness to Love.

13. The "subjective turn" in modern philosophy and the West's massive shift from religion to science demand a new synthesis of the faith to which the contemporary world can relate. Reading the "signs of the times," Karol Wojtyla set out on a bold philosophical project to integrate the faith with the insights of the modern philosophy of consciousness, without sacrificing anything essential to the traditional philosophy of being.

14. Wojtyla uses the philosophical method of phenomenology to retrieve the ordinary experiences of everyday life and study these phenomena *as we experience them* and, in this way, approach the reality of things-as-they-are. In turn, Wojtyla gives the mark of subjective experience to the objective science of ethics. He shows that the demands of the Gospel are not imposed from the "outside," but well up from "within" man.

15. Wojtyla shows an unstinting respect for persons and their freedom. A tyranny of truth has no place in the life of a personal subject created for "his own sake." Truth only has meaning for a person when he embraces it freely. The Church's reconciliation with freedom in this regard is essential if we are to understand John Paul II's pontificate, the Second Vatican Council, and the contemporary crisis in the Church.

16. By "making room" for subjectivity within an objective or realist philosophy, Wojtyla avoids the pitfalls of objectivizing rigorism and subjectivizing relativism. In this marriage of objectivity and subjectivity we encounter again the "nuptial mystery" of God's union with humanity in

Christ. A theological anthropology prevents the "subjective turn" from stagnating on man. It enables man (the Bride) to remain open to Christ (the Bridegroom).

17. The ecclesial crisis surrounding the encyclical *Humanae Vitae* points to the crucial need for a new context in which to understand the Christian sexual ethic. Nowhere does Wojtyla's philosophical project prove more fruitful than right here. As a corrective to antiquated explanations of sexual ethics that were often impersonal, legalistic, and authoritarian, John Paul II's theology of the body provides a winning personalistic affirmation of *Humanae Vitae*.

18. Paul VI stated that the teaching of *Humanae Vitae* must be viewed in light of a "total vision of man." John Paul II's catechesis on the body provides this "adequate anthropology" in its first three cycles: *Original Man*, *Historical Man*, and *Eschatological Man*. In the final three cycles, the Pope applies this "total vision of man" to the question of vocations—*Celibacy for the Kingdom* and *The Sacramentality of Marriage*—and then concludes with a reflection on *Humanae Vitae*.

PART I

WHO ARE WE?
ESTABLISHING AN ADEQUATE ANTHROPOLOGY

Cycle 1

Original Man

This first cycle consists of twenty-three general audiences delivered between September 5, 1979 and April 2, 1980. Although in this cycle John Paul primarily reflects on the creation accounts in Genesis, he explicitly begins with the words of Christ. By basing the three cycles of his "adequate anthropology" on the words of the Incarnate Word, he makes a deliberate anthropological statement. If his goal is to meditate on the human body in order to discover who man is as male and female, the "richest source for knowledge of the body is the Word made flesh. *Christ reveals man to himself.*"[1]

John Paul finds a source of great hope for all men and women in Christ's discussion with the Pharisees about marriage. If conflict, tension, jealousies, and divisions have tarnished the relationship of the sexes throughout history, Christ challenges his listeners to recognize that "from the beginning it was not so" (Mt 19:8). With these words, Christ calls all men and women burdened by the heritage of sin to a radical paradigm shift by reestablishing the original unity of the sexes as the norm for all who become "one flesh."

As the *Catechism* teaches, "According to faith the discord we notice so painfully [in the relationship of the sexes] does not stem from the *nature* of man and woman, nor from the nature of their relations, but from *sin*. As a break with God, the first sin had for its first consequence the rupture of the original communion between man and woman."[2] Yet the "good news" that Christ came to reconcile God and man means he also reconciles man and woman. "By coming to restore the original order of creation

---

1. *Letter to Families*, n. 19.
2. *CCC*, n. 1607.

disturbed by sin, [Christ] himself gives the strength and grace to live marriage in the new dimension of the Reign of God." Therefore, "by following Christ, renouncing themselves, and taking up their crosses...spouses will be able to 'receive' the original meaning of marriage and live it with the help of Christ."[3] Even if the heritage of sin carries with it the entire history of discord between the sexes, the roots of man and woman's relationship go deeper, and Christ enables us to tap into that deeper heritage.

The Church's teaching on marriage and sexuality can never be adequately understood apart from God's original plan, our fall from it, and our redemption in Christ. Many modern men and women find the Church's teaching on marriage and sexuality untenable because they remain locked in a fallen view of themselves and the world. This narrow horizon makes it easy to "normalize" disordered patterns of thinking and relating. The pain and conflict that inevitably ensue may lead people to yearn for something more, and such pain shows that we are created for something more. But without any reference to God's original plan and the hope of its restoration in Christ, people tend to accept the discord between the sexes as "just the way it is."

The following image may help frame our discussion. When we normalize our fallen state, it is akin to thinking it normal to drive with flat tires. We may intuit that something is amiss, but when everyone drives around in the same state, we lack a point of reference for anything different. In Christ's discussion with the Pharisees, he points them back to man and woman's "fully inflated" state. In turn, through his penetrating exegesis of the Genesis texts, John Paul seeks to reconstruct the experience of "full inflation." Just as tires are meant to be inflated, we know that we long for the original unity of man and woman. Pushing the analogy, the good news is that Christ did not come into the world to condemn those with flat tires. He came in love to fill our tires once again with air. To the degree that we experience this "re-inflation" (which is never perfect in this life), the Church's teaching on marriage and sexuality is no longer viewed as a rigid ethic imposed from "without." It is experienced as a liberating ethos welling up from "within."

---

3. *CCC*, n. 1615.

10. Christ Directs Us Back to "the Beginning"

September 5, 12, 19, 1979 (TB 25–30)[4]

Men and women of all times and cultures have raised questions about the nature and meaning of marriage. As John Paul observes, such questions are raised today "by single persons, married couples, fiancés, young people, but also by writers, journalists, politicians, economists, demographers, in a word, by contemporary culture and civilization" (87). The questions of modern men and women are charged with problems unknown to the Pharisees who questioned Jesus about the lawfulness of divorce. Even so, Jesus' response to the Pharisees is timeless. In it John Paul finds the foundation for establishing an adequate vision of who men and women are—or, more so—who they are called to be and, thus, how they are called to live when they join in "one flesh."

According to the Gospel of Matthew, the dialogue between Christ and the Pharisees took place as follows:

> And Pharisees came up to him and tested him by asking, "Is it lawful to divorce one's wife for any cause?" [Jesus] answered, "Have you not read that he who made them from the beginning made them male and female, and said, 'For this reason a man shall leave his father and mother and be joined to his wife and the two shall become one flesh'? So they are no longer two, but one flesh. What therefore God has joined together, let no man put asunder." They said to him, "Why then did Moses command one to give a certificate of divorce and to put her away?" He said to them, "For your hardness of heart Moses allowed you to divorce your wives, but from the beginning it was not so" (Mt 19:4–8, see also Mk 10:2–9).

A. Unity and Indissolubility

Moses allowed divorce as a concession to sin, but Christ can re-establish the original unity and indissolubility of marriage because he is "the Lamb of God who takes away the sin of the world" (Jn 1:29). Moses' reason for divorce, therefore, no longer holds sway. As the Holy Father says: "That 'let no man put asunder' is decisive. In the light of these words of

---

4. The dates of the audiences from which the content of a section is drawn will appear under each section heading along with the page numbers from the TB volume. The exact page from the TB volume will also follow each quote for quick reference. When quotes are pulled out of sequence from a future or previous audience, they will be referenced with a footnote. Recall that quotes are taken from the original Vatican translation and the one-volume copyedited version may vary slightly.

Christ, Genesis 2:24 [the two become 'one flesh'] sets forth the principle of the unity and indissolubility of marriage as the very content of the Word of God, expressed in the most ancient revelation" (26).[5] But as the Pope also points out, Christ does not merely use his authority to re-establish an objective norm. He invites his questioners to reflect on the beauty of God's original plan in order to awaken their consciences. This original plan is stamped in them. "The hardness of their hearts"[6] has obscured it, but it is still within them. Christ knows that if they traced the "echoes" of their hearts back to "the beginning," this norm would well up *from within*. They would understand *subjectively* the reason for the *objective* indissolubility of marriage. And if they lived from this deeper heritage of their hearts, they would desire nothing else.

The same holds true for the many people today who question the meaning of man and woman's relationship. If we are to provide adequate answers to contemporary questions, we too must take Christ up on his invitation to reflect on God's plan "in the beginning." Thus John Paul begins his investigation of the Genesis texts.

B. Two Creation Accounts

Many have been surprised by John Paul's concern to show that his biblical interpretation harmonizes with contemporary methods. For example, he seems to take for granted the view of many modern scholars that the two creation accounts in Genesis were written at different times by different authors (see 27–28).[7] The so-called "Elohist" account of Genesis 1 derives from "Elohim," the term used for God in this account. The "Yahwist" account of Genesis 2 and 3 (believed to be a much older text than the Elohist account) is so named because it uses the term "Yahweh" for God.

The Elohist account is loaded with a "powerful metaphysical content," defining man "in the dimensions of being and existence" (29). In fact, man is the only creature defined in relation to Being itself. He is the only creature defined *theologically*—not with a likeness to the other crea-

---

5. See *CCC*, n. 1644.

6. In the Hebrew, what we translate "hardness of heart" actually meant "non-circumcision of the heart." Since circumcision was the sign of the old covenant, John Paul notes later in his catechesis that non-circumcision meant "distance from the covenant with God" and "expressed unyielding obstinacy in opposing God" (8/6/80 first endnote, TB 184).

7. See also *CCC*, n. 289.

tures, but with a likeness to God. "In the seven-day cycle of creation...the Creator seems to halt before calling [man] into existence, as if he were pondering within himself to make a decision: 'Let us make man in our image, after our likeness'" (28). John Paul elaborates by saying that the first phrases of the Bible make it clear that man cannot be reduced to the elements of the world. He is certainly a physical creature, but he is also more than that; man is spiritual. The creative tension of the unity of body and soul defines him. This latter point is decisive for a theology *of the body.* "Man, whom God created 'male and female,' bears the divine image imprinted *on his body* 'from the beginning.'"[8] This establishes an "unassailable point of reference" in order to understand who we are (anthropology) and how we are to live (ethics).

Deeply imbedded in the truth of anthropology and ethics is man and woman's call to "be fruitful and multiply." This original divine blessing corresponds with their creation in God's image. As the prologue noted, the capacity to "pro-create" (not as a response to biological instinct but by the free choice proper to persons) enables them to participate in the creative, covenant love of God. Precisely in this context it is necessary to understand the reality of the good or the aspect of value. With God's affirmation that everything he created is "very good" (Gen 1:31), we can conclude that "being and the good are convertible" (29). This means that everything that exists is good in itself. Nothing that exists is evil in itself. Evil, by definition, is always and only the deprivation of what is good. Therefore, to exist—just to *be*—is very good. More specifically, to exist *as male and female* and to bring more males and females into existence ("be fruitful and multiply") is very good. To think otherwise is unbiblical. This philosophy of value (axiology) lies at the foundation of every Christian discussion about creation, and about human existence in particular.

In describing man's creation and his call to be fruitful and multiply, John Paul points out that the Elohist account contains only the objective facts and defines the objective reality. On the other hand, the Yahwist account seeks to penetrate man's psychology. In doing so it presents the creation of man especially in its subjective aspect. As the Pope states: "The second chapter of Genesis constitutes, in a certain manner, the most ancient description and record of man's self-knowledge, and together with the third chapter it is the first testimony of human conscience" (30). With such explicit attention paid to man's "interiority," John Paul says that the Yahwist account provides "in nucleo" nearly all the elements of analysis of man to which contemporary philosophical anthropology is sensitive.

---

8. 1/2/80, TB 58; emphasis added.

Here the Holy Father is referring to the modern "turn to the subject" of which we previously spoke.

Significantly, Christ referred to *both* creation stories when he directed the Pharisees back to "the beginning." In this way Christ's words confirm that both the objective and the subjective elements of the "one flesh" union are indispensable in establishing a proper understanding of man and woman's relationship. As an exegete seeking to penetrate man's "interiority" in order to confirm objective truth, John Paul will spend most of his time examining the subjective experiences of Adam and Eve from the Yahwist text. By doing so, he brings a dramatic development of thinking to our understanding of the Elohist teaching that man is made in the divine image.

11. Echoes of Our Original Experiences

September 19, 26; October 10, 24, 31, 1979 (TB 30–40)

The tree of the knowledge of good and evil marks the "boundary" between the state of original innocence (integral nature) and the state of historical sinfulness (fallen nature). Without any direct experience of it, "historical" men and women find it difficult to imagine what life was like on the other side of this boundary. Although we cannot actually cross this boundary, Christ orders us "in a certain sense to go beyond the boundary" (31).

A. An Essential Continuity

John Paul emphasizes that there is *"an essential continuity and a link* between these two different states or dimensions of the human being." The historical state "plunges its roots, in every man without any exception, in his own theological 'prehistory,' which is the state of original innocence" (32). Elsewhere he explains that there is imprinted in the experience of fallen man "a certain 'echo' of original innocence itself: a 'negative,' as it were, of the image, whose 'positive' had been precisely original innocence."[9] Although the negative of a photograph reveals something of the positive image, it needs to be "flipped over" for the colors to take on their true light. Thus even though we have no experience of original innocence, we can reconstruct it to a certain degree by "flipping over" our experience of innocence lost. If we listen, we can still hear the original experience

---

9. 2/4/81, TB 204.

echoing in our hearts. In fact, John Paul describes this echo as a "co-inheritance" of sin. Sin is only intelligible in reference to original innocence. If sin means literally to "miss the mark," the word implicitly refers to the mark we are missing: original innocence.

When that echo of innocence resounds in us, we experience a deep awareness of our own fallenness, of grace lost. But this should not cause us to despair, because it also opens us to the possibility of redemption, of grace restored. How tragic it would be if upon (re)discovering the beauty of God's original plan, we found no way to overcome sin in order to live it. Christ is the way! As we take up Christ's invitation to ponder our "beginning," we must keep in mind that there is *real power* in him to regain what was lost. Yes, we will always struggle with sin in this life because we have left the state of innocence irrevocably behind. Nonetheless, through "the redemption of the body" (Rom 8:23) won by Christ, we can come progressively to live as we were called to in the beginning. John Paul will continually return to this Pauline concept. By "redemption of the body" John Paul does not mean to single out one of the results of redemption. Rather, he intends to summarize the entire reality of Christ's Incarnation and paschal mystery. For John Paul, "the redemption of the body" is redemption itself. Man is always embodied man. Thus, just as a theological anthropology must be a theology of the body, so too must man's redemption be a redemption of the body.

"It is precisely this perspective of the redemption of the body that guarantees the continuity and unity between the hereditary state of man's sin and his original innocence" (34). In other words, if we could not begin reclaiming what was lost, the historical state would be hopelessly cut off from man's original vocation and destiny. The deepest longings of the heart would lead only to despair. But John Paul insists on this hopeful point: Historical man "participates not only in the history of human sinfulness as a...personal and unique subject of this history." He "also participates in the history of salvation, here, too, as its subject and co-creator" (33). Herein lies the meeting point of the remarkable gift of God with the mystery of human freedom. In the face of grace lost, God presents us with the sheer gift of salvation, but it remains up to us to accept the gift. As free agents, that is, as persons, we must cooperate with God in our own salvation. Through faith ("openness to the gift"), then, we become subjects and "co-creators" in salvation history.[10] From this perspective, historical man comes to view the "beginning" (original man) as his true fullness. The gift

---

10. See *CCC,* nn. 306, 2008.

of salvation gives birth to the hope of returning in some way to the beginning at the end (eschatological man) as a sort of homecoming.

B. Revelation and Experience

John Paul observes in an endnote that many people see a line of complete antithesis between God's revelation and human experience. The Holy Father readily recognizes that human experience is inadequate for understanding revelation. But he still affirms it as a legitimate means of theological interpretation and a necessary reference point. "In the interpretation of the revelation about man, and especially about the body, we must, for understandable reasons," the Pope stresses, "refer to experience, since corporeal man is perceived by us mainly by experience" (34). In the second endnote of this same address, John Paul asserts that we have a right to speak of the relationship between experience and revelation. Without this we ponder only "abstract considerations rather than man as a living subject" (94).

John Paul wants to unearth the "deep roots" of the Church's teaching on marriage and sexuality. Those deep roots are found in human subjectivity. Throughout his biblical exegesis, John Paul tries systematically to show how the dimension of man's personal subjectivity is an indispensable element in outlining a theology of the body. He says that "not only the objective reality of the body, but far more, as it seems, subjective consciousness and also the subjective 'experience' of the body, enter at every step into the structure of the biblical texts." Therefore, both subjective consciousness and experience must be considered and find their reflection in theology.[11] Here again John Paul seeks to justify his use of the phenomenological method in presenting the faith. We need not be suspicious of the philosophy of consciousness so long as we remain rooted in objective truth. Indeed, the original subjective experiences of man and woman prior to sin completely accorded with objective truth. By penetrating their consciousness we find reality reflected there. We find reality *experienced* and given its proper subjective resonance.

When John Paul speaks of "original human experiences," he has in mind not so much their distance in time but their basic significance. These original experiences did not take place in history as we understand it. As John Paul uses the word, "history" begins only with the "knowledge of good and evil," whereas the original experiences the Pope reflects on refer to a mysterious "prehistory." Furthermore, he attempts to reconstruct these experiences not so much to determine precisely who man and woman

---

11. See 4/15/81, TB 218.

were "then," but to help us better understand *who we are now*—more so, who we are meant to be. In the final analysis, we cannot know the events and experiences of our "prehistory" with any "historical" certainty—that is, not as we understand history today. We know that the human race sprang from one man and one woman, and that through "a deed that took place *at the beginning of the history of man,*"[12] they disobeyed God and fell into sin. However, we approach these primeval events and experiences only by pondering "the symbolism of the biblical language."[13]

Explicitly appealing to the contemporary philosophy of religion and of language, the Holy Father states that this biblical language is mythical. He clarifies that the term "myth," however, "does not designate a fabulous content, but merely an archaic way of expressing a deeper content."[14] Thus, John Paul is not conceding to the idea that the biblical creation stories are merely human fabrications. By describing these divinely inspired stories as "mythical," he is simply acknowledging that our "theological prehistory" is shrouded in mystery. Myth, symbol, and metaphor are the only means at our disposal if we wish to enter into the mystery of our "beginning."

Mysterious as our prehistory is, the original experiences of man and woman remain at the root of every human experience. "They are, in fact, so intermingled with the ordinary things of life that we do not generally notice their extraordinary character."[15] John Paul focuses on three such experiences: *original solitude, original unity,* and *original nakedness.* His analysis takes us to the extraordinary side of the ordinary. The first extraordinary thing we recognize is the depth of original insight that John Paul extracts from one of the most familiar stories in the Bible. The Holy Father brings the Scriptures to life—to each and every human life. By penetrating these original human experiences, John Paul enables us to see that the story of Adam and Eve, far from being abstract, is a story about each of us. His insights resound in us. This is the gift afforded by John Paul's incorporation of the modern "turn to the subject."

C. Original Solitude

"It is not good that the man should be alone; I will make him a helper fit for him" (Gen 2:18). These words of God-Yahweh form the basis of the Pope's reflections on *original solitude.* As we shall see, original solitude

---

12. *CCC,* n. 390.

13. *CCC,* n. 375.

14. 11/7/79, TB 43.

15. 12/12/79, TB 51.

will have an ample perspective in John Paul's reflections. To begin with, it has two basic meanings. The most obvious meaning derives from the male-female relationship. Man is "alone" without woman. But John Paul insists that this solitude has a more fundamental meaning, one derived from man's nature. He is "alone" in the visible world as *a person.*

It is significant that the first man (*'adam* in Hebrew), is not defined as a male *('ish)* until after the creation of woman *('ishshah).* So Adam's solitude is not only proper to the male. It is proper to "man" as such, to every human person. As John Paul says, this solitude is "a fundamental anthropological problem, prior, in a certain sense, to the one raised by the fact that this man is male and female" (36). It is prior not so much in the chronological sense but "by its very nature," since it is man's first discovery of his own personhood. In this way, being a body—being *some*body, a body-person—"belongs to the structure of the personal subject more deeply than the fact that he is in his somatic constitution also male or female."[16]

In other words, the "first" human experience is one of simply "being a body," not of being as a body male or female. Experience of sexuality, of being male or female, is in some sense "secondary" to this primary experience. The essential point is that, although sexual difference is fundamental to the meaning of our humanity, each human being (each body-person) stands with his own dignity as a subject *prior* to his call to live in communion with an "other" person via the gift of sexual difference. If one is to give himself away in an incarnate communion with an "other," he must first be the kind of creature capable of doing so; he must first be a "body-person." This is the essential significance and "priority" of original solitude.

Acknowledging Adam's need for a helper, God first creates the animals and brings them to the man to see what he will call them. Naming the animals is certainly to be seen as preparation for the creation of woman; however, John Paul demonstrates that it has a profound significance in itself. By naming the animals, Adam realizes he fundamentally differs from them. He looks for a "helper fit for him," but fails to find one among the animals. The experience only confirms his solitude. Adam's capacity to *name* the animals speaks of his fundamental difference from them. He has dominion over the earth and all its creatures. Adam's capacity to "till the earth" also reveals this. Tilling is a specifically human activity that seems to belong to the definition of man since no other living being is capable of it.

Adam realizes his unique capacity to "name" and to "till" through his experience of embodiment—through the unique relationship between his soul and body. In this psycho-somatic relationship, John Paul says "we

---

16. 11/7/79, TB 43.

touch upon the central problem of anthropology" (40). Through the experience of the body we penetrate man's self-consciousness, his experience and "discovery" of being a person. Adam is aware of himself; the animals are not. He has self-determination; the animals do not. He can consciously choose his acts; the animals cannot. He can consciously choose to *till* and *to name;* "and whatever the man called every living creature, that was its name" (Gen 2:19).

Thus, in naming or identifying the animals, he actually discovers his own "name," his own identity, his own freedom. "For created man finds himself, right from the first moment of his existence, before God as if in search of...his own 'identity'" (36). And man's self-knowledge "develops at the same rate as knowledge...of all the living beings to which man has given a name to affirm his own dissimilarity with regard to them" (37). In other words, to the extent that Adam realizes he differs from the animals, he realizes who he is as a person. Solitude, therefore, signifies man's subjectivity.

John Paul observes that naming the animals is a "test" of sorts through which man gains self-awareness. "Analyzing the text of...Genesis we are, in a way, witnesses of how man 'distinguishes himself' before God-Yahweh from the whole world of [animals] with his first act of self-consciousness." In this way Adam comes "out of his own being"; "he reveals himself to himself and at the same time asserts himself as a 'person' in the visible world" (37). Here it seems we already find a foreshadowing of the new Adam, Jesus Christ, who, according to the familiar passage from Vatican II, will fully reveal man to man himself. Later John Paul will say that the first Adam already bore the capacity and readiness to receive all that would become the second Adam, Jesus Christ.[17] From the beginning man was created as a Bride for Christ. Adam is already discovering this in his solitude, that he is made for communion.

Thus, human "dominion" over creation is essential not only to man in solitude, but also to man in the unity of male and female. In the Yahwist text, man needs a "helper" in his vocation to "till and keep" the garden. In the Elohist account, man and woman's vocation to fruitful union is coupled with their call to "subdue the earth" and to have "dominion over the fish of the sea, and over the birds of the air, and over every living thing that moves upon the earth" (Gen 1:28). In fact, man's experience of sexual difference and the call to communion will determine the way man exercises his dominion over creation. The loving communion of man and woman will facilitate a "loving" care of and for creation. But if love were

---

17. See 2/3/82, TB 253.

denied in the male-female relationship, responsible dominion over creation would lead to abuse of the visible world.[18]

12. Solitude Prepares Man for Communion

October 24, 31, 1979 (TB 38–42)

In just a few sentences from the creation narrative in Genesis 2, we can perceive with great depth the subjectivity of the human being. The Yahwist text makes it clear that man's creation as a person "is revealed not on the basis of any primordial metaphysical analysis, but on the basis of a concrete subjectivity of man" (40). This demonstrates the objective-subjective complementarity of the two creation stories. Adam's experience of solitude in the Yahwist narrative is his *subjective* realization of being created in God's image, as *objectively* described in the first creation account. In other words, what the Elohist account only observes externally (man is a person made in God's image), the Yahwist account confirms by penetrating man's interiority—his consciousness, his psychology, his experience.

In fact, the Holy Father says that without understanding Adam's subjective experience of solitude, we cannot understand who man is as a creature made in God's image. Recognizing this objective-subjective harmony is crucial to John Paul's entire project. Through this harmony, the anthropological definition of the Yahwist text approaches the theological definition of man from the Elohist text. Here, right from the start, we are pressing into the link between theology and anthropology. If in the Yahwist text solitude is the frontier of communion, communion too will shed light on the image of God in man that the Elohist text speaks of.

A. Partner of the Absolute

From the beginning, man was created to be, as John Paul describes, a "partner of the Absolute." As a personal subject, he was called to enter a covenant with God, a relationship of eternal communion. Above all, as "subject of the covenant," man's solitude "means that he, through his own humanity, through what he is [i.e., a person], is constituted...in a unique, exclusive, and unrepeatable relationship with God himself" (38). We cannot understand who man is apart from his supreme call to enter a covenant of love with his Creator. Of course, this call to communion with God is not man's due. It is a sheer, gratuitous gift,[19] but a gift that reveals man's great-

---

18. See *CCC*, n. 373; see also *Evangelium Vitae*, n. 42.

19. See *CCC*, n. 367.

ness. "The dignity of man rests above all on the fact that he is called to communion with God."[20] Our call to receive this gift explains who man is and why he aspires to "something more." St. Augustine said it well: "You have made us for yourself, O God, and our heart is restless until it rests in you."[21]

This call to be "partner of the Absolute" hinges on man's freedom, his ability to determine his own actions. For John Paul, the term "self-determination" encapsulates a lifetime of philosophical reflection. It enables us to approach the kernel of the human person, of what distinguishes man from the other "bodies" in the world. God did not command the animals not to eat from the tree of the knowledge of good and evil, only Adam. Why? God's command presents a choice, and only *persons* have the free will necessary to choose. Human beings are the only creatures in the visible world that can disobey God. A squirrel cannot commit a sin. Nor can a squirrel choose to open itself to an eternal covenant of love with God. Love presupposes freedom. In other words, if God gives us as human beings the choice of entering an eternal covenant with him (and one another), we also have the choice of rejecting that covenant. If Adam chose to eat the forbidden fruit, he would die. This "death" differs from the possibility of death for the animals, because human death reveals human personhood.

The Holy Father says that based on man's experience of his own freedom, he should have understood that the forbidden tree had roots not only in the garden of Eden, but also in his own humanity. "He should have understood, furthermore, that the mysterious tree concealed within itself a dimension of loneliness hitherto unknown" (41–42). This is not the loneliness of original solitude that confirmed man's personhood. This is the loneliness of *alienation* from God that would be man's death.[22]

B. Liable to Non-Existence

John Paul poses an interesting question. Could Adam even have understood the words "you shall die," since he had no experience of death, only life? He concludes that man, "who had heard these words, had to find their truth in the very interior structure of his own solitude" (41). In his solitude before God, Adam was totally aware of his dependence on God for

---

20. *Gaudium et Spes,* n. 19; *CCC,* n. 27.

21. See *CCC,* nn. 27, 30, 1718, 1024.

22. Mary Shivanandan describes this alienation as the third meaning of solitude. See *Crossing the Threshold of Love,* p. 101. See also §22.

his existence. In turn, he would have known that he was a limited being, by nature liable to nonexistence. Hence, he could have understood "death" in contrast to his original experience of having received life as a gift from his Creator. Here, just as historical man can envision original man's experience by contrasting it with his own, so too could original man envision the experience of "death" by contrasting it with his own experience of life.

In this way "the alternative between death and immortality enter, right from the outset, the definition of man and belongs 'from the beginning' to the meaning of his solitude before God himself"(42). One might say that man's solitude as a free creature suspends him, in some sense, between the tree of life and the tree of the knowledge of good and evil. He alone can choose his own destiny: death or immortality. No one can choose for him. And he *must* choose. Freedom, then, is man's capacity for eternity. It is his capacity for eternal life in communion with God *and* his capacity for eternal death in alienation from God.

In this way, original solitude enables us to understand that man is constituted in his very being by a relationship of *dependence* and *partnership* with God: dependence because man is a creature; partnership because man is a person created by a personal God who always extends to him a covenant of love. As we will learn, Satan's temptation to eat from the forbidden tree attacks this relationship of *partnership* and *dependence.* If God is not a God of love who extends a relationship of partnership to man, then dependence on this God comes to be seen as a threat to man's subjectivity. As a subject, man earnestly resists enslavement, and rightly so. Thus, the moment man perceives God as a domineering tyrant, he will shirk his dependence on him. Thus Satan attacks God's benevolent Fatherhood, as the prologue noted.

John Paul tells us that this original meaning of solitude, permeated by the alternative between death and immortality, has a fundamental meaning for the whole theology of the body. It already sums up man's fundamental vocation: love of God and love of neighbor (see Lk 10:27). Furthermore we shall see even more clearly in future reflections how original solitude already points man to his eschatological destiny of eternal communion with God. It already outlines the cosmic struggle involved if man is to claim that eternal destiny, a struggle that is always lived out in man's body.

C. The Body Expresses the Person

We might be tempted to think that man's knowledge of himself and his relationship to God was purely spiritual. But man was constituted as a specific unity of spirit and body. The Yahwist narrative expresses this by saying: "The Lord God formed man of dust from the ground, and breathed into his nostrils the breath of life; and man became a living being" (Gen 2:7). In the original language, the word "breath" is the same word for "spirit." Through his body (his "dust"), then, man lives "in the spirit"—his own spirit, and according to the Holy Spirit. Through the experience of his own body man comes to understand who he is and who God is.

The human body is so similar to animal bodies (especially other mammals) that, as John Paul observes, we might think that Adam would have reached the conclusion, based on the experience of his own body, that he was substantially similar to animals. However, while the animals were also created from the ground, the Yahwist text does not state that God breathed his Spirit into them. Hence, while in naming the animals, the man certainly realized that he was a "body among bodies," he also reached the conviction that he was alone.

The important point here is that everything we have been discussing about man's solitude—about his difference from the animals, his subjectivity as a person, his call to eternal communion with God, etc.—is revealed and experienced *through the body*. "This consciousness," the Pope says, "would be impossible without a typically human intuition of the meaning of one's own body" (40). If it is true that the "invisible" determines man more than the "visible," it is also true that the visible expresses the invisible. John Paul insists that "the body expresses the person. It is, therefore, in all its materiality, almost penetrable and transparent, in such a way as to make it clear who man is (and who he should be)" (41).

This is a remarkable assertion since we tend to think of personhood as a merely spiritual reality, not a material one. *Human* personhood is always a materialized-spiritual reality. Man's original solitude (the first realization of personhood) is revealed through the body: The body reveals that it is "not good for the man to be alone." The body reveals man's call to communion with "a helper fit for him." This is the more familiar meaning of original solitude. In naming the animals, Adam found many other "bodies." But none of these bodies revealed a person, as did his own body. Here we can sense Adam's deep longing for an-*other* body that reveals an-*other* person who is called to communion with him.

Man's experience of original solitude,[23] then, paves the way for the creation of this "other" and already anticipates the experience of *original unity*. In John Paul's mind, all this has deep implications for the meaning of our being created in the image of God.

---

23. *CCC*, n. 357 offers a concise summary of original solitude.

13. The Creation of Woman

November 7, 1979 (TB 42–45)

Man is not fully human—his creation is not complete—until he emerges in his "double unity" as male and female. Double unity speaks of a "two-in-oneness," which is man's completeness. Everyone knows the experience of "incompleteness." It drives us to seek communion with others. Not only do we want to be with others; we want to *know* another person and have our persons *known* by another person. Thus, we can all relate to the biblical expression that "it is not good to be alone." If man is to be fully himself, he needs a "helper."

Although only a few words describe woman's creation, John Paul shows that each one carries great weight. He remarks that the "mythical" language of the ancient narrative of Genesis leads us to that deep and mysterious content of woman's creation with ease. With the enthusiasm of a man in love with God's word, he adds that the text of woman's creation "is really marvelous as regards the qualities and the condensation of the truths contained in it" (43).

A. The Meaning of Adam's "Sleep"

We read in Genesis 2, "So the Lord God caused a deep sleep to fall upon the man, and while he slept took one of his ribs, and closed up its place with flesh; and the rib which the Lord God had taken from the man he made into a woman and brought her to the man." John Paul comments that contemporary men and women might immediately associate this "deep sleep" with a Freudian analysis of dreams and the subconscious, which, in Freud's mind, were always sexual. But "deep sleep" (*tardemah* in Hebrew) indicates not so much a passing from consciousness to subconsciousness, as a passing from consciousness to un-consciousness. For Adam, this deep sleep is "a specific return to non-being," since sleep almost annihilates man's conscious existence. As John Paul states in an endnote, this "emphasizes the *exclusivity of God's action* in the work of the creation of woman; the man had no conscious participation in it" (95).

■ *Tardemah,* John Paul notes, "is the term that appears in Holy Scripture when, during sleep or immediately afterwards, extraordinary events are to happen" (95). Interestingly, the Greek translation of the Hebrew Old Testament translates *tardemah* with *ekstasis*—"ecstasy" in English. While John Paul only makes passing reference to this, it is worth posing a possible meaning of Adam's sleep understood as a state of "ecstasy." Not only can we infer that Adam was "ecstatic" upon discovering the woman, but ecstasy literally means "to be outside oneself." And what is it that comes "outside" of the man? Woman. To go "outside oneself" also seems to connote the "sincere gift of oneself."

If by way of the analogy with sleep we can speak also of a dream, the content of Adam's dream, according to John Paul, is certainly that of finding a "second self" (in other words, someone who experiences solitude as a person and longs for communion). Yes, John Paul muses that Adam fell asleep dreaming of the perfect lover, you might say. Of course, we must not project onto Adam the way a fallen man might dream about an idealized and depersonalized body to suit his enjoyment. No, Adam dreamed in the purity of original innocence. He dreamed of an "other" body that revealed an "other" person, a person he could love as God loves. When he awoke, his dream had came true.

There "is no doubt," says the Holy Father, "that man falls into that 'sleep' with the desire of finding a being like himself. ...In this way the solitude of the man-person is broken, because the first 'man' awakens from his sleep as 'male and female'" (44). In this "sleep" the generic man is "recreated" to be sexually differentiated as a unity in two ("double unity"). Even if it is fraught with difficulties and confusion now due to sin, does not everyone come, in some sense, to a stage of sexual "awakening"?

B. The Meaning of Adam's Rib

The Holy Father observes that being fashioned from Adam's rib is an "archaic, metaphorical, and figurative way" of expressing woman's creation (44). While some have thought this demeans women, John Paul stresses that the biblical author intends to affirm the indispensable equality of the sexes and place it on a sure foundation. As the Pope expresses it, Eve's creation from Adam's rib indicates "the homogeneity of the whole being of both" (44). In other words, man and woman are made from the same "stuff." They share a common humanity. Later in his catechesis, John Paul states that "rib" also seems to indicate the heart—yet another affirmation that man and woman share the same humanity and the same dignity.[24]

Masculinity and femininity, then, are two "incarnations" of the same solitude before God and the world—two ways, in other words, of being a body-person made in God's image. Masculinity and femininity "complete each other." They are "two complementary dimensions...of self-consciousness and self-determination and, at the same time, two complementary ways of being conscious of the meaning of the body."[25]

---

24. See 5/23/84, TB 369.
25. 11/21/79, TB 48.

Recall that in naming the animal-bodies Adam realized he was "alone" in the world as a person. But upon sight of the woman-body he proclaims ecstatically, "This at last is bone of my bones and flesh of my flesh." With this exclamation the Holy Father explains that he seems to say: "Here is *a body that expresses another person.*"[26] For the Jews, bones meant simply "the human being."[27] "Bone of my bones," John Paul states in an endnote, "can therefore be understood in the relational sense, as 'being of my being'; 'flesh of my flesh' means that, though she has different physical characteristics, the woman has the same personality as the man" (96).

John Paul considers Adam's declaration the biblical prototype of the Song of Songs. The words of Genesis 2:23 are the original love song. They express "for the first time joy and even exaltation" (45). Later in his catechesis the Pope says that Adam's words "express wonder and admiration, even more, the sense of fascination."[28] "And if it is possible to read impressions and emotions through words so remote, one might also venture to say that the depth and force of this first and 'original' emotion of the male-man in the presence of the humanity of the woman...seems something unique and unrepeatable" (45). In short, the gift of woman enthralls Adam. At last, having named animal after animal only to remain "alone," he has found one who is *like himself* (yet also different in very important ways). He has found another person whom he can *know* as a person and be *known* by as a person. This is the rich significance of God creating woman from Adam's rib.

Because Adam's "awakening" entails the discovery of another person, John Paul says that the sense of original solitude becomes part of the meaning of original unity. In other words, the self-discovery of personhood enabled by man's solitude carries over into the experience of original unity. In fact, original unity will be, in some sense, the definitive discovery of what it means to be a person. The Holy Father says that the "key point" of original unity "seems to be precisely the words of Genesis 2:24...'the two shall become one flesh.' If Christ, referring to the 'beginning,' quotes these words, it is opportune for us to clarify the meaning of that original unity which has its roots in the fact of the creation of man as male and female" (42).

---

26. See 1/9/80, TB 61.
27. See Psalm 139:15, for example.
28. 5/23/84, TB 369.

14. Male-Female Communion: Icon of the Trinity

November 14, 1979 (TB 45–48)

In its primary meaning, the word "sex" refers to the differentiation of male and female, not to what they do together in becoming "one flesh." Thus, in the Yahwist account, prior to man's sexual "awakening" as male and female, man is in some sense "sexless" because he still lacks the "other." According to God's words, this "is not good," so sexual difference has an axiological meaning. In other words, masculinity and femininity have a *specific value* both before God and for each other. If it is "not good for man to be alone," it is good—*very* good—to exist as male and female, one *for* the other, and to join in the original unity of "one flesh."

A. Original Unity Overcomes and Affirms Solitude

The beauty and mystery of sexual difference specifically reveals man and woman's call to union. And sexual difference specifically allows that union to pass from an objective calling to an incarnate, subjective reality. "In this way, the meaning of man's original unity...is expressed as an overcoming of the frontier of solitude, and at the same time as an affirmation—with regard to both human beings—of everything that constitutes 'man' in solitude" (45).

What does the Pope mean by this? Recall that original solitude has two meanings. Original unity overcomes man's solitude without woman (and we can also speak of woman's solitude without man). But the experience of original unity *affirms* their solitude in the sense that they differ from the animals because their union also differs essentially from that of animals. As persons both man and woman have self-knowledge and self-determination. They are both subjects in the world and are conscious of the meaning of their bodies. This is the heart of the experience of man's solitude as a person in the visible world. Because this is common to man *and* woman, John Paul speaks not only of a "double unity," but also of a "double solitude." Only two *persons* are capable of rendering to each other that biblical "help." Only two *persons* are capable of love. "Double solitude," then, is the indispensable foundation of original unity. It is also the sure foundation of the true equality of man and woman.

In keeping with the Second Vatican Council, the Pope defines this unity as *communio personarum*—a "communion of persons."[29] John Paul says that the term "community" could also be used here if it were not ge-

---

29. See *Gaudium et Spes*, n. 12.

neric and did not have so many meanings. *"Communio"* expresses more and describes their unity with greater precision, he says, "since it indicates precisely that 'help' which is derived, in a sense, from the very fact of existing as a person 'beside' a person" (46). "In this communion of persons the whole depth of the original solitude of man...is perfectly ensured and, at the same time, this solitude becomes in a marvelous way permeated and broadened by the gift of the 'other.'"[30] In other words, their uniqueness as persons is not diminished in becoming "one" with the other. Instead, through communion, man and woman live *together, with,* and *for* each other in such a way that they rediscover themselves, affirming all that it means to be a person, affirming "everything that constitutes 'man' in solitude." John Paul says that this opening up to the other person (original unity) is perhaps even more decisive for the definition of man than his realization that he differed from the animals (original solitude).[31]

B. A Dramatic Development of Catholic Thought

Here we find ourselves at the threshold of a dramatic and long-needed development of Catholic thought in regard to how we image God. The function of this image, according to John Paul, "is to reflect the one who is the model, to reproduce its own prototype" (46). The model of course is the Trinity. Hence, traditional formulations posited man's imaging of God in various trinitarian breakdowns of an individual's soul (e.g., memory, understanding, and will). The divine model, however, is not one person divided in threes. The prototype of the image is, as John Paul describes it, "an inscrutable divine communion of Persons" (46).

Notice that God even refers to himself in the plural: "Let *us* make man in *our* image, after our likeness" (Gen 1:26). We "can then deduce that man became the 'image and likeness' of God not only through his own humanity, but also through the communion of persons which man and woman form right from the beginning" (46). In other words, not only as a rational individual does the human person image God (not only in the experience of original solitude), but also in the communion formed by man and woman (the experience of original unity).

This marks a bold theological move on the Pope's part. Positing the divine image in the male-female communion has not been the traditionally held perspective. But John Paul clearly affirms that "man becomes the im-

---

30. 2/13/80, TB 74.

31. See *CCC,* nn. 371–372 for a concise summary of the themes of original solitude and unity.

age of God not so much in the moment of solitude as in the moment of communion." He even states that this "Trinitarian concept of the 'image of God'...constitutes, perhaps, the deepest theological aspect of all that can be said about man." Furthermore, he makes the deliberate point of stating that on "all of this, right from 'the beginning,' there descended the blessing of fertility linked with human procreation" (47). This will forever mark a critical development in Christian anthropology. Through his Wednesday audiences, and even more authoritatively in later statements,[32] John Paul brings the previously dismissed idea[33] that man and woman image God *in and through their communion* into the realm of official magisterial teaching.

C. Incarnate Communion

Man's experience of solitude and unity as male and female brings us almost to the core of the anthropological significance of the body. The body reveals the mystery of man. But because man, even in his corporeality as male and female, is "similar to God," the body also reveals something of the mystery of God. Thus, the Pope explains that this core of the meaning of the body is not only anthropological, but also essentially theological. This is why he speaks of a theology *of the body*. The body reveals man and woman's call to communion and enables them to enter into it, thus imaging in some way the communion in God.

As John Paul stresses, this is an "incarnate communion"; it is from the beginning a communion in "one flesh" (Gen 2:24). Therefore, the "theology of the body, which right from the beginning is bound up with the creation of man in the image of God, becomes, in a way, also the theology

---

32. See, for example, *Mulieris Dignitatem*, nn. 6–7. See also *CCC*, nn. 357, 1702, 2205.

33. Although they framed the question somewhat differently, both Augustine and Aquinas (among others) rejected the idea that male-female unity and fruitfulness imaged the Trinity. See St. Augustine, *On the Trinity*, book 12, chapter 5 and St. Thomas Aquinas, *Summa Theologica*, question 93, article 6. However, Michael Waldenstein argues that, when read carefully, St. Thomas' and John Paul II's positions are not irreconcilable. He states that "according to both St. Augustine and St. Thomas one can speak, and speak properly, of a union of love between the divine persons in terms that are drawn from interpersonal love between human beings. This conclusion shows that the teaching of John Paul II about the image of God is implicitly contained in St. Augustine and St. Thomas, even though they do not state it explicitly" ("Pope John Paul II's Personalist Teaching and St. Thomas Aquinas: Disagreement or Development of Doctrine?", lecture presented at Thomas Aquinas College, January 12, 2001).

of sex." It becomes "the theology of masculinity and femininity" (47). A "deep consciousness of human corporeality and sexuality," the Pope even says, "establishes an inalienable norm for the understanding of man on the theological plane" (48). In other words, we cannot understand man theologically without understanding the meaning of sexual difference and our call to sexual communion. This call touches upon the core anthropological reality. As already stated, this core is also theological. From this perspective, sexual communion is an icon in some sense of the inner-life of the Trinity. Of course, this does not mean that God is sexual. When using this analogy we must always recall the infinite dissimilarity between God and his creature. But this does not mean the analogy is extrinsic. Sexual difference and the call to union intrinsically reveals something of the perfect distinction, unity, and fruitfulness within the Trinity.[34]

As such, John Paul says that Genesis 2:24 ("the two shall become one flesh") is a perspective text; that is, it "will have in the revelation of God an ample and distant perspective" (47). In fact, we can even recognize that in some sense the original unity of the sexes contains "in nucleo" all that God has to reveal to man about who God is (an eternal Communion of Persons), who we are (male and female in the divine image), and how we are to live (in a similar communion of persons). It even provides a glimpse into the nature of our ultimate destiny (the communion of saints in communion with the Trinity). We will learn that man and woman's incarnate communion right from the beginning foreshadows God's definitive revelation in Christ and his incarnate communion with the Church. *This* is why God created us as sexual beings—to prepare us as an eternal Bride for Christ.

Indicating the course of his future reflections, John Paul mentions two of the dimensions of the "one flesh" union that will demand attention: the *ethical* dimension and the *sacramental* dimension. These two "dimensions" are also interrelated. For we cannot understand the Christian sexual *ethic* unless we understand what the union of the sexes means as a *sacramental sign* of Christ's union with the Church (see Eph 5:31–32).

■ The whole reality of married life is, of course, a sacrament of sexual unity—the unity of male and female in a life-long bond. But as John Paul states, the "one flesh" union "is the regular sign of the communion of...husband and wife."[35] It serves as the sign that summarizes (or consum-

---

34. See *CCC*, nn. 42, 239, 370.

35. 9/27/80, TB 141.

mates) the whole reality of the giving of husband and wife to each other. As the Pope also says, "All married life is a gift; but this becomes most evident when the spouses, in giving themselves to each other in love, bring about that encounter which makes them 'one flesh.'"[36] Thus, John Paul affirms that by means of the "one flesh" union, the body "assumes the value of a sign, in a way, a sacramental sign."[37] Cycle 5 will further explore the multiform reality of the "sacramental sign" of marriage.

15. Relationality and the Virginal Value of Man

November 21, 1979 (TB 48–51)

We are trying to understand man, as John Paul says, in the "entire endowment of his being, that is, in all the riches of that mystery of creation, on which theological anthropology is based" (48). In this quest, the Pope affirms that the laws of knowing man correspond to those of his being.[38] And knowledge of man in the deepest essence of his being must always pass from solitude to communion.

Man is not fully himself when he is "alone." He can only find himself in relation. Thus, for John Paul, *relationality* enters the definition of the human person. As he says, to be a person "means both 'being subject' and 'being in relationship.'"[39] This starkly contrasts with the radical individualism promoted in the West today.

A. Relational Definition of Person

Mary Shivanandan notes that while "medieval philosophers did develop a relational notion of the Persons in the Trinity," they "did not translate this to their anthropology."[40] This had to wait for the insights of phenomenologists like Wojtyla. His *theological* anthropology makes this neglected translation with ease. It is precisely "as image of God [that] we live in relation."[41] Philosophical anthropology cannot ascertain the divine explanation of man's call to exist "in relation." John Paul bases his development on the following teaching of the Second Vatican Council:

---

36. *Letter to Families,* n. 12.

37. 10/22/80, TB 163.

38. See 9/26/79, TB 32.

39. 5/30/84, TB 371.

40. *Crossing the Threshold of Love,* p. 143.

41. *CCC,* n. 2563.

...the Lord Jesus, when praying to the Father "that they may all be one...even as we are one" (Jn 17:21–22), *opened up new horizons closed to human reason* by implying that there is a certain parallel between the union existing among the divine persons and the union of the sons of God in truth and love. It follows, then, that if man is the only creature on earth that God has wanted for its own sake, man can fully discover his true self only in a sincere giving of himself.[42]

This teaching brings us to the heart of the mystery of what it means to be a human "person." God creates us not for his sake. He does not need us for himself. God is totally complete in his own Trinitarian Communion. Nonetheless, love diffuses itself; it wants to share and give its own goodness, ever enlarging the circle of participation and communion. Hence, God creates us for *our own sake,* out of the sheer gratuitousness of his love. He creates us so that we might have the opportunity to participate in his own eternal goodness, in his own mystery of Communion. It is true that the world was made for the glory of God. However, as the *Catechism* (quoting St. Bonaventure) explains, this means that "God created all things 'not to increase his glory, but to show it forth and communicate it,' for God has no other reason for creating than his love and goodness."[43]

This is Gods' gift to us—his own love and goodness. But he does not force it on us. To do so would contradict the reality of "gift." It would contradict the reality of our being created for *our own* sake. Respecting us as persons, God leaves us in the freedom and power of our own counsel. We can participate in the gift of love and communion only by opening ourselves to receiving it *as a gift* (faith) and by making a sincere gift of ourselves in return. When we engage our freedom to open to "the gift," life itself becomes thanks-*giving (eucharistia)* for having been given so great a gift (see §7).

This clarifies the logic of the Council's teaching. Created for his "own sake," man can only fulfill himself through the "sincere gift" of self. In other words, man can only fulfill himself in authentic relation *to* and *with* other persons. A theology of the body shows us that this "relationality" is fundamentally revealed by sexual differentiation. Every human being—"with all his spiritual solitude, with the uniqueness, never to be repeated, of his person"—is either a "he" or a "she." Sex, then, and thus the call to communion, is "not just an attribute of the person," but is in this sense a "constituent part of the person" (49).

---

42. *Gaudium et Spes,* n. 24, emphasis added.
43. *CCC,* n. 293.

If men and women are to "find themselves," the solitude of every "he" or "she" must lead to the communion of a human "we" through the mutual self-giving of one to the other. The original unity and mutual enrichment of the sexes, therefore, marks "the whole perspective of [man's] history, including the history of salvation" (49). This, however, does not mean that everyone is called to the married state. It does mean that we are all called to live in communion with others through the sincere gift of self. According to God's original plan, marriage is the most fundamental expression of that call to communion, the paradigm or model in some sense of all human communion and self-giving. But in the context of his discussion about marriage with the Pharisees, Christ will reveal another way to live the fullness of the call to incarnate self-giving as male and female (see Mt 19:12).

In its course, John Paul's theology of the body will profoundly enrich our understanding of the celibate vocation, the basis of which we find already in man's solitude before God and in his call to be "partner of the Absolute." In the final analysis, the human desire for communion with an "other" can only be satisfied in union with *the* "Other" (God). Sexual love and communion is only a *temporal* response to man's yearning for an *eternal* love and communion. Wojtyla places all of this in its proper perspective in the following passage from *Love & Responsibility:*

> It is not sexuality which creates in a man and a woman the need to give themselves to each other, but, on the contrary, it is the need to give oneself, latent in every human person, which finds its outlet...in physical and sexual union, in matrimony. But the need...to give oneself to and unite with another person is deeper and connected with the spiritual existence of the person. It is not finally and completely satisfied simply by union with another human being. Considered in the perspective of the person's eternal existence, marriage is only a tentative solution of the problem of a union of persons through love.[44]

B. The Original Conjugal Act?

We find this "tentative solution" to man's yearning for communion revealed from the beginning in Genesis 2:24, in the two becoming "one flesh." According to John Paul, this unity "is undoubtedly what is expressed and realized in the conjugal act" (49). But, contrary to what some might imagine, this phrase is not a euphemism due to the biblical author's discomfort with sex. "One flesh" is an expression infused with meaning. It

---

44. *Love & Responsibility,* pp. 253–254.

goes far deeper than any surface understanding of sex, leading us into the depths of the "profound mystery" (see Eph 5:32) of interpersonal communion.

Several Greek Fathers (e.g., Gregory of Nyssa, John Chrysostom, Theodoret, and later John Damascene[45]) advanced the idea that in Paradise man and woman would not have joined in "one flesh." Following this line of thinking, the bodily union of the sexes almost seems to have resulted from sin. Not so for John Paul. The Pope stresses repeatedly throughout his catechesis that the "one flesh" union spoken of in Genesis 2:24 was instituted by the Creator *in the beginning.* The "words of Genesis 2:24 bear witness," the Holy Father says, to the "original meaning of unity." This unity, he continues, "is realized through the body [and] indicates right from the beginning...the 'incarnate' communion of persons—*communio personarum*—and calls for this communion right from the beginning."[46]

Of course this "beginning" refers to our "prehistory," which remains shrouded in mystery. Therefore, as John Paul's carefully nuanced statements indicate, the precise manner or mode of their original "incarnate communion" is inaccessible to us. We must avoid projecting our historical experience of bodily union on to the "beginning." Even so, the Holy Father affirms that man and woman "created in the state of original innocence [were] called in this state to conjugal union."[47]

■ If John Paul's statements on the original unity of the sexes leave room for interpretation, one could argue that he only affirms that conjugal union was part of the original plan and not that man and woman actually engaged in it prior to their knowledge of good and evil. In fact, John Paul states at one point that the man knows the woman for the first time in the act of conjugal union only in Genesis 4:1.[48] This is, of course, the first time they join together "in history" as we know it. John Paul always carefully distinguishes man's history from his theological prehistory. Again, original innocence would have afforded a manner of union beyond our comprehen-

---

45. See (as cited in Lawler, Boyle, and May, *Catholic Sexual Ethics,* second edition [Huntington, IN: Our Sunday Visitor, 1998], p. 266) Gregory of Nyssa *De Opificio Hominis,* 17 (PG 44.187); John Chrysostom, *De Virginitate,* 17 (PG 48.546); *Homilia in Genesi,* 18 (PG 80.136); Damascene, *De Fide Orthodoxa,* 2.30 (PG 94.976).

46. 11/14/79, TB 47, 48.

47. 10/13/82, TB 338.

48. See 3/12/80, TB 80.

sion. Whatever the "mode" of that union, John Paul wants to affirm that the experience of original unity was an incarnate, bodily experience and not merely a "spiritual" experience. Of course, in properly distinguishing between the spiritual and the physical, we must affirm that a spiritual unity takes precedence. A bodily union that was not preceded and informed by a spiritual union would be "animalistic." But, for the human person, spiritual love cannot (and must not) be divorced from the body. "In marriage, the physical intimacy of the spouses becomes a sign and pledge of spiritual communion."[49] John Paul speaks to this when he observes that "the most profound words of the spirit—words of love, of giving, of fidelity—demand an adequate 'language of the body.' And without that, they cannot be fully expressed." Man "cannot, in a certain sense, express this singular language of his personal existence and of his vocation without the body."[50]

By balancing the proper relationship of prehistory and history and of spiritual and physical unity, we approach the original, incarnate union of the sexes, which John Paul affirms is witnessed to by Genesis 2:24 (the two become "one flesh"). For John Paul it seems important to affirm the prehistorical existence of such bodily communion if only to shed light on that from which historical man has fallen and, therefore, to provide a measure for that to which Christ calls him. Remember that John Paul seeks to reconstruct what may have happened "then" specifically for our benefit now.

Despite John Paul's repeated affirmation that God instituted the union of the two in "one flesh" from the beginning, an important truth must be upheld in the thought of those who insisted on Adam and Eve's virginity prior to sin. In John Paul's mind it seems virginity is not first to be understood as the absence of a bodily union, but as the integrity of body and soul. In fact, the Pope states explicitly that when a couple unites in the conjugal act, they are meant to be "reliving, in a sense, the original virginal value of man" (49). What could this possibly mean? The Holy Father does not elaborate, so I offer the following interpretation.[51]

In the beginning man and woman experienced a perfect psychosomatic (soul-body) integration. They were "untouched" by the rupture of

---

49. *CCC*, n. 2360.

50. 1/12/83, TB 359.

51. In what follows, I am relying on the insights of a former professor, Monsignor Lorenzo Albacete.

body and soul that would defile them as a result of original sin. In this sense, the experience of original unity remained virginal (untouched by the disintegration of sin). Not only was this unity not a loss of personal integrity (virginity), it was the deepest possible affirmation of it. Sin, however, marks the loss of man's virginity (body-soul integrity) in the sense that it ruptured his psychosomatic unity. Thereafter, the lust that so often attends sexual union serves to accent and even exacerbate this body-soul rift. Lustful sexual union is always a dis-integrating experience, and, thus, a loss of virginity.

■ This sense of virginity helps us understand the virginity of the New Eve at a new level. Mary's title as the "Blessed Virgin" should not first bring to mind her choice to refrain from sexual intercourse. It is true, of course, that she never experienced sexual union. However, her particular blessing lies not in this fact *per se,* but in that she never experienced the rupture of body and soul. So it seems the title "Blessed Virgin" should first call to mind her Immaculate Conception. Being spared of all taint of original and personal sin, she is *perfectly integrated* in body and soul.

If lustful union effects a loss of virginity, are men and women now bound to lust? Even the holiest men and women must still contend with concupiscence, that disordering of the passions which resulted from original sin. Yet even if Baptism does not remove concupiscence, Christ "came to restore creation to the purity of its origins."[52] In Christ it is possible for husbands and wives progressively to conquer lust and thus relive in a real sense that original "virginal" experience of unity. In a certain sense this is the goal of Christian marriage—for husbands and wives to recover their "virginal value," not by foregoing sexual union, but by allowing it to be taken up and "recreated" in Christ's redeeming sacrifice. Quoting John Paul: "Man and woman, uniting with each other (in the conjugal act) so closely as to become 'one flesh' rediscover, so to speak, every time and in a special way, the mystery of creation. They return in that way to that union in humanity ('bone of my bones and flesh of my flesh') which allows them to recognize each other and, like the first time, to call each other by name." The Pope concludes that this "means reliving, in a sense, the original virginal value of man which emerges from the mystery of his solitude before God" (49).

---

52. *CCC,* n. 2336.

Thus, for spouses who—by continually surrendering their sexuality to Christ—experience a "real and deep victory" over lust,[53] sexual union becomes not a "loss" of anything, but a tremendous gain. They come fully to discover their true selves through the sincere gift of themselves to each other. Their communion confirms each of them in their virginal uniqueness, in the unrepeatability of their persons. Hence, to become "one flesh" returns in some sense to the "one reality" of the *humanum*—the "one reality" of man, which is the mystery of his solitude before God and all creation. Through "sex" (it seems we can take this to mean both sexual difference and sexual union) John Paul says that man and woman not only "surpass" their own solitude, but they assume the solitude of the other (the personhood of the other) as their own. If the body reveals the person, by becoming "one body" male and female become in some sense "one man" (almost "one human person") before God as in original solitude. In this way—in the sense that the experience of original unity also returns us in some way to the experience of original solitude—we can speak of the sexual act as an expression of or even a reliving of the "original virginal value of man."

To speak of male and female becoming in some way "one man," of course, implies a unity-in-distinction through which neither person is blurred as an individual, but becomes more fully him or herself. As John Paul observes: "The fact that they become 'one flesh' is a powerful bond established by the Creator, through which they discover their own humanity, both in its original unity, and in the duality of a mysterious mutual attraction" (49). Unity-in-duality, a two-in-oneness, is the key. This real unity and this real distinction is maintained in proper balance, however, only when man and woman's "mutual attraction" is integrated first with one's own subjectivity as a person and, in turn, is informed by an unwavering respect for the subjectivity of the other as a person.

Sexual attraction "in the beginning" summoned them to become a sincere gift for each other. It did not operate on its own, compelling a selfish indulgence at the expense of the other. Sexual attraction and desire was intimately bound up with choice and, therefore, with human subjectivity. Their ability to *choose* distinguished them from the animals. Human sexual activity, therefore, radically differs from the copulation of animals. If joining in "one flesh" was only a response to instinct and not the result of self-determination, their experience of unity would have indicated that

---

53. All of cycle 2 is devoted to discussing how Christ empowers us in just such a "real and deep victory" over lust. This phrase is taken from the audience of 10/22/80, TB 164.

they were similar to the animals rather than affirming their solitude. If historical man experiences sexual desire as an "instinct," this is the result of original sin. Therefore, if men and women of history are to become a "sincere gift" to one another, they *must* regain the integrity of self-mastery. The freely chosen, personhood-affirming communion of the first man and woman "must constitute the beginning and the model of that communion for all men and women who, in any period, are united so intimately as to be 'one flesh'" (50). This is what Christ confirms in his challenge to the Pharisees. Anything less does not correspond to our dignity as men and women made in the divine image. Anything less substitutes a counterfeit for the love and intimacy we long for.

C. The Vital Power of Communion

One of John Paul's goals in his theology of the body is to place the teaching of *Humanae Vitae* within the context of biblical anthropology. Man and woman's communion is not closed in on itself. When they become "one flesh," men and women submit their whole humanity to the original blessing of fertility.

As stated above, love diffuses itself. It seeks to increase its own circle of communion. God, who is love, is a *life-giving* Communion of Persons. We are made in this image as male and female. Thus, the original call to "be fruitful and multiply" is a call to live in the divine image. "Procreation," as John Paul expresses it, "is rooted in creation, and every time, in a sense, reproduces its mystery" (51). The mystery of creation is the mystery of God's overflowing Trinitarian Love, which shot us and the whole universe into being. When a man and woman become "one flesh" they renew this mystery "in all its original depth and vital power" (50). Or, at least, they are meant to do so. What might contraception, the deliberate sterilization of sexual union, do to this picture? In due time, John Paul will provide a startling answer.

16. The Key to Biblical Anthropology

December 12, 19, 1979 (TB 51–57)

The human experiences the Yahwist text speaks of have a basic significance for every man and woman in every age. Yet John Paul observes that these experiences so intermingle with the ordinary things of life that we tend to take them entirely for granted. Penetrating God's "revelation of the body" helps us to discover the extraordinary side of the ordinary. We discover that these experiences provide an interpretive key for understanding human existence.

A. Original Nakedness

Having examined the experiences of *original solitude* and *original unity,* we turn now to the third "fundamental human experience": *original nakedness.* As we read in Genesis 2:25, "the man and his wife were both naked and were not ashamed." In light of the biblical text analyzed so far, John Paul recognizes that, at first glance, this verse may seem misplaced, adding nothing more than a cursory detail. Of course, based on the riches he has already mined from the Yahwist narrative, we would not expect John Paul to stop at first glance. Far from being peripheral, John Paul shows us that the meaning of original nakedness is "precisely the key" for the "full and complete understanding" of the first draft of biblical anthropology (52). In other words, if we do not understand what it meant for the first man and woman to be naked without shame, we do not understand the original biblical meaning of our humanity.

Some might consider man's creation in the image and likeness of God as the more appropriate key to biblical anthropology. Original nakedness is nothing but the subjective reverberation and conscious reflection of this objective truth. As John Paul says, nakedness without shame "describes their state of consciousness; in fact, their mutual experience of the body...with the greatest precision possible." Thus, Genesis 2:25 "makes a specific contribution to the theology of the body...that absolutely cannot be ignored" (52).

The Pope observes that it is first necessary to establish that the experience of original nakedness involves a real non-presence of shame, and not a lack or underdevelopment of it. Original nakedness cannot be compared to the experience of young children, for example, who have yet to develop a sense of shame. Much less can nakedness *without* shame be compared to *shamelessness.* These are polar opposites. A shameless nakedness is immodest. It involves a lack or suppression of shame when shame is rightly called for (see Jer 3:2–3). Shame in one's nakedness is called for when nakedness poses a threat to the dignity of the person. The original experience of nakedness completely lacked shame because being naked posed no threat to the first couple's dignity. They *saw* the body as the revelation of the person and his (her) dignity. "Only the nakedness that makes woman an 'object' for the man, or vice versa, is a source of shame. The fact that 'they were not ashamed' means that the woman was not an 'object' for the man nor he for her."[54]

---

54. 2/20/80, TB 75.

On this side of the fig leaves, we can hardly imagine the experience of original nakedness. Original sin radically changed our experience of nakedness. Shame entered with sin, the shame that marks the "boundary" between original man and historical man. So how can we reconstruct the experience of original nakedness?

■ Karol Wojtyla provides a detailed, extremely rich, and well-balanced presentation of the problems of nakedness, shame, shamelessness, modesty, etc. in *Love & Responsibility*. Of particular interest is Wojtyla's discussion of "the law of the absorption of shame by love." He writes: "Shame is, as it were, swallowed up by love, dissolved in it, so that the man and the woman are no longer ashamed to be sharing their experience of sexual values. This process is enormously important to sexual morality."[55] He clarifies that this does not mean shame is eliminated or destroyed as in the case of shamelessness. Shame also has a positive role that is essential to love, for it protects the dignity of the person. Thus, the "swallowing of shame by love" does not mean removing the reserve or reverence that the inner mystery of the other person calls for. Still, Wojtyla writes that where there is genuine love, shame (in the negative sense) "as the natural way of avoiding the utilitarian attitude [toward the body] loses its *raison d'être* and gives ground. But only to the extent that a person loved in this way—and this is most important—is equally ready to give herself or himself in love."[56] In other words, nakedness does not offend nor elicit shame in relationships in which the persons are "conscious of the gift" given and have "resolved to respond to it in an equally personal way." Instead, in this situation, John Paul says, "The human body in its nakedness [becomes] a sign of trust and...the source of a particular interpersonal 'communication.'"[57]

B. Penetrating Their Experience

Some would claim we cannot know much about the interior experience of original nakedness. They say we can only use an objective approach (via traditional metaphysics) to arrive at an "exterior" understanding. An exterior perception of the world certainly gives us crucial insight. Thus, the Pope agrees that this dimension cannot be ignored. But he maintains that the "biblical expression 'were not ashamed' directly indicates the 'experience' as a

---

55. *Love & Responsibility,* p. 181.

56. Ibid., p. 183.

57. 4/29/81, TB 224.

subjective dimension."[58] Hence, we cannot arrive at the full meaning of original nakedness "without going down into the depths of man. Genesis 2:25 introduces us specifically to this level and wants us to seek there the original innocence of knowing" (56).

Here we see John Paul discussing the relationship between the traditional philosophy of being and the modern philosophy of consciousness. Original nakedness can be examined using metaphysical categories. In other words, it can be looked at from the perspective of "the truth of being or of reality," as the Pope puts it. This is indispensable and comes prior to any subjective investigation. However, if we stop at this level, we face the danger of abstraction. Phenomenological analysis allows us to penetrate the conscious, experiential reality of original nakedness, not in opposition to an objective view, but in tandem with it. For those who are skeptical of this approach, John Paul takes "the liberty of pointing out that the very text of Genesis 2:25 expressly requires that the reflections on the theology of the body should be connected with the dimension of man's personal subjectivity" (52).

Despite our state of hereditary sinfulness, our roots still lie in the garden of innocence (see §11). As John Paul states, by referring historical man to the beginning, "Christ indirectly establishes the idea of continuity and connection between those two states, as if allowing us to move back from the threshold of man's 'historical' sinfulness to his original innocence" (53). Our experience of shame connected with nakedness is the "flip side" of original nakedness. We have lost the full consciousness of the meaning of the body afforded by the state of original holiness. But by examining our own experience of shame and "flipping it over," we can see the "shape" of that fullness we lack. In this way we can "reconstruct," at least to some degree, the interior content of the experience of original nakedness.

C. The Phenomenon of Shame

John Paul begins his audience of December 19, 1979 with an important question: "What is shame and how can we explain its absence in the state of original innocence, in the very depth of the mystery of the creation of man as male and female?" First, we must recognize that shame is an inter-personal reality. Although John Paul will eventually demonstrate that shame has a meaning within each person (he will call this "immanent shame"; see §27), shame is generally experienced in relation to and with other persons. A person has no reason to be ashamed of his own nakedness when he is alone (so long as he is doing nothing shameful with his nakedness). But suppose a stranger were to walk in on you while you were get-

---

58. 1/16/80, TB 65.

ting out of the shower. Most people would instinctively feel a need to cover their nakedness. The phenomenologist cannot help but ask: Why?

According to John Paul, this "instinct" manifests a deep need of affirmation and acceptance as a person, and, at the same time, a fear that the "other" will not recognize and affirm the full truth of my person revealed by my nakedness (remember that the *body* reveals the person). We cover up to protect ourselves for fear that our dignity as "selves" (i.e., as persons) will not be upheld otherwise. Everyone, it seems, can attest to this phenomenon. If we can manage to take this fear of not being affirmed in the presence of another and "flip it over," we find ourselves at the threshold of the experience of original nakedness. We can almost enter in. We can almost "taste" it.

Original nakedness is precisely the experience of full consciousness of the meaning and dignity of the body. Based on this, there is no fear of standing naked before the other because, in doing so, both the man and the woman receive from the other the affirmation and acceptance they long for—the affirmation and acceptance that correspond perfectly with their dignity as persons. The Pope calls this experience the "original innocence of knowledge" (56). Such knowledge is based on a profound experience of intimacy and interpersonal "communication." John Paul notes that we have lost the deeper meaning of this word. True "communication," according to the Holy Father, is the experience of a "common union." Hence, to "communicate" means to establish a *communion* through the mutual and sincere gift of persons to each other.

■ Surveys of married couples and even clinical studies consistently report "poor communication" as a leading cause of marital breakdown. Most marriage preparation and/or enrichment programs, therefore, place heavy emphasis on teaching "communication skills." Typically these consist of various speaking and listening techniques that enable spouses to converse more effectively. They are certainly beneficial. However, the countless marriage preparation and enrichment programs I have surveyed pay little if any attention to teaching the skills necessary for this deeper and more essential meaning of communication. The essence of marriage consists in establishing a "common union" through the free and sincere gift of self. Lust is the prime enemy of the self-giving that affords authentic marital communication. Hence, among the many important "communication skills" in married life (and life in general), learning to overcome lust is most important. Without this liberation from lust we cannot express the "freedom of the gift," which is "the condition of all life together in truth."[59]

---

59. 10/8/80, TB 159.

The experience of original nakedness testifies to their authentic "communication," to the purity of their mutual self-giving. Such purity allows them to know one another via their nakedness since their nakedness itself "communicates" an intimate knowledge of the person. And it is a knowledge of each other's great dignity and goodness as male and female created in the image of God. As John Paul affirms: "'Nakedness' signifies the original good of God's vision. It signifies all the simplicity and fullness of the vision through which the 'pure' value of humanity as male and female, the 'pure' value of the body and of sex, is manifested."[60] The more we ponder the meaning of this original vision of nakedness—this "original innocence of knowledge"—the more the reality of sin and lust will make us want to weep. Those "garments of our misery" (Gregory of Nyssa's description of the fig leaves) constantly remind us of the tragedy of having lost sight of what God created our bodies to reveal—the spiritual mystery of our humanity and also, in some way, the mystery of his divinity.

When we realize the scandal of our blindness, we are led to our knees to beg God's mercy. And mercy *has* been revealed through the *body* of Christ. From the pulpit of the cross, Christ's naked body proclaims redemption to every man and woman who has ever lived under the inheritance of shame. "Fig leaves" will always be necessary in a fallen world. But as John Paul will demonstrate, even now we can regain something of the original good of God's vision.[61] Further analysis of original nakedness will enable us to understand the content of this vision more thoroughly.

17. The Body: Witness to Gift and Love
December 19, 1979; January 2, 9, 16, 1980 (TB 56–66)

According to St. Augustine, the deepest desire of the human heart is to *see* another and *be seen* by that other's loving look.[62] This sums up well the experience of original nakedness. Of course we are talking about more than the mere sensory experience of seeing a naked body with the eyes. We are talking about an interior "look" manifested through the eyes that knows and affirms the other as a person. As John Paul expresses it, in the experience of original nakedness "man and woman see each other even

---

60. 1/2/80, TB 57.

61. See *CCC,* nn. 1264, 1426, 2519, 2715.

62. See St. Augustine, *Sermon* 69, c. 2, 3.

more fully and distinctly than through the sense of sight itself.... They see and know each other, in fact, with all the peace of the interior gaze, which creates precisely the fullness of the intimacy of persons" (57). Original nakedness, then, indicates a total defenselessness before the other, a total absence of barriers, because of a total trust in the sincerity of their mutual exchange.

A. Exterior and Interior Nakedness

Total peace suffused the first man and woman's intimacy—their reciprocated interior gaze—precisely because, prior to sin, there was no rupture between the spiritual and the sensible. Gender difference and unity highlighted the spiritual-sensible difference and unity; it was where the spiritual-sensible difference and unity was most keenly "felt" and experienced. In this experience, it was as if the body was transparent. Exterior nakedness revealed an interior nakedness. As John Paul observes: "To this fullness of 'exterior' perception, expressed by means of physical nakedness, there corresponds the 'interior' fullness of man's vision in God, that is, according to the measure of the 'image of God'" (57). Man's perception of the world was in perfect harmony with God's. In beholding each other's nakedness, they saw not just *a* body, but *some*body—another *person* who radiated God's glory through his masculinity and her femininity. Seeing this and knowing this, they experienced no shame, only a deep peace and a profound awareness of their own goodness. In this way John Paul says that the human body acquires a completely new meaning that cannot remain "external." The body expresses the person, which is something more than the "individual." The body expresses the personal human "self" through an *exterior* reality perceived from *within*.

To look at a body and see only an "individual" is to perceive merely the exterior reality. The seeing of original nakedness is very different. It "is not just a participation in the 'exterior' perception of the world." It "has also an interior dimension of participation in the vision of the Creator himself—that vision [in which] 'God saw everything that he had made, and behold, it was very good' (Gen 1:31)" (57). The experience of the body, then, follows and indicates the experience of the heart.

■ I once heard the word "intimacy" defined as "into-me-see." This explains well that experience of original nakedness. There is no fear in being seen externally because there is no fear of being seen internally. In lectures when I discuss how the nakedness of Adam and Eve reveals the original good of God's vision, I often ask: "How many of you can stand naked in front of a mirror and say 'behold, it is very good'?" The laughs and bewildered looks point clearly to how far we have fallen from that original vision and experience of the human body. In some way, this reaction seems to indicate the extent to which we have normalized our "flat tires." Of course, our bodies do not look entirely the same as Adam and Eve's. Every grey hair, every blemish, every wrinkle reminds us that our bodies are on the road to decay. Prior to sin, Adam and Eve's bodies were not. They shone transparently with the glory of God. Even so, the corruption of sin has not triumphed; our bodies are "very good." We cannot live an authentic human life if we do not overcome those obstacles that keep us from embracing the fundamental truth of our own goodness.

B. The Reality of Gift

In these words of Genesis ("God saw everything that he had made, and behold, it was very good"), we glimpse not only the character of man and woman's interior gaze, but the divine motive behind creation itself, and behind our creation as male and female, in particular—Love. As the Pope points out, "only love, in fact, gives a beginning to good and delights in good. Creation, therefore, as the action of God, signifies not only calling from nothingness to existence,...but it also signifies...a fundamental and radical giving" (59).

Self-giving and love are synonymous in the mind of the Holy Father. Of course, "the concept of 'giving' cannot refer to a nothingness. It indicates the one who gives and the one who receives the gift, and also the relationship that is established between them" (59). God gives the gift of creation and man receives it. This establishes a "nuptial" relationship between them. In fact, the term "nuptial," according to the Holy Father, "manifests in a word the whole reality of that donation of which the first pages of the book of Genesis speak to us" (66). All creation has a nuptial character because it constitutes the original and fundamental gift. But in the visible world this gift can only be fully realized in and received by man because man alone is made in God's image. Only a person endowed with freedom and self-determination can receive "the gift" of God, which is love, and reciprocate that gift (i.e., loving God in return). This is the original covenant God establishes with man in creation.

How did man realize this gift? How did he experience this call to "nuptial" relationship with God (covenant) and enter into it? God stamped it in his *body* by creating man as male and female and calling them to be a nuptial gift to one another. John Paul says that the human body in all the original truth of its masculinity and femininity expresses the gift of creation. "This is the body: a witness to creation as a fundamental gift, and so a witness to Love as the source from which this same giving springs. Masculinity-femininity—namely, sex—is the original sign of a creative donation [by God] and of an awareness on the part of man, of a gift lived so to speak in an original way" (62).

We cannot understand human existence if we do not understand this reality of "gift." All is gift. God initiates the gift and creates man to receive the gift, which is God's divine Life and Love. This understanding of gift provides the interpretive key of the Pope's anthropology. Through this "hermeneutic of the gift" we approach "the very essence of the person." Man is created as a person first to receive the gift of God's gratuitous love, and then to recapitulate that love by being gift to others. In fact, this call to be gift is "the fundamental element of human existence in the world" (66). God inscribed it in the mystery of human sexuality. The complementarity of the body itself as male and female, as the revelation of the innermost being of man, of his subjectivity and freedom, summons man and woman freely to recapitulate the giving and receiving of the divine gift. Now the words of Genesis 2:24 take on their meaning: *For this reason*—to recapitulate the divine gift—"a man leaves his father and his mother and cleaves to his wife and they become one flesh." *This*, as John Paul says, is "the meaning with which sex enters the theology of the body" (62).

C. The Original Way of Living the Gift

When John Paul speaks of the "original way" of living the gift of God's love, he means precisely what we have been discussing regarding the experiences of original solitude, unity, and nakedness. In fact, "the dimension of the gift," according to John Paul, "decides the essential truth and depth of meaning of the original solitude-unity-nakedness" (58).

In its first meaning, that man is "alone" in the world as a person, original solitude reveals that man is a being capable of *receiving creation as a gift* of God's life and love. In its second meaning, original solitude reveals the need for a "helper," someone with whom the man can live in *a relationship of mutual gift*. Original unity reveals that this relationship of *mutual gift has been established*. And original nakedness reveals the *genuineness of the gift given*—that they are living with a full consciousness of the meaning of the body *as gift*. In this way, John Paul says that the two words "alone" and "helper" hold the key to understanding the essence of "the gift" as it manifests itself in man. The gift is first the human being's own creation as a person (original solitude; "alone"). Then, in receiving his own life as a gift, the person desires to become the same gift to an "other" that life is to him (original unity; "helper"). In turn, those two words reveal the essential content of man's existence as a creature made in the divine image. For man images God both as an individual ("alone") and in the male-female communion ("helper").

Hence, the words "alone" and "helper" summarize and reveal "the norm of existence as a person" by showing that the relationship of mutual gift fulfills man's original solitude. Not only that, but John Paul will say that the relationship of mutual gift fulfills the deepest meaning of man's being and existence. All of this is revealed through awareness of the meaning of the body and of sex, a meaning that John Paul will call "nuptial."

18. The Nuptial Meaning of the Body
January 9, 16, 1980 (TB 60–66)

The verses of Genesis 2:23–25 overflow with anthropological meaning. They express the joy of man's coming to be as male and female (v. 23), establish their conjugal unity (v. 24), and finally testify to the nakedness of both without shame (v. 25). This significant confrontation of man and woman in their nakedness allows us to speak of "the revelation and at the same time the discovery of the 'nuptial' meaning of the body in the very mystery of creation" (62).

The nuptial meaning of the body is one of the most important and synoptic concepts of the Pope's entire catechesis. From this point forward he will weave it throughout his addresses. But it is not simply a "concept" or intellectual idea. The nuptial meaning of the body speaks of man and woman's *conscious experience* of their bodies as a gift and symbol of God's love—and, in turn, their sharing this Love with one another in and through their bodies, their masculinity and femininity.

A. Incarnate Love

This *incarnate* concept of love points to the original integration and harmony of the interior and exterior dimensions of the human person. Man experiences his call to love from *within*. But the nuptial meaning of the body also confirms this *exteriorly* precisely because man is a unity of body and soul. Based on this anthropological truth of body-soul integration, speaking of the human person means simultaneously speaking of the human body and sexuality. "This simultaneousness is essential," the Pope says. For if "we dealt with sex without the person"—and we could also say if we dealt with the person without sex—"the whole adequacy of the anthropology...would be destroyed" (61).

The whole truth of the body and of sex, John Paul affirms, "is the pure and simple truth of communion between persons" (61). This communion is established through an integrated, incarnate love. Hence, John Paul defines the nuptial meaning of the body as the body's "capacity of expressing love: that love precisely in which the man-person becomes a gift and—by means of this gift—fulfills the very meaning of his being and existence" (63).[63] Here John Paul echoes that key text from the Second Vatican Council: "It follows then, that if man is the only creature on earth that God willed for its own sake, man can fully discover his true self only in a sincere giving of himself."[64] John Paul establishes here that this teaching of the Council is rooted not only in the spiritual aspect of man's nature, but also in *his body,* in the complementary difference of the sexes and their call to become "one flesh."

■ Of course, this does not mean that everyone is called to marriage and the "one flesh" union. Nor could it possibly mean that sexual union is required in order to understand and live the meaning of life. It does mean, however, that we are all called to some expression of "nuptial love"—to an incarnate self-giving. As Cycle 3 will explain, everyone, regardless of earthly vocation, finds the ultimate fulfillment of the nuptial meaning of the body in the "marriage of the Lamb," that is, in union with Christ. And everyone's journey toward this heavenly reality, regardless of earthly vocation, passes by way of our experience of sexual embodiment.

This interior law of the gift manifested in the exterior truth of the body is missed altogether by a purely naturalistic (or cosmological) view of man and his body. Since it does not penetrate the personal dimension, such an evaluation can only conclude that procreation is the primary end of sexual union. Without denying this truth, John Paul insists that the human body "is not only the source of fruitfulness and procreation, as in the whole natural order, but includes right 'from the beginning' the...capacity of expressing love" (63). John Paul holds the two meanings—love and procreation—in a fruitful togetherness. If traditional formulations have erred by stressing procreation to the neglect of nuptial love, many modern theories stress nuptial love to the neglect of procreation. If we seek to have an integral view of man, the two cannot be separated. Man loves *through his body,* which God blessed with the gift of fertility.

---

63. See *CCC,* n. 2331.

64. *Gaudium et Spes,* n. 24.

B. Revelation and Discovery of the Meaning of Life

Let us reflect for a moment on a particular aspect of the Pope's above quoted words. He says that if we live according to the true meaning of our bodies *we fulfill the very meaning of our existence.* How? The meaning of life is to love as God loves, and this is stamped in our sexuality. Anyone looking for the meaning of life has nowhere else to go. It is revealed in everyone's body—in masculinity and femininity. There lies the answer to the universal question: "What does it mean to be human?" There we find the law of the gift inscribed in our humanity. This is why misunderstanding and misuse of sexuality have such dire consequences for man and for society. A "culture of death" grows out of a world of people estranged from the nuptial meaning of their bodies. In fact, original sin marks precisely the subjective loss or obscuring of the nuptial meaning of the body.

As a result, for many people the experience of their body and sexuality—far from revealing life's meaning—seems inseparable from a gnawing sense of life's *meaninglessness.* Even many Christians who claim to have discovered life's meaning in a "spiritual" sense do not realize that that meaning is inscribed in *their bodies* as male and female, in their sexuality. Such persons may see the body as an annoying distraction, or even an inherent obstacle to living a Christian life. Not so! We cannot live an authentic Christian life apart from *the body.* God's revelation teaches us this. But we can also discover (or *re*discover) it in our own experience if we surrender our bodies to the grace poured out in the death and resurrection of Christ's body.

In his exegesis of Genesis 2, John Paul speaks repeatedly of the *revelation* and *discovery* of the nuptial meaning of the body. He does this to emphasize that the theological thread of the Yahwist text is also anthropological. In other words, prior to sin complete harmony reigned between God's revelation and human experience. God revealed the body's nuptial meaning, and man and woman discovered it and *consciously lived* it. Genesis 2:25 highlights this: "And the man and his wife were both naked and were not ashamed." As the inspired word of God, this is not only divine *revelation.* It speaks directly and specifically of man and woman's full and *conscious experience* of the nuptial meaning of their bodies. Even though we have lost this conscious experience of the original meaning of our bodies through sin, by taking on flesh the eternal Word *reveals* this meaning to us again. In his body given up for us, Christ offers us the redemption of our bodies, and with it the possibility of (re)*discovering* the body's nuptial meaning. Conscious experience of redemption in Christ leads precisely to this (re)discovery of life's meaning through the revelation of the nuptial meaning of the body of Christ.

C. The Freedom of the Gift

In the general audience of January 16, 1980, particularly rich in content, John Paul introduces another key concept: *the freedom of the gift.* If men and women are created for their "own sake," they cannot be possessed by another. They cannot be owned or taken-hold-of by another. They are "incommunicable." Thus, a problem arises: How can men and women communicate themselves to each other without violating the other's dignity as an incommunicable person? The answer lies in the freedom of the gift. Adam was under no compulsion to satisfy mere "instinct" at the sight of woman's naked beauty. As the Pope points out, such a concept implies an interior constraint, similar to the instinct that stimulates copulation in animals. Instead, Adam was free with the freedom of the gift. This means the sight of Eve's nakedness inspired nothing but the desire to make a "sincere gift" of himself to her. He could freely *choose* her for who she was. This is an experience far from merely succumbing to an instinctual attraction toward a generic nakedness. This is a desire and love for another person inspired by the genuine recognition of that person's authentic value—that person's unrepeatability.

Furthermore, recognizing that she is a person made for "her own sake," Adam knew he could not "take" Eve or "grasp" her. He had to trust that she—in her freedom—would desire to open herself to the gift he initiated and would respond freely with the gift of herself to him, which she did. In doing so, she also *chose* him. This is how incommunicable persons communicate their persons—by freely bestowing the mutual and sincere gift of self. In this way, John Paul says that the human body and sex are raised "to the level of 'image of God,' and to the level of the person and communion between persons" (63).

Freedom lies at the very basis of the nuptial meaning of the body and the experience of original nakedness. Man and woman can only be naked without shame, according to the Holy Father, when "they are free with the very freedom of the gift." The entrance of shame, therefore, indicates the loss of the freedom of the gift. Here John Paul means freedom as self-mastery or self-control. Such freedom "is indispensable in order that man... may become a gift, in order that (referring to the words of the Council) he will be able to 'fully discover his true self' in 'a sincere giving of himself'" (64). For man cannot give himself away if he does not first possess himself, if he is not in "control" of himself and his desires.

Self-control for original man, however, did not mean dominating unruly desires in order to keep them "in check." Such a concept can only stem from the projections of fallen man. In the beginning, man and woman experienced sexual desire as God created it, as the power and desire to love as God loves. Thus, they had no unruly desires to control. Free with the freedom of the gift, man and woman reveled in each other's goodness, in each other's beauty, according to the whole truth of their being as God revealed it to them in the mystery of creation. *This* reveling in each other's goodness enabled them to be naked without shame. This experience "can and must be understood as the revelation—and at the same time rediscovery—of freedom" (64). And precisely this freedom affords the revelation and the discovery of the nuptial meaning of the body. Hence, historical man's task will be to recover the truth of the body that sets him free. For this freedom, Christ has set us free (see Gal 5:1).

19. Chosen by Eternal Love

January 16, 1980 (TB 63–66)

That key anthropological statement of the Council (taken from *Gaudium et Spes,* n. 24) which we have been discussing has two main emphases. First, man is the only creature created "for his own sake." Second, man can only find himself "through the sincere giving of self."

God created the rest of creation for *our* sake. We are free to use (but not *ab*-use) creation for our benefit. The human person, however, since he exists "for his own sake," must *never* be used as a means to an end. He is an end in himself. Nonetheless, having been created for his own sake, man is not meant to live for his own sake, but to live for others. The human heart cannot find happiness in self-indulgent isolation. Hence, the second emphasis of the Council's statement: Man, if he is to find himself, must become a "sincere gift" to others. As Christ said, if you lose your life, you will find it (see Mk 8:35).

■ Secular humanism may seem to promote the idea that man is made for his own sake. However—and here it makes its tragic error—it concludes that he is meant to live for his own sake. This results in a radical individualism that actually denies the initial premise. Individualism inevitably treats others not as persons in their own right, but as a means or as an obstacle in the every-man-for-himself quest for fulfillment. Secular humanism does not believe in the reality of gift because it denies God who *is* Gift. But the selfless call to be gift to others is the only path to true communion and solidarity among persons, starting with the most fundamental communion of all, that of man and woman in marriage. As we shall learn, the denial of the gift is the essence of original sin. Hence, as George

Weigel keenly observes, through the original temptation the serpent "is the first and most lethal purveyor of a false humanism."[65]

The two emphases of the Council's statement ("own sake" and "self-gift") contain all the concepts that shed light on man's "beginning"—communion of persons; original solitude, unity, and nakedness; the gift; the nuptial meaning of the body; and the freedom of the gift. In the first meaning of *solitude* (i.e., man differs from the animals), Adam discovers that he is the only creature willed "for his own sake." In the second meaning of solitude (i.e., man is alone without the opposite sex), he realizes that he can only fulfill himself by giving himself away to another creature also willed "for his own sake" (or shall we say *her* own sake). *Original unity* is the "sincere giving" of man and woman to each other that forms the *communion of persons*. This call to be *gift* is revealed through their experience of *nakedness*. Our anatomy as male and female persons reveals the *body's nuptial meaning* which is fulfilled in the *freedom of the gift* of man and woman to each other.

A. Completing the Nuptial Meaning of the Body

In their first "beatifying meeting," man and woman discover their own selves in the gift of the other. In the purity of his love—in the purity of his sexual desire—man accepted woman as God willed her "for her own sake" in the mystery of her femininity. And in the purity of her love and desire, woman accepted man as God willed him "for his own sake" in the mystery of his masculinity. This purity affords the perfect integration of the interior and exterior dimensions of the person. The pure of heart see that the exterior beauty of the human body is "oriented interiorly by the 'sincere gift' of the person." They see "such a value and such a beauty as to go beyond the purely physical dimensions of 'sexuality'" (65). The body becomes the threshold to the transcendent reality of the spirit and even in some way to the ultimate mystery of the divine.

John Paul says that in this manner, awareness of the nuptial meaning of the body is in a way completed. Not only do the man and woman each become a sincere gift for the other, but the gift is completed when each *receives* the gift of self made by the other. The nuptial meaning of the body reveals both the call to become a gift, and "the capacity and deep availability for the 'affirmation of the person' [which] is nothing but acceptance of the gift" (65). It is precisely this reciprocal giving and accepting of the gift which creates the communion of persons. This communion

---

65. *Witness to Hope*, p. 338.

is constructed from within, from man's "interiority." But John Paul affirms that it also comprises "the whole 'exteriority' of man, that is, everything that constitutes the pure and simple nakedness of the body in its masculinity and femininity" (65).

John Paul also explains that this "affirmation of the person" means "living the fact that the other—the woman for the man and the man for the woman—is...someone willed by the Creator for his (or her) own sake." This someone is "unique and unrepeatable: someone chosen by eternal Love" (65). Is there any man or woman who does not ache in the depths of his or her being for such affirmation? And, according to John Paul, in God's plan this is all revealed and lived "by means of the body." This does not mean that everyone must experience sexual union to be affirmed as a person. But it does mean that sexual union is supposed to be *this:* the deep affirmation of our goodness as persons through the sincere giving and receiving of the gift of selves.

This is the language of the nuptial embrace: "I give myself totally to you, *all* that I am without reservation. Sincerely. Freely. Forever. And I receive the gift of yourself that you give to me. I bless you. I affirm you. *All* that you are, without reservation. Forever." This is an experience of being *chosen by eternal Love.* If sexual union does not say this, it does not correspond to the nuptial meaning of the body. It does not correspond to the dignity of the person and can never satisfy the longings of the heart. If sexual union does not say this, it is not an expression of love but only a cheapened counterfeit.

B. The Theme of Existence

John Paul says that man can never avoid this indispensable "theme" of his own existence. Man is made for nuptial love. It is stamped in his (and her) being, interiorly and exteriorly. Therefore, John Paul affirms that the nuptial meaning of the body is "the fundamental element of human existence in the world" (66). This means we can only find the happiness we seek if we discover this love, if we discover (or rediscover) the nuptial meaning of the body. Only their pure experience of the nuptial meaning of their bodies explains man and woman's original happiness. In the whole perspective of each person's history, man searches for happiness. In this quest John Paul says that man will not fail to confer a nuptial meaning on his own body. Even if many things distort his experience of sexuality, the desire for nuptial union will always remain at the deepest level of *the person.* John Paul cannot emphasize this point enough: "This 'nuptial' meaning of the human body can be understood only in the context of the person" (66).

Animals can copulate and reproduce, but their bodies do not have a nuptial meaning because they are not persons and they cannot love. We can also observe in this context that animals also cannot experience shame. We are the only "bodies" in the world that wear clothing. Why? Because our capacity for shame is the "flip side" of our capacity for love. Animals have neither capacity. Thus, what may seem somewhat similar in the copulation of animals and the copulation of humans is seen to be worlds apart when we consider the interior dimension of the person. This is why the nuptial meaning of the body "demands to be revealed in all its simplicity and purity, and to be shown in its whole truth, as a sign of the 'image of God'" (66).

Because of sin, we may feel far removed from experiencing the body as our first parents did in the state of original innocence. But only through that revelation of the original experience of the body can we understand that from which we have fallen *and* that to which we are called. In the fullness of time Christ took on flesh and was born of a woman so that we might experience the redemption of our bodies. In Christ we are called— and called *with power*—to recover that happiness that comes from living according to the full truth of our bodies.

20. The Grace of Original Happiness

January 30; February 6, 1980 (TB 67–72)

We have been trying to "reconstruct" the first man and woman's experience of the body in the state of original innocence before shame. As "historical man" we do this almost by means of a contrast with our own experience of shame. John Paul defines original innocence as that which "at its very roots excludes shame of the body in the man-woman relationship, radically eliminat[ing] its necessity in man, in his heart, that is, in his conscience" (68). This prompts a question: What in original man radically eliminates any experience of shame? John Paul has a one-word answer: *grace*. "The first verses of the Bible...speak not only of the creation of the world and of man in the world, but also of grace, that is, of the communication of holiness, of the radiation of the Spirit, which produces a special state of 'spiritualization' in man" (67). Of course, this state of "spiritualization" does not imply a distancing from the body. It means the *"in*-spiration" of our bodies with the gift of the Holy Spirit. It means the complete integration and original unity of soul and body, spirituality and sexuality.

A. The Radiation of Grace

John Paul states that if creation is a gift to man, then grace determines man's fullness and deepest dimension as a creature. Grace is God's self-gift to man; it is God's Spirit breathed into the dust of our humanity. The state of original innocence speaks above all of this gift of grace that God gives and man receives. This grace made it possible for human persons to experience the meaning of the world as God's primary gift or donation, and this grace enabled them to experience the mutual donation of masculinity and femininity as a recapitulation of this gift. Their original communion of persons, then, was a participation in grace. And grace, John Paul tells us, is "participation in the interior life of God himself, in his holiness" (67). It is "that mysterious gift made to the inner man—to the human 'heart'—which enables both of them, man and woman, to exist from the 'beginning' in the mutual relationship of the disinterested gift of oneself" (68).

"Disinterested" obviously does not mean that man and woman lacked interest in each other. They were deeply interested in each other, but not selfishly so. Their experience of "the radiation of God's love" (i.e., grace) enabled them to love one another sincerely, as God loves. In this we can understand the beatifying experience of the beginning connected with the awareness of the nuptial meaning of the body. This blissful awareness of the body's meaning speaks of their conscious experience of God with them and *within* them—of God's Spirit (i.e., his love) radiating *through their bodies.* "Happiness," John Paul says, "is being rooted in love. Original happiness speaks to us of the 'beginning' of man, who emerged from love and initiated love. ...This 'beginning' can also be defined as the original and beatifying immunity from shame as the result of love" (67).

If we allowed our hearts to enter into this "beatifying experience," we would taste the love for which we all long and the interior peace it brings. Perhaps we hesitate to imagine the experience of original happiness for fear of discovering that we cannot attain what we so earnestly long for. Why tantalize ourselves with false hopes? Is it not more realistic just to "make do" with the inheritance of our sinfulness?

Although we have left our original innocence irretrievably behind, John Paul stresses that the love God gave to man in the mystery of creation and in the grace of original innocence he gave irrevocably. In the fullness of time, Christ will bear witness to this irreversible love of the Father. His mission will be to proclaim that the grace of the mystery of creation was not lost forever, but becomes for anyone open to receiving it, the grace of the mystery of redemption.[66] "Where sin increased, grace abounded all the more" (Rom 5:20). This means that in Jesus Christ we can attain the happiness we long for. Even if we will always know suffering and tears in this life, we are alive with hope that in the end God will wipe away every tear from our eyes (see Rev 7:17). This is why we call the Gospel *good* news!

B. Purity of Heart and Man's Fidelity to the Gift

John Paul closes his address of January 30, 1980 by stating that original innocence can be understood as "purity of heart." Purity of heart manifests "a tranquil testimony of conscience" precisely because it "preserves an interior faithfulness to the gift according to the nuptial meaning of the body" (69). Preserving this "faithfulness to the gift," is the key to man and woman's happiness (beatitude).

In his following address, John Paul explains what original man's experience of fidelity to the gift looked like. Once again, he does it by way of contrast with historical man's experience of shame. He says that shame corresponds to a threat inflicted on the personal intimacy of man and woman's relationship and thus bears witness to the interior collapse of innocence. This "threat to the gift" results from a radical interior alteration of the content of sexual desire. When void of God's love, sexual desire seeks to appropriate the other rather than be a gift to the other. John Paul describes this appropriation as the "antithesis of the gift" and "the extortion of the gift." These vivid images *ex*-press the *in*-terior "content" of lust with pointed accuracy. To "extort" literally means "to twist" or to "turn out." Sexual desire "twisted" by sin does not trust in the freedom of the gift and refuses to risk becoming a gift. Instead it grasps at the gift and even seeks to snatch it by force or manipulation. This effectively and utterly drains the gift of its meaning. It is the antithesis of the gift and the antithesis of the nuptial meaning of the body.

But if we "untwist" this experience or "flip it over," we rediscover the content of the original experience of sexual desire. If shame expresses the above lack of fidelity to the gift and the nuptial meaning of the body, then we can conclude that nakedness without shame expresses an experience of total fidelity to the gift and the nuptial meaning of the body. If shame indicates "the extortion of the gift," nakedness *without* shame indicates *total freedom* in man and woman's self-giving. We have already described this as "the freedom of the gift."

---

66. See 10/29/80, TB 167.

Therefore, according to John Paul, fidelity to the gift consists in a moral participation in the eternal and permanent act of God's will that each should be loved and received for his or her own sake, and never reduced interiorly to a mere "object for me." This means that if man and woman are to find the happiness they desire in their relationship, they must freely give themselves to each other in the whole truth of their masculinity and femininity as the Creator wished them to be. Furthermore, at the same time they must fully accept and "welcome" each other, receiving each other precisely in the whole truth of their masculinity and femininity—body and soul—as the Creator wished them to be. In other words, sincere self-giving has no conditions or reservations. Since it participates in the love of God, the giving and receiving of nuptial love is *total* and *irreversible*.

C. Giving and Receiving Interpenetrate

John Paul adds: "These two functions of the mutual exchange are deeply connected in the whole process of 'the gift of self': the giving and the accepting of the gift interpenetrate, so that the giving itself becomes accepting, and the accepting is transformed into giving" (71). This observation provides an important window into the dynamism of sexual complementarity.[67] We previously quoted John Paul saying that the reality of "gift" implies that there is one who gives and one who receives, and a mutual relationship is established between them (see §17). This giving and receiving, which established the original covenant between God and man, finds a symbolic reflection in the covenant relationship of man and woman. The male, by virtue of the specific nuptial dynamism of his body, is disposed toward giving or initiating the gift. The female, by virtue of the specific nuptial dynamism of her body, is disposed toward accepting or receiving the gift. Nonetheless, "giving" does not belong exclusively to the male, nor "receiving" exclusively to the female. They interpenetrate so that in giving the male receives and in receiving the female gives.

---

67. The work of Sister Prudence Allen, RSM on sexual complementarity is of special import. See "Integral Sex Complementarity and the Theology of Communion," *Communio* (winter 1990): pp. 523–544. For greater depth of philosophical foundations on the issue of sexual complementarity, see the introduction to her books *The Concept of Woman: The Aristotelian Revolution (750 BC—1250 AD)* (Grand Rapids, MI: Eerdmans, 1997) and *The Concept of Woman: The Humanist Reformation (1250–1500)* (Grand Rapids, MI: Eerdmans, 2002).

In fact, in the order of creation, it seems to John Paul that the man, before giving himself to the woman, first *receives* her from the hand of God. This seems to indicate that every human being's first posture as a creature is one of *receptivity* to the gift of God. Indeed, it is impossible for a creature to give anything if he has not first received. Hence, only by receiving woman as a gift from God can the man then initiate the gift of himself to her. As John Paul says, "'From the beginning' the woman is entrusted [by God] to his eyes, to his consciousness, to his sensitivity, to his 'heart.' He, on the other hand, must, in a way, ensure the same process of the exchange of the gift, the mutual interpenetration of giving and receiving as a gift, which, precisely through its reciprocity, creates a real communion of persons" (71).

In this intimate communion, man and woman discover their true selves *in the other* through the sincere gift of themselves *to each other* and in the sincere acceptance of each other's gift. When the whole dignity of the giving and receiving is ensured, both man and woman experience the "specific essence" of their masculinity and femininity. At the same time the Pope says they reach the deep recesses of the "possession of self." This authentic self-possession enables them to give and receive each other in a way that corresponds to the essence of the gift. Furthermore, the Pope observes that this giving and receiving grows ever deeper and more intense. It grows as the finding of oneself in giving oneself bears fruit in a new and more profound giving of oneself. Here we approach the manner in which the sincere giving of male and female to each other reproduces in created form the Uncreated and Eternal spirating exchange of the Persons of the Trinity (keeping in mind, of course, the infinite difference between Creator and creature).

By living in the Trinitarian image, man and woman fulfill the meaning of their being and existence; they reach beatitude. As we shall see, this "beatifying communion" points us in some way right from the beginning to the beatific communion of heaven. There the created sign of Trinitarian Life will give way to its divine prototype, and man will participate in Trinitarian Life itself. Here we see the continuity between the experiences of original man and eschatological man. The experience of incarnate communion in the resurrection will be completely new. Yet John Paul also affirms that "at the same time it will not be alienated in any way from what man took part in 'from the beginning.'"[68] In this way we see that our origin foreshadows our destiny. Even if historical man will lose sight of this vision, the Anointed One will come preaching "recovery of sight to the blind" (Lk 4:18).

---

68. 1/13/82, TB 248.

21. Subjectivity and the Ethos of the Gift

February 13, 20, 1980 (TB 72–75)

John Paul devotes the audience of February 13, 1980 to a review of the main concepts he has outlined thus far. He points to the novelty of his project when he states that theology has traditionally "constructed the global image of man's original innocence...by applying the method of objectivization, proper to metaphysics and metaphysical anthropology. In this analysis," he continues, "we are trying rather to take into consideration the aspect of human subjectivity" (72).

John Paul knows that much of the Church's moral teaching (about sexuality in particular) seems "abstract" to modern man. People today do not think of the world in objective, metaphysical categories. They understand the world primarily through their own experiences. By penetrating the *experiences* of the first man and woman, John Paul wants to demonstrate that the Church's objective norms (ethics) actually correspond to the deepest subjective desires of the human heart (ethos). He wants to demonstrate that the Church's teachings are not hopelessly removed from real life experience. Nor are they imposed from "outside" of man, but, when properly understood, they actually well up from "within" him. John Paul believes that this approach to the Scriptures is actually more in keeping with the original texts.

A. The Future of the Human Ethos

Man and woman entered the world with complete knowledge of the nuptial meaning of their bodies and what that called them to ethically— that is, to participate in God's mystery by loving each other as God loves. They did not need an objective norm commanding them to love. Filled with the grace of creation, they desired nothing else. This was the *ethos* (the interior experience of the good) by which they freely lived. In fact, the Holy Father says that original innocence manifests and at the same time constitutes the perfect *ethos* of the gift—the perfect ethos of love.

Having lost the original grace of creation, historical man also lost this experience of the good. Deceived by a lie, he has become "disconnected" in his heart from what will make him truly happy. This is why John Paul insists that we must construct this theology of the body "from the beginning," carefully following Christ's words. Historical man must follow the trail of his heart back to the beginning in order to "reconnect" with God's original plan for his happiness—and this means reconnecting with the *ethos* of the gift inscribed in his body and in his heart. As we have stressed throughout, rediscovering the truth about the body and sexuality is no side issue. John Paul observes that man and woman were given to each other as a gift in the whole perspective of the existence of mankind and of the human family. He says that the "fundamental fact of human existence at every stage of its history is that God 'created them male and female.'...In this way a great creative perspective is opened: precisely the perspective of man's existence which is continually renewed by means of 'procreation'" (74). Man's existence and future obviously *depend* on the call of man and woman to become "one flesh."

This call is deeply rooted in the consciousness of humanity. Although "the man and the woman...emerge from the mystery of creation in the first place as brother and sister in the same humanity," John Paul also remarks that, according to Genesis 2:24, "man and woman were created for marriage."[69] Hence, understanding "the nuptial meaning of the body (and the fundamental conditionings of this meaning) is important and indispensable in order to know who man is and who he should be, and therefore how he should mold his own activity. It is an essential and important thing for the future of the human *ethos*" (74). Stated simply: If we do not understand the nuptial meaning of our bodies, we do not know who we are and, therefore, we do not know how to live. Ethics is rooted in anthropology. How we are to live is rooted in *who we are* as God created us to be. When we interiorize the truth of who we are, we (re)experience "the ethos of the gift," that is, we come more and more to desire subjectively only that which is objectively good.

If we fail to realize this, living a moral life will inevitably become an attempt to follow what seem like arbitrary and imposed "rules." Without a deep interior knowledge and understanding of the "why" behind the "ought," we become unconvinced of the "ought" and sooner or later abandon it. A morality that fails to recognize and respect man as a living subject inevitably leads to this crisis.

B. Ethos and the Subjectivity of Man

Through the ethos of the gift we can outline the "subjectivity" of man. "Subjectivity" refers to the self-experience of personhood. A person knows that he is not some*thing* but some*one*. In other words, a subject knows he cannot be reduced to an object. Man is a subject precisely because he is made in the image of the Divine Subject, God.

---

69. In a later reflection on the Song of Songs, John Paul will clarify what he means by saying man and woman are first brother and sister in the same humanity (see §88). He will also clarify that our creation for marriage does not mean marriage is the only path to fulfill the nuptial meaning of the body (see Cycle 4).

■ Traditional theological formulations often referred to God as "the divine object." As George Weigel reports in *Witness to Hope,* the young Father Wojtyla resisted using this phrase in his doctoral dissertation on John of the Cross. The renowned Father Garrigou-Lagrange, who directed young Wojtyla's dissertation, criticized him for his lack of conformity, but Wojtyla insisted that there was a danger in a formula that "objectivizes" God. For Wojtyla, God should not be thought of primarily as "the divine object," but as "the divine *Subject."* As Weigel writes, "We do not come to know God as we come to know an object (a tree, a baseball, an automobile). Rather, we come to know God as we come to know another person, through mutual self-giving."[70] Young Wojtyla's insistence on this point with the formidable Garrigou-Lagrange showed his determination and readiness as a young man to forge new paths in the Church's theological reflection.

A subject has the richness of an interior life that affords the freedom to act, to choose this or that—in a word, to love. A person feels stripped of his dignity when his freedom as a subject is denied and he is forced to act in a given way. Even if he is forced to act in a way that is objectively good, he will not experience it as good unless he makes that good *his own* by choosing it freely as a subject. Here we encounter the creative interplay of divine and human subjectivity. God does not force his will on us; we are not pawns in a cosmic scheme. God respects us entirely as the subjects he created us to be. He wants us to want *for ourselves* to participate in his plan. God initiates the gift—he proposes his loving plan—and invites us to participate. Then we, as subjects, must choose. This divine "respect" God shows toward his own creature defines man as "partner of the Absolute" (see §12).

Because the first man and woman interiorized the objective good by making God's will their own, they experienced the objective *ethic* as a liberating *ethos.* This is how the original ethos of the gift is to be understood. The first man and woman *experienced* the objective good as good precisely because they freely chose it in accord with their dignity as subjects. They desired nothing else. In this way John Paul says that "the subjective profile of love" was "objective to the depths" because man's subjective desires were nourished by the objective truth of the nuptial meaning of the body. And this interior orientation toward the good is precisely purity of heart.

70. *Witness to Hope,* p. 86.

C. Subjectivity and Purity

At this point we can recall what we stated previously: When it is pure, subjectivity is completely objective (see §8). Purity of heart connects a person's subjective desires (ethos) with the objective order of love (ethics). We know this link was established in the hearts of the first man and woman—in other words, we know they were pure—because of the experience of original nakedness. "The fact that they 'were not ashamed' means that they were united by awareness of the gift; they were mutually conscious of the nuptial meaning of their bodies, in which the freedom of the gift is expressed and all the interior riches of the person as subject are manifested" (75). The Holy Father explains that in a way purity of heart made it impossible for them to reduce each other to the level of a mere object. Shame enters precisely when man and woman lose purity of heart. Because of this loss, they fail to respect "the interior riches of the person as subject" and come to look upon the person as an object to be used. Because of this loss of purity, the demands of love no longer spontaneously well up from "within" man. In fact, they often appear now as a burden imposed from "without."

To use our previous image, when man is deceived by the "great lie," he actually prefers his flat tires and views any norm that calls him to inflate them as a burdensome imposition.

For historical man the discovery of the nuptial meaning of the body will cease to be a simple reality of revelation and grace. Nonetheless, the Holy Father maintains that the original nuptial meaning of the body "will remain as a commitment given to man by the ethos of the gift, inscribed in the depths of the human heart, as a distant echo of original innocence" (75). Even though he must now look through "the veil of shame," historical man must continually rediscover himself as "the guardian of the mystery of the subject" so as to defend every subject from being reduced in any way to a mere object.

This flows from "purity of heart," which is the fruit of being filled with grace. So if we are to live and love as we are called and thus fulfill the meaning of our being and existence, our only hope is to be filled again with grace. And grace has been poured out. When we open our hearts to it, we come gradually to (re)experience the ethos of the gift. Then, to the extent that we (re)experience this ethos, living according to the full truth of the nuptial meaning of the body becomes our deepest desire and longing—not imposed from the "outside" but welling up from "within." Then we recognize that our "tires" are made for air, we repent of ever thinking otherwise, and we allow Christ to inflate us.

22. The Primordial Sacrament

February 20, 1980 (TB 76–77)

Prior to their "knowledge of good and evil," man and woman "are immersed in the mystery of creation; and the depths of this mystery hidden in their hearts is innocence, grace, love, and justice" (76). They *experience* innocence, grace, love, and justice precisely through the awareness of the meaning of their bodies, their masculinity and femininity and their call to become "one flesh." Seeing themselves with God's own vision, they know they are good, very good (see Gen 1:31). With this lived awareness of the meaning of their bodies, John Paul says that both man and woman enter the world as subjects of truth and love. This means that, prior to sin, the first man and woman freely chose to act with their bodies only in truth and in love.

A. The First Feast of Humanity

It is hard to imagine the freedom and *pure* delight taken in the experience of original nakedness and unity. John Paul, poet that he is, seeks to fire our imagination when he describes the original fullness of the experience of the nuptial meaning of the body as "the first feast of humanity" (77). It is a feast of pure love, of God's and man's goodness. It is a feast of delight in the fact that "being and the good are convertible" (see §10). To be alive is good. To be created male and female is good. To become "one flesh" is very good. Even if historical man will find this "original feast" largely spoiled by sin and death, "right from the mystery of creation we already draw a first hope: that is, that the fruit of the divine economy of truth and love, which was revealed 'at the beginning,' is not death but life, and not so much the destruction of the body...as rather the call to glory (see Rom 8:30)" (77). "Glory," Wojtyla tells us, "is the irradiation of good, the reflecting of all perfection. And in one way it is also the inner atmosphere of the deity, the godhead. ...In a very special way God transmits this glory to man. The glory of God is living man; the glory of God is man alive."[71]

This "call to glory" is stamped in our body-persons as male and female. Sin and death *cannot* overcome it. God extends to man *forever* this divine gift of life and love. We can reject the gift, but God will never withdraw it. Even if we have rejected the gift, we can still "repent and believe in the good news" (Mk 1:15). We can always rediscover the divine gift. Despite sin, a "spark" of the divine gift always remains within man. As the Holy Father says, "Man appears in the visible world as the highest expres-

---

71. *Sign of Contradiction,* p. 181.

sion of the divine gift, because he bears within him the interior dimension of the gift" (76). With this statement, we approach the heart and essence of what John Paul means when he speaks of a "theology of the body." Man bears within himself the call to "be gift," that is, to love as God loves. This call to be gift is made *visible* through his body as male and female and through the call to life-giving communion in marriage.

B. John Paul's Thesis Statement

"Thus, in this dimension, there is constituted a primordial sacrament understood as a sign that transmits effectively in the visible world the invisible mystery hidden in God from time immemorial. And this is the mystery of truth and love, the mystery of divine life, in which man really participates" (76). This statement requires a careful explanation because it can be misunderstood. The Holy Father is speaking of marriage as a "sacrament"—a theological term that refers to the mediation of grace—in the context of the state of original innocence. Is there such a thing? Do not the sacraments as such begin with Christ and the Church? In what way can we speak of a "primordial sacrament"—a sacramental mediation of grace from the "beginning" before the Incarnation and before the seven sacraments Christ instituted?

Let us jump ahead for a moment to where John Paul's ever-deepening spiral of reflections will eventually take us. In his analysis of Ephesians (Cycle 5), the Holy Father takes St. Paul's words seriously that we are chosen in Christ "before the foundation of the world" (Eph 1:4). Based on this, John Paul says that "one must deduce that the reality of man's creation was already imbued by the perennial election of man in Christ." The primordial sacrament can only be properly understood in reference to Christ. The grace in which original man participated "was accomplished precisely in reference to him [Christ]...while anticipating chronologically his coming in the body."[72]

Therefore, the primordial sacrament, one might say, is a primordial preview of "the plan of the mystery hidden for ages in God" (Eph 3:9), which comes to fruition and is definitively revealed in Christ. St. Paul makes this explicit when he links the "one flesh" union of Genesis with the union of Christ and the Church. This is a "great mystery," he says (other translations say this is a "great sacrament"), and it refers to Christ and the Church (see Eph 5:31–32). John Paul says that Ephesians 5, in par-

---

72. 10/6/82, TB 335.

ticular, authorizes us to speak of "sacrament" in the wider and perhaps also more ancient and fundamental meaning of the term.[73] If sacrament in its restricted meaning refers to the seven signs of grace instituted by Christ, in this broader meaning "sacrament signifies the very mystery of God, which is hidden from eternity, however, not in an eternal concealment, but above all, in its very revelation and actuation."[74]

But what is this "great mystery" hidden in God? As the *Catechism* says, the "innermost secret" of God is that "God himself is an eternal exchange of love, Father, Son, and Holy Spirit, and he has destined us to share in that exchange."[75] This eternal plan is already set in motion through the primordial sacrament, which John Paul understands as a sign that transmits effectively in the visible world that innermost secret of God. How is the divine mystery made visible and effective in man's life? "The sacrament, as a visible sign, is constituted with man as a 'body' by means of his 'visible' masculinity and femininity" (76). Through their bodies— and through their call to become "one body"—man and woman in some way *participate* in the divine exchange of Trinitarian Life and Love.

■ "Participation" was an important theme in Wojtyla's book *The Acting Person* and was also developed in various essays published in *Person and Community*. By "participation" Wojtyla means "acting together with others."[76] But this does not simply mean "doing things" in conjunction with others. For Wojtyla, the essence of the *person* is revealed in the freedom of truly human action. Thus, when we truly act with others we participate in *"the very humanness of others."*[77] Participation takes place when subjects, acting together, experience "inter-subjectivity." This means living in communion with others *(communio personarum)* and in the broader sense building community. When John Paul speaks about "participating in the mystery of divine life," he is talking about sharing in the *very divinity of God.* He means participation in the divine nature (see 2 Pt 1:4); participation in the eternal *Communio Personarum.*[78] In fact, John Paul will

---

73. See endnote of 9/8/82 (TB 380–382) for a detailed discussion of the term "sacrament."

74. 10/20/82, TB 341.

75. *CCC,* n. 221.

76. *The Acting Person,* p. 261.

77. Ibid., p. 294.

78. See *CCC,* n. 2780.

eventually describe the communion of saints as the experience of the "perfect intersubjectivity of all."[79] In this way we can understand why Wojtyla concludes one of his essays with this striking statement: "The central problem of life for humanity in our times, perhaps in all times, is this: *participation or alienation?*"[80]

Here we encounter John Paul's thesis statement that the "body, in fact, and it alone is capable of making visible what is invisible: the spiritual and divine. It was created to transfer into the visible reality of the world the mystery hidden since time immemorial in God, and thus to be a sign of it" (76). *This* is why the Pope speaks of a theology *of the body.* Recalling all that we said earlier about the proper understanding of "sign" (see §2), the body, in the full beauty and mystery of sexual difference and the call to communion, is a sign—the primordial sign—of God's very own mystery. As the *Catechism* teaches, God "impressed his own form on the flesh...in such a way that even what was visible might bear the divine form."[81] Upon this incarnational mystery hinges the deepest essence of the *humanum*—of what is human. Upon this incarnational mystery hinges the incomparable dignity of every human being. Upon this incarnational mystery hinges everything that John Paul II proposes to the Church and the world about who man is and who he is called to be.

All of creation is sacramental, in that it reveals something of the mystery of its Creator. But John Paul tells us that this "sacramentality of the world" reaches its fulfillment in man created in the image of God as male and female.[82] Man, in turn, reaches his fulfillment through the sincere gift of self, which was realized in an original way through the incarnate union of Genesis 2:24. According to John Paul, in view of the sacramentality of the human body we fully understand those words of Genesis 2:24, "For this reason a man leaves his father and his mother and cleaves to his wife and the two become one flesh." The Pope says that these words "constitute the sacrament of marriage" (76). John Paul later states more explicitly that "the mystery hidden in God from all eternity ...became *a visible reality through the union* of the first man and woman in the perspective of marriage."[83] *The union* of man and woman, consum-

---

79. 12/16/81, TB 245.

80. *Person & Community: Selected Essays*, p. 206.

81. *CCC,* n. 704.

82. See *CCC,* nn. 41, 288, 315.

83. 10/13/82, TB 338 (emphasis in original).

mated according to the words of Genesis 2:24, in some way sums up or consummates the "sacramentality of creation."

The Holy Father explains that against this vast background we come to understand the rich significance of original nakedness. The words of Genesis 2:25 ("they were both naked and not ashamed") "express the fact that, together with man, holiness entered the visible world" (76). Holiness enabled man and woman *to see* the mystery of God revealed in and through each other's naked body. Through the original experience of the nuptial meaning of their bodies, man and woman gained awareness of the "sacrament of the body" (77). They were immune from shame because they were full of grace; that is, they were holy. It is "in his body as male or female," John Paul says, that "man feels he is a subject of holiness." He further explains that holiness "enables man to express himself deeply with his own body...precisely by means of the 'sincere gift' of himself" (76–77). In other words, holiness enables us to love with our bodies as God loves. It enables us to realize that our bodies bear the stamp of God's mystery of love. Holiness enables us to see, live, and experience God's plan of love and communion in our bodies.

23. The Deepest Essence of Married Life
March 5, 12, 1980 (TB 77–83)

In his closing remarks on original man, John Paul shifts gears in order to reflect on Genesis 4:1, "Adam knew Eve his wife, and she conceived and bore Cain, saying, 'I have gotten a man with the help of the Lord.'" Even though this takes place *after* original sin in the chronology of the Yahwist account, John Paul includes this in his reflections on original man. He does so because "the term 'knew' synthesizes the whole density of the biblical text analyzed so far" (80). Furthermore, he wants to stress the continuity and connection between original man and historical man. Finally, in closing his reflections on original man, John Paul wants to emphasize that sexual union, procreation, and moral choosing are intimately linked with man's creation in the image of God.

A. The Meaning of "Knowledge"

As John Paul notes, our contemporary language, although precise, often deprives us of the opportunity to reflect on the deeper meaning of things. The biblical word "knew," on the contrary, takes us beyond the surface of the sexual act to penetrate the rich experience of inter-personal unity. John Paul goes so far as to say that by speaking here of knowledge, "the Bible indicates the deepest essence of the reality of married life" (79).

"Knowledge" clearly distinguishes the sexual union of man and woman as persons from the copulation of animals. Animals do not "know" each other. Animals cannot "know" each other. Their mating and reproducing are determined by biological instinct, "by nature." For man, sexuality is not a passive biological determinant, but reaches "the specific level and content of self-conscious and self-determinant persons" (82). The term "knowledge" indicates that human sexuality decides man's concrete personal identity. Biblical knowledge "arrives at the deepest roots of this identity and concreteness, which man and woman owe to their sex. This concreteness means both the uniqueness and unrepeatability of the person" (79).

■ A word on this "unrepeatability" of the person: A husband and wife who truly "know" each other have arrived at the irreducible core of the person, and each loves this *person*—not merely physical or spiritual attributes of the person, but the person himself (herself). At this level, they continually recognize and affirm the unrepeatability of the other; he (she) is utterly unique and cannot be repeated or replaced. When the "one flesh" union expresses a love at this level—and it is always meant to do so—it becomes impossible to imagine replacing one's spouse with someone else, whether in thought or in deed. To do so would be adultery committed in action or in "the heart." However, if becoming "one flesh" only expresses a love for certain pleasing attributes or characteristics of the other, these can be easily recognized and desired in someone else, and often to a "more pleasing" degree. Thus, the intuition that one is only valued at the level of certain pleasing characteristics casts a permanent shadow of doubt over the relationship. Only when love reaches the level of the unrepeatability of the person is it built on a stable foundation. This foundation lasts "forever" because the value of the person itself is infinite. This is why marriage is indissoluble and why adultery is such a grave violation, because marriage is meant to be a relationship based on a love that reaches the unrepeatability of the person.

Although the text speaks only of the man's knowledge of the woman, it is clear that in becoming "one flesh" man and woman share a mutual knowledge of each other through the mutual gift of themselves. John Paul points out that according to the book of Genesis, *datum* (knowledge) and *donum* (self-gift) are equivalent. Man and woman are *given* to each other in order to be *known* by each other. They "reveal themselves to each other with that specific depth of their own human 'self'...by means of their sex" (79).

This mutual "knowledge" (which can only be freely given and received, never grasped) is so intimate and unifying that man and woman become "almost the one subject of that act and that experience, while remaining, in this unity, two really different subjects" (79). Biblical knowledge, then, speaks of unity in plurality, a two in oneness, or, in John Paul's personalist language, an "inter-subjectivity." In this unity neither person is lost or absorbed in the other, but discovers his or her true self through the sincere gift of self, that is, through the experience of *knowing* the other and *being known* by the other.

■ This gives us an accurate test of authentic love: In giving yourself to another, do you become more yourself or less yourself? Do you discover your true self, or do you feel absorbed by the other, lost in the other? True love always leads to self-discovery, never self-abasement. We see this reality of perfect unity and perfect distinction pre-eminently in the Trinity, the ultimate model of all love. Each Person of the Trinity is unique, unrepeatable, and distinct from the others. Yet each "is" himself in virtue of his relation to the others, that is, in virtue of the eternal mystery of self-giving and Communion at the heart of the Trinitarian Life.[84]

In view of this "knowledge," the Pope says that their conjugal union contains a new, and in a way, a definitive discovery of the meaning of the human body. The knowledge man gained of himself through naming the animals (i.e., he differed from the animals, he was a person called to love, he had self-awareness and self-determination), comes to its fulfillment in his knowledge of woman. "Knowledge, which was at the basis of man's original solitude, is now at the basis of this unity" (80). Since everyone must pass from solitude to unity through the sincere gift of self, John Paul can say: "Everyone finds himself again, in his own way, through that biblical 'knowledge'" (81). He adds "in his own way," because even if the one flesh union of marriage is the primary way, it is not the only way to enter into that biblical knowledge. Christ will call some men and women to forego sexual union "for the sake of the kingdom" (Mt 19:12).

B. Knowledge Leads to "a Third"

As we read in Genesis 4:1, man and woman also come to know each other in the "third," which springs from them both. Eve conceived and bore a son "with the help of the Lord." John Paul observes that fatherhood

---

84. See *CCC,* nn. 254–255, 689.

and motherhood manifests and completely reveals the mystery of human sexuality. Joining in "one flesh" always involves a particular consciousness of the meaning of the human body, bound up with fertility and procreation. In turn, the human power to generate new life—even if human generation remains radically "other"—is indissolubly bound up with the mystery of eternal generation in the Trinity. Through the mystery of procreation the embrace of man and woman is most clearly seen also as the embrace of God and man. John Paul says elsewhere that through their biblical "knowledge" man and woman share "in the great mystery of eternal generation. The spouses share in the creative power of God!"[85]

Fatherhood and motherhood point in some sense to the crowning of all that John Paul has said about the mystery of man and woman as persons made in the divine image. Recall that in discussing how man and woman image God in and through their communion, John Paul specifically stated that on "all of this, right from 'the beginning,' there descended the blessing of fertility linked with human procreation."[86] Now the Pope says that every time a man and a woman join in that communion of persons that makes them "one flesh," thereby opening themselves to the "blessing of fertility," it "confirms and renews the existence of man as the image of God" (83).

■ With good reason, John Paul never defines *how* the fruitful communion of man and woman images the Trinity in terms of who might represent whom. While it may be a legitimate question for speculative theology, lining up spouses and their offspring with specific persons of the Trinity must be approached cautiously lest we move too continuously from the gendered creature to the Uncreated (and un-gendered) God. Furthermore, the Trinity has not revealed itself as Husband, Wife, and Child, but as Father, Son, and Holy Spirit. This obviously has great import.[87]

Although hereditary sinfulness deprives man of God's likeness, he remains in God's image.[88] Thus, every time man and woman conceive a child "with the help of the Lord," they reproduce another image of God. The divine image constitutes a basis of "continuity and unity" between original man and historical man. Furthermore, man and woman not only reproduce another image of God, they also reproduce their own living im-

---

85. *Mulieris Dignitatem*, n. 18 (see also n. 8).
86. 11/14/79, TB 47.
87. See *CCC*, nn. 42, 239, 370.
88. See *CCC*, nn. 705, 2566.

age. They again recognize themselves, their own humanity, in the birth of "the third." With these profound reflections, John Paul concludes that the "words of the Book of Genesis, which are a testimony of the birth of man on earth, enclose within them at the same time everything that can and must be said about the dignity of human generation" (83). As the Pope observes, within this mystery, the Creator accords a particular dignity to the woman.

C. Eulogy of Femininity

John Paul is a man who loves woman with a purity as close to the beginning as it seems possible to reach in this life. It can even be said in light of the above analysis that he is a man who *knows* woman (in a celibate way, of course). He knows her distinctive beauty and dignity, and he stands in awe of the mystery of God's creative love revealed in her.

The Holy Father does not intend merely to state the obvious when he notes that the "constitution of the woman is different as compared with the man" (81). He believes it is of great significance, and of particular credit to woman, that God has chosen her body to be the place of conception, the shrine of new life. The whole constitution of woman's body is made for motherhood. Since the body reveals the person, John Paul believes that this speaks volumes, not only about feminine biology, but about the dignity and nature of woman as a person. This is why he takes special care to note that the Bible (and subsequently the liturgy) "honors and praises throughout the centuries 'the womb that bore you and the breasts you sucked' (Lk 11:27). These words," he continues, "constitute a eulogy of motherhood, of femininity, of the female body in its typical expression of creative love" (82).

In her joyous proclamation, "I have gotten a man with the help of the Lord," woman expresses the whole theological depth of the function of begetting and procreating. Furthermore, in giving birth the first woman is fully aware of the mystery of creation—of everything we have been discussing about man's "beginning"—which is renewed in human generation. Yes, according to the Holy Father, the entire mystery, dignity, goodness, vocation, and destiny of man as revealed "in the beginning" is reproduced in some sense every time a child is conceived under the heart of a woman.

24. Life Refuses to Surrender

March 5, 12, 26; April 2, 1980 (TB 77, 80–90)

John Paul drops the following dramatic statement in his audience of March 5, 1980 without any commentary: "Sin and death entered man's history, in a way, through the very heart of that unity which, from 'the be-ginning,' was formed by man and woman, created and called to become 'one flesh'" (77). We quoted this statement previously in the context of discussing the serpent's scheme to make the symbolic diabolic (see §5). Satan aims to alienate man from the life-giving Communion of the Trinity. As we have learned, the original unity of the sexes was to be a sign (or symbol) that would "effectively transmit" the Trinity's inner life to them. So Satan attacks "through the very heart of that unity which, from 'the be-ginning,' was formed by man and woman, created and called to become 'one flesh.'"

If Satan can convince man to distort this "primordial sacrament" (i.e., marriage, including the marital embrace), it will no longer effectively communicate God's life and love. It could even become a *counter-sign* of God's life and love. In such a case the symbolic would become diabolic. In other words, what was meant to unite God and man (and man and woman) would instead divide them. We already see the importance of the first chapters of Genesis for a proper understanding of the encyclical *Humanae Vitae*. For contraception is a specific attempt to defraud that bib-lical knowledge of its potential to generate a "third." It becomes a falsifi-cation of creative love and a marked affront to what John Paul calls the knowledge-generation cycle.

A. The Knowledge-Generation Cycle

Knowledge always precedes generation and remains intimately linked with it. The rich significance of the word "knowledge" indicates that "the third" who springs from their union is also "known" as a person who shares the same humanity as his parents. Bestowing the name "man" on the child ("I have gotten a man"), then, greatly differs from the experi-ence of naming the animals. They *know* what the name "man" expresses: this "third" is "bone of their bones and flesh of their flesh" (see 84). He is a body that expresses a *person*. In this way John Paul says that the biblical cycle of "knowledge-generation" comes to a close.

In the experience of this *knowledge* in which they give rise to another person, man and woman "are almost 'carried off' together," the Pope says, "by the humanity which they...wish to express again" (84). They wish to express their humanity again (in "the third") in order to affirm the good-ness of life and to overcome, in some sense, the inevitable prospect of death which now is part of their horizon due to sin. Man's awareness of the nuptial and generative meanings of his body comes into contact right from the beginning with awareness of death. Yet John Paul says that the fact that "Adam knew his wife and she conceived and bore" is like "a seal impressed on the original revelation of the body at the very 'beginning' of man's history on earth" (85). This seal ensures that God's original plan of life-giving communion has not been overcome by original sin.

In fact, as John Paul proclaims, "there always returns in the history of man the 'knowledge-generation' cycle, in which life struggles ever anew with the inexorable perspective of death, and always overcomes it" (85–86). What words of hope! We must all reckon with the reality of death. But man and woman's "knowledge" manifests the good news that life *refuses to surrender.* This is the "gospel of the body."

B. Affirming the Goodness of Life

"It is as if the reason for this refusal of life to surrender, which is manifested in 'generation,' were always the same 'knowledge' with which man goes beyond the solitude of his own being, and, in fact, decides again to affirm this being in an 'other'" (86). Man and woman affirm the goodness of life in their openness and readiness to beget a man with the help of the Lord. John Paul continues: "Man, in spite of all the experiences of his life, in spite of sufferings, disappointment with himself, his sinfulness, and, finally, in spite of the inevitable prospect of death, always continues, however, to put 'knowledge' at the 'beginning' of 'generation.' In this way he seems to participate in that first vision of God himself: God the Creator 'saw...and behold, it was very good.' And ever anew, he confirms the truth of these words" (86).

Historical man will find it difficult to confirm the truth of these words. Due to sin and the difficulties now inherent in human life, men and women often teeter between hope and despondency, between the "risk" of communion and the "safety" of solitude, between affirming life's goodness and cursing existence. This can bring them to prefer not to bring an "other" into the world. It can even lead to them to consider the original blessing of fertility (see Gen 1:28) as a curse.

Yet the man and woman who take that risk of love, surrendering their bodies to each other in *knowledge* and potential *generation,* stare death in the face and boldly proclaim: *"Life is good.* Communion is better than solitude. Life is better than death. Life, in fact, conquers death. Where, O death, is your victory? Where, O death, is your sting?" (see 1 Cor 15:55) Everyone must take his stand. Everyone must choose his posture. This will have far-reaching implications, particularly for John Paul's reflections on *Humanae Vitae.*

C. Christ's Words Remain Pertinent Today

Modern men and women have many pressing questions about the nature of marriage, much like the Pharisees who approached Jesus to ask him about divorce. Although many current problems were unknown to

Christ's contemporaries, John Paul believes that Christ's response remains just as pertinent today as it was two thousand years ago. In the last century, man has gained tremendous knowledge about his body from a scientific point of view. However, such knowledge has led man in many cases to reduce the human body to the level of an "object" to be manipulated. This greatly differs from the biblical "knowledge" that recognizes the human body as the revelation of a personal subject with inviolable dignity.

By pointing to the beginning, Christ "wishes man, male and female, to be this subject, that is, a subject who decides his own actions in light of the complete truth about himself" (88). John Paul seeks to help modern man do this through the theology of the body—to understand fully who man is so that he can decide on his actions in that light. To move beyond partial perspectives of man's being and construct a "total vision of man," we *must* return to the "beginning." There we find the first inheritance of every human being in the world. There we find the first proclamation "of human identity according to the revealed word, the first source of the certainty of man's vocation as a person created in the image of God himself" (86).

The archaic text of Genesis is completely "pre-scientific." Yet in the simplest and fullest way it reveals the truth so important for the "total vision of man." It is the truth of human subjectivity and "inter-subjectivity," that is, the communion between persons. The objective science of human sexuality is not inherently bad, and, as John Paul notes, we need not deprive ourselves of its results. Nonetheless, if a "science of the body" is to serve man, it must be informed by a "theology of the body." Without this John Paul insists that no adequate answer can be given to contemporary questions connected with marriage and procreation.

Modern man may find the idea of constructing a theology of the body incongruous. However, as John Paul points out, it should not surprise anyone familiar with the Incarnation. "Through the fact that the Word of God become flesh, the body entered theology," the Pope muses, "through the main door" (88–89). John Paul also adds that the Incarnation became the definitive source of the sacramentality of marriage.

D. Questions of Human Life

Questions about the body, marriage, and human sexuality, therefore, have a distinct religious and theological quality. They "are not only the questions of science, but, even more, the questions of human life" (89). We can observe here the title of Pope Paul VI's watershed encyclical, *Of Human Life (Humanae Vitae)*. The problems of marriage and procreation which Paul VI addressed in this encyclical take us to the heart of the mystery *of human life*. Here John Paul II recalls that Paul VI himself spoke of the need for a "total vision of man" if we are to understand the teaching of *Humanae Vitae*. Herein lies one of John Paul's main inspirations for developing the theology of the body.

So many men and women seek in marriage the way to salvation and holiness. If they are to find the fulfillment for which they are looking, John Paul maintains that they "are called, first of all, to make this 'theology of the body'...the content of their life and behavior. In fact, how indispensable is thorough knowledge of the meaning of the body, in its masculinity and femininity, along the way of this vocation!" This is so, the Holy Father continues, "since all that which forms the content of the life of married couples must constantly find its full and personal dimension in life together, in behavior, in feelings! And all the more so against the background of a civilization which remains under the pressure of a materialistic and utilitarian way of thinking and evaluating" (89).

By pointing back to "the beginning," Christ wishes to tell men and women of every age that true fulfillment in the relationship of the sexes comes only through the "redemption of the body." This means regaining "the real meaning of the human body, its personal meaning, and its meaning 'of communion'" (89). Only by understanding this personal and communal meaning of the body revealed "in the beginning" can we even begin to see the serious privation of a materialistic and utilitarian view. However, to give an exhaustive answer to our questions about marriage and sexuality, we must not stop only at man's beginning. We must also look at his history and ultimate destiny. We must look to Christ's words about lust in the "heart" (Mt 5:8) and about marriage in the resurrection (Mt 22:24–30). These words will form the basis of John Paul's subsequent reflections first on historical man and then on eschatological man.

Original Man—In Review

1. Christ's discussion with the Pharisees about marriage is John Paul's point of departure. Moses allowed divorce because of men and women's "hardness of heart." But in the beginning "it was not so." Thus, we must look to God's original plan for marriage as the model and norm of every relationship in which man and woman become "one flesh."

2. The Elohist account presents the seven-day story of creation. It defines man objectively in the dimensions of being and existence as the only creature of the visible world made in God's image and likeness. The

Yahwist account presents the subjective complement to the Elohist account. It penetrates man's psychology and defines him in the subjective dimensions of consciousness and experience.

3. The "redemption of the body" won for us by Christ guarantees the continuity between original man and historical man. The man who lives with the inheritance of sin cannot return to innocence, but neither is he entirely cut off from his origins. Each person, in fact, experiences a certain "echo" of original innocence. Christ calls us back to "the beginning" with the living hope that his gift of redemption has the power to restore what was lost.

4. Human experience is an indispensable element in constructing a theology of the body. John Paul examines three fundamental human experiences: *original solitude, original unity,* and *original nakedness.* He attempts to "reconstruct" these experiences of man's "prehistory" not so much to determine precisely who man and woman were "then," but to help us better understand who we are now—more so, who we are meant to be.

5. Original solitude is based on the words of Genesis: "It is not good that the man should be alone." This solitude means not only that man is "alone" without woman (and woman without man), but that man is "alone" in the visible world as a *person.* Adam discovers in naming the animals that he alone is aware of himself and is able to determine his own actions.

6. In his solitude man discovers that he is a "partner of the Absolute" and a "subject of the covenant" with God. This realization hinges on man's freedom, which is most fully revealed in the alternative between death and immortality. In short, solitude determines that man stands alone in the visible world as a creature made in God's image.

7. Man's spiritual solitude is discovered through the experience of his body. The body expresses the person. The body expresses man's difference from the animals, his subjectivity, and his call to communion with God and with an "other" like himself.

8. Genesis describes the creation of woman in archaic, metaphorical, and "mythical" language. Adam's deep sleep indicates his return to non-being and God's "re-creation" of man as male and female. Woman's creation from Adam's rib indicates that male and female share the same humanity. They are "bone of the same bone and flesh of the same flesh."

9. The experience of original unity is based primarily on the key text of Genesis 2:24—the two become "one flesh." Original unity overcomes original solitude (in the sense of being alone without the opposite sex) and affirms everything about man's solitude (in the sense that he is a personal

subject made in the divine image). The union of the sexes in "one flesh," then, is worlds apart from the copulation of animals.

10. John Paul defines the original unity as a "communion of persons" *(communio personarum)*. He brings a dramatic development of thinking to the Church by positing the divine image not only in man's humanity as an individual, but also in the communion of persons which man and woman form right from the beginning. The marital embrace itself is an icon in some sense of the inner life of the Trinity.

11. For John Paul, relationality enters the definition of the person. To be a person means "being subject" and "being in relationship." The beauty and mystery of sexual difference fundamentally reveals this relationality.

12. By joining in "one flesh" according to God's original plan, man and woman rediscover their "original virginal value." The virginity of "the beginning" cannot simply be equated with an absence of sexual union, but is more properly understood as the original integrity of body and soul. The grace of the sacrament of marriage allows husbands and wives progressively to rediscover the original integrity of the "one flesh" union.

13. Original nakedness is the experience of nakedness without shame. As the clearest subjective indication of their creation in the divine image, it is the key to understanding biblical anthropology. Original nakedness indicates a full consciousness of the original meaning of the body as the revelation of the person. It indicates a pure and transparent spiritual communication between the man and the woman "prior" to communication in the flesh.

14. The tranquility of original nakedness derives from "the peace of the interior gaze," which apprehends "the original good of God's vision" in the nakedness of the other. In God's declaration of the goodness of creation, we recognize that the motive of creation itself is love. Love and self-giving are synonymous. God initiates his own self-gift by creating us in his image. Man receives this gift and reciprocates it. In this way, the covenant of love between God and man is itself a relationship akin to nuptial self-giving and communion.

15. Man and woman recapitulate the gift of God in creation by becoming a gift to each other. This call to be gift is inscribed in the nuptial meaning of their bodies. The nuptial meaning of the body is the body's capacity of expressing love, that love in which the person becomes a gift and thus fulfills the very meaning of his being and existence.

16. Sexual desire was not experienced as an autogenous force. Rather, it was experienced as the desire to make a sincere gift of self, that

is, to love as God loves. The freedom of the gift indicates that man and woman respected one another as persons who were created for their "own sakes." They could not grasp or possess one another. If they were to live in communion, they had to bestow the gift of self freely.

17. The nuptial meaning of the body reveals both the capacity to become a gift to the other and the capacity for the deep affirmation of the other. Affirmation of the person means receiving the gift the other offers and respecting the other as a person created for his (her) own sake.

18. Man can never avoid the nuptial meaning of his body. It is the fundamental element of his existence in the world. Even if the nuptial meaning of the body undergoes many distortions because of sin, it will always remain at the deepest level of the person.

19. Man's fullest and deepest dimension is determined by the radiation of grace—that is, by God's gratuitous love poured into the human heart. Grace is participation in the interior life of God himself, in his holiness. And the original unity of the sexes was itself a participation in God's life and holiness. Grace enabled them to be naked without shame, which attests to the sincerity of the mutual gift of self.

20. Original happiness refers to the original beatifying experience of man and woman's communion with God and with each other. Original happiness is being rooted in love. It speaks of man's emergence from love and his participation in love. It is manifested by the experience of original nakedness.

21. The gift is lived through the complementarity of the sexes. Man, having first received woman as a gift from God, is disposed toward initiating the gift of himself to the woman. In turn, the woman is disposed toward receiving his gift. But the giving and receiving interpenetrate so that the giving becomes receiving and the receiving becomes giving. This is an ever-deepening exchange which in some way reflects the eternal exchange within the Trinity.

22. The ethos of the gift enables us to penetrate the subjectivity of man. It refers to the inner orientation of the first man and woman toward the objective good. They did not need an external ethic enforcing the law of the gift. They desired nothing else. God's law was not imposed from "outside" but welled up from "within" each of them.

23. Through the visibility of masculinity and femininity and their call to communion, the invisibility of the divine mystery of Love and Communion is made visible. In this way we understand marriage as the "primordial sacrament." The body, in fact, and it alone is capable of making

visible the invisible mystery of God. This is the mystery of truth and love in which man, male and female, really participates.

24. Original nakedness helps us understand that the primordial sacrament was efficacious; it truly communicated God's grace, his holiness, to man and woman. Holiness enabled them to be naked without shame. Holiness enabled man and woman to express themselves deeply with their bodies through the sincere gift of self.

25. "Knowledge" indicates the deepest essence of married life and synthesizes the whole depth of the original experiences of solitude, unity, and nakedness. Knowledge brings such a unity that spouses almost become the one subject of that act, while remaining two different subjects. Hence, knowledge speaks of a unity in plurality. Everyone finds himself, in his own way, through this biblical knowledge.

26. Knowledge leads to a "third." In her exaltation, "I have gotten a man with the help of the Lord," woman expresses the whole theological depth of procreation and begetting. The Bible and the liturgy express a eulogy of femininity by honoring and praising the womb that bore Christ and the breasts he sucked.

27. The "knowledge generation cycle" speaks to the goodness of human life that persists and continues to assert itself despite the tragedy of sin and death. Through knowledge and procreation, life struggles with the prospect of death and always overcomes it.

28. Questions about the body, marriage, and sexuality have a distinctive religious quality. They are not only questions of science but more so they are the questions about the meaning of human life. This is why we must reconstruct God's original plan for the body according to the words of Christ.

Cycle 2

Historical Man

Historical Man is the second of the three cycles that establish John Paul's "adequate anthropology." In forty general audiences delivered between April 16, 1980 and May 6, 1981, John Paul reflects on the reality of embodiment and erotic desire as man and woman experience them in history affected by sin. As we venture into these reflections, let us "be not afraid" to face honestly how far we have fallen from God's original plan. For only if we first realize how bad the "bad news" is, do we then realize how good the "good news" is. The "good news" is that historical man is not merely the man influenced by sin. He is also redeemed in Christ, who gives us *real power* to regain progressively—if arduously—what was lost. We must keep this in the forefront of our minds as we reflect on the effects of sin on our experience of the body and sexuality. Without this hope, we will be tempted to despair, or to minimize and even normalize sin.

Once again the Pope bases his reflection on Christ's own words, this time from the Sermon on the Mount regarding lust and adultery committed "in the heart." Many throughout history have seen in Christ's admonition a universal prohibition against eros. Yet John Paul demonstrates that Christ's words do not condemn the heart. Instead, they call us to reflect on the original meaning of sexual desire, our fall from it, and how Christ restores God's original plan through the "redemption of the body." If men and women have been driving with flat tires, Christ's words invite them to open their hearts to life "according to the Holy Spirit" so that they might come to experience eros according to its original "inflated" meaning.

Christ's words appeal to that "echo" in each of us of God's original plan. The more we tap into that echo, the more we realize that lust not only radically betrays authentic eros; it also radically betrays our authentic humanity. As the primordial plagiarization of love, lust can never satisfy our desire for communion with an "other." Love and all life together in truth, requires liberation from lust. Faced with the incessant and magnetic pull of lust, man seems helpless to overcome it. Based on his own resources, he is. But the good news of the Gospel is that "Jesus came to restore creation to the purity of its origins." "His grace restores what sin had damaged in us."[1]

Man cannot return to the state of original innocence. The redemption he experiences in Christ is more aptly a partial participation in the future resurrection. Historical man—that is, fallen and redeemed man—lives in the constant tension of "already, but not yet."[2] Regarding the "not yet," historical man will always battle with concupiscence. Regarding the "already," John Paul insists that historical man can experience a "real and deep victory" in this battle. Since Christ rose from the dead *within history*, we can affirm with Wojtyla that *"the 'redemption of the body' is already an aspect of human life on earth.* This redemption is not just an eschatological reality but a historical one as well. It shapes the history of the salvation of concrete living people, and, in a special way, of those people who in the sacrament of matrimony are called as spouses and parents to become 'one flesh' (Gen 2:24), in keeping with the intent of the Creator announced to the first parents before the fall."[3] This is the "good news" of Christ's words in the Sermon on the Mount. They announce that Christ came to liberate eros from the distortion of lust. As the Pope says in *Veritatis Splendor*, Christ's words are "an invitation to a pure way of looking at others, capable of respecting the spousal meaning of the body" (n. 15). So John Paul asks: "Are we to fear the severity of these words, or rather have confidence in their salvific content, in their power?"[4]

25. The New Ethos: A Living Morality
April 16, 23, 1980 (TB 103–107)

John Paul says that an adequate anthropology tries to understand and interpret man in what is "essentially human." It rests on essentially human experiences, as opposed to the "naturalistic reductionism" which often goes hand in hand with the theory of evolution concerning man's origin.[5]

---

1. *CCC*, nn. 1708, 2336.

2. See *CCC*, nn. 1002–1004.

3. "The Family as a Community of Persons," *Person & Community: Selected Essays*, p. 326.

4. 10/8/80, TB 159.

5. See 1/2/80, TB 58 and the first endnote of the same address (TB 97).

Not all theories of evolution contradict Catholic faith.[6] But theories of evolution that reduce man to a chance occurrence of nature no different than any other living thing certainly do. Such an interpretation of man misses altogether what is "essentially human" and contradicts human experience. Despite some modern propaganda to the contrary, we *know* we differ from the animals. Chickens do not look up at the stars with awe and wonder. Chickens do not question the meaning of their existence; they do not write music or poetry; they do not build cathedrals. Chickens do not have freedom and self-determination. Thus, they cannot love; nor can they sin. Only persons can sin. It is the "flip side" of our capacity to love.[7] In this sense, sin is an essentially human experience.

A. Adultery in the Heart

In the Sermon on the Mount, Christ says, "You have heard that it was said, 'You shall not commit adultery.' But I say to you that everyone who looks at a woman lustfully has already committed adultery with her in his heart" (Mt 5:27–28). John Paul points out that this is one of those passages that fundamentally revises the way of understanding and of carrying out the moral law of the old covenant. Like Christ's words that pointed us to the "beginning," John Paul says that the Lord's words about lust are pregnant with theological, anthropological, and ethical content.[8] They have "a key meaning for the theology of the body," a "global context," and an "explicitly normative character" (103–104). These words, then, are not only directed toward those who heard the Sermon on the Mount with their own ears. They are directed toward "every man" (male and female) of the past and of the future.

John Paul observes that adultery "in the heart" concerns a desire for sexual knowledge of someone who is not one's spouse. Although Christ's words apply just as much to women as they do to men, for the sake of example Christ speaks of the lust of a man toward woman and describes it as adultery committed "in the heart." As an interior act, this desire is expressed through the sense of sight, with mere looks. John Paul cites the case of David looking at Bathsheba as a prime example (see 2 Sam 11:2). How are we to understand this "new level" of the traditional commandment against adultery? In other words, why does Christ posit the immorality of

---

6. See John Paul II, "Truth Cannot Contradict Truth," Address to the Pontifical Academy of Sciences, October 22, 1996.

7. See *CCC*, n. 1861.

8. See 10/15/80, TB 160.

adultery first "in the heart" before and even without an act of adultery being physically committed?

B. Ethic and Ethos

Christ summarizes his teaching in the Sermon on the Mount by saying, "You, therefore, must be perfect, as your heavenly Father is perfect" (Mt 5:48). As the *Catechism* observes, "It is impossible to keep the Lord's commandment by imitating the divine model from outside; there has to be a vital participation, coming from the depths of the heart, in the holiness and the mercy and the love of our God."[9] Christ's words about committing sin "in the heart" call us to enter this "vital participation" in God's holiness, in his mystery of love and self-giving. They inaugurate the fulfillment of God's promise to Israel: "I will make a new covenant with the house of Israel.... I will put my law within them, and I will write it upon their hearts" (Jer 31:31–33).[10]

Living a mature moral life as a Christian does not mean begrudgingly submitting oneself to an external code of ethics. Scripture and our own experience attest that it is possible to live in strict accordance with laws yet never attain holiness. It is called "legalism" or "moralism." In such case, people keep to legalistic observance of the formula, but the spirit of the law does not abound in their hearts. Christ calls us to something very different. He appeals to the *interior* man.[11] "First cleanse the inside of the cup and of the plate, that the outside also may be clean" (Mt 23:26). With these words Christ proclaims the "new ethos" of redemption. *Ethos* refers to a person's inner-world of values—what attracts and what repulses him. It embraces in its content "the complex spheres of good and evil, depending on human will and subject to the laws of conscience and the sensitivity of the human heart."[12] Ethos, therefore, "can be defined as the interior form, almost the soul, of human morality...To reach it, it is not enough to stop 'at the surface' of human actions, it is necessary to penetrate inside" (104–105). We must penetrate the human "heart" where moral value is connected with the dynamic process of man's interior life—his "intimacy."

In the Sermon on the Mount, Christ speaks "about a certain human interpretation of the law which negates...the correct meaning of right and

---

9. *CCC*, n. 2842.

10. See *CCC*, n. 1965.

11. See *CCC*, nn. 1430–1432.

12. 11/5/80, TB 169.

wrong as specified by the will of the divine Legislator."[13] The typical interpretation of the law came to be "marked by an objectivism" which was "not concerned directly with putting some order in the 'heart' of man."[14] In fact, a faulty interpretation of the law had led the Israelites, in many cases, to compromise with lust.[15] Christ appeals to the interior man (ethos) in order to recover the original meaning of the law (ethic). In effect, Christ's teaching in the Sermon on the Mount expresses this: "You have heard the objective law and interpreted it *externally*. Now I tell you the subjective meaning of the law—what it calls you to *internally.*" In other words, "You have heard the *ethic*. Now I speak to you of its proper *ethos.*"[16]

■ Here we clearly see John Paul, as he himself states, drawing from the phenomenology of Max Scheler. For morality to be "real" to man, it must be connected with an experienced value. In emphasizing (or perhaps over-emphasizing) this valid point, however, Scheler failed to recognize man's responsibility toward objective moral values when his perceptions of value are misguided. In Christ's words in the Sermon on the Mount, we see the call to *purity* in one's subjective values. For when man's heart is purified, his subjective values correspond to that which is objectively true, good, and beautiful. But even the impure man has a duty toward the objective good. If Kant's ethical system was based on man's duty to the moral norm and Scheler's was based on man's experience of value, Wojtyla/John Paul II wants to draw the proper balance between duty and the experience of value.

C. Fulfillment of the Law

This emphasis on the subjective dimension of "ethos" does not do away with objective norms. On the contrary, the *new ethos* "makes us enter the depths of the norm itself" from the perspective of the personal sub-

---

13. 8/13/80, TB 133.

14. Ibid, TB 137.

15. See 8/20/80, TB 136.

16. There remains an organic relationship between the Law and the teaching of Christ which must be maintained while any sharp contrast between them avoided. The Christian ethos is certainly "new," but there is also a continuity with the Old Testament understood as "fulfillment." See Vatican Commission for Religious Relations with the Jews, *Notes on the Correct Way to Present the Jews and Judaism in Preaching and Catechesis in the Roman Catholic Church*. See also Pontifical Biblical Commission, *The Jewish People and Their Sacred Scriptures in the Christian Bible* (Boston: Pauline Books and Media, 2002).

ject and his *experience* of morality. As Christ himself said, "Think not that I have come to abolish the law and the prophets. I have come not to abolish them, *but to fulfill them"* (Mt 5:17). "According to Christian tradition, the Law is holy, spiritual, and good, yet still imperfect. Like a tutor, it shows what must be done, but does not of itself give the strength, the grace of the Spirit, to fulfill it."[17] In this sense, the law is sterile. By itself it cannot give man life. But Christ came that we might have life and have it *to the full* (see Jn 10:10). He came to fill-us-full with the Spirit of life and love that enables us not only to meet the law's demands, but to *fulfill* the law. Thus, Jesus' "message is new but it does not destroy what went before; it leads what went before to its fullest potential."[18]

Man fulfills the law through "the 'superabounding' of justice" in the human heart which re-orients the person's "interior perception of values" (105). This interior conversion creates a "subjective vitality"—that is, a heart *alive* (through the indwelling of the Holy Spirit) with the truth about what is good, what is just, what is holy. In effect, Christ is saying in the Sermon on the Mount: "You have heard the commandment not to commit adultery, but the problem is you *desire* to commit adultery." In turn, "Christ's faithful [are those who] 'have crucified the flesh with its passions and desires' (Gal 5:24); they are led by the Spirit and follow his desires."[19] When a person is led by the Spirit in this way, the law no longer constrains him. In other words, such a person no longer needs an objective norm constraining him (or her) from committing adultery. Led by the Spirit, he *does not desire* to commit adultery. Lust—even if he is still capable of it—no longer holds sway in his heart.

When a person experiences this "subjective vitality," not only is his will set on what is true, good, and beautiful, but his "upright will orders the movements of the senses...to the good and to beatitude"[20] as well. For such a person, avoiding adultery no longer means that the will has to overpower the desires of the heart. The very idea of committing adultery repels the senses and the inner movements of the heart. Such a person understands, as the *Catechism* teaches, that the "perfection of the moral good consists in man's being moved to the good not only by his will but also by his 'heart.'"[21]

---

17. *CCC,* n. 1963.

18. John Paul II, "Homily on the Mount of Beatitudes, Galilee," March 24, 2000.

19. *CCC,* n. 2555.

20. *CCC,* n. 1768.

21. *CCC,* n. 1775.

Certainly the road to such perfection is long and arduous. Even the holiest of men and women will always retain a remnant of their disordered passions (concupiscence[22]) on this side of the resurrection. Nonetheless a person *alive* with the truth about good is not fooled by the devil's plagiarizations. He sees them for what they are—the twisting of what God created to be true, good, and beautiful. And when we see the true, good, and beautiful with our own eyes, the counterfeits lose their allure. At this point the moral norm is not external. It is not "imposed" from without but wells up from within. This is "a living morality," the Pope says. It is a *new ethos* in which the subjective desires of the heart come in harmony with the objective norm. Such a lived understanding of morality is essential if man is to discover himself. As John Paul affirms, this is "the morality in which there is realized the very meaning of being a man" (105).

■ John Paul repeatedly stresses that this is a "new" ethos with regard to the Old Testament.[23] Of course this "living morality" which abounds in man's heart through the Holy Spirit was not entirely inaccessible to the people of the Old Covenant. Nor, as one can plainly recognize, is it "automatic" for those baptized into the New Covenant. As St. Thomas observed, "There were...under the regime of the Old Covenant, people who possessed the...grace of the Holy Spirit.... Conversely, there exist carnal men under the New Covenant, still distanced from the perfection of the New Law."[24] When Christians remain distanced from the "new ethos," they tend either toward rigoristic "angelism" or permissive "animalism" (see §5). While the "animalist" in particular might deny it, both poles, in fact, are working from the same faulty rule-obsessed morality. For rigorously adhering to the law and rebelliously breaking it are two sides of the same legalistic coin. The "new ethos" that Christ establishes—when it is truly lived—contains the truths that both of these poles are seeking to protect: freedom from the law on the one hand and the fulfillment of the law on the other. If you are led by the Holy Spirit, you are not under the law. You are free with the freedom for which Christ has set you free. But this freedom is not license. This freedom desires the good, only chooses the good, and thus fulfills the law (see Gal 5).

---

22. See *CCC*, n. 2515.

23. See 12/3/80, TB 174, for example.

24. Cited in *CCC*, n. 1964.

26. Original Sin and the Birth of Lust

April 23, 30; May 14, 28, 1980 (TB 107–116).

Christ's statement about adultery committed "in the heart" indicates something much more profound than one might first think. It has not only an ethical meaning, but also a profound anthropological meaning. If we "follow its traces" we learn who historical man is, or who he has become as a result of original sin. Christ's words call us back to who man was *before* sin. They "demand, so to speak, that man enter his full image" (107). Hence we can understand why the ethical and anthropological meaning of Christ's words remain in a mutual relationship. By understanding how we are to live (ethics) we learn who we are (anthropology). Conversely, by understanding who we are, we learn how we are to live.

A. The Heart

Christ's words in the Sermon on the Mount invite us to recognize that the demands of love are stamped in our hearts. "The heart is the seat of moral personality."[25] John Paul says that the "heart" is, in a way, the equivalent of personal subjectivity.[26] "With the category of the 'heart,' everyone is characterized individually, even more than by name." Each person "is reached in what determines him in a unique and unrepeatable way." Through the "heart" man "is defined in his humanity from 'within.'"[27] Will, emotion, thoughts, and affections originate in the heart. The heart, then, is where we know and experience the true meaning of the body, or, because of the hardness of our hearts, fail to do so. As John Paul says, "The heart has become a battlefield between love and lust. The more lust dominates the heart, the less the [heart] experiences the nuptial meaning of the body."[28]

Lust results from the breaking of the first covenant with the Creator. St. John speaks of a threefold lust: the lust of the flesh, the lust of the eyes, and the pride of life. These are not "of the Father" but "of the world" (1 Jn 2:16).[29] St. John's words also hold great importance for the theology of the

---

25. *CCC,* n. 2517.

26. See 12/3/80, TB 177.

27. 8/6/80, TB 132.

28. 7/23/80, TB 126.

29. Sexual lust obviously has particular importance for the theology of the body. However, the "man of lust" should be understood in the wider context of the "threefold lust."

body. The Holy Father carefully points out that "the world" St. John speaks of is not the world the Father created which is always "very good" (Gen 1:31). It is the world man deformed by casting the love of the Father from his heart.

In order to understand what lust is, or rather, who the "man of lust" is, we must return to Genesis and "linger once more 'at the threshold' of the revelation of 'historical' man." The mystery of sin marks the beginnings of human history. But this also marks the beginning of salvation history. Returning to Genesis "is all the more necessary, since this threshold of the history of salvation proves to be at the same time the threshold of authentic human experiences" (109). Through these experiences we establish an "adequate anthropology," including the experience of original sin. Original sin is certainly a mystery, but this does not mean it is abstract. There is perhaps no mystery of our faith confirmed more by human experience than the reality of sin. And, as John Paul will masterfully demonstrate, we can even reconstruct Adam and Eve's experience of original sin through a phenomenological examination of the Yahwist text.

B. Questioning the Gift

How did the "man of lust" take the place of the "man of original innocence"? Without completely analyzing the temptation and sin,[30] John Paul points to the "key moment" of the serpent's dialogue with the woman: "You will not die. For God knows that when you eat of it your eyes will be opened, and you will be like God, knowing good and evil" (Gen 3:4–5).

According to John Paul, this key moment "clearly includes the questioning of the Gift and of the Love from which creation has its origin as donation" (110). Man's existence, along with all of creation, was a gift of gratuitous love God gave to man. Created in the divine image and likeness, man could receive creation as a gift and reciprocate the gift of himself to God. Through this original covenant, God granted man the opportunity to participate in his very life, to be "like God" as a free gift (see §§15, 17). This is the deepest yearning of the human heart, to be "like God," to participate in his happiness (beatitude), in God's life. But Satan wants to keep this from us. One could read the serpent's temptation like this: "God does not love you. He does not want you to be like him, nor does he intend to make a *gift* of his life to you. In fact, he is specifically withholding it from you by forbidding you to eat from this tree. If you want life (happiness), if

---

30. See *CCC*, nn. 396–401.

you want to be 'like God,' then you have to reach out and grasp it for yourself because God won't give it to you."

Man determines the intentionality of his very existence by one of two fundamental and irreconcilable postures: *receptivity* or *grasping*.[31] The posture each person assumes depends upon his concept of God. If God is Love and the giver of all good things, then to attain the happiness we long for, we only need to *receive*. If God is a tyrant, then we will see him as a threat to our happiness, turn from our natural posture of receptivity, and seek to *grasp* life for ourselves. Certainly man also has the task of imaging God by taking the initiative and developing the world ("till [the earth] and keep it," Gen 2:15). But, as a creature, man becomes "like God" only by first *receiving* this likeness *from* God. In other words, as a creature, man's proper initiative always proceeds from his receptivity to the gift.

As the *Catechism* explains, "Constituted in a state of holiness, man was destined to be fully 'divinized' by God in glory." Man need only open himself to receive this as a gift. "Seduced by the devil, he wanted to 'be like God,' but 'without God, before God, and not in accordance with God.'"[32] Herein lies the denial of the gift and, in turn, the denial of man's receptivity before God. Man sets himself up as the initiator of his own existence and grasps at what God desired to give him freely.

■ The tendency to question the gift and "grasp" seems built-in to our fallen nature, as we can observe even in little children. For example, when my son asks for a cookie for dessert, before I can even get the cookie out of the box to present it to him as a gift, what does he do? He grasps at it. So I say to him, "Thomas, you're denying the gift. If you believed in the gift all you would need to do is hold your hands out in confidence and *receive* the cookie as a gift." When we believe in the gift and receive it as such, the natural response is to say "thank you" for the gift. The problem with man in his relationship with God is that he does not believe in the gift. So he grasps at it. "If you knew the gift of God...you would have asked him and he would have given you living water" (Jn 4:10). Not only is Christ the gift given, but he is also our example: "Have this mind among yourselves, which was in Christ Jesus, who, though he was in the form of God, did not count equality with God a thing to be grasped" (Phil 2:5–6).

---

31. For an excellent article on the nature of sin in relation to receptivity and grasping see Jean-Pierre Baput's "The Chastity of Jesus and the Refusal to Grasp" *(Communio,* Spring 1997, pp. 5–13).

32. *CCC,* n. 398.

Going further, the nuptial imagery of the Scriptures provides particular insight into this dynamic of original sin. It is of the bridegroom's masculine constitution to *initiate* the gift and of the bride's feminine constitution to *receive* the gift. Hence, in the spousal analogy of the Scriptures, God is symbolically "masculine" as the Heavenly Bridegroom, and man (male and female) is symbolically "feminine" as the Bride (this spousal analogy will come to fulfillment, of course, in the relationship of Christ and the Church). Using this nuptial imagery, it can be said that original sin consists in the rejection of the Bride's (man's) receptivity in relation to the Bridegroom (God). Do we not perhaps see in this reality why, according to the author of Genesis, the serpent approached the woman? He wanted man to reject his receptivity to the gift. As the one who embodies the "receptivity of the gift," woman stands as the archetype of all humanity.[33]

In succumbing to Satan's grievous lie, we detect the mystery of man who turns his back on "the Father." Man questions in his heart the deepest meaning of his existence as a gift from God; he doubts that Love was the origin of creation and the covenant. Conceiving God instead as a jealous tyrant goads man to do battle against him so as not to be enslaved. Thus, man turns his back on Love, casting "the Father" out of his heart.

At this point we penetrate the meaning of that gripping statement of John Paul's quoted earlier: *"This is truly the key for interpreting reality.... Original sin, then, attempts to abolish fatherhood."*[34] In its essence, original sin denies the Fatherhood of God, God's benevolent love that originates (i.e., "fathers") all of creation. We cannot understand who man is in creation, who he has become in history, and who he is destined to be in the eschaton—we cannot understand reality—unless we understand the mystery of God's Fatherhood *and* its denial. This is why "Christ, *through the revelation of the mystery of the Father and his love,* fully reveals man to himself and makes his supreme calling clear."[35]

■ This "key" for interpreting reality—that original sin attempts to abolish fatherhood—gives us the "key" for understanding the importance of the prayer Christ taught us. Is not the "Our Father" the specific antidote to the original lie of the deceiver? Does it not restore the truth about God and man denied by original sin? In the face of the devil's attack on God

---

33. See *Mulieris Dignitatem*, nn. 4, 27, 30. See also Edith Stein, *Essays on Woman* (Washington, D.C.: ICS Publications, 1987), pp. 62–63.

34. *Crossing the Threshold of Hope*, p. 228 (emphasis in original).

35. *Gaudium et Spes*, n. 22 (emphasis added).

and his love, the first man and woman should have proclaimed that God is "our Father—hallowed be his name!"[36] In the face of Satan's temptation to break away from God's reign and set their will in opposition to God's, the first man and woman should have proclaimed: "God's Kingdom come. *His* will be done on earth as it is in heaven!"[37] In the face of Satan's temptation to deny the gift, they should have proclaimed: "Our Father will *give* us our daily bread. We need not grasp at it!"[38] Finally, in this intense battle with the anti-Word, had the first man and woman only cried out in faith to the Father, "Spare us from yielding to temptation and deliver us from the evil one!"[39] God would surely have saved them. Perhaps we now understand more clearly why the *Catechism* asserts that the "Lord's Prayer 'is truly the summary of the whole gospel.'"[40] By denying the Fatherhood of God through original sin, man cut himself off from the original Covenant and lost sight of his own dignity and calling. Yet the "Lord's Prayer brings us into communion with the Father and with his Son, Jesus Christ. At the same time it reveals us to ourselves."[41]

By resisting the "rays of fatherhood," man almost cuts his heart off from what is "of the Father" so that all that remains in him is what is "of the world." In this moment John Paul says we are witnesses in a sense of the birth of human lust and the subsequent de-construction of man and woman's humanity. Recall that man and woman realized the gift of God's love precisely through the body and the experience of original nakedness. "This is the body: a witness to creation as a fundamental gift, and so a witness to Love as the source from which this same giving springs."[42] In this experience John Paul says that the human body bore in itself an unquestionable sign of the image of God. In fact, the original experience of the body provided the certainty that the whole human being was created in the divine image. In turn, the original acceptance of the body provided the basis for the acceptance of the whole visible world as a gift of God's love. What, then, would happen to their experience of the body if they questioned the gift and cast God's love from their hearts? Would they—could they—still experience the body as a "witness to Love"?

---

36. See *CCC*, nn. 2779–2815.

37. See *CCC*, nn. 2816–2827.

38. See *CCC*, nn. 2828–2837.

39. See *CCC*, nn. 2846–2854.

40. *CCC*, n. 2671.

41. *CCC*, n. 2799.

42. 1/9/80, TB 62 (see §17).

C. The Entrance of Shame

Lucifer promised Adam and Eve sight: "your eyes will be opened" (Gen 3:5). Yet all along that fallen "angel of light" desired to darken their vision. God had already freely given them not only sight, but the original good of his own vision. Satan dupes man into believing that God had created them blind and did not want them to see. Far from gaining anything by eating the forbidden fruit, man and woman lose what they had already been freely given. The Holy Father observes that, due to sin, man in some way loses the original certainty of the "image of God" expressed in his body. In fact, the body as a sign of the person and of the mystery of God's love "collapses," as the following words attest: "Then the eyes of both were opened, and they knew that they were naked; and they sewed fig leaves together and made themselves aprons" (Gen 3:7).

These words express the "frontier" between the man of original innocence and the man of lust. Shame is the boundary experience. Nakedness originally revealed the gift of God's love and enabled them to participate in it. It "represented full acceptance of the body in all its human and therefore personal truth" (113). Now nakedness reveals that they have been deprived of God's gift and are alienated from God's love. It reveals that they have lost sight of the body as the revelation of the person and of the divine mystery. A rupture and opposition now divide the spiritual and the sensible. This is what spawns shame. As John Paul expresses, shame enters when man "realizes for the first time that his body has ceased drawing upon the power of the spirit, which raised him to the level of the image of God" (115).

Since gender difference highlights man's spiritual-sensible (soul-body) polarity in a particular way, gender difference itself is now "blamed" in a sense for the rupture sin caused. This is where the rupture of sin is immediately "felt" and experienced. John Paul observes that man is ashamed of his body because of lust. Then he clarifies that man is ashamed not so much of his body as precisely of lust. In other words, man may attribute shame to the body and to gender difference, but this is almost always an excuse not to contend with the disorder of his own lustful heart.

The Pope explains that lust indicates the state of the human spirit removed from "the original fullness of values" that man possessed in the dimensions of God. Thus lust is a lack—the lack of God's love in the human heart. In the sexual realm (what St. John calls the "lust of the flesh"), lust refers to *un*-inspired sexual desire: sexual desire no longer informed by the Spirit, by God's love and grace.[43] In the Genesis text, shame rises because

---

43. See *CCC*, n. 2351.

even after sin man and woman still know they are called to love—to be a sincere gift for each other. They have not forgotten what they experienced before sin. But their ability to bring about that love has been shaken at its very foundations. Love no longer spontaneously wells up through their bodies as the expression of the heart. The heart, lacking the *in*-spiration of God's love, now tends to lust—to treating the other as an object created for "my sake" (i.e., for the sake of my own self-gratification), rather than as a subject created for his or her "own sake." Shame announces the uneasiness of conscience connected with this "new" experience.

Historical man experiences the lust of the flesh in two related ways. First, lust asserts itself almost as a predisposition resulting from original sin. When left to itself, man's fallen nature inclines him to treat others as objects of enjoyment rather than as subjects to love. This basic disorder—while it comes from sin (original sin) and inclines man to sin—is not itself a sin. Sin, in the proper sense, demands the engagement of the will. This is the second "experience" of lust. Only when a person engages his or her will to foster and follow that internal concupiscent impulse can one speak of lust as an "interior act," and therefore as a sin.[44]

If concupiscent desire is a "given" of man's fallen nature, does this mean that historical man is bound by his lusts? No! As John Paul boldly proclaims, *"Christ has redeemed us!* This means he has...set our freedom free from the *domination* of concupiscence. And if redeemed man still sins, this is not due to an imperfection of Christ's redemptive act, but to man's will not to avail himself of the grace which flows from that act."[45]

27. The Dimensions of Shame

May 14, 28, 1980 (TB 111–117)

As he continues his analysis, the Holy Father wants to penetrate the phenomenon of lust by examining the first man and woman's experience and their state of consciousness. "The Yahwist text," he says, "expressly enables us to do so" (112). The revelation of man and woman's first experience of shame takes us to the depths of man's "new" discovery of himself as a body in the world. Yet this time the Pope states that it is as if the man of lust felt that he had just stopped being above the animals. It is as if his experience of the body and sex was "driven back to another plane."[46]

---

44. See 10/8/80, TB 157.

45. *Veritatis Splendor*, n. 103 (emphasis in original).

46. See 7/23/80, TB 126.

What distinguished man from the animals? Man could freely determine his own actions. He was not led by instinct but was master of himself. For the person to live according to his own dignity requires such mastery. Because of sin, however, John Paul says that the structure of self-mastery is, in a way, "shaken to the very foundations" (115). Man suddenly realized that he had lost control of his body and its impulses. "It is as if he felt a specific break of the personal integrity of his own body, particularly in what determines its sexuality" (116).

Because of the rupture of the original covenant with God, man experiences almost a rupture of his original spiritual and material unity. Here we touch upon that "great divorce" spoken of previously (see §5). The perfect integration between the "breath" of the spirit and the "dust" of their bodies was now lost. Hence, the Pope observes that man not only lost the supernatural (and preternatural) gifts of grace which were part of his endowment before sin. He also "suffered a loss in what belongs to his nature itself, to humanity in the original fullness 'of the image of God'" (112). That "original fullness" is man's "natural" state.[47]

A. Shame Shakes the Foundations of Existence

The perfect integration of body and soul enabled the first man and woman to live in the perfect freedom of the gift. Since we tend to normalize our experience of disintegration, we can hardly imagine the "shock" of their new experience of having lost that freedom. Returning to our image, this would be akin to the shock of having driven with inflated tires and then having all four tires blow at the same time. Driving would be a totally different experience. As the Pope intuits, at the moment the first man and woman ate from the tree and fell from the original state of grace, "shame reaches its deepest level and seems to shake the very foundations of their existence" (111). So the man and his wife hid themselves from the presence of the Lord when they heard him walking in the garden (see Gen 3:8). The precision of the dialogue that then ensues between God and man, along with the whole narrative of the fall, is "overwhelming," the Pope says. "It manifests the surface of man's emotions in living the events in such a way as to reveal at the same time their depth" (112).

The "Lord God called to the man and said to him, 'Where are you?' And he said, 'I heard the sound of you in the garden, and I was afraid be-

---

47. See John Paul's endnote (TB 182–183) for an excellent summary of the Magisterium's treatment of various issues regarding nature and grace. Notice, too, that the Pope observes that these statements must be viewed according "to the needs of the age" in which they were made.

cause I was naked; and I hid myself'" (Gen 3:9–10). A certain fear always belongs to the essence of shame, but this is more than a fear of being physically naked. The experience of nakedness speaks of the interior movements of the heart. Nakedness before the Lord first indicated the unity established between God and man by the original covenant. Now, having eaten from the tree, man's own heart condemns him. He *knows* that he has broken the original covenant with God. He already feels the consequences *in his body*. In his state of fear and confusion, he can only "hide" in a fruitless attempt to escape the consequences of his actions. Here we have history's first "cover-up." As John Paul states, "Man tries to cover with the shame of his own nakedness the real origin of fear, indicating rather its effect, in order not to call its cause by name" (112). The real origin of man's fear is his "closing of his heart" to God's gift. Shame, therefore, keenly manifests the betrayal of the trust that God extended to man in the original covenant. But Adam refuses to admit this to himself or to God.

This new experience of his body not only indicates that sin shattered his original relationship with God and with the woman. It also reveals that sin ruptured his original and harmonious relationship with the rest of creation. "Original acceptance of the body was, in a way, the basis of the acceptance of the whole visible world" (113). Now, however, even the earth resists man and his task of "tilling the soil." The ground itself is "cursed" because of him (see Gen 3:17). Here we see that man's experience of his own gendered embodiment affects questions of ecology and questions of a society's work and economic structures. These issues are inseparable from sexuality, marriage, and family life. We must first reclaim the true meaning of these if we are to establish harmonious relationships with the environment, within the workplace, within culture at large, and between nations.

■ We see here the false dichotomy between the typically labeled "liberal" concern for social justice and the "conservative" concern for Church doctrine on sexual morality. John Paul is viewed as a man of contradiction because of his staunch support for both. Yet the contradiction does not lie in him. Social justice and sexual morality flow from the very same vision of the human person's dignity as a subject made in God's image and called to live in a communion of persons.[48] Furthermore, since man and woman's relationship is the deepest substratum of the social structure, there can be no social justice without a return to the full truth of the Christian sexual ethic.

---

48. See *CCC*, n. 2419.

Indeed, sin, injustice, and death entered the scene upon the denial of the gift revealed through masculinity and femininity: "You are dust and to dust you shall return" (Gen 3:19). Hence, the first man's fear also expresses "the sense of insecurity of his bodily structure before the processes of nature, operating with inevitable determinism" (114). In this way, John Paul suggests that man's fear in his nakedness implies a "cosmic shame." Man's sin disrupted the whole world order (see Rom 8:20–21). Man was created in God's own image as the crown of creation. He was called to have dominion over the earth and subdue it. Yet rather than the earth being subject to him, he is now subject to the earth. And all of this is felt *in his body*. The body represents man's "transcendent constitution." Man's body, which once shone with the glory of God, must now return to the earth. Man will either maintain hope and strive in his body to reclaim his transcendence, or he will surrender his body to decadence and decay. This is the battle for man that has raged in him and all around him since "the beginning."

B. Shame Is Immanent and Relative

Shame in relation to the cosmos makes way for the shame that is produced in humanity itself. Lust threatens man's dignity as a person made in God's image. John Paul affirms again that man was God's image both in his "personal ego" (original solitude) and in the interpersonal relationship of man and woman together (original unity/*communio personarum*). The shame that results from lust, then, is both *immanent* and *relative*.

Here we venture into the finer points of John Paul's analysis. Immanent shame refers to the shame experienced *within oneself* due to the loss of freedom (self-mastery) that resulted from the rupture of body and soul. This is the "flip side" of the experience of original solitude, in which man discovered his unique dignity as an integrated body-person. Immanent shame seems to indicate that man knew that the disintegration of body and soul threatened the value and dignity of his own personhood. The Pope remarks that this self-shame reveals a "specific humiliation mediated by the body." The person now finds it very difficult to embrace his own body, and he fails to perceive how essential his body is in understanding and embracing his own humanity. John Paul concludes that this shame is so acute "as to create a fundamental disquiet in the whole of human existence" (115).

Relative shame refers to the shame experienced *in relation* to the other. This is the "flip side" of the experiences of original unity and nakedness. Relative shame manifests a fear for one's own self in the presence of the other. This fear "obliges them to cover their own nakedness, to hide their own bodies, to remove from the man's sight what is the visible sign of femininity, and from the woman's sight what is the visible sign of masculinity" (114). Of course, this "visible sign" of masculinity and femininity refers most specifically to the genitals.

■ From all this we see that lust shatters the peace of the three original experiences of solitude, unity, and nakedness. Void of the gift, each experience is twisted into its negative form. Solitude becomes an experience of alienation. When the freedom of the gift is removed from communion, "commun-*ism*" is the only possibility—a coerced and, therefore, false unity that does not respect the dignity of the person as a self-determining subject. Finally, when lust is full-blown, nakedness without shame is twisted into shamelessness.

The negative form of the original experiences of solitude-unity-nakedness can also be understood in the following way. The person still desires to express his own "self" (original solitude), but void of the gift deforms this into an egotistical and alienating self-assertion (radical individualism). The person still desires others (original unity), but void of the gift deforms this into a "using" of others (radical exploitation). The person still desires to see and be seen by another (original nakedness), but void of the gift deforms this into voyeurism and exhibitionism (radical perversion). If the original experiences led to thanksgiving, worship, and beatitude, the deformed experiences lead to self-gratitude, idolatry, and despair. As we shall see, by the revelation of "the Gift" (of the mystery of the Father and his love), Christ will fully restore man to himself by restoring the grace that afforded the original experiences. This will be fulfilled definitively in the eschaton, but we also can begin to reclaim this restoration in the here-and-now.

Both immanent and relative shame have a sexual character. John Paul observes that the sphere of sexuality seems to highlight the interior imbalance connected with immanent shame. In a way, man feels lust *within himself* even before he experiences it *in relation* to the "other." When he actually directs this lust toward the other, we see the sexual character of relative shame. In this way, as John Paul observes, immanent and relative shame overlap. Just as the experience of solitude leads to unity, on the "flip side" lust does not merely stay *within*, but is always directed toward an "other." When this happens, even if it is only a lustful look as Christ indicates, the other feels threatened and instinctively wants to hide. This is why we cover our bodies—specifically those parts of our bodies that distinguish us from the opposite sex: to protect ourselves from the threat of lust. This is the "experience" of shame.

As John Paul indicates, we see here that shame and lust explain one another. Lust "explains" shame because lust gives rise to shame. Shame "explains" lust by revealing the injury caused by lust, both within the person lusting (immanent) and in regard to the person toward whom that lust is directed (relative). In this way, as the Pope tells us, we understand better why—and in what sense—Christ speaks of lust as adultery committed in the heart. Adultery is inherently non-marital. So is lust. Adultery is contrary to the dignity and value of the person. So is lust. Adultery is a counter-sign of the communion of love within the Trinity. So is lust.

C. Shame Has a Double Meaning

The need to cover the body in the presence of the other indicates that man and woman have lost "the peace of the interior gaze" (see §17). In a word, they have lost purity. They no longer see the other's body as a revelation of God's mystery. They no longer see the other's body as the revelation of the person. Instead, they see the other's body more as a "thing" to be used for their own selfish gratification. Sexual desire, void of the *in*-spiration of God, has become inverted, self-seeking.

■ It seems true, generally speaking, that men tend to experience their fallen sexual desires as geared toward physical gratification at the expense of a woman, while women tend to experience their fallen sexual desires as geared more toward emotional gratification at the expense of a man. We have all heard the expression that men will use love to get sex and women will use sex to get love (Wojtyla's book *Love & Responsibility* offers an in-depth analysis of these dynamics). It should also be mentioned here that some men and women experience sexual desires toward members of the same sex. While same-sex attractions—since they are almost never freely chosen—are not in themselves sinful, they are part of the disorder of the sexual appetite caused by original sin. In other words, if the men and women of history sometimes experience erotic desire toward their own sex, we can certainly say that "in the beginning it was not so."[49] The good news is that, whatever our individual distortions, we are all called to experience the ethos of redemption which has *real power* to restore God's original plan for sexuality in our hearts. This does not come easily nor completely in this life. Furthermore, the more deeply wounded a person is in his or her sexuality, the more time and effort it requires to experience

---

49. For a more thorough discussion of homosexuality in light of John Paul's theology of the body, see Christopher West, *Good News About Sex & Marriage: Answers to Your Honest Questions about Catholic Teaching,* chapter 8.

healing. Indeed some, like St. Paul, may experience a particular "thorn in the flesh" that, despite every sincere effort, is not removed in this life (see 2 Cor 12:7–10). On this point, we can observe that, through humble acceptance of one's cross, holiness can be compatible even with deep woundedness. That being said, we must also affirm that no one is exempt from what John Paul describes as the "task" Christ gives us of reclaiming God's original plan for the body and sexuality. As the *Catechism* states, "All Christ's faithful are to 'direct their affections rightly, lest they be hindered in their pursuit of perfect charity.'"[50] John Paul affirms that this task *"can* be carried out and is really worthy of man."[51] As we take up this task, our hope lies in knowing that "he who began a good work in [us] will bring it to completion at the day of Jesus Christ" (Phil 1:6).

Despite their "shock" at having lost their original purity, they did not completely lose a sense of their own dignity. They still realized that they were created "for their own sakes," and were never meant to be used. Contrary to the Lutheran idea, men and women are not "utterly depraved" as a result of original sin.[52] If they were, we could expect that they would have reveled shamelessly in their lusts. Instead, they clearly experienced lust as a threat. Thus, the Holy Father observes that shame has a double meaning, negative and positive. It indicates a threat to the value of the person (negative) and at the same time seeks to preserve this value interiorly (positive). In other words, shame indicates that man and woman have lost sight of the nuptial meaning of the body. But it also indicates an innate need to protect the nuptial meaning of the body from the threat of lust. This is precisely why they cover those parts of the body that reveal its nuptial meaning. The visibility of the sexual values of the body once revealed the truth of the person. In this new state of affairs, the sexual values of the body, ironically, are covered to ensure the value of the person.

This deeper penetration of shame as something positive and "protective" (this could also be called modesty) indicates a proper reverence for the mystery of the person in his or her "otherness." In this way, although the experience greatly differs, the Pope suggests that shame enables man and woman almost to remain in the state of original innocence.[53] This positive sense of shame, then, must always inform the relationship of the

---

50. *CCC,* n. 2545.

51. 11/12/80, TB 172.

52. See *CCC,* nn. 405, 406.

53. See 6/25/80, TB 122.

sexes. Even in marriage when the body is unveiled, a couple must maintain a proper reverence and respect for the value of the person, otherwise such unveiling would involve a certain shamelessness. The grace of marriage empowers couples to rediscover something of the original experience of nakedness without shame—a nakedness that does not elicit shame (in the negative sense) because the couple trusts in each other's pure intentions of love. But marriage in no way justifies shamelessness. That would involve degrading one's spouse without a corresponding experience of shame for having done so.

Understanding the positive sense of shame also helps us realize that lust is not of the essence of the human heart. It is not of the essence of the sexual relationship and sexual desire. Lust, rather, is a grave distortion of all these things. The heart goes deeper than these distortions, and still desires what is deeper. Shame indicates that the heart still senses an "echo" of God's original plan for sexuality and longs for it. Indeed, this distant memory of "the beginning" keeps shame alive in man's heart.

Hence, even though man's capacity for self-mastery has been "shaken to the very foundations," John Paul says that man still identifies himself with self-mastery and is always ready to "win" it. He is always ready to fight the distortions of lust in order to regain that freedom that was lost. Of course, lust fights back and, at times, man can be easily lured away from the truth (see Rom 7:22–23). But in the deeper part of his heart, *man still desires the truth*.[54] If we keep this in mind, the Pope tells us that we can understand better why Christ, speaking of lust, appeals to the human heart. Lust, no matter how base, can never snuff out the spark of goodness that always remains deeply imbedded in the human heart. In the Sermon on the Mount, Christ appeals to that spark, and through the gentle "breath" of the Holy Spirit, seeks to fan that spark into flame.

28. Lust Shatters the Original Communion of Persons

June 4, 18, 25; July 23, 1980 (TB 117–127)

John Paul continues his analysis by taking us to the further stage of the study of lust which he calls the "insatiability of the union" (117). The original unity the first couple experienced brought with it an explicit peace. But in man's heart lust distorted that original beatifying conjugal union of persons. After sin, the original capacity of communicating them-

---

54. See *CCC*, n. 1707.

selves to each other has been "shattered." Man and woman's relationship undergoes "a radical transformation." It no longer satisfies the longings of the heart as it once did, because they are crippled in their ability to love each other as they once did.

John Paul says that, as persons, man and woman are "called from eternity to exist in communion." This call defines us and reveals the deep meaning of our sexuality. We still desire communion even after sin. Yet we experience a "failure to satisfy the aspiration to realize in the 'conjugal union of the body' the mutual communion of persons" (121). This is sexual shame's deep meaning, what John Paul means by the "insatiability of the union."

A. The Second Discovery of Sex

The radical change in their experience of nakedness leads us to presume negative changes in the whole interpersonal man-woman relationship. Once again, the experience of the body gives us a window into the human heart. The role of the body, which was once the trustworthy foundation of their communion, is now "called in question" in man and woman's consciousness. Sexual difference, which had proclaimed and enabled the original communion of persons, "was suddenly felt and understood as an element of mutual confrontation of persons" (118). The Pope points out that they obviously did not stop communicating with each other through the body and its movements, gestures, and expressions. However, the simple and direct communion that flowed from the purity of original nakedness "disappeared."

The Pope calls this new experience "the second discovery of sex" and emphasizes that it differs radically from the first one. In this new situation, rather than finding themselves united by their sexual differences, the man and the woman are divided and even opposed because of their masculinity and femininity. In short, what was once the experience of male *and* female is now the experience of male *or* female. The Pope contends that in this new situation sexuality almost impedes their true inter-personal communion. Sexuality had once made visible the other's subjectivity and enabled a full communion of persons. Now it has become objectified. As the Pope expresses it, "The subjectivity of the person gives way, in a certain sense, to the objectivity of the body" (127). This means the body ceases to be incorporated into subjectivity. Now, if the man bound by lust is to retain a regard for the subjectivity of the other—and at the same time for his own subjectivity—he must cover the body; he must hide his nakedness to avoid being objectified by the other. This results from a new and fundamental lack of trust, which indicates the collapse of the original relationship of man and woman's communion.

This objectification leads men and women to seek "the sensation of sexuality" apart from a true communion of persons. This happens precisely because sexuality is now detached from the person and his call to image God through communion. This is the tragedy of lust: It exchanges a self-seeking gratification for the sincere gift of self; it *uses* the other as an object made for *my sake,* rather than loving the other as a subject made for his or her *own sake.* Yet, historical man often views this way of thinking and behaving as "normal."

B. *Sin's Effect on Woman*

At this point John Paul shifts his reflection to the words of Genesis 3:16 in which God says to the woman: "I will greatly multiply your pain in childbearing; in pain you shall bring forth children, yet your desire shall be for your husband and he shall rule over you." These words, like previous ones already analyzed, are loaded with content that can be mined through phenomenological analysis. The Pope says in typical form that these words reveal to us not only the exterior situation of man and woman, but enable us also to penetrate the deep mysteries of their hearts.

These words also have a "perspective character" that impacts all human history. As John Paul expresses, "The history of human consciences and human hearts will contain the continual confirmation of the words contained in Genesis 3:16" (120).[55] Because of sin, woman now has a particular "disability" as compared with man. Her special giftedness as woman—the fact that she embodies receptivity in relation to God, the man, and the gift of new life—will no longer be experienced as a gift but more as a burden, at times even a curse. The Pope clarifies that "there is no reason to understand [this] as a social disability or inequality." Instead, throughout history woman will experience a form of inequality manifested as "a lack of full unity precisely in the vast context of union with man, to which both were called according to Genesis 2:24" (120).

Has history not told an ongoing tale of male domination and prejudice against women? To varying degrees this has even manifested itself in some cultures as an explicit *hatred of woman,* a hatred of what is "feminine" (misogyny). It must be stated emphatically—if Genesis did not make it obvious enough—that male domination violates God's plan and is the specific result of sin.

■ It seems misogyny stems from the way woman constantly reminds the whole human race of what we have all rejected about ourselves through

---

55. For further development of these themes, see *Mulieris Dignitatem,* nn. 10, 24 and *Letter to Women.*

original sin—our *receptivity* in relation to God. Woman's particular receptivity to love and to life is her special "genius." Tragically, as a result of sin, woman's great blessing has come to be seen as a curse. Once again, nuptial imagery helps reveal the mystery. Because of Satan's deception, we have come to see God's "masculine-bridegroom" initiative as that of a tyrant with a will-to-rule over us. Hence, we reject our posture of receptivity as "feminine-bride" in favor of being our own "masculine" lords. We want to be "like God" but without God.[56] In this situation, we come to see the "feminine"—which symbolizes our true humanity—as a weakness to be dominated and controlled, even snuffed out. Does this not explain, perhaps, why there has been a tendency to favor "masculinity" over "femininity" throughout history? But this conception of God as tyrant-ruler—and in turn, this symbol of what is "masculine"—is a gross distortion. Where is this distortion lived out? Primarily in the relationship of the sexes. The man, rather than imaging the true initiative of God—rather than loving his wife "as Christ loved the Church" (Eph 5:25)—comes to image the gross distortion of the tyrant-ruler: "He shall rule over you" (Gen 3:16). In turn, the woman, under the weight of male domination and history's discrimination against her, is tempted to reject her own femininity and take to herself the distorted "masculine" will-to-power simply in order to survive. Are these not some of the deepest reasons behind the women's liberation movement and the gender confusion so prevalent in our world today? John Paul shows implicit respect for all that is good and just in the feminist movement. But he also calls women "to promote a 'new feminism' which rejects the temptation of imitating models of 'male domination,' in order to acknowledge and affirm the true genius of women in every aspect of the life of society, and overcome all discrimination, violence, and exploitation."[57]

C. Both Are Subject to Lust

The man's "rule" over the woman changes the whole dynamic of the original communion of persons. It indicates that lust has distorted the original masculine initiation of love. The man of lust seeks not to make a gift of himself to woman, but he seeks to dominate and control her, to possess her and use her for his own ends. As John Paul expresses it, "The relationship of the gift is changed into the relationship of appropriation" (127). Love "gifts." Lust "appropriates."

---

56. See *CCC,* n. 398.
57. *Evangelium Vitae,* n. 99.

Yet woman still "desires her husband." If the distortions of a man's heart lead him to disregard woman's dignity and *use her,* the distortions of a woman's heart can lead her, at times, to disregard her own dignity and *allow herself to be used.* Yet at other times the Pope notes that the instincts that the woman directs to the man precede his desire or even aim at arousing it and giving it impetus. In this way, woman also uses man for her own ends, treating him as an object and not as a person.

■ This dynamic in women is often lived out in an understandable retaliation against men and their lustful domination. A dramatic example of this was told to me by a counselor who had been working with a woman who was once a stripper in a "men's club." When the counselor asked her why she did it, she responded without hesitation: "Control." This woman, like the majority of women who compromise themselves in similar ways, had been sexually abused by older men as a child. Causing men to "lose control" by inciting their lusts was her way of "gaining control" over them. As she described it, "Every night I was able to put hundreds of desperate men at my mercy begging for more. And I'd very easily walk away each night with over one thousand of their hard-earned dollars."

Although the biblical texts seem to indicate the man's lust more specifically, John Paul clearly states that both the man and woman have become subject to lust. Shame, therefore, "touches the innermost recesses both of the male and the female personality, even though in a different way" (123). It is precisely this mutual lust that causes the opposition between the sexes. Obviously this "opposition does not destroy or exclude conjugal union, willed by the Creator (Gen 2:24), or its procreative effects; but it confers on the realization of this union another direction" (121). This direction is very different from that of "the beatifying beginning." Hence, if men and women are to rediscover what it means to be a sincere gift for each other and thus fulfill the very meaning of their being and existence,[58] they *must* overcome lust. Civilization itself depends on it.

29. Living the Body Flows from the Heart
June 25; July 23, 1980 (TB 124–127)

John Paul has been trying to reconstruct the original experience of shame and lust; the experience that clearly indicates the crossing over from the state of original innocence to the state of historical sinfulness. We

---

58. See 1/16/80, TB 63.

can penetrate the experience of both "states" by contrasting them with each other.

The Holy Father says that Genesis 2:24 speaks of the "union of bodies" in the sense of the authentic "union of persons." Becoming "one flesh," then, does not merely express the joining of two bodies. According to the Pope, this is a "sacramental expression" which corresponds to the communion of persons. "Where the flesh is one, one also is the spirit."[59] Living this, experiencing this, left no need for shame in their nakedness. The entrance of shame, therefore, indicates the loss of the original communion of persons in the image of God. Fear and shame replaced the absolute trust that man and woman had in each other in the state of original innocence. Fear and shame indicate the beginning of lust in man's heart, which John Paul describes as a "limitation, infraction, or even distortion of the nuptial meaning of the body" (124).

A. Living the Body

When the Holy Father speaks of the meaning of the body, he is referring in the first place to "the full awareness of the human being" (124). The body reveals the person. The body reveals, as in a "sacrament," the meaning and mystery of human life itself. But as John Paul stresses, the meaning of the body is not just something conceptual; it is not abstract. In gaining a full awareness of the human being through the body, we must include the actual lived experience of the body in its masculinity and femininity.

John Paul says that the meaning one attributes to his body determines that person's attitude in his way of "living the body." In other words, how we live as bodies—in particular, how we live out our sexuality—will flow from the attitude of our hearts regarding the meaning of our bodies, the meaning of our sexuality, the meaning of life itself. The body has an objective meaning, of course, which does not change based on subjective feelings. However, the Pope observes that this purely objective significance of the body and of sex is in a certain sense "a-historical." He means that, due to sin, historical man often experiences the objective meaning of the body as being "outside the system of real and concrete interpersonal relations between man and woman" (124). The Church's teaching, specifically regarding sexual morality, then comes to be seen as abstract and removed from real-life experience.

In Christ's words in the Sermon on the Mount, he appeals specifically to the *experience* of historical man. There is nothing abstract about "looking with lust." We all know immediately what that means in our own

---

59. *CCC*, n. 1642.

experience, in our own "hearts." This is why Christ's words sting so much. We *know* we are guilty. But Christ wants us to penetrate more deeply into our hearts where that "echo" of God's original plan still resounds. Tapping into that deeper heritage gives us the key to reconnecting the objective meaning of the body and sex with how we experience the body and sex subjectively. It gives us the key to "living the body" according to its true meaning and thus fulfilling the very meaning of existence.

Through the previous analysis of man and woman's experience before sin, we have discerned the body's nuptial meaning and rediscovered what it consists of as "a measure of the human heart." The heart is still measured by this objective meaning of the body, that is, by the call to sincere self-giving. Lust, however, attacks this sincere giving, depriving man and woman of the dignity of the gift inscribed in the beauty and mystery of sexual difference. So when the man of concupiscence "measures" his heart by the nuptial meaning of the body, he condemns himself. At this point he has three choices: normalize sin; fall into despair; or turn to Christ who came not to condemn, but to save (see Jn 3:17). As the Pope will repeatedly stress, Christ's words about lust do not so much condemn us but call us. They call us not just to force a subjectively lustful heart to submit to an objective ethic. They call us efficaciously to let the new *ethos* of redemption inform and transform our lustful hearts.

B. We Have Almost Lost the Capacity to Love

Due to concupiscence, the human body "has almost lost the capacity of expressing this love in which the man-person becomes a gift" (126). The Pope adds the word "almost" because a spark of God's plan remains in us. As he says, "The nuptial meaning of the body has not become completely suffocated by concupiscence, but only habitually threatened" (126). The Pope carefully maintains this essential point. Without this "almost" we would fall into Martin Luther's erroneous belief that man is "utterly depraved" due to sin.

■ The Lutheran idea of "utter depravity" may seem to diverge only slightly from the Catholic belief that man is tragically fallen, yet in some way retains his basic goodness. However, a notion of utter depravity has dangerous and far-reaching implications. For example, "dying to one's sinful nature" does not mean rooting out the weeds in one's soul so that the wheat can flourish. If we are utterly depraved, we are all weeds. This means all of our aspirations and desires are suspect. One who "dies to himself" in such a fashion will end up nullifying the unique mystery and giftedness of his own personhood. He will end up "dying" not only to sin, but also to the person God created him to be. Furthermore, if the human heart goes no deeper than its distortions, how can we hope to desire, let alone come progressively to experience, the restoration of God's original plan? In this case, the heart only desires corruption. Without the Pope's "almost," we come to see ourselves, to use one of Luther's images, as a "dung heap." Christ may cover us with a blanket of white snow. But even so, according to Luther's logic, we remain impure internally. Catholic anthropology insists that sin did not trump our "very good" creation. Hence John Paul maintains that the heritage of the human heart "is deeper than the sinfulness inherited."[60] Christ appeals to that deeper heritage of our hearts in order to reactivate it. Through the power of the Holy Spirit, he transforms us from within. This means that through ongoing conversion to Christ, through ongoing sanctification, we actually become pure as snow throughout. Historical man has this lifelong task: to give voice to the deepest aspirations of his heart by accepting the grace of ongoing conversion.

We must now battle against lust if we are to reclaim the freedom that enables us to make the sincere gift of self. This is difficult enough when lust manifests itself clearly. It is all the more difficult since lust "is not always plain and obvious; sometimes it is concealed, so that it passes itself off as 'love'" (126). Note John Paul's realism here. At times only a fine line divides authentic love and lust. When fooled by lust, the heart can even mistake it for love. John Paul asks: "Does this mean that it is our duty to distrust the human heart?" Then he responds without hesitation: "No! It only means that we must keep it under control" (126).

Far too many people, upon recognizing the distortions of their own hearts, succumb to the devil's trap by throwing out the baby with the bath water. We must certainly reckon with the forces of concupiscence within us. But concupiscence does not define the human heart. The heart goes deeper than its distortions. What, then, does the Pope mean by saying we must keep our hearts under control? We need to penetrate the dynamics of concupiscence to answer that question.

C. Regaining Self-Mastery

In short, John Paul tells us that concupiscence entails the loss of the interior freedom of the gift. Sexual desire is now "manifested as an almost autogenous force, marked by a certain 'coercion of the body,' operating according to its own dynamics" (126). In this way we have lost "control"

---

60. 10/29/80, TB 168.

of our own bodies and of the desires of our hearts. In a certain sense, this makes the interior freedom of self-giving impossible. "Concupiscence, in itself, is not capable of promoting union as the communion of persons. By itself, it does not unite, but appropriates" (127). Thus, concupiscent desire draws us away from affirming the person "for his or her own sake" and makes of that person an object of selfish gratification.

This also obscures our perception of the beauty that the human body possesses as an expression of the spirit. For the man of lust, "beauty" is now determined not by the visibility of *the person* in and through his or her body, but by what type or kind of body satisfies or appeals to concupiscence. This concept of beauty is often totally divorced from the person.[61]

For John Paul, keeping our hearts under control means regaining self-determination. It means controlling sexual impulses instead of being controlled by them. We should not conceive of this control, however, merely as the caging of a wild horse. While this approach may control the horse, it does not change it. If you opened the cage even for a moment, the horse would run wild. Caging the horse may be a necessary first step, but the ultimate goal is to tame (transform) the horse so that it no longer requires a cage. Applying this image, in regaining self-mastery it may well be necessary at first to "cage" concupiscent desire by force of will. But *this is only a first step*. If we remain here, the moral norm still operates as a constraint. Christ calls us to progress from constraint to freedom—from merely meeting the demands of the law to *ful*-filling those demands (see §25). As John Paul says, "This is a still uncertain and fragile journey as long as we are on earth, but it is one made possible by grace, which enables us to possess the full freedom of the children of God (see Rom 8:21)."[62]

For the Holy Father, the ultimate role of the will is not for it to tyrannize or repress the passions, but to direct them, with the transforming power of grace, toward the truth of self-giving love. "The upright will orders the movements of the senses it appropriates to the good and to beatitude." Within the ethos of redemption, "emotions and feelings can be taken up into the *virtues*."[63] In other words, Christ calls us to experience a real and deep victory over concupiscence so that what we desire subjectively becomes progressively more in tune with the objective meaning of

---

61. John Paul II will provide an intriguing and redeeming analysis of physical beauty in his cycle of reflections on the sacramentality of marriage.

62. *Veritatis Splendor,* n. 18.

63. *CCC,* n. 1768.

the body and sex. To the degree that we experience this transformation, we no longer need the "cage"; we come freely to desire the good. This is the freedom for which Christ has set us free (see Gal 5). This freedom enables us to live our bodies in holiness and honor liberated from lust's domination (see 1 Thess 4:4).

John Paul II's proclamation that the redemption of the body truly affords such freedom is one of the most important contributions of his entire catechesis on the body. It also seems to cause the most contention. An impulse-oriented view of the sexual appetite seems to have dominated traditional evaluations of sexuality. Without a personalistic understanding of human (and Christian) freedom, virtually all one can do to "manage" his sexual appetite is "cage" it. Christians who take on this view almost inevitably view marriage as a legitimate opportunity to allow the "caged horse" an occasional run. In turn, if a person thinks this way and constructs his or her life of "holiness" accordingly, it becomes almost impossible to imagine true freedom from the domination of concupiscence.

As Wojtyla observed in a pre-papal essay, the "very manner in which marriage [and the relationship of the sexes in general] is conceived must be from the start, to the greatest extent possible, freed from purely impulse-oriented, naturalistic presuppositions and shaped personalistically."[64] Within this deterministic, impulse-oriented view of sexuality, Wojtyla wrote elsewhere, "There seems to be a tendency to limit the possibility of virtue and magnify the 'necessity of sin' in this sphere. Personalism, with its emphasis on self-determination, would entail the opposite tendency." It "would perceive the possibility of virtue, based on self-control and sublimation."[65] For John Paul II, this possibility of real virtue in the sexual realm is an integral part of the "good news" afforded by the redemption of our bodies in Christ.

30. Maintaining the Balance of the Gift

July 30, 1980 (TB 128–130)

We have already observed that the difference between authentic love and lust, although at times subtle, can be understood as the difference between "gift" and "appropriation." We see precisely this contrast in the Yahwist texts that describe man and woman's experience before and after original sin. Genesis 2:23–25 expresses their experience of living the body

---

64. "Parenthood as a Community of Persons," *Person and Community*, p. 330.

65. "The Problem of Catholic Sexual Ethics," *Person and Community*, p. 286.

as gift. Genesis 3:7 and 16 express their experience of living the body as appropriation.

John Paul points out that the words of Genesis 3:16 ("he shall rule over you") "seem to suggest that it is often at the expense of the woman that this happens, and that in any case, she feels it more than man" (128). Experience seems to confirm this. Even so, it is a two-way street. As John Paul states, "If man in his relationship with woman considers her only as an object to gain possession of and not as a gift, he condemns himself thereby to become also for her only an object of appropriation and not a gift" (128). Yet even this statement seems to indicate a priority of action on the man's part. This does not mean woman is merely passive; she too acts. The masculine "priority of action," as we have described it, simply means that the man typically acts first. If woman embodies the "receptivity of the gift," it seems man embodies the "initiation of the gift" (note: these phrases are not found in the Pope's catechesis).

A. Man's Special Responsibility

This is why John Paul believes that, right from the beginning, man was charged with the particular responsibility of being "the guardian of the reciprocity of donation and its true balance" (128). As we discovered in the Yahwist text, "the woman is entrusted to his eyes, to his consciousness, to his sensitivity, to his 'heart.' He, on the other hand," the Pope continues, "must, in a way, ensure...the mutual interpenetration of giving and receiving as a gift, which, precisely through its reciprocity, creates a real communion of persons."[66]

All the man can do, according to John Paul, is "borrow" femininity as a gift, and only when the woman freely gives it. He cannot take hold of woman as his own possession. He can only take the "risk" of initiating the gift of himself. It is a risk because he puts his gift of self in the hands of her freedom without fully knowing how she will respond. To be true to the gift, he can only wait and trust that the woman, sensing the genuineness of the gift he initiated, will receive his gift and respond freely with the gift of herself to him (see §18).

Concupiscence wreaks havoc on this mutual exchange. Tainted by lust, what the man initiates is often not the "sincere gift of self," but the desire to appropriate the woman and gratify himself. Sensing this, the woman frequently recoils, and rightly so since she knows she is never meant to be used. The man, then, will often be tempted to extort from

---

66. 2/6/80, TB 71 (see §20).

woman her own gift. But this openly contrasts with the truth of love. Hence, although "the maintenance of the balance of the gift seems to have been entrusted to both, a special responsibility rests with man above all, as if it depended more on him whether the balance is maintained or broken or even—if already broken—re-established" (128–129). In other words, because the man embodies the "initiation of the gift," he has a particular responsibility to ensure that he initiates a genuine gift. He must ensure within his own heart and show the woman that he desires to make the sincere gift of himself and not to appropriate her. In other words, he must demonstrate that he has acquired an integral self-mastery. For if a man cannot control himself, he will inevitably seek to control woman in order to satisfy his own impulses and desires (we could also speak of a similar dynamic in women toward men).

John Paul recognizes that when discussing the diversity of men and women's roles, one has to realize that these have been conditioned to some degree by the social emargination of woman. He even says that the Old and the New Testaments give us sufficient proofs of such emargination. Nevertheless, the diversity of roles in man and woman's relationship is not merely the result of historical conditionings. Even when all exaggerations are purified (and we *must* seek to purify these), a fundamental and indispensable diversity of roles remains in the male-female relationship. One is not better than the other. They are merely different: different in a way that enables a true communion. Without *the difference* of the sexes, an incarnate, life-giving communion would be impossible.

B. Personal Analogy of Belonging

If a person can never be appropriated or possessed without offending human dignity, is it wrong, then, for lovers to speak of "belonging" to one another? Not if they understand the proper limits of using such language. In fact, John Paul recognizes that the possessive pronoun "my" has always belonged to the language of human love and cites nearly thirty examples of it in the Song of Songs. But when true lovers, such as in the Song of Songs, refer to each other as "mine," this certainly does not denote possession in the sense of appropriating and using. Rather, John Paul says that in the eternal language of human love, the term "my" indicates the reciprocity of the donation and the equal balance of the gift through which the mutual *communio personarum* is established.

Thus, man and woman can speak of belonging to each other only by way of analogy. When the man or the woman seeks to "possess" the other in the sense in which an object belongs to a person, the analogy of belonging breaks down and the communion of persons is impossible. Lust leads precisely toward this demeaning sense of possession. "From possessing a further step goes toward 'enjoyment': the object I possess acquires a certain meaning for me since it is at my disposal and I avail myself of it, I use it" (130). This radically violates the other's creation for his or her "own sake." In this case, the "other" only has value so far as she (from the male perspective) is "useful" for me. As soon as she is not, she is no longer "loved." At this point another more "useful" person will be sought—that is, another person from whom I can more easily get the enjoyment I seek.

In short, this is the underlying sickness of a divorce culture. John Paul states that because of concupiscence, this way of seeing, evaluating, and "loving" almost constantly threatens us. But this way of "loving" is not really loving at all, since selfish enjoyment excludes disinterested giving. Generally speaking, a divorce-mentality results from a counterfeit love that never reaches the great dignity and unrepeatability of the person (see §23), but only values those diminishable and repeatable attributes that bring self-gratification.

From John Paul's analysis we learn that if men and women are to "belong" to each other in the full expression of the communion of persons, they must first belong to Christ. They must first be in communion with him. The road to restored communion between the sexes passes by way of the death and resurrection of Jesus Christ. And there is no detour.

31. Christ's Words and the Old Testament Ethos
August 6, 13, 20, 27, 1980 (TB 131–142)

Christ's words about lust in the heart have both an anthropological foundation and a directly ethical character. So far John Paul has been sketching the anthropological foundation of Christ's words. In the address of August 6, 1980, he announces that the following stage of his analysis will develop their ethical meaning.

Before that, however, he devotes the five audiences between August 6 and September 3, 1980 to placing Christ's words from the Sermon on the Mount in the context of what he calls "the Old Testament ethos." The ethos of the Israelites was, of course, drawn from the law and the prophets. These provide the necessary frame of reference for understanding the nature of "the new ethos" Christ announced in the Sermon on the Mount. This "new ethos" is nothing other than the *fulfillment* of the law and the prophets (see §25). The interpretation of the law had become influenced by that "hardness of heart" Christ spoke of with the Pharisees. This brought about a situation contrary to God's original plan for the "one flesh" union. As John Paul says, only in the perspective of this break from the ethos of creation do we find the key to interpret the legislation of Israel regarding marriage and male-female relations as a whole. In the Sermon on the Mount, Christ also refers to the heart—to the "interior subject"— precisely because of man and woman's "hardness of heart."

A. Compromise in Legislation

Christ begins his teaching about lust with a reference to the law of Moses: "You have heard that it was said, 'You shall not commit adultery.'" As Christ indicates, all those gathered on the mount to hear his words were certainly familiar with this norm. However, Christ's further words, "But I say to you...," show that the norm alone was not enough. The norm itself could not change the lustful heart.[67]

John Paul points out with various examples that in the interpretation of the Old Testament, the prohibition of adultery was balanced by compromising with concupiscence. For example, while most people were expected to be monogamous, the lives of men like David and Solomon show the establishing of real polygamy, which, the Pope says, "was undoubtedly for reasons of concupiscence." In fact, "Old Testament tradition indicates that the real need for monogamy as an essential and indispensable implication of the commandment, 'You shall not commit adultery,' never reached the conscience and the ethos of the following generations of the chosen people" (134).[68]

Of course, the historical failures of the Jewish people in this regard are more of a commentary on fallen human nature than on the Jewish religion as such. God's revelation to Israel "endures forever."[69] Christ, however, as John Paul observes, does not accept the flawed interpretation of the law that became common in Israel. Men had subjected the law to human weakness and the limits of human willpower deriving precisely from the distortions of concupiscence. Hence, a compromised version of the law became superimposed on the original teaching of right and wrong connected with the law of the Decalogue.

When men compromise with concupiscence, a basic principle comes into play. Stated simply, the less the heart conforms to truth, the more the need arises for laws which must corral the people into maintaining some semblance of order. So we find numerous and detailed precepts in the Old

---

67. See *CCC*, n. 1963.

68. See *CCC*, n. 1610.

69. *CCC*, n. 1963.

Testament that evaluate sexual conduct in a particular and even peculiar way.[70] John Paul admits that it is "difficult to avoid the impression that such an evaluation was of a negative character," and often judged "the woman with greater severity" (137, 136). These laws were "not concerned directly with putting some order in the 'heart' of man, but with putting order in the entire social life, at the base of which stands, as always, marriage and the family" (137). However, some of these laws, while intending to maintain social order, actually protected the social dimension of sin.

Christ wants to rectify this situation. By appealing to men's hearts in the Sermon on the Mount, Christ indicates that the "discernment between what is right and wrong engraved on the human conscience can show itself to be deeper and more correct than the content of a norm" (135). The way to the "new ethos" passes through the rediscovery of the ethos of creation, which had been lost in the general Old Testament understanding and in the application of the commandment against adultery.[71]

B. Israel as the Adulterous Wife

If Israel's legislation at times obscured the correct content of the commandment against adultery, the prophets point to the true content of the norm when they denounce Israel's unfaithfulness to Yahweh by comparing it with adultery.[72] The legislative texts describe adultery as the violation of the right of ownership. Moreover, in keeping with the mentality of the time, this referred primarily to the man's legal "ownership" of his wife—often one of many—and the "right" he had to her body. However, John Paul demonstrates that in the text of the prophets, the background of real and legalized polygamy does not alter the ethical meaning of adultery. Nor do the prophets speak of adultery as a violation of rights over the body. For the prophets, adultery is a sin because it constitutes the breakdown of man and woman's covenant.[73]

The prophets recognize that monogamy is the only correct analogy or symbol of the "marital" covenant between God and the chosen people. Adultery then becomes "the antithesis of that nuptial relationship" and

---

70. For example, see Leviticus 18 and Deuteronomy 22:13–30; 25:11–12.

71. See 10/1/80, TB 153.

72. See Hosea 1—3 and Ezekiel 16, for example. In the text of the Pope's catechesis, he quotes Ezekiel 16 almost in its entirety because, as he says, "The analogy between adultery and idolatry is expressed therein in a particularly strong and exhaustive way" (139).

73. See *CCC,* n. 1611.

"the antinomy of marriage." In this way, the prophets paved the way for Christ and what he would teach about the foundations of sexual morality.

It is true that a man and woman who have established a marital covenant have a legal "right" to sexual union, and adultery violates this right. But sexual union in marriage is not merely a legal "right." John Paul's rich personalism will not allow him to stop at this juridical description. "Such bodily union," he says, is "above all...the regular sign of the communion of the two people" (140–141). It is the bodily expression of a covenant "born from love." Only such love establishes the proper foundation of that union in which man and woman become "one flesh." The Pope adds that it is precisely this nuptial love which gives a fundamental significance to the truth of "covenant"—both in the man-woman relationship, and, analogously, in the Yahweh-Israel (God-man) relationship. Adultery not only violates a legal right; John Paul describes it as a radical "falsification of the sign" of man and woman's covenant love. The prophets express precisely this aspect of adultery in describing the infidelity of the Israelites to their covenant with Yahweh.

C. Anthropology and Ethics of the Sign

John Paul bases his understanding of the bodily union as "the regular sign" of the communion of persons in marriage on his previous reflections from Genesis. He will also develop this idea more fully in cycle five when he reflects on Ephesians 5:31–32. For now he simply adds that this understanding of bodily union as the "sign" of married love is essential and important for the theology of the body, both from an ethical and an anthropological point of view.

From an anthropological point of view, understanding the one flesh union as the regular sign of the marital covenant helps us understand who man and woman are as incarnate persons called, in the mystery of creation, to exist in the communion of persons in the image of God.[74] From an ethical point of view, John Paul asserts that we "can speak of moral good and evil according to whether in this relationship there is a true 'union of the body' and whether or not it has the character of the truthful sign" (141–142). This key statement gives shape to the Holy Father's new context for understanding marriage and sexual morality. We will return to this statement several times.

The Pope is trying to help us see that Catholic teaching on sexuality is not rooted in arbitrary legislation. It is not based merely on the mainte-

---

74. See 7/23/80, TB 125.

nance of juridical rights and duties, as has been emphasized in the past.[75] Catholic sexual ethics rest on the firm foundation of anthropology. They rest on *who we are* and *who we are called to be* as men and women created in God's image. For John Paul, sexual morality is most clearly understood through the logic of "the truthful sign." In other words, in order to determine what is good, we only need to ask a simple question: Does this sexual attitude, thought, or action truly image God's free, total, faithful, and fruitful love? If it does not, it can never bring beatitude. It can never fulfill us. It is contrary to who we are and who we are called to be. This question transfers the discussion from legalism to liberty, from the prohibition and restriction of legislation to the empowerment and freedom of love. The question then shifts from, "How far can I go before I violate the law?" to, "What is the truth that sets me free and empowers me to love in God's image as male and female?" To this latter question John Paul gives a one-word answer: Christ!

32. Concupiscence and the Wisdom Literature

September 3, 10, 1980 (TB 142–146)

In the Sermon on the Mount, Christ established the "new ethos" by transferring the significance of adultery from the "body" to the "heart." Christ *knows* man's heart; "for he himself knew what was in man" (Jn 2:25). Although cultural conditions affect men and women of different times and places, the condition of man's heart—the "echo" of his original holiness and the tragedy of sin—remains the same in every time and place. As the Pope points out, the man of our time feels called by Christ's words about lust no less than the man of that time, whom the Master addressed directly.[76]

Even so, John Paul believes it is important to understand the context in which Christ's actual listeners received his revolutionary words. Thus, having looked briefly at the law and the prophets, John Paul points us now to the Wisdom literature of the Old Testament. Presumably Christ's listeners, upon hearing his words, would have related them to these books since they contain repeated admonitions about lust and also advice as to how to

---

75. One can note the difference in language between the 1917 Code of Canon Law and the new code of 1983. Canon 1081 in the 1917 Code speaks of marriage as a contract of yielding rights, first among them the *right to the body* (the *ius ad corpus*). Canon 1055 of the 1983 Code speaks of marriage in more personalist terms. It does not avoid the word contract, but it views marriage also as a "covenant" and "partnership of the whole of life" which is "ordered to the good of spouses and the procreation and education of children."

76. See 8/6/80, TB 132.

preserve oneself from it.[77] John Paul logically concludes that these books paved the way in a certain sense for Christ's words.

A. Wisdom, Experience, and True Salvation

True to their name, these books contain great wisdom. They reveal an intimate knowledge of the human heart and even develop a specific moral psychology. In this way, the Wisdom books "are close to that call of Christ to the 'heart' that Matthew has handed down to us" (144). Even so, John Paul says that with "one-sided" admonitions that often make woman out to be "a downright seducer of whom to be aware," the Wisdom texts do not change man's ethos in any fundamental way. "For such a transformation it is necessary to wait until the Sermon on the Mount" (144). For example, whereas the Wisdom texts offer understandable admonitions such as "Turn away your eyes from a shapely woman" (Sir 9:8), John Paul says that in the Sermon on the Mount Christ invites us "to a pure way of looking at others, capable of respecting the spousal meaning of the body."[78]

As experience attests, the battle with lust remains fierce. For the man bound by lust, "Turn away your eyes" retains all its wisdom. Christ, however, "speaks in the context of human experience and simultaneously in the context of the work of salvation." In the new ethos, these "two contexts are in a certain way superimposed upon and pervade one another" (143). This means that, although we all *experience* lust, we can also *experience* a real transformation of our hearts through the *salvation* Christ offers us. As the *Catechism* teaches, in the "Sermon on the Mount...the spirit of the Lord gives new form to our desires, those inner movements that animate our lives."[79]

Christ did not die on a cross and rise from the dead merely to give us coping mechanisms for sin (we already had plenty of those without a savior). Christ died and rose again *to set us free from sin.* The man whose heart has been transformed and *vivified* by the Spirit of the Lord need not merely "cope" with lust by turning his eyes away from a woman. Through continual death and resurrection, his desires take on "new form." As master of himself, he becomes empowered to look at others purely, with eyes of love, because—living from what the Pope calls "the deeper heritage of his heart"[80]—he does not desire to lust. This deeper place in his "heart"

---

77. See the endnotes of this general audience for a list of examples from Proverbs, Sirach, and Ecclesiastes (TB 185).

78. *Veritatis Splendor,* n. 15.

79. *CCC,* n. 2764.

80. See 10/29/80, TB 168.

will not let him lust. Lust, itself, although he still feels its "pull," becomes ever more distasteful to him.

To the degree that a man lives the ethos of redemption, he understands, as Karol Wojtyla says, that chastity "is not a matter of summarily 'annihilating' the value 'body and sex' in the conscious mind by pushing reactions to them into the subconscious." If chastity "is practiced only in this way, [it creates] the danger of...'explosions.'" Rather, the "essence of chastity consists in quickness to affirm the value of the person in every situation, and in raising to the personal level all reactions to the value of 'the body and sex.'"[81]

The truly pure man experiences a profound *integration* of sexuality and personality. From the male perspective, what he is attracted to and what *he sees* in a woman's feminine beauty is the dignity of her person. Her femininity becomes a sign that makes visible the invisible mystery hidden in God from time immemorial. He sees her body as a theology, a "theophany" of sorts—a revelation of the mystery of God. Such a man has "passed over" from the Old Testament ethos to the New Testament ethos. He is empowered not only to meet the law's demands, but to fulfill the law.

Attaining this level of purity is a task given to every man and woman.[82] It is certainly a fragile journey demanding a lifetime of diligent effort and arduous struggle. Victory does not come overnight, nor can one ever claim to have accomplished a permanent victory in this life.[83] Because lust will always be a reality in a fallen world, we will always need God's mercy. But the grace of his mercy *enables* us to attain a mature level of purity. No matter how deep our wounds and distortions go, the cross of Christ goes deeper, and John Paul continually insists that *real power* flows from Christ's death and resurrection to restore in us the purity that was lost through sin. Our struggle with concupiscence will only cease in the eschaton, but as the *Catechism* teaches: "Even now [purity of heart] enables us to see *according to* God." It "lets us perceive the human body— ours and our neighbor's—as a temple of the Holy Spirit, a manifestation of divine beauty."[84] The more we gaze with faith upon Christ, the more "his gaze purifies our heart." In turn, "the light of the countenance of Jesus illumines the eyes of our heart and teaches us to see everything in light of his truth."[85]

---

81. *Love & Responsibility,* pp. 170–171.

82. See *CCC,* nn. 2013, 2545; see also *Veritatis Splendor,* n. 18.

83. See *CCC,* n. 2342.

84. *CCC,* n. 2519.

85. *CCC,* n. 2715.

■ Although Christ did not come to give us coping mechanisms for sin, so long as we live in the historical tension of the "already, but not yet" of redemption, we still need them. But if traditional Christian wisdom seems to have focused on the "not yet," it seems John Paul wants to balance this with the "already." The more we tap into this "already," the more the beauty of the body rouses praise of God, not lust. As John Climacus wrote in *The Ladder of Divine Ascent*, "Someone, I was told, at the sight of a very beautiful body, felt impelled to glorify the Creator. The sight of it increased his love for God to the point of tears. Anyone who entertains such feelings in such circumstances is already risen...before the general resurrection."[86] The following story illustrates what mature Christian purity looks like. Two bishops walked out of a cathedral just as a scantily clad prostitute passed by. One bishop immediately turned away. The other bishop looked at her intently. The bishop who turned away exclaimed, "Brother bishop, what are you doing? Turn your eyes!" When the brother bishop turned around, he lamented with tears streaming down his face, "How tragic that such beauty is being sold to the lusts of men." Which one of these bishops was *vivified* with the ethos of redemption? Which one had passed over from merely meeting the demands of the law to a superabounding fulfillment of the law?

As an important clarification, the bishop who turned his eyes *did the right thing,* since he knew that if he had not done so he would have lusted. We classically call this "avoiding the occasion of sin" by "gaining custody of the eyes." This is a commendable and necessary first step on the road to a mature purity. But it is only a first step. We are called to more. The bishop who turned away desired the good with his will, but his need to turn away in order to avoid lusting demonstrates that concupiscence still dominated his heart. As the *Catechism* teaches, the "perfection of the moral good consists in man's being moved to the good not only by his will but also by his 'heart.'"[87] To the degree that our hearts are transformed through ongoing conversion to Christ, our purity matures, enabling us to see the body for what it is: a sign that makes visible the invisible mystery hidden in God from time immemorial. To the degree that we cannot see this, the distortions of sin still blind us. I am not suggesting the average man should look for opportunities to "test" his purity by gazing upon scantily clad women. Indeed, the large majority of men must heed the Old Testament admonition to "turn away your eyes." But for anyone who doubts that the

---

86. *The Ladder of Divine Ascent*, 15th step, 58, p. 168.
87. *CCC,* n. 1775.

purity of the "bishop who looked" is possible, I must add that the above example is adapted from the story of Bishop St. Nonnus of Edessa and the harlot Pelagia. Stories of their encounter differ and the details are sketchy. But it is generally reported that upon seeing the half-naked Pelagia parading through the streets of Antioch while his brother bishops turned away, Bishop Nonnus looked upon her with love and great delight. She noticed his look of love and was eventually converted through his counsel and preaching. She is known as St. Pelagia of Antioch.[88]

B. The Phenomenon of Lust

The Pope points out that the Wisdom literature offers some "classic" descriptions of carnal concupiscence. Sirach 23, for example, describes concupiscence as a "burning fire" that heats the soul and "will not be quenched until it is consumed." The man of lust "will never cease until the fire burns him up." John Paul develops this description with a remarkably keen phenomenological analysis of lust. This "flaring up in man," the Pope says, "invades his senses, excites his body, involves his feelings, and in a certain sense takes possession of his 'heart'" (145). It also causes the "external man" to reduce the "internal man" to silence. In other words, because passion aims at satisfaction, "it blunts reflective activity and pays no attention to the voice of conscience" (146).

Once the "external man" has suffocated the voice of conscience and given his passions free reign, he remains restless until he satisfies the insistent need of the body and the senses for gratification. One might think that this gratification should put out the fire, but on the contrary, as experience attests, it does not reach the source of internal peace. Since it only touches "the outermost level" of the person, the man who commits his will to satisfying the senses finds neither peace nor himself. On the contrary, as Sirach points out, he "is consumed."

John Paul can describe the phenomenon of lust with such vivid precision because he himself, no doubt, has battled it in his own heart. Lest anyone think that popes are exempt, this Pope would be the first to admit that, like the rest of us, he is a man of concupiscence. But unlike so many of us, he is also a tremendous witness to the fact that "where passion enters into the whole of the most profound energies of the spirit, it can also become a creative force" (146). If we allow our passions to "undergo a radical transformation," they can become, once again, the desire to love as God loves.

---

88. For an account of Nonnus and Pelagia see Helen Waddell, *The Desert Fathers* (Ann Arbor: University of Michigan Press, 1957), pp. 181–196.

C. External Modesty

Without this radical transformation of our passions we can only exhibit an "external modesty." The Holy Father relates that a merely external modesty provides an appearance of decency, but is really more a fear of the consequences of indecency rather than a fear of the evil in itself. In other words, the heart is not changed. The externally modest person still desires to gratify his (or her) disordered passions without regard for conscience. However, he might manage to refrain from acting on his disordered desires when he fears the consequences of doing so.

Here is a common example from the male point of view. Men of lust often seek to gratify their passions by looking lustfully at women. However, a man speaking to a woman at whom he would like to look lustfully will usually muster up the willpower to refrain from doing so in order to avoid getting caught. However, he will immediately shed this veneer of modesty as soon as she turns around and can no longer see the manner of his look. He will then allow lust to "flare up" in his heart since he is no longer in danger of being caught. In doing so, even though he does not commit adultery in the body, he commits adultery in his heart. Furthermore, according to a different translation, he makes that woman an adulteress in his heart.[89] Such an external modesty points all the more to the importance of allowing Christ's words in the Sermon on the Mount to penetrate our hearts and transform us.

33. Lust and the Intentionality of Existence

September 10, 17, 24, 1980 (TB 146–152)

Christ does not explain the meaning of lust in the Sermon on the Mount. He seems to presuppose knowledge of it in his listeners. John Paul says that if a person really does not know what lust is, then Christ's words do not apply to him. Yet everyone (male and female) *knows* these words apply to him because everyone experiences lust in his heart. We know it as an interior act that can express itself in a "look" even without expressing itself in a bodily act. Christ appeals to this common experience.

A. Behind the Lustful Look

John Paul wants to penetrate the significance of looking lustfully. In a fallen world, and particularly today in our media culture, temptations to

---

89. John Paul seems to favor this more ancient translation (see 4/16/80 and 9/3/80, TB 105, 142).

lust besiege man. Christ is not saying that a mere glance or momentary thought makes one guilty of adultery. Only when lust "sweeps the will along into its narrow horizon" can we speak of committing adultery in the heart. Concupiscence itself is not a sin. It comes from sin (original sin) and inclines us to sin, but merely recognizing its tug within us does not mean we have sinned. On this side of heaven, we will always be able to recognize the pull of concupiscence. It is what we do when we recognize it that matters. If we choose with Christ's help to struggle against concupiscence, we enter into the paschal mystery and grow in virtue and holiness. If, on the other hand, we choose to indulge concupiscent impulse, we choose to sin. Sin requires that man *acts* and is not merely acted upon. In other words, sin involves the subjective dimension of self-determination. Only then—that is, from that subjective moment and its subjective prolongation—can we say that a person has "looked lustfully" and, thus, committed adultery "in his heart."

When a man, having experienced the inclination to lust, activates his will (self-determination) to "look" at another in this way, he expresses what is in his heart; he expresses "the man within." "Christ in this case wants to bring out that the man 'looks' in conformity with what he is" (147). These are powerful words. In his theology of the body, John Paul wants to outline *who man is*. We gain crucial insight into this question by understanding how man looks at his own body and, even more so, how he looks at the bodies of others. The character of his look determines the way he formats or understands reality itself. According to John Paul, Christ "teaches us to consider a look almost like the threshold of inner truth" (147).

"In the beginning" man looked at the world as the gift that it was: He looked with respect toward all of creation and gratitude toward the Creator. Having distinguished himself from the animals, man looked at himself with deep awe and wonder, knowing that as a "partner of the Absolute" he was the crown of creation and was called to love (see §12). Man's respect for creation and deep wonder at himself crystallize, finally, in the peace of the original naked gaze of man and woman at each other. This gaze, this look, not only reveals that they know each other's worth, dignity, and goodness. It also reveals the deepest intention of their hearts with regard to existence. Their naked bodies witnessed to the truth that all of creation was a gift, and that Love was the source of that giving (see §17). This is what they saw when they "looked" at each other. Life, then, meant offering themselves—their bodies—to God and to each other in thanksgiving for so great a gift.

The entrance of lust in the heart affects *everything*. It changes, as John Paul says, "the intentionality of man's very existence" (150). If it did not concern such a deep change, Christ's words about the possibility of committing grave sin "in the heart" would have no meaning. The man who lives from lust no longer sees life as a gift to receive in thanksgiving from the hands of the Creator. Instead, lust indicates that man has denied the gift of God. From this perspective, life—if one is to attain it—must now be *grasped* (see §26).

The grave evil committed by the lustful look is precisely this: the denial of the gift expressed in the dignity of sexual difference. The man who lives "the gift" recognizes woman as a gift to be received both from the hands of the Creator and through the freedom of her own self-determination as a personal subject. But the man who denies the gift does not wait to receive woman as a gift. Instead, he extorts her gift; he *grasps* at her instead of *receiving* her. By doing so John Paul tells us that the man deprives the woman of her attraction as a person. He focuses merely on the attraction of her body as an object to satisfy the sexual need inherent in his fallen masculinity (we could say something similar with regard to the way a woman under lust's influence treats a man).

Lust, then, primarily has an axiological nature. In other words, it indicates a fundamental change in *the value* that man (male and female) assigns not only to sexuality, but to the whole universe. The man absorbed by lust no longer views creation with a sense of awe and wonder nor respects it as a gift from the Creator. Rather, creation and its goods are exploited and abused for selfish gain. They are grasped at rather than received with thanksgiving. In this way lust alters the intentionality of man's entire existence at its roots. We can recall here our previous discussion regarding the effects of man's new attitude toward his body on ecology and societal structures of labor and the economy (see §27).

B. Lust as Reduction

The Holy Father points out that the biblical/theological meaning of lust differs from the psychological meaning. The science of psychology speaks of lust as a desire for or intense attraction toward the sexual value of another person. It places no ethical meaning on the word. The biblical use of the word, however, has great ethical significance since it means a value is being impaired. This "value" is the value of the person revealed by the nuptial meaning of the body. Lust is sexual desire divorced from the nuptial (and procreative) meaning of the body. Lust has the internal effect of obscuring the true significance of the body, and hence, of the person itself. But the full value of the body-person can only be understood in light of the original call of man and woman as revealed in Genesis. Psychology by itself, then, does not have the context to understand lust as an impairment. It just seems "normal." Even if men and women can intuit that lust is contrary to their dignity, they cannot fully know why without the aid of revelation.

When we compare lust with what revelation tells us about the original mutual attraction of the sexes, we realize that lust is actually a rejection of true sexual desire. It involves an intentional "reduction" of God's original plan. In other words, lust entails a restriction or "closing down of mind and heart" to the full truth of the person and the perennial call to communion. Sex is part of all "the rich storehouse of values" with which man and woman relate to one another. In fact, the body in its sexuality is meant to reveal this rich storehouse of values. It is one thing to recognize this, and we *must* come to recognize this through the integration of sexuality and personality. But it is another thing altogether, the Pope points out, to reduce all the personal riches of the other's sexuality to an object of selfish enjoyment.

C. "Eternal" Sexuality

Sexuality provides an "invitation" and issues a "calling" to communion by means of mutual giving. John Paul states that this "dimension of intentionality of thought and heart" is so fundamental to humanity that it constitutes one of the main streams of universal human culture. In this universal sense John Paul speaks of the "eternal masculine," the "eternal feminine," and the "eternal attraction" between them. When man taps into this "eternal" dimension of sexuality, John Paul proclaims that it can free in him an entire gamut of spiritual-physical desires of an especially personal and "sharing" nature—all of which correspond to a proportionate pyramid of values regarding the person. This is mature, redeemed sexual attraction. Lust, on the other hand, does not have its sights on this "eternal" dimension. It seeks immediate gratification and thereby obscures the rich pyramid of values that marks the perennial attraction of the sexes. Lust turns from the man and woman's personal-sexual call to communion and pushes sexual attraction toward utilitarian dimensions, within which men and women use one another merely to satisfy their own needs.

In this utilitarian mode, sexuality "ceases being a specific language of the spirit; it loses its character of being a sign. It ceases," John Paul continues, "bearing in itself the wonderful matrimonial significance of the body[90]...in the context of conscience and experience" (149). In other words, while the body retains its nuptial meaning objectively speaking, man no longer readily experiences it. His conscience has become dulled to it. Using a precise, vivid image, John Paul says that lust "passes on the

---

90. In the English translation of the original Italian texts, the Pope's phrase *"significato sponsale del corpo"* is variously translated as "nuptial meaning of the body," "matrimonial" or "conjugal significance of the body," and "spousal meaning of the body."

ruins of the matrimonial significance of the body" and "aims directly at an exclusive end: to satisfy only the sexual need of the body, as its precise object" (149). The man of lust is not concerned with the body's nuptial/ procreative meaning. In fact, he often sees it as a nuisance since it impedes him from satisfying concupiscence. To his own demise, the man of lust will continually seek ways of eliminating this obstacle in his insatiable desire for gratification. John Paul stresses again that such an intentional and axiological reduction is completely contained in the way man "looks."

34. Adulterating Sexual Union within Marriage

October 1, 8, 1980 (TB 153–159)

John Paul II's revolutionary catechesis on the body garnered little media attention "in the beginning," so to speak. That all changed, however, with the general audience of October 8, 1980. Therein John Paul shows us "how deep-down it is necessary to go" if men and women are to adhere to Christ's words. In his prior address, John Paul states there is no doubt that, according to Christ, a man commits adultery in his heart when he looks with lust at a woman who is not his wife. However, the Pope says we can and even must ask whether or not Christ approves of a man looking with lust at his own wife. It was John Paul's answer to this question that immediately caught the attention of the international media.

A. The Typical Interpretation Requires a Deepening

Basic logic, when initially applied to this question, finds no problem with a man looking lustfully at his own wife. John Paul even stated early on in this cycle of reflections that "this lustful look, if addressed to his own wife, is not 'adultery in the heart,' precisely because the man's interior act refers to the woman who is his wife, with regard to whom adultery cannot take place."[91] If we stop at the surface, this reasoning seems entirely sound. However, as we have learned by now, John Paul II never stops at the surface. A deeper look at Christ's words indicates that "there remain good grounds for doubt whether this reasoning takes into account all the aspects of revelation, as well as of the theology of the body" (155).

As John Paul will explain, this interpretation of Christ's words (i.e., that it is acceptable to lust after one's own wife) fails to take into account

---

91. 4/23/80, TB 107.

the subjective dignity of the persons involved. John Paul's personalist understanding of ethics will not allow him to reduce the illicit to the illegal. As Christ insists, we must penetrate the heart. Hence, John Paul believes this typical interpretation requires "a deepening" in light of the anthropological and theological insights gained from his study of Christ's words. In classic personalist form, John Paul states that Christ not only considers the legal status of the man and woman in question. He also makes the moral evaluation of sexual desire depend above all on *the personal dignity* of the man and the woman. The Holy Father concludes, therefore, that the moral evaluation of sexual desire "has its importance both when it is a question of persons who are not married, and—perhaps even more—when they are spouses" (156).

When Christ speaks of committing adultery in the heart, it is significant that he does not refer to a woman who is not the man's wife. He simply refers to woman generically. As John Paul states, "Adultery 'in the heart' is committed not only *because* man 'looks' in this way at a woman who is not his wife, but *precisely* because he looks at a woman in this way." He thus concludes: "Even if he looked in this way at the woman who is his wife, he could likewise commit adultery 'in his heart'" (157).

This statement evoked a firestorm of criticism from the international media. Accusations flew that John Paul had such a negative evaluation of sex that he was condemning it even within marriage. The reaction was so widespread and severe that it prompted the Vatican newspaper *L'Osservatore Romano* to publish a response.[92]

Claudio Sorgi, the author of the Vatican response, suggested that certain media reports reflected "superficiality, lack of respect, and absence of attention" to what the Pope was saying, which led to "misunderstandings, we hope in good faith." Unfortunately, some comments were "so improvised and absurd as to be stupefying." Hence, the "suspicion arises," he concluded, "that not all the mistaken interpretations are in good faith." Furthermore, Sorgi pointed out that to adulterate a relationship simply means to distort it as compared with its original meaning. "Now what is it," he asks, "if not adultery, to reduce the conjugal relationship to a mere satisfaction of sexual need?" Appealing to modern sensibilities, Sorgi submits, "has it not been said and written plainly in recent years that marriage

---

92. See *L'Osservatore Romano*, October 12, 1980. The full text of this article was printed in *Blessed Are the Pure of Heart,* the second volume in the original four published by the Daughters of Saint Paul in 1983 (its inclusion immediately following the audience of October 8 has led some to mistakenly attribute 41 general audiences to this cycle of the theology of the body). It does not appear, however, in the one-volume edition of 1997.

often becomes a condition of slavery especially for the woman; that she is reduced to an erotic object or even that in certain cases the conjugal relationship is only masked prostitution?"

B. *Clarion Call to Uphold Woman's Dignity*

John Paul's statement about adulterating sexual union within marriage is nothing but a clarion call for men to uphold the dignity of their wives and vice versa. Both sexes are called to exist "for" the other sex through the free and sincere gift of self. Yet lust—in this case of the husband toward his wife—fundamentally changes the way in which woman exists "for" the man. It reduces the deep riches of her attractiveness as a female person to the mere satisfaction of the husband's need and thereby robs her of her dignity as a subject made in God's image. A man who uses woman's femininity to satisfy his own "instinct" has assumed this attitude "deep down," inwardly deciding to treat a woman in this way. This is precisely "adultery committed in the heart." So a man "can commit this 'adultery in the heart' also with regard to his own wife if he treats her only as an object to satisfy instinct" (157).

Simply getting married does not suddenly justify a man and woman using one another as a means of selfish gratification. For John Paul, using is the antithesis of love. Sexual union is only justified (i.e., made just, right, good, and holy) when—inspired by the love of God—man and woman give themselves to each other loving as God loves. Marriage, while an absolute prerequisite, does not automatically guarantee that this will happen. Spouses must commit themselves all the more to living according to the logic of "the truthful sign" (see §31). They must therefore guard against any thought or action that would make their union a *countersign* of God's love. Indulging concupiscent desire (like adultery) is just such a counter-sign.

■ How does this fit in with the traditional teaching that the "relief of concupiscence" is an end of marriage? This has often been interpreted to mean that marriage provides a legitimate outlet for indulging concupiscent desire. Such an interpretation all but gives men *carte blanche* to use their wives for their own selfish gratification. Because of this seriously misguided mindset, confessors and spiritual directors have often counseled wives that they are obligated to submit to their husbands' sexual needs upon request. But such "common wisdom" cloaks a terribly distorted anthropology. As Dr. John Crosby insists, "It is not too much to say that John

Paul abhors any such interpretation" of the relief of concupiscence.[93] Such a misguided view fails entirely to take into account the new ethos to which Christ directs men and women in the Sermon on the Mount. A look at the Latin provides a window into understanding John Paul's perspective on the issue. *Remedium concupiscentiae* is actually better translated *"remedy* for concupiscence." While "relief" implies mere indulgence of concupiscent desire, "remedy" implies that the grace of marriage offers a healing of concupiscent desire. Through the healing power of the redemption of the body, men and women can progressively (re)experience sexual desire as God created it to be—the desire to love as he loves in the sincere gift of self. Only this understanding of *remedium concupiscentiae* is compatible with a personalist understanding of sexual ethics. As Cardinal Wojtyla wrote in a 1974 essay on marriage, "If it is true that marriage may also be a *remedium concupiscentiae* (see St. Paul: 'It is better to marry than to burn'—1 Cor 7:9), then this must be understood in the integral sense given it by the Christian Scriptures, which also teach of the 'redemption of the body' (Rom 8:23) and point to the sacrament of matrimony as a way of realizing this redemption."[94]

C. The Cause of Misunderstanding

For those who have understood John Paul's thought up to this point, his teaching about the possibility of committing "adultery in the heart" within marriage makes complete sense. However, for those who are locked in a fallen view of sex John Paul's statement seems to disqualify all sexual expression—hence, the media's barrage of criticism. Indeed, John Paul affirms that it is impossible to arrive at the second interpretation of Christ's words if we confine ourselves to the purely psychological interpretation of lust. Christ's words in the Sermon on the Mount call us to a theological understanding of lust as a reduction of God's plan "in the beginning."

A psychological understanding of lust sees the selfish sting of concupiscence as "normal." Yet, as John Paul insists in this crucial statement, Christ's words in the Sermon on the Mount demonstrate that "Christian ethos is characterized by a transformation of the conscience and attitudes

---

93. See *The Legacy of John Paul II*, ed. Geoffrey Gneuhs (New York, NY: Crossroads, 2000), p. 57.

94. "The Family as a Community of Persons," *Person & Community: Selected Essays*, p. 327.

of the human person, both man and woman, such as to express and realize the value of the body and sex according to the Creator's original plan, placed as they are in the service of the 'communion of persons.'"[95] Psychology knows nothing of this "original plan" or the real hope of transforming the heart in this regard. Psychology knows only the reduction of lust. If *that* is wrong—if *that* is "adultery in the heart"—then men and women, husbands and wives, have no hope. They can only fear the severity of Christ's words and clamor against the Pope's interpretation of them.

In this sense, the Pope's critics understood John Paul correctly. Left solely to the forces of (fallen) nature, there is no hope for husbands and wives *not* to adulterate their own relationship, at least to some degree. But certain media reports completely missed that Christ's words (and John Paul's interpretation of them) are deeply imbued with the hope and *the real possibility* of redemption from lust. As John Paul expresses in the concluding comments of this most contentious address, "Are we to fear the severity of [Christ's] words, or rather have confidence in their salvific content, in their power?" (159)

■ The *Washington Post* article which reported on this address shows how much the secular media missed the "good news" of John Paul's call to sexual redemption. Judy Mann, in her article "A Lesson on Lust for the Vatican," grants that the Pope's remarks on lust were "motivated only by the best of intentions." However, she then goes on to inform the Pope that "he may not be familiar with the role lust plays in the American family....From the time Americans reach adolescence, lust is the life force." Mann seems to favor marriage and family life, but she seems blind to the real possibility of any alternative to lust as the foundation for marriage. She reports that in her day "one of the first things you learned at your mother's knee was that boys had only one thing on their minds—which was you-know-what—and that the road to the altar was paved with firm denials. I know for a fact," Mann says, "that in my generation lust led to hundreds of thousands of American marriages." Not only does lust lead to marriage, according to Mann, it can also aid marital fidelity. She concludes that "the Pope might want to bear in mind" that if "a man has lust in his heart for his wife, chances are he won't have adultery on his mind for somebody else."[96] These are the sad conclusions of a merely psychological

---

95. 10/22/80, TB 163.

96. Judy Mann, "A Lesson on Lust for the Vatican," *Washington Post,* October 10, 1980, pp. B–1 and B–2.

interpretation of lust. Not only does it normalize lust, it asserts it as a good. Interestingly, however, Mann's tone hints that she may wish things were different. Unfortunately, she has resigned herself to the lesson (and attendant world-view) learned at her mother's knee: Lust is just the way it is. In light of this "lesson on lust for the Vatican," John Paul boldly calls Mann (and her mother) to "another vision of man's possibilities."[97]

35. Lived Morality and the Ethos of Human Practice

October 8, 15, 22, 1980 (TB 158–165)

We have already devoted many pages to John Paul's analysis of Christ's words about lust, yet the spiral continues to deepen. Christ's words are exacting, to say the least. To fulfill them, we must undergo a radical paradigm shift with regard to the way we think of and experience sexuality and sexual desire. We must allow "the recesses of the heart" to be thoroughly revealed. We must come to perceive anew the lost fullness of our humanity, and want to regain it. In other words, we must perceive the true, liberating meaning of "purity of heart" and open ourselves to receive it as a gift of grace flowing from Christ's death and resurrection.

Of course, virtue does not come to fallen man without toil. If a person desires authentic liberation from lust, he must work in tandem with grace and firmly reject everything that stems from lust. As Christ figuratively states, he must "pluck out his eye" and "cut off his hand" if these cause him to stumble. For "it is better that you lose one of your members than that your whole body go into hell" (Mt 5:29–30). Why are Christ's words so harsh and foreboding? One might observe in this context that lust and hell can both be defined with the same five words: *the absence of God's love.* This is why lust is so serious. If God's love constitutes man's origin, vocation, and destiny, then lust constitutes the antithesis of man's very existence.

A. The Pure and Simple Fabric of Existence

Christ takes such a firm stand against lust because lust is the first and most tenacious obstacle to an authentic communion between the sexes—and man and woman's call to form a communion of persons "is the deepest substratum of human ethics and culture" (163). Humanity stands or falls on this point since all moral disorder, according to John Paul, comes

---

97. 10/29/80, TB 168.

from the impurity of a lustful heart. Such impurity "distorts both sexual life and the operation of social and economic life and even cultural life."[98]

■ This statement certainly contradicts the idea that a person's "private" sexual behavior has no bearing on anyone outside the bedroom. Journalist Philip Lawler confirmed the Pope's statement when, writing in 1997, he observed that "the public consequences of 'private' sexual behavior now threaten to destroy American society. In the past thirty-five years the federal government has spent four trillion dollars—that is, $4,000,000,000,000,000—on a variety of social programs designed to remedy ills which can be attributed, directly or indirectly, to the misuse of human sexuality."[99] Along the same lines, a Jewish proverb recounts the story of a man on a boat drilling a hole beneath his seat. When the man sitting next to him protests, he replies, "Why should you care what I'm doing? It's under *my* seat."

John Paul observes that human life is by its nature "co-educative." This means that the common life of men and women "constitutes the pure and simple fabric of existence." Thus, the dignity and balance of human life "depend at every moment of history and at every point of geographical longitude and latitude on 'who' she will be for him and he for her" (159). In short, a culture of lust degenerates into a culture that does not respect life—a culture of death. Only when men and women are freed from the grip of lust that strangles the spirit can they fulfill themselves "in the freedom of mutual giving." And this freedom in giving "is the condition of all life together in truth" (159). Only in freedom can men and women realize "the sacramental unity" that the Creator himself willed (see Gen 2:24). Without this internal liberation from lust, a life together in truth cannot exist. And the new dimension of ethos, John Paul says, "is always connected with the revelation of that depth, which is called 'heart,' and with its liberation from 'lust,' in order that man, male and female in all the interior truth of the mutual 'for,' may shine forth more fully in that heart" (158).

B. Ethos and Praxis

In his audience of October 15, 1980, John Paul shifts to a more practical analysis of Christ's words. If humanity stands or falls on purity of heart, how do we live so that we might stand? If we accept Christ's words, how are we to think? How are we to feel regarding sexuality, sexual attraction, and desire? Can anything in us reliably guide our thinking, feeling,

---

98. 12/17/80 third endnote, TB 230–231.
99. "The Price of Virtue," *Catholic World Report*, July 1997, p. 58.

and acting in this regard? If Christ's words do not merely accuse the human heart but also call us to good—what, exactly, is that good? "These questions are significant for human 'praxis,' and indicate an organic connection of 'praxis' itself with *ethos*. Lived morality is always the *ethos* of human practice" (160). In other words, as Christ himself indicated (see Mt 15:19), human actions (praxis) flow from the orientation of the human heart (ethos). "Lived morality," then, is a morality beyond mere duty. It flows from the super-abounding love in one's heart. With John Paul's shift to a more practical analysis, he wants to show the way to attain that proper orientation of heart so that what flows from our hearts in practice will be a fulfillment of Christ's words.

The "how to's" of living according to Christ's words in the Sermon on the Mount have found multiform expressions throughout history. Currents of thought have drawn nearer to or moved further from the true ethos of Christ's words based on various historical factors. They have passed "from the pole of pessimism, to the pole of optimism, from puritan severity, to modern permissiveness. It is necessary to realize this," according to John Paul, "in order that the *ethos* of the Sermon on the Mount may always have due transparency with regard to man's actions and behavior" (161).

With this statement, John Paul sets the stage for the proper interpretation of Christ's words in the field of human praxis. Having learned from the currents of history that have swung the pendulum from rigorism to license and back, it seems we can now penetrate Christ's words with more balance and accuracy. It seems we are now better prepared to establish the proper "ethos of human practice" in this vexing field of morality.

C. The Grave Error of Manichaeism

John Paul knows that if we are to understand the proper sense of Christ's words, we must contend with the "Manichaean demon" that has plagued Catholic moral theology throughout much of Christian history. In its original form, Manichaeism saw the source of evil in matter, in the body, and therefore condemned everything corporeal in man. Since our bodiliness, as John Paul notes, "is manifested in man mainly through sex," Manichaeism particularly devalues all things sexual.[100]

John Paul knows that—like a wolf in sheep's clothing—such heretical thinking has seeped into many Christians' minds and hearts and must be uprooted. Some would even claim that the harshness of Christ's words in the Sermon on the Mount harmonize with a Manichaean devaluation of

---

100. John Paul offers a further explanation of the Manichaean ethos in the endnote of this address (see TB 185–186).

sex. Hence, the Holy Father firmly and repeatedly stresses that "the Manichaean way of understanding and evaluating man's body and sexuality is essentially alien to the Gospel" (165). Therefore, anyone who wants to see in Christ's words a Manichaean perspective would be committing an essential error. "The appropriate interpretation of Christ's words," as John Paul unambiguously affirms, "must be absolutely free of Manichaean elements in thought and in attitude" (163).

While the unaccustomed ear might equate the severity of Christ's words with the severity of Manichaeism, the essential difference lies in the assignment of evil. Manichaeism assigns evil to the body and sex itself. Christ assigns evil to man's heart, and not even to man's heart itself, but only to the distortion of lust. Lust devalues the body. Christ's statement in the Sermon on the Mount, then, springs "precisely from the affirmation of the personal dignity of the body and of sex, and serves only this dignity" (165). Thus, Christ's words in no way condemn the body and sex or deny their value. Instead they express a deep and mature affirmation of the body and sex. Christ calls his listeners to understand the body's divine dignity and value both objectively and subjectively. John Paul poetically observes that Christ impresses this mature dimension of ethos on the pages of the Gospel in order to impress it subsequently in human life and human hearts. Only when the truth about good penetrates the heart—that is, only when ethic becomes ethos—can we speak of a "real" and a "human" morality.

D. Irreconcilable Difference in Mentality

John Paul summarizes the irreconcilable difference in mentality this way: "Whereas, for the Manichaean mentality, the body and sexuality constitute, so to speak, an 'anti-value'; for Christianity, on the contrary, they always constitute a 'value not sufficiently appreciated'" (163–164). Far from devaluing the body and sex, Christianity assigns to the body and sex a value beyond compare. Recall John Paul's thesis that the "body, in fact, and it alone, is capable of making visible what is invisible: the spiritual and divine. It was created to transfer into the visible reality of the world, the mystery hidden since time immemorial in God, and thus to be a sign of it."[101] Now, in the context of countering Manichaeism, John Paul returns to his thesis and states that the "body, in its masculinity and femininity, is called 'from the beginning' to become the manifestation of the spirit. It does so also by means of the conjugal union of man and woman when they unite in such a way as to form 'one flesh.'" In this way the body "assumes the value of a sign—in a way, a sacramental sign" (163).

---

101. 2/20/80, TB 76 (see §22).

This is the value that the Manichaean mentality "insufficiently appreciates" (or fails to appreciate altogether): The body and sex are sacramental—in some way through the veil of a sign they make the divine mystery visible. Christ calls men and women to rediscover this value and live according to the logic of "the truthful sign" both in thought and in action. Hence, the Pope insists that Christian praxis in this regard only concerns detaching oneself from the evil of lust. It *never* means transferring the evil of lust to its object. "Such a transfer would mean a certain acceptance—perhaps not fully conscious—of the Manichaean 'anti-value.' It would not constitute a real and deep victory over the evil of the act...; on the contrary, there would be concealed in it the great danger of justifying the act to the detriment of the object" (164).

In other words, in seeking to live according to Christ's words in the Sermon on the Mount, we must be sure that we are battling the true evil—lust. We must never project the evil in question onto the body and sexuality of the person toward whom our lusts are directed. Christ certainly demands detachment from the evil of lust, but John Paul insists that this never means that the object of that desire, that is, the woman who is "looked at lustfully," is an evil.[102] In fact, so long as man redirects the assignment of evil from his own lusts to the woman, he exempts himself from any need to overcome the evil in his heart. We can see, then, that the Manichaean condemnation of the body "might—and may always be—a loophole to avoid the requirements set in the Gospel" (162).

John Paul reproaches those who condemn the body and sexuality in the name of holiness, when, in fact, such "holiness" stems from a resistance of the demands of holiness. Mature holiness demands of men and women "a real and deep victory" over the evil of lust. It demands transformation of the deep impulses of the heart. It demands purity of vision, which is not only the ability to turn away from a potential object of lust. Even more so it is the ability, through the ongoing maturation of purity, to affirm positively with one's look that "object," which is always also a subject, a person.

■ This assignment of the Manichaean "anti-value" to the body can be seen in the tendency to describe sex or certain body parts as "dirty." No body part is "dirty." Nor is it ever accurate to call sex itself dirty. For God looked at all he had made and called it *very good*. What may be unclean or impure is the human heart and its view of certain body parts or its manner of engaging in sex. It would be misguided, for example, for a mother who

---

102. John Paul notes that this important clarification seems to be lacking in some Wisdom texts. See, for example, Proverbs 5:1–6; 6:24–29 and Sirach 26:9–12.

catches her son with a *Playboy* magazine to scold him for looking at "dirty pictures." While it may be unconscious and unintentional on the mother's part, the assignment of evil is then on the body (since they are pictures of the body) instead of on the evil of lust behind the production and the viewing of pornography. As John Paul says, pornographic portrayals of the body "arouse objection...not because of their object, since the human body in itself always has its inalienable dignity—but because of the quality or way of its reproduction,"[103] which is intended to incite lust. This distinction is not just a matter of semantics but has to do with the proper assignment of evil. It has to do with conforming our language to authentic Christian teaching on the body. Consider also the common question asked when knocking on someone's bedroom door before entering: "Are you decent?" In light of the above, the only proper response to such a question—even if one is entirely naked—is an unequivocal "yes!" The body is *always* decent. Only the manner of another's "look" may lack decency. Thus, we cover the body out of reverence for its goodness, its decency—not to hide any supposed indecency.

36. The Interpretation of Suspicion

October 22, 29, 1980 (TB 163–168)

For those who desire purity, the sexual body *is not the evil with which we must contend.* The Holy Father insistently repeats this point because he knows many Christians have fallen prey to this grave Manichaean error. Far from being evil or even tainted, the body, and sexual union itself, contain a value and dignity that we can barely fathom. But we *must* fathom this value and dignity if we are to live according to the true ethos of Christ's words.

A. True Victory Over Lust

Sexuality is "deeply penetrated" by the mystery of the "redemption of the body" (see Rom 8:23). Only in this light can we properly understand Christ's words. If Christ accuses the heart of lust, he also calls man to experience a "real and deep victory" over the evil of lust in order that man may rediscover and live according to the true value of the nuptial meaning of the body. On the other hand, John Paul says that the Mani-

---

103. 5/6/81, TB 228.

chaean attitude leads to "annihilation" and "negation" of the body and of sex, or at best to their "mere toleration" because of the necessity of procreation.

■ The idea that the Church thinks sex is bad, even if she grants the one reluctant exception of condoning it for procreation, is widespread. Many people, Catholics and non-Catholics alike, might actually believe that such heretical thinking is official Church teaching! Even some of the Church's otherwise esteemed thinkers have said things that lend credence to these ideas. In these addresses, John Paul II's ardent desire to set the record straight almost seems to leap off the page.

John Paul says that in trying to overcome lust, man must contend with the "inveterate habits" springing from Manichaeism in his way of thinking and evaluating things. A man struggling with lust, for example, can easily blame the woman after whom he is lusting rather than look deeply into his own heart. As John Paul observes, true victory over lust in this case would stem from the man's effort to "rediscover the true values" of the woman's body and sexuality and "to reassert them" so that the Manichaean "anti-value" does not take root in his conscience and in his will. This means much more than simply turning away in order to avoid looking with lust. Containing lustful impulse is the essential first step. But if a person's purity stops here it is only a "negative" purity, so to speak. It is only a "turning away." As such, it carries the danger of slipping into the Manichaean error of assigning an "anti-value" to that from which a man is continually turning, that is, a woman, a person.

To gain a true victory over lust, John Paul says that purity must mature from the "negative" turning away, to the more "positive" recognition and assertion of the real beauty, dignity, and value of the body and of sex.[104] This can only happen through the concerted effort, in this case, of the man, guided by grace, to see the woman's *personhood* revealed through her feminine body. Through the indwelling of the Holy Spirit, such "seeing" becomes not only a concept accepted by the mind, but a living reality "felt" by the heart. Indeed, the ethos of redemption enables man to be "moved to the good not only by his will alone, but also by his sensitive appetite."[105] This is the task that Christ gives us and this is what the "redemption of the body" affords: the gradual reintegration of body and

---

104. John Paul speaks of the "negative" and "positive" dimensions of purity more explicitly in his audience of 1/28/81, TB 200–201.

105. *CCC*, n. 1770.

soul, of personality and sexuality, and the ability to *see* this and *experience* it—not perfectly in this life, but more and more effectively as we allow all of our diseased ways of thinking about the body and sexuality to be crucified with Christ.

■ From the moment of the very first sin, men have tended to blame women for their own disordered hearts (see Gen 3:11–12). Certainly women have a responsibility not to play on men's weaknesses. But whether women live responsibly in this regard or not, men have their own *prior* responsibility to battle lust and continually mature in purity to the point that they can see and assert *every* woman's true value and dignity.[106] If men do not take this responsibility seriously, they will almost inevitably project an air of blame toward women for their own lusts. And women, it seems, have antennas for picking up on this. This dynamic was exemplified in the comments of a young person who heard a talk of mine on woman's dignity. She attended a Catholic college where students, for the most part, genuinely desire to grow in holiness. She shared with me the emotional effects of having men for three years continually turn away or look at the sidewalk whenever she walked across campus. Those men may have needed to do this in order to avoid lusting. But was there not one man on that campus pure enough to look at her, and in so doing affirm her dignity rather than lust after her? Every human being is crying out to be seen and loved—to be acknowledged positively as a person of value and worth. One can easily imagine that over time a woman in such circumstances might come to believe that there was something wrong with her—that *she* was responsible for causing men to stumble simply by being a woman. This woman said that what struck her most about the talk was that *she was good;* that she, herself, as a woman was not the problem. For she had a God-given dignity that shone in her femininity, whether the men on campus could see that or not. This is obviously a delicate situation since it is better for a man not to look at a woman than to look at her with lust. But it is better yet to mature to the point where a man can look at a woman and, keeping his heart under control, assert in positive affirmation the true dignity and value of the person.

B. Masters of Suspicion

We are approaching the crux of the matter for historical man: the crux of human practice. How is man to live? He is to live according to the purity of his origins. That is the norm; that is the standard; that is man's

---

106. See the concluding paragraphs of *Mulieris Dignitatem,* nn. 10 and 14.

task. Through the ethos of redemption, he is called to regain what was lost. As Christ's words indicate in both his discussion with the Pharisees and in the Sermon on the Mount, man and woman are called progressively to reclaim the nuptial meaning of the body as it was revealed "in the beginning."

This may sound a bit unrealistic. After all, in the state of original innocence—which, as the Church teaches, man has left irrevocably behind—man and woman did not need to contend with concupiscence. In the experience of historical man, however, the lust of the flesh always weighs him down and casts a shadow on all things sexual. Given that, it seems the best a man can hope for in this fallen world is to learn somehow to manage his unruly impulses and avoid the near occasion of sin. We have become so wounded and twisted that lust, as common experience attests, will always have the upper hand in man's heart—at least in this life.

Will it? Those who believe that lust inevitably determines man's experience of the body and sexuality can count themselves among those whom John Paul labels "the masters of suspicion." A master of suspicion is a person who does not know or does not fully believe in the transforming power of the Gospel. Concupiscence holds sway in his own heart, so he projects the same onto everyone else. In his mind the human body will always rouse concupiscence, especially if it is partially exposed, and all the more so if it is totally naked. It can do nothing else. So he holds the human heart in a state of continual and irreversible suspicion.

■ The story of the two bishops previously mentioned (See §32) illustrates the interpretation of suspicion. The bishop who turned away readily assumed that his brother bishop was looking with lust. Having never experienced a real and deep victory over lust, he could not imagine any other way to look at the woman and he immediately accused his brother bishop of indulging lust. In this way, he held his brother's heart in a state of suspicion.

The Protestant scholar Paul Ricoeur coined the phrase "masters of suspicion" in describing the thinking of Freud, Marx, and Nietzsche. As John Paul points out, these thinkers have significantly influenced the way modern man understands himself and interprets morality. John Paul admits that we see a significant convergence in each of their systems of thought with a Scriptural analysis of man, but we see also a fundamental and unmistakable divergence. Like Christ in the Sermon on the Mount, these men also "accuse" the human heart. The Holy Father even sees a particular correspondence in each of these thinkers' systems with one of the three forms of lust described by St. John. John Paul suggests that Nietzschean thought corresponds in some sense with "the pride of life"; Marxist thought with "the lust of the eyes"; and Freudian thought, of course, with "the lust of the flesh."

But convergence ends here because these men make lust "the absolute criterion of anthropology and ethics"; they place lust at the core of their interpretation of man. The Pope stresses that biblical anthropology does not allow us to stop here, but opens us to the ethos of redemption. This is the fundamental divergence: the "masters of suspicion" see no hope of redemption from lust. "This interpretation is very different, it is radically different from what we rediscover in Christ's words in the Sermon on the Mount. These words reveal not only another ethos, but also another vision of man's possibilities" (168).

It is certainly true, as John Paul observes, that if man leaves himself at the mercy of the forces of fallen nature, he cannot avoid the influence of lust. But it is equally true that man is not merely at the mercy of the forces of his fallen nature. The Pope insists that in Christ, fallen nature is always at the same time *redeemed* nature. With full confidence in the power of Jesus' death and resurrection to free us from sin, the Vicar of Christ asserts: "Man cannot stop at putting the 'heart' in a state of continual and irreversible suspicion due to the manifestations of the lust of the flesh.... Redemption is a truth, a reality, in the name of which man must feel called, and 'called with efficacy'" (167). Yes, *real power* gushes forth from Christ's crucified and risen body to *set us free from the domination of concupiscence*. As the Holy Father proclaims, we are "called to rediscover, nay more, to realize the nuptial meaning of the body [through] that spiritual state and that spiritual power which are derived from mastery of the lust of the flesh" (167).

Again it must be emphasized that the mature form of such mastery is not akin merely to reigning in a wild horse (see §29). Certainly to the degree that concupiscence seeks to rear its ugly head, it must be "caged." But as one's mastery over lust matures, grace operatively transforms the horse so it no longer needs the cage. Mature self-mastery enjoys the fruits which grace has wrought by transforming the content and character of sexual desire from lust to love, making one truly free with "the freedom of the gift."

C. The Meaning of Life Is at Stake

Perfect freedom from concupiscence is reserved for the eschaton when we will be forever united with Christ in his resurrection. Until then we remain on the difficult and fragile pilgrimage of "becoming."[107] Yet "in

---

107. See *Veritatis Splendor,* n. 18.

a certain way...by virtue of the Holy Spirit, Christian life is already now on earth a participation in the death and Resurrection of Christ."[108] If we do not believe that men and women—even while still on the journey toward perfection—can die to lust and be raised to a new life of victory over it, then it seems that we do not fully believe in (or are not fully aware of) the *good news* of Christ's death and resurrection and how it can effectively operate in our lives.

Sin has wounded us deeply. Even so, as the Pope stresses, the original meaning of our humanity is "indestructible," and the "new man" risen with Christ is called with power to rediscover it. Hence, a continuity is established between "the beginning" and the perspective of redemption.[109] Christ does not invite man to return to the state of original innocence, since humanity has left it irrevocably behind. Nevertheless, in Christ, we *can* live and love as God intended in the beginning. But a key difference exists between the original and historical state: Living the truth came naturally to original man, while historical man must engage in an arduous spiritual battle in order to see the body as God created it to be. But if we are willing to die with Christ, we too can come to share his victory over sin. We can *experience* and *know* this victory deep within our hearts—not easily, and not overnight, but progressively through suffering for the truth, we are purified inwardly and the lies lose their power over us.

Doubt in this regard comes easily. Doubt, after all, takes us off the hook. If we consider Christ's appeal in the Sermon on the Mount hopelessly unrealistic, we do not have to challenge ourselves to grow or to change. It gives us a quick and easy detour around the cross (if such a thing exists). John Paul warns us not to detach Christ's appeal from the context of concrete existence. The expectation that Christ places on us in the Sermon on the Mount (i.e., that we would not lust) is entirely realistic in light of who he is, who we are, and what he came to do for us. If it seems hopelessly unrealistic, we need to ask ourselves what we really believe about who Christ said he is and what his death and resurrection mean in our lives. We must not fall into the trap of "holding the form of religion" while "denying the power of it" (2 Tim 3:5).

Much is at stake. In fact, even though Christ's appeal to overcome lust refers to a limited sphere of human interaction, within this sphere it always means "the rediscovery of the meaning of the whole of existence, the meaning of life" (168). If we close ourselves to the possibility of a real

---

108. *CCC,* n. 1002.

109. See 12/3/80, TB 175.

transformation of our hearts, we lock ourselves into "the interpretation of suspicion." And, as John Paul clearly states, "The meaning of life is the antithesis of the interpretation 'of suspicion'" (168).

37. Grace, Faith, and Man's Real Possibilities

October 29, 1980 (TB 165–168)

Above we quoted John Paul saying that Christ's words in the Sermon on the Mount "reveal not only another ethos, but also another vision of man's possibilities" (168). Most people who contest Christ's teaching about lust in the Sermon on the Mount (and Christian teaching on sexuality in general) do so specifically because they do not believe it corresponds with the concrete possibilities of man. John Paul responds:

> But what are "the concrete possibilities of man"? And of *which* man are we speaking? Of man *dominated* by lust or of man *redeemed by Christ?* This is what is at stake: the *reality* of Christ's redemption. *Christ has redeemed us!* This means he has given us the possibility of realizing the *entire truth* of our being; he has set our freedom free from the *domination* of concupiscence. And if redeemed man still sins, this is not due to an imperfection of Christ's redemptive act, but to man's will not to avail himself of the grace which flows from that act. God's command is of course proportioned to man's capabilities, but to the capabilities of the man to whom the Holy Spirit has been given; of the man who, though he has fallen into sin, can always obtain pardon and enjoy the presence of the Holy Spirit.[110]

This bold papal proclamation brings us to the heart of the matter. John Paul, Christ's modern-day apostle, echoes the words of the Apostle Paul: "Do not empty the cross of its power!" (see 1 Cor 1:17) If we accept the Pope's challenge to ponder the *full power* of Christ's death and resurrection, we come to realize that this "other vision of man's possibilities" opens before us vistas of freedom and joy of which few men and women ever dream.

Returning to our image of the flat tires—despite the dysfunction of driving through life with the rubber shredding off the rims, many of us have become so accustomed to this that life with inflated tires might seem threatening. Such a vision demands that we re-evaluate perhaps an entire lifetime of the diseased ways of thinking and relating we had grown accustomed to and may even have assimilated into a "deflated" notion of holiness. "Be not afraid!"

---

110. *Veritatis Splendor*, n. 103 (emphasis in original).

A. Grace Restored

As John Paul indicates above, only grace—life in the Holy Spirit—enables us to experience true liberation from lust and the joy that freedom brings. In the beginning, the grace given to man and woman constituted them in a state of original holiness and justice. This "beatifying gift" enabled them to see each other as God saw them, as evidenced by original nakedness (see §20). In the redemption, grace is given first for the remission of sins, yet it abounds in such a way that man can gradually reclaim God's original plan for human life. Christ's words in the Sermon on the Mount "bear witness that the original power (therefore also the grace) of the mystery of creation has become for each of [us] power (that is, grace) of the mystery of redemption" (167). Recall that grace is "participation in the interior life of God himself, in his holiness." It is "that mysterious gift made to the inner man—to the human 'heart'—which enables both of them, man and woman, to exist from the 'beginning' in the mutual relationship of the disinterested gift of oneself."[111] To be full of grace, then, means to be full of the Holy Spirit, of the very Love and Life of the Trinity, who *in*-spires the dust of our humanity with the capacity to love according to the image in which we are made.

The first Adam rejected this gift at the prompting of the deceiver. The New Adam restores this gift in fidelity to the Father. To experience this restoration we need faith. For *"faith*, in its deepest essence," according to John Paul II, "is *the openness* of the human heart to the gift: *to God's self-communication in the Holy Spirit.*"[112] We must open our hearts—yes, those same hearts accused and found guilty of lust—to Christ our Bridegroom. With utter trust and genuine humility we must submit our hearts to his judgment, to his justice. When we do, Christ returns to us a heart not condemned, but restored. The more we surrender our hearts in this way, the more we experience the Holy Spirit impregnating our sexual desires "with everything that is noble and beautiful" with "the supreme value which is love" (168).

The need for this transformation wrought by grace is essential. According to John Paul it "concerns the very 'nature,' the very substratum of the humanity of the person, the deepest impulses of the 'heart'" (167). To be filled with God's grace is—in a less strict sense of the term—man's "natural" state, the way God created man to be "in the beginning." Without this transformation, without this grace, we cannot live according to the ethos of the Gospel. Without this transformation, the best we can do is "cope" with our lusts. Christ's words call us to so much more!

---

111. 1/30/80, TB 67–68.

112. *Dominum et Vivificantem*, n. 51.

B. Christ's Call Wells Up from Within

Furthermore, as John Paul states, "The words of Christ uttered in the Sermon on the Mount are not a call hurled into emptiness" (167). They find a home in man's heart precisely because man is not completely absorbed by the lust of the flesh. He can seek another form of mutual relations in the sphere of the perennial attraction of the sexes. In fact, even when experiencing lust, man feels within his own heart a deep need to preserve the dignity of the mutual relations of the sexes. The word of the Gospel calls him to this, so man experiences this call from "outside" himself. Yet at the same time the Holy Father insists that man also experiences this call from "inside" himself. This is what he means by saying Christ's words are not hurled into emptiness. When we let Christ's words act in us, they tap into that "echo" of our beginning deep within our hearts—that beginning that was "very good"; that beginning in which man and woman knew and lived the full truth of the body and, hence, were naked and felt no shame.

The more a person allows the echo of that good beginning to resound in his heart, the more he will realize, as John Paul says, that "the heritage of his heart" is deeper than the sinfulness inherited; *it is deeper than lust.* What cause for rejoicing! Lust is not the final word on man. Lust is not at man's core. The heritage of the human heart is deeper than all its distortions. And the "words of Christ, set in the whole reality of creation and redemption, re-activate that deeper heritage and give it real power in man's life" (168).

To use an image, if the heart is a "deep well," the water—having been cut off from its source—often appears stagnant and murky. But beyond the mud and mire remains a remnant of the grace of our creation—a spring with the capacity of yielding crystal clear waters. Christ reactivates that spring! Tapped into, these waters well up in us to purify our whole hearts. Indeed, they well up in us to eternal life (see Jn 4:14). Despite our many sins and distortions, at our core, behold: we *are* very good!

38. Longing for the True, Good, and Beautiful

November 5; December 3, 1980 (TB 168–171, 176–177)

In his audience of November 5, 1980, John Paul begins an analysis of the relationship between "ethos" and "eros," that is, between the ethical and the erotic. Do the words of Christ in the Sermon on the Mount condemn the erotic? Do they warn severely against eros? To answer these questions, we must clarify what we mean by "eros."

The Holy Father recounts that the Greek term "eros" passed from mythology into Plato's philosophy, then into romantic literature, and finally into its common usage today. He acknowledges that eros has a vast range of meanings according to its usage in different periods and cultures. Each of these shades of meaning points in its own way to the "complex riches of the heart" to which Christ appealed in the Sermon on the Mount. Yet the sensual and sexual nature of eros forms the common thread woven in all these meanings.

John Paul defines "erotic phenomena" as "those mutual actions and ways of behaving through which man and woman approach each other and unite so as to be 'one flesh'" (170). The main point of the Pope's catechesis is to analyze these "erotic phenomena" and understand them in light of biblical revelation. John Paul wonders if the term "eros" leaves room for the ethos Christ announced. Does eros merely refer to the lust which Christ condemns? Or can eros also refer to that good and beautiful attraction of the sexes revealed "in the beginning" by the nuptial meaning of the body?

A. Plato's Definition of Eros

Ever determined to establish the fundamental goodness of sexual desire and sensuality, John Paul refuses to surrender the term eros to the distortion of lust. He creatively rehabilitates eros by appealing to Plato's philosophy. In Platonic usage, eros means the interior force that attracts man to the true, good, and beautiful. Within this sphere, the way opens toward what Christ expressed in the Sermon on the Mount. The Pope believes that people often see Christ's words about lust merely as a prohibition against eros without trying to discover "the really deep and essential values" that this prohibition covers and ensures. If we would open our hearts to the deeper meaning of Christ's words, we would find that Christ desires to liberate us to experience the true meaning of eros.

The Holy Father never tires of explaining that Christ not only accuses the heart of lust, but also appeals to the heart to rediscover the goodness of God's original plan for sexuality. The ethos of redemption, then, "means the possibility and the necessity of transforming what has been weighed down by the lust of the flesh" so that we might experience eros as the desire for "what is true, good, and beautiful" (170–171). John Paul firmly establishes that eros and ethos do not differ from each other. They are not opposed to one another as many presume. Instead, through the transforming power of redemption, eros and ethos "are called to meet in the human heart, and, in this meeting, to bear fruit" (171). When eros and ethos meet, they bear fruit in purity. Pure sexual desire leads us in truth.

Those with a mature purity of heart simply do not "look with lust." Even if concupiscence still tugs at us, the pure of heart can recognize it, resist it, and allow grace to "untwist" it. In this way man and woman come to participate to a significant degree in the original good of God's vision. Perfection in this regard comes only in the eschaton. Yet even now purity enables us to see with God's vision, to view the body as a manifestation of divine beauty.[113] Men and women, husbands and wives, who acquire this purity actually "taste" something of that experience of original nakedness. Yes, for the pure of heart, the erotic is true. It is good. It is beautiful.

The more we come to see this, the more the cloud of negativity and shame that tends to hover over all things sexual dissipates in our hearts. We no longer tend to condemn manifestations of sexuality with a sense of suspicion. Instead, we experience the very meaning of life and understand the fundamental place of sexuality in it. And we know it is *very good.*

B. Growing in Holiness

Experiencing this mature kind of purity is not theory for John Paul; it manifests an aspect of true holiness. And such holiness is truly attainable. But as already stated, a mature purity of heart does not come automatically. It is a gift of grace to be sure, but we must diligently cooperate with this grace. The Holy Father observes that when a person often yields to the lust of the flesh, turning from it is not only difficult, but may give the impression of suspending sexual desire "in emptiness." This is especially true, he says, when a person must make up his mind to deny lust for the first time. "However, even the first time, and all the more so if he then acquires the capacity, man already gradually experiences his own dignity." He "bears witness to his own self-mastery and shows that he is carrying out what is essentially personal in him. And, furthermore, he gradually experiences the freedom of the gift" (176).

Notice John Paul's emphasis on experience. Man is capable of *experiencing* his own dignity. He does so precisely when he exercises his freedom to choose the good, true, and beautiful. When someone acts against lust rather than allowing lust to act against him, he activates his self-determination and, hence, "what is essentially personal in him." This is the battle for the dignity of our own personhood: will we *act* for the good; or will we forfeit our self-determination and let evil *act upon us?* Lust is always ready to invade our hearts, dominate our senses, and assault our self-determination. We can acquiesce. Or we can *act* from our essence. This is the quintessential moment of truth. Much is at stake here, for in this moment

---

113. See *CCC,* n. 2519.

man determines *the intentionality of his very existence* (see §33). Do man's passions determine what is good, or is there an objective reality (God) outside him to which he must submit himself and toward which he must, with the help of grace, direct his passions?

If in this moment man conquers the enticing illusion of lust and acts in conformity with who he is as a creature made in God's image, he regains his original dignity as a person. In fact, John Paul says that overcoming lust is a "reminiscence" of original solitude. The man who does so *experiences* his transcendence, his subjectivity, his freedom, and his call to live in a communion of persons (see §§11, 12). The more we overcome lust, the more we can be a real gift to another. And we come to desire nothing else.

C. Redemption, Not Repression

This greatly differs from begrudgingly conforming one's behavior to an external norm. Of course, one only acquires this freedom in stages. If a person begins with the deception that views lust as a "good" to be pursued, the first essential stage of conversion is to recognize lust as an evil to avoid. The objective norm serves its essential purpose here. As St. Paul says, a man engrossed in sin does not know what sin is without the law (see Rom 7:7). Such a man will avoid lust only begrudgingly at first out of obedience to the law. If he perseveres, however, lust itself becomes more and more distasteful to him. His subjective desires come more and more in tune with the true, the good, and the beautiful. In this way, the negative and prohibitive ethic of Christ's words in the Sermon on the Mount becomes a positive and liberating ethos.

This is how we appropriate the gift of our redemption. It is very different than repressing our lusts or merely seeking distraction from sexual temptations. John Paul's anthropological vision seeks to reclaim everything that is authentically human—everything that God created man to be "in the beginning." But this cannot happen if man ignores or represses his sexual desires.[114] Lust is the deceiver's plagiarization of the original power to love, the "twisting" of the fundamental drive within man to become a sincere gift to another. Man's sexual desires must be reclaimed according to this truth, "untwisted" and integrated within an adequate vision of the dignity and meaning of the human person. This means not running from our desires, but facing them and continually surrendering them to Christ—right at the moment lust flares up in us—so that he might set our desires aright.

---

114. See *Love & Responsibility*, pp. 170–171.

■ When a person struggling with lust seeks guidance, he will often hear from spiritual directors, confessors, and even otherwise sound chastity educators something like: "Just try to distract yourself from lustful thoughts. Try to ignore them. Do something constructive. Take a walk. Take a bike ride. If need be, take a cold shower." While such advice may offer a helpful starting point—indeed, in the heat of a powerful temptation an immediate distraction is often essential—this approach offers only a temporary solution at best. Even when a person successfully distracts himself, that lust still lies "within" him. It will come back, and probably with more intensity. The Pope's anthropology of redemption offers us a way of getting to the root of the problem. If we surrender our lustful desires to Christ, he can transform them by the power of the Holy Spirit. The *Catechism* proclaims that in the Sermon on the Mount "the Spirit of the Lord gives new form to our desires, those inner movements that animate our lives. Jesus teaches us this new life by his words; he teaches us to ask for it by prayer. The rightness of our life in him will depend on the rightness of our prayer."[115] As I wrote in my previous book, "When sexual feelings, desires, and temptations present themselves, as they inevitably do, instead of trying to ignore them or 'stuff' them by pushing them down and under, we need to bring them up and out. Not up and out in the sense of indulging them, but up and out and into the hands of Christ our Redeemer. You might simply say a prayer like this: *Lord Jesus, I give to you my sexual desires. Please undo in me what sin has done, so that I might know freedom in this area and experience sexual desire as you intend. Amen.*"[116]

The man who continues diligently on this road of redemption—not repression—eventually sees lust for what it is: a cosmic tragedy that masks and even dismantles the very meaning of existence. At this point, lust no longer has "hold" of him. He begins to experience the freedom for which Christ has set him free (see Gal 5:1). Even if he continues to feel the pull of concupiscence, it does not deceive him or lure him away. He knows concupiscence is a cheap counterfeit for authentic eros. And he knows that it can never satisfy.

---

115. *CCC*, n. 2764.

116. *Good News About Sex & Marriage*, p. 81.

39. Drawing Pure Waters from a Hidden Spring

November 12; December 3, 1980 (TB 171–176)

We have been discussing the "how to's" of growing in holiness according to the ethos of the Sermon on the Mount. Christ clearly indicates that the way to attain this holiness must be the way of temperance and mastery of desires. As John Paul explains, if we are to achieve "an adequate way of being and acting," we must first allow our hearts to be transformed from "within." Caught up in our society's non-reflective, results-oriented mentality, we are often tempted to modify externals without addressing the deeper issues of the heart. Yet the only path to holiness is to open one's deepest self to grace and accept the slow and often painful process of inner transformation. It is called taking up the cross daily and following Christ (see Lk 9:23). That alone produces "results."

A. Discerning the Movements of Our Hearts

If we are to progress on the road to holiness, if eros and ethos are to meet in our hearts and bear fruit, John Paul says that we must succeed in being an "interior man." We must "be able to obey correct conscience; to be the true master of [our] own deep impulses, like a guardian who watches over a hidden spring" (172) Only then are we free to draw from all those impulses what is fitting for purity of heart. In this way we continually "rediscover in what is 'erotic' the nuptial meaning of the body and the true dignity of the gift. This is the role of the human spirit," John Paul says, and it is "a role of an ethical nature. If it does not assume this role, the very attraction of the senses and the passion of the body may stop at mere lust, devoid of ethical value." If man stops here, he "does not experience that fullness of 'eros'—which means the aspiration of the human spirit toward the true, good, and beautiful—so that what is 'erotic' also becomes true, good, and beautiful" (171).

John Paul shows himself to be a true "interior man" with the penetrating insight he offers those who wish to watch over their "hidden spring" and draw pure waters from it. Paraphrasing a lengthy passage, he says that we must learn with perseverance and consistency the meaning of our bodies and of our sexuality. We must learn this not only in the abstract (although this, too, is necessary), but above all in the interior reactions of our own "hearts." This is a "science," he says, which cannot be learned only from books, because it concerns deep knowledge of our interior life. Deep in the heart we learn to distinguish between what, on the one hand, composes the great riches of sexuality and sexual attraction, and what, on the other hand, bears only the sign of lust. Although these internal movements of the heart can sometimes be confused with one another, Christ calls us to acquire a mature and complete evaluation. And, as the Pope concludes, "it should be added that this task *can* be carried out and is really worthy of man" (172).

We have already noted the Pope's realism in this regard (see §29). Sometimes we can easily confuse love and lust. To be sure, on this side of perfection we will always recognize mixed motives in our hearts. This should not stifle us, however. In fact, the Holy Father affirms that the discernment we are speaking of has an essential relationship with spontaneity. It is often thought, as the Pope points out, that living according to Christ's words in the Sermon on the Mount puts a serious dent in the spontaneity of man and woman's relationship. Spontaneity is here understood as "doing what comes naturally" or acting immediately on what moves and attracts a person. Someone moved and attracted by lust views the moral path as a real impediment to eros. "But this opinion is erroneous and, in any case, superficial. Obstinately accepting it and upholding it, we will never reach the full dimensions of eros" (172).

The full dimension of eros comes when men and women are free with the freedom of the gift; when they are free from the chains of lust that compel them to indulge concupiscence and degrade the true, good, and beautiful. One experiences this full dimension of eros, therefore, when he is moved and attracted by that which is true, good, and beautiful—by the rich storehouse of values contained in sexuality as a God-given path to an authentic gift of self and communion of persons. Such a person chooses the truth *spontaneously*. The moral norm no longer acts as a constraint because his heart is in conformity with the truth. Here we encounter the transforming power of Christ's words about lust. They do not only prohibit. As John Paul says, whoever accepts Christ's words about lust "must know that he is also *called to a full and mature spontaneity* of the relations that spring from the perennial attraction of masculinity and femininity. This very spontaneity is the gradual fruit of the discernment of the impulses of one's own heart" (172).[117]

B. Mature Spontaneity and Noble Gratification

Sexual excitement derived from concupiscence flares up in the immediate reactions of the heart with a "subjective intensity" which extends its dominion over man's emotional sphere and involves his whole body.[118] Such a flaring up of lust demands immediate or "spontaneous" gratification. But this type of "sexual excitement is very different from the deep emotion with which not only interior sensitivity, but sexuality itself reacts

---

117. See *CCC,* n. 1972.
118. See 11/5/80, TB 170.

to the total expression of femininity and masculinity" (173). Through the gift of redemption, through the meeting of eros and ethos, the character of sexual excitement is transformed and integrated with the dignity of the person and the supreme value of love. The more we experience this transformation, the more the desire to make a sincere gift of ourselves wells up from within us—and with an intensity much more refined and grand than mere lust can ever rouse.

> ■ The image of the burning bush can illustrate the difference between lust and redeemed sexual desire. When lust flares up in us, it consumes us with such an intense heat that it devours any fuel we supply it. The heat not only chars the bush but reduces it to ash. Christ wants to raise us up from our ashes! He wants to impregnate our sexual desire with the fire of his own passionate love. When we experience the fire of redeemed sexual desire, we "burn" but are not consumed. Indeed we rediscover our own humanity. We rediscover our primordial call to love and communion. We rediscover that we are made in the image of a God who revealed himself to Moses in a blazing bush that was not consumed.

Genuine erotic spontaneity actually leads, as John Paul says, to "a noble gratification" of sexual desire. It taps into that original beatifying experience because it forms man and woman in a true communion of persons. This deep and mature spontaneity is virtually unknown to the man who indulges concupiscence. Such a man refuses to pay the price of gaining self-control. And, paradoxically, the authentic spontaneity to which Christ calls us all comes precisely at the cost of self-control. Only by exercising such control can the human heart rediscover "the spiritual beauty of the sign constituted by the human body in its masculinity and femininity" (173). This is the epiphany of the body referred to previously (see §2). When we see and experience the body as a sign of God's eternal mystery of communion, this conviction comes to permeate our conscience and our very being. The value of the sign then *spontaneously* guides both our choices and our desires. Hence, John Paul concludes that this mature spontaneity of the human heart does not suffocate its noble desires and aspirations, but, on the contrary, it frees them, and even facilitates them.

40. The Perspective of the Whole Gospel

December 3, 10, 1980 (TB 174–180)

In the audience of December 3, 1980, John Paul begins drawing his reflections on Matthew 5:27–28 to a close. He recaps the context in which Christ is speaking and summarizes some of the previous themes. He opens by stressing several times that this is a *new* ethos. It is new not only in regard to the Old Testament, but new in regard to every man of every period and culture. By stressing this "newness," it seems as though he is challenging us to recognize that even after 2,000 years of Christian history, the new ethos still has not firmly established itself in human hearts. People are still relying on their own resources in trying to live a Christian life. We have only two options in this case: repress our disordered desires in a misguided attempt to attain "holiness" (this leads to "angelism" and rigorism), or abandon the real demands of the Gospel for a watered-down version that allows us to indulge our disordered desires ("animalism" and laxity).

The new ethos fundamentally differs from both approaches. It demands a *radical* paradigm shift from typical perspectives and manners of living. Radical, of course, means "to the root." The new ethos is meant to do precisely this: return us to our roots, to the purity of our origins. As John Paul says, in the new ethos "the original ethos of creation will have to be taken up again" (175). This is why Christ refers to the beginning in discussing the problems surrounding man and woman's relationship. The new ethos, then, is "the 'ethos of redemption' and, more precisely, the ethos of the redemption of the body" (174). Only the perspective of redemption justifies Christ's reference to "the beginning." Without this perspective, we have only our own resources. We have only lust in its three forms. Even if a spark of God's original plan still remains in us, without the perspective of redemption, we have no hope of fanning that spark into flame.

A. The Whole Mission of Christ

By calling the man of lust back to "the beginning" through the redemption of the body, Christ establishes a continuity between original man and historical man. Moreover, as we shall learn, the redemption of the body will be fully revealed only in the final resurrection, of which Christ speaks on another occasion. Hence, life in the body for historical man not only calls him to live in continuity with his origins. Life in the body here and now is meant to lead him in continuity (while maintaining the important discontinuity) to his ultimate destiny: the consummation of all things; the resurrection of the body.

What John Paul is speaking about in terms of experiencing the restoration of God's plan for the body and sexuality is no footnote in the Christian life. Indeed, it pertains to the whole spectrum of God's plan for us. According to the Holy Father, this redemption of the body "is, in fact, the perspective of the whole Gospel, of the whole teaching, in fact of the whole mission of Christ" (175). Of course we will never open ourselves to the gift of redemption if we do not first have a profound realization of our *need* for redemption. John Paul reminds us that to aspire to virtue, purity of heart, and Christian perfection requires an awareness of our own sinfulness as a necessary starting point and an indispensable condition.

To grow in this perfection, we must "enter into an alliance" with the new ethos. We must give our entire selves to it. We must sell everything (see Mt 13:44), put our hands to the plow, and never look back (see Lk 9:62). When we do that, our "deepest and yet most real possibilities" are manifested and "the innermost layers of [our] potentialities acquire a voice" (176). John Paul points out that a person who surrenders to lust, to suspicion, and/or to the Manichaean anti-value has no knowledge of those innermost layers of his own heart. The ethos of redemption, on the other hand, is based on a close alliance with those layers of the human heart. It is those layers of the heart that can recognize the value of the nuptial meaning of the body. Those layers can see in the body "the value of a transparent sign." This sign, in turn, reveals "the gift of communion, that is, the mysterious reality of [God's] image and likeness" (176).

This is precisely the manner by which we experience "the whole mission of Christ" according to the call of the Sermon on the Mount. It means rediscovering and living according to the dignity and value of the human body as a sign of (and calling to) communion. And communion is man's origin, vocation, and destiny. *This* is the perspective of man's whole life, of Christ's whole teaching and mission. Those who have the purity to see it realize that this "whole perspective" is contained in and revealed through the human body in its creation and redemption.

B. Analysis of Purity

John Paul concludes his analysis of Christ's words in the Sermon on the Mount with a closer analysis of purity of heart. Such an analysis is "an indispensable completion" of Christ's words. Purity is a requirement of love; it is the dimension of love's interior truth in man's heart. Hence, purity concerns the innermost layers of man's being. It concerns his subjectivity and his realization in *solitude* of his call to *communion*—his call to love. Thus, as the Pope states, "purity of heart is explained, finally, with regard for the other subject, who is originally and perennially 'co-called'" (177). Purity of heart enabled Adam to recognize Eve as the one who was called with him ("co-called") to live in a communion of persons. This same purity enabled them to experience nakedness without shame. Purity, then, is what man and woman lost due to sin, and it is what Christ came to restore in our hearts.

John Paul points out that when we speak of purity as a moral virtue, we use the word in an analogous sense with physical cleanness. Something pure contrasts with something unclean or polluted. The Old Testament tradition greatly valued physical cleanliness, as the abundance of ritual cleansings demonstrates. Many of these rituals concerned the cleansing of the body in relation to sexual impurity (see Lv 15). However, sexual impurity was understood almost exclusively in relation to physiology and its organic processes. John Paul suggests these may have corresponded to hygienic prescriptions according to the state of medicine at that time. But such heightened attention to physical purity led to an erroneous way of understanding moral purity, which was often taken in the exclusively exterior and material sense.

Christ radically opposes this. His words indicate that none of the aspects of sexual uncleanness in the strictly physiological sense falls by itself into the definition of purity or impurity in the moral sense.[119] As John Paul stresses, referring to Christ's words from Matthew 15:11, "Nothing from 'outside' makes man filthy, no 'material' dirt makes man impure in the moral, that is, interior sense. No ablution, not even of a ritual nature, is capable in itself of producing moral purity. This has its exclusive source within man: it comes from the heart" (178).

■ We can observe here the meaning of the rich symbolism of the wedding feast of Cana (see Jn 2:1–11). This is one of the few pertinent Scripture passages John Paul does not discuss in his theology of the body. Briefly we can recognize that, if wine is a symbol of grace, running out of wine speaks of the married couple's need for new life in Christ. If they are to love one another purely, they must drink deeply of the "new wine" that Christ gives and allow it to change them interiorly. The water Christ changed to wine was intended for the Jewish rites of purification. Christ's miracle symbolizes the fulfillment of Israel's ritual ablutions. Christ's "new wine" has the ability to purify our hearts. Furthermore, Christ, in referring to his "hour," points us to the marriage consummated on the cross.[120] There he will give himself up for his Bride to make her holy and without blemish (see Eph 5:25–27). The water and wine at Cana, therefore, prefigure the blood and water that flow from Christ's side on Calvary. Like the first Adam, Christ is put into a "deep sleep" on the cross. As figures of Baptism and Eucharist, the water and blood symbolize the life of God flowing from the side of the New Adam as the birth of the New Eve (remember that the "rib" symbolized the common life shared by the first

---

119. For example, a woman's menstrual flow does not make her "unclean" in any moral sense (see Lev 18:19).

120. See *CCC*, nn. 1335, 2618.

Adam and Eve).[121] Like the first Adam, the New Adam calls the New Eve "woman" (compare Gen 2:23 and Jn 19:26). This evokes the re-creation or "resurrection" of man and woman's original relationship. And it is all prefigured at a *wedding feast* that takes place *on the third day*. All those who are "born again" through the waters of Baptism become the spiritual children of the New Adam and the New Eve—born not of a husband's seed, but born of God (see Jn 1:13). And all those who drink the "new wine" of the Eucharist are purified and empowered from within to love others according to "the new ethos of redemption."[122]

Christ's shift of focus from external purity to "purity of heart" marks the turning point to the new ethos. Here we encounter the crux of the matter both for Christ and his Vicar. *This* is why John Paul II places so much emphasis on the subjectivity of man. This is why he uses the phenomenological method in coming to an adequate understanding of man. Purity certainly places objective demands on us. But to fulfill those demands, *we must be purified from within*. When we are, subjectivity becomes completely objective (see §§8, 21). That suspicion toward the human heart previously mentioned tends also to oppose John Paul II's emphasis on "subjectivity." If the heart is always suspect and can never be transformed, a gulf will always remain between objective truth and subjective human desire. But to remain locked in this perspective is to empty the cross of its power. It is the antithesis of the meaning of life (see §36).

41. Purity of Heart and Life According to the Spirit

December 17, 1980; January 7, 1981 (TB 191–194)

John Paul devotes nine of his final audiences on historical man to a Scriptural analysis of purity of heart. Most of his reflection examines various passages from the Pauline Letters important for understanding purity. However, in typical form, he begins with the words of Christ: "Blessed are the pure in heart, for they shall see God" (Mt 5:8). Here, as in Matthew 5:27–28, Christ appeals to the human heart, to the "interior man." His words remind us of that "beatifying beginning" in which man and woman, in beholding each other "naked without shame," saw the uniqueness and

---

121. See *CCC,* nn. 766, 1067, 1225.

122. For an excellent discussion of the Cana account in light of nuptial symbolism, see *Mary in the Mystery of the Covenant*, (Alba House, 1992), pp. 157–208.

unrepeatability of the person from "within" (see §17). Not only that, but in the visibility of their naked bodies they saw a sign that revealed the invisible mystery of God. Purity of heart specifically enabled them to *see* the body in this way, as a theology.

If we have been following the Pope's train of thought, we can say this: Blessed are the pure in heart, for they shall see God's mystery revealed in the human body. For, according to the Pope's thesis, the body, and it alone, is capable of making God's invisible mystery visible to us. And "in the beginning" nakedness manifested "the 'pure' value of humanity as male and female, the 'pure' value of the body and of sex."[123] The Pope tells us that purity "is the glory of the human body before God. It is God's glory in the human body, through which masculinity and femininity are manifested."[124] Of course, Christ's words do not limit purity merely to sexual morality. The Pope expresses that all moral good manifests purity, and all moral evil manifests impurity. Nonetheless, in a way sexual purity lies at the basis of all moral good since all moral disorder, according to John Paul, stems from the impurity of a lustful heart.[125]

A. The Flesh and the Spirit

To recover the beatifying experience of purity, we must contend with the tension and conflict between the flesh and the Spirit that St. Paul outlined: "The desires of the flesh are against the Spirit and the desires of the Spirit are against the flesh" (Gal 5:17). As the Holy Father says, "It is not a question here only of the body (matter) and of the spirit (soul)." These "constitute from the beginning the very essence of man" (191). Their union and integration make man "very good" (Gen 1:31). As John Paul says elsewhere: "From the context it is clear that for the Apostle it is not a question of discriminating against and condemning the body, which with the spiritual soul constitutes man's nature and personal subjectivity."[126] What St. Paul is talking about in the opposition between the flesh and the Spirit is that disposition of forces formed in man with original sin.[127]

John Paul is careful to use a capital "S" for Spirit to indicate that the real opposition we experience "in the flesh" is with the Holy Spirit and what he desires for us. In an endnote, the Pope also points out that "flesh" for St. Paul "is not to be identified with sex or with the physical body"

---

123. 1/2/80, TB 57.

124. 3/18/81, TB 209.

125. See 12/17/80 third endnote, TB 230–231.

126. *Dominum et Vivificantem*, n. 55 (see also *CCC*, n. 2516).

127. See *CCC*, nn. 2525–2516.

(229). In Pauline terminology, "flesh" seems almost to coincide with the threefold lust of which St. John speaks. Thus, for Paul, the flesh indicates not only the "exterior" man, but also the man who is "interiorly" cut off from what is of the Father so that he lives according to what is of the world. To live according to the flesh, then, means to live according to our "un-inspired" desires. It means to live according to the "dust" of our humanity not filled with God's Spirit. John Paul says that the same idea is expressed in modern ethics and anthropology by terms like "humanistic autarchy" (man unto himself), "secularism," and "sensualism."

The person who lives "according to the flesh" lives almost at the opposite pole as compared to how the Spirit would lead him. The Spirit of God wants a different reality from the one that the flesh desires. The Holy Spirit, who is the "Person-Love" and the "Person-Gift" within the Trinity,[128] wants to fill our bodies with himself so that we might be a sincere gift in love to others. In other words, the Spirit wants to *in*-spire us to live according to the nuptial meaning of our bodies. We could even say that by virtue of the Holy Spirit *in*-spiring our flesh, our bodies acquire a nuptial meaning. In respect for our freedom, however, the Spirit never forces his own gift. We are free to reject the Spirit. If we do (and we have in some sense through the inheritance of original sin), we live according to our *un*-inspired "flesh." In this state we become bent on our own selfish gratification even at the expense of others. This is the antithesis of the nuptial meaning of the body; it is the antithesis of love, and the antithesis of life. As St. Paul expresses, "to set the mind on the flesh is death, but to set the mind on the Spirit is life and peace" (Rom 8:6).

B. Justification by Faith

The Holy Father observes that Paul's words regarding "life according to the flesh" and "life according to the Spirit" are at the same time a synthesis and a program. They synthesize very realistically the "fight" in man's heart between good and evil. But they do not simply leave man at the mercy of these interior forces. They provide a program for victory. "In this struggle between good and evil, man proves himself stronger, thanks to the power of the Holy Spirit" (194).

St. Paul speaks of the interior battle between flesh and Spirit in the context of his discussion of justification by faith (see Rom 7, 8; Gal 5). Man cannot justify himself by observance of the law. If he seeks to, Christ is of no advantage to him and he misses altogether the necessity and purpose of redemption. "You are severed from Christ, you who would be jus-

---

128. See *Dominum et Vivificantem*, n. 10.

tified by the law; you have fallen away from grace" (Gal 5:4). Condensing Paul's teaching, the *Catechism* says:

> The law entrusted to Israel never sufficed to justify those subject to it; it even became the instrument of "lust" (see Rom 7:7). The gap between wanting and doing points to the conflict between God's Law which is the "law of the mind," and another law "making me captive to the law of sin which dwells in my members" (Rom 7:23).
>
> "But now, the righteousness of God has been manifested apart from law, although the law and the prophets bear witness to it, the righteousness of God through faith in Jesus Christ for all who believe" (Rom 3:21–22). Henceforth, Christ's faithful "have crucified the flesh with its passions and desires"; they are led by the Spirit and follow the desires of the Spirit (Gal 5:24).[129]

Justice super-abounds in man's heart by faith in Jesus Christ. This is man's victory. This is how he *experiences* the power of the Holy Spirit— by faith. We have previously quoted John Paul's definition of faith: *"Faith,* in its deepest essence, is *the openness* of the human heart to the gift: *to God's self-communication in the Holy Spirit."*[130] Therefore, "'justification by faith' is not just a dimension of the divine plan of man's salvation and sanctification, but is, according to St. Paul, a real power that operates in man and is revealed and asserts itself in his actions" (193). It is "the power of Christ himself operating within man by means of the Holy Spirit" (192).

St. Paul speaks of this justification when he says: "He who raised Christ Jesus from the dead will give life to your mortal bodies also through his Spirit which dwells in you" (Rom 8:11). This "life" given to our mortal bodies does not just refer to the eschaton. It is also intended for "historical man"—for every man of "yesterday, today, and tomorrow," in the history of the world and of salvation. History, even if it remains the domain of struggle and ambiguity, is also the domain in which salvation is given and received. This means that historical man can truly be *vivified* by the Holy Spirit; he can begin to live a resurrected life even now.[131]

In this way the Pauline theology of justification expresses faith in "the anthropological and ethical realism" of redemption. In other words, Christ's redemption bears real fruit in changing man's heart (anthropological realism) and, consequently, changing his behavior (ethical realism). As the *Catechism* teaches, "Justification is not only the remission of sins, but

---

129. *CCC,* nn. 2542, 2543.

130. Ibid, n. 51.

131. See *CCC,* n. 1092.

also the sanctification and renewal of the interior man....It frees from the enslavement to sin, and it heals."[132] In this way, justification, carried out by the Holy Spirit, enables justice to abound in man and in his behavior "to the extent that God himself willed and which he expects" (194). This divine expectation is not only that man would meet the law's demands, but that he would "fulfill" them through the super-abounding justice poured into his heart through the Holy Spirit. This justification "is essential for interior man, and is destined precisely for that 'heart' to which Christ appealed, when speaking of 'purity' and 'impurity' in the moral sense" (193). Through the justification of the Holy Spirit, man "becomes himself" and enters his authentic ethos. Through the indwelling Spirit, objective reality enters human subjectivity and what was once felt as an external law wells up as an intimate demand of the person. In this way, the Christian "incarnates" the Gospel; *logos*—that which is objective Truth—becomes *ethos*.

C. Fruits and Works

In his Letter to the Galatians, St. Paul says that "the works of the flesh are plain: fornication, impurity, licentiousness, idolatry, sorcery, enmity, strife, jealousy, anger, selfishness, dissension, party spirit, envy, drunkenness, carousing, and the like" (5:19–21). "But the fruit of the Spirit is love, joy, peace, patience, kindness, goodness, faithfulness, gentleness, self-control" (5:22–23). John Paul points out, as have many biblical scholars, that Paul distinguishes "works" of the flesh from "fruits" of the Spirit. For Paul, "works" are the specific acts of man, whereas the term "fruit of the Spirit" emphasizes God's action in man. As John Paul says in an endnote, "This 'fruit' grows in him like the gift of a life whose only Author is God; man can, at most, promote suitable conditions, in order that the fruit may grow and ripen" (231). In other words, everything that comes from "the flesh" is not of the Father but of the world. The goodness that springs from man's heart, on the other hand, is of the Father and not of the world. It is the fruit of the indwelling Holy Spirit. Only from this perspective can we clarify fully the nature and structure of the ethos of redemption.

Reclaiming the purity of our origins does not mean pulling ourselves up by our boot straps. We "are speaking of a possibility opened up to man exclusively by grace."[133] The ethos of redemption is born in man when he forms an alliance with the Holy Spirit, allowing him to guide all his thoughts and behaviors. Behind each of the moral virtues that St. Paul out-

---

132. *CCC*, nn. 1989–1990.
133. *Veritatis Splendor*, n. 24.

lines as a fruit of the Spirit lies a specific choice, an effort of the will, which is the fruit of the human spirit permeated by the Spirit of God. This cooperative action of the divine and human is always manifested in choosing that which is true, good, and beautiful. Again we see how this differs from merely following an external norm or law. "Healing the wounds of sin, the Holy Spirit renews us interiorly through a spiritual transformation. He enlightens and strengthens us to live as 'children of the light' through all that is 'good and right and true.'"[134] In other words, the Holy Spirit, operating deeply within man's heart, orients his desires rightly so that he comes to desire freely what the law demands of him. This is why St. Paul can say that "if you are led by the Spirit, you are not under the law" (Gal 5:18). You naturally live in love, joy, peace, patience, kindness, goodness, faithfulness, gentleness, and self-control. As St. Paul points out, no law forbids these things (see Gal 5:22 – 23).

■ In my lectures, to demonstrate what "freedom from the law" looks like, I will often ask a married man in the audience if he has any desire to murder his wife. A man with no desire to murder his wife does not need the commandment "Thou shalt not murder thy wife," because he has no desire to break it. He is free from this law. Similarly, men and women who have attained a mature level of sexual purity do not need a laundry list of sexual "thou shalt nots." They freely fulfill the law with the freedom for which Christ has set them free. Christ did not die and rise from the dead to give us more laws to follow. His purpose was to purify our hearts so that we would no longer need the law. As the *Catechism* states, "The Law of the Gospel...does not add new external precepts, but proceeds to reform the heart, the root of human acts, where man chooses between the pure and the impure."[135]

42. The Freedom for which Christ Has Set Us Free

January 7, 14, 1981 (TB 194–197)

As we have already seen, John Paul will at times drop a statement of great significance into his text with little or no comment. Evidently he thought it important to insert these points even if he could not elaborate on them in a brief general audience. One such example is his passing reference to the "cosmic dimension" of the redemption of the body in his address of

---

134. *CCC*, n. 1695.

135. *CCC*, n. 1968.

January 7, 1981. This seems to represent another lap in his previous reflection on the cosmic dimension of shame (see §27). Is it too much to say that the way we live our bodies has ramifications for the entire universe? St. Paul does not think so. He says that the whole creation has been groaning in travail since the beginning, awaiting the redemption of our bodies (see Rom 8:22–23). Implication: The whole universe is affected when we live, or fail to live, according to the truth of our bodies. This perspective stands as the biblical antithesis to the notion that "private" sexual behavior has no bearing on anyone or anything outside the bedroom. But onto other themes.

A. Impurity and the Death of the Spirit

We have been reflecting on the opposition between the body and the spirit (or Spirit in reference to the Holy Spirit) in relation to reclaiming purity of heart. Of course, this antagonism between body and spirit is not "natural" to man. It results from the interior rupture caused by original sin.[136] When we turned our backs on God, the breath of God's life died in us. We only had recourse to our *un*-inspired dust, what St. Paul calls "the flesh." The Apostle tells us that if we live according to the flesh we will die. But if by the Spirit we put to death the deeds of the body we will live (see Rom 8:13). According to the Pope, this putting to death the deeds of the body expresses precisely what Christ spoke about in the Sermon on the Mount, appealing to the human heart and exhorting it to control lustful desires. This mastery, this putting to death the deeds of the flesh is an indispensable condition of the "life according to the Spirit." In other words, we must die with Christ if we are to live with him in the power of the resurrection.

Life according to the flesh, as St. Paul describes it, effects the "death" of the Spirit in man. So, as John Paul explains, the term "death" means not only the death of the body, but also the reality of mortal sin. Mortal sin is that which "kills" God's life, his Spirit, within us. Those who live according to the flesh (unless they repent and are filled once again with the Spirit) "shall not inherit the Kingdom of God" (Gal 5:21). Elsewhere, as the Holy Father points out, St. Paul says that no fornicator or impure man has any inheritance in God's Kingdom (see Eph 5:5). Only the pure man is capable of seeing God. That is the very definition of purity. Hence, impurity can be defined as the *inability* to see God. God desires to reveal his mystery in and through the mystery of our humanity as male and female, but the impure man cannot see it. The sexual sinner

---

136. See 1/2/80, TB 57; 5/28/80, TB 115.

closes his eyes to it. It is not that God will throw him into hell because of his sin. It is more accurate to say that because of his impurity he is *ipso facto* incapable of the beatific vision.

How then does the impure man become pure? How does the blind man regain his sight? He does so by opening his flesh once again to the life of the Holy Spirit. As much as lust blinds man and woman to the truth of the body and deprives the heart of genuine desires and aspirations, so much does "life according to the Spirit" permit man and woman to regain the freedom of the gift and recover purity of heart.[137] Regaining purity, then, is not first a matter of "doing," but a matter of "letting it be done." Like the Immaculate one—that is, the woman totally pure of heart—we must offer our *fiat* to the Holy Spirit. Only then will Christ be "conceived" in our flesh.

John Paul concludes that justification comes "from the Spirit" (of God) and not "from the flesh." In other words, it comes from God's action in us as a fruit of the Spirit, not as a work of our own. Those who seek justification in following laws (in "doing" rather than "letting it be done") have been alienated from Christ. They have cut themselves off from the grace given by the Holy Spirit that empowers us to fulfill the law (see Gal 5:4–5). St. Paul therefore exhorts the Galatians to free themselves of the erroneous "carnal" concept of justification, and to follow the true one, the "spiritual" one. In this sense he exhorts them to consider themselves free from the law, and even more to be free with the freedom for which Christ "has set us free."

B. Freedom and Purity

According to John Paul, we experience true purity of heart according to the measure that we experience the freedom for which Christ "has set us free." This is the crux of the new ethos: *freedom!* The Pope states that St. Paul touches the essential point right here, revealing the anthropological roots of the Gospel ethos. The "dimension of the new Gospel ethos is nothing but an appeal to human freedom, an appeal to its fuller implementation and, in a way, to fuller 'utilization' of the potential of the human spirit" (197).[138] We have the potential to be *free* from sin. We have the potential to be *free* to desire and choose only what is good. We have the potential to be *free* with the freedom of the gift—not perfectly in this life, but progressively and substantially.[139] "For freedom Christ

---

137. See 12/1/82, TB 349.

138. See *CCC*, nn. 1730–1748.

139. See *Veritatis Splendor*, n. 17.

has set us free; stand fast therefore, and do not submit again to a yoke of slavery" (Gal 5:1).

For St. Paul, freedom is inextricably linked with love. "For you were called to freedom, brethren; only do not use your freedom as an opportunity for the flesh, but through love be servants of one another" (Gal 5:13). Notice, too, that St. Paul knows that the freedom necessary for love also provides the opportunity to indulge "the flesh." This is a key point. In our attempts to live the Gospel, we often seek to eradicate sin by eradicating our freedom to commit it. We must not remove the freedom we have to sin. For in the same stroke we eradicate the freedom necessary to love. To squelch freedom in order to avoid sin is not living the Gospel ethos of freedom at all. This approach knows not the freedom for which Christ has set us free. If we must chain ourselves in order not to commit sin, then we are just that—*in chains*. A person in this state remains bound in some way to his desire to sin and has yet to tap into the mature ethos of redemption. He has yet to experience in a sustained way life according to the Holy Spirit. For "where the Spirit of the Lord is, there is freedom" (2 Cor 3:17).

Here we put our finger on the pulse of the human mystery. Freedom is God's gift to man, a gift given as the capacity to love. But the flip side of the capacity to love is the capacity to sin. God respects our freedom. This means he respects our freedom to sin. He did not stay Adam and Eve's hands when they reached out to eat the fruit of the tree of the knowledge of good and evil. He told them what would happen, and then entrusted that to their freedom. Had God stayed their hands, he would have denied them the dignity he had bestowed on them. As the *Catechism* states, "God does not want to impose the good, but wants free beings." Thus, the *"right to the exercise of freedom*, especially in moral and religious matters, is an inalienable requirement of the dignity of the human person."[140] We inevitably sense the compromise of our dignity when we are forced to conform to the will of others. Even if the will of others is good, it can never be imposed. We must engage our freedom in choosing good if we are ever to experience that which *is* good *as* good.

■ This dynamic operates pointedly in the relationship of parents and children, especially when the children come of age. Parents have the delicate task of promoting the good without forcing it on their children. This means that, within appropriate limits, parents (like God the Father) must allow their children to choose wrongly, to sin. If parents "force" their children *not* to sin, they set up an unfortunate dynamic in which their children

---

140. *CCC,* nn. 1738, 2847.

may feel compelled to rebel against what is good in order to assert their own dignity as self-determining persons. In such situations, the Church calls parents to "recognize the fragment of truth that may be present in some forms of [their children's] rebellion."[141] A valuable lesson can be learned in this regard from John Paul II's struggle with Communism. Not all of the goals of Communism are evil. For John Paul, it seems the primary evil of Communism (and all totalitarian systems) lies in the way it annihilates human freedom to achieve its goals. Papal biographer George Weigel reports a conversation between John Paul II and General Pinochet (Chile's dictator) as follows: "Pinochet pressed the Pope: 'Why is the Church always talking about democracy? One method of government is as good as another.' John Paul politely but firmly disagreed. 'No,' he said, 'the people have a right to their liberties, even if they make mistakes in exercising them.'"[142] In other words, according to John Paul's read on the dignity of the person as a self-determining agent, a higher value is maintained when one exercises his freedom wrongly, than when one is forced to do something objectively good.[143] In human affairs, the greatest good is the realization of the person, and this cannot come about without a steadfast respect for human freedom, which always implies (within due limits) respecting the freedom of others to choose wrongly. This deeply personalist affirmation of freedom, as expressed primarily in *Dignitatis Humanae*, is one of the main contributions of the Second Vatican Council.

43. An Adequate Image of Freedom and Purity

January 14, 28, 1981 (TB 198–202)

Society has much to say about sexual liberation. But society generally views it as the freedom to indulge one's lusts without restraint. It means never having to say no. This does not promote genuine freedom. This promotes bondage to libido. John Paul observes that the antithesis and, in a way, the negation of freedom occurs when freedom becomes a pretext for man to live according to the flesh. Man chooses to indulge lust because he feels bound by lust. The man of lust cannot *not* lust. Hence, in his view the moral law that condemns lust oppresses him. He must be

---

141. *The Truth & Meaning of Human Sexuality*, n. 50.

142. *Witness to Hope*, p. 533.

143. See *Karol Wojtyla: The Thought of the Man Who Became Pope John Paul II*, pp. 181–182.

"liberated" from it so he can live in his bondage to lust unhindered.[144] In essence, he wants to be free *from freedom* in order to embrace slavery without retribution.

A. Authentic Freedom

The man described above is utterly deceived. To him, good is evil and evil good. Slavery is freedom and freedom slavery. Such a man will never find the happiness he seeks. As John Paul says, he "ceases to be capable of that freedom for which 'Christ set us free'; he also ceases to be suitable for the real gift of himself which is the fruit and expression of this freedom. He ceases, moreover, to be capable of that gift which is organically connected with the nuptial meaning of the human body" (198). Therefore, so long as he lives in his bondage to lust, he can never fulfill the meaning of his being and existence.

Oh, the tragic deception of thinking Christ is against us! If the man of lust would but open himself to the gift of redemption, through ongoing conversion Christ would liberate his liberty from the oppression of lust. He would free him with a freedom so real that he would be free indeed. He would free him with the freedom of the gift—the freedom of receiving the gift of God (the Holy Spirit) and, in turn, the freedom of being a real gift to others. *This* is the meaning of life. *This* is the freedom for which we all long. This is the freedom for which Christ has set us free. To attain it, we must die to the lusts of the flesh and be raised to the love of the Spirit.

■ I will never forget the first time I realized that I was truly free. Prior to returning to my faith as a young adult, I had dated a girl for four years. I could not *not* lust after her. Whenever I was with her I was a man on a mission—not to love her as Christ loves, but to "get" what I wanted. Of course, I thought this was liberation because I had thrown off the oppressive "rules" of my Catholic upbringing and was indulging my lusts unhindered. I was utterly duped: even more so because, like everyone else, I called this love. I started dating my now-wife Wendy after about five years of deep purgation and healing from the indulgences of my past (discovering John Paul's theology of the body was instrumental in this healing). One day, early on in our relationship, Wendy and I were sitting on a mountainous ledge overlooking a river in Pennsylvania. Holding her in my arms, I had a flashback to my previous "mode of operation." And it dawned on me: I was free. *I was truly free!* My freedom had been set free from the

---

144. See *Veritatis Splendor,* n. 18.

domination of lust. I *did not desire* to "get" something from Wendy or to use her for my own gratification. I desired to be a gift to her, to bless and affirm her. Oh, what a feeling to be free with the freedom of the gift! I was flying. I was walking on water! I *knew* the power of redemption. I *knew* the power of the death and resurrection of Christ. I *knew* the power of the Holy Spirit. I felt his breath vivifying *my flesh* and impregnating my desires with everything noble and beautiful, with the supreme value of love.

B. Purity and Self-Control

St. Paul contrasts fornication, impurity, and licentiousness as works of the flesh with the self-control that is a fruit of the Spirit. According to John Paul, this self-control is closely linked with purity of heart. This becomes more explicit in Paul's First Letter to the Thessalonians: "For this is the will of God, your sanctification: that you abstain from unchastity; that each one of you know how to control his own body in holiness and honor, not in the passion of lust like the heathens who do not know God" (4:3–5). "God has not called us for uncleanness [i.e., impurity], but in holiness. Therefore, whoever disregards this, disregards not man, but God, who gives his Holy Spirit to you" (4:7–8).

According to John Paul, every word in this formulation has a particular meaning. It is a "deeply right, complete, and adequate" image of the virtue of purity, which emerges from the eloquent comparison of the function of "abstaining from unchastity" with that of "controlling one's body in holiness and honor." The Pope further observes that these two functions—abstention and control—are closely connected and dependent on each other. One cannot control his body "in holiness and honor" if he cannot abstain from lust and that which leads to it. In turn, that recognition of the "holiness and honor" of the body gives adequate meaning to abstention from lust.

John Paul shows his Thomistic foundations when he draws from the Angelic Doctor's teaching on virtues in order to compare it with St. Paul's image of purity. For Thomas, purity is a form of the virtue of temperance. Rooted in the will, it consists primarily in containing the impulses of sensitive desire, which has as its object the corporeal and sexual in man. But, as John Paul observes, the same Pauline text turns our attention to another "more positive" role of the virtue of purity. The task of purity is not only a "turning away" from unchastity. This is a "negative," less mature purity. As St. Paul describes it, purity is also, and even more so, a "turning toward" the holiness of the body—a holiness that calls for our honor, admiration, and respect (see §36). Only when we have such honor for the body are we empowered from within to control the impulses of concupiscence that, if left unchecked, would degrade the nuptial meaning of the body.

As John Paul expresses, "The honor that arises in man for everything that is corporeal and sexual, both in himself and in any other person, male and female, is seen to be the most essential power to control the body 'in holiness'" (201). When this honor toward the body imbues us, we immediately sense when impulses of concupiscence rise up in us. And precisely that honor toward the body and sexuality makes us ready and willing to submit our disordered desires to Christ, so that he might continually order them rightly. The Pope believes that this concept of honor is perhaps the essential thread of the Pauline doctrine on purity. So, in search of a more thorough understanding of what Paul means by honor, the Holy Father turns his attention to Paul's description of the body in 1 Corinthians 12:18–25.

44. Purity Stems from Piety as a Gift of the Holy Spirit

February 4, 11; March 18, 1981 (TB 202–209)

Although Paul's description of the human body in 1 Corinthians 12 is intended to outline an image of the Church as the Body of Christ, it also has a fundamental meaning for the Pauline doctrine on purity. There St. Paul says:

> God arranged the organs in the body, each one of them, as he chose...[T]he parts of the body which seem to be weaker are indispensable, and those parts of the body we think less honorable we invest with the greater honor, and our unpresentable parts are treated with greater modesty, which our more presentable parts do not require. But God has so adjusted the body, giving the greater honor to the inferior part, that there may be no discord in the body, but that the members may have the same care for one another (vv. 18–25).

Paul's description here is obviously pre-scientific. His goal is not to present a biological study on the human organism. In fact, the Pope says that such a description cannot be adequate since it is not just a question of the body as an organism but of the human person who expresses himself through that body and in this sense "is" that body. All descriptions of the body must take this into account. Portraying the body is, in fact, "one of the tasks and one of the perennial themes of the whole of culture: of literature, sculpture, painting, and also of dancing, of theatrical works, and finally of the culture of everyday life, private or social" (203). The Pope believes it is necessary to say how right it is to evaluate and portray the body in these various ways. However, all portrayals of the human body must have a proper spiritual attitude of reverence and respect, recognizing its holiness which, as Christians know, springs from the mysteries of creation and redemption.

A. Restoring Harmony in the Body

John Paul observes that St. Paul's description of the body seems to correspond perfectly with the analysis of our creation, fall, and redemption that he has been outlining in the theology of the body. God's arrangement of the body and all its parts is "very good." The experience of original nakedness was a participation in this original good of God's vision. Hence, prior to sin, man and woman experienced no discord in the body whatsoever, but a perfect harmony. The Pope adds that this harmony is precisely "purity of heart." Adam and Eve readily bestowed the "greater honor" on those parts of their bodies that revealed their call to communion. Nakedness, therefore, was entirely modest. Furthermore, this purity "enabled man and woman in the state of original innocence to experience simply (and in a way that originally made them both happy) the uniting power of their bodies." This uniting power of their bodies was "the 'unsuspected' substratum of their personal union or *communio personarum*" (204). In other words, the whole dynamic of attraction and arousal that led them to become "one flesh" was so integrated with their dignity as persons as to be taken for granted. There was no question of using one another. They had no need to hold one another in a state of "suspicion" when it came to the arousal of the body. For they lived their bodies "in holiness and honor." Hence, they were naked and felt no shame.

St. Paul observes that we now consider some parts of our bodies "weaker," "less honorable," and "unpresentable." This corresponds to the shame Adam and Eve experienced after they ate from the forbidden tree. However, the Pope quickly affirms that in this same description of man's experience of shame, Paul indicates the path which leads to the gradual victory over that "discord in the body"—a victory which John Paul insists can and must take place in man's heart.

The key to rediscovering purity is to recognize that there is imprinted on our experience of shame "a certain 'echo' of man's original innocence itself: a 'negative,' as it were, of the image, whose 'positive' had been precisely original innocence" (204). We have already compared this concept to the negative of a photograph (see §11). The negative provides a clue of the positive image. Similarly, that shame which leads us to consider our genitals "less honorable" and "unpresentable" is the negative. But shame's direct relation to our genitals provides a clue for understanding the true meaning and profound dignity of our creation as male and female. If we develop this negative or "flip it over," we realize that these parts of our bodies—far from being "less honorable"—deserve all "the greater honor." For these parts of our bodies distinguish the sexes and thus reveal our call to image God in life-giving communion.

B. The Need for a Pure Purity

Therefore, for St. Paul, purity and modesty must be centered on the dignity of the body—on the dignity of the person who is always expressed through the body, through his masculinity and her femininity.[145] Thus, if one's "purity" is based on anything but a sincere appreciation for the value and dignity of the body, it is not authentic purity. Likewise, if one's modesty is based on a fear or devaluation of all things sexual, it is not authentic modesty. What, then, is the path to a pure purity and an authentically modest modesty? As we have been stressing all along, it is openness to the gift of redemption. As John Paul says, the man of lust must be "entirely enveloped by the 'redemption of the body' carried out by Christ." He "must open himself to 'life according to the Spirit...in order to rediscover and realize the value of the body, freed through redemption from the bonds of lust.'"[146]

■ As the future pope observed in *Love & Responsibility*, modesty is certainly connected with the way people dress, but the connection is not what most people tend to think. The following question can help us assess whether we have a proper understanding of purity and modesty in dress. If covering the sexual values of the body in public is a virtually universal manifestation of modesty, are we led to do so out of a sense that these parts of our body are "dishonorable"? Or do we cover our sexual values out of a profound sense of "the greater honor" they deserve because of the dignity God bestowed on them? Do we cover our sexual values because we attribute to them an "anti-value," or because we realize they manifest "a value not sufficiently appreciated" (see §35)? Understanding this distinction is essential for an authentic modesty and for our purity to be just that—pure. Tapping into some of the confusions regarding modesty, Karol Wojtyla clearly states that accenting sexual values by dress is inevitable, and it can remain compatible with sexual modesty. Immodesty in dress, he says, is that which displaces the dignity of the person and aims deliberately to elicit lust in others. He also observes that partial and even total nakedness cannot simply be equated with immodesty. "Immodesty is present

---

145. See *CCC*, nn. 2517–2527.

146. 4/1/81, TB 213.

only when nakedness plays a negative role with regard to the value of the person, when its aim is to arouse concupiscence, as a result of which the person is put in the position of an object of enjoyment." What happens then he calls "*depersonalization by sexualization*." But he adds that this is not inevitable.[147] Only a "master of suspicion" would conclude that the naked body always and *inevitably* leads to lust. In summary, authentic modesty is a natural fruit of a proper—that is, a pure—understanding of the divine dignity God has bestowed on the body and sexuality. It cannot simply be equated with a certain manner of dress or lack thereof. As the *Catechism* states: "Teaching modesty to children and adolescents means awakening in them respect for the human person."[148] If a mother and father were concerned about the way their teenaged daughter was dressing, rather than focusing only on the clothes, they would do better to instill in her a sense of awe and wonder for the divine dignity of her body and the gift of her sexuality. A person who consciously understands this *does not want to be cheapened by lust.* A woman who consciously understands this, for example, will (aided with a little education in male psychology) come to *know* interiorly when the attention she draws by her dress invites lust, and she will naturally want to dress in a way that protects her dignity.

As with all virtues, attaining purity certainly requires a personal effort. Ultimately, however, a man cannot make himself pure. Purity is also a gift to which a person must open himself. The Holy Father describes purity as "a new capacity of the human being, in which the gift of the Holy Spirit bears fruit" (206). Thus, purity has not only a moral dimension as a virtue. Purity also has a charismatic dimension as a gift of the Holy Spirit.[149] These two dimensions of purity are present and closely connected in Paul's message. Among the seven gifts of the Holy Spirit (see Is 11:1–2), John Paul points out that the one most compatible with purity is piety.[150] Pi-

---

147. See *Love & Responsibility*, pp. 186–193.

148. *CCC*, n. 2524.

149. See *CCC*, n. 1810.

150. Piety, the Pope says, "is a part of the theology of the body which is little known, but which deserves particular study" (209). He will later devote a portion of his catechesis to explaining the role of piety in living out the truth of the body, specifically in relation to living the truth of sexual union.

ety is the gift of respect for what is a work of God.[151] Piety, then, "seems to serve purity in a particular way, making the human subject sensitive to that dignity which is characteristic of the human body by virtue of the mystery of creation and redemption" (208).

St. Paul is trying to awaken in us a sense of awe and respect for the great dignity that God has bestowed on our bodies when he says:

> The body is not meant for immorality, but for the Lord, and the Lord for the body...Do you not know that your bodies are members of Christ? Shall I therefore take the members of Christ and unite them to a prostitute? Never!... Shun immorality. Every other sin which a man commits is outside the body; but the immoral man sins against his own body.... Do you not know that your body is a temple of the Holy Spirit within you, which you have from God? You are not your own; you were bought with a price (1 Cor 6:13–20).

These words "stigmatize" unchastity as the sin against the holiness of the body, the sin of impurity. They are severe words, "even drastic," according to John Paul. But St. Paul, full of the Holy Spirit and, hence, alive with the gift of piety, knows whereof he speaks. He knows that the "redemption of the body involves the institution, in Christ and through Christ, of a new measure of holiness of the body" (207). By virtue of the Incarnation the human body has been admitted, together with the soul, to union with the Person of Christ, and, in turn, to union with the Father through the Holy Spirit.

John Paul says that the Holy Spirit dwells in man—in his soul and in his body—as fruit of the redemption carried out by Christ. Through the gift of redemption, every man has received himself and his own body again from God as a new creation. So in redemption we receive a "double gift"—the gift of the Holy Spirit and the gift of our own restored humanity. Sins of the flesh (or "carnal sins") not only entail a "profanation of the body"—of our own humanity—but a "profanation of the temple" of the Holy Spirit. As St. Paul's tone indicates, *this is very serious.* Some might be tempted to see in the sternness of Paul's words a devaluation of the body and sexuality. Quite the contrary, his austere tone stems from his desire to protect and ensure the incomparable dignity which God has bestowed on the body and sexuality. By virtue of the Incarnation, the human body obtains "a new supernatural elevation, which every Christian must take into account in his behavior with regard to his 'own' body and, of course, with regard to the other's body: man with regard to woman and woman with regard to man" (207).

---

151. See 11/21/84, TB 417.

45. God's Glory Shining in the Body

February 11; March 18, 1981 (TB 205–210)

"Do you not know that your body is a temple of the Holy Spirit within you, which you have from God? You are not your own; you were bought with a price" (1 Cor 6:19–20). It is precisely a living awareness of our redemption, a living awareness that we were "bought with a price" that enables us to "control our bodies in holiness and honor." St. Paul calls us to "shun immorality." We must certainly do so if we are to learn how to control our bodies. Yet St. Paul calls us to so much more. Tapping into that "holiness and honor" of which he speaks "always bears fruit in deeper experience of that love which was inscribed 'from the beginning,' according to the image and likeness of God himself, in the whole human being and therefore also in his body" (209). Thus, Paul's words "acquire the eloquence of an experience of the nuptial meaning of the body and of the freedom of the gift connected with it" (208).

Let us recall that freedom is the crux of the new ethos (see §42). We only know true purity of heart to the extent that we are free from the domination of lust. But freedom in Christ is not so much freedom *from* as freedom *for*—freedom *for love*. Only in freedom is the profound aspect of purity and its organic link with love revealed. As we have already quoted John Paul saying, "Purity is a requirement of love." Purity "is the dimension of [love's] interior truth in man's 'heart.'"[152] And love is impossible if we are not free with the freedom to be a sincere gift to others.

■ Since the freedom to which Christ calls us is so rarely proclaimed, we may think it impossible. Take a sincere engaged couple who honestly wants to save sexual intimacy for marriage. They will often think that in order to stay "chaste," they should never spend any extended time alone together. They fear, of course, that if they *were* alone, they could not refrain from sex. This may be the case, but this is not a mature experience of the freedom for which Christ has set us free. Attaining Christian freedom is obviously a process. A couple with a proper awareness of their own weaknesses will certainly act in respect for those weaknesses. To do so is commendable.

However, if the only thing that kept a couple from having sex before marriage was the lack of opportunity, what does that say about the desire

---

152. 12/3/80, TB 177.

of their hearts?[153] Are they free to choose the good? Are they free to love? To use an image, if a man and woman need to chain themselves to two different trees in order to avoid sin, they are not free; they are in chains. As stated previously, if we chain our freedom to sin, with the same stroke we chain the freedom necessary to love (see §42). All the more dangerous in such an approach is the implicit attitude that marriage will somehow "justify" the couple's lack of freedom. The wedding night then becomes the moment when the couple are supposedly "allowed" to cut the chains loose, disregarding their previous need for constraints. Yet if this couple were not free to choose the good the day before they got married, standing at the altar will not suddenly make them free.

As John Paul has already made abundantly clear, marriage does not justify lust, and lust is precisely sexual desire void of the freedom of the gift. For most people, to live as the free men and women we are called to be demands a radical paradigm shift in ways of thinking, living, and evaluating. Trusting our own freedom to control concupiscence and to choose the good can be very threatening. It is much easier to distrust ourselves and hold our hearts in continual suspicion. But this is the antithesis of the meaning of life. We are called to set our eyes on Christ, get out of the boat, and walk on water. Many Christians, it seems, stay in the boat for fear of sinking if they were to get out. This may seem like a "safer" approach. We can't sink if we never leave the boat. But neither can we walk on water. The truth of human life does not reside in the boat! It can only be found on the water amidst the wind and the waves—in the drama of putting faith to the test and learning to walk with our eyes set on the Lord. Learning to love always involves risk. There is nothing "safe" about it. But it is better to get out of the boat and accept the risk of sinking than to lock up our freedom and throw away the key. As with Peter, Christ says, "Come!" Yes, we might sink. If we do, we have a merciful Savior ready to save us, as did Peter.

A. Glorify God in Your Bodies

After stating, "You are not your own; you were bought with a price," St. Paul ends his passage in 1 Corinthians 6 with a significant exhortation: "So glorify God in your bodies" (v. 20). John Paul states that purity—in both its dimensions as a virtue and as a gift of the Holy Spirit—brings about in the body such a fullness of dignity in interpersonal relations that God himself is thereby glorified. Hence, purity "is the glory of the human

---

153. See *CCC,* nn. 1768, 1770, 1775, 1968, 1972.

body before God. It is God's glory in the human body" (209). Men and women who relate with one another purely truly glorify God in their bodies. Far from stifling their relationship, purity enables them to enter that authentic communion they both long for—a communion that images the divine communion. They experience that "extraordinary beauty" which permeates every sphere of their mutual and common life. This beauty makes it possible to express themselves in "simplicity and depth, cordiality, and the unrepeatable authenticity of personal trust" (209). In this way, purity enables men and women, husbands and wives, to rediscover something of that "beatifying beginning" in which the first man and woman were both naked and felt no shame.

Everything tainted by sin becomes pure when we are entirely enveloped by the redemption of the body carried out by Christ. When purity swallows that sense of suspicion with which we so often consign our own hearts to irreversible lust, we see the entire universe with new eyes. We significantly regain that original good of God's vision and realize that *everything* God has made is "very good."

B. To the Pure All Things Are Pure

St. Paul demonstrates that Christ's words about purity as the ability to "see God" not only have an eschatological meaning, but bear fruit already in time. As he writes in his Letter to Titus: "To the pure all things are pure, but to the corrupt and unbelieving nothing is pure; their very minds and consciences are corrupted. They profess to know God, but they deny him by their deeds" (Ti 1:15–16). The Pope points out that these words can refer to purity in the general sense of all moral good, but also to the more specific sense of sexual purity. Either way, in these two short sentences, St. Paul shows that our view of the whole universe shifts according to our purity of heart or lack thereof.

Impurity causes blindness. It prevents us from seeing God's glory in his creation—least of all, it seems, in manifestations of sexuality and the nakedness of the body. In turn, blindness can lock us into such suspicion toward the heart that purity seems impossible. When we see the freedom of those who are pure, we condemn it outright as an indulgence in sin. It could be nothing else. For, according to this mindset, sin can only be avoided when we chain freedom. To let freedom "loose" is *ipso facto* to fall into sin. This approach toward the body may seem consonant with Christian holiness. But it denies what John Paul calls "the supernatural realism of faith" (208) and "the anthropology of rebirth in the Holy Spirit" (210).

Such blindness shows a lack of wisdom that fails to recognize reality. As John Paul says, "Purity is, in fact, the condition for finding wisdom and following it" (209). The Pope then quotes from the Book of Sirach: "I directed my soul to her [that is, to Wisdom], and through purification, I found her" (51:20). The pure see reality as it is—as *very good*. This instills in them a deep sense of awe and wonder toward the Creator. This instills in them that wholesome "fear of the Lord," which, as that famous line from Proverbs expresses, is the beginning of all wisdom (see Prov 1:7).

In this manner, John Paul points out that the Wisdom Books of the Old Testament prepare in some way for the Pauline doctrine on purity of heart. In fact, the double meaning of purity as a virtue and as a gift of the Holy Spirit already takes shape in the Wisdom texts. The virtue of purity is in the service of wisdom, and wisdom is a preparation for receiving the gift of the Holy Spirit. This divine gift strengthens a person's virtue and makes it possible for that person to enjoy, in wisdom, the fruits of a pure life.

46. The Most Suitable Education in Being Human

April 1, 8, 1981 (TB 210–217)

In the audience of April 1, 1981, John Paul recaps his reflections up to this point. Christ's words about God's plan for marriage "in the beginning," as well as his words about lust in the Sermon on the Mount, have enabled us to outline the true theology of the body. We have learned that our humanity has a theological basis. It is founded on the truth about God and, more specifically, the truth about God made man in Jesus Christ. An adequate anthropology, then, must ultimately be a theological anthropology. An adequate anthropology must be a "theology of the body." For only in the mystery of *the Word* (theology) *made flesh* (of the body) does the mystery of man take on light.[154] As John Paul says, man's vocation "springs from the eternal mystery of the person: the image of God incarnate in the visible and corporeal fact of the masculinity or femininity of the human person" (211). *This* is the body's great dignity: it incarnates God's mystery, which is love. Man's vocation is to love as God loves, and it is revealed through the nuptial meaning of his body.

A. The Joys of Purity

Summarizing his reflections on purity, John Paul says that purity constitutes the opposite of adultery committed in the heart. It constitutes the deep recognition and affirmation of the goodness of the body and of sexuality according to the original good of God's vision. Christ's words

---

154. See *Gaudium et Spes*, n. 22.

about man and woman's union in "the beginning" and his words about "looking lustfully" recall to the man of lust the original experience of the body with an "expressive evangelical eloquence." The Pope affirms that Christ's words are entirely realistic. They do not try to make the human heart return to the state of innocence, but they indicate the way to a purity of heart that *is* possible and accessible to man even in the state of hereditary sinfulness.

The purity Christ calls us to is not just abstention from unchastity (temperance). At the same time, Christian purity opens the way to an ever more perfect discovery of the original dignity of the human body. If purity is first manifested as temperance, it eventually "matures in the heart of the man who cultivates it and tends to reveal and strengthen the nuptial meaning of the body in its integral truth. Precisely this truth must be known interiorly; it must, in a way, be 'felt with the heart,' in order that the mutual relations of man and woman—even mere looks—may re-acquire that authentically nuptial content of their meanings" (213). In mature purity man experiences the "efficacy of the gift of the Holy Spirit," which enables him to reach the mystery and subjectivity of the person through his or her body. He thus enjoys the fruits of the victory won over lust. This victory restores to our experience of the body "all its simplicity, its explicitness, and also its interior joy" (213).

Such joy is *very different* from any momentary satisfaction that comes by indulging lust. John Paul compellingly expresses this reality in a passage that seems to summarize all his reflections on Christ's words about lust. He writes: "The satisfaction of the passions is, in fact, one thing, and the joy that man finds in mastering himself more fully is another thing, since in this way he can also become more fully a real gift for another person. The words spoken by Christ in the Sermon on the Mount direct the human heart precisely toward this joy. We must entrust ourselves, our thoughts and actions to them, in order to find joy and give it to others" (213–214).

B. Pedagogy of the Body

In his audience of April 8, 1981, John Paul closes his reflections on historical man. We have been reflecting on the human heart, in which there is inscribed, John Paul says, "the most interior and, in a way, the most essential designs of history. It is the history of good and evil...and, at the same time, it is the history of salvation, whose word is the Gospel and whose power is the Holy Spirit, given to those who accept the Gospel with a sincere heart" (214).

John Paul has been constructing an adequate anthropology which he calls the "theology of the body." His catechesis provides an education or a pedagogy in being human. Pedagogy aims at educating man, setting before him the requirements of his own humanity and pointing out the ways that lead to the fulfillment of his humanity. This is precisely the goal of the theology of the body. The words of Christ that John Paul has analyzed (concerning the man of innocence and the man of lust) contain a pedagogy of the body, expressed in a concise and also extremely complete way. By analyzing Christ's words "to their very roots," we have learned that the Creator has assigned the body and the gift of sexuality to man as a task. It is the task of discovering the truth of our humanity and the dignity of the person. It is the task of embracing our redemption and growing in purity so that we can fulfill ourselves and bring joy to others through the sincere gift of ourselves—the sincere gift of our bodies which affords a true interpersonal communion. This is lived out particularly in marriage, but marriage is not the only way to live the sincere gift of self.

The task of the body and sexuality is, in fact, the task of discovering the truth and meaning of life and living it. It is the task of embracing "the perspective of the whole Gospel, of the whole teaching, in fact of the whole mission of Christ."[155] As we have learned, if we follow through with this "task" of the body, if we follow all the traces of our hearts and all the stirrings of our sexuality to their source, we find ourselves at the edge of eternity catching a glimpse of the Mystery of the Trinitarian God. By way of this journey men and women discover who they are. Ultimately, there is no other way but via God's revelation in the body. This is why John Paul asserts that "it is this theology of the body which is the basis of the most suitable method of the pedagogy of the body, that is, the education (in fact, the self-education) of man" (215).

Here we encounter one of those key quotes that demonstrates the scope and purpose of the Pope's catechesis. It is not "just" a catechesis on sex and marriage. The truth about sex and marriage, in fact, provides the key for understanding what it means to be human. John Paul says that the pedagogy of the body, understood as "theology of the body," speaks not only of the sacramentality of married life, but of human life itself. However, we cannot understand and live the truth about life if lust fills our hearts and our behavior contradicts the dignity of the person. A pedagogy of the body, therefore, must provide an anthropology that adequately explains the moral order regarding human sexuality. John Paul's catechesis heads precisely in this direction.

---

155. 12/3/80, TB 175.

C. Spirituality of the Body

Perhaps the greatest threat facing man today is the ideology of disembodiment. As a person, man is spiritual. But the body must be understood "as a sign of the person, a manifestation of the spirit" (215). The body, in fact, in the full truth of its masculinity or femininity is given as a task to the human spirit. This is why John Paul speaks of a specific "spirituality of the body." Living a "spiritual" life *never implies disparagement for the body*. Instead, growing in spiritual maturity always means becoming more and more integrated with the gift of one's masculine or feminine body. It means growing closer and closer to that original, rich, and far-reaching experience of holiness evidenced, as John Paul says, by the fact that the man and woman were both naked without shame. Holiness is certainly spiritual, but it is "felt" in the body.[156] Spiritual maturity, then, is intimately connected with rediscovering the nuptial meaning proper to the body. The spiritually mature person comes to *see* the nuptial meaning of the body, to *know* it, to *feel* it in his heart, and to *live* it. This is how men and women—and not only married men and women—*incarnate* the Gospel message.

This radical embodiment starkly contrasts with the modern view of things. An interior divorce between body and spirit is virtually taken for granted in our world today. In fact, the Pope points out that the whole development of modern science, despite its many contributions to human welfare, is based on the separation in man of body and spirit. This deprives the body of its personal meaning and dignity, and man, in turn, ceases to identify himself subjectively with his own body. In this milieu, the human body comes to be treated as an object of manipulation.

In this context, John Paul makes a statement applicable to sex education. He says that purely biological knowledge of the sexual functions of the body can help people discover the true nuptial meaning of the body only if an adequate spiritual maturity of the person accompanies this knowledge. Otherwise, as experience attests, it can have quite the opposite effect. We can gain two main points from this. First, the Holy Father does not condemn outright instruction in the sexual functions of the body. But it would be unwise to inundate those who are not spiritually mature with purely biological knowledge. Second, helping those who are not spiritually mature grow in such maturity requires that we help them discover the nuptial meaning of the body. Thus, true education in sexuality is always an education in the theology of the body, which is always the most suitable education in the meaning of being human.

---

156. 2/20/80, TB 76–77.

D. The Church Applies Christ's Words Today

The Pope says that precisely in these divergent views of the body we touch upon the crux of the modern controversies surrounding the Church's teaching on marriage and sexual morality. And the controversy grows most pointed in the teaching of the encyclical *Humanae Vitae*. The Church's teachings aim at applying Christ's words to the here and now. Hence, "it is necessary to consider prudently the pronouncements of the modern Church. Their adequate understanding and interpretation, as well as their practical application (that is, precisely, pedagogy) demands that deep theology of the body which, in a word, we derive mainly from the key words of Christ" (216).

With this statement, the Pope reveals the essence of his project: to provide an adequate understanding of the Church's teaching on sexuality, particularly her teaching on contraception, which is the linchpin of all sexual morality.[157] Furthermore, he makes the explicit point that this adequate understanding derives *from the words of Christ*. It is rooted not only in natural law, on which the traditional emphasis has been placed in understanding sexual morality. It is rooted also in divine revelation. In this way, as John Paul says in an endnote from a previous audience, "the concept of natural law also acquires a theological meaning."[158]

But the above statement on the importance of the theology of the body not only reveals the essence of the Pope's project. It also outlines John Paul's great commission for the Church. The Church must plumb the depths of "that deep theology of the body" if she is practically to apply Christ's words and help the world incarnate the Gospel in a new evangelization. At the heart of the new evangelization, at the heart of building a civilization of love and a culture of life, is marriage and the family. And at the heart of marriage and the family is the truth about the body and sexual-

---

157. While this might seem like an exaggeration to many modern minds, wise men and women throughout history have recognized the fact that once sexual pleasure is divorced from its intrinsic link with procreation, any sexual behavior can be justified. We previously noted Sigmund Freud's statement that the "abandonment of the reproductive function is the common feature of all sexual perversions" *(Introductory Lectures in Psychoanalysis,* p. 266). The inner logic is clear. If sexual relations need not be inherently related to procreation, why should sexual climax be limited to genital intercourse between a husband and wife? The logic that accepts intentionally sterilized intercourse, if it is to remain consistent with itself, must end by accepting any and every means to orgasm: from masturbation, to fornication and adultery, to sodomy, etc.

158. 4/23/80 first endnote, TB 181. As exemplified in his encyclical *Veritatis Splendor* (see especially n. 19), one of John Paul's seminal contributions to moral theology has been to reunite moral doctrine with faith in Christ. This reunion has been termed by some "a Christological approach to natural law."

ity. John Paul made the theology of the body the first catechetical project of his pontificate because it is the only adequate starting point for the renewal of the family, the Church, and the world. As he knew so well in starting here, such renewal cannot possibly happen if we do not go to the "deepest substratum of human ethics and culture," if we do not embrace the truth of sexual morality, particularly the truth taught in the encyclical *Humanae Vitae.*

Plumbing the depths of the theology of the body means reconnecting with our own embodiment. It means living the very dynamism of the Incarnation by allowing the Word of the Gospel to penetrate our flesh and bones. It means realizing that our bodies are sacramental, that they reveal the mystery of our humanity and also point to the infinitely greater mystery of God's divinity. When this incarnation of the Gospel takes place in us, we see the Church's teaching on sexual morality not as an oppressive list of rules, but as the foundation of a liberating ethos, a call to redemption, a call to rediscover in what is erotic the original meaning of the body which, in turn, reveals the very meaning of life. This is the first step to take in renewing the world.

47. Portraying the Naked Body in Art

April 15, 22, 29; May 6, 1981 (TB 218–229)

In his encyclical *Humanae Vitae*, Pope Paul VI speaks of the need of creating an atmosphere favorable to education in chastity.[159] John Paul II closes his cycle on historical man by devoting four audience addresses to this need in relation to what he calls "the ethos of the image" (228). By this he means the portrayal of the human body in art and in the culture of the mass media. When dealing with such portrayals, he says that we find ourselves continually within the orbit of the words Christ spoke in the Sermon on the Mount.

Is it possible to portray the naked body artistically without offending the dignity of the person? This is a very delicate problem, the Pope says, which intensifies according to various motives and circumstances. In the first three of these four audiences, as John Paul outlines the problem he seems so apprehensive at times that one might think he condemns nakedness in art altogether. Not so! In the restoration of the Sistine Chapel, he insisted on removing several of the loincloths that prudish clerics had had painted over Michelangelo's original nudes. In turn, when he dedicated the

---

159. See *Humanae Vitae*, n. 22.

restored Sistine Chapel he described it as *"the sanctuary of the theology of the human body."* It seems Michelangelo, he said, had been guided by the evocative Word of God in Genesis 2:25, which enabled him, "in his own way," to see the human body naked without shame. For "in the context of the light that comes from God, the human body also keeps its splendor and its dignity. If it is removed from this dimension, it becomes in some way an object, which depreciates very easily, since only before the eyes of God can the human body remain naked and unclothed, and keep its splendor and beauty intact."[160] The question then becomes: Is it possible to see the human body with the eyes of God? The perfect vision is reserved for the eschaton. But, quoting again from the *Catechism* in this regard: "Even now [purity of heart] enables us to see *according to* God...; it lets us perceive the human body—ours and our neighbor's—as a temple of the Holy Spirit, a manifestation of divine beauty."[161]

John Paul says that just because portraying the body in art raises a very delicate problem, it does not mean that the naked human body cannot become a subject of works of art. It only means that this problem is not purely aesthetic, nor morally indifferent. Therefore, John Paul does not intend to question the right to this subject in art. He aims merely at demonstrating that its treatment is connected with a special responsibility.

A. A Perennial Object of Culture

The Pope notes first that the human body is a perennial object of culture. Sexuality and the whole sphere of love between man and woman has been, is, and will continue to be a subject of art and literature. Indeed, the Bible itself contains that wonderful narrative of the Song of Songs which celebrates the intimate love of man and woman without shame.[162] The body and sexuality's frequency in art and literature indicates their fundamental importance in each person's life and within culture at large. It speaks of that deep yearning we all have to understand the nuptial meaning of masculinity and femininity which is inscribed in the whole interior—and at the same time visible—structure of the human person.

Herein lies the challenge for artists. If they are to portray *the visible structure of the person* (i.e., the human body), they must do so in a way that does not obscure but brings to light *the interior structure of the per-*

---

160. Homily preached by John Paul II at the Mass celebrating the restored Sistine Chapel, April 8, 1994 (published in *L'Osservatore Romano*, April 13, 1994).

161. *CCC,* n. 2519.

162. The Song of Songs will be the subject of future audiences in the Pope's catechesis.

son. In other words, art must integrate the body and soul of the person portrayed by bringing to light the body's nuptial meaning. "The human body—the naked human body in the whole truth of its masculinity and femininity—has the meaning of a gift of the person to the person" (220). Artists must work within this "nuptial system of reference" if they are not to offend the dignity of the body, which is always the dignity of a person. The ethical norms that govern the body's nakedness are therefore inseparable from the personal truth of the gift.

John Paul affirms that this norm of the gift is even deeper than the norm of shame—understood as the need for privacy regarding the body. Therefore, so long as the norm of the gift is properly and diligently respected, the body can be uncovered without violating its dignity. A person of "developed sensitivity" can overcome the limits of shame, but the Pope observes that this is accomplished only "with difficulty and interior resistance" (222). In other words, even if this demands overcoming the interior pull of concupiscence, a mature person can see the body in its nakedness and not violate the dignity of the gift. But the Holy Father carefully distinguishes "overcoming" the limits of shame from "overstepping" the limits of shame. In the latter case, concupiscence is not conquered, but shamelessly indulged. Nakedness then entails a violation of the personal dignity of the body.

B. The Danger of Anonymity

A real danger exists of objectifying the naked body through artistic portrayal. John Paul describes this as the danger of anonymity, which is a way of "veiling" or "hiding" the identity of the person reproduced. Through photography in particular, the Pope observes that the body very often becomes an "anonymous" object, especially when the images of a person's body are diffused on the screens of the whole world. Despite their similarities, John Paul notes an important difference between photographing the naked body and portraying it in the plastic arts. In painting or sculpture, the body undergoes a specific elaboration on the part of the artist, whereas in photography an image of an actual, living person is reproduced. Thus photography has even greater need of ensuring the visibility of the interior person. When this fails to happen, "the human body loses that deeply subjective meaning of the gift and becomes an object destined for the knowledge of many" (221). Hence, both the artist who portrays the body and those who view the artist's work must be aware of their obligation to uphold the dignity of the body as a sign of the gift of persons. From this perspective, John Paul speaks not only of the "ethos of the image," but also the "ethos of the viewing" (226).

Creating an atmosphere favorable to chastity in the media and the arts, then, involves recognizing "a reciprocal circuit" which takes place between the image and the seeing. This can be explained by the reciprocity found in actual interpersonal relationships. In genuine relationships, John Paul says that the human body in its nakedness becomes the source of a particular interpersonal "communication." It is "understood as a manifestation of the person and as his gift"—as "a sign of trust and donation to the other person." Thus, we can conclude with the Holy Father that nakedness does not offend nor elicit shame when man and woman are "conscious of the gift" given and have "resolved to respond to it in an equally personal way" (224).

■ This dynamic can be keenly observed within a loving marriage, but also in other rare situations. For example, I once heard the following story of a woman who modeled for art students. Having disrobed before the students, she immediately covered herself when she noticed that the shade had not been drawn on the window. When the teacher apologized and drew the shade, she again disrobed. This demonstrates that her nakedness before the students was not "shameless," but a form of "nakedness without shame." She trusted the students to respect her "gift," and to respond to it in an equally personal way. However, shame immediately manifested itself (and rightly so) when she realized her nakedness was being potentially exposed to an unknown (and, therefore, untrusted) audience.

A further problem arises, however. Even when an artist portrays the human body intending to illuminate its true nuptial meaning, he cannot always know how the recipient of his work will respond. "In fact, that 'element of the gift' is, so to speak, suspended in the dimension of an unknown reception and an unforeseen response" (225). In this way it is threatened in the sense that it may become an anonymous object of appropriation and abuse. "It cannot be forgotten," as John Paul reminds us, "that the fundamental interior situation of 'historical' man is the state of threefold lust" (222). Through the ethos of redemption this lust can be gradually overcome. Unfortunately, however, not everyone embraces the ethos of redemption. In our fallen world, that "original shame, known already from the first chapters of the Bible, is a permanent element of culture and morals" (222). Furthermore, even if the negative sense of shame can, with fervent effort, be gradually overcome, we must not forget the positive function of shame which always maintains a certain veil of respect for the dignity and mystery of others as persons.

C. True Art Versus Pornography

Some works of art portray the naked body in a manner that does not arouse lust but "makes it possible to concentrate, in a way, on the whole truth of man, and the dignity and beauty—also the 'suprasensual' beauty—of his masculinity and femininity" (227). The Pope says that such works of art "bear within them, almost hidden, an element of sublimation" (227). A masterful artist can lead us through the naked body to the whole personal mystery of man and allow us to comprehend the nuptial meaning of the body in purity of heart.[163] In contrast to these, other works of art—and perhaps even more often photographic images—epitomize man's degradation rather than sublimation. The Pope insists that this is not because of their object, since the human body in itself always has its inalienable dignity, but because of the quality or way of its reproduction and portrayal.

The difference between an authentic portrayal of the naked body in art and a pornographic[164] portrayal, then, lies in the artist's intention. Since the body itself always maintains an objective dignity, John Paul observes that the body can only be violated in the intentional order. An artist's work manifests "his interior world of values" (227). The artist who not only understands the nuptial meaning of the body in the abstract, but also lives it himself interiorly, can transfer this reality to his work. As experience confirms, the intentions of an artist are usually easy to ascertain. However, we must be careful not to project our own impurity onto artists whose intentions are pure. Those who subscribe to the "interpretation of suspicion" will tend to question the intentions of any artist who portrays the naked body. They will tend to label any portrayal of the naked body as obscene. Such was the case when various clerics, upon viewing Michelangelo's work in the Sistine Chapel, accused him of obscenity and subsequently covered his nudes with awkward drapes and loincloths. Doing so only demonstrated in some sense their own impurity; that is, their own *inability* to see the body as a theology, a revelation of the mystery of God.[165]

---

163. For a fascinating and provocative study of nakedness in Renaissance art that strove to reveal a theology of the body, see Leo Steinberg's *The Sexuality of Christ in Renaissance Art and in Modern Oblivion* (Chicago, IL: University of Chicago Press, 1996).

164. John Paul actually distinguishes between "pornography" which refers to literature and "pornovision" which refers to images. In common English usage, of course, the term pornography usually refers to both.

165. A documentary on the restoration of the Sistine Chapel reported this story: Apparently, Michelangelo liked to use the faces of actual people in painting his figures. It was already known that Michelangelo used the face of a cleric who condemned his nude

Michelangelo's nudes are not pornographic because he intended to reveal the nuptial meaning of the body as a revelation of the Trinitarian Mystery. It is quite clear, however, that this is *not* the intention of pornographers, who portray the naked body with the explicit intention of rousing lust in men. By doing so, they explicitly violate "those deep governing rules of the gift and of mutual donation" which are inscribed in the human being (223).

■ The juxtaposition of the nudity on the billboards just outside the Vatican and the nudity portrayed in the art inside the Vatican vividly illustrates the difference between pornography and a respectful portrayal of the body in art (shall we call it "nuptial-ography"?). On this point, those who subscribe to the "interpretation of suspicion"—and think it holy or "Catholic" to do so—simply cannot justify their position after touring the Vatican. It would be virtually impossible to count the number of depictions of the body that prudery would quickly label "obscene" in St. Peter's Basilica and the Vatican museum.

As the Pope says, pornographers will retort that they act in this way in the name of the realistic truth about man. Furthermore, they demand the right to "everything that is human" in works of art. But, as John Paul insists, the problem with pornography is precisely that *it fails to portray everything that is human*. Precisely this truth about man—the whole truth about man—makes it necessary to condemn pornography. The Holy Father confirms that this condemnation "is not the effect of a puritanical mentality or of a narrow moralism, just as it is not the product of a thought imbued with Manichaeism. It is the question of an extremely important, fundamental sphere of values, before which man cannot remain indifferent because of the dignity of humanity [and] the personal character and the eloquence of the human body" (225). For John Paul, we could say that the problem with pornography is not that it reveals too much of the person, but that it reveals far too little. Indeed, it portrays the naked human body without revealing *the person* at all.

With these refreshingly balanced reflections, John Paul closes his cycle on historical man. We have reflected on man's origins and on the

---

paintings as the model for the demon in the lower right-hand corner of the Last Judgment. However, only when the loincloth on this demon was removed during the restoration did the modern world glimpse the full extent of Michelangelo's disdain for this cleric's prudery. What may have seemed like a vine coiled around this demon was actually revealed to be a serpent. Not only that—it was taking a generous chomp out of his genitals!

historical drama of sin and redemption. Now, in order to complete the outline of an "adequate anthropology," we must look to the reality of embodiment and sexuality in the dimension of man's eternal destiny.

Historical Man—In Review

1. Christ's words, which equate "looking lustfully" with committing "adultery in the heart," announce the "ethos of redemption." Merely following an external ethic is not enough. It is necessary to penetrate inside the human heart (ethos) where man *experiences* the truth about good or fails to do so.

2. Fulfilling the law cannot be equated only with meeting the law's demands. It involves a super-abounding justice in man's heart that readily goes beyond the demands of law out of genuine love for the truth. This is a "living morality" in which we realize the very meaning of being human.

3. The "heart" defines our humanity from "within." In a way it is equivalent with personal subjectivity. The heart is where we come to know and live the true nuptial meaning of the body or fail to do so. For historical man, the heart is a battlefield between love and lust.

4. John Paul describes original sin as the "questioning of the gift." Man denies that "God is love" and therefore casts the Father from his heart. When the heart is *un*-inspired by God's love, it gives birth to lust. Lust, then, is sexual desire devoid of God's love. Shame rises in the heart because man realizes that his body has ceased drawing from the power of the spirit.

5. Shame is cosmic (experienced in relation to all creation), immanent (experienced within oneself), and relative (experienced in relation to the "other"). Shame also has a double meaning. It manifests that man and woman have lost sight of the nuptial meaning of the body, and it also indicates an inherent need to protect the nuptial meaning of the body from the degradation of lust.

6. In the "second discovery of sex," what had once enabled man and woman's communion was suddenly felt to impede communion. It seems that the woman bears a particular disability in this new situation. Both man and woman are subject to lust, but the male tendency to dominate and control woman now places her in an apparent position of inequality.

7. The nuptial meaning of the body continues to serve as the "measure of the heart" for historical man. This means that through the grace of redemption, Christ gives man the task of reclaiming the truth of the body and sexuality. Lust has not completely suffocated the nuptial meaning of the body, only habitually threatened it. Recognizing the distortions of our hearts should not lead us to distrust ourselves, but should spur us on to reclaim self-mastery.

8. Maintaining the balance of the gift has been entrusted to both men and women, but it seems the man has a particular responsibility in this regard. If he is called in some sense to initiate the gift, he must ensure that the gift he initiates is genuine. He cannot seek to "possess" the woman's femininity, only "borrow" it. If men and women are to "belong" to each other, this can only come about through the sincere gift of self and never through lustful desire.

9. Old Testament legislation compromised with concupiscence, but the prophets point to the integrity of the covenant of marriage and to its sign. The bodily union of spouses is the regular sign of married love. Understanding this is essential for the entire theology of the body, both from an ethical and an anthropological point of view. For John Paul, sexual morality is understood through the logic of "the truthful sign."

10. The Wisdom literature of the Old Testament contains classic descriptions of carnal concupiscence and admonitions to avoid indulging it. However, it does not change ethos in any fundamental way. For such a change, we must wait for the gift of redemption in Christ.

11. A man "looks" in conformity with what he is. A "look" determines the intentionality of man's very existence. If a man looks with lust, he confirms his denial of the gift of God's love, the gift of the other person, and the gift of life itself. He reduces the value of the person to an object of self-gratification.

12. Marriage in no way "justifies" lust. Thus, a man can commit adultery in his heart with his own wife if he treats her as nothing but an object to satisfy his own instinct. A merely psychological definition of lust, however, cannot arrive at this conclusion, since it does not take man and woman's beginning as the normative point of reference.

13. The common life of men and women "constitutes the pure and simple fabric of existence." Their call to communion "is the deepest substratum of human ethics and culture." Hence, the freedom of the gift afforded by liberation from lust "is the condition of all life together in truth."

14. To understand Christ's words about lust properly, we must contend with the "inveterate habits" of Manichaeism in our ways of thinking and evaluating. While the heresy of Manichaeism assigns to the body and sex an "anti-value," Christianity recognizes in the body and sex a value not sufficiently appreciated. The Manichaean condemnation of the body often serves as a loophole to avoid the demands of Christian purity.

15. If we are to gain a true victory over lust, purity must mature from the "negative" turning away to the more "positive" assertion of the value and dignity of the body and sex. The "masters of suspicion" do not believe in the power of redemption to transform the heart in this way. But we must not stop at putting the heart in a state of irreversible suspicion. Redemption is a truth that calls man with efficacy to transformation of heart. The meaning of life, then, is the antithesis of the interpretation of suspicion.

16. Christ's call to overcome lust is not "hurled into emptiness" but taps in to that "echo" of our beatifying beginning that remains within each of us. The heart is deeper than lust, and Christ's words reactive that deeper heritage giving it real power in our lives. The grace of creation becomes renewed for each of us in the grace and gift of redemption.

17. The erotic and the ethical do not differ from each other. *Eros* and *ethos* are not inherently opposed. In fact, they are called to meet in the human heart and bear fruit. Eros is meant to be redeemed, transformed, sanctified—not repressed or snuffed out. Through purification the erotic becomes true, good, and beautiful.

18. Like a "guardian who watches over a hidden spring," we are called to discern the deep impulses of our hearts so we can draw forth what is fitting for the dignity of the gift and the communion of persons. Living this ethos of redemption, far from stifling eros, affords a mature spontaneity and a noble gratification.

19. Christ spoke his words about lust in the perspective of the redemption of the body, which is "the perspective of the whole Gospel, the whole teaching, in fact the whole mission of Christ." Christ's emphasis on purity of heart brings the Old Testament ethos to fulfillment in the New.

20. "Blessed are the pure of heart, for they shall see God." The pure can see the body as a making visible of God's mystery. Yet to attain this vision we must contend with the system of forces within us, which St. Paul describes as a battle between the flesh and the Spirit. The "flesh" does not refer to the human body, as such, but to the man of lust—the man who has cut his heart off from the love and vision of God.

21. Justification by faith is not just a dimension of the divine plan of salvation, but is a real power at work in man to free him from the bonds of

sin and, in this case, lust. Justification by faith enables man to experience the power of "life according to the Spirit," which bears fruit in purity of heart and of action.

22. We experience purity of heart to the measure that we experience the "freedom for which Christ has set us free." The ethos of redemption is nothing but an appeal for the full flowering of human freedom. Freedom to sin is the "flip side" of freedom to love. If we seek to eradicate sin by eradicating our freedom to commit it, we also eradicate the freedom that is necessary to love.

23. Freedom is negated when it becomes a pretext for indulging "the flesh." Such a man is not free, but enslaved by his disordered passions. Freedom and purity come as we learn to refrain from unchastity and, more so, when we control our bodies "in holiness and honor."

24. Authentic purity recognizes that those parts of the body we may think are "less honorable" actually deserve greater honor. Purity has a moral dimension as a virtue, but it also has a charismatic dimension as a gift of the Holy Spirit. It is connected with piety, which is respect for the work of God. Unchastity is a violation of piety because the body is a temple of the Holy Spirit.

25. St. Paul exhorts us to glorify God in our bodies. Purity is God's glory radiated in the human body. Christ's words about purity as the ability to "see God" have not only an eschatological meaning but bear fruit here and now. "To the pure all things are pure, but to the corrupt and unbelieving nothing is pure." The latter deny the "supernatural realism of faith" and the "anthropology of rebirth in the Spirit."

26. This theology of the body is at the basis of the most suitable education of man in the meaning of his own humanity. It calls him to an authentic Christian spirituality, which is *always* a spirituality of the human body. Furthermore, understanding and practically applying the pronouncements of the Church's Magisterium regarding marriage and sexuality demand that deep theology of the body which we derive from the words of Christ.

27. Portrayal of the naked body in art is connected with a special responsibility. It demands respect for the "nuptial system of reference," which reveals the body as an intimate gift of the person. The body can be portrayed in its nakedness in a way that elicits awe and respect for the mystery of our humanity, but it can also be portrayed in a way that degrades our humanity. Pornography does not reveal too much of the person. It reveals far too little.

Cycle 3

Eschatological Man

In our quest for a "total vision of man" we have looked at our origin and our history, now we must look to our destiny. We must reflect upon the experience of embodiment for the man of the eschaton. As the *Catechism* affirms, "'On no point does the Christian faith meet with more opposition than on the resurrection of the body.' It is very commonly accepted that the life of the human person continues in a spiritual fashion after death. But how can we believe that this body, so clearly mortal, could rise to everlasting life?"[1] Christ's resurrection is the definitive word on the subject. Thus St. Paul attests that he who raised Christ from the dead will give eternal life to our mortal bodies as well (see Rom 8:11).

John Paul bases this cycle on Christ's discussion with the Sadducees. The Lord announces that men and women "neither marry nor are given in marriage" in the resurrection (see Mt 22:30; Mk 12:25; Lk 20:35). At the surface, Christ's assertion may seem to undermine all that the Pope has already said about the surpassing dignity of nuptial union and the "eternal attraction" between the sexes (see §33). Certainly we know by now that John Paul's exegesis never remains at the surface. As we shall learn, Christ's words reveal a completely new dimension of the human mystery, and thus point to the crowning glory of all the Pope has said.

Eschatological Man is the shortest cycle—only nine addresses delivered between November 11, 1981 and February 10, 1982. But it is perhaps the most profound cycle and, thus, the most difficult at times to follow. Yet it is well worth every ounce of mental energy it requires. If we could but take in what this pontiff tells us about the joys to come, it would set us ablaze! John Paul weds his Carmelite mysticism with his phenomenological insights for an unsurpassed vision of the eschaton. To be sure, reflecting on the resurrection of the body stretches the Pope's philosophical method to the limit. How can we possibly talk about subjective experience

---

1. *CCC*, n. 996.

in relation to the final resurrection when we have no experience of it whatsoever? We can do so in the same way we talk about original innocence—based on the principle of continuity. Christ, in his "revelation of the body," calls historical man to look in two directions. In Christ's conversation with the Pharisees, he calls us to look to the beginning. In his conversation with the Sadducees, Christ calls us to look to the future resurrection.

Even if a "discontinuity" separates the experience of original man, historical man, and eschatological man, as John Paul says, "What the human body is in the sphere of man's historical experience is not completely cut off from those two dimensions of his existence, which are revealed through Christ's words." Hence, these two "extensions of the sphere" of the experience of the body "are not completely beyond the reach of our understanding." Based on the principle of continuity, "we can make a certain theological reconstruction of what might have been the experience of the body on the basis of man's revealed 'beginning,' and also of what it will be in the dimension of the 'other world.'"[2]

Applying this principle, we can say that if our origin and our history have something to do with the experience of Trinitarian love in the human reflection of nuptial union, then our destiny will also have something to do with that same experience. Of course, this "will be a completely new experience," as the Pope says. Yet "at the same time it will not be alienated in any way from what man took part in from 'the beginning' nor from what, in the historical dimension of his existence, constituted in him the source of the tension between spirit and body, concerning mainly the procreative meaning of the body and sex."[3]

Returning to our image of the tires: If in his discussion with the Pharisees and in the Sermon on the Mount, Christ calls historical man to reflect on "the beginning" when our tires were fully inflated—then in his discussion with the Sadducees, Christ calls us to reflect on the future when tires will lose their *raison d'être* and will give way to flight.

48. An Infinite Perspective of Life

November 11, 18, 1981 (TB 233–237)

Like the Pharisees who approached Jesus to question him about divorce, the Sadducees also tried to trap Jesus. The Sadducees did not be-

---

2. 12/16/81, TB 245.

3. 1/13/82, TB 248.

lieve in the resurrection. Appealing to the levirate law (see Deut 25:5–10), they brought a case to Jesus to prove their position. "'There were seven brothers; the first took a wife, and when he died left no children; and the second took her, and died, leaving no children; and the third likewise; and the seven left no children. Last of all the woman also died. In the resurrection, whose wife will she be? For the seven had her as wife'" (Mk 12:20–23). The Pope remarks that the Sadducees unquestionably treat the question of resurrection as a theory or hypothesis that can be disproved. Furthermore, as John Paul adds in an endnote, the Sadducees insinuate "that faith in the resurrection of the body leads to admitting polyandry, which is contrary to God's law" (258).

A. The Power of God

The Sadducees considered themselves highly educated experts in the Scriptures. But Jesus—an "uneducated," renegade prophet—responds:

> You are wrong, for you know neither the scriptures nor the power of God. For in the resurrection they neither marry nor are given in marriage, but are like angels in heaven. And as for the resurrection of the dead, have you not read what was said to you by God, 'I am the God of Abraham, and the God of Isaac, and the God of Jacob?' He is not God of the dead, but of the living (Mt 22:29–33).[4]

John Paul says that Christ's response is "stupendous in its content." It forms the third element of "the triptych" of Christ's words which are essential for the theology of the body. His response, in fact, completes "the revelation of the body" and "is one of the answer-keys of the Gospel." It reveals "another dimension of the question [which] corresponds to the wisdom and power of God himself" (234).

Christ will eventually answer all doubts about the resurrection with the miracle of Easter. For now, however, he wants to demonstrate the truth about resurrection from the testimony of the Old Testament. Mark's account reports more details: "'And as for the dead being raised, have you not read in the book of Moses, in the passage about the bush, how God said to him, "I am the God of Abraham, and the God of Isaac, and the God of Jacob"? He is not God of the dead, but of the living; you are quite wrong'" (Mk 12:26–27). John Paul mentions in an endnote that the immortality of their souls could seemingly explain why the Patriarchs are still "living." In other words, it need not prove the resurrection of the body. But Jesus was addressing himself to the Sadducees who accepted

---

4. See *CCC,* nn. 988–1008.

"only the biblical psycho-physical unity of man who is 'the body and the breath of life.' Therefore, according to them the soul dies with the body" (259). For the Sadducees, Jesus' affirmation that the Patriarchs were "alive" could only have been understood in reference to the resurrection of the body.

Each of the synoptic accounts of the discussion "contains two essential elements: 1) the annunciation about the future resurrection of the body; 2) the enunciation about the state of the body of the risen man" (235). The Holy Father examines each element. Regarding the simple truth of the resurrection, Jesus first shows the Sadducees "an error of method: they do not know the Scriptures." Then he shows them "an error of substance: they do not accept what is revealed by the Scriptures—they do not know the power of God, they do not believe in him who revealed himself to Moses in the burning bush" (236). Jesus demonstrates that mere literal knowledge of the Scripture is not enough. In other words, just to be a Scripture scholar does not suffice. "The Scriptures, in fact, are above all a means to know the power of the living God who reveals himself in them, just as he revealed himself to Moses in the bush" (236). If we "know" the Scriptures inside and out but have not encountered the mystery of the living God within them, we have missed the whole point.

B. The God of Life

To reread the Scriptures correctly "means to know and accept with faith the power of the Giver of life, who is not bound by the law of death which rules man's earthly history" (236). As John Paul says, "He who is—he who lives and is Life—is the inexhaustible source of existence and of life, as was revealed at the 'beginning' in Genesis" (237). Although we have turned our backs on Life by breaking the original covenant, and thus lost access to the "Tree of Life," John Paul affirms that throughout the Scriptures the living God continually extends his covenant of Life to man and desires to renew it. "Christ is God's ultimate word on this subject," the Pope says. The covenant which Christ establishes between God and mankind "opens an infinite perspective of life." In Christ, "access to the Tree of Life—according to the original plan of the God of the covenant—is revealed to every man in its definitive fullness. This will be the meaning of the death and resurrection of Christ; this will be the testimony of the Paschal Mystery" (237).

More than that, as we shall learn, the sacrament of marriage testifies to this, that sacrament which is consummated when husband and wife become "one flesh." If husband and wife are faithful to the truth of the sign of their covenant, they image and participate in that definitive covenant

between Christ and the Church. Then their marriage too opens to "an infinite perspective of life." Tragically, spouses can, like the Sadducees, close
themselves to this perspective of life. They can, like the Sadducees, "deprive" God of his life-giving power. Then, rather than becoming a truthful
sign of the covenant of life, they (knowingly or unknowingly) become a
counter-sign of it. And God, as in the case with the Sadducees, becomes
"the God of their hypotheses and interpretations" rather than "the true God
of their fathers" (237).

49. Anthropology of the Resurrection

December 2, 1981 (TB 238–240)

John Paul defines marriage as "that union in which, according to the
words of Genesis, 'a man cleaves to his wife and they become one flesh.'"
He further states that if this union is "characteristic of man right from the
'beginning'" it does not "constitute, on the other hand, the eschatological
future of man" (238). Indeed, Christ's words about the resurrection affirm
that the "one flesh" union of marriage belongs exclusively to "this age"
(Lk 20:34).

Many have thought Christ's words disparage sexuality and marital
love. Some have seen his statement as proof positive that sexual love is
inherently tainted and unfit for the holiness of heaven. Others have feared
that it means an eternal sadness of separation from their spouses.[5] But, like
the Sadducees, those who accept these interpretations "know neither the
scriptures nor the power of God" (Mt 22:29).

A. The Fulfillment of Marriage

The resurrection will not eradicate marriage. Rather, marriage will be
brought to its ultimate fulfillment in "the Marriage of the Lamb" (Rev
19:7). From the beginning, the "great mystery" of nuptial union was given
to us to anticipate and prepare us for the "great mystery" of eternal union
with Christ. This is why John Paul describes marriage as the *primordial
sacrament*. But precisely as a sacrament—an earthly sign of a heavenly reality—marriage is not the final word on man. Man's ultimate end is
heaven. Sacraments will not exist in heaven because they will have come
to fruition.[6] When Jesus says men and women will not be given in marriage in the resurrection, it is as if he is saying, "You no longer need a sign

---

5. See St. John Chrysostom's quote in *CCC,* n. 2365.

6. See *CCC,* n. 671.

to point you *to* heaven when you are *in* heaven." This is why the Pope says that in the resurrection, marriage and procreation "lose, so to speak, their *raison d'être*" (238). The reason they exist is to prepare us for heaven as the fruitful Bride of Christ.

In John Paul's vision of the resurrection, nothing essentially human is mitigated or eliminated. Everything we have learned about who the human person is as a subject (original solitude) and his perennial call to live in an incarnate communion of persons (original unity) reaches its ultimate realization. As the Pope says, the future age "means the definitive fulfillment of mankind." At the same time, however, this entails "the quantitative closing of that circle of beings, who were created in the image and likeness of God" through conjugal union (237).

In other words, man's destiny is fulfilled only when the age in which men and women multiply through the union of their bodies comes to a close. This "closing" must never be perceived as a loss over which to lament. What a tragic misconception! This closing opens to the fulfillment of every human desire which from the beginning was written in man's heart and stamped in his body as male and female. In fact, as John Paul points out, Christ reveals the new condition of the human body in the resurrection precisely by proposing a reference and a comparison with the condition in which man had participated since the beginning.

B. Like the Angels?

The Pope carefully clarifies that when Christ says we will be "like angels in heaven" (Mt 22:30) he *does not* mean that we will be *dis*-incarnated or otherwise dehumanized. The context in which Christ is speaking, John Paul says, "indicates clearly that man will keep in 'that age' his own human psychosomatic nature. If it were otherwise, it would be meaningless to speak of the resurrection" (239). Unfortunately, Plato's belief that the body is the earthly prison of the soul has significantly influenced the thinking of some Christians. As the Pope insists, "The truth about the resurrection clearly affirms, in fact, that the eschatological perfection and happiness of man cannot be understood as a state of the soul alone, separated (according to Plato: liberated) from the body." This idea is essentially alien to orthodox Christianity. Instead, man's ultimate beatitude "must be understood as the state of man definitively and perfectly integrated through such a union of the soul and the body, which qualifies and definitively ensures this perfect integrity" (240).[7]

---

7. See *CCC,* n. 650.

■ Philosopher Peter Kreeft writes: "A soul without a body is exactly the opposite of what Plato thought it is. It is not free but bound. It is in an extreme form of paralysis." The human soul *needs* the body to express itself—not only on earth but in heaven as well. "The body is the matter of the soul, and the soul is the form of the body. That is why the resurrection of the body is internal to the immortality of the soul, not a dispensable extra. When death separates the two," Kreeft continues, "we have a freak, a monster, an obscenity. That is why we are terrified of ghosts and corpses, though both are harmless: they are the obscenely separated aspects of what belongs together as one. That is why Jesus wept at Lazarus' grave: not merely for his bereavement but for this cosmic obscenity."[8]

John Paul mentions that faith in the resurrection of the body played a key role in the formation of theological anthropology. In fact, he says that theological anthropology could be considered simply as the "anthropology of the resurrection." For only in light of the resurrection of the body do we fully understand who man is theologically and what he is destined for as a body-person. In fact, the Pope says that St. Thomas' reflections on the resurrection led him to draw closer to the conception of Aristotle. Unlike Plato, Aristotle taught that, together with the soul, the body constitutes the unity and integrity of the human being. Christian belief in the resurrection of the body confirms this.

But another question arises: Will we be raised as male and female? Some, granting the resurrection of the body, envision a sexless heaven based on St. Paul's teaching that in Christ "there is neither male nor female" (Gal 3:28). The Pope believes that our bodiliness belongs to our humanity more deeply than the fact that in our bodiliness we are either male or female. In other words, the experience of being a body-person (original solitude) is deeper than and "prior" to the experience of sexual differentiation and the call to communion (original unity).

That being said, John Paul mentions three times in his audience of December 2, 1981 (and on other occasions throughout this cycle) that in the resurrection we reacquire our bodies *in their masculinity and femininity*. Sexual difference is the perennial sign and summons of the human race to communion. The resurrection fulfills not only the bodily experience of solitude, but also the bodily experience of communion. As John Paul expresses it, in the resurrection we rediscover not only "a new, per-

---

8. Peter Kreeft, *Everything You Ever Wanted to Know about Heaven* (San Francisco: Ignatius Press, 1990), p. 93.

fect subjectivity of everyone" as individuals. At the same time we rediscover "a new, perfect intersubjectivity of all,"[9] that is, communion with
other persons.

Based on the Pope's modern philosophical language, we come to understand that sexual difference is not only retained, but is in some way essential to the communion of saints. Of course the resurrection means a
completely new state of human life. Both the reality of sexual difference
and the mystery of communion will be experienced in an entirely new
way. As the *Catechism* says, "This mystery of blessed communion with
God and all who are in Christ is beyond all understanding and description."[10] We must not, therefore, conceive of the eternal communion that
awaits us as an expansion into infinity of the earthly reality of the male-
female communion. Nonetheless, nothing genuinely human will be done
away with or annihilated. All that is essentially human in the original experiences of solitude-unity-nakedness will be brought to ultimate fulfillment. Heaven, therefore, will be the experience of a great multitude of
solitudes living in perfect unity without any fear of being seen and known
by each and by all.

■ Does this mean we will we be naked in heaven? Those who claim to
have caught glimpses of the blessed report that it is hard to classify them as
either clothed or naked.[11] The experience is simply "other" than we can
imagine. If clothed, the blessed wear a "nuptial garment."[12] If naked, there
is no fear because the original *raison d'être* of shame (in the negative
sense) has ceased utterly. Interestingly, both the Gospel of Luke (24:12)
and of John (20:5–7) mention that Christ's burial coverings were left behind in the tomb after his resurrection. The *Catechism* teaches that, together with the empty tomb, this signifies that "Christ's body had escaped
the bonds of death and corruption."[13] Michelangelo sought to convey this
truth by portraying his famous *Risen Christ* naked without shame. It seems
fitting that the New Adam would come forth from the ground just as the
first Adam did. It also seems significant that Christ would come forth from
the virgin tomb (see Jn 19:41) just as he came forth from the virgin womb.
Yet in doing so, Christ's risen body was mysteriously "different," so much
so that his own disciples did not immediately recognize him.

---

9. 12/16/81, TB 245.

10. *CCC,* n. 1027.

11. See *Everything You Ever Wanted to Know about Heaven,* p. 43.

12. See *CCC,* n. 1682.

13. *CCC,* n. 657.

The Book of Revelation speaks of the saints in heaven wearing "white robes" (Rev 7:9). White is the color of light. When Christ was transfigured, his garments "became white as light" (Mt 17:2). Light reveals rather than conceals. In heaven, all is revealed by the light of Christ. "For nothing is hid that shall not be made manifest, nor anything secret that shall not be known and come to light" (Lk 8:17). Many Church Fathers speak both of Adam and Eve in paradise and of the blessed in heaven as being clothed in glory. "They shall have no need of woven raiment," says Ignatius of Antioch, "for they shall be clothed in eternal light."[14] John Paul II describes purity as "the glory of the human body before God. It is God's glory in the human body, through which masculinity and femininity are manifested."[15] White robes and nakedness are *both* symbols that the Church has used to convey Christian purity and new birth in Christ. St. Cyril of Jerusalem describes the symbolism of the once common practice of nude Baptism as follows: "As soon as you entered [the baptismal font] you divested yourself of your garment; this gesture symbolized the divesting yourself of the old man in you with all his practices.... O marvelous thing, you were naked before everyone and yet you did not blush for shame. Truly you represented in this the image of the first man, Adam, who in paradise was naked but was not ashamed."[16] The resurrected state will recover whatever was essentially human in Adam's original experience of nakedness, but in an entirely new dimension "beyond all understanding and description."[17]

50. Penetration of the Human by the Divine

December 2, 9, 1981 (TB 239–243)

If the resurrection signifies man's perfect realization, the Pope affirms that this cannot consist in a mutual opposition of spirit and body, but only in a deep harmony between them. Of course, according to the "system of forces" within man, the spirit has primacy over the body. But original sin disrupted this system of forces in man, and the body often rebels against the spirit. St. Paul expressed this so well: "I see in my members another law at war with the law of my mind" (Rom 7:23). However, in the

---

14. *Epistle to the Philippians,* series 2, v. 13.

15. 3/18/81, TB 209.

16. *Mystagogical Catecheses,* 2:2.

17. *CCC,* n. 1027.

"other world," the primacy of the spirit will be realized and manifested in a "perfect spontaneity" without any opposition from the body. John Paul carefully points out that this must not be understood as a definitive "victory" of the spirit over the body. That would imply some remaining tension: an extrinsic domination of the spirit and a reluctant submission of the body. In the resurrection, however, no tension will exist. The body will return to perfect unity and harmony with the spirit. Thus, opposition between the spiritual and the physical in man will cease. John Paul says, "We could speak here also of a perfect system of forces in mutual relations between what is spiritual in man and what is physical" (241).

A. Divinizing Spiritualization of the Body

Christ's comparison of men and women to angels points to a perfect "spiritualization" of the body. This means that the spirit "will fully permeate the body, and that the forces of the spirit will permeate the energies of the body" (241). Man and woman knew something of this in the beginning (see §20). Indeed, the rupture of the harmony of body and spirit specifically caused the entrance of shame (see §27). Furthermore, through the redemption of the body, historical man "can, as the result of persevering work," regain that harmony and "express a personality that is spiritually mature" (241). Even so, Christ's words about the resurrection refer to a dimension of spiritualization different from that of earthly life. John Paul adds that this is a spiritualization even different from that of the "beginning" itself.[18]

One of the main differences, John Paul says, is that the eschatological spiritualization of the body precludes any opposition between body and spirit. Original man, although fully integrated, had the possibility of disintegration (as original sin attests). Historical man can progressively regain integration, but he can still and often does fall prey to concupiscence. Eschatological man will experience a "perfect spiritualization," which makes it impossible that "another law" would be at war with the law of the mind (see Rom 7:23). Hence, this state "is differentiated essentially (and not only with regard to degree) from what we experience in earthly life" (241).

---

18. Here we gain insight into the soteriological principle (principle of salvation) that through Christ's redemption we gain even more than what we had in the state of original innocence. Hence, in the liturgy of the Easter Vigil, the Church exults in the "happy fault" of Adam.

Furthermore, the spirit that will totally permeate the body is not only man's own spirit. It is the Holy Spirit. So the Pope speaks of a "divinizing spiritualization."[19] For "the sons of the resurrection" in Luke 20:36 are not only "equal to angels." They are also "sons of God." This is why "the degree of 'spiritualization' characteristic of 'eschatological' man will have its source in the degree of his 'divinization'" (242). This means man's destiny is to participate in the very divinity of the Trinity through the *in*-spiration of his body by the Holy Spirit's power. And this is all revealed in our corporality and sexuality. In the beginning, man's creation as male and female and his call to conjugal communion "constituted a primordial sacrament understood as a sign that transmits effectively in the visible world the invisible mystery hidden in God from time immemorial. And this is the mystery of truth and love, the mystery of divine life, in which man really participates."[20]

Through their experience of original unity, man and woman participated in the *very humanness* of each other. This was an effective sign of their call to participate in the *very divinity* of God (see §22). But the divinization to come will not be mediated by an earthly sign.[21] Hence, the future divinization is "incomparably superior to the one that can be attained in earthly life." It "is a question not only of a different degree, but, in a way, of another kind of 'divinization'" (242).

This means that the consummate union of earth is consummated, so to speak, only in the consummate union of heaven. As the *Catechism* teaches, *"For man*, this consummation will be the final realization of the unity of the human race, which God willed from creation...Those who are united with Christ will form the community of the redeemed, 'the holy city' of God, 'the Bride, the wife of the Lamb.'"[22] In the Lamb's gift of self to his Bride, John Paul says that "penetration and permeation of what is essentially human by what is essentially divine, will then reach its peak so that the life of the human spirit will arrive at such fullness which previously had been absolutely inaccessible to it" (242). This is man's ultimate "participation in divine nature." It is man's ultimate "participation in the interior life of God himself." It is his ultimate participation in *grace* (see §§20, 37). This grace is "the communication of God in his very divinity, not only to man's soul, but to his whole psychosomatic subjectivity"

19. 1/13/82, TB 248.

20. 2/20/80, TB 76.

21. See, *CCC*, nn. 1023, 1136.

22. *CCC*, n. 1045.

(242). By virtue of this grace, man will "conceive" divine life within him and bear it continually in the Holy Spirit. Of course the spousal analogy is ultimately inadequate in conveying the mystery. Nonetheless, we see something of the mystery "stamped" in our very being as male and female and in our call to nuptial union.

■ How can we not, at this point, be reminded of Mary as the model of the Church and the archetype of humanity? She is the one who in this life was impregnated with divine life! She is the one who in this life allowed her entire person—body and soul—to be permeated by the Holy Spirit. Hence, she is our eschatological hope. For in her, the redemption of the body is already brought to completion.

B. Nuptial Meaning of the Beatific Vision

John Paul speaks of this divine communication to man's "psychosomatic subjectivity" (his soul-body personhood) and not only to a generic "human nature" in order to emphasize the personal and communal dimension of God's heavenly gift. Heaven is a "union with God in his Trinitarian mystery and of intimacy with him in the perfect communion of persons. This intimacy—with all its subjective intensity—will not absorb man's personal subjectivity, but rather will make it stand out to an incomparably greater and fuller extent" (242). In other words, each person's uniqueness will not be lost or absorbed into the Trinity. Each person will shine in the full glory of his or her unrepeatability.

Once again, all of this was foreshadowed in some way through that original, beatifying union of man and woman who, full of grace, did not know shame in their nakedness. By surrendering themselves to each other, each person was not lost or absorbed in the other but, in fact, discovered his (her) true self through the sincere gift of self (see §23). In an infinitely greater dimension—in the definitive fulfillment of every human longing for union—we will discover our true selves in the resurrection when we respond to the gift of God with the sincere gift of ourselves to him.

From the beginning, human embodiment—connected as it is with erotic desire for union with an "other"—was meant to be a sign of and a preparation for that ultimate union with the ultimate Other. John Paul concludes that in "this 'spiritualization' and 'divinization' in which man will participate in the resurrection, we discover—in an eschatological dimension—the same characteristics that qualified the 'nuptial' meaning of the body" (243). This time, however, all those characteristics (the complementarity of the sexes; the call to life-giving communion; the desire to see another and be seen by that other) are fulfilled "in the meeting with the mystery of the living God, which is revealed through the vision of him 'face to face'" (243). The *Catechism* speaks of this fulfillment when it says that the Church "longs to be united with Christ, her Bridegroom, in the glory of heaven" where she "will rejoice one day with [her] Beloved, in a happiness and rapture that can never end."[23]

John Paul asks whether it is possible to think of this eschatological experience of the nuptial meaning of the body above all as the "virginal" meaning of being male and female—of the "virginal" experience of nuptial union and communion. To answer this question, the Holy Father says we must first penetrate more deeply into the "very essence" of the beatific vision.[24]

51. The Body: Witness to the Eschatological Experience

December 9, 16, 1981 (TB 241–244)

"Divinization" in the future world, the Pope says, "will bring the human spirit such a 'range of experience' of truth and love such as man would never have been able to attain in earthly life." If we are to penetrate "into the very essence" of this divinization, into the very essence of the beatific vision, it is "necessary to let oneself be guided by that 'range of experience' of truth and love which goes beyond the limits of the cognitive and spiritual possibilities of man in temporality" (242). With these words, John Paul shows himself to be a mystic. Only a mystic can let himself be guided by "a range of experience" beyond time while still living in time. In other words, beyond the principle of continuity (see §48), a phenomenological analysis of man's destiny can only be attempted by someone who has mystically experienced something of life beyond the veil. It seems John Paul has. He stretches words and ideas to their maximum capacity in his attempt to communicate to us something of an "eschatological experience."

A. The Eschatological Experience

As stated previously, from the beginning man was created to be a "partner of the Absolute" (see §12). He was called to enter a covenant with God—a relationship of eternal communion analogous to the union of spouses (see §17). Man broke this original covenant with God by eating from the forbidden tree. Yet God's gift of himself to man is irreversible (see §20). Christ's coming is the ultimate testimony of God's irreversible

---

23. *CCC*, n. 1821.
24. See *CCC*, n. 1028.

gift. If historical man is willing to pass by way of the cross, not only can he recover that original communion with God, but he opens himself to the living hope of the eschatological fulfillment of this communion.

In this eschatological fulfillment, we will know "in a deep and experiential way, the 'self-communication of God' to the whole of creation." In particular, we will know and experience the self-communication of God to us. This "is the most personal self-giving by God in his very divinity" because we are "that being who, from the beginning, bears within himself the image and likeness of God" (243). We are that being who bears within him the interior dimension of the gift (see §22). In this eschatological experience, the interior dimension of the gift in man—expressed and made visible "in the beginning" through the nakedness of the body—will meet its divine prototype "face to face." All our energies will be concentrated on receiving the Gift of the living God and reciprocating that love by giving ourselves back to him. This "eschatological communion *(communio)* of man with God," the Pope says, "will be nourished by the...contemplation of that more perfect communion—because it is purely divine—which is the trinitarian communion of the divine Persons in the unity of the same divinity" (243).

In other words, our union with the living God springs from the beatific vision of his unity and Trinitarian Communion. Beholding the total, perfect, and incessant reciprocal giving of the Trinity will inspire us to give ourselves incessantly to God in response to his eternal gift to us. In this way, the object of the beatific vision "will be that mystery hidden in the Father from eternity, a mystery which in time was revealed in Christ, in order to be accomplished incessantly through the Holy Spirit" (243).

B. The Body as a Witness to Love

In a word, that mystery we shall behold "face to face" is love (see 1 Jn 4:8). Love is gift; and gift is grace; and grace received is communion—*with the divine*. Recalling John Paul's thesis, this mystery of love and gift (and grace and communion) hidden in God from all eternity and definitively revealed in Christ was made visible from the beginning by the sign of the body in its masculinity and femininity (see §22). Man and woman embody the reality of gift. Hence, the body has a nuptial meaning. As previously quoted (see §17), John Paul says, "This is the body: a witness to creation as a fundamental gift, and so a witness to Love as the source from which this same giving springs. Masculinity-femininity—namely, sex—is the original sign of a creative donation [by God] and of an awareness on the part of man, of a gift lived so to speak in an original way."[25]

---

25. 1/9/80, TB 62.

This "original way" of living the gift of God's love (grace) was revealed in the experiences of original solitude, unity, and nakedness. The "historical way" of living the gift seeks to recover the grace of creation through the redemption of the body. Finally, the "eschatological way" of living the gift not only fully recovers the original purity, but takes us infinitely beyond to an entirely new dimension—to an immediate *bodily* participation in the Trinitarian mystery of love and gift. This Trinitarian mystery of love and gift will become "the content of the eschatological experience and the 'form' of the entire human existence in the dimension of the 'other world'" (243). Therefore, the Pope says that eternal life in the resurrection must be understood as the full and perfect experience of grace.

Our first parents experienced the original dimension of this grace in the beginning. We participate in it as well through faith and the sacraments. However, this grace will only "reveal itself in all its penetrating depth to those who partake in the 'other world.'" There, the grace already given in creation and restored in redemption will "be experienced in its beatifying reality" (243).

C. The Perfection of Subjectivity

This ultimate participation in grace, in the very life and love of God, is what enables all that is physical in man to participate perfectly in all that is spiritual in him. At the same time this experience will consist in the perfect realization of what is personal in man. According to the great "nuptial mystery," we are created to be Bride of Christ. In giving ourselves totally to Christ, we do not lose ourselves. We discover ourselves (see Mk 8:35). In submitting ourselves as a Bride to our eternal Bridegroom, we are not dominated; we are not abased. We are loved (see Eph 5:25). We are served (see Mt 20:28). We are filled to the full with life (see Jn 10:10). If we doubt that surrendering totally to God provides the key to our freedom and the fulfillment of our personal subjectivity, we are still duped by the father of lies. We are still "questioning the gift" (see §26). If we only knew the gift of God and who it is that offers it to us (see Jn 4:10)!

Not only will participants in the other world rediscover their authentic subjectivity, but the Pope repeatedly affirms that they will acquire it to a far more perfect extent than in earthly life. By living in "perfect communion with the living God," they will enjoy a perfectly mature subjectivity. This confirms what John Paul calls "the law of the integral order of the person." According to this law, as a personal subject, man is created for his own sake (solitude), but he is not called to live for his own sake. He can only perfect his subjectivity through the sincere gift of self, that is, through a perfect experience of inter-subjectivity (unity). In turn, the perfection of communion is conditioned by the spiritual maturity of the subjects who enter that communion. We can see this clearly in the case of marriage. A marriage is only as healthy as those who enter it. However, at the same time, and according to the same law of the integral order of the person, the perfection of communion determines the perfection of the participants in that communion. In marriage, as the spouses' communion grows in perfection, so do the spouses.

Man and woman knew the earthly model (the primordial sacrament) of this perfect communion in the beginning. To the extent that we allow the ethos of redemption to permeate us, we can rediscover and live according to this original earthly model. But in the resurrection, the earthly model will give way to the divine prototype, and human subjectivity will be perfected through an immediate experience of inter-subjectivity with the divine Subject who, himself, lives an eternal mystery of divine inter-Subjectivity. *This* is why men and women are no longer given in marriage in the resurrection. Their call to communion will be fulfilled in an eternal communion with *the* Eternal Communion.

52. The Eschatological Authenticity of the Gift

December 16, 1981; January 13, 1982 (TB 244–249)

In his exchange with the Pharisees, Christ speaks of the state of marriage "in the beginning." In his exchange with the Sadducees, he speaks of the state of marriage in the future. These two "words" of Christ are linked together almost as bookends in John Paul's "total vision of man."

A. A New Threshold for Understanding Man

John Paul says that Christ's words about the resurrection enable us to understand the meaning of that original "one flesh" unity in a whole new dimension. Recall that John Paul described Genesis 2:24 ("the two shall become one flesh") as a perspective text, indicating that it "will have in the revelation of God an ample and distant perspective."[26] Here the Pope says that Christ's words about the resurrection and the state of male and female in the resurrection are of decisive importance "not only as regards the words of the book of Genesis," but "in what concerns the entire Bible" (249).[27]

Christ's words on the resurrection "enable us, in a certain sense, to read again—that is, in depth—the whole revealed meaning of the body,

---

26. 11/14/79, TB 47.

27. Recall that what we learn in the theology of the body is no side issue. It concerns "the perspective of the whole Gospel, of the whole teaching, in fact, of the whole mission of Christ" (see §§9, 40).

the meaning of being a man, that is, a person 'incarnated,' of being male or female as regards the body" (249). In the beginning, the meaning of our creation as male and female was revealed as "gift." Man and woman were created first to receive the gift of God's gratuitous love, and then to recapitulate that love by being gift to each other (see §17). "Therefore," as Genesis 2:24 proclaims, "a man leaves his father and his mother and cleaves to his wife, and they become one flesh." This was the consummate expression of the gift in the beginning, which established that incarnate communion of persons (see §14).

The words of Genesis 2:24 refer "especially to this world," the Pope says, but "not completely" (249). These are "the words that constitute the sacrament of marriage."[28] Hence, like all sacraments, the "one flesh" unity of marriage points in some way to the "other world." There, the gift will be consummated in an eternal, eschatological dimension of "incarnate communion" inclusive of all who respond to the wedding invitation of the Lamb. If, as John Paul says, the words of Genesis (and from the context it seems the Pope is speaking specifically of Genesis 2:24) "were almost the threshold of the whole theology of the body," Christ's words about the resurrection present almost "a new threshold of this complete truth about man, which we find in God's revealed Word. It is indispensable to dwell upon this threshold," the Pope says, "if we wish our theology of the body—and also our Christian 'spirituality of the body'—to be able to use it as a complete image" (249).

B. Divine-Human Communion

John Paul explains the absence of marriage in the resurrection not only with the end of history, but also—and above all—with what he calls the "eschatological authenticity" of man's response to God's self-giving. In the consummation of the gift in the resurrection, the divine Subject (God) will give himself to the human subject (man) in a beatifying experience "absolutely superior to any experience proper to earthly life. The reciprocal gift of oneself to God...will be the response to God's gift of himself to man" (244). By virtue of the eternal Word made flesh, this too will be an *incarnate* gift, an incarnate communion.

Keeping in mind the ever greater dissimilarity in the analogy while also focusing on the intrinsic similarity, we are talking about the ultimate consummation of the marriage of divinity and humanity. We are talking about the eternal, beatifying experience of a perfect divine-human intersubjectivity; a perfect divine-human *communio personarum*. We are talk-

---

28. 2/20/80, TB 76.

ing about the eschatological fulfillment of that "perspective text" of Genesis 2:24. As St. Paul says, the union in one flesh is a "great mystery," and it refers to the union of Christ and the Church (see Eph 5:31–32). Christ left his Father in heaven; he left the home of his mother on earth—to give up his body for his Bride so that we, the Bride of Christ, might become "one flesh" with him. What was foreshadowed from the beginning in the incarnate communion of man and woman (marriage) and definitively revealed in the incarnate communion of Christ and the Church (Eucharist) will be lived eternally in the resurrection.

This is the ultimate meaning of "being a body"; of being male and female in the divine image. Sexual difference and our longing for union reveal that we are created for eternal communion with *the* eternal Communion: Father, Son, and Holy Spirit. Participation in this eternal Communion will be a completely new experience, but it will not be alienated from the earthly experience of communion. The earthly communion, then, will not be eradicated—it will be definitively fulfilled.

Again, we can see Satan's reason for attacking man and woman's communion in the beginning and throughout history. It is the primordial sign in creation of God's plan to take on flesh and be one with us. This is precisely what Satan wants to thwart. But all he can do in his attempts to counter God's plan is plagiarize the sacraments. All he can do is twist what God created to be true, good, and beautiful. This means all of the sexual confusion in our world—and in our own hearts—is simply the human desire for heaven gone berserk. Untwist it and we rediscover the image of God in every human being; we rediscover the deep human longing—that God put there—for union with him. G. K. Chesterton expressed the same idea when he wrote: "Every man who knocks on the door of a brothel is looking for God."[29]

C. Knowledge of God

John Paul speaks of the beatific vision as "a concentration of knowledge and love on God himself." This knowledge "cannot be other than full participation in the interior life of God, that is, in the very trinitarian reality" (244). We can recall at this point our previous discussion of biblical "knowledge" (see §23). Through their knowledge of each other in Genesis, man and woman came to know "a third." In some sense they came to participate in a created version, so to speak, of the uncreated relations of the Trinity (see §20).

29. Dooley, David, ed. *The Collected Works of G. K. Chesterton* Volume I (San Francisco: Ignatius, 1986).

The entire cosmos, in fact, bears the mark of its Creator; the mark of trinitarian relations.[30] John Paul says the knowledge of God in heaven will be at the same time the discovery, in God, of "the whole world of relations" that are part of God's perennial order in the cosmos. In other words, the eschatological experience will not only be man's full participation in the *uncreated* world of relations (the Trinity). It will also be a full participation in the *created* world of relations. This includes a full participation in man's original harmony with creation[31] *and* a full participation in the original created communion of persons.

This means that created relations will not be annulled or overridden by participation in the uncreated relation. As John Paul says, "The concentration of knowledge and love on God himself in the trinitarian communion of Persons can find a beatifying response in [man] only through realizing mutual communion adapted to created persons. And for this reason," he says, "we profess faith in the communion of saints" (244).[32]

53. Fulfillment of the Nuptial Meaning of the Body

December 16, 1981; January 13, 1982 (TB 244–249)

Christ's words do not fall in a void, whether he speaks of the beginning or of the future resurrection. If we experience an "echo" of our beginning deep within our hearts, we also experience a kind of "premonition" of our destiny. In fact, the earthly experience of the body "supplies the substratum and the base" of the heavenly experience of the body (246). Although "it is difficult to construct a fully adequate image of the 'future world,'...at the same time there is no doubt that, with the help of Christ's words, at least a certain approximation to this image is possible and attainable" (248).

---

30. See *CCC,* n. 237. See also *Dominum et Vivificantem,* n. 50 for a concise statement of the cosmic dimensions of Trinitarian relations as manifested by the Incarnation.

31. See *CCC,* nn. 1047–1048. As St. Paul says, "We know that the whole creation has been groaning in travail [awaiting] the redemption of our bodies" (Rom 8:22–23). Despite the exaggerations of some environmentalist and "animal rights" groups, there is nonetheless a fundamental rightness in man's concern and love for creation (see *CCC,* nn. 2415–2418). When we untwist the distortions, we rediscover a fundamental longing for harmony with creation that was part of God's original plan. John Paul previously described the "cosmic shame" that manifests the breaking of this harmony with creation (see §27).

32. See *CCC,* nn. 1474–1477.

The nuptial meaning of the body gives John Paul the key for constructing an image of the "future world." The call to be gift (to love as God loves) is inscribed in the interior and exterior structure of the human person from "the beginning." This primordial truth finds its eschatological realization in the reciprocal gift of God and man to each other in an eternal divine-human communion of persons. However, as mentioned above, man's participation in the uncreated Communion of the Trinity is also a perfect realization of the created communion of persons. Not only will we be "one" with God; we will be "one" with everyone who responds to the wedding invitation of the Lamb.

A. A Union of Communion

Paraphrasing John Paul, the communion of saints consists of many created communions united with each other by contemplating the vision of that Uncreated Communion (the Trinity). In turn, man's beatific vision of the Trinity constitutes a real communion with this Uncreated Communion. This "union of communion," as the Pope describes it (244), is an eternal and mysterious unity of created communions with the Uncreated Communion. In this ultimate reality we will see all and be seen by all. We will know all and be known by all. And God will be "all in all" (Eph 1:23).

If you find yourself lost in the communion of these communions, drawing from the logic of the nuptial meaning of the body, we can say this. In the eschatological experience, we who are many as male and female will form one body (see 1 Cor 10:17). In a manner beyond our present comprehension,[33] all that is masculine in humanity will be in union with all that is feminine in humanity. In turn, this "one body" will form the one Bride of Christ who, through eternal union with her Bridegroom, will live in eternal communion with the Trinity. As the Pope says, and we have already quoted, we must think of this reality in terms of "the rediscovery of a new perfect subjectivity of everyone and at the same time of the rediscovery of a new perfect intersubjectivity of all." This reality, the Pope continues, "signifies the real and definitive fulfillment of human subjectivity, and, on this basis, the definitive fulfillment of the 'nuptial' meaning of the body. The complete concentration of created subjectivity, redeemed and glorified, on God himself, will not take man away from this fulfillment; in fact—on the contrary—it will introduce him into it and consolidate him in it." Finally, the Pope concludes that "in this way, eschatological reality will become the source of the perfect realization of the trinitarian order in the created world of persons" (245).

---

33. See *CCC,* nn. 1000, 1027.

When the Pope speaks of "the trinitarian order," he is speaking of unity-in-plurality, oneness-in-multitude, a communion-of-solitudes. In the beginning, biblical "knowledge" signified a communion so intimate and unifying that man and woman became "almost the one subject of that act and that experience, while remaining, in this unity, two really different subjects."[34] In a similar way, the great multitude of subjects that form the communion of saints in communion with the Trinity will be almost the one subject of that act and experience of eternal self-giving, while remaining, in this unity, a multitude of different subjects (both human and divine). Human participation in the "trinitarian order" means a participation in the perfect unity and distinction found within the Trinity itself.[35] "That nuptial meaning of the body will be realized, therefore," according to John Paul, "as a meaning that is perfectly personal and communitarian at the same time" (247–248).

B. *Virginal Communion*

Harkening back to that original "virginal value of man," John Paul says that in man's beatifying gift of himself to God, "as a response worthy of a personal subject to God's gift of himself, 'virginity,' or rather the virginal state of the body will be totally manifested as the eschatological fulfillment of the 'nuptial' meaning of the body" (244). Recall that virginity in the state of innocence was not first to be understood as the absence of bodily union, but as the integrity of body and soul—as the state of man in "solitude" before God. Hence, the original incarnate communion of man and woman did not rob them of virginity, but affirmed it, because it also affirmed man in "solitude" before God (see §15).

Therefore, if man's destiny is to be understood as the definitive fulfillment of his origin, the incarnate communion of saints in union with the Trinity must be understood as a virginal communion. For, as we have already quoted John Paul saying, man's ultimate beatitude "must be understood as the state of man definitively and perfectly integrated through [the] union of the soul and the body."[36] According to the Pope, virginity is "the specific sign and the authentic expression of all personal subjectivity" (244) because it is the specific sign of man's psychosomatic integration. "In this way, therefore, that eschatological situation in which they 'neither marry nor are given in marriage' has its solid foundation in the future state of the personal subject" (244); that future state of perfect "virginal" integration.

---

34. 3/5/80, TB 79.

35. See *CCC*, nn. 254–255, 689.

36. 12/2/81, TB 240.

Again, this does not mean absence of union but, rather, perfection of union. The "'nuptial' meaning of the body in the resurrection to the future life will correspond perfectly both to the fact that man, as male and female, is a person created 'in the image and likeness of God,' and to the fact that this image is realized in the communion of persons" (247). And the Pope affirms that this will be a "union which is proper to the world of [human] persons in their psychosomatic constitution" (244).

C. Perfect Freedom of the Gift

"This will be a completely new experience," the Pope says. Yet "at the same time it will not be alienated in any way from what man took part in from 'the beginning' nor from what, in the historical dimension of his existence, constituted in him the source of the tension between spirit and body, concerning mainly the procreative meaning of the body and sex. The man of the 'future world' will find again in this new experience of his own body precisely the completion of what he bore within himself perennially and historically" (248). In the beginning the body was a sign of the person and his call to communion. Throughout history, the original meaning of that sign has been obscured. John Paul observes that the heritage of concupiscence has weighed us down with endless limitations, struggles, and sufferings. In the resurrection, however, that original sign will not only be restored; it will be fulfilled. The body, as it was created to do from the beginning, will reveal the eternal mystery hidden in God and enable us to participate in it.

"The perennial meaning of the human body...will then be revealed again, and will be revealed in such simplicity and splendor when every participant in the 'other world' will find again in his glorified body the source of the freedom of the gift" (248). What was the source of the freedom of the gift in the beginning? Grace, the indwelling of God's breath in the dust of our humanity, the spiritualization of the body, the perfect integrity of body and soul (see §§18, 20). Therefore, the "glorification of the body, as the eschatological fruit of its divinizing spiritualization, will reveal...the perfect 'freedom of the sons of God' (see Rom 8:14)." This "freedom lies precisely at the basis of the nuptial meaning of the body" and "is indispensable in order that man...may become a gift."[37] Thus, in the eschatological fulfillment of the nuptial meaning of the body, the perfect freedom of the gift will nourish "each of the communions which will make up the great community of the communion of saints" (248).

---

37. 1/16/80, TB 63, 64.

54. A Development of the Truth about Man
January 13; February 3, 1982 (TB 247, 254)

Man and woman's call to marriage and procreation is fundamental in the mystery of creation. It touches upon the core anthropological reality (see §14). Christ presents "a development of the truth about man himself" when he explains that in the resurrection we neither marry nor are given in marriage. Yet, according to the Pope, "man will always be the same, such as he came from the hands of his Creator and Father" (247). Christ does not state that eschatological man will no longer be male and female as he was "from the beginning." He merely indicates that the meaning of being male or female in the eschaton must be sought outside marriage and procreation. However, John Paul affirms that "there is no reason to seek it outside that which...derives from the very mystery of creation and which subsequently forms also the deepest structure of man's history on earth, since this history has been deeply penetrated by the mystery of redemption" (247).

A. Communion Is Fundamental

What is it that derives from the very mystery of creation, forms the deepest structure of man's history on earth, and will, therefore, also form the basis of the meaning of the body in the resurrection? Man is created as male and female to form a "unity of the two." The Pope says that in his solitude, man is revealed to himself as a person in order to reveal, at the same time, the communion of persons. In both states (solitude and communion) the human being is constituted as an image and likeness of God.

In the purity of original nakedness, man discovered his fundamental call to communion in the nuptial meaning of the body. Throughout history the primary way man has entered into this communion is through the call to marriage and procreation. However, as those crucial words of Christ make clear, this will not be the case in the resurrection. Summarizing his previous reflections, John Paul says that this "indicates that there is a condition of life without marriage in which man, male and female, finds at the same time the fullness of personal donation and of the intersubjective communion of persons, thanks to the glorification of his entire psychosomatic being in the eternal union with God."[38] He also summarizes his vision of the eschaton when he says that "the divinizing profundity" of the vision of God "face to face" will enable men and women to live the nuptial meaning of their bodies in a simultaneous experience of "perpetual

---

38. 3/10/82, TB 262.

'virginity'" *and* "perpetual 'intersubjectivity'" (254). The Holy Spirit dwelling *in our flesh* will be "the inexhaustible source" of this perfect, eternal, virgin-union.

For historical man, this means that earthly marriage is not his end-all and be-all. It is given only to prepare for and anticipate the "marriage" to come. John Paul expresses the same idea in this striking statement: "Marriage and procreation in itself did not determine definitively the original and fundamental meaning of being a body, or of being, as a body, male and female. Marriage and procreation merely give a concrete reality to that meaning in the dimensions of history" (247). If historical man has lost his bearings due to sin and has been adrift on a meaningless sea, this statement guides him back to shore. Even more, disembarking from his wayward vessel, the truth contained in this statement is the *terra firma* on which man stands in order to be rightly oriented in *his-story* between the echoes of his origin and the premonitions of his destiny.

■ It is entirely human to yearn for marital love. Yet we must be careful never to "hang our hats on a hook that cannot bear the weight." Anyone who looks to marriage as his ultimate fulfillment is setting himself up for serious disillusionment. Realizing that earthly marriage is only a sign of the heavenly marriage to come, and that the union to come is a gift extended to everyone without exception, takes a tremendous burden off people's expectations for ultimate happiness through marriage in this life. Only within this perspective does marriage even take on its authentic purpose and meaning. Only within this perspective will a person who enters marriage be able to avoid suffocating his spouse with his expectations and hopes for ultimate fulfillment. Then and only then can marriage bring the true measure of happiness and joy it is intended to bring. As a married man, I will be the first to extol the joys of married life. But these are only a foretaste, only a foreshadowing of the eternal joys to come.

B. Icon or Idol?

As soon as man steps off this *terra firma*, he forgets that marriage is only a temporal icon of an eternal reality. Then the "one flesh" union becomes an idol. When this happens, paraphrasing St. Paul, God gives us up in the lusts of our hearts to impurity. We dishonor our bodies, worshiping them instead of the Creator. Claiming to be wise, we become fools, exchanging the glory of the immortal God for its mere image (see Rom 22–25).

The image is only that—an image, an icon. Icons are meant to point us to something far greater than themselves. When we lose sight of this, we worship the icon itself. To use another image, that deep spiritual-physical craving that man experiences for union in "one flesh" is like the energy of a rocket that, when rightly directed, launches us into the stars and even to the edge of eternity itself. When nuptial union is understood and lived in this way, even the beatifying joys of the marital embrace are experienced as a kind of earthly foreshadowing of the eternal joys of heaven.[39] But what would happen if we inverted the rocket's engines, aiming them away from the stars and back upon ourselves? The rocket could only backfire in a blast of self-destruction. And we would be left trying desperately to make sense out of the charred remains of our lives and our deepest aspirations.

In many ways, it seems this icon-idol distinction summarizes the cultural crisis that the sexual revolution ignited. The greater the gift (human sexuality), the greater the temptation to idolize it. However, when we exchange the truth for a lie—that is, when we exchange the icon for an idol—love becomes lust and we experience all the tragic consequences sin brings.[40] As we shall learn, viewing the "one flesh" union of marriage in light of the celibate vocation is the sure remedy for the world's false, idolatrous cult of the body and sex.

55. St. Paul's Teaching on the Resurrection

January 27; February 3, 10, 1982 (TB 249–257)

John Paul concludes his reflections on eschatological man by devoting three audience addresses to what he calls "the anthropology of the resurrection according to St. Paul" (255). St. Paul expresses his faith in the resurrection throughout his letters, but primarily in chapter fifteen of First Corinthians. Christ's response to the Sadducees was "pre-paschal." He appealed only to the truth of the Old Testament to demonstrate the resurrection—to the truth that the living God "is not the God of the dead, but of the living" (Mk 12:22). Paul, however, in his "post-paschal" argumentation refers above all to the reality of Christ's own resurrection. In fact, Paul defends this truth as the foundation of the Christian Faith in its integ-

---

39. See *CCC,* n. 1642.

40. Who cannot think in this context of the self-inflicted proliferation of sexually transmitted diseases (some fatal, such as AIDS), the abortion holocaust, and the social plague of divorce that has resulted from the idolatry of lust promoted incessantly by the culture of death? And these are only some of the measurable consequences. Although we see the symptoms all around us, the havoc wrought on the souls of hundreds of millions of people cannot be quantified.

rity: "If Christ has not been raised, then our preaching is in vain and your faith is in vain.... But, in fact, Christ has been raised from the dead" (1 Cor 15:14, 20).

A. God's Reply to Death

John Paul describes Christ's resurrection as "the reply of the God of life to the historical inevitability of death." It "is the last and the fullest word of the self-revelation of the living God as 'not God of the dead, but of the living' (Mk 12:27)" (250). St. Paul presents Christ's resurrection as the beginning of our own eschatological fulfillment, our own victory over death. Paul, in fact, following the other Apostles, experienced the state of Jesus' glorified body in his meeting with the risen Christ on the road to Damascus (see Acts 9). When Paul proclaims resurrection, he knows of what he speaks. If we are to live according to the full truth of our bodies— to live according to the image in which we are made—we too must have our own "meeting with the risen Christ." Indeed, the road to human happiness begins and ends in this meeting.

Admitting that it is difficult to sum up here and comment adequately on Paul's "stupendous and ample argumentation" (249), the Pope focuses primarily on the following passage:

> What is sown is perishable, what is raised is imperishable. It is sown in dishonor, it is raised in glory. It is sown in weakness, it is raised in power. It is sown a physical body, it is raised a spiritual body. If there is a physical body, there is also a spiritual body. Thus it is written, "The first man, Adam, became a living being"; the last Adam became a life-giving spirit. But it is not the spiritual which is first but the physical, and then the spiritual (1 Cor 15:42–46).

This teaching is essentially consistent with Christ's words on the resurrection. However, whereas Christ called us to reflect on the resurrected state of the male-female communion, Paul's teaching seems to remain in the sphere of the individual person's interior structure. Paul focuses on that interior "system of forces"; that tension between the flesh and the spirit well known to him (see Rom 7:17–25). However, through the "divinizing spiritualization" of the body, he demonstrates that this "system of forces" will undergo a radical change in the resurrection.

Taking account of various misinterpretations, John Paul carefully points out that Paul's seemingly pejorative description of the body cannot be interpreted in the spirit of dualistic anthropology. This would imply an inherent dishonor to man's bodily constitution contrary to the original good of God's vision. When Paul writes that the body is "weak," "perishable," and "in dishonor," he speaks from the experience of historical man whose body is weighed down by concupiscence. These descriptions, as John

Paul says, indicate what revelation describes as the consequence of sin—what Paul himself will call elsewhere "bondage to decay" (Rom 8:21).

However, according to St. Paul, this "bondage to decay" also conceals within itself the hope of resurrection, just as a woman's labor pains portend the hope of new life (see Rom 8:22). Paul can make this connection between "decay" and "hope" because he understands that the Holy Spirit has been poured out upon us for the redemption of our bodies (see Rom 8:23). As John Paul says, "Redemption is the way to resurrection. The resurrection constitutes the definitive accomplishment of the redemption of the body" (252).[41]

B. The First Adam Bears Potential for the New Adam

It is quite significant that Paul unites man's eschatological perspective with reference to the "first Adam" as well as a deep awareness of man's historical situation. As the Pope points out, by doing so St. Paul synthesizes all that Christ had announced in his three "key words" about "the beginning," about lust in the "heart," and about the "resurrection of the body." Paul's synthesis "plunges its roots into the revealed mystery of creation and redemption as a whole." Man's creation is "the enlivening of matter" or "the animation of the body" by the Spirit (251). In this way, as St. Paul says, "Adam became a living being" (1 Cor 15:45). Man's redemption-resurrection is to be understood in the same way. If the Spirit "died" in us due to sin so that we return to dust (see Gen 3:19), our redemption-resurrection must be the (re)quickening of our dust with the breath of the Spirit. Hence, we see again that St. Paul does not negate the body but speaks of its ultimate dignity as the temple of the Holy Spirit (see 1 Cor 6:19).

■ Notice that in the New Adam's resurrection he, like the first Adam, comes forth from the ground at the moment of the Spirit's *in*-spiration. Describing the earth as a "mother" has a definite element of truth. Significantly, both John and Luke mention that Christ was put in a tomb not previously used (see Jn 19:41 and Lk 23:53). As stated earlier, Christ was born of a virgin womb and "born again" of a virgin tomb. Similarly, on the last day, at the moment of the Spirit's *in*-spiration, the earth will in some sense "give birth" virginally to all those who have returned to dust in joyful hope of the coming of their Savior, Jesus Christ.[42]

The re-quickening of the body by the Spirit does not only restore man's original state before sin. According to the Pope, that would not "cor-

---

41. See *CCC,* n. 1026.
42. See *CCC,* n. 1683.

respond to the internal logic of the whole economy of salvation, to the most profound meaning of the *mystery* of the redemption." The re-inspiration of the flesh in the redemption-resurrection "can only be an *introduction* to a *new fullness"* (see §50). "This will be a fullness that presupposes the whole of human history, formed by the drama of the tree of the knowledge of good and evil" (255 – 256).

In contrasting the first Adam with the last Adam (Christ), Paul tries to show that historical man has been placed in a sort of tension between two poles. John Paul says that between these two poles—between the first and the second Adam—takes place the process that St. Paul expresses as follows: "As we have borne the image of the man of earth, so we will bear the image of the man of heaven" (1 Cor 15:49). Yet the Pope stresses that the "man of heaven" is not an antithesis and negation of the "man of earth." He is above all his completion and confirmation. Already in our creation, our humanity "bears in itself," the Holy Father says, "a particular potential (which is capacity and readiness) to receive all that became the 'second Adam,' the Man of heaven, namely Christ: what he became in his resurrection" (253).

Viewing this through the lens of the "nuptial mystery," we can say that just as a bride is made in her very being as a woman to receive her bridegroom, so too is man (male and female) made to receive Christ. John Paul observes that among all the bodies in the cosmos, the human body bears in itself the "potentiality for resurrection"—that is, it bears the aspiration and capacity to become definitively "incorruptible, glorious, full of dynamism, spiritual." This is possible because right from the beginning man is made in the image of God as male and female, body and soul. In this way John Paul says that man "can receive and reproduce in this 'earthly' image and likeness of God also the 'heavenly' image of the second Adam, Christ" (254).

Since "every man bears in himself the image of Adam," it can be said that "every man is also called to bear in himself the image of Christ, the image of the risen One." This reality will only be consummated in the other world. "But in the meantime it is already in a certain way a reality of this world, since it was revealed in this world through the resurrection of Christ" (254).

C. The Spiritual Body

Christ's resurrection is a reality "ingrafted" in our humanity. Even though our bodies are sown "in weakness" and are "perishable," we bear in ourselves at the same time, the Pope says, "the interior desire for glory" (253). God put it there "in the beginning"—not to frustrate us by dashing our hopes, but to lead us to fulfillment in him. All hopes, therefore, must be placed in our resurrection. Then the body that we experience as perishable will be raised imperishable. The body that we experience as weighed down in dishonor and weakness will be raised in glory and power. For what is sown a physical body is raised a spiritual body.

"Body" in this sense refers to the whole person in his psychosomatic subjectivity. Thus, Paul is not contrasting a material reality with a non-material reality. The "physical body" is the whole person inasmuch as he resists and opposes the Holy Spirit. It is the man who lives "according to the flesh" (see §41). The "spiritual body" is the whole person inasmuch as he remains under the influence of the vivifying Spirit of Christ. As the Pope states in an endnote, in contrast to any dualistic notion of the person, St. Paul "insists on the fact that body and soul are capable of being...spiritual" (261). While spirituality has a just supremacy over sensuality, we must not think that the sensual life fundamentally opposes the spiritual life.[43] If we experience sensuality as "a force prejudicial to man," this is due only to sin. Man's senses are "often attracted and, as it were, impelled toward evil" (256) only because of concupiscence.

At the same time he denies the lustful cravings of disordered sensuality, the man of concupiscence must open sensuality to the total penetration and permeation of the Spirit. Then he experiences the "fundamental function of the senses that serves to liberate spirituality" (256). This is what Paul means by the "spiritual body." It is, as the Holy Father expresses, "precisely *the perfect sensitivity of the senses, their perfect harmonization with the activity of the human spirit* in truth and liberty" (256). Thus, as the *Catechism* says, "The virtuous person tends toward the good with all his sensory and spiritual powers."[44] For those who have entered an alliance with the Holy Spirit, this spiritual-sensual unity is a reality already developing in them toward final completion.

■ With the dualistic worldview we have inherited from Descartes, it is very difficult for modern men and women to understand the Pauline concept of a "spiritual body." As Peter Kreeft observes: "'Spiritual' to premodern cultures did not mean 'immaterial.' Pre-Cartesian cultures did not divide reality into two mutually exclusive categories of purely immaterial spirit and purely nonspiritual matter. Rather, they saw all matter as *in-*

---

43. As Wojtyla said in *Love & Responsibility*, "An exuberant and readily roused sensuality is the stuff from which a rich—if difficult—personal life may be made. It may help the individual to respond more readily and completely to the decisive elements in personal love" (p. 109).

44. *CCC,* n. 1803.

formed, *in*-breathed by spirit." Kreeft elaborates: "Descartes initiates 'angelism' when he says, 'My whole essence is in thought alone.' Matter and spirit now become 'two clear and distinct ideas.'...This is *our* common sense; we have inherited these categories, like nonremovable contact lenses, from Descartes, and it is impossible for us to understand pre-Cartesian thinkers while we wear them. Thus we are constantly reading our modern categories anachronistically into the authors of the Bible."[45] Proof of Kreeft's assertion is that St. Paul's "spiritual body" seems like a pure contradiction in terms to most moderns.

D. In Conclusion

Having reflected on the triptych of Christ's words about man's experience of embodiment and erotic desire in his origin, history, and destiny, John Paul concludes his outline of an adequate anthropology. But how is this total vision of man meant to inform the vocational path of men and women in this life? How can historical man respond to the truth of his creation as male and female in God's image? How is historical man to live out the redemption of the body as he awaits its final consummation? As John Paul will continue to demonstrate in his next cycles, there are two basic ways of doing so: celibacy for the kingdom and marriage. Each in its own way is an adequate response to an adequate anthropology.

Eschatological Man—In Review

1. When the Sadducees questioned Jesus about the resurrection with a marriage case which they thought would lead to the admission of polyandry, Christ responded by saying that in the resurrection, men and women "neither marry nor are given in marriage." This stupendous response is the third element in the "triptych" of Christ's words which constitute and, in this case, complete "the revelation of the body."

2. God is the God of the living, not of the dead. He is the God of life! Christ's resurrection is the ultimate word on the subject. Marriage and its consummate expression also testify to God as the God of life. But in the resurrection, marriage and conjugal union lose their *raison d'être*. They exist "from the beginning" to point us to the Marriage of the Lamb. When

---

45. *Everything You Ever Wanted to Know about Heaven*, pp. 86–87.

this marriage is consummated, the primordial sacrament will give way to the divine prototype.

3. When, in referring to the resurrection, Christ says we will be "like angels in heaven," this does not mean we will be disincarnated. Since man was constituted "from the beginning" as male and female in a unity of body and soul, his eschatological perfection cannot be understood as a state of the soul alone. His body will be raised and glorified in an infinitely perfected masculinity and femininity.

4. In our resurrected integration, the mutual opposition between body and soul that resulted from original sin will cease utterly. The forces of the spirit will fully permeate the energies of the body. This eschatological "spiritualization of the body" will differ essentially (and not only in degree) from what we experience in earthly life. It is different even from what man and woman experienced "in the beginning."

5. The spirit totally permeating the body is not only man's spirit, but the Holy Spirit. Hence, the eschatological "spiritualization" is also a "divinization." In the Marriage of the Lamb, "penetration and permeation of what is essentially human by what is essentially divine, will then reach its peak." God will communicate himself in his very divinity not only to man's soul, but to his whole embodied personhood. This will be man's ultimate participation in grace, in the divine nature.

6. In the "divinizing spiritualization" of the resurrection, we rediscover—in an eschatological dimension—the same nuptial meaning of the body in the beatific vision, which is a meeting with the mystery of the living God "face to face." This "is the most personal self-giving by God in his very divinity." All of our energies will be concentrated on receiving this divine gift and reciprocating it through the gift of ourselves to God.

7. Christ's words about the resurrection enable us to reread with new depth the meaning of that perspective text of Genesis 2:24 (the two become "one flesh"). These words refer especially to "this world," but they also point in some way to the "other world"—to the eschatological dimension of communion. The ultimate meaning of our creation as male and female is found in our call to incarnate communion with the Trinity in and through the Incarnate Christ.

8. If in the eschaton we are to participate in the Uncreated relations of the Trinity, this participation must be adapted in some way to the communion of created persons. For this reason we profess belief in the communion of saints. Not only will we be "one" with the divine Persons. We will also be "one" with every human person who responds to the wedding invitation of the Lamb.

9. We must think of the resurrection in terms of "the rediscovery of a new perfect subjectivity of everyone" (fulfillment of original solitude) and at the same time "of the rediscovery of a new perfect intersubjectivity of all" (fulfillment of original unity). This reality "signifies the real and definitive fulfillment of human subjectivity, and, on this basis, the definitive fulfillment of the 'nuptial' meaning of the body."

10. The eschatological state "will become the source of the perfect realization of the trinitarian order in the created world of persons." This implies a participation in the perfect unity and distinction found within the Trinity itself. Thus the nuptial meaning of the body will be experienced in a way that is "perfectly personal and communitarian at the same time."

11. In the resurrection, the body will be experienced in its perfect "virginal" state due to the perfect integration of body and soul. As in the beginning, there will be no contradiction between virginity and communion. The resurrected nuptial meaning of the body will correspond perfectly both to man and woman's creation in the image of God as individuals and to the fact that this image is realized through the incarnate *communio personarum*.

12. The eschatological communion of persons will be a completely new experience, yet it will not be alienated in any way from the original and historical dimension of the procreative meaning of the body and sex. The perennial meaning of the human body will be revealed in an eschatological splendor when men and women rediscover in their glorified bodies the perfect freedom of the gift. In turn, this freedom will nourish "each of the communions which will make up the great community of the communion of saints."

13. Christ's response to the Sadducees presents a profound development of the truth about man. It teaches us that marriage "did not determine definitively the original and fundamental meaning of being a body, or of being, as a body, male and female. Marriage and procreation merely give a concrete reality to that meaning in the dimensions of history." In other words, earthly marriage is not man's end, but only preparation for the heavenly marriage yet to come.

14. In St. Paul's teaching on the resurrection in First Corinthians 15, he unites the "last Adam" with the "first Adam" in the context of a deep awareness of the effects of sin. By doing so the Apostle synthesizes all that Christ said in his three "key words" about man's origin, history, and destiny.

15. Historical man lives in a sort of tension between the poles of the first and the last Adam. Since every man bears the image of the first Adam, every man is called to bear the image of Christ. Already in creation our humanity bears the potential to receive Christ, just as a bride bears in herself the potential to receive her bridegroom.

16. According to St. Paul, the body that historical man experiences as perishable will be raised imperishable. What we experience as weighed down in dishonor and weakness will be raised in glory and power. For what is sown a physical body is raised a spiritual body. Paul is not contrasting a material reality with a non-material reality. He is speaking of the spiritualizing divinization of the whole man, body and soul. In the resurrection, the dust to which we have returned will be re-quickened by a new fullness of the breath of God which is the Holy Spirit.

PART II

HOW ARE WE TO LIVE?
APPLYING AN ADEQUATE ANTHROPOLOGY

Cycle 4

Celibacy for the Kingdom

We are shifting gears now to part two of John Paul's Wednesday catechesis on the body. Having outlined a "total vision of man" based on the words of Christ, the Holy Father now seeks to apply that anthropology to the Christian vocations. In other words, having thoroughly answered the question "Who are we?" he now addresses the question "How are we to live?" He wants to demonstrate how his "adequate anthropology" is *actualized* in the Christian vocations.

The human mystery is one of love and gift. The Creator gives man his very being as a gratuitous gift of love. He is created in the image of God as male and female and endowed with freedom (self-determination) in order to recapitulate the mystery of love and gift. "Therefore a man leaves his father and his mother and cleaves to his wife, and they become one flesh" (Gen 2:24). Yet in the same discussion in which Christ reestablishes God's original plan for marriage, he also invites some to sacrifice marriage "for the sake of the kingdom of heaven" (Mt 19:12). Thus, as John Paul says in *Familiaris Consortio*, "Christian revelation recognizes two specific ways of realizing the vocation of the human person, in its entirety, to love: marriage and virginity or celibacy. Either one is in its own proper form an actuation of the most profound truth about man, of his being 'created in the image of God.'"[1]

This cycle on celibacy for the kingdom consists of fourteen general audiences delivered between March 10, 1982 and July 21, 1982. For good reason John Paul reflects on the celibate vocation prior to his cycle on the marital vocation. As we shall learn, only by understanding the meaning of Christian celibacy can we understand the sacramentality of marriage. For celibacy is a more immediate participation (even if only by way of anticipation) in what marriage signifies sacramentally—the eternal "virgin-union" of Christ and the Church.

---

1. *Familiaris Consortio*, n. 11.

Using our former image, Christians called to the marital vocation are in some way meant to reclaim the "inflated tires" of the beginning as a sacramental sign of man's ultimate end. In a sense, Christians called to the celibate vocation move in the other direction. They look to the future, anticipating in the here-and-now the life of flight "beyond tires." In this way they shed light on God's ultimate plan right from the beginning. Recall the Pope's provocative statement that marriage "in itself did not determine definitively the original and fundamental meaning of being a body, or of being, as a body, male and female. Marriage and procreation merely give a concrete reality to that meaning in the dimensions of history."[2] In a way, men and women who are celibates "for the sake of the kingdom of heaven" step outside the dimensions of history—while living within its dimensions—and proclaim to the world that "the kingdom of God is here."

56. Some Make Themselves Eunuchs
March 10, 17, 24, 31, 1982 (TB 262–272)

The "call to an exclusive donation of self to God in virginity and in celibacy thrusts its roots deep into the Gospel soil of the theology of the body" (262). Based on our reflections on the resurrection, we can see clearly that this vocation "is a charismatic orientation toward that eschatological state in which men 'neither marry nor are given in marriage'" (263).[3] However, as John Paul demonstrates, it is very significant that Christ does not refer to celibacy in his discussion with the Sadducees about the resurrection. Instead, he refers to it in his conversation with the Pharisees about God's plan for marriage "in the beginning."

When Christ firmly established the indissolubility of marriage, his disciples said: "If such is the case of a man with his wife, it is not expedient to marry" (Mt 19:10). Christ does not respond to their line of reasoning. Instead, he takes the discussion to a new level by introducing an even more radical way of living according to God's plan for creating us male and female. He replies:

---

2. 1/13/82, TB 247.

3. See *CCC,* nn. 1618, 1619.

Not all men can receive the precept, but only those to whom it is given. For there are eunuchs[4] who have been so from birth, and there are eunuchs who have been made eunuchs by men, and there are eunuchs who have made themselves eunuchs for the sake of the kingdom of heaven. He who is able to receive this, let him receive it (Mt 19:11–12).

A. Christ's Words Mark a Turning Point

As concise as these words are, John Paul states that they are "admirably rich and precise, rich with a number of implications both of a doctrinal and pastoral nature" (276). At the same time, it is hard to overestimate how incomprehensible these words would have been to the Israelites. In the tradition of the Old Testament, marriage was a religiously privileged state, privileged by revelation itself. Marriage had acquired a "consecrated significance" because of God's covenant with Abraham and the promise of countless offspring. The Pope observes that only persons with physical impotence could constitute an exception. Such people (eunuchs) were seen as outcasts, accursed by God because they could not participate in fulfilling the promise given to Abraham. In such a climate it would have been inconceivable for someone actually to *choose* to "make himself a eunuch." And for the kingdom of heaven? Outlandish!

Christ certainly acknowledges this difficulty in the way he introduces the idea to his listeners. As John Paul puts it, it is as if Christ wished to say: "I know that what I am going to say to you now will cause great difficulty in your conscience, in your way of understanding the significance of the body. In fact, I shall speak to you of continence, and, undoubtedly, you will associate this with the state of physical deficiency, whether congenital or brought about by human cause. But I wish to tell you that continence can also be voluntary and chosen by man 'for the sake of the kingdom'" (266).

John Paul says that from the viewpoint of theology—that is, of the revelation of the body's significance—Christ's words mark a decisive turning point for historical man and his call to marriage. However, they "do not express a command by which all are bound, but a counsel which concerns only some persons" (263). Therefore, the Holy Father says that continence is a kind of exception to the general rule of this life, which is to marry.

---

4. A eunuch is a person who, either by birth defect or acquired malady, is physically incapable of engaging in sexual intercourse. Definitive and perpetual impotence is to this day a canonical impediment to marriage (see canon 1084). See Christopher West, *Good News About Sex & Marriage,* pp. 54–57 for an explanation of this.

B. Voluntary, Supernatural, Virginal Communion

The Pope stresses that celibacy is a "personal choice" empowered by a "particular grace." Hence, this vocation must be understood as *voluntary* and *supernatural*. Without these two specific characteristics, it does not fall within the scope of Christ's words. On the one hand, this means continence for the kingdom can never be imposed on anyone. It is a gift given by God that must be received and freely chosen.[5] On the other hand, even if freely chosen, if continence is not "for the kingdom" it would not correspond to Christian celibacy. Thus, Christ's phrase "for the kingdom" expresses not only the *objective* orientation of this vocation. It also indicates the need for a *subjective* motivation "that corresponds adequately and fully to [this] objective finality" (270). For example, if a person were to choose celibacy out of a fear of marital intimacy or a disdain for sexuality, this would not be celibacy for the kingdom.

At the same time, while Christ stresses the supernatural dimension of this vocation, he wishes to root the vocation to such continence "deep in the reality of earthly life" (264). In some sense the celibate person steps *beyond* the dimensions of history into that state of the body where men and women are no longer given in marriage. But all the while he remains grounded *within* the dimensions of history and, in this way, becomes a prophetic witness *in his body* to the future resurrection. In other words, the celibate man or woman witnesses to the definitive accomplishment of the "redemption of the body" while still awaiting its ultimate consummation.

Christian celibacy, therefore, exists in the heart of that tension of "already, but not yet." For, as the Holy Father points out, this vocation is a question "not of continence *in* the kingdom of heaven, but of continence *'for* the kingdom of heaven'" (264). It is an anticipation and "eschatological sign" of the life to come. Thus, an essential difference exists between celibacy for the kingdom as an earthly vocation and that glorified state of the body in which all men and women will "neither marry nor be given in marriage." Because in this world marriage remains part of man's normal and noble inclination, the celibate choice "is joined to renunciation and also to a particular spiritual effort" (267). However, if celibacy anticipates the future world, the virginal state of the future world does not indicate an absence of real interpersonal communion. Virginity and bodily communion are not opposed to one another. Rather, in the eschatological reality—as in the beginning—they are fulfilled in each other (see §§15, 53). Thus, the celibate vocation—while renouncing the genital expression of incarnate communion—does not renounce the human vocation to live in a *communio personarum*.

---

5. See *CCC,* n. 1599.

Continence for the kingdom is *"a charismatic sign* [that] indicates the eschatological 'virginity' of the risen man, in whom there will be revealed," the Pope says, "the absolute and eternal nuptial meaning of the glorified body in union with God himself through the 'face to face' vision of him." At the same time the body will be "glorified also through the union of a perfect intersubjectivity, which will unite all who 'participate in the other world,' men and women, in the mystery of the communion of saints" (267). In this way "that continence 'for the kingdom of heaven'— as an unquestionable sign of the 'other world'—bears in itself especially the interior dynamism of the mystery of the redemption of the body" (271). Through that dynamism we will all recover our "original virginal value" in an eschatological dimension through the perfect integration of body and soul in union with the Word made flesh. All the saints will live in the eternal "virginal" communion of one body. *This* is what the celibate vocation anticipates.

57. Continence, Spiritual Fruitfulness, and the Ethos of Redemption
March 24, 31; April 7, 1982 (TB 267–275)

Earthly continence for the kingdom "is a sign that the body, whose end is not the grave, is directed to glorification. Already by this very fact," John Paul says, "continence 'for the kingdom of heaven' is a witness among men that anticipates the future resurrection" (267). In this state, men and women no longer marry—not because the deep truth of marriage is eradicated, but because it is eternally fulfilled in the union of Christ and the Church. In this sense, those who are celibate for the kingdom are "skipping" the sacrament in anticipation of the real thing. They wish to participate in a more direct way—here and now—in the "Marriage of the Lamb."

■ The term "celibacy" speaks more about what this vocation is not rather than what it is. It seems that some of the confusion and negativity surrounding this vocation could be avoided if it were defined more in terms of what it embraces—the heavenly marriage—instead of what it gives up.

John Paul says that he "who consciously chooses such continence, chooses, in a certain sense, a special participation in the mystery of the redemption (of the body). He wishes in a particular way to complete it, so to say, in his own flesh (see Col 1:24)." In doing so, the celibate person finds a distinctive "imprint of a likeness to Christ" who himself was continent for the kingdom (271). The Pope observes that the departure from the Old Testament tradition, in which marriage and procreation were a religiously privileged state, had to be based on the example of Christ himself. From the moment of his virginal conception, Christ's whole earthly life, in fact, was a witness to a new kind of fruitfulness. This mystery, however, remained hidden from those to whom Christ first spoke about continence for the kingdom. The Pope points out that only "Mary and Joseph, who had lived the mystery of his conception and birth, became the first witnesses of a fruitfulness different from that of the flesh, that is, of a fruitfulness of the Spirit: 'That which is conceived in her is of the Holy Spirit' (Mt 1:20)" (268). The miracle surrounding Christ's virgin birth would only gradually be revealed to the eyes of the Church on the basis of Matthew and Luke's Gospels.

A. Joseph and Mary's Virginal Marriage

John Paul remarks, "Though [Christ] is born of her like every other man,...nonetheless Mary's maternity is virginal. To this virginal maternity of Mary there corresponds the virginal mystery of Joseph" (268). Joseph and Mary's virginity is certainly in keeping with that continence for the kingdom which Christ will one day announce to his disciples. However, at the same time, they were a legitimate husband and wife.[6] As John Paul says, "The marriage of Mary and Joseph conceals within itself, at the same time, the *mystery* of the perfect communion of the persons, of the man and woman in the conjugal pact, and also the mystery of that singular continence for the kingdom of heaven: a continence that served, in the history of salvation, the most perfect 'fruitfulness of the Holy Spirit.' Indeed," the Pope continues, "it was in a certain sense the absolute fullness of that spiritual fruitfulness, since precisely in the...pact of Mary and Joseph in marriage and in continence, there was realized the gift of the Incarnation of the Eternal Word" (268).

■ It seems John Paul II may be developing the Church's understanding of St. Joseph's role in the Incarnation. For John Paul, St. Joseph is not a kind of "tack-on" provided to lend some legitimacy in the public eye to what would have been perceived as Mary's single motherhood. For John Paul, it seems Joseph's virginal "yes" to God (and virginal love for Mary) played an essential role in the mystery of the Incarnation. Mary responded to the Annunciation with her *fiat*. John Paul writes in *Redemptoris Custos*

---

6. For those interested in the finer points of canon law, the Church teaches that a couple must be capable of consummating their marriage at the time they enter marriage (see canon 1084), but they are not absolutely obligated to consummate their marriage.

that *"at the moment of Joseph's own 'annunciation'* he said nothing; instead he simply *'did* as the angel of the Lord commanded him' (Mt 1:24)."[7] This typically masculine "doing" could be considered the nuptial counterpart to Mary's feminine "let it be done." And this virginal complementarity of Joseph and Mary expressed the absolute fullness of spiritual fruitfulness. Although we typically refer to Joseph as Jesus' "foster father," John Paul insists that Joseph's fatherhood is not less real because of his virginity. In a way, it is even more real. The Pope writes: *"In this family, Joseph is the father: his fatherhood* is not one that derives from begetting offspring; but neither is it an 'apparent' or merely 'substitute' fatherhood. Rather, it is one that *fully shares in authentic human fatherhood."*[8] Human fatherhood becomes all the more authentic to the degree that it becomes a transparent sign of God's Fatherhood. Joseph's fatherhood is the most transparent sign of God's Fatherhood and is, therefore, all the more real.

In a profound paradox which simultaneously embraces the heavenly marriage (i.e., continence for the kingdom) *and* the earthly marriage, Joseph and Mary's virginal-communion of persons literally effected the marriage of heaven and earth. This is the grace of the hypostatic union—the marriage of the human and divine natures in the Person of Christ. And this grace is connected precisely with the absolute fullness of the spiritual fruitfulness that comes from embracing continence for the kingdom. John Paul concludes that every man and woman who authentically embraces continence for the kingdom in some way participates in this super-abounding spiritual fruitfulness.

B. Marriage and Celibacy Stem from the Same Ethos

The marriage of Joseph and Mary sheds a bright light on both Christian vocations. The Pope observes that it helps us to understand the profound sanctity of marriage *and* a certain personal "disinterestedness" in marriage on the part of those who prefer to remain continent for the kingdom. John Paul will go to great lengths reflecting on the sanctity of marriage in his next cycle. For now let us linger on this question, posed from the common perspective of our day: "Why would a Christian be 'disinterested' in marriage? After all, for the Christian, this is the only legitimate opportunity for sex, right? Who in his right mind would actually prefer a life without sex?"

---

7. *Redemptoris Custos,* n. 17.

8. Ibid, n. 21.

This widespread perspective can only stem from a failure to understand the redemption Christ won for us. So much confusion about the Church's teaching—not just on sex, but on the whole economy of salvation—stems from the tunnel vision that results from normalizing concupiscence. For those whose hearts are bound by lust, the idea of choosing a life of total continence is absurd. But for those who have been liberated from lust by the ethos of redemption, the idea of sacrificing the genital expression of their sexuality "for the sake of the kingdom of heaven" not only becomes a real possibility—it becomes quite attractive.

When authentically lived, the Christian call to life-long continence witnesses dramatically to the freedom for which Christ has set us free. Of course, a truly chaste marriage witnesses to the same freedom. Contrary to the tunnel vision perspective mentioned above, marriage *does not* provide a "legitimate outlet" for indulging one's lusts (see §34). Thus, whoever has an authentic Christian understanding of marriage at the same time gains an authentic Christian understanding of life-long celibacy. Such an understanding comes from the ethos of redemption. As John Paul says, behind the call to continence in Matthew 19 and the call to overcome lust in Matthew 5 "are found the same anthropology and the same ethos" (274). In other words, both vocations (marriage and celibacy) flow from the same vision of the human person and the same call to experience the redemption of our bodies, which includes the redemption of our sexual desires.

In the invitation to celibacy for the kingdom, John Paul says that the prospects of the ethos of historical man are "enlarged upon" in light of the future anthropology of the resurrection. This does not mean that the anthropology of the resurrection replaces the anthropology of historical man. Men and women who choose celibacy for the kingdom, just like those who choose marriage, must contend with concupiscence. But historical man is also redeemed man. "Redemption is a truth, a reality, in the name of which man must feel called, and 'called with efficacy.'"[9] Only the man or woman living this efficacy is prepared to embrace a life of continence for the kingdom. Lest we fall into the trap of thinking marriage legitimizes concupiscence, we must insist that living the efficacy of redemption is also required of those who embrace marriage. The Holy Father expresses this when he says that the person who chooses continence for the kingdom "must put this decision into effect, subjugating the sinfulness of his [fallen] nature to the forces that spring from the mystery of the redemption of the body. He must do so just as any other man does...whose way remains that of matrimony. The only difference," the Pope says, "is the type

---

9. 10/29/80, TB 167.

of responsibility for the good chosen, just as the type of good chosen is different" (275).

The difference between marriage and continence for the kingdom must *never* be understood as the difference between having a legitimate outlet for concupiscence on the one hand and having to repress concupiscence on the other. Christ calls *everyone* to overcome the domination of concupiscence through the redemption of the body. Only upon experiencing a true level of freedom in this regard do the Christian vocations (celibacy *and* marriage) make sense. For *both* flow from the same experience of the redemption of the body and of sexual desire. Both flow from the same nuptial meaning of the body and the call to become a gift in and through masculinity and femininity. Without experiencing the freedom of the gift for which Christ has set us free (see §§42, 43), celibacy is seen as hopelessly repressive and marriage as legitimately indulgent. How far from the Gospel ethos these perspectives are!

58. Celibacy for the Kingdom Is an Exceptional Calling
March 31; April 7, 14, 28, 1982 (TB 270–278, 282–284)

History has seen some serious distortions of the Church's teaching that celibacy is a "higher" calling than marriage. Tragically, many Catholics have thought that this means marriage is only a second-class vocation for those who "can't handle" celibacy. The sentiment often goes like this: "If celibacy is so good, marriage must be so bad. If refraining from sex makes one pure and holy, having sex must make one dirty and unholy." Yet nothing could be further from the mind of the Church in promoting the value of celibacy. Such a belief smacks of the Manichaean heresy.

A. Celibacy Does Not Devalue Marriage

In response to such distortions, John Paul stresses that the "'superiority' of continence to matrimony in the authentic Tradition of the Church never means disparagement of marriage or belittlement of its essential value. It does not even mean a shift, even implicit, on the Manichaean positions, or a support of ways of evaluating or acting based on the Manichaean understanding of the body and sexuality, matrimony and procreation" (275). He continues by saying that Christ's words about celibacy point to a "superiority" of this vocation only by virtue of its motive "for the kingdom of heaven." We may admit only this superiority. In Christ's words "we do not find any basis whatever for any disparagement of matrimony" (275).

In Christ's words about continence "there is no reference to the 'inferiority' of marriage with regard to the 'body,' or in other words with regard to the essence of marriage, consisting in the fact that man and woman join together in marriage, thus becoming 'one flesh'" (276). This is God's *good* and *holy* design. Hence, the "superiority" of continence *does not* rest on the mere fact of abstinence from sexual union. The Pope insists that "Christ's words on this point are quite clear." Christ proposes continence not "with prejudice against conjugal 'union of the body,' but only 'for the sake of the kingdom of heaven'" (276).

How, then, are we to understand the exceptional value of celibacy in relation to the marriage vocation? John Paul points out that if marriage "is fully appropriate and of a value that is fundamental, universal, and ordinary," then it makes sense that continence for the kingdom "possesses a particular and 'exceptional' value" (270). From the context of Christ's words, John Paul says that "it can be seen sufficiently clearly that here it is not a question of diminishing the value of matrimony in favor of continence" (273). Marriage certainly has a *great* value as an earthly sacrament of the eternal communion of heaven. But celibacy is not a sacrament of heaven on earth. Because it directly anticipates the eschatological reality, it *is* (if only in this anticipatory sense) "heaven on earth." It is a sign that the kingdom of God is here. Celibacy could be understood as "higher" than marriage, then, in the same way that heaven is higher than earth. In this way Christian celibacy "is particularly efficacious and important for 'the kingdom of heaven.' And so should it be," John Paul says, "seeing that Christ chose it for himself" (270).

Those who choose celibacy as their Christian vocation must do so, the Pope says, not because of "a supposed negative value of marriage, but in view of the particular value connected with this choice" (263). Those men and women to whom this calling is given must discover and welcome this value as their own personal vocation. Marriage with its own value always remains the normal calling in this life. It is in this sense that the value of celibacy is exceptional; it is the exception to the rule.

B. A True Sacrifice, But Not a Rejection of Sexuality

As our study of the Genesis texts revealed, men and women are "made" for marriage according to the normal and noble inclinations of their nature. The Pope describes continence as a conscious decision to "break away from" these noble inclinations in anticipation of their eschatological fulfillment. Because of the great good that marriage entails as a divine institution, choosing to renounce marriage demands real self-sacrifice. As John Paul expresses: "That break also becomes the beginning of successive self-sacrifices that are indispensable if the first and funda-mental choice [is to] be consistent in the breadth of one's entire earthly life" (274).

The Pope remarks that Christ, in calling some men and women to re-nounce marriage, has no desire to "conceal the anguish" that continence and its enduring consequences can bring. In some sense, those who choose continence are choosing to remain in the "ache" of man's original solitude before God. They are choosing to devote their yearning for communion di-rectly toward God. As John Paul says, "continence must demonstrate that man, in his deepest being, is...'alone' before God, with God" (273). Never-theless, John Paul stresses that "what is an invitation to solitude for God in the call to continence for the kingdom of heaven at the same time respects both the 'dual nature of mankind' (that is, his masculinity and femininity) and the dimension of communion of existence that is proper to the person" (273). Recall that the eschatological reality is not only man's perfect com-munion with God. It is also the perfect communion of all men and women with each other (see §§52, 53). Thus, John Paul says that the continent per-son, anticipating the perfect communion of saints, "is capable of discover-ing in his solitude...a new and even fuller form of intersubjective commun-ion with others" (273).

Christ, therefore, while calling some to renounce marriage, does not thereby call the continent person to renounce his nature as a sexual being. As John Paul says, the continent person, like everyone else, remains "'dual' by nature (that is, directed as man toward woman and as woman toward man)." We recognize this in the "trinitarian meaning" of our cre-ation as male and female in God's image. Whoever properly "compre-hends" Christ's call to continence "preserves the integral truth of his own humanity without losing along the way any of the essential elements of the vocation of the person created in 'God's image and likeness'" (273). And this trinitarian image is *always* fulfilled in man through the nuptial mean-ing of the body, which calls man to the sincere gift of self and establishes a true communion of persons.

Far from renouncing this most fundamental meaning of sexuality, the celibate person is able "to fulfill himself 'differently' and, in a certain way, 'more' than through matrimony, [by] becoming a 'true gift to others'" (273–274). Differently in that the celibate person does not become a gift via the one flesh union; and "more" in that the celibate person can partici-pate to a higher degree in the "intersubjectivity of all." Hence, John Paul says that celibacy for the kingdom "comes about on the basis of full con-sciousness of the nuptial meaning which masculinity and femininity contain in themselves. If this choice should come about by way of some artificial 'prescinding' from this real wealth of every human subject, it would not appropriately and adequately correspond to the content of Christ's words" (284). In fact, the Holy Father insists that only in relation to a "profound and mature knowledge of the nuptial meaning of the body...does the call to voluntary continence 'for the sake of the kingdom of heaven' find full warranty and motivation." Then he adds: "Only and exclusively in this perspective does Christ say, 'He who is able to receive this, let him receive it' (Mt 19:12)" (283).

59. Marriage and Celibacy Explain and Complete Each Other

April 14, 21, 28; May 5, 1982 (TB 276–286)

Papal biographer George Weigel has described John Paul as a clergyman with a "lay soul."[10] He also observes that perhaps no more priestly priest has sat in the chair of Peter than Pope John Paul II. Yet Weigel's point is that in some sense this Pope has the heart of a layman. For John Paul, the focal point of the Church's life is not found inside the Vatican. The focal point of Christian life resides where lay men and women live out their call to holiness: in the home, the family, the streets, the fields, the factory, the office.

A. Perfection Is Measured by Charity

Having internalized his own call to holiness as a layman, Wojtyla was one of the main forces behind the Second Vatican Council's emphasis on the universal call to holiness. Prior to this renewed emphasis, many Catholics thought that only priests and nuns were called to sanctity. Since those who bound themselves by the evangelical counsels (poverty, chastity, and obedience) embraced what is traditionally called "the state of perfection," lay people often felt consigned to "the state of imperfection." John Paul's "lay soul" shows itself in his efforts to transcend this false dichotomy. He insists that marriage and celibacy do not "divide the human (and Christian) community into two camps [as if there were] those who are 'perfect' because of continence and those who are 'imperfect' or 'less perfect' because of the reality of married life" (276). Perfection in the Christian life is not measured by whether or not one is celibate. Instead, the Pope asserts that it "is measured with the rule of charity"(277).

This means that "perfection is possible and accessible to every man, both in a 'religious institute,' and in the 'world'" (277). The Holy Father

---

10. George Weigel, "The Soul of John Paul II." Lecture delivered at Oxford, March 6, 2001.

even says that a person who does not live in "the state of perfection" can nonetheless "reach a superior degree of perfection—whose measure is charity—in comparison to the person who does live in the 'state of perfection' with a lesser degree of charity" (277). Far from being opposed to one another, John Paul demonstrates at great length the profound complementarity between these vocations which is essential to the life and health of the Church. Marriage and continence, the Pope says, are meant to "explain and complete each other" (276). Marriage reveals the nuptial character of the celibate vocation just as the celibate vocation reveals the sacramentality of marriage. He even says that in "the life of an authentically Christian community the attitudes and values proper to one and the other state...in a certain sense interpenetrate each other" (277).

B. Marriage Reveals the Nuptial Character of Celibacy

John Paul says that the conjugal fidelity of spouses and the irrevocable gift they make to each other provide the foundation of celibacy for the kingdom. Marriage, in fact, reveals the very nature of the love expressed by the person who is continent for the kingdom. Thus "the nature of one and the other love is 'conjugal,' that is, expressed through the total gift of oneself" (277).

Christ is the ultimate example of conjugal love lived in a celibate way. While remaining celibate, Christ revealed himself as Spouse of the Church by giving himself "to the very limit" in the paschal and Eucharistic mystery. In this way, Christ gave the ultimate revelation of the nuptial meaning of the body. Through the light which marriage sheds on this vocation, we come to realize, as John Paul says, that celibacy for the kingdom "has acquired the significance of an act of nuptial love." Continence for the kingdom is "a nuptial giving of oneself for the purpose of reciprocating in a particular way the nuptial love of the Redeemer" (282). Furthermore, since conjugal love is ordered by its nature toward fatherhood and motherhood, the Pope says that continence for the kingdom must lead in its normal development to fatherhood and motherhood in a spiritual sense. Thus the familial terms husband, bride, father, mother, brother, and sister are applicable to marriage and family life *and* to the celibate vocation.

This means that the choice of marriage *and* the choice of celibacy for the kingdom require and suppose "the learning and the interior acceptance of the nuptial meaning of the body, bound up with the masculinity and femininity of the human person" (284). For *both* vocations flow from the true meaning of human sexuality and the deepest meaning of sexual desire. To the degree that sexual desire is freed from the distortion of concupiscence, it becomes the desire to make a sincere gift of one's body (one's very self) to another. As the Holy Father expresses it: "On the basis of the same disposition of the personal subject and on the basis of the same nuptial meaning of being, as a body, male or female, there can be formed the love that commits man to marriage for the whole duration of his life, but there can be formed also the love that commits man to a life of continence 'for the sake of the kingdom of heaven'" (284). According to John Paul, this is the significance of Christ's words in Matthew 19 where he speaks of marriage according to God's original plan *and* celibacy for the kingdom.

The point is that no one can escape the nuptial meaning of his or her body. Every man, by virtue of the nuptial meaning of his body, is called in some way to be both a husband and a father. And every woman, by virtue of the nuptial meaning of her body, is called in some way to be both a wife and a mother. This is lived on earth either through marriage or, in a different way, through the celibate vocation.[11] But, according to Christ's words, John Paul says that anyone who chooses marriage must do so just as it was instituted by the Creator "from the beginning." Similarly, anyone who pursues continence for the kingdom of heaven must seek in it the proper values of this vocation.

■ What about the place of the single person in living out the nuptial meaning of the body? Many more people are in this situation today than was typical in the past. This "new" reality calls for a pastoral response from the Church that has yet to be adequately developed. In brief, I would say that there is a difference between one who is single by choice in order to devote himself to worthy causes[12] and a person who is single not by choice but by circumstance.[13] The former has made a definitive vocational choice in some ways parallel to the celibate vocation. The latter is still waiting to make a definitive vocational choice. This does not mean such a person's life need remain "on hold." He or she can live a very fruitful life serving others while maintaining the hope of finding a spouse or continuing to discern a call to consecrated celibacy.[14] In every way that single men and women give and receive the "sincere gift of self"—through prayer, work, leisure, service of friends, families, neighbors, the poor, etc.—they

---

11. See *CCC*, n. 923.

12. See *CCC*, n. 2231.

13. See *CCC*, n. 1658.

14. See *Good News About Sex & Marriage*, p. 166.

are living the truth of the nuptial meaning of their bodies. In any case, the ultimate fulfillment of the nuptial meaning of the body for everyone is to be found, not in any earthly vocation, but in the heavenly marriage of Christ and the Church.

C. Celibacy Reveals the Sacramentality of Marriage

Christian celibacy is not a sacrament. Why? Sacraments mediate heavenly realities on earth. But in the future world the sacraments lose their *raison d'être* because we will participate in the divine mystery *immediately* (without sacramental mediation).[15] Celibacy is not a sacrament because it is a more direct participation (if only by way of anticipation) in the life to come. It anticipates the life *beyond* sacraments. It is precisely "with regard to this dimension and this orientation," John Paul says, that "continence 'for the kingdom of heaven' has a particular importance and special eloquence for those who live a married life" (277). Because celibacy is *not* a sacrament, it demonstrates why marriage *is* a sacrament. It demonstrates that marriage's ultimate purpose is to point men and women toward their eschatological destiny—toward the consummation of the Marriage of the Lamb, which immeasurably exceeds anything possible in earthly life. John Paul says we must "not forget that the only key to understanding the sacramentality of marriage is the spousal love of Christ for the Church" (286). This is the primordial value and meaning of man and woman's call to become "one flesh" (see Eph 5:31–32).

Hence, the Holy Father says that renouncing conjugal union at the same time affirms the deepest meaning of conjugal union because it "highlights that meaning in all its interior truth and personal beauty" (285). The Pope admits that this may seem paradoxical. Yet many truths of the Gospel are paradoxical—and these are often the most profound truths. The personal beauty and interior truth of conjugal union lies in its establishment of a true communion of persons so intimate and profound as to image something of the interior life of the Trinity and the marriage of Christ and the Church. *This* is what celibacy—as a more direct participation in the heavenly marriage—affirms about the union of husband and wife.

Celibacy's affirmation of marriage arises when we discover the dimension of "gift" proper to each vocation. In this way, the Pope says that the celibate gift of self indirectly serves to highlight what is most lasting and most profoundly personal in the marriage vocation. It highlights the

---

15. See *CCC*, n. 1023.

fact that conjugal union—in its totality and in its consummate expression—is the temporal manifestation of the eternal reality of "gift." Furthermore, the spiritual fruitfulness of celibacy even reveals something about the physical fruitfulness of marriage. John Paul says that physical procreation fully responds to its meaning only if it is completed by fatherhood and motherhood in the spirit. This spiritual counterpart to physical procreation is expressed in all that the parents do to educate the children born from their conjugal union.

For all these reasons, as John Paul says, continence "is in a certain sense indispensable, so that the very nuptial meaning of the body can be more easily recognized in all the ethos of human life and above all in the ethos of conjugal and family life" (286). Without the eschatological reminder of the celibate vocation, the call to become "one flesh" easily turns in on itself and loses its orientation toward the eternal union yet to be consummated. In this way, celibacy provides an essential remedy for the world's false, idolatrous cult of the body (see §54).

60. Celibacy Anticipates the Maximum Fullness of God's Bounty
April 21, 28; May 5, 1982 (TB 278–287)

Before he begins reflecting on St. Paul's teaching on the celibate vocation, John Paul offers some concluding remarks on Christ's words about eunuchs for the kingdom. In his audience of April 21, 1982, the Pope reviews and summarizes previous themes. He reiterates that Christ wants to impress on his disciples that because continence entails renouncing a great good, it demands great sacrifice. But in this instance John Paul nuances his statement by adding that celibacy is a renunciation only when "viewed in the light of temporal categories" (281). We must remember that celibacy makes no sense apart from those key words of Christ: *"...for the sake of the kingdom of heaven."*

A. Man's Definitive Fulfillment

Christ established the kingdom of heaven in time and also foretold its eschatological fulfillment. All are called to participate in and prepare for the coming of the kingdom (the Pope points to the parable of the wedding banquet in Matthew 22 as an illustration of this). Yet John Paul concludes that those who are continent for the kingdom are called "to participate in a singular way in the establishment of the kingdom of God on earth, through which the definitive phase of the 'kingdom of heaven' is begun and prepared" (279).

Taking up one's cross every day and following Christ can reach the point of renouncing marriage and raising a family of one's own. If Christ calls some to sacrifice so great a good—a good which God established from the beginning as a sign of his own Covenant Love—this sacrifice must involve an even greater realization of *the same great good* which marriage and family life serves. It must involve a supernatural potential for realizing the kingdom of God both in its earthly dimension and in its ultimate consummation. Masculinity and femininity reveal that the human person is created "for" another—to be a gift "for" the other. Christ's words about celibacy "consequently show that this 'for,' present from the beginning at the basis of marriage, can also be at the basis of continence 'for' the kingdom of heaven" (284).

Being "for" another always implies a nuptial relationship of sorts. Thus, "in order to clarify what the kingdom of heaven is for those who choose voluntary continence for the sake of it, the revelation of the nuptial relationship of Christ with the Church has a particular significance" (280). A decisive text for John Paul in this regard is Ephesians chapter 5. The Pope says that the "profound mystery" of nuptial union outlined there by St. Paul (see vv. 21–32) is equally valid both for the theology of Christian marriage and for the theology of Christian celibacy. The kingdom of heaven is the consummation of Christ's union with the Church. As John Paul reminds us, this is "the definitive fulfillment of the aspirations of all men, to whom Christ addresses his message: it is the fullness of the good that the human heart desires beyond all that can be his lot in this earthly life; it is the maximum fullness of God's bounty toward man" (280).

When viewed in this light, celibacy is not a renunciation at all (and it *must* be viewed in this light if is to concur with Christ's words). It is embracing in the here and now—if only by anticipation—the ultimate reality of communion, that maximum fullness of God's bounty toward man. As previously mentioned, we live in the tension of "already, but not yet" in relation to the coming of the kingdom. One could say that Christian celibacy emphasizes the "already," whereas Christian marriage emphasizes the "not yet." In order for a person to discern properly if he is called to celibacy (and, equally so, to discern the call to marriage), he must have a mature understanding of this "tension" emphasized by the complementarity of celibacy and marriage in the life of the Pilgrim Church.

In view of the "already," celibacy is not a renunciation. In view of the "not yet," however, celibacy demands not only a real sacrifice but also a weighty responsibility. Even so, the Pope says, "Undoubtedly throughout all this, through the gravity and depth of the decision, through the severity and the responsibility that it bears with it, love appears and shines through: love as the readiness to give the exclusive gift of oneself for the sake of 'the kingdom of God'" (281).

"It is natural for the human heart to accept demands," the Pope observes, "even difficult ones, in the name of love for an ideal, and above all in the name of love for a person." Then he adds that "love, in fact, is by its very nature directed toward a person" (281). And for those who choose celibacy for the kingdom, that person is Christ himself.

B. Liberation from Concupiscence

The Holy Father recognizes that a proper examination of the way in which the celibate vocation is formed, or rather "transformed" in a person would require an extensive study beyond the scope of his analysis. Suffice it to say that it is impossible to receive the "gift" of this vocation if one accepts the modern view that man has a sexual instinct akin to animals. Applying this naturalistic concept to man, John Paul says, "is not at all appropriate and adequate." It greatly limits the full truth of human subjectivity revealed and expressed through the nuptial meaning of the body. The nuptial meaning of the body, deduced from the first chapters of Genesis (especially Gen 2:23–25) is the "only appropriate and adequate concept" in which to discover man's personhood and subjectivity in the sphere of sexuality. As revealed in the experience of original solitude, man, even when he is understood from the viewpoint of species, "cannot even basically qualify as an *animal*, but a *rational animal"* (283).

Man is a subject because he is free to determine his own actions. He is not bound by instinct like an animal. If he feels that he is, then he does not experience the truth of his own humanity, but the domination of concupiscence that greatly diminishes the truth of his humanity. Only when a person has experienced a significant liberation from concupiscence—and is, thus, in possession of his own sexual subjectivity— can he properly receive the vocation of celibacy as a gift. This is why John Paul says that the celibate vocation is a matter not only of formation but of *transformation.*

Anyone who has doubts or reservations about God's plan for sexuality and marriage should not undertake the vocation of celibacy. For only when a person adequately understands the beauty and sacredness of God's plan for sex and marriage can he fully understand what it means to renounce them for the kingdom. John Paul concisely expresses this when he says: "In order for man to be fully aware of what he is choosing (continence for the sake of the kingdom), he must also be fully aware of what he is renouncing." He adds parenthetically that "it is a question here really of knowledge of the value in an 'ideal' sense; nevertheless," he concludes, "this knowledge is after all 'realistic'" (285).

The Holy Father stresses that Christ explicitly requires this full and mature understanding when he says, "He who is able to receive this, let him receive it" (Mt 19:12). Only with this *full* understanding do Christ's words convey what John Paul calls their "convincing mark and power" (281). Only with this *full* understanding do we comprehend why John Paul says that the call to continence "has a capital significance not only for Christian ethos and spirituality, but also for anthropology and for the whole theology of the body" (287).

61. Analysis of St. Paul's Teaching on Celibacy

June 23, 30; July 7, 14, 1982 (TB 287–297)

John Paul devotes four of his final five audiences of this cycle to a reflection on St. Paul's teaching on celibacy as outlined in chapter seven of his First Letter to the Corinthians. Paul answers some concrete questions that troubled the first generation of Christians in Corinth regarding the relationship of celibacy and marriage. The Pope reflects that he might have been responding to the concerns of a young man who wanted to marry, or a newlywed who wanted to give direction to his married life. It might also have been a father or guardian who asked Paul for counsel regarding whether or not his daughter should marry. As the Pope reminds us, Paul was writing in a time when marriage decisions belonged more to parents than to young people. He also notes that a particular asceticism then existed in Corinth that may have been influenced by dualistic currents of thought that devalued the body. This may have led some to question whether marriage itself was a sin. If such ideas were circulating in the Corinthian community, this certainly would have led to troubled consciences for the married and for those who wished to marry.

Understanding this context helps us better appreciate not only the content of Paul's response but also his manner and style. He demonstrates a keen understanding of the human condition and counsels his audience with the greatest realism. Furthermore, Paul presents the truth proclaimed by Christ in all its authenticity, yet at the same time, the Pope says, "he gives it a stamp of his own." He offers opinions and accents "totally his own" while carefully distinguishing them from the Lord's commands. Although moralists often turn to Paul's teaching in 1 Corinthians 7 seeking resolutions to difficult questions, the Pope reminds us that ultimate resolutions must be sought in the life and teaching of Christ himself. This is significant since, as we shall see, Paul seems to make concessions which we do not find in the life and teaching of Christ. Paul's letter to the Corinthians certainly demands full respect as the word of God. Nonetheless, the life and words of Christ in the Gospels hold pre-eminence,[16] and Paul's teaching must be interpreted in light of Christ's teaching.

A. Paul Does Not Devalue Marriage

It can appear as though Paul paints a rather negative picture of marriage in this passage from First Corinthians. Based on some of the Apostle's statements, John Paul himself asks at one point if Paul might not express a personal aversion to marriage. "I wish that all were [celibate] as I myself am" (v. 7). "Do not seek marriage" (v. 27). "[L]et those who have wives live as though they had none" (v. 29). The married man's "interests are divided" (v. 34). Admittedly, it can seem difficult to reconcile John Paul II's personalist vision with statements like these. It can even appear as though St. Paul were leaning toward a Manichaean view of marriage. But John Paul asserts that in a thoughtful reading of the whole text "we find no introduction to...'Manichaeism'" (297).

Paul obviously wants to spare his flock the "troubles in the flesh" that marriage brings with it (see v. 28). But the Holy Father maintains that Paul's desire is not based on any supposed negative value of marriage. It is a "realistic observation," the Pope says, in which "we must see a just warning for those who—as at times young people do—hold that conjugal union and living together must bring them only happiness and joy. The experience of life shows that spouses are not rarely disappointed in what they were greatly expecting" (290). The Holy Father rightly observes that conjugal love—that love precisely by virtue of which the two become "one flesh"—is a difficult love. It places serious moral demands on the couple. If this is what St. Paul intends to say, John Paul argues that "he certainly remains on the grounds of evangelical truth and there is no reason here to see symptoms of...Manichaeism" (290).

The Pope finds a personalist key to interpreting Paul's teaching in verse seven. There the Apostle states in relation to the choice of vocation that "each has his own special gift from God, one of one kind and one of another." The Holy Father places great weight on this statement. He believes that it leads us to see differently St. Paul's teaching as a whole. With this assertion as our interpretive key, we realize that, according to St. Paul, both celibacy *and* marriage stem from a special grace given by God.[17] While Paul clearly encourages abstention from marriage to the Corinthians, this most definitely does *not* stem from a view that marriage is

---

16. See *CCC,* nn. 125–127.

17. See *CCC,* n. 1620.

somehow evil. Paul explicitly wants to counter the idea seemingly circulating in Corinth that marriage is a sin (see vv. 28, 36). To this end he states explicitly, as the Pope repeatedly reminds us, that in both vocations "there is operative that 'gift' that each one receives from God" (297). This gift is the grace that makes the body a "temple of the Holy Spirit," as St. Paul stated in the previous chapter of his letter (see 1 Cor 6:19). This gift remains in both vocations (celibacy and marriage) if the person remains faithful to his gift and, according to his state, does not "dishonor" this temple of the Holy Spirit, which is his body.

B. Outlet for Concupiscence?

Various distortions were prevalent in the Corinthian community that dishonored the temple of the Holy Spirit. St. Paul writes "fully aware of the weakness and sinfulness to which [they were] subjected, precisely by reason of the concupiscence of the flesh" (297). It even seems he is willing to concede to some weakness for the sake of avoiding a greater dishonor to the body. For instance, he says that couples should "come together again, lest Satan tempt you through lack of self control." And then he adds: "I say this by way of concession" (v. 6). And also: "But if they cannot exercise self-control, they should marry. For it is better to marry than to be aflame with passion" (v. 9).

John Paul asks if Paul, based on these words, might not view marriage as an ethical outlet for concupiscence. To this legitimate question, the Pope, in my opinion, fails to give an altogether satisfying answer. Do we not find here the basis of that traditional understanding that one of the ends of marriage was "relief of concupiscence" in the sense of *indulging* lustful desire? (see §34) Again it may seem difficult to reconcile John Paul's teaching with St. Paul's. The Holy Father has insisted throughout his entire catechesis that there is "real power" in Jesus Christ's death and resurrection to *set men free* from the domination of concupiscence. Based on the ethos of redemption which Christ preached in the Sermon on the Mount, John Paul has held out this freedom as the norm and the task for all Christians and stressed that marriage does *not* justify indulging concupiscence.

This, it seems, is why John Paul reminds us that we must look to the teaching of Christ himself for ultimate resolutions to these difficult questions. He also rightly cautions against making judgments about what the Apostle was thinking or teaching about marriage solely based on his statements in 1 Corinthians 7. For example, we can recognize that indulging concupiscence at the expense of one's wife would blatantly contradict Paul's call for husbands to love their wives "as Christ loved the Church" in Ephesians 5. Recall John Paul's pre-papal statement quoted previously: "If it is true that marriage may also be a *remedium concupiscentiae* (see St. Paul: 'It is better to marry than to burn'—1 Cor 7:9) then this must be understood in the integral sense given it by the Christian Scriptures, which also teach of the 'redemption of the body' (Rom 8:23) and point to the sacrament of matrimony as a way of realizing this redemption."[18]

Despite the qualifications the Pope offers, the reader of his exegesis is left desiring more explanation for the apparent incongruity between the Sermon on the Mount (and John Paul's interpretation thereof) and Paul's teaching that it "is better to marry than to burn." The Pope does say that Paul certainly characterizes marriage "on the human side" based on the particular struggles with concupiscence found among the Corinthians. But John Paul believes, based on the Apostle's statement about the "gift" in verse seven, that "he at the same time, with no less strength of conviction, stresses...also the action of grace in every person—in one who lives in marriage no less than in one who willingly chooses continence" (295). This statement seems to indicate that John Paul believes there is no incongruity in what he has been teaching and in what Paul says to the Corinthians. In the final analysis, there may not be. Unfortunately (although the Pope does revisit this issue in cycle 5), John Paul does not take us to that stage of the discussion.

■ It does not seem to me that Paul holds out the power of grace to set the Corinthians *free* from the domination of concupiscence with equal strength of conviction. It seems more plausible to me that Paul offers some concessions to human weakness (specifically, lack of self-control caused by the domination of concupiscence) without a bold proclamation of the full power of redemption because, as he said earlier in his letter, they were not ready for it. He could only feed them with milk, not with solid food, because they were still "babes in Christ"; they were still "of the flesh" (see 1 Cor 3:1–3).

62. Why Celibacy Is "Better" According to St. Paul

June 23, 30; July 7, 14, 1982 (TB 289–299)

As previously noted, Paul is responding to various questions and erroneous ideas found among Christians in Corinth. Paul counters the idea

---

18. "The Family as a Community of Persons," *Person & Community: Selected Essays*, p. 327.

that marriage is itself sinful by stating explicitly that he who marries "does well." But he encourages celibacy because he believes that "he who refrains from marriage will do better" (v. 38). To clarify any confusion on this point, John Paul stresses that Paul is not speaking of the difference between good and evil, but only between good and better. But why does he say that refraining from marriage is "better"? While he affirms the reasons we already discussed (see §58), he adds some personal insights.

A. Anxious About the Affairs of the Lord

First, Paul clearly states that celibacy is better than marriage only given the appropriate circumstances. In keeping with the words of Christ, celibacy must be a voluntary response to a special grace (see v. 7), and it must be chosen because "the form of this world is passing away" (v. 31). In other words, it must be chosen for the sake of the kingdom (which does not pass away).

The Holy Father spends much time reflecting on the following words as the basis of Paul's teaching that celibacy is "better" than marriage. "The unmarried man is anxious about the affairs of the Lord, how to please the Lord; but the married man is anxious about worldly affairs, how to please his wife, and his interests are divided" (vv. 32–34). John Paul says this passage indicates the spousal nature of the celibate vocation. We try to please the people we love, especially a spouse. A form of spousal love, then, is at the foundation of the celibate's desire to "please the Lord." Of course, as the Pope notes, every Christian who lives his faith is anxious to please the Lord. But the celibate person, free from the obligations of marriage and family life, can devote himself to the affairs of the Lord in an exclusive or "undivided" way. Furthermore, John Paul observes that people can "be anxious" only about what occupies their hearts. The "affairs of the Lord" occupy the hearts of those who are celibate for the kingdom. They have chosen the "better part," the "one thing necessary" (see Lk 10:41).

What are the "affairs of the Lord"? John Paul says they signify in the first place the building up of Christ's Body, the Church. But they also signify "concern [for] the whole world" (291). For, as St. Paul says, "the earth is the Lord's and everything in it" (1 Cor 10:26). According to John Paul, this love that Paul has for the Lord, his Church, and his whole world—and his ability to devote himself totally to their service—motivates him to write that "I wish that all were as I myself am" (v. 7).

The Holy Father says that a celibate person with such love and devotion to Christ is marked by an "interior integration"—a unification that allows him to dedicate himself completely to the service of God's kingdom in all its dimensions. Do we not see here, perhaps, an echo of that "original virginal value of man" who was characterized by a perfect interior integration (see §15)? In any case, it is not celibacy *per se* that enables such "virginal" integration. John Paul notes that an unmarried person can also experience an interior "division." When a celibate lacks a clear goal for which to sacrifice marriage, he often faces a certain emptiness. At the same time, as John Paul has already affirmed, a married couple devoted to Christ can rediscover in some sense that original "virginal" integrity.

B. Both Vocations Are a Call to Holiness

Paul mainly desires to help the Corinthians live in "undivided devotion to the Lord" (v. 35). Marriage in itself is no obstacle to Christian devotion. But, as experience attests, married men and women can easily get distracted by the "affairs of the world." As John Paul says, "The Apostle seems to know all this very well, and takes pains to specify that he does not want to 'lay any restraint' [v. 35] on one whom he advised not to marry" (293). His overall point is to call the Corinthians to holiness in body and spirit (see v. 34).

"In order to grasp adequately the whole depth of Paul's thought," John Paul says, "we must note that 'holiness,' according to the biblical concept, is a state rather than an action. It has first of all an ontological character and then also a moral one" (294). In other words, holiness is not first a matter of "doing." It is first a matter of "being." Holiness is first a gift that we must *receive,* not a commodity that we must *produce.* The moral goodness of our actions then flows forth as a fruit of and response to the gift we have received.

■ Recall John Paul's statement that "holiness is measured according to the 'great mystery' in which the Bride responds with the gift of love to the gift of the Bridegroom."[19] Holiness is a gift of love given by the Bridegroom to which we give our consent, our *"fiat."* This is why the *Catechism* teaches that "Mary goes before us all in the holiness that is the Church's mystery as 'the bride without spot or wrinkle.'"[20]

Furthermore, as St. Paul states and John Paul emphasizes, both celibacy *and* marriage are a special *gift* from God. When received as such, both are vocations to holiness. However, as the Apostle to the Gentiles stresses, in a sense the married person finds it more difficult to understand

---

19. *Mulieris Dignitatem,* n. 27.
20. *CCC,* n. 773.

and live this. As Christ affirmed in his discussion with the Sadducees, marriage is part of what Paul calls "the form of this world [which] is passing away" (v. 31). And if man is to be holy, he cannot become too attached to the goods of a perishable world. "Desire for true happiness frees man from his immoderate attachment to the goods of this world"—including marriage—"so that he can find his fulfillment in the vision and beatitude of God."[21] Thus, for marriage to lead to holiness, the Christian must live it in light of his definitive vocation. In other words, he must not let it tie him down to "earthly affairs." He must live it as a sacrament of the life to come. This is what St. Paul means when he says "let those who have wives live as though they had none" (v. 29). Obviously, a celibate for the kingdom is not locked in the world's transience in the same way a married person is. "It is for this very reason," John Paul asserts, "that the Apostle declares that one who chooses continence 'does better'" (296).

C. The Grace Operative in Married Life

John Paul closes his reflections on Paul's First Letter to the Corinthians with some comments on the operation of grace in the conjugal union. The Pope observes that Paul writes about it with the same realism that marks the advice he gives throughout the seventh chapter of this letter. "The husband should give to his wife her conjugal rights, and likewise the wife to her husband. For the wife does not rule over her own body, but the husband does; likewise the husband does not rule over his own body, but the wife does" (vv. 3–4).

John Paul notes that this language of "rights" and "ruling over the body" has passed from Paul's vocabulary into the whole theology of marriage. Unfortunately, these phrases have not always been understood in a way that upheld the dignity of the spouses and the personal nature of the one flesh union. The contractual "rights" and "duties" of spouses have been emphasized at times to the neglect of the love proper to a personal covenant. Hence, ever on guard against anything that obscures the dignity of the person, John Paul insists that these Pauline phrases "cannot be explained apart from the proper context of the marriage covenant" (297). In his catechesis up to this point, the Holy Father has tried to clarify precisely this deeply personal nature of conjugal relations. And he will clarify it even more fully in his next cycle of reflections.

John Paul also has an intriguing and original way of applying the following passage from St. Paul's letter: "Do not refuse one another except

---

21. *CCC*, n. 2548.

perhaps by agreement for a season, that you may devote yourselves to prayer; but then come back together again" (v. 5). According to the Holy Father, "St. Paul clearly says that conjugal common life and the voluntary and periodic abstinence by the couple must be the fruit of this 'gift of God' which is their 'own.'" By knowingly cooperating with this gift, the couple "can maintain and strengthen that mutual personal bond and also that dignity conferred on the body by the fact that it is a 'temple of the Holy Spirit who is in them' (see 1 Cor 6:19)" (298). With these statements, the Holy Father is clearly laying the foundation for his future reflections on the value of periodic abstinence to an authentic marital spirituality (see cycle 6).

Furthermore, he interprets Paul's call to periodic abstinence as an indication of "the need to take into consideration all that in some way corresponds to the very different subjectivity of the man and the woman" (298). All the subjective richness of man and woman is expressed differently, John Paul indicates, according to their different levels of sensitivity. If these differences are to produce harmony rather than discord, they must remain under the influence of that particular gift (grace) given to married people. Based on the subject matter of the Pauline passage, the Pope's statements seem a clear reference to the different rise in sexual arousal in man and woman of which he (as Karol Wojtyla) wrote in detail in *Love & Responsibility*. Because the man typically experiences a more rapid rise in sexual arousal than the woman, the virtue of continence is necessary if the man is to respond tenderly and lovingly toward his wife.[22] Such tenderness is aided by the practice of periodic abstinence and prayer, of which St. Paul spoke. Here again we see John Paul applying familiar Scripture passages in excitingly innovative ways.

63. The Redemption of the Body and the Hope of Every Day
July 14, 21, 1982 (TB 299–302)

John Paul closes his cycle on celibacy in his audience of July 21, 1982 with a summary of his reflections up until this point. "Everything we have tried to do in our meditations in order to understand Christ's words," the Pope says, "has its ultimate foundation in the mystery of the redemption of the body" (302). Historical man can begin to reclaim God's original plan for his humanity only in this context. And it is the only basis for man's hope to attain ultimate fulfillment in his eschatological destiny.

The Holy Father reminds us that St. Paul speaks of the redemption of the body in both an anthropological and a cosmic dimension. It is anthro-

---

22. See *Love & Responsibility*, p. 275.

pological because "it is the redemption of man." It is cosmic because, at the same time, the Pope says, "it radiates, in a certain sense, on all creation, which from the beginning has been bound in a particular way to man and subordinated to him (see Gen 1:28–30)" (299–300). According to John Paul, "All visible creation, all the universe, bears the effects of man's sin" (299). As St. Paul writes, "creation was subjected to futility." But it was subjected "in hope: because the creation itself will be set free from its bondage to decay and obtain the glorious liberty of the children of God" (Rom 8:20–21). The hope of man and the hope of the entire universe, then, rests on the redemption of the body.

A. Christ Fulfills the Proto-evangelium

Recalling the *proto-evangelium* (i.e., the first announcement of the Gospel) in Genesis, John Paul says that the hope of the body's redemption was planted in man's heart immediately after the first sin. The Lord said to the serpent, "I will put enmity between you and the woman, and between your seed and her seed; he shall bruise your head, and you shall bruise his heel" (Gen 3:15). The Church sees in these words a foreshadowing of the New Adam and the New Eve, of Jesus and Mary.[23] Satan will continue to attack the woman and her call to bear life (e.g., see Rev 12). The devil will wound the woman's offspring (Jesus). Yet in the very process of what seems like a victory for Satan, Christ will deal a fatal blow to his head and restore man and woman (and all creation) to the purity of their origins.

Through John Paul's theology of the body we come to realize that this cosmic battle between good and evil, while fought on a spiritual plane (see Eph 6:12), is always a battle for the truth of the body. It is an attack on the nuptial meaning of the body. This is why "the redemption of man" is the redemption of his body. In fact, what the *proto-evangelium* announces is the nuptial meaning of the body's restoration. For Christ defeats the devil and fully reveals man to himself precisely through the nuptial gift of his body on the cross and the "rebirth" of his body in the resurrection.

The triptych of Christ's words upon which John Paul has been reflecting (i.e., Christ's words about the beginning, about the man of lust, and about the resurrection) flow "from the divine depths of the mystery of redemption." And this redemption "finds its specific 'historical' subject precisely in Christ himself [because] the redemption of the body has already been accomplished in Christ" (300). Christ fulfills the hope of the *proto-evangelium* "not only with the words of his teaching, but above all with the testimony of his death and resurrection" (300).

---

23. See *CCC*, n. 411; for the Marian interpretation see *Lumen Gentium*, n. 55 and *Redemptoris Mater*, nn. 7, 11, 24.

B. The Hope of Every Day

St. Paul indicates that the redemption of the body is something we "wait for...with patience" (Rom 8:25). We are saved in hope. But who hopes for what he has already attained (see v. 24)? In this sense Paul speaks of the ultimate fulfillment of the redemption of the body—the eschatological victory over death, to which Christ gave testimony above all by his resurrection. Those who limit themselves to this sense of Paul's words might resign themselves merely to coping with concupiscence until Christ returns. We will certainly always feel the pull of concupiscence in this life, but John Paul insists that the redemption of the body can and *must* bear fruit in the here-and-now of historical man's life. Recall from our reflection on historical man that "*the 'redemption of the body' is already an aspect of human life on earth.* This redemption is not just an eschatological reality but a historical one as well. It shapes the history of the salvation of concrete living people...in keeping with the intent of the Creator announced to the first parents before the fall."[24] Thus, in the Sermon on the Mount, Christ calls historical man to overcome concupiscence not only by observing external norms of behavior, but "even in the uniquely interior movements of the human heart" (301). This call "is a question not of the eschatological hope of the resurrection, but of the hope of victory over sin." With humble faith and buoyant optimism, John Paul calls this "the hope of every day." The "hope of every day," the Pope observes, "manifests its power in human works and even in the very movements of the human heart, clearing a path, in a certain sense, for the great eschatological hope bound with the redemption of the body" (301).

Whether man chooses marriage or celibacy for the kingdom, he must daily give a living witness of fidelity to his choice. For both vocations, such fidelity is only possible when man draws "from the mystery of the redemption of the body the inspiration and the strength to overcome the evil that is dormant in him under the form of threefold concupiscence." This victory comes from "the hope of every day, which in proportion to the normal duties and difficulties of human life helps to overcome 'evil with good' (Rom 12:21)." Thus, as John Paul affirms, "the 'redemption of the body' is expressed not only in the resurrection as victory over death. It is present also in Christ's words addressed to 'historical' man" (301).

---

24. "The Family as a Community of Persons," *Person & Community: Selected Essays,* p. 326.

C. The Theology of the Body Is Fundamental

John Paul states that there is a "bond that exists between the dignity of the human being (man or woman) and the nuptial meaning of his body." The more we live and experience daily a victory over concupiscence, the more we "discover and strengthen that bond" (301). As this bond establishes itself firmly in man's conscience, he discovers the true dignity of every human being by readily recognizing the nuptial meaning of that person's body. In fact, we could even say that to the extent that concupiscence binds us, we are blind to the dignity of the person precisely because we are blind to the nuptial meaning of his or her body. Or, perhaps more aptly, to the extent that we are bound by concupiscence, the dignity of the person remains only an idea, a concept we may well accept, but which we do not *feel* and *experience* in the movements of the heart.

The triptych of Christ's words affords us that "hope of every day" which enables us progressively to rediscover and, more, to experience in our hearts the nuptial meaning of the body. Through the mature freedom of the gift, we can fulfill our body's nuptial meaning either through marriage or celibacy for the kingdom. "Both [vocations] furnish a full answer to one of man's fundamental questions, the question about the significance of 'being a body,' that is, about the significance of masculinity and femininity" (299). "In these different ways," John Paul says, enlisting his anthem from Vatican II, "Christ fully reveals man to man, making him aware of 'his sublime vocation'" (302). What is man's sublime vocation? It is to be taken up into the eternal ecstasy of the Trinitarian mystery through a union with the eternal Word, which St. Paul compares to the union of spouses (see Eph 5:31–32). And this vocation, the Holy Father reminds us, "is inscribed in man according to all his psycho-physical makeup, precisely through the mystery of the redemption of the body" (302).

Apart from the redemption of the body, all interpretations of man— or, what John Paul calls "anthropological hermeneutics"—inevitably fall short of the full truth of man's greatness, of his sublime calling. Thus, John Paul boldly proclaims that the "theology of the body is shown to be something truly fundamental and constitutive for all anthropological hermeneutics" (299). In other words, unless we understand the truths of the theology of the body, we do not—and cannot—understand fundamentally and adequately who man is and who he is meant to be. Nor can we understand how he is meant to live. For the theology of the body is "equally fundamental for ethics." And, if we are to penetrate man's subjectivity, it is fundamental in constructing a "theology of the human ethos" (299).

With this concise review of his reflections up to this point, John Paul prepares his audience for the next cycle of reflections on the sacramentality of marriage.

Celibacy for the Kingdom—In Review

1. Christ's words about those who make themselves eunuchs "for the sake of the kingdom" form the basis of the Pope's reflection on the celibate vocation. This voluntary and supernatural calling serves as a charismatic sign of the future resurrection when men and women "neither marry nor are given in marriage" but participate eternally in the marriage of the Lamb. Based on the covenant with Abraham, preferring to be a eunuch was virtually unthinkable for a Jew.

2. The departure from the Old Covenant was effected especially in the celibate example of Christ. The celibate lives of Joseph and Mary also speak to this new dimension. In a profound paradox, they simultaneously embrace the marriage of earth and the marriage of heaven. By doing so, they effect the most fruitful marriage of the cosmos—the union of the human and divine natures in the Person of Christ. All those who live an authentic celibate vocation participate in some way in this new superabounding spiritual fruitfulness.

3. Behind both marriage and the celibate vocation "are found the same anthropology and the same ethos." In other words, both vocations flow from the same vision of the human person and the same call to experience the redemption of our bodies, which includes the redemption of our sexual desires. Without understanding the ethos of redemption, life-long continence is viewed as hopelessly repressive and marriage as a "legitimate outlet" for lust.

4. An authentic understanding of the "superiority" of continence never means disparaging marriage. It is not based on any prejudice toward the "one flesh" union which, as the essential element of marriage, is part of God's good and holy design. The celibate vocation is "superior" only in its more direct orientation toward man's superior heavenly destiny.

5. Christ does not wish to hide the real sacrifice involved in choosing life-long continence. Historical man is "made" for marriage. However, continence in no way rejects man's dual nature as a sexual being. It participates in the ultimate purpose and meaning of masculinity and femininity. The celibate person fulfills the nuptial meaning of his body differently and even "more" than the married person by being a sincere gift to others.

6. Marriage and celibacy do not divide the Church into two camps of those who are "perfect" and "imperfect." Perfection is measured by charity, not by whether or not one is celibate. Celibacy and marriage, in fact, explain, complete, and in some sense interpenetrate each other.

7. Marriage reveals that continence, too, is an expression of conjugal love which leads to a spiritual fatherhood and motherhood. Continence, by anticipating the heavenly union of Christ and the Church, reveals that marriage is a sacramental participation in the same mystery. Each vocation, in its own way, expresses the reality of "gift" inscribed in the body.

8. Masculinity and femininity reveal that the human person is created to be a gift "for" another. Christ's words reveal that men and women can express this in choosing celibacy "for" the kingdom. This is only a renunciation when viewed in temporal categories. The kingdom for which some choose celibacy expresses the fullness of God's bounty toward man and is the ultimate fulfillment of all that man desires.

9. The celibate vocation is not only a matter of formation but of *transformation*. Only when a person is liberated from lust and is in possession of his own sexual subjectivity can he be a gift to others—whether in the celibate vocation or in marriage. Only one who understands and embraces the beauty and sacredness of God's plan for sex and marriage can renounce them in the mature sense that Christ requires.

10. In 1 Corinthians 7, St. Paul presents the truth about celibacy proclaimed by Christ, yet at the same time he employs a style "totally his own." It can seem as though Paul has a rather negative view of marriage, but in a thoughtful reading of the text we see no introduction to Manichaeism. In fact, Paul insists that both marriage and the celibate vocation are a special "gift" (grace) from God.

11. Many have thought that Paul's statement "it is better to marry than to burn" justifies indulging concupiscence within marriage. It may seem difficult to reconcile John Paul II's teaching with St. Paul's. Yet Paul's words cannot be interpreted apart from Christ's words about lust nor apart from Paul's teaching as a whole, which includes "the redemption of the body" and the call of husbands to love their wives "as Christ loved the Church."

12. The Apostle writes that he who marries "does well," but he who refrains "does better" since he can devote himself in an undivided way to "the affairs of the Lord." Marriage itself is a vocation to holiness and therefore concerns the "affairs of the Lord." But experience attests that the responsibilities of marriage and family life can distract men and women from their ultimate vocation and tie them down to "earthly affairs." It is in this sense that Paul exhorts married people to live as though they were not married.

13. When Paul speaks of granting "conjugal rights" and spouses "ruling over the body" of the other, these expressions cannot be explained

apart from the context of the love proper to the marriage covenant. Grace is poured out on the couple in their conjugal life to harmonize their different levels of sensitivity. The periodic abstinence which Paul recommends can aid this.

14. Christ fulfills the *"proto-evangelium"* of Genesis not only in his teaching, but especially with his death and resurrection. In this way Christ "re-creates" man and woman and redeems the nuptial meaning of the body. This redemption is not only a hope for the eschaton, but is also a "hope of every day." It already begins here-and-now and clears a path for future glory.

15. A deep bond exists between the dignity of the person and the nuptial meaning of his or her body. To the extent that concupiscence binds us, the dignity of the person is not "felt." Thus, the theology of the body and the redemption to which it calls us is fundamental for all interpretations of man and for constructing an adequate and authentic human ethos.

Cycle 5

The Sacramentality of Marriage

The theology of the body has emerged along the lines which Christ provides in the triptych or three-part "revelation of the body." Having reflected on this "total vision of man" and then applied it to the vocation of celibacy for the kingdom, we are now prepared to penetrate the "great mystery" of the sacramentality of marriage. For what Christian celibacy participates in by immediate anticipation, Christian marriage participates in by sacramental mediation.

We are speaking, of course, about the marriage of the Lamb—the ultimate fulfillment of both the celibate vocation and the sacrament of marriage. But in what way does Christian marriage participate in the spousal relationship of Christ and the Church? The answer lies in this fifth cycle of John Paul II's theology of the body. These twenty-two general audiences delivered between July 28, 1982 and February 9, 1983[1] are perhaps more densely packed with far-reaching theological insight than the other cycles. So it will take a bit more ink to unpack this cycle than the others.

Cycle 5 provides a fresh analysis of what John Paul calls another "key" and "classic" text of Scripture: Ephesians 5:21–33. The mystery of God's spousal love for humanity, John Paul says, was only "half opened" by the prophets of the Old Testament. In Ephesians 5:21–33 "it is fully revealed."[2] St. Paul speaks of the "great mystery" of man and woman's communion in "one flesh" as a perennial foreshadowing of Christ's incarnate communion with the Church. Hence, this text brings our understanding of the body and nuptial union to a "mystical" level. We can mine the great

---

1. John Paul postponed his catechesis for a year after closing this cycle. He resumed in May of 1984 with a reflection on the Song of Songs, the story of Tobiah and Sarah, and a review of Ephesians 5. Some divisions of the Pope's catechesis include these (five) addresses in cycle 5. However, as John Paul indicates, these addresses are better situated as an introduction to his cycle on *Humanae Vitae* (see 5/23/84, TB 368).

2. 9/22/82, TB 329.

riches of this passage only in light of Christ's "revelation of the body." The Pope wants to understand how the sacramentality of marriage emerges in this "classic" text. He wants to understand how it is expressed and confirmed there. He adds that the answers he seeks cannot be attained quickly, but only through a gradual, "long-term" effort. These answers, he says, "must pass through the whole sphere of...the theology of the body."[3]

Using our former image, when spouses allow their "tires" to be inflated with the "great mystery" proclaimed in Ephesians 5, they come to experience marriage as it was created to be. The deep longings and worthy desires of the heart for love—for giving and receiving affirmation, tenderness, mercy, and compassion, for life-long commitment and fidelity of heart, mind, and body—are not left frustrated, but are met in true measure. In short, marriage works when both spouses are committed to the "great mystery" of redemption in Jesus Christ. The road of married life will always have its bumps, but couples with tires inflated by the "breath of God" are supremely equipped to handle them.

64. Marriage and the "Great Mystery" of Ephesians
July 28; August 4, 1982 (TB 304–309)

One would be hard-pressed to find a passage in the Scriptures that has been more maligned and dismissed by today's "politically correct" society than Ephesians 5. In light of such polemics—which have even seeped into the Church—John Paul is at pains to resurrect the true meaning of St. Paul's[4] words and to show their fundamental importance. Here is the full passage:

> Be subject to one another out of reverence for Christ. Wives, be subject to your husbands, as to the Lord. For the husband is the head of the wife as Christ is the head of the church, his body, and is himself its Savior. As the church is subject to Christ, so let wives also be subject in everything to their husbands. Husbands, love your wives, as Christ loved the church and gave himself up for her, that he might sanctify her, having cleansed her by the washing of water with the word, that he might present the

---

3. 7/28/82, TB 305.

4. The Holy Father acknowledges in an endnote that some exegetes question the Pauline authorship of Ephesians. John Paul provides a provisional solution to the dispute "by means of a median supposition which we accept here as a working hypothesis: namely, that St. Paul entrusted some concepts to his secretary, who then developed and refined them" (7/28/1982, endnote; TB 380). For this reason he alternately references "the author of the letter to the Ephesians," the "Apostle," and "St. Paul."

church to himself in splendor, without spot or wrinkle or any such thing, that she might be holy and without blemish. Even so husbands should love their wives as their own bodies. He who loves his wife loves himself. For no man ever hates his own flesh, but nourishes and cherishes it, as Christ does the church, because we are members of his body. "For this reason a man shall leave his father and mother and be joined to his wife, and the two shall become one flesh." This is a great mystery, and I mean in reference to Christ and the church; however, let each one of you love his wife as himself, and let the wife see that she respects her husband.

A. The Crowning of the Themes of Scripture

When this controversial passage from Ephesians is correctly understood in the full biblical context, we realize that it contains "central themes and essential truths" that cannot be dismissed. John Paul even says in his poetic fashion that we should consider this passage "as the 'crowning' of the themes and truths which, through the word of God revealed in Sacred Scripture, ebb and flow like long waves" (305). He reiterates this and even goes a step further in his *Letter to Families* by describing this passage from Ephesians as "the compendium or *summa*, in some sense, *of the teaching about God and man* which was brought to fulfillment by Christ."[5] John Paul wants to penetrate this "summa" to help us "understand possibly 'to the very depths' how much richness of the truth revealed by God is contained in the scope of [this] wonderful page" (306). To do so we must presuppose the triptych of Christ's words about the human body in the beginning, in history, and in the resurrection.

As John Paul points out, the words of Ephesians 5 "are centered on the body." They speak of the body in both the analogous sense of the Body of Christ, which is the Church, and the concrete sense of the human body in its sexual complementarity and its "perennial destiny for union in marriage"(305). The convergence of these two meanings of the body gives us the key to understand the "great mystery" St. Paul speaks of in verses 31–32. There the Apostle links the primordial meaning of the "one flesh" union of spouses with the union of Christ and the Church. What is the relationship between these two holy communions? John Paul will provide a "studied" answer.

Precisely at this point—in the relationship of that perennial union in "one flesh" with the union of Christ and the Church—we find ourselves on the threshold of the meaning and mystery of the universe. We find ourselves on the threshold of discovering the glory and greatness that God has bestowed on us by creating us as male and female and calling us to incarnate

---

5. *Letter to Families*, n. 19.

communion. This is why, using again his anthem from *Gaudium et Spes*, John Paul says that this passage from Ephesians "reveals—in a particular way—man to man, and makes him aware of his lofty vocation" (306).

B. The Experience of the Incarnate Person

By linking this passage from Ephesians with the key anthropological statement of Vatican II, we glimpse from yet another angle the exceptional importance John Paul places on St. Paul's words here. However, a person can only see this link with *Gaudium et Spes* 22 "inasmuch as he shares in the experience of the incarnate person" (306). This phrase "the experience of the incarnate person" in some way describes the Pope's entire catechesis. This is what the theology of the body—and this passage from Ephesians—are all about. They seek to ground man in the *experience* of his own *incarnate personhood*. The modern view of man, however, has effectively severed man from his body. In the often vehement dispute over Ephesians 5, we glimpse the great clash of two competing humanisms and, in particular, their respective views of the human body and the meaning of sexuality.

In the modern view, the body has been relegated to the realm of sub-human nature. It may serve as a biological reference point, but it has nothing to say about the human person and the order of human relationships. Much less does the body say anything about theology—about the nature of the divine mystery and God's love for humanity. In this view, the person stands over and against his body. The body does not call him to anything. It makes no demands on him. Modern man owns his body like a thing and he can do whatever he wants with it. The body and sexuality are then used as tools and as a means to selfish pleasure, even profit. The "word" (or anti-word) inscribed in the body for modern man is "self-gratification."

St. Paul, on the other hand, is deeply rooted in a sacramental, theological view of the body. He knows the body "speaks" a mystical language. It speaks not only about the truth of the human person as male and female. It speaks about the "great mystery" hidden in God from all eternity. For St. Paul, the truth about who man is as male and female can only be understood in light of this "great mystery." Recalling God's incarnate plan for man and woman in Genesis, he links it with the analogy of the spousal love of God for his chosen people. In doing so, he calls man and woman to embrace the sublime vocation inscribed in their bodies from "the beginning"—to love as God loves. The Word inscribed in the body in Ephesians 5 is "self-donation."

The modern view of man and of human sexuality cannot tolerate and, in fact, radically opposes this "great *incarnational* mystery." Such a grand vision places far too many demands on man and challenges his utilitarian view of the body at its roots. Thus, those who embrace the vision of the body and of marriage proclaimed in Ephesians 5 should expect fierce attacks. It is no coincidence, as John Paul indicates, that St. Paul's proclamation of the "great mystery" is followed by "a stupendous encouragement to the spiritual battle (see 6:10–20)" (308). It is also important to realize that St. Paul began his letter by presenting the eternal plan of man's salvation in Christ (see Eph 1). This is the battle we are fighting—the battle of salvation. It is a *spiritual* battle but it is waged against the truth of the *body*. And, as we learn from the Letter to the Ephesians, the sacramentality of marriage stands at the center of the clash. If we are to win this battle, the first piece of armor we must don is to "gird our loins with the truth" (Eph 6:14).

65. The Body Enters the Definition of Sacrament

July 28; August 4, 11, 1982 (TB 305–311)

In his audience of August 4, John Paul outlines the overall structure of the Letter to the Ephesians before analyzing chapter 5. This helps us position St. Paul's detailed instructions to husbands and wives in the broader context of the moral obligations of the family, the larger Christian community, and society as a whole. It also helps us understand the spiritual climate which the Apostle believes should animate the lives of Christians. Sinful humanity is called to new life in Jesus Christ. Only by living this "new life"—that is, only through the encounter with the risen Christ—are men and women empowered to live as St. Paul exhorts them to live.

For this reason the Apostle bends his knee "before the Father" and asks him to grant that the readers of his letter would "be strengthened with might through his Spirit in the inner man, and that Christ may dwell in your hearts through faith; that you, being rooted and grounded in love, may have power to comprehend with all the saints what is the breadth and length and height and depth, and to know the love of Christ which surpasses knowledge, that you may be filled with the fullness of God" (3:14–19). If the Apostle holds husbands and wives to a high standard, he assures his readers that the "fullness of God" and the love of Christ within us affords a "power" that can do far more in us than anything we could ask or imagine (see Eph 3:20).

A. God's Plan of Salvation Is Rooted in the Body

The union of man and woman in one flesh is a "great mystery" that refers to Christ's union with the Church (see 5:31–32). Even at first glance we see that this truth proclaimed by Ephesians 5 confirms John Paul's thesis statement (see §22). The Apostle is speaking here of that "great mystery" hidden in God from time immemorial that, according to John Paul, the body "and it alone" is capable of making visible to us. It is the mystery of divine love and life—of Trinitarian Communion—in which man and woman are called to participate through the intimacy of a quasi-nuptial union with Christ. This is the very essence of what this passage from Ephesians reveals about the sacramentality of marriage and its consummate expression of conjugal intercourse. The Pope seeks gradually to unfold precisely this point.

The Pope reiterates his thesis when he affirms that "in some way, even if in the most general way, the body enters the definition of sacrament, being 'a visible sign of the invisible reality,' that is, of the spiritual, transcendent, divine reality. In this sign—and through this sign—God gives himself to man in his transcendent truth and in his love. The sacrament is a sign of grace, and it is an efficacious sign." In other words, the Pope says, "Not only does the sacrament indicate grace and express it in a visible way, but it also produces it." The sacrament "effectively contributes to having grace become part of man, and to realizing and fulfilling in him the work of salvation, the work begun by God from all eternity and fully revealed in Jesus Christ" (305–306).

This is a grand statement of incarnational theology. It grounds God's plan of salvation *in the body* by grounding the action of God's grace in the body. It beautifully echoes Tertullian's famous saying: "the flesh is the hinge of salvation."[6] Man is an incarnate person. This is the only way he can encounter God and be himself. This means that, contrary to popular opinion, in his quest for transcendence man need not shed his skin. In an act of utter *kenosis* (self-emptying), Transcendence himself took on man's skin, thus *divinizing the body*. In the Bridegroom, Jesus Christ, "the whole fullness of deity dwells bodily" (Col 2:9). The Incarnation, then, as John Paul said at the conclusion of his first cycle, "is the definitive source of the sacramentality of marriage."[7] The Incarnation, in fact, is the definitive and ultimate "nuptial" union. It is the union of divinity and humanity in the Person of the Word. It is the indissoluble sign of the Father's covenant love for humanity, of the super-abounding grace bestowed upon the incarnate—that is, the human—person.

---

6. See *CCC*, n. 1015.

7. 4/2/80, TB 89 (see §24).

This is precisely the affirmation of the body and of nuptial union found in St. Paul's proclamation of the "great mystery" in Ephesians 5. John Paul will explore the meaning of sacrament (particularly the sacrament of marriage), as he says, first in the dimension of covenant and grace (this is the divine reality of sacrament), and then in the dimension of the sacramental sign (this is the human reality of sacrament).

B. Modern Sensitivities and St. Paul's Interpretive Key

Since he became pope, John Paul has repeatedly proclaimed, "Be not afraid." We can certainly apply this to St. Paul's words in Ephesians 5. We need not be afraid of what this passage reveals about man and woman's relationship. John Paul certainly is not. He presses into it without hesitation. In the process he shows that far from promoting an imbalance or inequality between spouses, this passage provides the only means of ensuring the proper ordering of love between them—reverence for the mystery of Christ revealed through their bodies.

In speaking of the wife's subjection to her husband, the Holy Father affirms that the "author of the letter to the Ephesians does not fear to accept those concepts which were characteristic of the mentality and of the customs of the times.... Nowadays our contemporary sensitivity is certainly different; quite different, too," the Pope continues, "are the mentality and customs, and also the social position of women in regard to men" (310–311). But when we dismiss St. Paul's words out-of-hand because of modern sensitivities, we miss his evangelical genius altogether. Like any great evangelist, he seeks to inject the cultural customs of his day with the Christian mystery. Since the first chapter of his letter the Apostle has been outlining the divine plan of man's salvation—that mystery hidden in the Father which has been made known through Christ's union with the Church. He has also been seeking to outline the vocation of those who are baptized into this mystery. According to John Paul, these are the two principal guidelines of the entire letter, and St. Paul's "classic" teaching on marriage appears at the meeting of these guidelines. The mystery of Christ's union with the Church and the vocation of Christians to "walk in love, as Christ loved us" (5:1–2) provide the interpretive key to Paul's teaching. This is *crucial* to a proper understanding of the passage.

The Apostle insists that those who accept their vocation in Christ "must no longer live as the Gentiles do, in the futility of their minds; they are darkened in their understanding, alienated from the life of God...due to their hardness of heart" (4:17–18). Then he exhorts his readers: "Put off your old nature which belongs to your former manner of life and is corrupt through deceitful lusts, and be renewed in the spirit of your minds, and put on the new nature, created after the likeness of God in true righteousness and holiness" (4:22–24). Do we not see here reference to that same "hardness of heart" and that same "lust" Christ referred to in his words about God's original plan for marriage and in the Sermon on the Mount? Do we not also see the call to a radical transformation of the conscience and attitudes of men and women according to the image and likeness of God in which they were made?

In light of the ethos of redemption, St. Paul's exhortation to husbands and wives takes on a revolutionary meaning. Indeed, it turns the typical interpretation (i.e., that St. Paul is justifying male domination) on its head. Knowing that male domination flows from sin (see Gen 3:16), the Apostle is actually calling husbands and wives to live according to God's original plan in which there was a perfect balance, complementarity, and equality between the sexes.

C. Mutual Subjection

Based on the Holy Father's exegesis, we might conclude that Paul is saying something like this to his readers: "You are accustomed to subordination within marriage. This means one thing to the Gentiles who are darkened in their understanding and corrupted by lust. But here is how this looks in light of the mystery of Christ. Here is what this means for the vocation of Christians."

The first thing St. Paul calls spouses to do is to be "subject to one another out of reverence for Christ" (5:21). John Paul emphasizes this passage in order to highlight the often overlooked fact that subjection within marriage, according to St. Paul, is *mutual*. It is not, as often thought, a unilateral subjection of the wife to the husband. At this point the questions multiply. What does it mean to be "subject" to one another? And why out of reverence for Christ? Furthermore, does it not seem like Paul then stresses the wife's subjection to her husband more than the husband to his wife? As we shall see, these questions can only be properly answered if we believe in "the gift." They can only be properly answered if we understand that the truth of masculinity and femininity lies in the sacramental ability of the body to convey the covenant relationship of God and man. "The gift" is the love which the Heavenly Bridegroom gives to humanity as Bride. But men and women must *believe* in the gift if they are to *receive* it and *recapitulate* it in their love for one another.

Remove this element of "gift" and, in relation to divinity, humanity can only assert itself in the face of a supposed tyranny. In turn, this same dynamic will be played out in the relationship of the sexes. "Subjection" then means a self-abnegating surrender to domination, particularly in the relationship of the wife to the husband. Void of "the gift," the feminist re-volt against Ephesians 5 is quite understandable. But we are not void of the gift! *The gift has been given in superabundance* through the "great mystery" of which Ephesians 5 speaks. But we must "believe in the good news" (Mk 1:15). We must reclaim the original meaning of the body—of masculin-ity and femininity—and the original way of living the body as a gift.

Recall one of John Paul's key statements from his reflections on Gen-esis: "This is the body: a witness to creation as a fundamental gift, and so a witness to Love as the source from which this same giving springs. Mas-culinity-femininity—namely, sex—is the original sign of a creative dona-tion [by God] and of an awareness on the part of man, of a gift lived so to speak in an original way."[8]

The original way of living "the gift" was manifested in the perfect balance of love between the sexes as exhibited by the peace of original na-kedness. As we all know from experience, however, original sin shattered this "original way." Concupiscence does not live the reality of gift. In-stead, it appropriates and dominates the other. This is felt in a particularly pointed way by woman in relation to man (see §28). But through the power of the Holy Spirit, the author of Ephesians calls spouses to put off their old nature corrupted by lust and put on the new nature made in God's image (see 4:22–24). In other words, through the mystery of redemption, St. Paul calls spouses back to that "original way" of living the gift.

66. Reverence for Christ Must Inform the Love of Spouses

August 11, 18; September 1, 1982 (TB 309–314, 320)

Only when the Apostle's words are imbued with the mystery and fi-delity of the "gift" does his teaching about "subjection" within marriage take on its authentic meaning. From this perspective we come to under-stand with John Paul that to be "subject" to one's spouse means to be "completely given" (312). In turn, mutual subjection means "a reciprocal donation of self" (310). In other words, to be subject to one another means to live the sincere gift of self "in everything" (v. 24) according to the nup-tial meaning of the body, of masculinity and femininity.

A. Reverence for Christ

This is the radical paradigm shift St. Paul calls for by informing the customs of the day (which concupiscence certainly influenced) with the

---

8. 1/9/80, TB 62 (see §17).

mystery of Christ. In this way, John Paul says that Christian marriage, according to Ephesians, "excludes that element of the pact which was a burden and, at times, does not cease to be a burden in this institution" (310). Husbands and wives are called to mutual subjection *out of reverence for Christ*. This means that their mutual relations should flow from their common relationship with Christ. They should flow from a profound and lived experience of the redemption of the body and, in this way, reclaim something of that original harmony of the beginning.

This reverence for Christ, John Paul points out, is analogous to "fear of the Lord" or piety. Such "fear" is not a defensive attitude before God as if he posed a threat. It is a gift of the Holy Spirit that inspires a profound respect for the holy, the sacred, and the expression of this gift is love. The mystery of Christ is, in fact, inscribed in the very bodies of husband and wife and in their "one flesh" union. This is what makes marriage a sacred mystery. As John Paul says, when "awe" for this mystery penetrates the spouses' hearts it engenders in them that holy "reverence for Christ" and leads them to be "subject to one another." This confers a profound and mature character on the conjugal union.

With Christ as both the source and the model of their subjection (of their giving), the Holy Father observes that the psychology and moral nature of the spouses is so transformed as to give rise to "a new and precious fusion" of their relations and conduct (310). Husband and wife become "fused" in this sense not only with one another, but also with the Holy Spirit who inspires them to live the "sincere gift of self." Filled with the Spirit (see v. 18), husbands are inspired to love their wives "as Christ loved the church" (v. 25); and wives are inspired to be subject (or given) to their husbands "as the Church is subject to Christ" (v. 24).

B. The Spousal Analogy

Christian spouses must model their relationship after the relationship of Christ and the Church. According to the great "spousal analogy," the wife is an icon of the Church as Bride and the husband is an icon of Christ as Bridegroom. Hence we read: "Wives, be subject to your husbands *as* to the Lord. For the husband is the head of the wife *as* Christ is the head of the church" (vv. 22–23). John Paul stresses, "In saying this, the author does not intend to say that the husband is 'lord' of the wife [in any way that would imply] that the interpersonal pact proper to marriage is a pact of domination of the husband over the wife" (310). Recall that Christ says any proper "headship" among his followers must not be modeled after the Gentiles who lord it over their subjects and make their authority felt. Instead the "lord" must serve others in love and in self-sacrifice (see Lk 22:25–26).

St. Paul could not be clearer on this point when he says: "Husbands, love your wives *as* Christ loved the church." How did Christ love the Church? He "gave himself up for her" (v. 25). Christ said that he came not to *be* served but *to serve,* and to lay down his life for his Bride (see Mt 20:28). Thus, John Paul insists that the love to which St. Paul calls husbands clearly "excludes every kind of subjection whereby the wife might become a servant or a slave of the husband, an object of unilateral domination. Love makes the husband simultaneously subject to the wife, and thereby to the Lord himself, just as the wife to the husband" (310).

But one might still ask why St. Paul, having called spouses to a mutual subjection, subsequently specifies the wife's subjection to her husband, whereas he calls the husband to "love his wife." The Holy Father might respond that in this manner the Apostle maintains the complementarity of the sexes that is indispensable in living "the gift." Husband and wife are certainly called to a mutual subjection, but, according to the nature of sexual difference, each lives this subjection in different, complementary ways.

■ The feminist debate arises precisely here, in the admission that any fundamental and meaningful *difference* between the sexes exists. But, again, it arises only in a paradigm void of the "the gift" (see §65). In the face of man's historical domination of woman, many feminists think that the only way to claim their equality with men is to level sexual difference. They prefer words like "mutuality" to "complementarity" when discussing the inter-relationship of the sexes. Of course, there is a proper place for "mutuality," such as in the expression "mutual self-donation." But the original call of mutual self-donation is only possible in and through the beauty, mystery, and complementarity of sexual *difference*. The point is that equality between the sexes does not and must not mean "sameness." As John Paul expresses, the equal dignity of man and woman results from their "specific diversity and personal originality.... Consequently, even the rightful opposition of women to what is expressed in the biblical words, 'He shall rule over you' (Gen 3:16) must not under any condition lead to the 'masculinization' of women." He continues, "In the name of liberation from male 'domination,' women must not...*deform and lose what constitutes their essential richness*."[9] Tragically, by leveling sexual difference we also eradicate the nuptial mystery proclaimed by our humanity. In other words, we blind ourselves to the theology of the human body in its maleness and femaleness.

9. *Mulieris Dignitatem*, n. 10.

C. Giving and Receiving the Gift

As John Paul stated in his reflections on original man, the reality of gift "indicates the one who gives, the one who receives the gift, and also the relationship that is established between them."[10] The Pope was referring specifically to the covenant of creation established between God and man. But it also applies to the nuptial relationship of man and woman which images and participates in God's covenant love with humanity. As John Paul expresses, in imaging the nuptial mystery of Christ's love for the Church "the husband is above all *he who loves,* and the wife, on the other hand is *she who is loved"* (320). In other words, it corresponds to the nuptial meaning of the husband's body to "initiate the gift," whereas it corresponds to the nuptial meaning of the wife's body to "receive the gift." This complementary, sacramental reality is written in our very anatomy— and, thus, because the body is the "sacrament" of the person, it is written in our very personality as male and female.

> ■ This giving and receiving of the gift is *not* to be equated with "activity" and "passivity." Nor is it correct to limit "giving" to the masculine and "receiving" to the feminine. Recall John Paul says that "the giving and the accepting of the gift interpenetrate, so that the giving itself becomes accepting, and the acceptance is transformed into giving."[11] We could qualify the complementarity of the sexes in their giving and receiving, as Dr. William E. May expresses it, by stating that the man "gives in a receiving way," whereas the woman "receives in a giving way."[12]

Through our analysis it comes to light, as the Holy Father proposes, that "the wife's 'submission' to her husband, understood in the context of the entire passage of the letter to the Ephesians, signifies above all 'the experiencing of love.' All the more so since this 'submission' is related to the image of the submission of the Church to Christ, which certainly consists in experiencing his love" (320).

By drawing this analogy between spousal love and Christ's love for the Church, we realize that, despite modern sensitivities and cultural differences, the fundamental moral principle of the Letter to the Ephesians remains the same for all times and cultures. When properly understood and lived, the Pope observes that it always produces that profound and

---

10. 1/2/80, TB 59 (see §17).

11. 2/6/80, TB 71.

12. See *Marriage: The Rock on which the Family Is Built* (San Francisco, CA: Ignatius Press, 1995), p. 50.

solid structure of the true communion of persons in marriage. It enables men and women to live the sincere gift of self stamped in the nuptial meaning of their bodies. In this way, husband and wife, in their own complementary ways, image God and thus fulfill the very meaning of their being and existence.

67. Carnal Love and the Language of Agape

August 11, 18, 25; September 1, 1982 (TB 311–320)

As we are seeing, the sacramentality of marriage emerges in the Letter to the Ephesians via the spousal analogy of Christ's love for the Church. The Pope tells us that St. Paul inserts his teaching on marriage into the very reality of the mystery hidden from eternity in God and revealed to mankind in Jesus Christ. In this way we are "witnesses of a particular meeting of that mystery with the very essence of the vocation to marriage" (311). This means that the sacramentality of marriage is not merely some holy thing tacked onto marriage as a natural institution. Marriage's participation in the divine mystery is of its very essence. Of course, in the strict sense of the term, marriage is only a sacrament when both spouses are already baptized in Christ. Yet even in the marriages of non-Christians there remains a "figure" in some sense of the primordial sacrament,[13] a certain—even if not sacramentally efficacious—sign of Christ's union with the Church.

John Paul observes that marriage clarifies and illuminates the mystery of Christ and the Church, at least to a certain degree. Yet at the same time, the mystery of Christ and the Church "unveils the essential truth about marriage" (312). Thus John Paul tells us that the spousal analogy operates in two directions. In analyzing the text of Ephesians 5, we must look at both. Here we can recall what we stated in the prologue about reading the human spousal analogy from the perspective of the divine "katalogy." This means that the movement upwards ("ana") from the human spousal union to the union of Christ and the Church implies a prior downward ("kata") movement from Christ's union with the Church to the union of spouses (see §4).

A. Marriage Emerges from the Mystery of Christ

When we reread St. Paul's analogy "inversely"—that is, beginning with Christ's relationship with the Church and then moving to husband

---

13. See 10/13/82, TB 336.

and wife ("katalogy")—we realize that "marriage, in its deepest essence, emerges from the mystery of God's eternal love for man and for humanity: from the salvific mystery which is fulfilled in time through the spousal love of Christ for the Church " (313). As John Paul asserts, this means "that marriage corresponds to the vocation of Christians only when it reflects the love which Christ the Bridegroom gives to the Church his Bride, and which the Church...attempts to return to Christ. This is redeeming love, love as salvation, the love with which man from eternity has been loved by God in Christ" (312).

This is quite a lofty calling. Who by his own strength can live this divine love? Only the grace of salvation makes it possible. And the sacrament of marriage affords precisely this. As John Paul says, marriage "is a revelation *and a realization* in time of the mystery of salvation, of the election of love, hidden from eternity in God" (312).[14] So once again we learn that "at the basis of an understanding of marriage in its very essence is the spousal relationship of Christ to the Church" (313). From the beginning, marriage found its *raison d'être* as a visible sign of the divine eternal mystery, as an image and foreshadowing of Christ's union with the Church. In this way, John Paul says that the Letter to the Ephesians leads us to the very foundations of the sacramentality of marriage.

Accordingly, we must conclude that in the spousal analogy St. Paul does not find merely a coincidental or extrinsic resemblance that affords a convenient way of making his point. This is not the wistful thinking of a dreamy evangelist. Instead, "one must admit," according to the Holy Father, "that in the very essence of marriage a particle of the mystery is captured. Otherwise, the entire analogy would hang suspended in a void." It "would be without a real basis, as if it had no ground beneath its feet" (313). The cross of Christ is planted in the ground beneath the feet of this spousal analogy. Here we witness the totality of Christ's spousal love for the Church. "That gift of himself to the Father by obedience unto death (see Phil 2:8) is contemporaneously, according to the Letter to the Ephesians, a 'giving himself up for the Church.' In this expression, redeeming love is transformed," the Pope says, "into spousal love: Christ, giving himself up for the Church, through the same redeeming act is united once and for all with her, as bridegroom with the bride, as husband with his wife" (314).

In this way we can see that "the mystery of the redemption of the body conceals within itself, in a certain sense, the mystery of 'the marriage of the Lamb'(see Rev 19:7)." Through the Bridegroom's sincere gift of

---

14. Emphasis added.

self "the entire salvific gift of the redemption penetrates the Church as the Body [of Christ], and continually forms the most profound, essential substance of her life" (314). This is the mystery stamped in our bodies, in the gift of sexual difference and our call to become "one flesh." Hence, we can understand why in *Familiaris Consortio* John Paul describes spouses as "the permanent reminder to the Church of what happened on the cross." "Their belonging to each other," he says, "is the real representation, by means of the sacramental sign, of the very relationship of Christ with the Church."[15]

B. Head and Body Analogy

All of this is confirmed and deepened by the head and body analogy St. Paul also uses.[16] The Pope suggests that this analogy seems even more central to the Apostle in his proclamation of the truth about Christ's relationship with the Church. However, John Paul says we must equally affirm that St. Paul has not placed the head-body analogy alongside or outside of the spousal analogy. In fact, the Apostle speaks as if in marriage the husband is also the "head of the wife" and the wife "the body of the husband." These two images are so interrelated that, according to the Holy Father, the analogy of head-body actually becomes the analogy of groom-bride. We see the link between these two analogies in the "one flesh" union the Apostle speaks of, quoting from Genesis. Speaking of the spousal relationship in terms of the head-body relationship, it is as if St. Paul is saying that spouses, in becoming "one body," are united so intimately as to form "one organic union"—one "organism."

And since the body is the expression of human subjectivity, John Paul goes so far as to say that, by becoming "one body," spouses also become in some manner "one subject." The Apostle indicates this when he says, "He who loves his wife loves himself" (v. 28). The Holy Father quickly clarifies, however, that this does not blur the spouses' individuality. An essential and dominant "bi-subjectivity" always remains at the basis of "uni-subjectivity." Otherwise, spouses would be lost or swallowed up in the other, rather than finding their true selves through the sincere gift of self (see §23).[17]

---

15. *Familiaris Consortio,* n. 13.

16. See *CCC,* nn. 787–796.

17. These reflections are closely related with the themes of solitude being "prior" to unity (see §§11, 49), of double-solitude as the foundation for unity (see §14), of unity-in-plurality (see §§23, 53), and of the rediscovery of a perfect subjectivity and inter-subjectivity (see §§49, 53).

We can see this distinction clearly in the relationship of Christ with the Church. John Paul states that there "is no doubt" that Christ is a subject different from the Church. Nonetheless, he is united with her in a particular relationship as in one organic union of head and body, or, as the *Catechism* expresses, as "one mystical person."[18] Even so, the unity of Christ and the Church, like the unity of husband and wife, does not remove their distinction.[19] Precisely in the tension of unity-in-plurality, the Trinitarian mystery is manifested in a real way, and man's own mystery is revealed to himself.

C. Unity through Love

The Holy Father further specifies that the spouses' "uni-subjectivity" does not have a "real character" but only "intentional." It is a "unity through love" established not in an ontological sense but in a moral sense. Still, in this moral sense, conjugal love is so unifying that it allows spouses "to be mutually interpenetrated, spiritually belonging to one another to such a degree that the...'I' becomes in a certain sense the 'you' and the 'you' the 'I'" (320). In other words, spousal love makes the "I" (that is, the subjectivity) of the other person his own. "The 'I' of the wife," the Pope suggests, "becomes through love the 'I' of the husband" (319). Hence, at the close of his passage, St. Paul reiterates that each husband is to "love his wife as himself" (v. 33).

As John Paul stresses, all of this is rooted in and expressed through the body. "The body is the expression of that 'I' and the foundation of its identity. The union of husband and wife in love is expressed also by means of the body " (319). So, in loving their wives "as Christ loved the Church" (v. 25), husbands are to "love their wives as their own bodies" (v. 28). For this is how Christ loves the Church, which is his Body. John Paul says that the body of the "other" becomes "one's own" in the sense that one cares for the welfare of the other's body as he cares for his own. "For no man ever hates his own flesh, but nourishes and cherishes it, as Christ does the church, for we are members of his body" (vv. 29–30). All of these references to the body (see vv. 23, 28, 29, 30, 31) find their logic in "the motive of one flesh" that Paul presents as a "great mystery." This *bodily love* which unites the spouses expresses "the most general and at the same time the most essential content" of the entire passage of Ephesians 5. This incarnate love signifies divine love. In this way, John Paul demonstrates that "carnal love"—far from being base or innately corrupt as often suspected—is meant to express "the language of 'agape'" (320).

---

18. See *CCC,* nn. 795, 1119, 1474.

19. See *CCC,* n. 796.

■ In *Love & Responsibility*, Karol Wojtyla offers a practical application for how a husband is to care for his wife's body as he does his own within the intimacy of marital relations. In the final chapter entitled "Sexology and Ethics," the future pope tells us that if a man is truly to love his wife, "it is necessary to insist that intercourse must not serve merely as a means of allowing [his] climax." Love, he says, "demands that the reactions of the other person, the sexual 'partner,' be fully taken into account." He continues: "Sexologists state that the curve of arousal in woman is different from that in man—it rises more slowly and falls more slowly.... The man must take this difference between male and female reactions into account...so that climax may be reached [by] both...and as far as possible occur in both simultaneously." The husband must do this, Wojtyla insists, "not for hedonistic, but for altruistic reasons." In this case, if "we take into account the shorter and more violent curve of arousal in the man, [such] tenderness on his part in the context of marital intercourse acquires the significance of an act of virtue." Wojtyla is speaking here not so much of the "technique" of marital relations, but of an atmosphere of tenderness, communication, and affection that creates the proper "culture" of marital relations. This culture of love reflects Christ's tender, incarnate love for the Church.[20]

68. Baptism Expresses Christ's Spousal Love for the Church

August 25; September 1, 1982 (TB 317–321)

The Pope tells us that St. Paul's teaching in Ephesians 5 provides us with a profound sense of the sacredness of the human body in general, and especially in marriage. We can already see from our analysis that St. Paul had a keen grasp of the human body's capacity to signify sacred mysteries—to convey theology. The head-body and groom-bride analogies he employs can carry the tremendous load he places on them because the human body, in the mystery of sexual difference and the call to union, "was created to transfer into the visible reality of the world, the invisible mystery hidden in God from time immemorial, and thus to be a sign of it."[21] From this perspective, St. Paul does not place an excessive load on the body at all. God created the body to carry this "load." God created the body as a theology—as a visible sign of his own divine mystery.

---

20. *Love & Responsibility,* pp. 272, 274, 275.

21. 2/20/80, TB 76 (see §22).

This sign in no way exhausts the mystery; it is not a complete or adequate image. As stated previously, we must be careful never to reduce the spiritual and divine mystery to its physical and human sign. This would involve a dangerous and heretical blurring between Creator and creature. Nonetheless, with that understood, the body is an *efficacious* sign and in a real way communicates the divine mystery it symbolizes.

A. The Nuptial Character of Baptism

In examining the spousal character of Christ's love for the Church in Ephesians 5, we notice that the scope and goal of Christ's love is the Church's sanctification: "Christ loved the church and gave himself up for her, that he might sanctify her, having cleansed her by the washing of water with the word, that he might present the church to himself in splendor, without spot or wrinkle or any such thing, that she might be holy and without blemish" (vv. 25–27).

The Church understands this "washing of water" as a reference to Baptism. John Paul describes Baptism as "the first and essential fruit of Christ's giving himself for the Church." In this way Baptism takes on a nuptial character. It "is an expression of spousal love," the Pope says, "in the sense that it prepares the Bride (Church) for the Bridegroom [and] makes the Church the spouse of Christ" (317). Baptism, of course, is applied to individual persons. But within the spousal analogy, St. Paul speaks of this "washing" in reference to the Church as a whole. As John Paul affirms, "The spousal love of Christ is applied to her, the Church, every time that a single person receives in her the fundamental purification by means of Baptism. He who receives Baptism becomes at the same time— by virtue of the redemptive love of Christ—a participant in his spousal love for the Church" (317).

To accent the spousal character of Baptism, the Pope points to an intriguing insight of various biblical scholars. They observe that the washing with water recalls the ritual of the nuptial bath which at one time commonly preceded a wedding. This was an important religious rite, John Paul notes, even among the Greeks.[22]

B. Physical Beauty Is an Image of Holiness

Baptism, however, is only the beginning of our nuptial relationship with Christ. St. Paul also points to Baptism's eschatological fulfillment when he speaks of the Church "in splendor without spot or wrinkle or any such thing" (v. 27). Christ will "present the Church to himself" in radi-

---

22. See *CCC*, n. 1617.

ance. The Pope says that this "seems to indicate that moment of the wedding in which the bride is led to the groom, already clothed in the bridal dress and adorned for the wedding." John Paul continues: "The text quoted indicates that the Christ-spouse himself takes care to adorn the spouse-Church; he is concerned that she should be beautiful with the beauty of grace, beautiful by virtue of the gift of salvation in its fullness, already granted from the moment of the sacrament of Baptism" (317).

It is significant, according to the Holy Father, that St. Paul presents the image of the Church in splendor as a bride "all beautiful in her body"—as a bride without spot, wrinkle, blemish, or "any such thing." This is certainly a metaphor, but the Pope pauses to demonstrate its eloquence in showing how deeply important the body is in the analogy of spousal love. According to John Paul, "'spot' can be understood as a sign of ugliness, and 'wrinkle' as a sign of old age or senility" (318). Both terms, according to the metaphor, indicate not a defect of the body, but a defect of the spirit, a moral defect. The Pope also adds that, according to St. Paul, the "old man" signifies the man dominated by sin (see Rom 6:6). Therefore, Christ's redemptive and spousal love "ensures that the Church not only becomes sinless, but remains 'eternally young'" (318).

Recall that the body is the outward expression of the person. With this deeply integrated understanding of body and soul, physical beauty is understood as a sign of spiritual beauty. Spiritual beauty is goodness and purity—in a word, it is holiness. And what is holiness? Holiness "is measured according to the 'great mystery' in which the Bride responds with the gift of love to the gift of the Bridegroom."[23] Having received the Bridegroom's (Christ's) love, the Bride (each member of the Church as well as the Church understood as a corporate person) can respond also with that same love. And this holiness is manifested *in the body*. Holiness, John Paul affirms, "enables man to express himself deeply with his own body...precisely by means of the sincere gift of himself." It is "in his body as male or female, [that] man feels he is a subject of holiness."[24] For St. Paul, then, the physical beauty of the body without spot, wrinkle, or blemish is an image of the holiness to which we are all called as the Bride of Christ.

■ In our day and age, the desire for youthfulness and beauty has spawned its own religion. This false "cult of the body"[25] is saturated with a

---

23. *Mulieris Dignitatem,* n. 27 (see also *CCC,* n. 773).

24. 2/20/80, TB 76–77 (see §22).

25. See *CCC,* n. 2289.

million and one "sacraments" that promise the "grace" of remaining forever young and attractive. Thousands of beauty aids promise skin without spot or wrinkle or "any such thing." Thousands of creams, soaps, scrubs, and medications pledge to free us from our blemishes. Thousands of other products—from power shakes to thigh-busters—guarantee to reshape our metabolisms and our figures in order to restore our shapeliness and youthful vigor. Untwist this distorted cult of bodily youth and beauty, and what do we have? Our desire for holiness; our desire for sanctification, for purity and innocence; our desire for heaven, where we will share in the radiant beauty and eternal youth of Christ's Bride.

By using the image of physical beauty to convey holiness, St. Paul shows a masterful understanding of the sacramentality of the body. For him, the human body indicates "attributes and qualities of the moral, spiritual, and supernatural order" (318). By virtue of this "sacramentality," St. Paul can explain the mystery of sanctification, the mystery of Christ's redemptive love, and the mystery of humanity's union with the divine all "by means of the resemblance of the body and of the love whereby husband and wife become 'one flesh'" (318–319).

Yet again we must clarify that this is not a wishful projection of the Apostle's ideals on the body and sexual union. The body and sexual union are meant to convey this. God inscribed this in our humanity by creating us as male and female and calling us to become "one flesh." It all proclaims the mystery of Christ—not adequately and perfectly, but wonderfully, beautifully, and efficaciously. In this way we "see how profoundly the author of the letter to the Ephesians examines the sacramental reality, proclaiming its grand analogy: both the union of Christ with the Church, and the conjugal union of man and woman in marriage are in this way illuminated by a particular supernatural light" (318).

69. Spousal Love and the Recognition of True Beauty

September 1, 1982 (318–321)

Using St. Paul's image of the Bride's beautiful body as a metaphor for holiness, and following the logic of the spousal analogy in which husbands and wives are to mirror the love of Christ and the Church, we discover a remarkable truth that helps us understand the attractiveness of the human body. Of course our attraction toward the body has been confused by concupiscence. If we are to understand beauty and attractiveness in its proper perspective, we must listen to that "echo" of God's original plan still deep within us; we must recognize the distortions of sin; and we must trust in the power of redemption to restore holiness in our lived experience of the body. With that in mind, let us open our hearts to absorb what the Holy Father has to say.

A. The Husband Must Desire His Wife's Beauty

If Christ, in his self-giving love for his Bride, desires her beauty—that beauty of interior holiness which is also manifested in the body—then husbands, in loving their wives "as Christ loved the Church," must also desire their beauty. "Love obliges the bridegroom-husband," according to John Paul, "to be solicitous for the welfare of the bride-wife; it commits him *to desire her beauty* and at the same time *to appreciate this beauty and to care for it*" (319).[26] Of what beauty is the Pope speaking? Calling us again, not to be merely more "spiritual" but more *incarnational,* John Paul adds that this "is a case of visible beauty, of physical beauty" (319). Precisely at this point we must recall the tension and conflict that exist between the manner of appreciating the beauty of the body for original man, and the manner of appreciating the beauty of the body for the man of lust. Right in the crux of that tension the man of lust is called to faith in the power of redemption.

We could say that for original man, the appreciation of the other's beauty was disinterested. In appreciating the beauty of Eve's body, Adam was not seeking *his own* gratification. He was appreciating her beauty for "her own sake" as a marvel and image of God's beauty. Nakedness without shame enables us to discern this. Likewise, the entrance of shame enables us to recognize a profound change in man and woman's understanding of and appreciation for the beauty of the other's body. A spark still flickers within us of that original, holy appreciation of the beauty of the body, but we must contend now with self-seeking. We have lost the self-mastery that afforded "the peace of the interior gaze" (see §§17, 27).

Woman feels the resulting pain of this distortion in a particularly keen way. It seems the beauty of woman is more often objectified and exploited in society. And men with their disordered attractions seem more to blame for society's false standard of "beauty" than women. In turn, this illusory standard contributes to a deep-seated sense of inadequacy and even self-loathing in many women because they fail to meet it. And those women who come closer to society's impossible standard of beauty must continuously stake the claim of their own dignity in the face of men's lustful attractions in order to avoid constant degradation. In both situations, men fail to recognize, desire, appreciate, and care for the true beauty of woman.

---

26. Emphasis added.

■ Two personal stories might illustrate how grace can enable men to appreciate woman's true beauty. The first regards a woman who seemed to capture society's standard of beauty, and the other regards a woman who was far from it. Several years ago, during a Mass at the National Shrine of the Immaculate Conception, I noticed a very beautiful woman sitting a few pews ahead of me. At one point she casually flipped her red hair over her shoulder. Whoa! This gesture tapped into some deep well in my soul. It captured all that was so beautifully "feminine" about her. "Lord, what was *that?*" I prayed. Rather than repress the stirrings of my heart, I surrendered them to Christ so he could purify them and show me their true meaning. As I prayed, it dawned on me that the beauty of woman—if we have the purity to see it—lies in her being a living, incarnate symbol of heaven, of the New Jerusalem, of God's dwelling place. Is not woman's womb the dwelling place of the Lord? And yes, when all is purified, man's desire to enter woman's gates seems to point in some way to his desire to dwell in the house of the Lord. This is what purity of heart affords and how grace reorients us when we let it. The deepest truth of my attraction to this woman confirmed my desire for heaven. Some might suspect that my attraction to this woman during Mass would be a source of distraction—or worse, an occasion of sin. Yet as I allowed the distortions to be crucified, this woman helped me enter into true worship. She helped me understand what the Mass is all about. I realized that right then and there, in that Basilica dedicated to Mary, I was already in "woman's womb" and I was about to witness the Word being made flesh. In this realization the words of John Paul II ring out: Christ instituted the Eucharist to express in some way "the relationship between man and woman, between what is 'feminine' and what is 'masculine.'"[27]

The next story is closely related. Several months later I was vacationing at the beach. Seeing many shapely, bikini-clad women, I found myself engaged in a lively battle to reclaim this heavenly vision of woman's body.[28] Then I noticed a very overweight woman and my initial thought was, "Oh, what a relief. No struggle there." But then I realized that my reaction to her was simply another dimension of a distorted view of the per-

27. *Mulieris Dignitatem,* n. 26.

28. By telling this story I do not mean to give license to those who might be so bound by lust that going to a beach would be an "occasion of sin." For the man bound by lust, the admonition "Turn away your eyes from a shapely woman" (Sir 9:5) retains all its wisdom (see §32).

son. My heart sank. The dignity of the person is so great that he—or, in this case, she—is never meant to be used as a means of selfish gratification. Again, in the case of this heavy woman, "No problem there." But wait! Is a person meant to be disregarded and discarded, pushed aside as if inconsequential? I did have a problem there: a big problem. As I had been praying to see the true personal beauty in all of the "shapely" women at the beach, so too did I begin to pray to see the true personal beauty in all the "unshapely" women at the beach. Coming to do so is another dimension of our struggle to see others as Christ sees them. By God's grace I experienced a new level of integration that day, a new level of purity of heart. "Even now...[purity of heart] enables us to see *according to* God...; it lets us perceive the human body—ours and our neighbor's—as a temple of the Holy Spirit, a manifestation of divine beauty."[29]

B. True Love Recognizes Woman's True Beauty

How, then, is that "appreciation of beauty," to which John Paul calls husbands, to be lived out? Only the man who experiences freedom from the domination of concupiscence through ongoing conversion to Christ can look beyond the illusory measures of beauty to woman's true beauty—a beauty in which *every* woman shares. It is the beauty of the human story, the beauty of the mystery of humanity. For, as John Paul says elsewhere, woman is "the archetype of the whole human race: she *represents the humanity* which belongs to all human beings, both men and women."[30] Woman's body, then, in a unique way—and even more particularly according to the personal characteristics of each woman—bears testimony to the original good of creation, the tragedy of the fall, and the hope of full redemption.

■ We see this pre-eminently in *the* woman—Mary, the Mother of God. Without a doubt, *this woman* is the most beautiful creature God has ever created. Her body radiates the glory of God, the splendor of holiness like no other body (next to Christ's own body which, of course, originates from his mother's body). For she lives in her body, like no other human person, the mystery of the human drama of creation and redemption. As the *Catechism* expresses, "Mary goes before us all in the holiness that is the

---

29. *CCC,* n. 2519.
30. *Mulieris Dignitatem,* n. 4.

Church's mystery as the 'bride without spot or wrinkle.'"[31] In this sense we speak of Mary as "our hope." For she lives already in her body what we hope for—the fullness of redemption. In this light we can also understand the interconnectedness of Mary's Immaculate Conception and bodily Assumption into heaven. One who has received the fullness of redemption (Immaculate Conception) does not experience decay but lives the final resurrection "already" (Assumption).[32]

The husband who believes wholeheartedly in the human story (in other words, the husband who believes wholeheartedly in the Gospel) embraces his wife's humanity *as she is.* He sees even in her blemishes and disfigurations an "echo" of the beginning and the hope of eternal glory. Such a husband, the Pope says, "examines his bride with attention, as though in a creative loving anxiety to find everything that is good and beautiful in her." This is what "he desires for her" (319). He desires that all that is good and beautiful in her would blossom and radiate through her body. This is what he *sees* in her. This *is* his wife's beauty—the radiation of her goodness. In this way he reclaims something of the original good of God's vision (see Gen 1:31).

The Holy Father even says that the husband's love in some sense "creates" the goodness that he sees in the one he loves. In this way the husband imitates the love of *the* Creator whose love "gives a beginning to good and delights in good."[33] The husband's ability to see that good, the Pope continues, "is like a test of that same love and its measure" (319). In other words, the husband who does not recognize this good, this beauty in his wife, cannot be said to love his wife. In any case, he does not love his wife "as Christ loved the Church."

■ Is beauty definable? Is it not in the eye of the beholder? Certainly every man and woman—whether they meet the idealized standard of beauty or not—reflects something of the beauty of God. Granting this, why do we find some bodies more "attractive" than others? Research indicates that even infants will stare at an "attractive" face longer than an "unattractive" one.[34] What mystery of our humanity is revealed by the spectrum of physical appearances we find in the human family? Obviously standards of beauty are deeply influenced by cultural conditioning. Even so, I would

---

31. *CCC*, n. 773.

32. See *CCC*, n. 2853.

33. 1/2/80, TB 59.

34. See Cathy Newman, "The Enigma of Beauty," *National Geographic* (January 2000), pp. 95–121.

imagine every culture could relate, each in its own way, to a general scale of "normally attractive," "unattractive," and "very attractive." Extending the Pauline metaphor of physical beauty as an image of holiness, I would hazard the idea that within this scale or spectrum we see something of original man, historical man, and eschatological man. Furthermore, recognizing that Christ fully reveals man to himself, I would suggest that in this spectrum we can see something of a parallel in Christ's own life. Christ was *figured* to our "normally attractive" humanity in the Incarnation, *disfigured* by our sin in his passion, and *transfigured* by God's glory in his resurrection. It seems in some way we all bear this spectrum in our bodies, some visibly emphasizing one element of the spectrum more than other elements. Yet recall the continuity in the human drama. In Christ, the "figure" of original man, the "disfigure" of historical man, and the "transfigure" of eschatological man are all one man, one mystery which is the final Adam—and this one mystery is radiantly beautiful! We fail to see authentic human beauty when we fail to recognize how the body of historical man, with all its blemishes and disfigurations, contains the echo of the beginning and the hope of eternal glory. Without this "total vision of man"—with the final Adam's death and resurrection at the center of it all—real human beings are not beautiful. We much prefer fantastic images and air-brushed ideals. Without Christ at the center of the human drama, not only do we prefer fantasy, we actually become repulsed by the real. Many a man who has indulged his fantasy in the illusionary world of pornography has found it terribly difficult to love the real flesh and blood he married. Those who cannot love a person with blemishes grasp at glory. They fail to reckon with the "mystery of iniquity" and grope in some sense for eschatological man without the cross of history. Perfect human beauty will come, but not as the world desires. The radiance of the "spotless Bride" is given as a gift, but we must be willing to be *configured* to the whole Adam (Christ) in his figure, disfigure, and *then* his transfigure.

C. Spousal Love and the Eucharist

Covered with the blemishes, spots, and wrinkles of sin—Christ loved his Bride all the more. He saw her goodness, her beauty still, and longed to tell her of it by the testimony of his death on the cross. "God shows his love for us in that while we were yet sinners Christ died for us" (Rom 5:8). Thus, the husband who commits himself to "nourishing" and "cherishing" the beauty of his wife's body must give himself to her in the most disinterested way "as Christ does the Church" (v. 29). This is the measure of love, as St. Paul tells us and as the Pope reiterates.

According to many Scripture scholars, this "nourishment" the Apostle refers to is "a reference to the Eucharist with which Christ in his spousal love nourishes the Church" (321). In this way we glimpse how this nourishment (the Eucharist) indicates, even though in a minor key, "the specific character of conjugal love, especially," the Pope observes, "of that love whereby the spouses become 'one flesh'" (321).[35]

We will later return to the Eucharistic character of marital love and conjugal union. It will profoundly influence the rest of John Paul's reflections on the body, specifically his reflections on *Humanae Vitae*. For now, the Pope merely states that the expressions of nourishment and caring for the body help us to understand in a general way the dignity of the body and the moral imperative to care for its good. They also give us a profound sense of the sacredness of man and woman's relationship and their call to become "one flesh."

70. Mystery, Sacrament, and the Climax of the Spousal Analogy
September 8, 1982 (TB 321–324)

In his audience of September 8, 1982, the Holy Father launches into a specific analysis of the riches of sacramental theology. In one of the most interesting endnotes of the entire catechesis, John Paul helps us understand the multi-layered texture of the word "sacrament" by tracing its history and usage.[36] This term "has traveled a long way in the course of the centuries" (380). The journey begins with the Greek word *"mysterion"* ("mystery"), which in the Book of Judith referred to the king's secret military plans (see Jdt 2:2). In the book of Wisdom (2:22) and in the prophecy of Daniel (2:27), however, "mystery" came to signify God's creative plans for man and the purpose which he assigns to the world. St. Paul's usage marks a turning point. For him "mystery" is not merely God's eternal plan, but the accomplishment on earth of that plan in Jesus Christ (see Eph 3:4; Col 2:2, 4:3).

It was not until the third century that the most ancient Latin versions of the Scriptures translated *mysterion* with the word *"sacramentum."* Interestingly, this term originally referred to the military oath taken by the Roman legionaries. Tertullian pointed out that since these soldiers were initiated into a new form of life, made a commitment without reserve, and pledged faithful service even unto death, the term "sacrament" was fitting

---

35. See *CCC,* n. 1621.

36. See *CCC,* n. 774.

for those sacred rites of Christian initiation: Baptism, Confirmation, and Eucharist. St. Augustine emphasized that sacraments are sacred signs which contain and confer in some way what they symbolize. St. Thomas then further specified that not all sacred signs are sacraments, but only those signs which actually sanctify our humanity. From this point forward, the word "sacrament" was restricted to mean one of the seven sources of grace instituted by Christ.[37]

A. Recovering the Broader Meaning of "Sacrament"

Only in the last century have theologians sought to recover that broader and more ancient understanding of sacrament as the revelation and accomplishment of the mystery hidden in God from time immemorial. John Paul asks, "Is not 'sacrament' synonymous with 'mystery'" (323)? Given the particular nuance of these synonyms, we can understand the reality of "mystery-sacrament" in the tension of that "hidden-revealed" marvel that is God and his plan for humanity. Within this tension, "mystery" signifies primarily what is hidden, whereas "sacrament" signifies primarily what is revealed.[38] The *good news* of the Gospel is found precisely here. What has been *hidden* from time immemorial in God has been definitively *revealed* to us in Jesus Christ (see Rom 16:25–26).

Yet, even so, in the age of the sacraments (that is, on this side of the resurrection) this "hidden-revealed" tension will always remain. For the divine mystery so far exceeds the human capacity of comprehension that, as the Pope reminds us, "even after its proclamation (or its revelation) it does not cease to be called 'mystery'" (323). "For now we see in a mirror dimly, but then face to face. Now I know in part; then I shall understand fully, even as I have been fully understood" (1 Cor 13:12).

John Paul speaks of the sacrament—or "sacramentality"—of the body in this broader sense. He points out that the Fathers of the Second Vatican Council also revived this meaning of the word when they described the Church in *Lumen Gentium* as "the universal sacrament of salvation." Earlier in the same document they proclaimed that the "Church is in Christ in the nature of a sacrament—a sign and instrument, that is, of communion with God and of unity among all men."[39] The Pope observes that the phrase "in the nature of a sacrament" was used to recover that

---

37. See *CCC*, n. 1117.

38. See *CCC*, nn. 774, 1075. See also Gerard Beigel, *Faith and Social Justice in the Teaching of Pope John Paul II* (New York, NY: Peter Lang, 1997), p. 35.

39. *Lumen Gentium*, nn. 1, 48; See *CCC*, nn. 747, 774–776, 780, 1045, 1108, 1140.

broader sense of the term without confusing this with the seven sacraments. Speaking in this way, the Council Fathers indicate that the Church, in her existence as Bride and Body of Christ, proclaims and accomplishes the mystery of salvation. This is the mystery hidden in God from eternity: that all members of the human race would live in fruitful communion with the Trinity and with one another through communion with Christ. This is the "great mystery" of nuptial communion of which St. Paul speaks in Ephesians. This "great mystery," John Paul tells us, "as God's salvific plan in regard to humanity, is in a certain sense the central theme of the whole of revelation, its central reality. It is this that God, as Creator and Father, wishes above all to transmit to mankind in his Word" (322).

B. Keystone of the Spousal Analogy

As St. Paul indicates, marriage has participated in this "great mystery" as a sign and proclamation from the beginning. Hence, while the sacramentality of the Church is related to each of the seven sacraments, "it must be said that the sacramentality of the Church remains in a particular relationship with marriage: the most ancient sacrament" (324). This "particular relationship" comes to full light in verses 31–32 of St. Paul's marvelous passage. Directly following his words about the Eucharistic gift through which Christ "nourishes" the Church with his own body, St. Paul references the original biblical call to spousal self-donation. "For this reason a man shall leave his father and mother and be joined to his wife and the two shall become one flesh" (v. 31). Then, in a stroke of inspired theological genius, St. Paul immediately links this to the Eucharistic mystery of which he just spoke. The two becoming one flesh "is a great mystery, and I mean in reference to Christ and the church" (v. 32). John Paul says that here St. Paul writes not only of the great mystery hidden in God, but also, and above all, of the mystery which Christ accomplishes through his act of redemptive-spousal love. In this act of love, Christ gives his body up for the Church and is thereby united with her "in a spousal manner, as the husband and wife are reciprocally united in marriage instituted by the Creator" (323). Thus, the Pope observes that the Apostle's reference to Genesis 2:24 is necessary not so much to recall the "one flesh" unity of spouses, but to present the mystery of Christ's union with the Church.

This linking of the union of marriage with the union of Christ and the Church is, according to John Paul, "the most important point of the whole text, in a certain sense, the keystone" (321). Only by comprehending this linking can we understand how Ephesians 5 "reveals man to himself and makes his supreme calling clear" (see §64). In this linking, St. Paul "unites marriage, as the most ancient revelation ('manifestation') of the [divine] plan in the created world, with the definitive revelation and 'manifestation'" of that plan in Jesus Christ (321–322). In this way "St. Paul sets in relief the continuity between the most ancient covenant...and the definitive covenant." God established the original covenant "by constituting marriage in the very work of creation," according to Genesis 2:24. And he established the definitive covenant in Christ, who, "having loved the Church and given himself up for her, is united to her in a spousal way, corresponding to the image of spouses. This continuity," the Pope continues, "constitutes the essential basis of the great analogy contained in the letter to the Ephesians" (322). We might even say that through this linking of the incarnate union of spouses with the incarnate union of Christ and the Church, the spousal analogy reaches its climax.

71. The Foundation of the Whole Sacramental Order

September 8, 29, 1982 (TB 321–324, 332–333)

"Therefore a man leaves his father and his mother and cleaves to his wife, and they become one flesh" (Gen 2:24). These are the words John Paul spoke of early in his catechesis, saying they will have in God's revelation "an ample and distant perspective."[40] This ample and distant perspective comes into sharp focus in Ephesians 5:31–32. In view of the entire Bible, John Paul says that the words of Genesis 2:24 can be considered "the fundamental text on marriage" (321). These are also "the words that constitute the sacrament of marriage."[41] Becoming "one flesh," then, does not merely express the joining of two bodies. According to the Holy Father, this is "a 'sacramental' expression which corresponds to the communion of persons."[42]

A. The Sacrament Proclaims and Accomplishes the Mystery

Summarizing our previous reflections, "sacrament" (in the broader and more ancient sense of the term) refers to the revelation of the divine mystery. The Pope adds that it also presupposes man's acceptance of the mystery by means of faith. At the same time, however, John Paul says that "sacrament" is something more than this. Sacramental reality is such that the mystery proclaimed is also effectively *accomplished* in those who be-

---

40. 11/14/79, TB 47 (see §14).

41. 2/20/80, TB 76 (see §22).

42. 6/25/80, TB 123 (see §29).

lieve. Man *really participates* in the mystery of divine life signified by the sacrament. "The sacrament consists in the 'manifesting' of that mystery in a sign which serves not only to proclaim the mystery, but also to accomplish it in man. The sacrament is a visible and efficacious sign of grace. Through it, there is accomplished in man that mystery hidden from eternity in God, of which the letter to the Ephesians speaks" (323).

John Paul asks if St. Paul might be speaking of marriage as a sacrament in the sense that we understand sacraments today (i.e., the seven sacraments). He concurs, however, with the widespread opinion of Biblical scholars and theologians that Paul is not. Nonetheless, John Paul says, "it seems that in this text he is speaking of the bases of the sacramentality of the whole of Christian life and in particular the bases of the sacramentality of marriage." Even if he speaks of marriage as a sacrament in an indirect way, still he does so "in the most fundamental way possible" (323). The keystone of the sacramentality of marriage in Ephesians 5 is, once again, found in verses 31–32 where St. Paul links the "one flesh" union of the first Adam and Eve with the union of the New Adam and Eve (Christ and the Church). Here we witness the salvific initiative of God toward man in the different phases of its revelation. St. Paul is speaking of the revelation of the "great mystery" in its most ancient phase and in the phase of "the fullness of time" (Gal 4:4).

Through "the image of the conjugal union of husband and wife, the author of [Ephesians] speaks...of the way in which that mystery is expressed in the visible order, of the way in which it has become visible, and therefore has entered into the sphere of sign" (332). By "sign" John Paul simply means the visibility of the Invisible. According to St. Paul, two intimately related "signs" make the divine Reality visible. The union of husband and wife is the most ancient sign of the mystery. And the union of Christ and the Church is the definitive sign of this mystery revealed in "the fullness of time." John Paul credits St. Paul with "a special merit" for bringing "these two signs together, and [making] of them one great sign— that is, a great sacrament" (333).

Here we find the surest foundation for speaking of the Eucharistic— or "liturgical," as John Paul will later say (see §90)—nature of marital love and of the "nuptial" nature of the Eucharist. The love of husband and wife (consummated when the two become "one flesh") and the love of Christ and the Church (consummated sacramentally in Eucharistic communion) are so intimately related as to form, according to St. Paul and as John Paul II expresses, "one great sign." This sign not only reveals to man the mystery hidden for ages in God that all would be one in Christ (see Eph 3:9, 1:10). It also accomplishes it in man.

B. Conjugal Union in Light of the Incarnation

Since this is the most important point and "keystone" of the entire text, we should try to penetrate even further the inter-relationship of these two "signs" which form "one great sign." The Pope has already described the conjugal union of spouses as the original and "most ancient" revelation of the mystery. Given this, his following statement might seem odd. The Holy Father asserts that the divine mystery "has become visible *first of all* in the very historical event of Christ" (332).[43] This is puzzling within the confines of historical chronology. However, by recalling the first sentence of John Paul II's first encyclical, we solve the puzzle: "The Redeemer of man, Jesus Christ, is the center of the universe and of history."[44]

History is measured by Christ. In a sense, history does not begin "in the beginning" and move forward in time. The human drama, we could say, "begins" with the Incarnation at its center and moves outward in both directions. The point here is that, as Pope Leo XIII said in his encyclical on marriage, the "one flesh" union of man and woman "has been even from the beginning a foreshadowing of the Incarnation of the Word of God."[45] Conjugal union, therefore, can only be fully understood in light of Christ's union with the Church. For it is the "relationship of Christ to the Church," John Paul emphasizes, which "constitutes the fulfillment and the concretization of the visibility of the mystery itself" (332). Looking backward in time from the vantage point of Christ's incarnate union with the Church, John Paul says our attention turns "to what was already presented previously—in the context of the very mystery of creation—as the 'visibility of the Invisible,' to the very 'origin' of the theological history of man" (332).

Here John Paul wants us to recall his thesis: "The body, in fact, and it alone is capable of making visible what is invisible: the spiritual and divine. It was created to transfer into the visible reality of the world the mystery hidden since time immemorial in God, and thus to be a sign of it."[46] This sacramental understanding of the body is constituted by means of man's visible masculinity and femininity. Therefore, the body also communicates the mystery "by means of the conjugal union of man and woman when they unite in such a way as to form 'one flesh.'" In this way, through the unity of masculinity and femininity, John Paul tells us that the body "assumes the value of a sign—in a way, a sacramental sign."[47]

---

43. Emphasis added.

44. *Redemptor Hominis,* n. 1.

45. *Arcanum.*

46. 2/20/80, TB 76 (see §22).

47. 10/22/80, TB 163 (see §35).

C. Foundation and Summit of the Sacramental Order

Now a key text of the Holy Father's comes to light—a text which in some way captures the full weight of glory that the Pope believes God has ascribed to marriage and to the consummate union of spouses. "It can be said," John Paul asserts, "that the visible sign of marriage 'in the beginning,' inasmuch as it is linked to the visible sign of Christ and of the Church...transfers the eternal plan of love into the 'historical' dimension and makes it the foundation of the whole sacramental order" (332–333). This is another one of those stunning statements that the Pope plants in his catechesis without commentary. It may well become one of those texts that theologians chew on for centuries, only gradually unpacking its implications.

In this context, John Paul stresses that Christ's union with the Church is "the summit of the salvific economy of God" (333). With this image in mind, we might say that at the trail-head marking the path to this summit, we have marriage and its consummate expression of conjugal intercourse. Inasmuch as this "trail-head" points to the summit, the visible sign of marriage is the foundation upon which God reveals and actuates his hidden designs—revealing his plan for man and for the universe that all things in heaven and on earth might be "one" in fruitful union with Jesus Christ (see Eph 1:10). This is the deepest essence and meaning of human embodiment, of erotic desire, and of nuptial love. They are meant to point us to Christ and to God's hidden designs for the universe. Thus, inasmuch as the spousal union points us (analogically) to Christ's union with the Church, the visible sign of marriage constitutes "the foundation of the entire sacramental order"—that order by which God *incarnates* his own mystery, making it visible in the order of "signs."

Perhaps now we can sense with what awe and reverence St. Paul referred to the "one flesh" union as "a profound mystery." Perhaps now we can better understand what St. Paul means when he calls spouses to submit to one another *out of reverence* for Christ. Words fail when we come in contact with such a mystery. The only proper response is silence offered as praise and tears offered in reparation for the desecration of this sacramental mystery so prevalent in our world and often in our own hearts.

72. Christ Reveals the Mystery of Divine Love

September 15, 22, 1982 (TB 324–330)

In his audience of September 15, 1982, the Holy Father reflects once again on the first chapter of the letter to the Ephesians. There St. Paul outlines the revelation of "the mystery...set forth in Christ" (1:9). The Pope tells us that in the rest of the letter St. Paul exhorts those who have received this revelation and accepted it in faith to model their lives according to the truth they have received. This truth is not a concept, but a person. This Truth is Jesus Christ.

A. The Centrality of Christ

The greater part of Paul's letter provides moral instruction (or *parenesis*). But John Paul stresses that the Apostle's moral instructions are intimately intertwined with the "great mystery" revealed in Christ. They are given to those in whom the grace of redemption is efficaciously at work by virtue of the sacraments, especially Baptism. The point is that the moral life can never be divorced from life in Christ. Christian morality is not a sterile ethical code but a living ethos vivified by the resurrected life of Jesus Christ.

This indispensable truth has a particular bearing on the moral life of husbands and wives since their union is a sign and actuation of the mystery of salvation. In that climactic moment of Ephesians 5:31–32, we learn that "the mystery hidden for ages in God" (3:9) was foreshadowed "from the beginning" in the union of Adam and Eve. But it is the New Adam who definitively reveals the mystery by leaving his Father in heaven, and leaving the home of his mother on earth, to "cleave to his wife" (the Church) and become "one flesh" with her. Christ is the meaning of embodiment. Christ is the meaning of morality. Christ is the meaning of marriage. Throughout this audience (and throughout the entire catechesis on the body), the Holy Father underscores the centrality of Christ.

Christ stands at the heart of the "great mystery" proclaimed by St. Paul. "In him—precisely in him—humanity has been eternally blessed 'with every spiritual blessing.' In him—in Christ—humanity has been chosen 'before the creation of the world.'" When "this eternal mystery is accomplished in time, this is brought about also in him and through him: in Christ and through Christ. Through Christ there is revealed the mystery of divine love. Through him and in him it is accomplished" (325). We have been chosen in Christ to "be holy and blameless before him"; to be part of God's family; to be adopted as "his sons through Jesus Christ." This is possible despite humanity's fall because we now "have redemption through his blood, the forgiveness of our trespasses, according to the riches of his grace which he lavished upon us." This is "the mystery of [God's] will"; this is his "plan for the fullness of time": to "unite all things in [Christ]" (Eph 1:3–5, 7–10).

B. The Mode of Gift and the Veils of Faith

This eternal mystery is accomplished in time in the mode of "gift"—the gift God gives to man in Jesus Christ. St. Paul likens this divine gift to the gift of spouses who through mutual self-donation become "one flesh."[48] In Ephesians 5 the "supernatural conferring of the fruits of redemption acquires...the character of a spousal donation of Christ himself to the Church similar to the spousal relationship between husband and wife. Therefore, not only the fruits of redemption are a gift. Christ himself is a gift. He gives himself to the Church, as to his spouse" (325).

John Paul says that when we accept the gift offered to us through faith in Christ, we really become participants in the eternal mystery, even though it works in us under the veils of faith. The "veils of faith" can also be described as the veils of sacramental signs. For, as John Paul said in his previous audience, participation in the eternal plan of God "becomes a reality in a mysterious way, under the veil of a sign; nonetheless, that sign is always a 'making visible' of the supernatural mystery which it works in man under its veil."[49]

Various saints have observed that God veils his mystery in sacramental signs out of mercy, for if we saw his glory as he is we would die. No one can see God's glory and live (see Ex 33:20). But herein lies our privileged calling. God's gift to us is his own self-disclosure: his own self-communication. We shall see his face and live! Indeed, we are called with "unveiled face," St. Paul tells us, to behold the glory of the Lord. This vision transforms us into God's likeness "from one degree of glory to another" (2 Cor 3:18).

Through this ongoing transformation we reclaim and experience the sacramentality of our bodies. Even if it does so in a veiled way, the human body is meant to proclaim God's eternal mystery. The more we are transformed "from glory to glory" according to the likeness of God, the more we can see the divine mystery stamped in our bodies—in every*body*. Furthermore, we come to understand, just as spouses come to experience, that the communion of male and female in "one flesh" participates in God's glory as well.

---

48. See *CCC*, n. 772.

49. 9/8/82, TB 323.

73. The Spousal Analogy Helps Penetrate the Essence of the Mystery

September 22, 29, 1982 (TB 327–333)

In order to help us better understand the letter to the Ephesians and the great spousal analogy, the Holy Father reminds us that the idea of the spousal love of God for humanity does not appear in the abstract. Instead, it is in continuity with the spousal analogy employed throughout the Old Testament. Here the Pope reminds us of the many passages from Isaiah, Hosea, and Ezekiel and of the vivid celebration of spousal love presented in the Song of Songs.

St. Paul preserves the spousal analogy of the Old Testament while transforming it and deepening it according to the "great mystery" now revealed through Christ's union with the Church. This "Christological" and "ecclesiological" dimension, John Paul says, was found only as an "embryo" in the Old Testament. It was only foretold. But what was "scarcely outlined," only "half-open," is now "fully revealed" in the letter to the Ephesians. Fully revealed, but of course, the Pope reminds us, "without ceasing to be a mystery" (329–330).

A. Your Maker Is Your Husband

To show the continuity and development of the spousal analogy from the Old to the New Testament, John Paul II devotes an entire audience (9/22/82) to analyzing the following text from Isaiah in light of that classic passage from Ephesians 5.

> [Y]ou will forget the shame of your youth, and the reproach of your widowhood you will remember no more. For your Maker is your husband, the Lord of hosts is his name; and the Holy One of Israel is your Redeemer, the God of the whole earth he is called. For the Lord has called you like a wife forsaken and grieved in spirit, like a wife of youth when she is cast off, says your God. For a brief moment I forsook you, but with great compassion I will gather you,...with everlasting love I will have compassion on you, says the Lord, your Redeemer....For the mountains may depart and the hills be removed, but my steadfast love shall not depart from you, and my covenant of peace shall not be removed, says the Lord, who has compassion on you (Is 54:4–8, 10).

The Pope states that this text "has theological content of extraordinary richness." "These words brim over with an authentic ardor of love," he says. And this "is perhaps the strongest 'declaration of love' on God's part, linked up with the solemn oath of faithfulness forever." Furthermore, these words indicate "the very character of the gift, which is the love of

God for the spouse-Israel." It is "a gift which derives entirely from God's initiative...indicating the dimension of grace, which from the beginning is contained in that love" (328).

■ Recall that God's initiative as Bridegroom and humanity's response as Bride are essential in understanding how the bodies of male and female reveal the nuptial mystery. The nuptial meaning of the man's body calls him to image God's initiation of the gift, whereas the nuptial meaning of the woman's body calls her to image humanity's receptivity and response to the gift (see §66). This is why the Pope describes woman as the "archetype of the whole human race."[50] Of course this does not mean that it is "wrong" for wives to initiate the gift of self. It is also crucial that husbands learn how to receive and respond. Even so, since the body is the revelation of the person, initiation and receptivity speak not only of male and female anatomy, but of male and female personality. It is not mere social convention, for example, that men most often propose marriage to women. It speaks of the masculine call to image God in the initiation of the gift. Whatever resistance we might have to this truth ultimately stems, it seems, from a failure to believe in and live the reality of gift. As soon as the element of the "sincere gift" is removed, the initiation of God, and, in turn, the initiation of the male, is seen (understandably so) as a threat. In turn, woman retreats (understandably so) from her natural receptivity.

John Paul comments that the "shame of your youth" and the "reproach of your widowhood" mentioned by Isaiah indicates the mentality of the time when it was disreputable for a marriageable woman to remain unmarried. While the Holy Father does not mention this, we might also recognize an echo of that shame of Eden which man and woman experienced having broken their covenant with God. Only through the love of our Redeemer and the restoration of the covenant can a man and woman regain something of that original vision of the body that enables them to "forget" their shame. Indeed, authentic love "swallows shame," as Wojtyla expresses it.[51]

B. New "Moments" of Revelation

Comparing the text of Isaiah with that of Ephesians, we certainly recognize a continuity, but we also recognize "new revealed moments"—the trinitarian, Christological, and eschatological moments. Isaiah obviously

---

50. *Mulieris Dignitatem*, n. 4

51. See *Love & Responsibility*, p. 181.

could not consciously speak to these new "moments." God as a Trinity of Persons; Christ as the Incarnate Son, Bridegroom, and Redeemer; and the ultimate consummation of the nuptial mystery in which Christ's Bride will be "holy and blameless before him" (Eph 1:4) are realities only revealed in their fullness in the historical event of Christ. From this perspective, St. Paul can distinguish the work of the Father, the Son, and the Holy Spirit throughout his letter in a way that Isaiah could not.

In fact, John Paul points out that in Ephesians St. Paul presents the mystery hidden for ages in God first in the dimension of paternal love rather than conjugal love. The Father "destined us in love to be his sons through Jesus Christ, according to the purpose of his will" (Eph 1:5). Of course the prophets also spoke of the paternity of God (see Hos 11:1–2; Is 64:8; Mal 1:6). But what Isaiah did not and could not know in speaking of God as Redeemer was that the "figure of the Redeemer is...proper to him who is the first 'beloved Son' of the Father (Eph 1:6)" (329). According to John Paul, God as "spouse" in some way parallels God as "redeemer." Christ the Redeemer is the heavenly Bridegroom. Without knowing the full implications, Isaiah himself spoke to this reality. In fact, Isaiah uses the analogy of spousal love only when the Creator and the "Holy One of Israel" is manifested as redeemer.

Thus the Holy Father observes that St. Paul no longer repeats: "your Maker is your Husband." Instead St. Paul reveals Christ the Son as Redeemer and Bridegroom. Christ's salvific love "consists in giving himself up for the Church." In this way St. Paul reveals redemptive love "as spousal love whereby [Christ] espouses the Church and makes it his own Body" (329). Thus John Paul says that Christ's giving himself up for the Church is equivalent to carrying out the work of redemption. In this way the "Creator Lord of hosts" spoken of by Isaiah becomes the "Holy One of Israel" as her Redeemer. But John Paul adds that in this case, we are speaking of "the new Israel," the Church. Here we see the continuity and the deepening of the spousal analogy from the old covenant to the new covenant.

C. The Radical Character of Grace

Through the different phases of the spousal analogy—from the embryo of the old covenant, to the full revelation of the new—we come to see both the full extent and limitations of this analogy. John Paul believes that "the analogy of spousal or conjugal love helps to penetrate the very essence of the mystery"—but, of course, only "up to a certain point" and only "in an analogical way." The Pope continues: "It is obvious that the analogy of earthly...spousal love cannot provide an adequate and complete understanding of that absolute transcendent Reality which is the divine mystery....The mystery remains transcendent in regard to this analogy as in regard to any other analogy, whereby we seek to express it in human language" (330).[52] That being said, the Pope believes that the "analogy of spousal love contains in itself a characteristic of the mystery which is not directly emphasized by...any other analogy used in the Bible" (331). He also mentions that this even includes the analogy of paternal love.

What specific characteristic does John Paul mean? "The analogy of spousal love," he says, "permits us to understand in a certain way the mystery...as a love proper to a total and irrevocable gift of self on the part of God to man in Christ." John Paul points out that this is a question of "man" both in the personal and in the communal sense. Isaiah expresses the community dimension as "Israel" and St. Paul expresses it as "Church." In both cases these terms indicate a "reduction of the community to the person"—Israel and the Church are considered as "bride-person" in relation to the "bridegroom-person" (Yahweh and Christ). Thus every "concrete 'I' should find itself in that biblical 'we'" (331). That biblical "we" is the one bride who has received God's irrevocable gift of self.

John Paul says that this gift of God to man is certainly "radical" and therefore "total." He adds, however, that we cannot speak of this "total" giving of God to man in its transcendental fullness. As a creature, man cannot receive divinity as such. Such a "total" and uncreated gift "is shared only by God himself in the 'triune communion of the Persons'" (331). Nevertheless, through God's gift of self—which by virtue of the Incarnation is a bodily gift, and, analogously, a nuptial gift—we do *participate* in the divine nature (see 2 Pet 1:4). As the Eucharistic prayer indicates, we "come to share in the divinity of Christ who humbled himself to share in our humanity." According to this measure, God's self-gift *is* "total" in that he gives all that he can give of himself to us considering our limited faculties as creatures.

In this way the spousal analogy, like no other analogy in the Bible, indicates the radical character of grace. John Paul says that it helps us understand the mystery of grace both as an eternal reality in God and as an historical fruit of mankind's redemption in Christ. This is how marriage as a human reality "incarnates" spousal love in the image and likeness of the divine Mystery.

---

52. See *CCC*, n. 42.

74. Original Unity: A Fruit of Eternal Election in Christ

October 6, 1982 (TB 333 – 336)

In his audience of October 6, 1982, John Paul begins to re-examine marriage's "beginning" in light of what we have learned in Ephesians about the "great mystery." The Pope says that the letter to the Ephesians authorizes us to do this because the Apostle himself refers to the "beginning." He refers specifically to the words of Genesis 2:24, which instituted marriage as a sacramental reality right from the beginning. The Holy Father wants to return to these words regarding the "one flesh" union in order to understand better how they illuminate marriage as the primordial sacrament.

A. Imbued with Christ before Original Sin

"The letter to the Ephesians opens up before us the supernatural world of the eternal mystery, of the eternal plans of God the Father concerning man. These plans," the Pope reminds us, "precede the 'creation of the world,' and therefore also the creation of man. At the same time those divine plans begin to be put into effect already in the entire reality of creation" (334). This sheds new light on the nature and origin of the grace of original innocence. "The letter to the Ephesians leads us to approach this situation—that is, the state of man before original sin—from the point of view of the mystery hidden in God from eternity" (333 – 334). According to this mystery, God chose us in Christ not only after we sinned and in order to redeem us from sin. God chose us in Christ "before the foundation of the world" (Eph 1:4). This means that "before sin, man bore in his soul the fruit of eternal election in Christ" (334).

It seems that John Paul cannot stress this point enough. Comparing the testimony of the "beginning" with the testimony of Ephesians, he says that "one must deduce that the reality of man's creation was *already* imbued with the perennial election of man in Christ....Man, male and female, shared *from the 'beginning'* in this supernatural gift." And again he says that this supernatural endowment in Christ "took place *before* original sin" (334– 335).[53] Rereading the account of creation in light of the New Testament, we realize that man's destiny in Christ is already implied in his creation in the image of God. For it is Christ who "is the image of the invisible God." Thus, it is in Christ that we image God right from the beginning (see Col 1:15 –16).[54]

---

53. Emphasis added.

54. See *CCC,* nn. 280, 1701.

With these statements, the Holy Father appears to be adding his input to a centuries-old theological debate: Would Christ have come had man not sinned? In any case, this pope's opinion on the matter seems clear. For him, Jesus Christ—the *incarnate* Christ—"is the center of the universe and of history."[55] For him, it seems even to entertain the idea of a universe without an incarnate Christ is to miss a central point of the "great mystery" of God's love for humanity.[56]

Christ is "the first-born of all creation" (Col 1:15). Everything—especially man in his original unity as male and female—was created for him, through him, and in expectation of him. When we reread man's beginning in view of the "great mystery" of Ephesians, we can see that Christ's *incarnate* communion with the Church is already anticipated and in some sense "contained" in the original incarnate communion of man and woman. And this original unity in "one flesh" was constituted by God *before* sin. Man and woman's original unity, therefore, was a beatifying participation in grace (see §20). This grace made original man "holy and blameless" before God. Here John Paul reminds us that their primordial (or original) holiness and purity were also expressed in their being naked without shame. The Holy Father then asserts that this original bounty was granted to man in view of Christ, who from eternity was "beloved" as Son, "even though—according to the dimensions of time and history—it had preceded the Incarnation" (334).

B. The Continuity of God's Plan

If this is the case, the Incarnation is not an afterthought—a second plan intended to rectify the first, supposedly thwarted when man sinned. Of course sin put man on a major detour, one might say, in realizing God's plan. But sin is not an insurmountable roadblock. Sin is not more powerful than God's eternal plan to unite us with Christ. God's plan for man and for the universe continues in spite of sin.

The grace of original innocence, John Paul tells us, "was accomplished precisely in reference to [Christ] while anticipating chronologically his coming in the body" (335). And, recalling our reflections on Genesis, that grace was given "in an irrevocable way, despite the subsequent sin and death."[57] It is true that man lost this grace as a result of sin. The entrance of shame attests to this. But he did not lose it forever. Christ's

---

55. *Redemptor Hominis,* n. 1.

56. See *CCC,* nn. 280, 381, 653.

57. 1/30/80, TB 67 (see §20).

resurrection bears witness that the grace of the mystery of creation becomes, for anyone open to receiving it, the grace of the mystery of redemption.[58] "The redemption was to become the source of man's supernatural endowment after sin and, in a certain sense, in spite of sin" (335). In this way God's eternal plan for man—remaining the same yesterday, today, and forever—is definitively accomplished in his beloved Son.

John Paul wants to stress the *continuity* between God's plan in the mystery of creation and his plan in the mystery of redemption. But at the same time we can deduce a "new" dimension to God's self-gift—the revelation of his mercy.[59] After sin, in order to fulfill "the mystery hidden for ages in God" (Eph 3:9), Christ would first have to reconcile man to the Father. This means that his Incarnation and his bodily gift of self would now entail his suffering and death. "In him we have redemption through his blood, the forgiveness of our trespasses" (Eph 1:7). This forgiveness is essential to Christ's mission. Still, it is not the only purpose of his mission. Forgiveness of our sins is only part of "the riches of his grace which he lavished on us" (Eph 1:7–8). One might call it the necessary prerequisite for the fulfillment of God's eternal plan for us "to be his sons through Jesus Christ" (1:5). From the perspective of the spousal analogy, if spouses have been at enmity with each other, they must first reconcile before they re-unite in "one flesh." Christ's self-gift on the cross is the reconciliation of estranged spouses that opens the way for their eternal consummate communion.

75. Marriage Is the Central Point of the Sacrament of Creation

October 6, 1982 (TB 333 – 336)

We spoke above of the eternal plan of God the Father to unite us in an incarnate communion with Christ. These plans precede the creation of the world and therefore also our creation as male and female. Furthermore, man's sin did not and could not thwart God's plan. The Father continues to carry out the mystery of his will to unite all things in Christ despite sin. John Paul asks: "In what way is the reality of the sacrament, of the primordial sacrament, verified in this context?" (335) We will now seek to answer this question.

---

58. See 10/29/80, TB 167.

59. See *Dives in Misericordia*, n. 7.

A. The Body Pervaded by Grace

The Holy Father says that the following phrases sum up his entire analysis of the creation accounts in Genesis. He quotes himself: "'Man appears in the visible world as the highest expression of the divine gift, because he bears within himself the interior dimension of the gift. And with it he brings into the world his particular likeness to God....Resulting from this likeness there is also the primordial awareness of the conjugal significance of the body, pervaded by the mystery of original innocence'" (333).[60]

God *is* "gift" just as "God *is* love" (1 Jn 4:8). Man is the highest expression of the divine gift in the visible world because he is created as a person who is called *from within* to love. This is "the interior dimension of the gift." But in the perfect integration of body and soul, this "interior dimension" is also manifested outwardly in the body—in the nuptial meaning (here translated "conjugal significance") of the body. To say that their awareness of the nuptial meaning of the body was "pervaded by the mystery of original innocence" is to say their experience of the body was "pervaded by grace." This is that grace of election in Christ which was already granted in the mystery of creation. The effect of that grace is, as John Paul says (quoting again from his earlier catechesis on Genesis), "'that man feels himself, in his body as male and female, the subject of holiness.' 'He feels' himself and he is such from the 'beginning'" (335).

And what is holiness? "The holiness of God is the inaccessible center of his eternal mystery."[61] Human holiness is our participation in this mystery enabled by God's utterly gratuitous gift of himself to us. Therefore, human holiness is measured according to the response of the Bride (man) to the gift (grace) of the Bridegroom (Christ). In turn, holiness "enables man to express himself deeply with his own body...precisely by means of the 'sincere gift' of himself."[62] In this way we see how the *invisible* divine reality of gift-grace-holiness (in a word, love) was originally made *visible* through the human body and in the incarnate self-gift of man and woman to each other. Therefore the Holy Father adds that the holiness that the Creator conferred originally on man pertains to what he calls the "sacrament of creation."

---

60. This quote from the audience of February 20, 1980 (see TB 76) is translated differently here.

61. *CCC,* n. 2809.

62. 2/20/80, TB 76–77.

B. The Sacrament of Creation

When John Paul speaks of the "sacrament of creation" he indicates that all of the created universe in some way makes the invisible mystery of its Creator visible. As the psalmist proclaims: "The heavens are telling the glory of God" (Ps 19:1). The sacrament of creation reaches its highest expression in the crown of creation: man, male and female. Man, in turn, reaches his fulfillment through the sincere gift of self which was realized in an original way through that rich personal union of man and woman in "one flesh." It is the *incarnate communion* of man and woman that in some way sums up or *consummates* the "sacrament of creation" (see §22).

The Holy Father expresses this when he says: "The words of Genesis 2:24, 'a man...cleaves to his wife and they become one flesh,'...constitute marriage as...a sacrament inasmuch as it is an integral part, and," the Pope believes, "the central point of the 'sacrament of creation.' In this sense it is the primordial sacrament" (335). Quoting himself again, the Pope reminds us that the primordial sacrament is to be "'understood as a sign which effectively transmits in the visible world the invisible mystery hidden from eternity in God. And this is the mystery of truth and love, the mystery of the divine life in which man really shares'" (333). Thus, John Paul tells us that "the institution of marriage, according to the words of Genesis 2:24, expresses not only the beginning of the fundamental human community." At the same time it expresses "the salvific initiative of the Creator, corresponding to the eternal election of man [in Christ], of which the letter to the Ephesians speaks" (335).

Here we reach the summit of the "great mystery" of our creation as male and female and our call to become "one flesh." Here we touch the deepest essence of the body and of nuptial union *as theology*. It is this: When we allow the grace of redemption to "untwist" what is disordered in our sexuality, we realize that our entire incarnate personalities as male and female—lived in the current of our erotic desire for union—proclaim, express, and summon us to receive as utter "gift" our eternal election in Jesus Christ. This election invites us to dwell in the glory of the divine self-giving for all eternity. This divine life of triune self-giving is "the mystery hidden from eternity in God." And this is what the body—through its visible masculinity and femininity—proclaims and in what it summons us to participate. The Holy Father recalls his thesis: "'The body in fact, and only it, is capable of making visible what is invisible: the spiritual and divine. It was created to transfer into the visible reality of the world the mystery hidden from eternity in God, and thus to be its sign'" (335).[63]

---

63. In the audience of February 20, 1980, the English translation stated that the body becomes "a" sign of the divine mystery. Here the translation states that the body becomes "its" sign. The Italian *("e cosi esserne segno")* says "a" sign.

The primordial sacrament as instituted in Genesis 2:24 contains a supernatural efficacy because already in creation man was "chosen in Christ."[64] In this way the Pope says we must recognize that the original "sacrament of creation" draws its efficacy from Christ. John Paul indicates that St. Paul speaks of this grace in Ephesians 1:6—the "grace which [the Father] freely bestowed on us in the Beloved." Marriage—this primordial sacrament of sexual love—is intended, therefore, not only to advance the work of creation through procreation. God also intends that it serve "to extend to further generations of men the same sacrament of creation, that is, the supernatural fruits of man's eternal election on the part of the Father in the eternal Son" (336).

■ Based on this, is it any wonder why Satan attacks right here? Recall that sin "and death entered man's history, in a way, through the very heart of that unity which, from 'the beginning,' was formed by man and woman, created and called to become 'one flesh.'"[65] Satan's goal is to keep man from his eternal election in Christ. He does so by plagiarizing the primordial sacrament. Satan wants to twist man and woman's union into an "anti-sacrament"—an effective denial of the gift of God's life and love. He plagiarizes the Word inscribed in the body ("self-donation") and makes it his own anti-word ("self-gratification"). At this point we are getting closer to understanding why Karol Wojtyla, just a few months before his election as Pope John Paul II, described the teaching of *Humanae Vitae* as a "struggle for the value and meaning of humanity itself."[66]

76. Marriage: Platform for the Actuation of God's Designs
October 6, 13, 1982 (TB 334–337)

We have been chosen in Christ "before the foundation of the world to be holy and blameless before him" (Eph 1:4). This is the mystery of God's will St. Paul announced in the first chapter of Ephesians: to unite us (and all things) with Christ according to the riches of his grace (see vv. 4, 8–9). According to John Paul, this is all actuated by the "great mystery" proclaimed in Ephesians 5.

---

64. See *CCC*, n. 257.

65. 3/5/80, TB 77 (see §24).

66. Cited in *Crossing the Threshold of Love*, p. 113.

We have learned that marriage—instituted by the union of male and female in "one flesh"—was already "in the beginning" an image of and a participation in this eternal election in Christ. This lofty theological concept may seem hopelessly removed from the "real life" experience of ordinary men and women. From the experience of men and women dominated by concupiscence, yes. But for husbands and wives who are being freed from the domination of concupiscence through ongoing conversion to Christ, this "lofty theology" gradually becomes what they *live* and *experience*.

In what way? How actually is marriage and its consummate expression supposed to image and participate in our eternal election in Christ? To answer this question we must attune ourselves to that "echo" of our origins deep within us. We must recall the original experiences we reconstructed in our analysis of Genesis—solitude, unity, and nakedness—and believe in the power of the grace "which God lavishes on us in his Beloved" to restore what was lost.

A. Being Chosen and Being Able to Choose

The Holy Father recalls that in all of creation, the election to the dignity of adopted sonship was proper only to the "first Adam"—to the man created in the image and likeness of God as male and female. This "Adam" realized he was alone in the visible world as a *person*. The deepest meaning of this solitude is that Adam was constituted "in a unique, exclusive, and unrepeatable relationship with God himself." He alone among all the body-creatures was a "partner of the Absolute."[67]

The experience of original solitude, then, was an experience of "being chosen" and of "being able to choose." God *chose* Adam in love. He chose him *in Christ*. For, as John Paul's favorite passage from Vatican II tells us, "Adam, the first man, was a figure of him who was to come, namely Christ the Lord."[68] Furthermore, in "being chosen," Adam was also given the ability *to choose* to love God in return *and* to choose to love another human person in order to recapitulate the love God had given to him. In this way original solitude leads to the experience of original unity (see §12). For it is not good for the man to be alone.

But the experience of original nakedness in particular enables us to see how man and woman's original unity was an image of and participation in man's eternal election in Christ. Nakedness without shame revealed that they were "free with the very freedom of the gift." Adam had no compulsion to satisfy an "urge" at the sight of woman's nakedness. Her body

---

67. 10/24/79, TB 38 (see §12).

68. *Gaudium et Spes*, n. 22.

inspired nothing in Adam but the desire to make a "sincere gift" of himself to her: to *choose* her in freedom as his bride, as God had chosen him in Christ "before the foundation of the world." Furthermore, knowing that she was a person made for "her own sake," he knew he could not "take" her or "grasp" her. He had to trust that she—in her freedom—would desire to open herself to the gift he initiated and respond freely with the gift of herself to him, which she did (see §18). Free from any compulsion and selfish sting, their marital union was a mutual choice—a choice made *for* the good of the other and *because of* the good of the other. It was a participation in that original good of God's vision which, as John Paul says, affirms his choosing of us.

In this way their conjugal union was a "beatifying experience," imaging and participating in their having been "elected" or chosen by eternal Love (see §19). John Paul describes this participation as the "supernatural efficacy" of the primordial sacrament. In other words, the experience of original unity truly communicated God's life and love to man and woman.

B. Sin and the Loss of Supernatural Efficacy

This reality, however, as experience attests, became dimmed by the heritage of original sin. As John Paul expresses, "the heritage of grace was driven out of the human heart at the time of the breaking of the first Covenant with the Creator." In this way "marriage, as a primordial sacrament, was deprived of that supernatural efficacy which at the moment of its institution belonged to the sacrament of creation in its totality. Nonetheless," the Pope continues, "even in this state, that is, in the state of man's hereditary sinfulness, *marriage never ceased being the figure of that sacrament* we read about in the letter to the Ephesians." Despite sin, John Paul suggests that "marriage has remained the platform for the actuation of God's eternal designs" (336).

Even if crippled in its ability to do so, man and woman's longing for marital union has spoken in some way of the "great mystery" to all the generations of history. The universal cultural heritage of romantic poetry, literature, music, and art often points to a basic intuition that the love of the sexes is meant to be a merging of the human and the divine.[69]

While marriage entails many trials under the inheritance of sin, a "spark" of that beatifying beginning remains. In fact, this spark prepares men and women for the gift of redemption. The heart longs for "something more" than life can offer under sin's influence. To tap into that desire for "something more" is to tap into that "echo" deep within our hearts of

---

69. See *Gaudium et Spes,* n. 49.

God's original plan for us. Despite formidable foes that seek to snuff it out, that yearning cannot and will not be repressed.[70] It is a yearning to live in the grace of our eternal election in Christ. It is a yearning to live in the eternal embrace of the Marriage of the Lamb. Nothing else can satisfy. Nothing else can fulfill. And all else is destined to pass away.

■ It is precisely this yearning that Satan targets and toys with in order to manipulate us in his direction. The myriad pleasures of this world which he parades before us as "the prince of the power of the air" (Eph 2:2) purport to satisfy our longings but leave us empty. Still, we must always keep in mind that all Satan can do to attract us is plagiarize the joys God created for us in this world to foreshadow the joys of heaven. All the authentic pleasures of this world are in some way sacramental, whereas all the counterfeit pleasures of this world are in some way sacrilegious. This is where the battle is fought: between sacraments and their counterfeits, between icons and idols, between signs and anti-signs. One foreshadows an eternity of fulfillment and communion, the other an eternity of emptiness and alienation.

77. Sacrament of Creation Fulfilled in Sacrament of Redemption
October 13, 1982 (TB 336–339)

The "echo" of God's original plan that resounds in the human heart despite sin is irrepressible. We might call this an echo of the sacrament of creation. And this echo prepares men and women to receive the sacrament of redemption. John Paul speaks to this when he suggests that "the sacrament of creation had drawn near to men and had prepared them for the sacrament of redemption, introducing them into the work of salvation" (336). What does the Pope mean by the "sacrament of redemption"? To answer this, let us first recall what he means by the sacrament of creation.

A. Sacraments of Creation and Redemption

The sacrament of creation is that which in the totality of creation makes visible the mystery hidden in God from all eternity. This is the mystery of divine life and love—of *communion*—in which original man really participated through the grace of the sacrament of creation.[71] Marriage as

---

70. See Lorenzo Albacete, *God at the Ritz: Attraction to Infinity* (New York: Crossroads, 2002).

71. See *CCC,* n. 375.

instituted by the words of Genesis 2:24 is the central and consummate point of the sacrament of creation. In this sense it is the primordial sacrament which was at work in man and woman with supernatural efficacy. Marriage, however, lost its efficacy as the central point of the sacrament of creation with the dawn of sin. When man broke his covenant with the Creator, the "life" with which he had been *in*-spired, *ex*-spired in his heart. Shame in their nakedness attests to this loss of grace and holiness. Even so, as John Paul suggests, "marriage has remained the platform for the actuation of God's eternal designs" (336). "In fact, the original 'unity in the body' of man and woman does not cease to mold the history of man on earth, even though it has lost the clarity of...the sign of salvation, which it possessed 'at the beginning.'"[72]

When St. Paul links this "unity in the body" of the first Adam and Eve with the incarnate communion of the New Adam and Eve (Christ and the Church), he speaks of it as a "great mystery." According to the Holy Father, this linking of Genesis 2:24 with Christ and the Church "seems to indicate not only the identity of the mystery hidden in God from all eternity, but also that continuity of its actuation" (336–337). This continuity "exists between the primordial sacrament connected with the supernatural gracing of man in creation itself, and the new gracing which occurred when 'Christ loved the Church and gave himself up for her to make her holy...' (Eph 5:25–26)." It is this "new gracing," the Pope emphasizes, "*that can be defined in its entirety as the sacrament of redemption*" (337).

According to St. Paul, Christ gives himself *for* the Church and *to* the Church in the image of the nuptial union of husband and wife in marriage. In this way John Paul says that in some sense the sacrament of redemption takes on once again "the figure and form of the primordial sacrament." The marriage of the first man and woman was a sign of the supernatural gracing of man in the sacrament of creation. To this "there corresponds the marriage, or rather the analogy of the marriage, of Christ with the Church as the fundamental 'great' sign of the supernatural gracing of man in the sacrament of redemption" (337). This "new gracing" definitively renews the covenant of the grace of election, which was broken in the beginning by sin. The Pope also says that this "new gracing" of the sacrament of redemption is "a new actuation" of that mystery hidden in God from all eternity. It is new in relation to the sacrament of creation because this new grace is in a certain sense a "new creation." As St. Paul proclaims: "Therefore, if anyone is in Christ, he is a new creation; the old has passed away, behold, the new has come" (2 Cor 5:17).

---

72. 11/24/82, TB 345.

While John Paul stresses the continuity between the original gracing and the new gracing, he also notes an important difference. The original gracing given in the sacrament of creation constituted man in the state of original innocence. The new gracing given in the sacrament of redemption is given first for the remission of sins. But, as discussed previously (see §74), forgiveness of sins is only part of "the riches of his grace which he lavished on us" (Eph 1:7–8). In this context the Holy Father quotes from Romans 5:20: "Where sin increased, grace abounded all the more."

B. Signs of Creation and Redemption

But in what manner is the grace of the sacraments of creation and redemption actuated? John Paul stresses that *"in speaking about the eternal mystery being actuated* we are speaking *also about the fact that it becomes visible with the visibility of the sign"* (338). There is a sign that actuates the sacrament of creation by making the mystery of creation visible. And there is a sign that actuates the sacrament of redemption by making the mystery of redemption visible. What are these signs? John Paul himself tells us that "the mystery hidden in God from all eternity...in the sacrament of creation, became *a visible reality through the union* of the first man and woman in the perspective of marriage." This same mystery "becomes in the sacrament of redemption *a visible reality [through] the indissoluble union of Christ with the Church,* which the author of the letter to the Ephesians presents as the nuptial union of spouses" (338).

As John Paul said: "It is a special merit of [the Apostle] that he brought these two signs together, and made of them one great sign—that is, a great sacrament."[73] When we speak of these signs—of the union of spouses and of the analogous union of Christ and the Church—according to John Paul, "we are speaking also about the *sacramentality* of the whole heritage of the sacrament of redemption, in reference to the entire work of creation and redemption" (338–339). This is the power of sacramental signs. They actualize that which they symbolize. In the beginning marital unity was created to symbolize the eternal mystery of life-giving Communion in the Trinity. "As the 'first Adam'—man, male and female—created in the state of original innocence and called in this state to conjugal union (in this sense we are speaking of the sacrament of creation) was a sign of the eternal mystery, so the 'second Adam,' Christ, united with the Church through the sacrament of redemption by an indissoluble bond, analogous to the indissoluble bond of spouses, is a definitive sign of the same eternal mystery" (338).

---

73. 9/29/82, TB 333.

From this perspective John Paul tells us that the Church itself is the "great sacrament," the new sign of the covenant and of grace. Just as marriage emerged from the sacrament of creation as a primordial sign of the covenant and of grace, now the new sign of the covenant and of grace "draws its roots from the depths of the sacrament of redemption." Thus, the "primordial sacrament is realized in a new way in the sacrament of Christ and the Church."[74]

John Paul is talking about the profound interrelationship of the marriage of the first Adam and Eve and the marriage of the New Adam and Eve (Christ and the Church). We could even say these two marriages are married to each other. In this way they form "one great sign" which reveals the "great mystery." Of course sacramental signs do not fully explain the mystery. As an object of faith the mystery remains veiled even in the expression of its sign. Yet grace is communicated with power under the veil of the sign.

C. Christ's Spousal Love Is Unitive and Life-Giving

In this densely packed audience of October 13, 1982, John Paul stresses that the nuptial gift of Christ to the Church, as the analogy indicates, has both a unitive and a "life-giving dimension." We see the unitive dimension in the reciprocity of the gift between Christ and the Church. Christ initiates the sacrament of redemption by giving up his body for the Church with the desire of "uniting himself with her in an indissoluble love, just as spouses, husband and wife, unite themselves in marriage" (338). But the gift given must also be received. Through her response to the gift, the Church "in her turn completes this sacrament as the wife, in virtue of spousal love, completes her husband." This "completion" of the husband by his wife was already pointed out, the Pope says, when the first man found in woman "a helper fit for him."

Recall that the wife's mystery "is manifested and revealed completely by means of motherhood" (see §23). Hence, along with the "unitive dimension" of Christ's spousal love for the Church we also recognize the "life-giving dimension." In this context John Paul says "we can add also that the Church united to Christ, as the wife to her husband, draws from the sacrament of redemption all her fruitfulness and spiritual motherhood" (338). St. Peter testifies to this in some way when he writes that we have been "reborn not from a corruptible, but from an incorruptible seed, through the living and enduring word of God" (1 Pet 1:23).

---

74. 10/27/82, TB 342.

At this point we are close to understanding the importance of the encyclical *Humanae Vitae*. The "one flesh" union of spouses is meant to be a sign of the "great mystery" of Christ's union with the Church. And, as John Paul has already said, we can speak of moral good and evil in the sexual relationship "according to whether...or not it has the character of the truthful sign."[75] Anyone can recognize that an attack on the unitive dimension of sexuality—for instance, physical abuse inflicted on one's spouse—would contradict utterly the sign of Christ's love for the Church. Why then is it so difficult to recognize that an attack on the life-giving dimension also utterly contradicts this sign of Christ's love for the Church? This is the context in which the Holy Father will reflect on the issue of contraception in his next cycle.

78. Marriage: Prototype of All the Sacraments

October 20, 27, 1982 (TB 339 – 342)

John Paul II's analysis of Ephesians demonstrates the profound inter-relationship of creation and redemption in the human drama. In this same context it also demonstrates the profound inter-relationship of nature and grace. Some conceive of man as capable of a purely "natural fulfillment" apart from grace. Grace is then "added on" to man's nature, it seems, as if it were a two-story structure. But based on John Paul II's analysis of Genesis and Ephesians, we know that God gave grace to man in his creation *as man*. To be full of grace, then, is man's natural state—if by "natural" we mean God's one and original plan for man.

Just like a bride is created in her very being to receive her husband, so too is man created in his very being to receive grace; to receive divine life as the Bride of Christ (see §55). This insight is found already in the work of St. Thomas Aquinas, who taught that man is naturally capable of grace because he is made in God's image.[76] In this sense we cannot speak of a purely "natural" state of man detached or divorced from grace. The only natural state is that willed by God in the beginning. When man fell

---

75. 8/27/80, TB 141–142.

76. See *Summa Theologiae,* I–IIae, q. 113, a. 10. Fathers Hogan and LeVoir also point this out in their discussion of nature and grace in their book *Covenant of Love: Pope John Paul II on Sexuality, Marriage, and Family in the Modern World* (San Francisco, CA: Ignatius Press, 1992), p. 35. For a discussion of Wojtyla's intervention at the Council on the issue of nature and grace, see Rocco Buttiglione, *Karol Wojtyla: The Thought of the Man Who Became Pope John Paul II,* pp. 195–199.

from grace, he did not become a "natural" man. He stooped lower than his nature. This is why Christ, in revealing the mystery of the Father and his love—that is, in revealing the mystery of grace—fully reveals man to himself. This grace, of course, is not man's due, any more than being created in the first place is his due (see §12). We need not dissociate nature and grace, as some might imagine, in order to maintain this important truth. Man's creation—and his creation with a graced nature—is not owed him. It is a sheer gift.[77]

A. Grace of the Primordial Sacrament Restored

We see this "marriage" of nature and grace in Ephesians 5:31–32 where St. Paul weds the consummate sign of the sacrament of creation with the consummate sign of the sacrament of redemption. Quoting from Genesis he says: "For this reason a man shall leave his father and mother and be joined to his wife, and the two shall become one flesh." Then he adds: "This is a great mystery, and I mean in reference to Christ and the church."

According to the Holy Father, a careful analysis of this key text shows that the Apostle's linking of the original union of spouses with the union of Christ and the Church "is not merely a comparison in a metaphorical sense." This passage speaks "of a real *renewal* (or of a 're-creation,' that is, of a new creation) of *that which constituted the salvific content* (in a certain sense, the 'salvific substance') of the primordial sacrament" (341). In other words, the grace of the primordial sacrament which was lost through sin is now re-stored, re-created, or *resurrected* in the sacrament of redemption.

Marriage regains its efficacy—its power to actualize that which it symbolizes. This time, however, it draws this efficacy not from the sacrament of creation, but from the sacrament of redemption. With this efficacy, John Paul points out that marriage is not merely a model and figure of Christ's union with the Church. It "constitutes also an *essential part* of the new heritage" (339). "Christ in his conversation with the Pharisees (Mt 19) not only confirms the existence of marriage instituted from the 'begin-

---

77. This brief sketch barely begins to introduce a very complex debate that lies at the heart of the theological problem of our time. At the core of the contemporary controversy regarding the relationship between nature and grace is the teaching of the French Jesuit theologian Henri de Lubac. For a summary of the debate as it centers on his thought see David Schindler's introduction to de Lubac's book, *The Mystery of the Supernatural* (New York: Crossroad Herder, 1998), pp. xi–xxxi. For a more comprehensive discussion, see Hans Urs von Balthasar's *The Theology of Karl Barth* (San Francisco, CA: Ignatius Press/Communio Books, 1992), especially part III, pp. 251–358.

ning' by the Creator, but he declares it *also an integral part of the new sacramental economy"* (340). The new sacramental economy is the new order of "salvific signs" which derives its origin and efficacy from the sacrament of redemption.

B. Marriage Provides the Basic Structure of Salvation

In referring to these new "salvific signs" John Paul moves from the broader sense of "sacrament" to the more specific sense in which sacrament refers to those signs instituted by Christ and administered by the Church (see §70). The Pope emphasizes that this new sacramental economy differs from the original economy in that it is directed not to the man of original innocence, but to the man burdened with the heritage of original sin. This new economy has seven sacraments instituted to give grace to the man of concupiscence. In the original economy, John Paul says that marriage was "the unique sacrament" instituted for man in the state of innocence. Based on the integral relationship of creation and redemption, we can conclude that the primordial sacrament already foreshadowed the grace that was to become the gift of redemption. This grace is now given to the man of concupiscence through the spousal union of Christ and the Church poured forth in each of the seven sacraments. It is given for the remission of sins but also in superabundance for the sake of eternal communion with Christ.

Recall that God's original plan for man is in a sense continuous. Sin did not thwart it. Accordingly, marriage—which was the central point of the sacrament of creation in its totality—also provides the figure according to which we construct "the basic main structure of the new economy of salvation and of the sacramental order which draws its origin from the spousal gracing which the Church received from Christ" (339). In other words, Christ assumes into the whole economy of redemption the same nuptial imprint which permeated creation. As the *Catechism* teaches, "The entire Christian life bears the mark of the spousal love of Christ and the Church."[78] Therefore John Paul observes that marriage, as a primordial sacrament, is "assumed and inserted as it were from its very bases" into the integral structure of the new sacramental economy. Thus, marriage arises from redemption, as the Holy Father emphasizes, *"in the form of a prototype."* "Reflecting deeply on this dimension, one would have to conclude that all the sacraments of the new covenant find in a certain sense their prototype in marriage as the primordial sacrament" (339).

---

78. *CCC,* n. 1617.

This idea is closely related with what the Holy Father said earlier when he described the visible sign of marriage as "the foundation of the whole sacramental order" (see §71). Marriage is in some sense the foundation, the model, and the prototype of all of the sacraments because all of the sacraments draw their essential significance and their sacramental power from the spousal love of Christ the Redeemer. John Paul points out that Ephesians 5 shows the spousal character of Baptism (v. 26) and the Eucharist (v. 29) in a particularly graphic, if somewhat allusive, manner. Moreover, we can recognize that each of the seven sacraments is imbued with a nuptial meaning. Each of the sacraments, in its own way, unites us *in the flesh* with Christ our Bridegroom. When we as Bride are open to the gift, the sacraments infuse (pushing the analogy, we might say "impregnate") us with divine life.

> ■ A person can go through the motions of receiving the sacraments while denying the life-giving grace they afford; an example of this would be a person who receives the Eucharist in a state of defiance toward God. This would be a serious sacrilege. A question then arises. If the consummate expression of the sacrament of marriage is meant to symbolize the gift of Christ and the receptivity of the Bride to divine life, what does contraception do to this picture?

The "great mystery" of Christ's union with the Church was foreshadowed from the beginning in our creation as male and female and in our call to become one flesh. As if this has not been emphasized enough, we shall say it again: Sexuality—when given its full biblical, theological-sacramental, and anthropological meaning—is all about Christ. And Christ "is the center of the universe and of history."[79]

79. An Adequate Anthropology and an Adequate Ethos

October 20, 27; November 24, 1982 (TB 340 – 347)

In keeping with his circular style of writing, in his audiences of October 27 and November 24, 1982,[80] John Paul revisits those key words of Christ about God's original plan for marriage and his words about lust as "adultery committed in the heart." We can now understand the power and

---

79. *Redemptor Hominis*, n. 1.

80. No audiences were delivered as part of the catechesis between these two dates.

importance of these key texts with even more precision in light of the "great mystery" of Ephesians 5. John Paul reminds us that these words have a profound theological, anthropological, and ethical significance. "Christ speaks from the depths of that divine mystery. And at the same time he enters into the very depths of the human mystery" (347). In this way the God-Man witnesses to a theological-anthropology. Christ "fully reveals man to himself" by unveiling the God-like dignity bestowed on men and women in the mystery of creation and redemption. It is a dignity that calls men and women to greatness. In other words, it makes demands on them—ethical demands.

A. The Anthropology of Redemption

When Christ refers to God's original plan for man and woman's joining in "one flesh," as well as when he condemns the lust in man's heart, his words penetrate "into that which man and woman are (or rather into *who* man and woman are) in their original dignity of image and likeness of God." John Paul immediately stresses that historical man inherits this same dignity in spite of sin. In fact, the dignity of original man is "continually 'assigned' to man as a duty through the reality of redemption" (346).

Christ's key words flow "from the divine depth of the 'redemption of the body' (Rom 8:23)" (343). Christ thereby opens marriage (and male-female relations in general) "to the salvific action of God, to the forces which...help to overcome the consequences of sin and to constitute the unity of man and woman according to the eternal plan of the Creator" (345). John Paul says that redemption, in fact, signifies a "new creation." It assumes all that is created to express it anew according to "the fullness of justice, of equity, and of sanctity designated by God"—especially in man who is created as male and female in the divine image. Thus, the "salvific action which derives from the mystery of redemption assumes in itself the original sanctifying action of God in the very mystery of creation" (345). Christ's words bear within them the leaven of this hope. The Pope reminds us that this is not only a hope reserved for our state in the final resurrection. This is also a hope that can be progressively realized "in the dimension of daily life" (343)—"the hope of every day" (see §63).

John Paul insists that it is truly possible for historical man to "find again the dignity and holiness of the conjugal union 'in the body,' on the basis of the mystery of redemption" (346). What hope! Man and woman need not be continually wounded by the blades of concupiscence which stab at the heart of their dignity and their communion. Married life need not be only an ongoing coping with or mere channeling of wounded and wounding desires. The Pope says that marriage invites us to participate *consciously* in the redemption of the body. Spouses who are committed to doing so (Christian spouses are supposed to commit to this) can progressively rediscover, reclaim, and live according to their original dignity. They can—by daily taking up the redeeming cross of Christ—experience a real measure of the harmony, peace, and happiness of original unity. As the *Catechism* teaches, "By coming to restore the original order of creation disturbed by sin, [Christ] himself gives the strength and grace to...'receive' the original meaning of marriage and live it."[81]

B. The Ethos of Redemption

Christ's words about marriage not only show us who we are in the mystery of creation and redemption. They have at the same time an "expressive ethical eloquence." In other words, Christ's words provide the foundation both for an "adequate anthropology" and for an "adequate ethos." John Paul has already described this as "the ethos of redemption."

Christ not only confirms marriage as a primordial sacrament. In referring to "the beginning," he also draws moral conclusions: "Whoever divorces his wife and marries another commits adultery against her" (Mk 10:11). The Pope points out that St. Paul also places his teaching on marriage in the context of moral exhortations, which outline the ethos that should characterize the life of Christians. John Paul then defines what a Christian is: "Christians [are those] people aware of the election which is realized in Christ and in the Church" (340). Precisely *these* people have been empowered by grace to understand and to live the "ethos of redemption." Those who have not been so empowered will inevitably see the demands of Christian morality as an imposition. They will see an external ethic that burdens rather than an internal ethos that liberates (see §25).

■ It seems that few people who fill the pews of our churches are "aware of the election which is realized in Christ and in the Church" (340). More specifically, my experience in sharing the theology of the body with Christians around the world indicates that most people who fill the pews do not realize that this election—the mystery of the Gospel itself—is stamped mysteriously in their own bodies as male and female. Hence, as John Paul II repeatedly insists, a crucial need exists for a "new evangelization"—new because it is largely directed to the baptized.[82]

---

81. *CCC*, n. 1615.

82. The epilogue will address how John Paul II's theology of the body provides a foundation, both in substance and methodology, for the new evangelization.

While the Christian ethos can be explained philosophically (and John Paul adds through a *personalist* philosophy)—nonetheless, Christian ethos is essentially theological since it is an ethos of redemption. More specifically, according to John Paul, it is an ethos of the redemption of the body. Ultimately, the Christian ethos is only fully tenable to those who are living their election in Christ—to those who are living the grace of a redeemed life in the body. Redemption is "the basis for understanding the particular dignity of the human body, rooted in the personal dignity of the man and the woman" (345). This dignity forms the basis of all morality.

All of the Church's teachings on sexual morality, then, are a call for men and women to embrace and uphold their own greatness. As the Holy Father says, in defining the ethos of sexual morality in the Sermon on the Mount, Christ "assigns as a duty to every man the dignity of every woman; and simultaneously (even though this can be deduced from the text only in an indirect way), he also assigns to every woman the dignity of every man. Finally," the Pope concludes, "he assigns to everyone—both to man and woman—their own dignity" (346). John Paul defines this dignity as the *"sacrum"*—the "sacredness"—of the person. And he specifically adds that this sacredness of men and women is "in consideration of their femininity or masculinity, in consideration of the 'body'" (346). The body reveals man's greatness—man's dignity.

C. The Struggle with Concupiscence

Living according to our own dignity is a continuous and often arduous struggle. In this context Christ speaks of the heart—"that 'intimate place' in which there struggle in man good and evil, sin and justice, concupiscence and holiness" (347). However, if Christ wants all men and women to realize that they are subject to concupiscence, he also wants them to realize that he makes the grace of redemption available to them with *real power* to transform their hearts.

Redemption "is given to man as a grace of the new covenant with God in Christ—and at the same time it is assigned to him as an ethos" (345). This is a demanding ethos, to be sure. Christ assigns it to man's heart and, as John Paul adds, "to his conscience, to his looks, and to his behavior" (347). If the man of concupiscence feels powerless in himself to meet these demands, he need only remember his election in Christ.

Here John Paul reminds us that the new ethos is "the form of the morality corresponding to God's action in the mystery of redemption" (345). What was God's action in the mystery of redemption? It was grace poured out in superabundance to conquer sin (see Rom 5:20). It was the death of our sinful nature "so that as Christ was raised from the dead to the glory of the Father, we too might walk in newness of life" (Rom 6:4). If we once yielded our bodies to impurity, now the Spirit enlivens our mortal bodies and empowers them for righteousness (see Rom 6:19; 8:11). When the power of the Holy Spirit vivifies us in this way, we come to *know* the sacredness of the body and of conjugal relations. Living from this awareness—even if we still recognize the tug of concupiscence—we simply do not desire to profane the sacred. We would prefer to be crucified.

As St. Peter learned, if we keep our eyes on Christ we can walk on water. Even if our faith wanes and we begin to sink, Christ always reaches out to save us if we but turn to him again (see Mt 14:25 – 31). But we must first *believe* in the power of Christ and step out of the boat. As we observed previously, the drama of redemption—in this case the drama of conquering concupiscence in our hearts, our looks, and our behavior—lies not in the "safety" of the boat, but amidst the wind and the waves. That is where Christ is, and he beckons us, "Come!"

80. Marriage Reveals the Salvific Will of God
November 24; December 1, 1982 (TB 344 – 349)

The Church firmly believes that Christ instituted each of the seven sacraments. Traditionally theologians have pointed to Christ's presence at the wedding feast of Cana as the biblical evidence of Christ's institution of marriage as a sacrament.[83] John Paul II also points to Christ's discussion with the Pharisees as such evidence. Based on these words, the Pope concludes that marriage is not only a sacrament from the very "beginning," but it is also a sacrament arising from the mystery of the "redemption of the body." Elsewhere in the same audience John Paul says that "Christ's words to the Pharisees refer to marriage as a sacrament, that is, to the primordial revelation of God's salvific will" for man (344).

A. Gaudium et Spes *24 Linked with Genesis 2:24*

This definition of the sacrament of marriage deserves comment. What is God's salvific will for man? Christ summarizes it when he says: "This is my commandment, that you love one another as I have loved you" (Jn 15:12). This is the meaning of our creation as male and female and our call to become "one flesh." It is a call to love as God loves "from the beginning." John Paul then links this call revealed already in Genesis 2:24 with the teaching of *Gaudium et Spes* n. 24:

---

83. See *CCC*, n. 1613.

...the Lord Jesus, when praying to the Father "that they may all be one...even as we are one" (Jn 17:21–22), opened up new horizons closed to human reason by implying that there is a certain parallel between the union existing among the divine persons and the union of the sons of God in truth and love. It follows, then, that if man is the only creature on earth that God has wanted for its own sake, man can fully discover his true self only in a sincere giving of himself.

In virtue of God's salvific will, John Paul says that "man and woman, joining together in such a way as to become 'one flesh,' were at the same time destined to be united 'in truth and love' as children of God" according to the above teaching of *Gaudium et Spes*. John Paul continues by saying that Christ directs his words about marriage as the primordial sacrament "to this unity and toward this communion of persons, in the likeness of the union of the divine persons" (344–345), as the above teaching of the Council also indicates. In his *Letter to Families*, John Paul states that every man and woman "fully realizes himself or herself through the sincere gift of self. For spouses the moment of conjugal union constitutes a very particular expression of this. It is then that a man and a woman, in the 'truth' of their masculinity and femininity, become a mutual gift to each other."[84]

John Paul illuminated for us early on that this teaching of the Council on communion among persons through the sincere gift of self is rooted in the body—in the nuptial meaning of the body (see §18). The human model for all the "sons of God" who are united "in truth and love" is the union of husband and wife in "one body." For we are all "one body" in Christ (see 1 Cor 12:12–13). This reflects what was already said about the conjugal union shedding light on all genuine expressions of love (see §4).

B. Dominion Over Concupiscence

When husband and wife are united "in truth and love," marriage becomes "an efficacious expression of the saving power of God." This "saving power" enables man and woman to overcome concupiscence and gain dominion over the tendency toward an egoistic gratification. "The unity and indissolubility of marriage are the fruit of this dominion, as is also a deepened sense of the dignity of woman in the heart of a man (and also the dignity of man in the heart of woman)." This deepened appreciation for the dignity of the opposite sex becomes evident "both in conjugal life together, and in every other circle of mutual relations" (348).

John Paul already said that "the freedom of the gift" afforded by liberation from lust "is the condition of all life together in truth."[85] If we want

---

84. *Letter to Families*, n. 12.

85. 10/8/80, TB 158–159 (see §35).

to build a culture that respects life and acknowledges human dignity, we must begin by overcoming concupiscence in our own hearts. There is no other starting point. There is no other solution. It all begins right here. But how can we do it? Concupiscence is ever-ready to rear its ugly head and blind us to our great dignity. True enough. But when we open our flesh to the life of the Holy Spirit, we find a power at work in us infinitely greater than the force of concupiscence. Listen to these words of hope: "As much as 'concupiscence' darkens the horizon of the inward vision and deprives the heart of the clarity of desires and aspirations, so much does 'life according to the Spirit'...permit man and woman to find again the true liberty of the gift, united to the awareness of the spousal meaning of the body in its masculinity and femininity" (349). John Paul specifies that this "life according to the Spirit"—while available to everyone—is also the specific grace poured out in the sacrament of marriage.

As a sacrament of the Church, the Pope says that marriage is also "a word of the Spirit" which exhorts man and woman to model their whole life together by drawing power from the mystery of the redemption of the body. In this way, man and woman "are called to chastity as to a state of life 'according to the Spirit'" (348). Marriage, then, is a sacrament of redemption given to the man of concupiscence as a grace and at the same time as an ethos. In this case John Paul says that the redemption of the body signifies the "hope of daily life, the hope of temporal life" which overcomes the domination of concupiscence.

C. Better to Marry than to Be Aflame with Passion

In this context, the Holy Father wishes to stress again that the chaste love of husband and wife excludes the idea that marriage provides a "legitimate outlet" for indulging concupiscence (see §34). To this end he turns again to St. Paul's words in 1 Corinthians 7 in order to clarify the common but—in John Paul's mind—erroneous interpretation of the Apostle's teaching.

There St. Paul recommends marriage "because of the temptation to immorality" (v. 2). He would prefer that his readers remain single as he is. "But if they cannot exercise self-control, they should marry. For it is better to marry than to be aflame with passion" (v. 9). On first reading, this passage clearly seems to justify the indulgence of concupiscence in marriage. We previously asked if an incongruity exists between the teaching of St. Paul and the teaching of John Paul II on this point. It was my opinion that John Paul's explanation of the apparent incongruity was not altogether satisfying (see §61). This time, however, the Pope's explanation is a bit more convincing.

The Holy Father again stresses the Apostle's teaching that Christian marriage, like Christian celibacy, is a special gift of grace (see v. 7). For John Paul, grace always signifies the new ethos. Hence, he concludes that St. Paul "expresses in his striking and at the same time paradoxical words, simply the thought that marriage is assigned to the spouses as an ethos" (348). To demonstrate this, the Pope points out that in Paul's words, "it is better to marry than to be aflame with passion," the verb *ardere* ("to be aflame") signifies a disorder of the passions deriving from concupiscence. But "to marry" signifies the ethical order which Paul consciously introduced in this context. So, according to this reasoning, St. Paul is saying that the ethos of marriage (which transforms the desires of the heart into sincere self-giving) is better than being ruled by concupiscence.

John Paul reminds us that marriage is meant to be "the meeting place of eros with ethos and of their mutual compenetration in the 'heart' of man and of woman, as also in all their mutual relationships" (348). Purity of desire is the fruit born when eros and ethos meet in the human heart (see §38). Such purity excludes the indulgence of concupiscence altogether. Such purity has no desire whatsoever to appropriate the other for one's own selfish gratification—only to love the other as God loves, in the sincere gift of self.

81. Conjugal Union According to the Holy Spirit
December 1, 1982 (TB 349–351)

In the beginning, the body and erotic desire was the trustworthy foundation of man and woman's communion. Due to the distortions of concupiscence, however, men and women often question the trustworthiness of the body and of erotic desire (see §28). Concupiscence, one might say, has put a multi-pronged thorn into the relationship of the sexes. This jagged barb has pricked and pierced many men and women so often that they have become numb to their aspirations for authentic love and communion in marriage. In such case, "double solitude"—rather than leading toward a "unity of the two" in which the sexes really *participate* in each other's humanity—stagnates, leading them to withdraw into what could be called a protective "double alienation" (see §§12, 14).

Nonetheless, men and women who mutually overcome the concupiscence of the flesh through "life according to the Spirit" can rediscover marriage as "the sacramental alliance of masculinity and femininity." Through this ongoing transformation, the same "flesh" that is held suspect due to concupiscence "becomes the specific 'substratum' of an enduring and indissoluble communion of the persons...in a manner worthy of the persons" (348–349). This means that Christ gives us hope of healing. To continue with the above image, can we not recognize in Christ's own thorn-pierced flesh his willingness to take upon himself those very wounds that keep the sexes from true unity and communion? The Bridegroom's gift of self on the cross proclaims at the same time both the depth of our woundedness *and* the possibility of re-establishing a true life-giving marital communion.

A. Sexual Gratification "in the Spirit"

We should highlight again that living "according to the Spirit" does *not* mean eschewing the body (see §§2, 41, 46). It means the integration of body and spirit. It means opening our flesh to the Holy Spirit's *in*spiration. For spouses, this also means opening the "one flesh" they become in marital intercourse to the indwelling of the Spirit. John Paul does not hesitate to say that "life 'according to the Spirit' is also expressed in the mutual 'union' whereby the spouses [become] 'one flesh.'" He does not even shy away from describing "the consciousness of the gratification" that spouses experience as an expression of life according to the Spirit. And this "life according to the Spirit," the Pope says, is "the grace of the sacrament of marriage" (349). Husband and wife are meant to experience this grace when, through the sincere gift of self, they become "one flesh."

Sexual union, then, is meant to be not only the union of husband and wife, but also of God and man. In this way, sexual pleasure itself (understood integrally) is meant to be a participation in God's own mystery—in the joy of loving as God loves (see §§20, 54, 67). Recall that Christ gave us the commandment to love as he loves so that his joy might be in us and that our joy might be complete (see Jn 15:11). Of course this pleasure and gratification greatly differs from the "egoistic gratification" toward which concupiscence tends. John Paul tells us that authentic sexual gratification always corresponds to the dignity of the spouses themselves. The husband and wife who are fully aware of their dignity as expressed in the nuptial meaning of their bodies strive to uphold it in all of their expressions of intimacy and affection.

Furthermore, when conjugal gratification is "in the Holy Spirit," it is never closed in on itself. Spouses, in opening their flesh to the Holy Spirit, are also conscious that this Spirit is "the Lord and Giver of Life." If their sexual union is to be "according to the Spirit," spouses must trustingly "submit their masculinity and femininity to the blessing of procreation" (349). As John Paul explicitly affirms, the spouses' dignity cannot be divorced from their potential to become parents. The pulse and intensity of authentic gratification in conjugal union is naturally integrated with "the profound awareness of the sanctity of the life...to which the two [might] give origin, participating—as progenitors—in the forces of the mystery of creation" (349). Would not any intentional divorce from these "forces of the mystery of creation," in fact, be a specific closing off of one's flesh to the Lord and Giver of Life—a closing off to "life according to the Spirit"?

B. Procreation: An Integral Part of Creation and Redemption

Since the mark of nuptial love permeates both the mystery of creation and the mystery of redemption (see §78), so too does its fruitfulness. As the Scriptures demonstrate, procreation is an integral part of both the mystery of creation (see Gen 1:28) and the mystery of redemption (see Lk 1:35; 1 Tim 2:15). Recall John Paul's statement that every conception of a child reproduces the mystery of creation (see §15). Now he also states that every child conceived is a testimony to the hope of redemption. He relates this once again to St. Paul's words about the hope of the redemption of the body (see Rom 8).

In light of this hope, John Paul says that each "new human life, [each] new man conceived and born of the conjugal union of his father and mother, opens to 'the first fruits of the Spirit' (Rom 8:23) 'to enter into the liberty of the glory of the children of God' (v. 21)" (349). In other words, every time a child is conceived, the very mystery of that child's conception proclaims the work of the Spirit. It proclaims the mystery of Trinitarian love and the mystery of our being chosen in Christ to be children of God in communion with him for all eternity.

Because of sin, however, this hope that the child represents is not realized without suffering. Since the dawn of man's shame, an element of the cross has also been written into the mystery of nuptial union and procreation. Authentic love between the sexes is determined right here: Will men and women embrace the cross or run from it? Love leads to redemptive suffering. Lust leads to resisting suffering. Sexual sin, in fact, always involves a specific attempt to divorce love from the cross of Christ. In all truth, there is no love apart from this cross.

C. Lust, Love, and Suffering

When spouses "take up their cross and follow" Christ, the suffering of nuptial love and procreation is redemptive. Indeed, it plunges men and women—husbands, wives, and their offspring—headfirst into the mystery of Christ's death and resurrection. Spouses who believe in the "good news" of redemption are not crippled by fear of the sufferings they must endure. They are not afraid to surrender their "one body" to the Lord and

Giver of Life. In fact, when they do, they effect in some way what their sacrament symbolizes. They recapitulate the entire mystery of creation and redemption (see §77).[86] For the marital embrace "bears in itself the sign of the divine mystery of creation and redemption."[87]

When husband and wife are aware of the "great mystery" which their union symbolizes and in which it participates, marriage "constitutes the basis of hope for the person, that is, for man and woman, for parents and children, for the human generations" (350). John Paul speaks of this hope when, quoting again from Romans 8, he declares: "And if 'the whole creation has been groaning in travail together until now' (v. 22), a particular hope accompanies the pains of the mother in labor." This is "the hope of the 'revelation of the sons of God' (v. 22)" (350). Every newborn babe who comes into the world bears within himself a spark of this hope. Recognizing this spark, however, can be difficult in a world engulfed by darkness. John Paul affirms with St. Paul that the hope of redemption is "in the world." It penetrates all creation. However, this hope is not "of the world." It is of the Father. Herein lies the struggle. In order to live in the hope of redemption, we must trust in the Father's love. But man has called the Father's love into question since "the beginning."

Recall that original sin is the mystery of man turning his back on the Father. *"Original sin attempts, then, to abolish fatherhood*, destroying its rays which permeate the created world, placing in doubt the truth about God who is Love."[88] Through original sin, man casts God out of his heart, detaching himself from what is "of the Father" so that all that remains in him is what is "of the world." In this way, we witness the birth of human lust (see §26). As the Apostle John tells us, lust "is not of the Father but is of the world" (1 Jn 2:16). However, the Pope tells us that marriage, including the sexual love proper to spouses, is not "of the world" but "of the Father." Deep in the human heart a battle rages for dominance between the two—between that which is of the Father and that which is of the world. A battle rages between love and lust, between hope and despondency, between life and all that opposes it.

Genesis tells us with certainty that fertility is a blessing from the Father (see Gen 1:28). However, because of the suffering it entails, men and

---

86. If we do not hesitate to describe spouses as co-creators with God, could we not also describe them in this sense as "co-redeemers" with God? (I owe this provocative idea to my friend and colleague Steve Habisohn, founder and president of the GIFT Foundation.)

87. 11/14/84, TB 416.

88. *Crossing the Threshold of Hope,* p. 228.

women often question the value of bringing another life into the world. Without a living faith in Christ's resurrection, the suffering connected with procreation can even lead people to the point of counting the original blessing of fertility itself as a curse (see §24). Such people will often seek to avoid procreation not by avoiding sexual intercourse, but by defrauding this sacred act of its procreative potential. Closing their union in this way to the Lord and Giver of Life, they close themselves to that which is "of the Father," and there remains what is "of the world." There remains sexual desire *un*-inspired by God. This cannot *not* be lust (see §26).

D. Procreation and the Eschatological Hope

In this way we see that the blessing of fertility forces us to choose between that which is "of the Father" and that which is "of the world." This choice has eternal consequences. The Holy Father quotes again from the Apostle John: "On the one hand, indeed, 'the world passes away and the lust thereof,' while on the other, 'he who does the will of God abides forever' (1 Jn 2:17)" (350). John Paul then states that the grace of "marriage as a sacrament immutably ensures that man, male and female, by dominating concupiscence, does the will of the Father. And he 'who does the will of God remains forever' (1 Jn 2:17). In this sense marriage as a sacrament also bears within itself the germ of man's eschatological future" (350–351). In other words, the chaste love of spouses, as proof of the indwelling of the Holy Spirit, becomes a foreshadowing and even a "guarantee" in some sense of eternal life (see Eph 1:13–14). As the *Catechism* says, "Chastity is a promise of immortality."[89]

In this context John Paul briefly revisits Christ's words about the future resurrection. Recall that Christ's exclusion of marriage in the resurrection does not mean that the deep truth of marriage will be done away with. It means it will be fulfilled in the Marriage of the Lamb (see §49). Earthly marriage serves as the indispensable precursor to heavenly marriage. Of course, in order for marriage to prepare people for heaven, the earthly model must accurately image the divine prototype. John Paul describes marriage as "the sacrament of the human beginning." As man's origin, conjugal union enables man to have a future not merely in the historical dimensions, but also in the eschatological. Thus John Paul observes that every man brings into the world his vocation to share in the future resurrection because his origin lies in the marriage (more specifically, the sexual union) of his parents. In this way marriage fulfills an "irreplaceable service" with regard to man's ultimate destiny.

---

89. *CCC*, n. 2347.

Hope of eternal life—this is the living hope in which spouses participate when they become "one flesh" and open their bodies to life according
to the Spirit. They choose what is of the Father. In the face of all that as-
sails their hope, they choose life—not only in its earthly temporal dimension, but also in its heavenly, eternal dimension.

82. The Fusion of Spousal and Redemptive Love

December 15, 1982 (TB 351– 354)

In his audience of December 15, 1982, John Paul summarizes and
concludes his analysis of that classic text from Ephesians 5. In doing so,
he takes us for yet another lap in his ever deepening spiral of reflections.
The Pope tells us that the "great mystery" St. Paul speaks of is above all
the mystery of Christ's union with the Church. But, according to the continuity of God's saving plan, the Apostle links this "great mystery" to the
primordial sacrament in which the two become "one flesh." Here John
Paul says we find ourselves in "the domain of the great analogy" which
presupposes and rediscovers the sacramentality of marriage. Marriage is
presupposed as "the sacrament of the human beginning" linked with the
whole mystery of creation. But it is "rediscovered as the fruit of the spousal love of Christ and of the Church linked with the mystery of the redemption" (351).

A. The Unity of Spousal Love and Redemption

Presupposing the original meaning of marriage, St. Paul calls spouses
to "learn anew" this sacrament in light of the spousal unity of Christ and
the Church. This means modeling their lives and their unity not only on
the original unity of man and woman, but also and more so on the unity of
Christ and the Church. As John Paul states: "That original and stable image of marriage as a sacrament is renewed when Christian spouses—conscious of the authentic profundity of the 'redemption of the body'—are
united 'out of reverence for Christ' (Eph 5:21)" (352). This is not just an
abstract theological concept. It is meant to be *lived* and *experienced* by
couples. Uniting "out of reverence for Christ" means uniting with a deep
respect and awe for the "great mystery" stamped in and revealed through
the nuptial meaning of the male and female body.

But notice the Pope says this is possible only when spouses are "conscious of the authentic profundity of the redemption of the body." In other
words, they must be conscious of the gift of the Holy Spirit poured out in
Christ's death and resurrection. They must allow the life and love of Christ

to vivify their entire body-soul personalities. To the extent that men and women are not vivified in this way, the distortions of concupiscence will continue to obscure the "great mystery" inscribed in their bodies. But to the degree that spouses allow their lusts to be "crucified with Christ" (see Gal 5:24), the grace poured out in and through the sacraments (including, if not especially, the sacrament of marriage) can free spouses (and men and women in general) from the blinding effects of concupiscence. The more we cooperate with this grace, the more the scales fall off our eyes. As this happens, we come more to see, experience and "feel" the true dignity and nuptial meaning of the body as a revelation of the mystery of Christ. Precisely in this way we gain that "reverence for Christ" of which St. Paul speaks. In fact, John Paul boldly observes that this "reverence for Christ" is nothing but a spiritually mature form of sexual attraction.[90]

This is what authentic marital love affords. Spousal love is itself redemptive. The Pauline image of marriage "brings together the redemptive dimension and the spousal dimension of love. In a certain sense it fuses these two dimensions into one. Christ has become the spouse of the Church, he has married the Church as a bride, because 'he has given himself up for her' (Eph 5:25)" (352). In the sacrament of marriage, both the spousal and redemptive dimensions of love "permeate the life of the spouses." In this way, the nuptial meaning of the body—and an authentic reverence for it—is confirmed and in some sense, John Paul says, "newly created." At the same time husband and wife—via their spousal-redemptive love—"participate in God's own creative love. And they participate in it both by the fact that, created in the image of God, they are called by reason of this image to a particular union *(communio personarum)*, and because this same union has from the beginning been blessed with the blessing of fruitfulness" (352).

B. Understanding Human Existence

John Paul says that the linking of the spousal significance of the body with its "redemptive significance" is obviously important with regard to marriage and the Christian vocation of spouses. But then he adds that it also "is equally essential and valid for the understanding of man in general: for the fundamental problem of understanding him and for the self-comprehension of his being in the world" (352–353). This is another one of those striking statements that almost stops the reader in his tracks. According to John Paul II, the meaning of human existence is contained right

---

90. See 7/4/84, TB 379.

here: in Ephesians 5 where St. Paul links the spousal significance of the body from Genesis 2:24 (the two become "one flesh") with the redemptive significance of the body revealed by Christ's union with the Church. John Paul believes that the "great mystery" of Christ's union with the Church "obliges us" to link the spousal significance of the body with its redemptive significance. In this link, John Paul reiterates that all men and women "find the answer to the question concerning the meaning of 'being a body'"—which is the meaning of being a human being (353).

Our creation as male and female—our sexuality—is inextricably intertwined with the question we all have about the meaning of life. Sexuality, as John Paul says, is "profoundly inscribed in the essential structure of the human person" (353). And it is a call "from the beginning" for men and women to participate in the divine nature by loving as God loves—in a fruitful communion of persons *(communio personarum)*. This is the deepest meaning of human existence: We are created *by* eternal Love and Communion, to participate *in* eternal Love and Communion. This is the spousal significance of the body. Yet, because of sin, we cannot fulfill the meaning of our existence unless we are redeemed. Christ's incarnate union with the Church affords this redemption and this is the redemptive significance of the body. Thus in the spousal-redemptive significance of the body lies the very meaning of human existence.

Love, in a word, is man's origin, vocation, and destiny. While Love in its divine mystery is purely spiritual, in its revelation and human realization it is always *incarnational*. This mystery of love and communion was revealed in the original spousal significance of the body. But the body's original meaning is only "completed," John Paul tells us, in the redemptive significance of Christ's incarnate union with the Church. Christ initiates his spousal-redemptive love as a gift. We are created to receive it, but never forced to do so. If we engage our freedom and open ourselves to the gift, like a bride we conceive that gift within us. Life then becomes thanksgiving *(eucharistia)* for the gift received, and we experience an incessant desire to extend the divine-human *communio personarum* to the ends of the earth.

C. Spousal Love Embraces the Universe

The "great mystery" of spousal and redemptive love is clearly recapitulated (although differently) in the vocations to marriage and celibacy. However, John Paul stresses that the spousal and redemptive meanings of the body pertain to everyone in every human situation. They are not only lived in marriage and celibacy for the kingdom, he says. They are lived in many "diverse ways of life and in diverse situations:...for example, in the many forms of human suffering, indeed, in the very birth and death of man" (354). Spousal love marks all of human life, and marriage provides the paradigm for all of human life. No one is excluded from this "great mystery." It embraces "every man, and, in a certain sense, the whole of creation" (353). John Paul goes so far as to say that through "the new covenant of Christ with the Church, marriage is again inscribed in that 'sacrament of man' which embraces the universe" (354).

Everyone without exception is called to the "great sacrament" of Christ's union with the Church. Marriage is organically inscribed in this new sacrament of redemption just as it was inscribed in the sacrament of creation. This means that the sacrament of marriage remains "a living and vivifying part" of the process of salvation "to the measure of the definitive fulfillment of the kingdom of the Father" (354).

In all of this John Paul wants to underscore yet again the profound unity—the marriage of sorts—between creation and redemption. When we take this unity and continuity seriously, the implications multiply: We recognize a profound and original unity between nature and grace (see §78), between God and man (see §12), between man and woman (see §14), and between man and all creation (see §52). We also recognize that *all* of these unities—all of these marriages—find their foundation and draw their efficacy from the ultimate unity, the ultimate marriage: that of the divine and human natures in the incarnate person of Christ. He is "the center of the universe and of history."[91] Christ "fully reveals man to himself and makes his supreme calling clear."[92] Only when we take the profound link between creation and redemption seriously does the meaning of our humanity and our lofty vocation as men and women come into focus.

As John Paul states: "Man, who 'from the beginning' is male and female, should seek the meaning of his existence and the meaning of his humanity by reaching out to the mystery of creation through the reality of redemption. There one finds also the essential answer to the question on the significance of the human body, and the significance of the masculinity and femininity of the human person" (354). It is Christ. We were created from the beginning as male and female and called to communion to prepare us for communion with Christ.

---

91. *Redemptor Hominis,* n. 1.

92. *Gaudium et Spes,* n. 22.

83. The Language of the Body and the Sacramental Sign

January 5, 12, 19, 1983 (TB 354–363)

Early in this cycle of reflections John Paul said he would explore the meaning of sacrament, particularly the sacrament of marriage, first in the dimension of covenant and grace (this is the divine dimension), and then in the dimension of the sacramental sign (this is the human dimension) (see §65). Having explored the former, the Holy Father now devotes the five remaining audiences in this cycle to the latter. Of course, John Paul has already said much about the nature of marriage as a sacramental sign. Still, he wants to penetrate more deeply into the very "structure" of the sign and define it more specifically. By doing so it seems he brings a welcome resolution to a centuries-old theological discussion. What *visible* reality of marriage (human dimension) symbolizes and effects the *invisible* mystery (divine dimension) of grace?

A. Debate About the Sign

Theological debates about what constituted marriage as a sacramental sign came to the fore around the tenth and eleventh centuries when marriage was placed more fully under the jurisdiction of the Church. Most theologians and canonists followed the lead of Hugh of St. Victor who posited the sign of marriage in the words of consent (the wedding vows) and their mutual exchange in the rite of marriage. Other currents of thought posited the sign in the bodily act of consummation. The latter view was resisted for various reasons. For example, how would such a view account for the virginal marriage of Joseph and Mary? Furthermore, emphasis on consummation was resisted, no doubt, at least in some cases, because of the "interpretation of suspicion" and its inability to imagine the sexual act as a participation in grace.

■ This debate was closely related with the question about what established the indissoluble bond of marriage. Roman law recognized the mutual consent as the "contractual moment" of marriage. However, the various cultures of northern Europe being evangelized in the tenth and eleventh centuries recognized marriage either at the moment of betrothal (when the father handed the bride over to the husband) or at the moment of consummation. In light of these debates, Pope Alexander III decreed that marriage is ratified at the moment of consent. However, marriage is not constituted in its full reality until the moment of consummation. In some cases, therefore, prior to sexual union a marriage can be dissolved by papal dispensation.[93]

---

93. See canons 1061, 1142. For an overview of the history outlined here see Peter J. Elliot, *What God Has Joined* (Homebush, Australia: St. Paul/Alba House, 1990), pp. 73–117.

John Paul's faith in the *real power* of the redemption of the body removes the taint of suspicion from the sexual act. For him, there is no question that the sexual union of spouses is meant to be a participation in grace. He has already affirmed that God intends the "one flesh" union and its accompanying pleasure as a vehicle of the Holy Spirit in married life—of the specific grace of the sacrament of marriage (see §81).

Does this mean he simply sides with those more daring theologians who posited the sign of marriage in the act of consummation? For John Paul conjugal intercourse certainly plays a fundamental role in understanding the sacramental sign of marriage. He has already said as much in various ways throughout his catechesis (see §§22, 29, 31, 35, 77). But John Paul does not resolve the debate by picking sides. He creatively demonstrates that, in effect, both "sides" are correct. The key to this innovation lies in understanding the rich and mysterious "language of the body."

B. Words of the Spirit Expressed in the Flesh

All that John Paul has said about the body and its nuptial meaning is expressed through the body's "language." According to John Paul, the body "speaks." It speaks the deepest truth of man's personal existence as male and female and of his call to love as God loves in a life-giving communion of persons. And man "cannot, in a certain sense, express this singular language of his personal existence and of his vocation without the body" (359). From the beginning, man was constituted in such a way as to express spiritual realities in and through his flesh. This means that "the most profound words of the spirit—words of love, of giving, of fidelity—demand an adequate 'language of the body.' And without that, they cannot be fully expressed" (359). To divorce the language of the spirit from the language of the body, as John Paul says elsewhere, breaks "the personal unity of soul and body [and] strikes at God's creation itself at the level of the deepest interaction of nature and person."[94]

What bearing does this have on determining the structure of the sacramental sign of marriage? John Paul says that the exchange of wedding vows gives an intentional expression on the level of intellect and will, of consciousness and of the heart to the spiritual reality of love, of giving, and of fidelity. However—if, according to the Pope's thesis, the body *and it alone* is capable of making spiritual realities visible—the spoken language of the vows is not "complete" without an adequate and corresponding language of the body. The spiritual expression of intellect and will *must* have a corresponding bodily expression. What is that corresponding bodily expression? Conjugal intercourse.

---

94. *Familiaris Consortio*, n. 32.

The marital embrace, one might say, is where the words of the wedding vows *become flesh*. The "language" inscribed in sexual intercourse and expressed by those who perform the sexual act is and should always be the language of wedding vows. John Paul states: "Indeed the very words 'I take you as my wife—my husband'...can be fulfilled only by means of conjugal intercourse." With conjugal intercourse "we pass to the reality which corresponds to these words.[95] Both the one and the other element," he says, "are important in regard to the structure of the sacramental sign." And this sign, the Pope reminds us, "expresses and at the same time effects the saving reality of grace and of the covenant" (355).

> ■ St. Bonaventure offered a profound reflection on the interrelationship of the exchange of vows and consummation in marriage. He taught that in the moment of consent when spouses commit their will to marriage, they are with Christ in his agony in the garden. There Christ committed his will to "giving himself up" for his Bride. In the moment of consummation, spouses are with Christ on the cross, living out in their bodies what they committed to at the altar, just as Christ is living out what he committed to in the garden.[96]

John Paul concludes that the "sacramental sign is constituted in the order of intention insofar as it is simultaneously constituted in the real order" (355). He continues by saying that the words spoken by the bride and groom "would not, *per se,* constitute the sacramental sign of marriage" unless these words corresponded to the awareness of the body, linked to their masculinity and femininity. Here we must recall the whole series of our previous analyses of Genesis. Most specifically, the Holy Father recalls that the Creator himself instituted conjugal intercourse from the very beginning according to those familiar words of Genesis 2:24. Hence, the Pope affirms that the structure of the sacramental sign remains essentially the same as "in the beginning." It is expressed in "'the language of the body' inasmuch as the man and the woman, who through marriage should become one flesh, express in this sign the reciprocal gift of masculinity and femininity as the basis of the conjugal union of the persons" (356). Through their mutual exchange of vows, in fact, "the man and the woman express their willingness to become 'one flesh' according to the eternal truth established in the mystery of creation" (355). Recall John Paul's

---

95. See *CCC,* n. 1627.

96. See St. Bonaventure, "On the Integrity of Matrimony," *Reviloquium,* Part VI, chapter 13.

statement that marriage only corresponds to the vocation of Christians if they chose it just as the Creator instituted it "from the beginning" (see §59). This means the exchange of vows is a sacramental sign by reason of its content—by its expressed willingness to actuate the vows in "one flesh." However, John Paul tells us that in and of itself the exchange of consent is "merely the sign of the coming into being of marriage. And the coming into being of marriage is distinguished from its consummation to the extent that without this consummation the marriage is not yet constituted in its full reality" (355). While marriage is contracted at the moment of consent, it is not fully constituted as a marriage until the moment of consummation.

C. The Interplay of Form and Matter

According to the scholastic tradition, sacraments are constituted by the creative interplay of the words spoken (the "form") and the physical reality (the "matter").[97] The vows make up the "form" of the sacrament of marriage and the bodies of husband and wife make up the "matter." Accordingly, as John Paul says: "Both of them, as man and woman, being the ministers of the sacrament in the moment of contracting marriage constitute at the same time the full and real visible sign of the sacrament itself" (356).

The words spoken correspond to the "human subjectivity of the engaged couple" in their masculinity and femininity and in their call to become "one flesh." In the marital embrace the "form" and the "matter" (their vows and their bodies) in some sense become one and the same sacramental mystery—one and the same sacramental sign. "In this way," John Paul says, "the enduring and ever new 'language of the body' is not only the 'substratum' but, in a certain sense, the constitutive element of the communion of the persons" (356). Of course, the communion of persons in marriage does not refer only to the specific moment of joining in "one flesh." Conjugal intercourse is meant to be a sign that encompasses and sums up (*con*-summates) the whole reality of married life. "The man and woman, as spouses, bear this sign throughout the whole of their lives and remain as that sign until death." At the beginning of their lives together, the "liturgy of the sacrament of marriage gives a form to that sign: directly, during the sacramental rite...; indirectly, throughout the whole of life" (357).

So, does the liturgical exchange of vows make up the sign? Do the man and woman themselves make up the sign? Does conjugal intercourse make up the sign? Does the whole of married life make up the sign? Yes, yes, yes, and yes. The entire reality of the gift of man and woman to each

---

97. See 10/20/82, TB 341.

other "until death" is the unrepeatable sign of marriage. And, as John Paul says, this is a "sign of multiple content" (363). It is first established by the liturgical rite in the exchange of consent, and it is then embodied and brought to fulfillment in marital intercourse. In turn we come to realize that this "is not a mere immediate and passing sign, but a sign looking to the future which produces a lasting effect, namely the marriage bond, one and indissoluble" (363). In its multiple content, the sacramental sign of marriage "is a visible and efficacious sign of the covenant with God in Christ, that is, of grace which in this sign should become a part of them as 'their own special gift' (according to the expression of the 1 Corinthians 7:7)" (356).

84. The Prophetism of the Body
January 12, 19, 26, 1983 (TB 357–365)

The sacramental sign of marriage is expressed through the language of the irrevocable self-giving of man and woman to each other. It is a gift given "in good times and bad, in sickness and in health,...all the days of my life." This language of the spirit—of the heart, will, and intellect—has a corresponding "language of the body." This body-language is expressed throughout married life, but especially in the act of marital intercourse. As the Holy Father says in his *Letter to Families:* "All married life is a gift; but this becomes most evident when the spouses, in giving themselves to each other in love, bring about that encounter which makes them 'one flesh.'"[98] This confirms the Pope's statement that "the 'language of the body' also enters essentially into the structure of marriage as a sacramental sign" (357). Just as the body is the visible sign of a person's soul, the "one body" that spouses become serves in some way as the visible sign of their marriage's "soul." In turn, if the whole of married life is a sign, we might say that conjugal intercourse is the sign of that sign.

A. The Body Proclaims God's Covenant Love

Although John Paul gives a fresh voice to this idea of the body possessing a language, he points out that it has a long biblical tradition. This tradition begins in Genesis (especially 2:23–25), passes through the prophets, and finds its definitive culmination in Paul's Letter to the Ephesians (see Eph 5:21–33). John Paul believes that the prophetic books of the Old Testament have a particular importance for understanding marriage in the dimension of sign. In the text of the prophets the body speaks

---

98. *Letter to Families,* n. 12.

the language of God's covenant love for his people. Based on this tradition, John Paul says we can even "speak of a specific 'prophetism of the body' both because of the fact that we find this analogy especially in the prophets, and also in regard to its very content. Here, the 'prophetism of the body' signifies precisely the 'language of the body'" (357).

The analogy the prophets use seems to have two levels. "On the first and fundamental level, the prophets present the Covenant between God and Israel as a marriage (which also permits us to understand marriage itself as a covenant between husband and wife)" (357–358). If other books of the Old Testament tend to present Yahweh as the Lord of absolute dominion, the prophets present "the stupendous dimension of this 'dominion,' which is the spousal dimension. In this way, the absolute of dominion is the absolute of love" (358). Thus, in the prophets, a breach of the Covenant involves not only a breaking of the law of the supreme Legislator, but infidelity and betrayal of God's love. This "is a blow which even pierces his heart as Father, as Spouse and as Lord" (358).

This more fundamental level of the analogy reveals a second level which is precisely the language of the body. If God's covenant love is presented as a spousal love, the language of the body is meant to express faithfully that same covenant love of God. It is in this way that the language of the body is understood as prophetic. As John Paul points out: "A prophet is one who expresses in human words the truth coming from God, one who speaks this truth in the place of God, in his name and in a certain sense with his authority" (361). This is precisely what God created the human body to do. From the beginning God created the body to proclaim his own truth, his own mystery of life and love—of communion.

B. Man: The Author of His Own Language

However, John Paul points out several times that the body itself is not the author of this prophetic language. The language of the body, to be sure, has an objective dimension—a meaning given by God which is pre-inscribed in the body, so to speak. However, man must take up this language as its subject. In this way, John Paul says, he becomes the "author" of the language of his own body. If he is to speak the truth with his body, every man must ensure that the *subjective* language he authors corresponds with its *objective* meaning.

Here we glimpse the very foundations of morality for man. Throughout his catechesis, John Paul—in accord with modern sensitivities—fully recognizes man as a personal subject. In this context he affirms it again: "Man...is a conscious and capable subject of self-determination. Only on this basis can he be the author of the 'language of the body'" (367). However, man's liberation as a subject comes not by a self-assertive divorce from objective reality. It comes by wedding himself to it—not because it is imposed upon him, but because he trusts in it and desires it freely. He subjects himself to it as a subject (see §§8, 9, 21, 25, 38, 46). If man's "authorship" of the language of his own body speaks of his freedom to choose between good and evil, it does not thereby give him authorship over what *is* good and evil. This is a tree from which man cannot eat, lest he die (see Gen 2:17). The moment man divorces himself from the objective good and seeks to author his own reality is precisely the moment of abuse of his own subjectivity. It is the moment of broken trust in his Creator and of infidelity to the covenant (see §26).

Recall that the prophets use the language of the body both in praising God's fidelity to his covenant and in condemning Israel's infidelity as "adultery." In this way the prophets outline ethical categories, setting moral good and evil in mutual opposition. This has immediate implications for the union of man and woman. In their relationship "it is the body itself which 'speaks'; it speaks by means of its masculinity and femininity, it speaks in the mysterious language of the personal gift, it speaks...both in the language of fidelity, that is, of love, and also in the language of conjugal infidelity, that is, of 'adultery'" (359).

What does all this mean? If man, as a self-determining subject, is the author of his own body's language, he can choose to speak the truth. But he can also choose to speak lies. In other words, if the body is prophetic, the Pope points out that we must carefully distinguish between true and false prophets. John Paul remarks that the categories of truth and falsity are essential to every language. Everyone can recognize that it is possible to speak a lie with the body. The Scriptures give a plain example in Judas' kiss. Here an expression of love became instead an act of betrayal.

C. Speaking the Language of the Body in Truth

John Paul says that when spouses exchange the words of consent they explicitly confirm the essential "truth" of the language of the body and implicitly exclude any "falsity." In other words, they commit to being true prophets according to the original biblical meaning of joining in "one flesh." The body speaks the truth "through conjugal love, fidelity, and integrity." It speaks lies "by all that is the negation of conjugal love, fidelity, and integrity" (360–361). John Paul says that in this way the essential truth of the sign will remain organically linked to the morality of the spouses' marital conduct. Recall that we can speak of moral good and evil in the marital/sexual relationship "according to whether...or not it has the character of the truthful sign."[99]

---

99. 8/27/80, TB 141–142.

In this context, John Paul specifically reminds us that the language of consent in marriage—to which the language of the body in sexual intercourse corresponds—must include an affirmative answer to the following question. As an essential part of the liturgical rite, the priest or deacon asks the couple: "Are you willing to accept responsibly and with love the children that God may give you...?" If the language of the consent says "yes" but the language of the body says "no" to this question, would we not encounter a specific negation of conjugal love, fidelity, and integrity?

As the author of his own body's language, man must learn to reread the nuptial meaning of the body as integrally inscribed in each person's masculinity or femininity. "A correct rereading 'in truth' is an indispensable condition to proclaim this truth, that is, to institute the visible sign of marriage as a sacrament" (361). Indeed, John Paul says that "the essential element for marriage as a sacrament is the 'language of the body' in its aspect of truth. It is precisely by means of that, that the sacramental sign is, in fact, constituted" (360).

Through the whole "ensemble of the 'language of the body'...the spouses decide to speak to each other as ministers of the Sacrament of Marriage" (363). They not only proclaim the truth coming from God. John Paul even says that in some sense they proclaim this truth in God's name. In constituting the marital sign in the moment of consent and fulfilling it in the moment of consummation, the spouses "perform an act of prophetic character. They confirm in this way their participation in the prophetic mission of the Church received from Christ" (361).

By speaking the language of the body in truth, spouses "also arrive in a certain sense at the very sources from which that sign on each occasion draws its prophetic eloquence and its sacramental power. One must not forget," the Pope insists, "that the 'language of the body,' before being spoken by the lips of the spouses, the ministers of marriage as a sacrament of the Church, was spoken by the word of the living God, beginning from the book of Genesis, through the prophets of the Old Covenant, until the author of the letter to the Ephesians" (362). Hence, John Paul reaffirms that this enduring language of the body carries within itself all the richness and depth of the divine-human mystery: first of creation and then of redemption.

85. Constituting the Sign in Love and Integrity
January 19, 26; February 9, 1983 (TB 363–368)

The entire question of the sacramental sign of marriage has "a highly anthropological character," the Holy Father tells us. "We construct it on the basis of theological anthropology and in particular on...the 'theology of the body'" (365). In turn, the understanding of the sacramental sign as John Paul presents it confirms his theological anthropology, his specific interpretation of man.

The body is understood as a "theology" specifically because God created it from the beginning to be a sign of his own divine mystery. He created it as such in its sexuality—its masculinity and femininity—and the call to form "one body." We know, however, that with original sin the body almost lost its capacity to reveal the divine mystery. The man of concupiscence is almost blind to the value of the body as a sacramental sign. How then is he to "reread" the language of the body in truth? Precisely at this point we stand at the thresholds of two competing and irreconcilable anthropologies. We either open to the possibility of rebirth in the Holy Spirit, or we condemn man with an irreversible suspicion.

A. Man Is Not Determined by Lust

Rereading the language of the body in truth is given as a task to the man of concupiscence. But is such a man up to the task? Is the man of lust not bound to falsify the language of the body? At this point John Paul recalls his reflections on "the masters of suspicion," who believe man is determined by lust and has no alternative but to lust (see §36). John Paul insists again that the redemption of the body is not only a divine mystery, but also—in Christ and through Christ—a human reality in every man. Christ does not merely accuse the heart of lust in the Sermon on the Mount. Above all, Christ *calls* the man of concupiscence to overcome the lust in his heart through the ethos of redemption (see §29). Christ calls man with tenderness and compassion, with mercy and forgiveness.

We see this foreshadowed already in the prophets. John Paul points out that Hosea in particular "sets out in relief all the splendor of the Covenant—of that marriage in which Yahweh manifests himself as a sensitive, affectionate Spouse disposed to forgiveness, and at the same time, exigent and severe."[100] Christ's words about lust are indeed severe. However, are "we to fear the severity of these words, or rather have confidence in their salvific content, in their power?"[101] They have power to save us because the man who speaks them is the Lamb of God who takes away the sin of the world. This means that the man of concupiscence need not be determined by lust. If such were the case, man would "be condemned to essential falsifications." He would be "condemned to suspect himself and others

---

100. 1/12/83, TB 359.

101. 10/8/80, TB 159 (see §34).

in regard to the truth of the language of the body. Because of the concupiscence of the flesh he could only be 'accused,' but he could not be really 'called'" (367).

However, John Paul assures us that "the 'hermeneutics of the sacrament'"—that is, the interpretation of man in light of the grace poured out through the sacrament—"permits us to draw the conclusion that man is always essentially 'called' and not merely 'accused'" (368). The Pope insists, therefore, that concupiscence does not destroy the capacity to reread the language of the body in truth. In fact, the light of the Gospel and of the New Covenant revealed in Christ's body enables us to reread the true language of the body "in an ever more mature and fuller way" (366). Thus, John Paul affirms that despite the heritage of original sin, men and women are able—from the evangelical and Christian perspective of the problem—to constitute the sacramental sign in fidelity and integrity. And they are able to do so "as an *enduring sign:* 'To be faithful to you always in joy and in sorrow, in sickness and in health, and to love and honor you all the days of my life'" (367).

B. Speaking the Truth Day by Day

Spouses establish this enduring sign at the moment of their consent in the exchange of vows. However, that initial sign will be continually completed by the "prophetism of the body." The spouses' bodies will continue to speak "for" and "on behalf of" each of them—in the name of and with the authority of each of the spouses. In this way, in and through the language of their bodies, husband and wife will carry out "the conjugal dialogue" proper to their vocation. They will continually and mutually speak of their commitment to their marital covenant (or their lack thereof).

John Paul says that spouses are called to form their life and their living together as a communion of persons on the basis of that language of the body. And, as he exclaims, "it is necessary that it be reread in truth!" (364) In this sphere John Paul says that the spouses are both the cause and the authors of conjugal actions which have "clear-cut meanings." These "conjugal actions" refer, of course, to the acts of conjugal intercourse. But they also refer to the whole "ensemble of the 'language of the body' in which the spouses decide to speak to each other as ministers of the Sacrament of Marriage" (363). The Pope observes that all the meanings of the language of the body are initiated and synthesized in the content of conjugal consent. Day by day, the spouses draw from that synthesis the same sign, identifying themselves with it throughout their lives. In all that they do—and especially in the consummate expression of their union—the spouses remain faithful to their original consent, or they fail to do so. They deepen their love and fidelity, or they cheapen it.

In this way we see that there "is an organic bond between rereading in truth...the 'language of the body' and the consequent *use* of that language in conjugal life" (364). Spouses "are called explicitly to bear witness—by using correctly the 'language of the body'—to spousal and procreative love, a witness worthy of 'true prophets.' In this consists the true significance and the grandeur of conjugal consent in the sacrament of the Church" (365). "If concupiscence...causes many 'errors' in rereading the 'language of the body'...nevertheless in the sphere of the ethos of redemption there always remains the possibility of passing from 'error' to the 'truth'...the possibility of...conversion from sin to chastity as an expression of a life according to the Spirit" (366–367).

With these words of hope from the Holy Father, we conclude our reflections on the fifth cycle of the theology of the body. Now we are well prepared to understand the crucial importance of *Humanae Vitae*.

The Sacramentality of Marriage—In Review

1. In Cycle 5 of his catechesis on the body, John Paul seeks to resurrect the true meaning of Ephesians 5 and to demonstrate its fundamental importance not only for understanding the sacramentality of marriage, but for understanding the entire Christian mystery and the very meaning of human existence.

2. The Apostle's outline of the nuptial mystery in Ephesians 5 reveals man to himself in a particular way and makes him aware of his lofty vocation. But man can only see the importance of Ephesians 5 for his own existence to the extent that he participates in the experience of the incarnate person. Modern rationalism, with its radical split between body and soul, is perpetually at odds with the "great mystery" of Ephesians 5.

3. In a general way the body enters the very definition of "sacrament" as a visible sign of the invisible. The body, then, through its sacramentality, is an efficacious sign of grace; it is "the hinge of salvation." Thus, man need not shed his skin in his quest for transcendence. He need not eschew his body and sexuality. This is the affirmation of Ephesians 5—bodiliness and nuptial union are a "great mystery" that refer to Christ and the Church.

4. In calling wives to "be subject" to their husbands, St. Paul appeals to the custom of the day in order to inject this mentality with the mystery of Christ's love for the Church and the vocation of Christians to "walk in love,

as Christ loved us." In this light, the Apostle calls spouses to "be subject to one another out of reverence for Christ." Subjection within marriage, then, is not one-sided, but mutual. And it must be modeled on the love of Christ.

5. When viewed through the paradigm of the "gift," we come to understand that to be "subject" to one's spouse means to live the sincere gift of self. In turn, mutual subjection means reciprocal self-donation. According to the spousal analogy, the husband must image Christ in his self-giving and the wife is called to image the Church in her receptivity to the gift, and in her giving of herself back to her husband.

6. Since the husband is to love his wife "as Christ loved the Church," this clearly excludes male domination. This results from original sin. When properly understood, the wife's "submission" to her husband signifies above all the experiencing of love. This seems even more obvious because the wife's "submission" is related to the submission of the Church to Christ, which certainly consists in experiencing his love.

7. The spousal analogy operates in two directions. To a certain degree marriage illuminates the mystery of Christ and the Church. At the same time Christ's relationship with the Church unveils the essential truth about marriage. The very essence of marriage captures a particle of the Christian mystery. If it were otherwise, the analogy would hang suspended in a void.

8. The spousal analogy is intimately related with the head-body analogy. In becoming "one body," the spouses almost form "one organism," like a head and a body. In this way they almost become "one subject" while maintaining an essential "bi-subjectivity." This is a unity-in-plurality through the mystery of love in which the "I" of the other in some sense becomes one's own. In this way "carnal love" images the Trinity and expresses the language of agape.

9. Ephesians 5 shows that the purpose of Christ's self-gift is our sanctification. Christ cleanses us "by the washing of water with the word." This is a reference to the "nuptial bath" of Baptism, which applies and extends the spousal and redemptive love of Christ to all who are bathed so that we might become a glorious bride, "without spot or wrinkle or any such thing."

10. By using physical beauty as a metaphor for holiness, St. Paul demonstrates a masterful understanding of the sacramentality of the body. For him, the human body indicates attributes of the moral, spiritual, and supernatural order. St. Paul explains the mystery of sanctification, the mystery of Christ's redemptive love, and the mystery of humanity's union with the divine by means of the resemblance of the body and of the spousal union in "one flesh."

11. Love obliges the husband to desire his wife's beauty, to appreciate it and to care for it. A husband who loves his wife "as Christ loved the Church" wants all that is good in her to blossom and radiate through her body. He sees even in her blemishes and disfigurations an "echo" of the beginning and the hope of eternal glory. Christ saw his Bride covered with the blemishes and disfigurations of sin and loved her all the more.

12. The "nourishment" Christ offers his Bride is his own body in the Eucharist. Thus, in Ephesians 5 we glimpse the manner in which the Eucharist indicates the specific character of nuptial love, especially of that gift of self in "one flesh."

13. Since the time of Aquinas, the term "sacrament" has referred almost exclusively to the seven signs of grace instituted by Christ. Only in the last century have theologians sought to recover the broader and more ancient understanding of "sacrament" as the revelation and accomplishment of the mystery hidden in God from eternity. If "sacrament" is synonymous with "mystery," mystery connotes that which is hidden, and sacrament that which is revealed.

14. The "great mystery" revealed by the sacrament is God's plan of salvation for humanity. In some sense this is the central theme of divine revelation. St. Paul indicates that the "one flesh" union of spouses has participated in this "great mystery" from the beginning. His linking of Genesis 2:24 with Christ's union with the Church is the keystone of Ephesians 5. It establishes the continuity between the most ancient covenant and the definitive covenant.

15. The sacrament manifests the divine mystery in a sign which serves not only to proclaim the mystery, but accomplish it in man. The image of conjugal union in Genesis 2:24 speaks of the most ancient way in which the divine mystery was made visible while the union of Christ and the Church speaks of the definitive sign of this mystery given in the fullness of time. To his special merit, St. Paul makes of these two signs one great sign.

16. Conjugal union foreshadowed the Incarnation right from the beginning. Thus, the visible sign of marriage—inasmuch as it is analogically linked to the visible sign of Christ and the Church, the summit of God's revelation—transfers God's eternal plan of love into history and becomes the "foundation of the whole sacramental order."

17. Christ is at the heart of the "great mystery" proclaimed in Ephesians. In him we have been blessed "with every spiritual blessing" and chosen "before the creation of the world." The eternal mystery is accomplished in Christ and through Christ. Christ reveals the mystery of divine

love. Christ is the meaning of embodiment and marriage. Christ is the meaning of the moral instruction given by Paul. Christ is the center of *everything*.

18. The "great mystery" is accomplished in the mode of gift, of the spousal donation of Christ himself to his Bride. We participate in the eternal mystery of love and communion when we open ourselves to the gift and accept it through faith. The divine mystery is at work in us under the veil of faith and the veil of a sign that makes the Invisible visible.

19. The spousal love of God for humanity was only "half open" in the Old Testament. In Ephesians 5 it is fully revealed. Paul presents new revealed moments unknown prior to Christ. We now learn with clarity what Isaiah already intuited: that there is a certain parallel between God as "spouse" and God as redeemer. Christ's spousal gift of self to his Bride is equivalent to carrying out the work of redemption.

20. The spousal analogy is certainly not adequate or complete, yet it contains a characteristic of the mystery not emphasized by any other analogy in the Bible—the aspect of God's "total" gift of self to man. In Christ, God gives all that he can give of himself to man considering man's limited faculties as a creature. In this way, the spousal analogy provides a vivid image of the radical character of grace.

21. Man was chosen in Christ "before the foundations of the world." Thus, the grace of original innocence was accomplished in reference to Christ, while anticipating chronologically his coming in the body. Christ's coming, therefore, is not merely the result of sin. God's eternal plan for man in Christ remains the same yesterday, today, and forever. The redemption became the source of grace for man after sin and, in a certain sense, in spite of sin.

22. Genesis 2:24 constitutes marriage as the primordial sacrament inasmuch as it is the central point of the "sacrament of creation." All creation makes God's mystery visible in some way. Yet the "sacrament of creation" reaches its highest expression in man, male and female, who fully realizes himself through the sincere gift of self. The interior dimension of the gift in man is revealed through the grace-filled awareness of the nuptial meaning of the body.

23. The primordial sacrament contains a supernatural efficacy because already in creation man was "chosen in Christ." Hence the original "sacrament of creation" draws its efficacy from Christ. Marriage is intended, therefore, not only to advance the work of creation through procreation. God also intends that it serve to extend his eternal plan of love and election in Christ to further generations.

24. The heritage of sin dimmed the beatifying experience of original unity. As the primordial sacrament, marriage was deprived of its supernatural efficacy. Yet even in the state of man's hereditary sinfulness, marriage always remained the figure of that sacrament—the platform for actuating God's eternal designs. The original unity in the body still molds human history, even though it lost the clarity of the sign of salvation.

25. The "sacrament of redemption" refers to the totality of the new gracing of man in Christ. St. Paul links it with Genesis 2:24, showing that it takes on the same form in some sense as the primordial sacrament. The sacraments of creation and redemption are actuated in the visibility of their signs—*through the union* of the first Adam and Eve in creation, and *through the union* of the New Adam and Eve (Christ and the Church) in redemption. These signs, which St. Paul made one "great sign," refer to the entire work of creation and redemption.

26. Christ's spousal relationship with the Church, as the analogy would indicate, has both a unitive and a life-giving dimension. The unitive dimension is completed when the Church receives and responds to the gift of her Bridegroom, just as Eve completed her husband as a "helper fit for him." In turn, the Church manifests the life-giving dimension in her fruitfulness and spiritual motherhood.

27. The Apostle's linking of the original union of spouses with the union of Christ and the Church is not merely a metaphor, but speaks of a real renewal of that which constituted the salvific content of the primordial sacrament. In other words, the grace of the primordial sacrament, which was lost through sin, is now *resurrected* in the sacrament of redemption.

28. In some way Christ assumes into the whole economy of redemption the same nuptial imprint which permeated creation. As a primordial sacrament, marriage is assumed and inserted from its very bases into the integral structure of the new sacramental economy. Thus, marriage arises from redemption *in the form of a prototype*. In some way all of the sacraments find their prototype in marriage as the primordial sacrament.

29. Marriage constitutes an exhortation to participate *consciously* in the redemption of the body. Spouses who are committed to doing so can progressively rediscover, reclaim, and live according to their original dignity. They can—by daily taking up the redeeming cross of Christ—experience a real measure of the harmony, peace, and happiness of original unity.

30. Christian ethos can be explained philosophically but, ultimately, it is only fully tenable to those who are living the grace of a redeemed life in Christ. Christ assigns the ethos of redemption to man's heart, his conscience, his looks, and behavior. The sacred and personal dignity of the

body forms the basis of all morality, sexual or otherwise. When we are vivified by the Holy Spirit, we are consciously aware of this sacred dignity and do not desire to profane it.

31. There is a deep link between the call to become "one flesh" in Genesis 2:24 and the teaching of *Gaudium et Spes* 24 that man can only find himself "through the sincere gift of self." The egotistic gratification of concupiscence is incompatible with such self-giving. Yet as much as concupiscence distorts the heart and its desires, so much does "life according to the Holy Spirit" permit men and women to find again the true freedom of the gift in their bodily union.

32. St. Paul's words—"it is better to marry than to be aflame with passion"—do not justify indulging concupiscence. "To be aflame" signifies a disorder of the passions, whereas "to marry" signifies the ethical order and the ethos of redemption. Marriage is meant to be the meeting place of eros with ethos—a meeting which bears fruit in purity of heart.

33. The mutual union in "one flesh" and its accompanying gratification is meant to be an expression of "life according to the Spirit"—of the specific grace of the sacrament of marriage. Authentic gratification, however, is not egoistic, nor is it ever closed in on itself. If conjugal union is to be "according to the Spirit," spouses must open their union to that Spirit who is the Lord and Giver of Life.

34. Every child conceived of conjugal union not only reproduces the mystery of creation, but also proclaims the hope of redemption. Openness to life in conjugal intercourse, therefore, has not only a temporal dimension, but also an eternal dimension. The blessing of fertility forces men and women to choose between what is "of the Father" and what is "of the world." "The world passes away and the lust thereof; but he who does the will of God abides forever" (1 Jn 1:17).

35. In light of Ephesians 5, spouses are called to model their lives not only on the original unity of man and woman, but even more so on the unity of Christ and the Church. In this way the original meaning of marriage is presupposed and rediscovered, but only if spouses consciously experience the redemption of the body. Authentic spousal love is itself redemptive. St. Paul, in some sense, fuses these two dimensions of love into one.

36. The linking of the spousal significance of the body with its redemptive significance is obviously important with regard to marriage, but it is equally essential if man is to comprehend the very meaning of his existence in the world. Man is called *in his body* to love as God loves. This is the spousal significance of the body. Yet, because of sin, he cannot fulfill the meaning of his existence unless he is redeemed. Christ's union with the Church affords this redemption, and this is the redemptive significance of the body.

37. By reaching out to the mystery of creation through the reality of redemption, we discover the meaning of human existence, the meaning of sexuality, and the meaning of marriage. Spousal love marks all of human life. In Christ's union with the Church, marriage is again inscribed in that "sacrament of man" which embraces the universe.

38. The wedding vows give an intentional expression to the spiritual reality of marital love and fidelity. Yet, these profound words of the spirit demand a corresponding "language of the body." The words of the wedding vows, in fact, can be fulfilled only by means of conjugal intercourse. Only in the act of consummation is marriage constituted in its full reality. Both the vows and the marital embrace, then, are important in regard to the structure of the sacramental sign of marriage.

39. The sacramental sign of marriage is a sign of multiple content. It is first established by the liturgical rite in the exchange of consent and is then consummated in marital intercourse. In turn, the sacramental sign endures in the man and woman themselves and their indissoluble bond throughout their lives.

40. Since the language of the body proclaims the mystery of God's life and love, we can speak of a specific "prophetism of the body." Man, as a subject, becomes the author of this language. He can choose to speak the truth with his body, but he can also choose to speak lies. If the body is "prophetic," we must carefully distinguish between true and false prophets.

41. Spouses must learn to reread and "speak" the language of their bodies truthfully. Indeed the essential element of the sacramental sign of marriage is the language of the body spoken in truth. During the liturgical rite of marriage, the priest or deacon asks the couple if they promise to receive children lovingly from God. If the language of consent says "yes" but the language of the body says "no," this falsifies the sacramental sign.

42. All the meanings of the language of the body are initiated and synthesized in the content of conjugal consent. Day by day, spouses draw from that synthesis the same sign, identifying themselves with it throughout their lives. In all that they do—and especially in the consummate expression of their union—the spouses remain faithful to their original consent, or they fail to do so. They deepen their love and fidelity or they cheapen it.

43. Rereading the language of the body in truth is given as a task to the man of concupiscence. Even if concupiscence causes many "errors" in rereading the language of the body and gives rise to sin, man is not determined by concupiscence. Through the ethos of redemption the possibility always remains of passing from "error" to the "truth"—the possibility of conversion from sin to chastity through life according to the Holy Spirit.

Cycle 6

Love and Fruitfulness

The Holy Father postponed his catechesis on the body during the Holy Year of Redemption in 1983. He resumed the next year with his sixth and final cycle, consisting of twenty-one addresses delivered between May 23 and November 28, 1984. After some reflections on the Song of Songs, the book of Tobit, and some new themes gleaned from Ephesians 5, John Paul II applies his "adequate anthropology" to the teaching of Pope Paul VI's landmark encyclical *Humanae Vitae.* As he states: "The reflections we have thus far made on human love in the divine plan would be in some way incomplete if we did not try to see their concrete application in the sphere of marital and family morality." Taking this further step "will bring us to the completion of our now long journey."[1]

It has been a long journey indeed. Every step has led us to this point. In fact, John Paul sees his entire catechesis on the body as "an ample commentary on the doctrine contained in the encyclical *Humanae Vitae.*"[2] Questions come from this encyclical which, according to John Paul, "permeate the sum total of our reflections." Therefore, it "follows that this last part is not artificially added to the sum total but is organically and homogeneously united with it."[3] In his introduction to this cycle, the Holy Father states: "It seems to me, indeed, that what I intend to explain in the coming weeks constitutes as it were the crowning of what I have illustrated."[4]

The fierce denunciation of the encyclical's teaching had inspired John Paul II to develop his theology of the body in the first place. He made this the first major catechetical project of his pontificate because it is absolutely impossible to build a civilization of love and a culture of life if we

---

1. 7/11/84, TB 386.

2. 11/28/84, TB 420.

3. Ibid, TB 422.

4. 5/23/84, TB 368.

do not understand and embrace the teaching of *Humanae Vitae*. And it is impossible to understand the full importance of *Humanae Vitae* without a "total vision of man." As Paul VI himself recognized: "The problem of birth, like every other problem regarding human life is, to be considered beyond partial perspectives." It must be seen "in light of an integral vision of man and of his vocation, not only his natural and earthly, but also his supernatural and eternal vocation."[5] This was John Paul's cue. This "integral vision of man" is precisely what the theology of the body provides for us. This biblical–theological–sacramental–personalistic vision of man and of conjugal union not only provides a new and winning context for understanding the Church's constant teaching on the immorality of contracepted intercourse. It also places it on the surest foundation possible: that of divine revelation itself.[6]

Some divisions of the catechesis place the Pope's reflections on the Song of Songs and the marriage of Tobiah and Sarah at the conclusion of the Sacramentality of Marriage. However, not only does John Paul indicate that these five audiences are a preface to his analysis of *Humanae Vitae*,[7] the importance of these audiences is also "felt" more when seen in this light. His stated goal is to help us understand in a more adequate and exhaustive way the sacramental sign of marriage. "The spouses in the Song of Songs, with ardent words, declare to each other their human love. The newlyweds in the book of Tobit ask God that they be able to respond to love. Both the one and the other find their place in what constitutes the sacramental sign of marriage. Both the one and the other share in forming that sign."[8] As we shall see, these biblical couples help us understand how vital the teaching of *Humanae Vitae* is if spouses are to "form the sign" of marriage according to its divine prototype.

86. The Biblical Ode to Erotic Love

May 23, 1984 (TB 368–370)

"All scripture is inspired by God and profitable for teaching, for reproof, for correction, and for training in righteousness" (2 Tim 3:16). Unfortunately, some churchmen throughout history have seemed to think these words of St. Paul do not apply to the erotic love poetry of the Song

---

5. *Humanae Vitae*, n. 7.

6. See 7/18/84, TB 389; 11/28/84, TB 421.

7. See 5/23/84, TB 368.

8. 6/27/84, TB 377.

of Songs. As John Paul admits, the reading of this apparently "profane" book of the Bible has often been discouraged. Yet he also points out that the greatest mystics have drawn from this source, and its verses have been inserted into the Church's liturgy.

For those who have comprehended the theology of the body thus far, a biblical ode to erotic love is not the least bit troubling. It only affirms John Paul's thesis that God created the human body and the mystery of erotic love as a primordial sign of his own divine mystery. A conundrum only arises, it seems, when we accept the "interpretation of suspicion" (see §36). The Song's unabashed celebration of erotic love does not permit such suspicion. It teaches us to love human love with the original good of God's vision.

A. Interpreting the Song of Songs

But how are we to understand the Song of Songs? In three extensive endnotes, John Paul discusses many studies and hypotheses regarding this book. Quoting from various scholars, John Paul seems critical of those who rush to disembody the Song of Songs, seeing it only as an allegory of God's "spiritual" love. It certainly serves to illuminate the prophets' description of God's spousal love for Israel. In turn, the Song of Songs also sheds light on Christ's union with the Church as St. Paul describes in Ephesians 5. Nonetheless, John Paul expresses the view of Alonso-Schockel that to "forget the lovers" or to "petrify them in fictions" is not the right way to interpret the Song of Songs (384).

It is "the conviction of a growing number of exegetes," the Pope insists, that the Song of Songs (quoting biblical scholar J. Winandy) is "'to be taken simply for what it manifestly is: a song of human love'" (383). The Pope quotes Alonso-Schockel again: "'Anyone who does not believe in the human love of the spouses, who must seek forgiveness for the body, does not have the right to be elevated....With the affirmation of human love instead, it is possible to discover in it the revelation of God'" (384).

This confirms an essential element of incarnational/sacramental reality. Grace—the mystery of God's life and love—is communicated *through* the "stuff" of our humanity, not despite it. Presenting the position of the scholar A. M. Dubarle, John Paul says that "a faithful and happy human love reveals to man the attributes of divine love" (385). This means, as D. Lys notes, "that the content of the Song of Songs is at the same time sensual and sacred" (385). If we ignore the sacred, the poetry of the Song is seen as a purely lay erotic composition. But when we ignore the sensual, we fall into "allegorism." Thus, integrating the sensual and the sacred is essential—not only to a proper interpretation of the Song of Songs, but also to a proper interpretation of what is authentically human.

B. Mutual Fascination with the Body

Integrating the sensual and the sacred is precisely the goal of a theology (sacred) of the body (sensual). Hence, the Song of Songs evokes all the themes already discussed in the Pope's catechesis. John Paul says that the entire Song testifies to that "beginning" Christ referred to in his decisive conversation with the Pharisees. It demonstrates all the richness of the language of the body whose first expression is already found in Genesis 2:23–25.

Recall John Paul's description of Adam's fascination with woman as the biblical prototype of the Song of Songs (see §13). Now he says that what "was expressed in the second chapter of Genesis (vv. 23–25), in just a few simple and essential words, is developed here in full dialogue." It is expressed "in a duet, in which the groom's words are interwoven with the bride's and they complement each other." A wonder, admiration, and fascination similar to Adam's "runs in a peaceful and homogeneous wave from the beginning to the end of the poem" (369). And just like in the beginning, the "point of departure as well as the point of arrival for this fascination—mutual wonder and admiration—are in fact the bride's femininity and the groom's masculinity in the direct experience of their visibility." The body reveals the person and the body summons them to love. Thus, their words of love are "concentrated on the 'body'" (369).

Fascination with the human body in its masculinity and femininity—often considered innately prurient—is entirely biblical. Concupiscence has certainly distorted our vision and our sentiments. Yet, when we tap into that deep well of human desire and fascination that remains beyond the distortions of concupiscence, we discover that our attraction to the body is God-given. And it is very good (see Gen 1:31). Of course attraction to the body in an integral sense must always be and always is attraction to a person. It is a vision of another person not only with the eyes but with the heart. A look determines the heart within the one who looks, and it determines whether or not he sees the heart of the person at whom he looks. When one's heart is pure, so is his look. When he looks, he sees not just *a* body, but *some*body. Seeing the person, he cannot use the person as an object of egoistic gratification. As we continue reflecting on the Pope's analysis, this is precisely what we will learn about the "look" of the lovers in the Song of Songs.

87. Integrating Eros and Agape

May 23; June 6, 27, 1984 (TB 368–370, 373–376)

John Paul continually emphasizes that in the inspired duet of the Song of Songs, the body itself constitutes the source of the lovers' mutual fascination. It "is on the body that there lingers directly and immediately that attraction toward the other person, toward the other 'I'—male or female—which in the interior impulse of the heart generates love" (369). Or, we could say that it is *meant* to generate love. Tragically, for the man of concupiscence, the visibility of the body often generates lust. Of course, through the gift of redemption, historical man can overcome the domination of concupiscence, but not without a lively spiritual battle.

John Paul observes that it is as if the spouses of the Song live and express themselves in an ideal world in which the struggle in the heart between good and evil did not exist. "The words of the spouses, their movements, their gestures correspond to the interior movement of their hearts" (368). The movement of their hearts is purity, freedom, and love. "Is it not precisely the power and the interior truth of love that subdues the struggle that goes on in man and around him?" (376) The more that love purifies the heart, the less concupiscence can deceive us.

A. Experience of the Beautiful

In turn, this "love unleashes a special experience of the beautiful, which focuses on what is visible, but at the same time involves the entire person" (369). An integrated understanding of beauty always involves the whole person. The lover exults: "Behold, you are beautiful, my love, behold, you are beautiful! Your eyes are doves behind your veil. Your hair is like a flock of goats moving down the slopes of Gilead" (Song 4:1). The Pope acknowledges that such metaphors of beauty may surprise us today since we are not familiar with the life of shepherds and goat herders. Nonetheless, they show us how the language of the body seeks support and corroboration "in the whole visible world."

As John Paul tells us, the groom rereads this "language" at one and the same time with his heart and with his eyes. In other words, the groom is entirely integrated internally and externally. If a "look" determines the very intentionality of existence (see §33), the lover has determined to live in the truth of the *gift*. He respects woman as a gift. His look concentrates "on the whole female 'I' of the bride." He sees her as a *person*—a subject—created for her own sake. And her personhood "speaks to him through every feminine trait, giving rise to that state of mind that can be defined as fascination, enchantment" (370).

In this way the language of the body finds a "rich echo" in the groom's words. He speaks in poetic transport and metaphors, which attest to the experience of beauty, what the Pope calls "a love of satisfaction" (370). Yet in the end the lover's metaphors fall short. Leaving them behind, the groom says, "You are all beautiful, my beloved, and there is no blemish in you" (Song 4:7). Even though their duet precedes the time of

Christ, here we see that the husband loves his wife "as Christ loved the Church" (Eph 5:25). Recall John Paul's statement that Christ-like love obliges the husband to desire his wife's beauty, to cherish it and care for it, desiring all that is good for her (see §69). For Christ gave himself up for his bride that she might be "holy and without blemish." Likewise, John Paul tells us that the husband's aspiration in the Song of Songs is "born of love" on the basis of the language of the body. It "is a search for integral beauty, for purity that is free of all stain: it is a search for perfection that contains...the synthesis of human beauty, beauty of soul and body" (373–374).

B. Eros Purified by Love

This is true erotic love! According to John Paul, eros is to be understood as the heart's aspiration toward what is true, good, and beautiful (see §38). But for eros to be experienced in this way, it must be integrated with love. "This love has been called 'agape' and agape brings the eros to completion by purifying it" (375). We might even say that we witness this purification of eros in the strophes of the Song of Songs. Here "'the language of the body' becomes a part of the single process of the mutual attraction of the man and woman, which is expressed in the frequent refrains that speak of the search that is full of nostalgia, of affectionate solicitude (see Song 2:7), and of the spouses' mutual rediscovery (see Song 5:2). This brings them joy and calm, and seems to lead them to a continual search" (373). John Paul observes that in their search for each other and even in their meeting and embracing they ceaselessly "tend toward something." Their duet clearly shows their readiness to respond to the call of eros. But it also intimates that they desire to surpass the natural limits of eros—to infuse it with something more. That "something more" is agape.

"In the Song of Songs the human eros reveals the countenance of love ever in search and, as it were, never satisfied. The echo of this restlessness runs through the strophes of the poem: 'I opened to my lover, but he had departed, gone. I sought him but I did not find him; I called to him but he did not answer me' (Song 5:6)" (374). John Paul asks whether or not such restlessness is part of the nature of eros. Then he adds that if it is, it would indicate the need for self-control. It seems that here John Paul refers to an experience of eros that has yet to be integrated with agape. Restlessness in this sense seems related to John Paul's idea of the "insatiability of the union" (see §28). Yet if such is the case, eros need not be abandoned, repressed, or held in suspicion. It need only be opened to the infusion of agape.

Above we quoted John Paul saying that the lovers of the Song in some sense seem "outside" the battle between good and evil. This is true in most of the Song. Nonetheless their restless need to integrate eros with agape seems to point to just such a battle. The Song describes love in terms of a jealousy as "cruel as the grave" (Song 8:6). St. Paul, however, will say that love "is not jealous" (1 Cor 13:4). How do we account for the discrepancy? John Paul does not venture an analysis other than to suggest that when human eros "closes its horizon," it remains opened to another "horizon of love" that in Paul's words speaks another language. It is the language of agape.

If love is stern as death (see Song 8:6), according to John Paul this means that love "goes to the furthest limits of the 'language of the body' in order to exceed them" (374). The language of erotic love is only a sign—a sacrament—of Trinitarian love, of agape. Ultimately even spouses must "break away," the Pope says, from those earthly means of expressing eros-agape in order to enter into "the very nucleus of the gift from person to person" (374). The ultimate reality of gift can be none other than the eternal mystery of the Trinity itself. That Communion alone can satisfy the love that is ever seeking and (in this life) never satisfied.

John Paul's exegesis of the Song of Songs touches each of the themes of his catechesis up to this point. We see signs of original man, historical man, and eschatological man. We see the truth about married love and even the meaning of "breaking away" from such love as expressed in the celibate vocation.

88. Mutual Entrustment and the Truth of the Person

May 30; June 6, 1984 (TB 370–374)

John Paul tells us that it is vitally important for the theology of the body and for the theology of the sacramental sign of marriage "to know *who the female 'you' is for the male 'I'* and vice versa" (370). This is also vitally important for life in general. Recall the Pope's statement that the dignity and balance of human life depend at every moment of history and at every point on the globe on who woman will be for man and who man will be for woman (see §35). The poetic duet of the lovers in the Song of Songs expresses with particular eloquence who man and woman "are" for each other. John Paul focuses on two themes or plots from the Song which exemplify this.

A. My Sister, My Bride

The first could be called the "fraternal" theme. Several times throughout the Song, the lover refers to his bride first as his sister. "You have ravished my heart, my sister, my bride, you have ravished my heart with one glance of your eyes.... How sweet is your love, my sister, my bride!" (4:9–10) According to John Paul, these expressions say much more than if he had called her by name. They illustrate how love reveals the other person. "The fact that in this approach that female 'I' is revealed for her groom as 'sister'—and that precisely as both sister and bride—has a special eloquence" (371). It reveals that he sees her not as a thing to be appropriated, but as a *person* to be loved. To be a person "means both 'being subject' and 'being in relationship'" (371). The term "sister" denotes this.

The word "sister" speaks of their common humanity. We can recall the meaning of "double solitude" (see §14). Both man and woman share the same solitude, the same humanity. It is as if they "were descended from the same family circle, as though from infancy they were united by memories of a common home...From this there follows a specific sense of common belonging." Furthermore, through the name "sister," the groom's words tend to reproduce as the Pope poignantly expresses, "the history of the femininity of the person loved. They see her still in the time of girl-hood and they embrace her entire 'I,' soul and body, with a disinterested tenderness" (371).

The word "sister" also speaks of their being in relationship. It speaks of the two different ways in which masculinity and femininity "incarnate" the same humanity (see §13). At this point, however, the term "sister" gives way to the term "bride"—but without losing what is essential in the groom's recognition of his bride as "sister." The transition from "sister" to "bride" maintains—and it must maintain—the same recognition of her personhood. This is the special eloquence of calling her "sister" *before* calling her "bride." It reveals that the lover's *modus operandi* in desiring her as bride is love, not lust.

John Paul observes that recognizing one's beloved first as a "sister" challenges the man to assess the sincerity of his love. The groom of the Song readily takes up this challenge. In turn, the Holy Father says that the sincerity of their love allows them to live their mutual closeness in security and to manifest it without fearing the unfair judgment of others. They are not ashamed of their love because they are confident in its purity. From this experience of selfless love a deep interior tranquility arises, reminiscent of the "peace of the interior gaze" in the experience of original nakedness (see §17). "So I was in his eyes as one who finds peace" (Song 8:10). While this is a peace found deep in the human heart, nonetheless John Paul says it is also a "peace of the body." Above all, John Paul describes it as the peace of the encounter of man and woman as the image of God by means of a reciprocal and disinterested gift of self. This is the richness and the challenge of the words "my sister, my bride."

■ I have observed differing reactions between men and women when I have presented the "sister-bride" concept at seminars. For whatever reason, most women, it seems, tend to respond readily, as if such an idea confirms their deepest hopes for a romantic relationship. Men, on the other hand, often seem taken aback. To consider a potential "sex-partner" as a "sister" cuts right at the heart of what most men seem to desire in a relationship. A man revolts at the idea of indulging lust with his "sister." This is precisely the point! Women certainly have their own distortions to contend with, but coming to recognize woman first as "sister" compels men in a particular way to face the distortions of lust and to seek grace in "untwisting" those distortions. I also offer the following observation. The whole concept of "dating" in popular culture today—with its expectations of immediate romantic involvement if not immediate sexual intimacy—serves to skip the "fraternal plot" of man and woman's relationship altogether. Men and women who have never come to love one another fraternally are without a proper foundation for spousal love. They are in grave danger of mistaking concupiscence for spousal love. Building a marriage on such a foundation is equivalent to building a house on sand.

B. A Garden Enclosed

John Paul uncovers the second plot of the Song of Songs in the following passage of the poem: "A garden locked is my sister, my bride, a garden enclosed, a fountain sealed" (4:12). These expressions also have a profound contribution to make in determining who man and woman "are" for each other. The Holy Father intuits that these words reveal the man's respect for the woman as "master of her own mystery" (372). She is her own person with her own will to choose, and as such she is inviolable. Recognizing this, the lover knows he cannot "take" her or "grasp" her. If they are to live in a common union *(communio personarum),* it must be based on the freedom of the gift (see §18). As John Paul expresses it: "The 'language of the body' reread in truth keeps pace with the discovery of the interior inviolability of the person" (372).

When we fail to reread the language of the body truthfully—that is, when we lust—we inevitably violate the mystery of the person. We take what is not given. We become master over another person. And persons—precisely because they are persons—are meant to be their own masters. Their dignity demands it. John Paul stresses that the person "surpasses all measures of appropriation and domination, of possession and gratification" (374). If the man were to barge into this "locked garden" (in deed or thought), or if he were to manipulate her into surrendering the key, he would not be loving her, he would be raping her.

Declaring her an "enclosed garden" and a "sealed fountain" attests to the sincerity of his own gift of self. He is knocking at the door, not breaking in. He presents himself to her as a gift, placing himself in her hands and entrusting himself to her freedom. He puts "his hand to the latch" (Song 5:4) only with her "yes"—a yes given in total freedom, without any hint of coercion. Indeed the bride knows that the groom's "longing" is for her—for her whole feminine person, not merely her body—so she goes to meet him, as the Pope describes, with the "quickness" of the gift of herself. She answers him with the entrustment of herself. As master of her own mystery (that is, with the full freedom of her own choice) she says: "I belong to my lover." The freedom of the gift is the bride's response to the deep awareness of the sincere gift expressed by the groom's words. In this way their love is built up. And as the Pope affirms, "It is authentic love" (372).

C. My Lover Belongs to Me and I to Him

Authentic love, as proclaimed by the Song of Songs, means "the initiation into the mystery of the person, without, however, implying its violation" (373). We have described this initiation into the mystery of the person as "participation" in the other's humanity (see §§22, 52). The lovers of the Song approach this participation through the duet of an ever growing nearness between them. In this way they discover each other as a gift and, as John Paul says, they even "taste" each other as a gift. The "love that unites them is at one and the same time of a spiritual and a sensual nature" (373). In other words, their spiritual love is integrated with and even rooted in their bodies—in their sexuality and sensuality. The pining of their hearts for authentic love is expressed in the pining of their bodily senses without the disturbance and "disconnect" of concupiscence.

■ The erotic poetry of the Song of Songs is full of sensual references to foods and fragrances, to smelling, tasting, eating, and drinking each other's goodness (see, for example, 1:12–14; 2:3–6; 4:10—5:1). This indicates a profound interconnection between nuptial love, smelling, tasting, eating, and drinking. Are not these senses (and, in fact, all of the senses) fully engaged in erotic love? What does the passionate kiss of lovers say if not in some sense "I want to taste you; I want to take you into myself and consume you; 'eat' you; 'drink' you"? Furthermore, does not the very fragrance of the body stir men and women to love? Perhaps we look on the senses with suspicion because they often rouse concupiscence. But to the degree that men and women live from that vivification of the Holy Spirit, all things sensual stir them to love. Yes, our senses—all of our senses— were created by God to inspire love! This is the nature of incarnational/

sacramental reality. We see these interconnections between nuptial love, smelling, tasting, eating, and drinking very clearly—even if only analogously—in the Eucharistic liturgy. Here, more than in any earthly encounter, Christ invites us to "taste and see" his own goodness (see Ps 34:8). Fragrances of incense, oils, and candles all add to the sensual experience of the union of Bridegroom and Bride. And how is the marriage of Christ and the Church sacramentally consummated? The deepest desire of the Heavenly Bridegroom is that we, his Bride, might *eat his flesh* and *drink his blood.*

Concupiscence alone violates the person, never love. If a person's "love" violates the one loved, then *it is not love* and should not be called love. It is love's counterfeit—lust. If lust seeks to grasp and possess the other, true love "expresses the authentic depth of the mutual belonging of the spouses" (372). John Paul observes that the spouses in the Song are aware of "belonging" to each other, of being "destined" for each other: "My lover belongs to me and I to him" (Song 2:16). But recall the "personal analogy of belonging" of which the Holy Father previously spoke (see §30). In the language of authentic love, when spouses speak of "belonging" to each other it "indicates the reciprocity of the donation, it expresses the equal balance of the gift...in which the mutual *communio personarum* is established."[9] As John Paul states: "When the bride says, 'My lover belongs to me,' she means at the same time, 'It is he to whom I entrust myself,' and therefore she says, 'and I to him' (Song 2:16). The words 'to me' and 'to him' affirm here the whole depth of that entrustment, which corresponds to the interior truth of the person" (372).

■ In man and woman's being "destined" for each other we can even see a sign of our being destined in Christ (see Eph 1:4). Similarly, if a Christian speaks of "belonging" to Christ, this is not an "ownership" on Christ's part. God may indeed have a "right of ownership" over his creatures. But here is the mystery of the "divine respect" he shows toward humanity—he does not assert such a right of ownership. He, too, respects us—his Bride—as "masters of our own mystery." Wojtyla makes this point unambiguously in the following provocative statement: "Nobody can use a person as a means toward an end, no human being, nor yet God the Creator. On the part of God, indeed, it is totally out of the question, since, by giving man an intelligent and free nature, he has thereby ordained that each man alone will decide for himself the ends of his activity, and not be a

9. 7/30/80, TB 129.

blind tool of someone else's ends. Therefore, if God intends to direct man toward certain goals, he allows him to begin with to know those goals, so that he may make them his own and strive toward them independently. In this amongst other things resides the most profound logic of revelation: God allows man to learn his supernatural ends, but the decision to strive toward an end, the choice of course, is left to man's free will. God does not redeem man against his will."[10]

89. Sacrificial Love Conquers Death

June 27, 1984 (TB 375–377)

To deepen further the meaning of the sacramental sign of marriage, in his audience of June 27, 1984, the Holy Father begins to analyze the marriage of Tobiah and Sarah in the book of Tobit. Setting the stage for his reflections, the Holy Father recalls to his audience that Sarah had already been married seven times, but because of a demon each man died before having intercourse with her (see Tob 6:13–14). John Paul II—man of keen observation that he is—says that in taking Sarah as his wife, young Tobiah had reason to be afraid. In fact, upon giving his daughter to Tobiah in marriage, Sarah's father proceeded to dig Tobiah's grave (see Tob 8:9). But an angel said to Tobiah: "Do not be afraid, for she was destined for you from eternity. You will save her, and she will go with you, and...you will have children by her." Then we read: "When Tobiah heard these things, he fell in love with her and yearned deeply for her" (Tob 7:17).

A. Love Is Victorious in the Test of Life and Death

Here we see all the components of good and evil gearing up for a great spiritual battle: angels and demons; life and death; God's eternal salvific will and man's rebellious designs; love and all that is opposed to love. In what context does this great clash take shape? In the joining of a man and woman in "one flesh." Precisely in this union, John Paul tells us, "the choices and the actions [of men and women] take on all the weight of human existence" (376).

These are weighty words, but they should not surprise us. We have seen that the weight of human existence rests on man and woman's union from the outset of our reflections. The first pages of Genesis reveal that sexuality and procreation are intimately linked with the great contest of

---

10. *Love & Responsibility.* p. 27.

good and evil, life and death (see §24). As John Paul starkly expresses: Spouses, "in fact, becoming one as husband and wife, find themselves in the situation in which the powers of good and evil fight and compete against each other" (376).

Husbands and wives live this great *spiritual* contest in their *bodies*. We see this vividly in the case of Tobiah and Sarah. John Paul observes that from the very first moment their love had to face the test of life and death. He continues: "The words about love 'stern as death,' spoken by the spouses in the Song of Songs...assume here the nature of a real test" (376). Tobiah knows that if he is to conquer death through love, he must turn to the Lord in prayer:

> When the door was shut and the two were alone, Tobiah got up from the bed and said, "Sister, get up, and let us pray that the Lord may have mercy upon us." And Tobiah began to pray, "Blessed art thou, O God of our fathers, and blessed be thy holy and glorious name for ever...Thou madest Adam and gavest him Eve his wife as a helper and support. Thou didst say, 'It is not good that the man should be alone; let us make a helper for him like himself.'...And now, O Lord, I am not taking this sister of mine because of lust, but with sincerity. Grant that I may find mercy and grow old together with her." And she said with him, "Amen" (Tob 8:4–8).

Tobiah's prayer "situates the 'language of the body' on the level of the essential terms of the theology of the body" (377). Notice that, just as Christ will eventually direct the Pharisees to do, Tobiah and Sarah set their hearts on God's original plan for marriage. Notice Tobiah calls her "sister" like the lover in the Song of Songs. Notice that he contrasts lust with the "sincere gift of self." Notice that he intends to spend his whole life with her ("What therefore God has joined together let no man put asunder" [Mt 19:6]). And notice that Tobiah knows they cannot live this sublime calling without the help of God's mercy.

The prospect of proclaiming and *choosing* the truth of God's original plan for marital union "opens up before them with the trial of life and death, already during their wedding night" (377). Yet Tobiah and Sarah are confident in love's victory. They "unhesitatingly face this test. But in this test of life and death, life wins because, during the test on the wedding night, love, supported by prayer, is revealed as more stern than death." Yes, love "is victorious because it prays" (376).

If Tobiah had "reason to be afraid" in taking Sarah as his wife, as St. John tells us: "There is no fear in love, but perfect love casts out fear" (1 Jn 4:18). In a clarion call for all men and women to embrace that perfect love—almost repeating his signature phrase "be not afraid"—John Paul declares: "The truth and the power of love are shown in the ability to place oneself between the forces of good and evil which are fighting in man and around him, because love is confident in the victory of good and is ready to do everything so that good may conquer" (376).

B. Tobiah Lives!

No sacrifice is too great for true lovers—no suffering too much to bear—when it is needed to ensure the victory of good over evil. This is precisely the testimony of the cross, of Christ's spousal love for the Church. This is precisely the perfect love in which every husband and wife is called to participate. And this is precisely what the teaching of *Humanae Vitae* calls spouses to embrace.

As the Holy Father reminds us, marriage "is, in fact, the image...of that covenant which takes its origin from eternal Love." It is "the original sacrament of the Covenant of God with man, with the human race." Hence, "the 'language of the body' becomes the language of the ministers of the sacrament, aware that in the conjugal pact there is expressed and realized the mystery that has its origin in God himself" (377). This mystery is that God is Love and that God is Life! Because of their prayer and their love, Tobiah and Sarah can "see with the glance of faith the sanctity of this vocation." Through "the unity of the two, built upon the mutual truth of the 'language of the body'—they must respond to the call of God himself which is contained in the mystery of the Beginning. And this is why they ask: 'Call down your mercy on me and on her'" (377). In receiving this mercy, they consummate their marriage and Tobiah lives!

If the demon in Sarah's previous marriages wrote death into the plan of man and woman's relationship, the angel's message to Tobiah restored life to that plan. Inspired by God's designs for marriage, Tobiah's sacrificial (Christ-like) love conquered death. In the face of authentic nuptial love, death has no chance. Life refuses to surrender (see §24). Because of the eros-agape love that united them in "one flesh," Tobiah and Sarah witness to God as the God of Life. Their union joyously proclaims: "Where, O death, is your victory? Where, O death, is your sting?" (see 1 Cor 15:55)

90. Conjugal Life Becomes Liturgical

June 27; July 4, 1984 (TB 377–380)

In both the Song of Songs and the story of Tobiah and Sarah we see the spouses rereading the language of the body in truth. Both couples witness to the deepest meaning of the sacramental sign of marriage. They understand the truth of this sign not only in an *objective* sense. They also desire it *subjectively*. They long for it in their hearts. When this profound integration between objective reality and subjective experience occurs, John Paul says that spouses experience the language of the body for what it is. They experience it as the language of the liturgy.

A. The Liturgical Language of the Body

In his audience of July 4, 1984, John Paul develops the idea that by living according to the ethos of redemption, conjugal life itself becomes liturgical. In some sense this audience brings us to the climax of John Paul's dramatic proposal about the "greatness"—the God-likeness—of nuptial love. Here we cross the threshold and enter into the most profound integration of the sensual and the sacred. But what, exactly, does it mean to describe conjugal life as liturgical?

Turning to the *Catechism*, we learn that in Christian tradition, liturgy "means the participation of the People of God in 'the work of God.'"[11] The work of God refers above all to the "great mystery" of our redemption in Jesus Christ accomplished through his death and resurrection. To say that conjugal life is liturgical is to say that it participates in this "great mystery." As such, the union of man and woman in conjugal love is meant to sanctify the world as a living sign of redemption—a constant reminder of what happened in the death and resurrection of Christ. "It is this mystery of Christ that the Church proclaims and celebrates in her liturgy so that the faithful may live from it and bear witness to it in the world."[12] Spouses do precisely this when they live in fidelity to the language God inscribed in their bodies as male and female.

The *Catechism* also says that liturgy is the Church's "celebration of divine worship." In fact, it is "a participation in Christ's own prayer addressed to the Father in the Holy Spirit."[13] So, too, is conjugal life. When lived according to the "great mystery" of God's designs, even the marital embrace itself becomes a profound prayer. It becomes Eucharistic (see §71) as an act of thanksgiving offered to God for the joyous gift of sharing in his life and love. Pushing the analogy, we might even view the marital bed as an altar upon which spouses offer their bodies in living sacrifice, holy and acceptable to God. This is their spiritual act of worship (see Rom 12:1).

Liturgy also refers "to the proclamation of the Gospel and to active charity" carried out by the Church "in the image of her Lord."[14] So does conjugal life. Conjugal life is a profound and continuous proclamation of

---

11. *CCC*, n. 1069.
12. *CCC*, n. 1068.
13. *CCC*, n. 1070, 1073.
14. *CCC*, n. 1070.

the "Gospel of the body" lived in the image of Christ's love for the Church. Quoting from the Second Vatican Council, the *Catechism* concludes: "The liturgy then is rightly seen as an exercise of the priestly office of Jesus Christ. It involves the presentation of man's sanctification under the guise of signs perceptible by the senses and its accomplishment in ways appropriate to each of these signs."[15] In conjugal life, the sanctification of spouses is presented and appropriately accomplished through the sign of their faithful union, lived out day-to-day and consummated in becoming one flesh. In this way spouses are initiated into the mystery of Christ through an ongoing marital-liturgical catechesis which proceeds "from the visible to the invisible, from the sign to the thing signified, from the 'sacraments' to the 'mysteries.'"[16]

The idea that conjugal life is in some way liturgical is not surprising when we consider that the whole liturgical life of the Church revolves around the sacraments.[17] Marriage is not only one of the sacraments, but is in some sense the prototype or model of all the sacraments (see §78). Hence, not only is conjugal life liturgical. When we read the spousal analogy in the other direction, we realize that the Church's liturgical life is in some sense conjugal. "The entire Christian life bears the mark of the spousal love of Christ and the Church."[18] According to this analogy, the Church's liturgical life is where she enters into the "great mystery" of nuptial union with Christ. It is where the Bride receives the spousal love of her Bridegroom in an eternally fruitful embrace *(fiat)* and offers endless praise and thanksgiving for so great a gift *(magnificat)*.

B. The Mystical Language of the Body

The Holy Father looks once again to that marvelous passage of Ephesians 5 for corroboration of the body's liturgical language. "This text," he says, "brings us to such a dimension of the 'language of the body' that could be called 'mystical.' It speaks of marriage, in fact, as a 'great mystery'" (378). It is true that St. Paul says this "great mystery" refers to Christ's union with the Church. Nevertheless, St. Paul extends that mystical analogy to the sacramental sign of marriage. He extends it "to the 'language of the body' reread in the truth of the spousal love and the conjugal

---

15. Ibid.

16. *CCC,* n. 1075.

17. See *CCC,* n. 1113.

18. *CCC,* n. 1617.

union of the two." It is the liturgy which "elevates the conjugal pact of man and woman, based on the 'language of the body' reread in truth, to the dimensions of 'mystery,' and at the same time enables that pact to be fulfilled in these dimensions through the 'language of the body.' It is precisely the sign of the sacrament of marriage that speaks of this." (378).

If we ponder this "great mystery," John Paul observes that the text of Ephesians 5 radically frees our thinking both from elements of Manichaeism and from a non-personalistic view of the body. At the same time it "brings the 'language of the body,' contained in the sacramental sign of matrimony, nearer to the dimension of real sanctity" (378). The great sign of married love expresses not only "an interpersonal event laden with intense personal content." It also expresses "a sacred and sacramental reality, rooted in the dimensions of the Covenant and grace—in the dimension of creation and redemption. In this way," John Paul continues, "the liturgical language assigns to both [spouses] love, fidelity, and conjugal honesty through the 'language of the body.' It assigns them the unity and indissolubility of marriage in the 'language of the body.' It assigns them as a duty all the *sacrum* (holy) of the person and of the communion of persons, and likewise their femininity and masculinity—precisely in this language" (379). The language of the body—expressed in the whole of married life and consummated in becoming "one flesh"—is sacred. It is holy. It is mystical and liturgical!

When we let these truths sink in, we cannot persist in our suspicion toward the body. We cannot persist in the heretical belief that the body and sexuality are somehow inherently tainted (Manichaeism). We cannot persist in the dualistic error that views the body as an inherent obstacle to the spiritual life. Instead we realize that our male and female bodies are the vehicle of the Holy Spirit, in all of life, but especially in married life. Our bodies are created to be infused with holiness, with grace. Even if we have lost this grace due to sin, we can receive it once again through the sacraments. As John Paul evangelically proclaims: "The sacraments inject sanctity into the plan of man's humanity: they penetrate the soul and body, the femininity and masculinity of the personal subject, with the power of sanctity" (378).

This is not an abstract theological concept. John Paul insists that we can *experience* this in the depths of our subjectivity. He adds that all of this is expressed in the body and brought about through the language of the liturgy. When spouses understand marriage as an integral part of the liturgical life of the Church, they are empowered to live their sacrament as the vocation to holiness that it is. They experience and express the true language of their bodies not only in the moments of joining in "one flesh," but in "an uninterrupted continuity of liturgical language"—in the whole series of acts and duties that make up their daily lives as spouses.

When spouses strive with God's grace to speak the liturgical language of the body honestly in the consummate sign of their union, the whole ensemble of their conjugal dialogue becomes an extension of that fidelity. Living the true language of the body becomes a way of life, a liturgical way of life, a life of prayer. Every sacrifice, every diaper change, every meal cooked, every commute to work, every duty and responsibility carried out day-to-day is understood and lived as a continuation of the faithful gift, that unconditional "yes" spoken by the body in the marital union of bodies. It all becomes an offering to God as an ongoing participation in the Church's liturgy. It all serves to sanctify the family and the world.[19]

C. Spiritually Mature Sexual Attraction

A profound sense of the holiness of the body and of conjugal union—of the person and the communion of persons—must form the essential "ethos" and "spirituality" of married life. St. Paul calls spouses precisely to this when he exhorts them to be "subject to one another out of reverence for Christ" (Eph 5:21).

In fact, John Paul says that this Pauline image of reverence for Christ "is none other than a spiritually mature form of that mutual attraction: man's attraction to femininity and woman's attraction to masculinity" (379). The Pope remarks that this is the same sexual attraction which the book of Genesis revealed for the first time (see 2:23–25) and which "seems to flow like a wide stream" through the verses of the Song of Songs. It also finds a concentrated expression in the story of Tobiah and Sarah. This spiritually mature sexual attraction "is none other than the blossoming of the gift of fear"—that reverence and awe for the sacred which John Paul reminds us is one of the seven gifts of the Holy Spirit (see §66). Chaste thought and action stem precisely from this spiritually mature attraction. As the Pope concludes, chastity is not only a human virtue, but a divine gift (grace)—a gift of the Spirit dwelling in our flesh.[20]

Through the virtue and gift of a mature chastity, men and women find that lust no longer deceives them. The desires of their hearts conform to the truth, dignity, and sacredness of the body and the call to communion. As the Holy Father says: "Both the man and the woman, getting away from concupiscence, find the proper dimension of the freedom of the gift,

---

19. See *CCC*, nn. 1368, 2031.

20. See *CCC*, nn. 1810, 1811, 2345.

united to femininity and masculinity in the true spousal significance of the body." In this way they experience the mysterious language of the body "in a depth, simplicity and beauty hitherto altogether unknown" (380). Such a statement is not a projection of a celibate pontiff, but an observation continually confirmed by a pastor who has worked intimately and extensively with married couples.

John Paul concludes that this seems to be the integral significance of the sacramental sign of marriage. "In that sign—through the 'language of the body'—man and woman encounter the great 'mystery' in order to transfer the light of that mystery...to the 'language of the body.'" The Pope affirms that through the ethos of redemption married couples are able to transfer "the light of truth and beauty, expressed in liturgical language," to their "practice of love, of fidelity, of conjugal honesty" (380). Through the gift of redemption, man and woman are called, just as they were "in the beginning," to be the visible sign of God's creative love. Ephesians 5 fully discloses the "great mystery" of this sign, but it "sinks its roots...in the mystery of the creation of man: male and female in the image of God" (379).

If redeemed man, joining as male and female so intimately as to be "one flesh," is called to image God as the visible sign of his creative love, what happens to this "sign" if the spouses rob it of its procreative potential? If the lovers of the Song of Songs proclaim the joy of living the true sign of marital love while Tobiah and Sarah face a test of life and death to reclaim the truth of that sign, what light does this shed on the teaching of *Humanae Vitae?*

91. *Humanae Vitae* and the Truth of the Sacramental Sign

July 11, 1984 (TB 386–388)

As Cardinal Wojtyla wrote in his book *Sources of Renewal,* "The key problem of life as actually lived by Christians is that of the link between faith and morals." We discover "Christian morality understood in all its fullness"—that is, "not only in the field of behavior and its governing norms, but still more in the field of...*ethos*"—only by participating "in the priestly and kingly mission of the Redeemer." Christian morality, therefore, "combines the element of sacrifice, proper to a priesthood, with the kingly element of victory, of man's dominion over himself and the world of nature. These two elements," Wojtyla concludes, "constitute the very root of [Christian] morality."[21]

---

21. *Sources of Renewal,* p. 99.

These two elements—sacrifice and victory—also constitute the root of the teaching of *Humanae Vitae*. Only those willing to embrace the *sacrifice* required by authentic conjugal love will ever taste the *victory* over concupiscence that comes through the redemption of the body. Only through such sacrifice and victory can man and woman's union shine as a transparent sign of God's love in the world. Our long study of John Paul's catechesis on the body shows what is at stake in the Church's teaching on the regulation of births—the very essence of the human vocation to mirror God's love in the world as male and female.

A. The Summit of the Issue

In an essay published soon after the release of *Humanae Vitae*, Wojtyla observed that the teaching of the encyclical hinges on a basic theological proposition concerning conjugal love. Conjugal love takes its origin from God—from the God who has revealed himself to us at one and the same time as "Love" and as "Father."[22] According to Wojtyla, this is "the very summit of the issue. The theological view of conjugal love must lead us to this summit." Thus, Wojtyla observes that Paul VI's encyclical *"responds basically to a single question:* what must conjugal love be like in order to discover God's eternal plan of love in it? Under what conditions does conjugal love reflect its prime exemplar, God as Love and God as Father? This is the level upon which we must consider the entire encyclical and the teaching on conjugal love contained therein."[23]

In this light, before we venture into John Paul II's specific analysis of this most contested encyclical, we will do well to remember the Pope's "key" for interpreting reality: *"Original sin attempts...to abolish fatherhood."*[24] Does not contraception, in a given act of intercourse, attempt to do the same? "Called to give life, spouses share in the creative power and fatherhood of God." Indeed, the "divine fatherhood is the source of human fatherhood."[25]

The question then arises: Can an act of sexual intercourse that the couple renders sterile possibly image and communicate to the world the eternal mystery of God who has revealed himself to us at one and the same time as "Love" and as "Father"? What might this say about the one who is ultimately behind the scheme to sterilize conjugal love? Who is behind the original temptation to "abolish fatherhood"?

---

22. See *Humanae Vitae*, n. 8.

23. "The Teaching of the Encyclical *Humanae Vitae* on Love," *Person & Community: Selected Essays,* pp. 303, 304.

24. *Crossing the Threshold of Hope,* p. 228.

25. *CCC,* nn. 2214, 2367.

B. *Two Inseparable Meanings of the Conjugal Act*

John Paul begins his analysis of *Humanae Vitae* in his audience of July 11, 1984. The Pope's appeal to human subjectivity throughout his catechesis makes it clear that he believes it virtually impossible to explain the Church's teaching on sexual morality without incorporating the way modern men and women think. *Humanae Vitae,* in fact, is one of the first documents of the Church's Magisterium to draw from modern philosophy's "subjective turn" in its approach to married life and conjugal morality. John Paul relates that the Fathers of the Second Vatican Council had already discussed the necessity for a deepened analysis of human subjectivity in this regard.[26] In turn, the Council clearly integrated personalist language into its teaching on marriage.[27] Even prior to that, there were a few seeds of personalism in Pope Pius XI's *Casti Connubii* of 1930.[28] Still, *Humanae Vitae* is the first Magisterial document which attempts to frame a major moral pronouncement in largely personalist terms.

■ Here it is easy to recognize the influence of a certain Polish prelate in the paragraphs of Paul VI's encyclical. In fact, historians and other commentators on Church affairs often credit Karol Wojtyla as the main architect behind *Humanae Vitae*. Papal biographer George Weigel, however—while recognizing Wojtyla's influence—argues that the encyclical did not adopt in full the rich personalist context that Wojtyla proposed to his predecessor. Weigel even suggests that the encyclical might have been better received and the aftermath not so ugly had Paul VI more fully heeded Wojtyla's advice.[29]

Humanae Vitae reaffirms the constant teaching of the universal Church that in each and every marriage act "there must be no impairment of its natural capacity to procreate human life."[30] There is nothing new here. The novelty of Paul VI's encyclical, however, is that it bases this teaching "on the inseparable connection, established by God which man on his own initiative may not break, between the unitive significance and the procreative significance which are both inherent to the marriage act."[31] Without analyzing the whole encyclical, John Paul focuses primarily on this passage.

---

26. See 10/31/84, TB 411.

27. See *Gaudium et Spes,* nn. 47–52.

28. See *Casti Connubii,* n. 24, for example.

29. See *Witness to Hope,* pp. 209–210.

30. *Humanae Vitae,* n. 11. This passage is typically and less accurately translated: "...each and every marriage act must remain open to the transmission of life."

31. Ibid, n. 12.

This new basis of defense for the Church's teaching marks a clear turn to the subject. To focus on the "significance" (or meaning) of the act rather than its "end" is to evaluate the sexual act from the interior perspective of the persons performing it. As Wojtyla wrote in a pre-papal essay, "One can detect in this part of the encyclical *a very significant passage from what some might call a 'theology of nature' to a 'theology of person.'*"[32] The purpose is not to separate "nature" from "person," but to link them in a deep and organic way. In an integral "theology of person," an appeal to the "meaning" of the conjugal act does not imply that persons are free to assign their own meaning to the act. Paul VI avoids the pit of "subjectivism" by linking this subjective turn with objective reality. These two meanings of sexual intercourse, he says, are rooted in "the fundamental structure" of the act and "the actual nature of man and of woman."[33] Through this "fundamental structure" and because of the "actual nature" of the persons engaging in the act, anyone can observe that sexual intercourse both "unites husband and wife in the closest intimacy" and at the same time "makes them capable of generating new life" (387). Logic recognizes both meanings as essential to the integrity of the act as nature (God) designed it. Thus, it logically follows—unless we have a split view of nature and person, body and soul (as most of the "modern world" does, and herein lies the precise problem)—that both meanings of the act are essential to the integrity of the subjects themselves who are performing the act.

Here John Paul insists that morality is not based merely on evaluating an "act" in the abstract. It is based on the truth of the acting person(s) and their dignity.[34] Only persons, in fact, are capable of morality. In evaluating sexual morality "we are dealing with nothing other than reading the 'language of the body' in truth" (388). He also stresses, therefore, that the inseparability of the unitive and procreative meanings of intercourse "is closely connected with our previous reflections on *marriage in its dimension as a (sacramental) sign*" (386). The sacramental sign is based on the faithful and ongoing *incarnation* of the vows freely professed at the altar—vows of fidelity, permanence, and openness to children (see §§83, 84). "In fact, the man and the woman, living in the marriage 'until death,' repropose uninterruptedly," the Pope suggests, "that sign that they made—through the liturgy of the sacrament—on their wedding day" (387).

---

32. "The Teaching of the Encyclical *Humanae Vitae* on Love," *Person & Community: Selected Essays*, p. 308.

33. *Humanae Vitae*, n. 12.

34. It is significant to note that the very first line in the section of the *Catechism* that deals with morality is "Christian, recognize your dignity..." (*CCC,* n. 1691).

C. Signs and Counter-Signs

If all of married life constitutes the sacramental sign, there is also a consummate moment in which spouses renew and express this sign in a very particular way—the moment of the marital embrace. Here couples are called to speak and renew the vows they made at the altar *with their bodies*. As John Paul stresses: "Precisely *at such a moment so rich in significance,* it is also especially important that the 'language of the body' be reread in truth. This reading," he continues, "becomes the indispensable condition for acting in truth, that is, for behaving in accordance with the value of the moral norm" (387). Notice the words "value" and "moral norm." John Paul observes that in Paul VI's encyclical, the Church not only wants to recall an objective moral norm, but also demonstrate its subjective value and foundation. In his theology of the body, John Paul frames the objective truth and the subjective value of the norm in terms of the sacramental sign, that is, in terms of the objective language of the body and its subjective "rereading in truth."

Recall that statement we have repeated several times: We can speak of moral good and evil in the sexual relationship according to "whether or not it has the character of the truthful sign."[35] John Paul reasonably maintains that "the 'language of the body' should express, at a determinate level, the truth of the sacrament. Participating in the eternal plan of love ('Sacrament hidden in God'), the 'language of the body' becomes, in fact, a kind of 'prophetism of the body.'"[36] In other words, the language of the body—throughout all of married life, but especially in the conjugal act—is meant not only to proclaim the mystery of God's life and love, but to enable spouses to participate in it. From this perspective, as professor Mary Rousseau has expressed, morally upright sexual behavior is simply another way of saying "sacramentally efficacious" sexual behavior.[37]

For sacramental signs to be efficacious they must accurately symbolize the spiritual reality they are intended to communicate. The "one flesh" union of husband and wife—inasmuch as it is a sign of Christ's union with the Church (see Eph 5:31–32)—is meant to symbolize "the entire work of creation and redemption."[38] It is meant to be a sign of the Trinitarian mys-

---

35. 8/27/80, TB 141–142.

36. 8/22/84, TB 397.

37. See Mary Rousseau, "Eucharist & Gender" *Catholic Dossier* (September/October, 1996): pp. 19–23. This article is an insightful and provocative treatment of sacramental efficacy as applied to sexual morality and especially the reservation of priestly ordination to men.

38. 10/13/ 82, TB 338–339.

tery hidden in God from all eternity. This is the mystery of eternal life-giving Love and Communion in which man is called to participate through the "great mystery" of Christ's union with the Church—a union that gives life and gives it to the full (see Jn 10:10).

But what does a contracepted act of intercourse—that is, an act of intercourse that the spouses themselves defraud of its procreative potential—do to this sacramental picture? We can certainly argue against contraception purely from natural law (i.e., human reason). But John Paul's catechesis on the body demonstrates the ultimate *theological* reason for the immorality of contraception: it is fundamentally sacrilegious. It profanes the "great mystery"—the "great sacrament" by falsifying the sign.[39] As the Pope says, by virtue of their sacrament, spouses have a divine mission "fundamental for all humanity" to "witness to Love and to Life." But if marital love is falsified "communion is broken, the mission destroyed."[40]

■ In his insightful book *Sex & Sacredness (A Catholic Homage to Venus)* Christopher Derrick frames his entire discussion of sexual morality in terms of the profane and the sacred. In doing so, he takes the insights of John Paul's theology of the body to their logical conclusions. To "profane," he observes, "refers to whatever we find in front of the temple *(pro fanum)*, and therefore outside it, to whatever lacks the religious kind of importance. The 'sacred' will then be whatever *does* have the religious kind of importance." As the Church sees it, sex is supremely sacred. "If the word 'sacrament' means anything at all in this connection," Derrick writes, "it means that the symbolic is here the actual—that God is actively present in the marital bedroom and deeply involved in what happens there.... He's right in there where the action is; and we, on our side, are correspondingly involved with him." In response to the notion that the Church harps disproportionately on sexual sin, Derrick responds that we may well be tempted to commit any number of sins. "But unless we go in for Satanism and the Black Mass, there is only one kind of sin which allures us powerfully and constantly and which (if committed) will involve the profanation of a sacrament." This applies particularly, Derrick believes, to contraception. "In order to avoid the Cross, we shall be separating love from creativity." Contracepted intercourse "will still have a theological meaning. But this will now be Manichaean instead of Christian: we shall be enacting [not faith in Christ, but] the faith of those who denied the possibility of any di-

---

39. See *CCC,* n. 2120.

40. Homily on the Feast of the Holy Family, December 30, 1988.

rect relationship between God's love and the existence of this troubled world. The Venus whom we then serve will be daemonic in the rather specialized sense of being heretical or worse."[41]

Sexual union is not only a *biological* process; it is also a *theological* process. When we override the divine Word written in our bodies with contraception, we speak *against* (we *contra*-dict) the "great mystery" of God's life and love that our bodies were created and redeemed to proclaim. Insert contraception into this sacramental symbol of married love, and (knowingly or unknowingly) a couple engages in a *counter-sign* of the "great mystery" of creation and redemption. Their union becomes an objective *denial* of God's creative and redemptive love. In this way, the objective language of the body turns the spouses (knowingly or unknowingly) into "false prophets." In contracepted intercourse, the language of the body is akin to blasphemy. It speaks not the *symbolic* Word, but the *diabolic* anti-Word (see §5).

Such are the logical, moral, practical, and pastoral conclusions of an authentic theology *of the body*. If we are to embrace our own greatness—our own God-like dignity—as revealed in the Scriptures, we must also embrace the demands incumbent upon our dignity. For those who come to understand the "great mystery" of joining in one flesh, contraception is simply *unthinkable*. As John Paul will say in the course of his reflections: such couples have a "salvific fear" of ever "violating or degrading what bears in itself the sign of the divine mystery of creation and redemption."[42]

92. The Harmony of Authentic Love with Respect For Life
July 11, 18, 25; August 8, 22, 1984 (TB 386–392, 396–399)

John Paul acknowledges that the moral norm taught by *Humanae Vitae* is not found literally in Sacred Scripture. Nonetheless, we find the basis for this teaching in the Scriptures, "especially," the Pope says, "in biblical anthropology." Hence, while some would claim the Bible has little or nothing to say on the matter of contraception, the Holy Father believes that it is "totally reasonable" to look precisely in a biblical "theology of the body" for the foundation of the truth taught by *Humanae Vitae*. Precisely within this full biblical context we realize that the norm upheld by the encyclical

---

41. *Sex & Sacredness*, pp. 23, 97, 99, 100.

42. 11/14/84, TB 416.

belongs not only to the natural moral law, but also, John Paul stresses, "to the *moral order revealed by God"* (389). It is an integral part of the "ethos of redemption." The "the norm of the natural law, based on this 'ethos,' finds not only a new expression, but also a fuller anthropological and ethical foundation in the word of the Gospel and in the purifying and corroborating action of the Holy Spirit" (390).

In other words, the immorality of contraception is not the teaching of men, but the teaching of God, a teaching based on God's revelation. Therefore, as the Magisterium has stated, "This teaching is to be held as definitive and irreformable."[43] It cannot be changed, nor is it open for theological debate. Furthermore, insofar as it is a norm of natural law, it concerns all men and women everywhere—not only members of the Church. Yet the Church, in particular, is called to witness to this norm before men. In this context, John Paul appeals to "every believer and especially every theologian" to "reread and ever more deeply understand the moral doctrine of the encyclical in this complete context" (390). Then he adds that his own catechesis on the body is precisely an attempt at this rereading.

A. Theology of the Body Not Merely a Theory

Having built his theology of the body on the solid foundation of Christ's own words, the Pope concludes: "The theology of the body is not merely a theory, but rather a specific, evangelical, Christian pedagogy of the body" (396). It is an education—and the most suitable method of education—in the meaning of being human.[44]

John Paul says that the importance of the theology of the body derives from its source—the Bible, especially the Gospels and the words of Christ himself. The Gospel, "as the message of salvation, reveals man's true good, for the purpose of modeling...man's earthly life in the perspective of the hope of the future world." This is what the encyclical *Humanae Vitae* proclaims. It points to "the true good of man as a person, male and female" (396). By doing so it shows how the problem of birth regulation can be addressed in a way that corresponds to man's true dignity and lofty vocation.

It is an entirely biblical idea that God has inscribed his own "language," his own Word, in the body in order to reveal his mystery to the world. Every human being proclaims this mystery through his (or her) own body. If we are to be ourselves, we must learn to read this divine

---

43. *Vademecum for Confessors Concerning Some Aspects of the Morality of Conjugal Life,* n. 4.

44. See 4/8/80, TB 215.

body-language "in truth." John Paul says: "It is a question here of the *truth* first *in the ontological dimension* ('fundamental structure') and then—as a result—in the subjective and psychological dimension ('significance')" (388). Here the Pope stresses the primacy of objective reality but also indicates its link with subjective experience. Through this linking, *Humanae Vitae* attempts to demonstrate how its moral norm is not imposed from "outside," but wells up from "within" man. In other words, it is in accord with the deepest truth about man and, hence, his deepest desires.

■ Many would argue that *Humanae Vitae* did not persuasively demonstrate this. It is no injustice to Paul VI to recognize that his personalistic argument, although groundbreaking, needed refinement. But John Paul II's theology of the body compensates in abundance for whatever might have been lacking in Paul VI's argument. It imbues precisely that rich and developed personalism that makes the teaching of *Humanae Vitae* ring true.

Recall that moral norms are not hurled into emptiness (see §37). When we learn to read the objective truth of the body, it then enters the person's consciousness (his subjective dimension) and finds a home there. We are created for truth, and the honest person knows it when he finds it. Demonstrating his trust in people's good will, Paul VI writes: "We believe that our contemporaries are particularly capable of seeing that this teaching [on the immorality of contraception] is in harmony with human reason."[45] John Paul adds that we should also be capable of seeing its profound conformity with all that Tradition has given us, which stems from biblical sources.

B. Development of the Council's Teaching

Many claim that the teaching of *Humanae Vitae* was a step backward from the forward-looking teaching of Vatican II. On the contrary, the Council issued strong statements affirming the constant teaching of the Church on the immorality of contraception. In this context the Council also referenced some of the most authoritative statements of the modern Magisterium in this regard, Pius XI's *Casti Connubii* being first on the list.[46] As John Paul states: *Humanae Vitae* "is not only found to be along the lines of the Council's teaching, but it also constitutes the development and completion of the questions contained there, particularly regarding the question of the 'harmony of human love with respect for life'" (390).

---

45. *Humanae Vitae,* n. 12.

46. See *Gaudium et Spes,* n. 51, endnote 14.

■ Endnote 14 of *Gaudium et Spes* n. 51 reveals part of the reason why so many people were expecting the Church's teaching to change. The Council Fathers stated that they reserved judgment on certain "questions which need further and more careful investigation." These "have been handed over...to a commission for the study of population, family, and births, in order that, after it fulfills its function, the Supreme Pontiff may pass judgment." The point in question was the birth control pill. Faulty natural law arguments that posited the immorality of contraception primarily in the physical obstruction of semen (i.e., barrier methods and withdrawal) found no grounds against the pill. This new historical situation raised new considerations. It also pointed to the need for a renewal in moral theology—away from a physicalist interpretation of natural law to a personalist one. Just such a renewal was already underway in Poland with the guidance of Karol Wojtyla. The personalist understanding of the moral law which he helped develop at the University of Lublin left no doubt about the immorality of the pill. But the Council's tacit admission of uncertainty on this point gave people the idea that the Church was considering a change in her teaching. Indeed, as the familiar story goes, the papal commission rendered a split decision to Paul VI: the majority advocating not only acceptance of the pill, but a complete change in teaching on contraception. In turn, this "majority report" was leaked to the press, fueling false hopes that an unprecedented Catholic about-face was imminent. So a maelstrom of opposition was poised and ready when Paul VI, inspired, we must believe, by the Holy Spirit, saw the wisdom of the "minority report" and issued *Humanae Vitae*.

Perhaps the most common argument for contraception is that it enables couples to foster their love for one another when conception is undesirable. With this argument in mind, John Paul recalls the Council's statement that "a true contradiction cannot exist between the divine laws pertaining to the transmission of life and those pertaining to the fostering of authentic conjugal love."[47] In fact, since the unitive and procreative meanings of the sexual act are truly *inseparable*, if the couple violates one, they also damage the other.

The *raison d'être* of joining in "one flesh" is for the spouses to form a true *communio personarum* in the image of divine Love and Communion. However, as John Paul says, when a couple engages in contracepted intercourse, they may engage in a union of bodies, but they fail to achieve a true communion of persons. In fact, contraception introduces a divorce

---

47. Ibid.

at the very heart of the spouses' body-soul integrity. By doing so, it "strikes at God's creation itself at the level of the deepest interaction of nature and person."[48] If contracepted intercourse claims to express love for the other person, it can only be a *dis*-embodied person. It is not a love of the person for his or her "own sake" (see §19). It is not a love for the person as God created him or her to be in the full truth of masculinity and femininity. Instead, by contracepting, spouses implicitly (or even explicitly) reject the way God made them as persons. More specifically, they reject the God-ordained unity of body and soul. In this way, by attacking the procreative meaning of the sexual act, contracepted intercourse "ceases also to be an act of love" (398).

C. The Essential Evil of Contraception

Truth and love go hand-in-hand. "As ministers of a sacrament which is constituted by consent and perfected by conjugal union, man and woman are called to express that mysterious 'language' of their bodies in all the truth which is proper to it." At this point the Holy Father presents his most vivid image of sexual love: "By means of gestures and reactions, by means of the whole dynamism, reciprocally conditioned, of tension and enjoyment—whose direct source is the body in its masculinity and its femininity, the body in its action and interaction—by means of all this, man, the person, 'speaks'" (397–398).

What does the body-person say? Based on the Pope's teaching on the prophetism of the body we can conclude that if the husband loves his wife "as Christ loved the Church," he says: "This is my body which is given for you" (Lk 22:19). And if the wife responds in love to her husband as the Church responds to Christ, she says (as the model of the Church says): "Let it be done to me according to your word" (Lk 1:38). By speaking this prophetic language honestly, spouses faithfully and continually minister their sacrament to each other in the true image of the union of Christ and the Church. By joining in "one flesh" in this way "man and woman reciprocally express themselves in the fullest and most profound way possible to them." They "express themselves in the measure of the whole truth of the human person" (398). Then the whole "dynamism of tension and enjoyment" which they experience is a participation in the joy Christ promised when we love as he loves (see Jn 15:11). Indeed, the whole dynamism of tension and enjoyment is a vehicle of the Holy Spirit, a participation in divine life, the very grace of the sacrament of marriage.

---

48. *Familiaris Consortio,* n. 32.

But insert contraception into this picture and it changes everything. Void of the sincere gift of self, the whole dynamism of tension and enjoyment becomes an end in itself rather than a fruit of love. In the final analysis, contracepted intercourse amounts to little more than an act of mutual (or at least one-sided) use and self-seeking. In this regard, contracepted intercourse is closer to an act of (mutual) masturbation than to an act of spousal love and self-donation.

Rendering the sexual union sterile effectively scrambles the sacramental language of the body. Continuing with the above image, by refusing to give his own potency, the husband declares: "This is my body *not* given for you." And by denying the fruitfulness of her own womb, the wife declares: "Let it *not* be done to me according to your word." Right at the great mystery's "moment of truth," the truth is exchanged for a lie. Far from imaging the union of Christ and the Church, in some sense contracepted intercourse becomes a "counter-sign" of the great mystery—we might even say an *"anti-*sacrament."

Is this not the deceiver's goal from the beginning? The father of lies wants us to speak his own language! He wants the Word of the Gospel inscribed in our bodies (self-donation) to become his anti-word (self-gratification). He wants us to *lie* with our bodies. According to the Holy Father: "Such a violation of the interior order of the conjugal union, which is rooted in the very order of the person, constitutes the essential evil of the contraceptive act" (398). He adds that the reflections on the "sign" of marriage as a sacrament are of "special validity for this interpretation" (399).

■ In an address entitled "The Church: a Bride Adorned for Her Husband," John Paul contrasted the biblical, feminine figure of Christ's Bride with "the hostile and furious presence of another female figure, 'Babylon,' the 'great harlot' (see Rev 17:1, 5)." John Paul points out a major difference between the two: the Bride of Christ (the Church) "is endowed with an inner fruitfulness by which she constantly brings forth children of God.... These are the children who form that 'assembly of the first-born who are enrolled in heaven.'" Thus, in union with the Holy Spirit (the Lord and Giver of Life), the Bride cries, "Come, Lord Jesus!" (Rev 22:20) In contrast, John Paul says we recognize the "great whore" of Babylon as the one who embodies "death and inner barrenness." With an understanding of the symbolic language of the body gained from John Paul's catechesis on the body, we might ask which figure from Revelation does contracepted intercourse symbolize—the life-giving Bride of Christ, or the adulterous one who *chooses* barrenness? The desire to avoid a pregnancy (when there is sufficient reason to do so) is not what vitiates contracepted intercourse. What vitiates the act is the specific choice to *render sterile* a potentially fertile union. This changes entirely (*contra*-dicts) the symbolic meaning of the act. When spouses have sufficient reason to avoid a pregnancy, it is entirely possible to do so without ever rendering a potentially fertile act sterile, without ever adulterating the sacramental meaning of the act.

93. *Humanae Vitae:* A Call to Liberation and Responsible Parenthood

July 25; August 1, 22, 1984 (TB 392–394, 397)

Marriage is the primordial sacrament of God's eternal mystery in the world. God gives it to us as a gift—as a means of entering a covenant relationship not only with an earthly spouse, but also with him. But God does not force us to participate in the marriage covenant according to his designs. He sets forth his designs in creation and confirms them in Christ and in the teachings of his Church. Then he places us in the freedom of our own counsel.

A. Interpreting the Eternal Plan of Love

As John Paul says, God calls every husband and wife "to be a witness and interpreter of the eternal plan of love" (397). These expressions indicate a profound and even stunning act of entrustment on God's part. God places the primordial revelation of his own mystery in human hands and then he "lets go." In turn, every couple interprets this mystery—faithfully or unfaithfully—"by becoming the minister of the sacrament which 'from the beginning' was constituted by the sign of the 'union of flesh'" (397).

Why such self-abandoned trust on God's part? He knows we will be unfaithful to his plan. Yes, but he also knows that a spark of our "beatifying beginning" remains despite the distortions of concupiscence, and he is always looking for ways to fan that spark into flame. The trusting gift of self is the only way to "revive" our authentic humanity. He is willing to take that risk of entrusting himself to us even if we take advantage of that trust: even if we shun him—*even if we crucify him*—in his very act of entrustment. Some might ask: "Why does God even give us the possibility of spoiling his plan?" Here again we contemplate the mystery of human freedom. If we did not have the ability to forsake God's plan—to twist, distort, and malign it—we would not have the ability to enter into it. For love to be love, it must be free. In other words, as discussed previously, without the possibility of sin there is no possibility of love (see §§12, 25, 42).

Every time a husband and wife form that "sign" of the union of flesh, God is wooing them to open up to him and his eternal designs. But if a husband and wife are detached from that "spark" of God's original plan, they will have difficulty recognizing that their sexual union is a "sign" of anything beyond their own desire for a gratifying experience of shared pleasure. They will want to call this "love," but in reality, what is often called love, "if subjected to searching critical examination turns out to be, contrary to all appearances, only a form of 'utilization' of the person"[49] stemming from concupiscence. When man and woman are cut off from their own dignity and lofty calling, concupiscent "love" seems quite normal to them. Sadly, it may be all they know and all they have ever known. Such a couple may desire a few children along the way. But prior to that, or once they have the desired number, they will almost inevitably view contraception or even surgical sterilization as the most expedient way to continue "loving" one another without fear of an "unwanted pregnancy."[50] If they are Catholic, they will probably brush off the Church's teaching as "out of touch," impractical, and not "pastoral."

B. True Pastoral Concern

John Paul II responds to such accusations by defining the true nature of pastoral concern. "Pastoral concern," he insists, "means the search for the true good of man, a promotion of the values engraved in his person by God." In this context, there is indeed a "rule of understanding." But this does not consist in watering down the true dignity of man. Instead, the rule of understanding "is directed to the ever clearer discovery of God's plan for human love, in the certitude that the only true good of the human person consists in fulfilling this divine plan" (392).

John Paul remarks that whoever believes that *Humanae Vitae* does not sufficiently take into account the difficulties present in concrete life

---

49. *Love & Responsibility*, p. 167.

50. Dr. William E. May is keen to point out that the slogan of contraception and abortion proponents is "No unwanted child ought ever to be born." However, the truth proclaimed by the Church in the name of Christ is that "No person ought to be unwanted" (see The John Paul II Institute 1993–1995 Academic Catalogue, p. 41). This sums up well the disparity between secular and Christian humanisms.

does not understand the pastoral concern at the origin of the document. Throughout his encyclical, Paul VI is solicitous of the real problems and questions of modern man in all their import and states explicitly that he has no desire to pass over these concerns in silence. He acknowledges that some might find the encyclical's teaching "gravely difficult" if not "impossible to observe." He states plainly, in fact, that men and women cannot live this teaching "unless God came to their help with that grace by which the good will of men is sustained and strengthened."[51] If God makes serious demands on us, at the same time he pours out all the grace needed for men and women not only to meet those demands, but fulfill them super-abundantly.

Paul VI's choice was either to trust in God's grace, or to compromise the truth. What is the truly loving, the truly "pastoral" thing to do? As Paul VI stated in his encyclical: "To diminish in no way the saving teaching of Christ constitutes an eminent form of charity for souls."[52] *Humanae Vitae,* in fact, is nothing other than a call for men and women to embrace their own "greatness"—to embrace the full truth of what it means to be created in the image and likeness of God and redeemed in Jesus Christ. Is this not pastoral? Is this impractical? Is this only an ideal that needs to be adjusted in light of man's concrete possibilities? We have already recorded John Paul's response to this question:

> But what are "the concrete possibilities of man"? And of *which* man are we speaking? Of man *dominated* by lust or of man *redeemed by Christ?* This is what is at stake: the *reality* of Christ's redemption. *Christ has redeemed us!* This means he has given us the possibility of realizing the *entire truth* of our being; he has set our freedom free from the *domination* of concupiscence. And if redeemed man still sins, this is not due to an imperfection of Christ's redemptive act, but to man's will not to avail himself of the grace which flows from that act. God's command is of course proportioned to man's capabilities; but to the capabilities of the man to whom the Holy Spirit has been given; of the man who, though he has fallen into sin, can always obtain pardon and enjoy the presence of the Holy Spirit.[53]

---

51. See *Humanae Vitae,* nn. 3, 20, 25.

52. *Humanae Vitae,* n. 29.

53. *Veritatis Splendor,* n. 103 (emphasis in original).

Humanae Vitae, then, is a call to faith in the *real power* of redemption. It is a call to a radical paradigm shift in which we listen attentively to that "echo" of God's original plan deep within us and refuse to normalize concupiscence. Yes, *Humanae Vitae,* so often viewed as oppressive, calls us to liberation! It calls us to live in the true freedom of love. It calls us to respond to the unreserved gift God gives to us with the unreserved gift of ourselves to him.

C. Responsible Parenthood

Does this mean that couples are to leave the number of children they have entirely to "chance"? No. Both the teaching of Vatican II and *Humanae Vitae,* in calling couples to a responsible love, call them also to a responsible parenthood.

As John Paul II expresses, "responsible parenthood requires that husband and wife, 'keeping a right order of priorities, recognize their own duties toward God, themselves, their families and society' (*HV,* 10). One cannot therefore speak of 'acting arbitrarily.' On the contrary the married couple 'must act in conformity with God's creative intention' (*HV,* 10)" (394). This, of course, implies a mature ability on the part of husband and wife to discern God's intention for the size of their family. The counsel of a priest or spiritual director can certainly assist them in this regard. However, the Church wisely teaches that it "is the married couple *themselves* who must in the last analysis arrive at these judgments before God."[54] No one else can make this judgment for them. And John Paul states that this point is "of particular importance to determine...the moral character of 'responsible parenthood'" (393).

The Council limits the guidance it gives to couples to the following: Husband and wife should consider "their own good and the good of the children already born or yet to come." They should "read the signs of the times and of their own situation on the material and spiritual level." Finally, they should consider "the good of the family, of society, and of the Church."[55] One couple might prudently make these considerations and choose to have a large family. Another couple might prudently make these considerations and choose to limit their family size. So long as both couples are acting in a way that respects the meaning of sexual union—in a way that never falsifies the language of the body—the Church teaches that they are *both* exercising responsible parenthood.[56]

---

54. *Gaudium et Spes,* n. 50; emphasis added.

55. Ibid.

56. See *Humanae Vitae,* n. 10.

94. The Natural Regulation of Births

August 1, 8, 22, 1984 (TB 393–399)

It is a myth that the Catholic Church teaches that couples must have as many children as is physically possible. The Church readily recognizes, particularly in our day and age, that in the course of married life couples might have just reason to avoid a pregnancy. As John Paul points out, *Humanae Vitae* admits that even those who use contraception can be motivated by "acceptable reasons" for avoiding pregnancy. However, the Holy Father also emphasizes that the end never justifies the means. Contraception remains a grievous violation of the sacramental sign of married love regardless of the motives for using it. In this context John Paul refers to the following teaching of the Council:

> When it is a question of harmonizing married love with the responsible transmission of life, it is not enough to take only the good intention and the evaluation of motives into account; objective criteria must be used, criteria drawn from the nature of the human person and human action, criteria which respect the total meaning of mutual self-giving and human procreation in the context of true love; all this is possible only if the virtue of married chastity is seriously practiced.[57]

"The relative principle of conjugal morality is, therefore, fidelity to the divine plan manifested in the 'intimate structure of the conjugal act' and in the 'inseparable connection of the two significances of the conjugal act'" (394).

B. Non-Procreative versus Anti-Procreative

Suppose a couple has just reasons for avoiding a pregnancy. What could they possibly do that would in no way violate the objective meaning of conjugal intercourse?

Every time a couple engages in the marital embrace they must speak the language of their bodies in truth. In other words, they must renew honestly (with their bodies) the commitments they freely made at the altar—commitments of fidelity, permanence, and openness to children. But are couples always obligated to engage in intercourse? Indeed, on various occasions in life a couple may have good reason to refrain from intercourse. In such cases, abstinence itself becomes an expression of love. The need to avoid a pregnancy is just such an occasion. In itself, refraining from marital union to avoid a pregnancy in no way violates the truth of intercourse as a "sign." In order actively and directly to violate the sign of intercourse, you must first engage in it. Only then can you defraud it of its meaning.

---

57. *Gaudium et Spes*, n. 51.

Furthermore, what if a couple who were abstaining from intercourse to avoid a pregnancy were to discover—based on the very way God designed human fertility—that an act of intercourse on a given day would be naturally infertile. Would they be doing anything that objectively violated the sign of conjugal union by engaging in intercourse then? Would they be contracepting? In other words, would they be doing anything to impede the procreative potential of that act of intercourse?

Herein lies the specific moral difference between contraception and the natural means of regulating fertility. It is true, as *Humanae Vitae* recognizes, that "in each case married couples, for acceptable reasons, are both perfectly clear in their intention to avoid children." Paul VI even states that "they mean to make sure none will be born."[58] However, in the one case, infertile intercourse is an act of God. In the other case, the couple take the powers of life into their own hands with the intent of thwarting God's creative designs.

Anyone who thinks the moral difference here is a matter of splitting hairs must answer the following question. What is the moral difference between a miscarriage and an abortion? The result is the same—a dead baby. But one is an "act of God," and in the other, man takes the powers of life into his own hands. As John Paul says elsewhere: "Contraception is to be judged so profoundly unlawful as never to be, for any reason, justified. To think or to say the contrary is equal to maintaining that in human life, situations may arise in which it is lawful not to recognize God as God."[59]

Married couples who recognize God as God realize, as Paul VI points out, that they are not the masters of the sources of life, but rather the ministers of the design established by the Creator.[60] As Creator, God calls married couples to be *procreative* (see Gen 1:28). Spouses may at times have a just reason to be *non*-procreative. But it would violate the very essence of married love to be *anti*-procreative. Abstaining from intercourse and engaging in naturally infertile intercourse are both *non*-procreative behaviors. In this way, as *Humanae Vitae* states, couples can "control birth without offending moral principles."[61] However, to render an act of intercourse infertile is to engage in *anti*-procreative behavior. One harmonizes with the nature of man and of marital love, while the other grievously contradicts both.

---

58. *Humanae Vitae,* n. 16.

59. *L'Osservatore Romano,* October 10, 1983, p. 7.

60. See *Humanae Vitae,* n. 13.

61. Ibid, n. 16.

■ We speak of "natural" family planning (NFP) specifically because of this—it harmonizes with the *nature* of man and of marital intercourse. NFP is morally acceptable not because it is not "artificial," but because it is not contraceptive. Couples who use NFP morally *never* impede the procreative potential of any of their acts of intercourse. In this way, the value of the "sign" of intercourse remains objectively intact. Likewise, artificial birth control is not immoral *because* it is artificial, but because it is contraceptive—because it objectively violates the sign. In my opinion, the term "artificial" should be dropped from the discussion altogether as it only confuses the issue. Most confusing of all is the phrase "artificial contraception," as it implies that NFP is somehow "natural contraception." NFP is not contraception at all! This, in fact, is the key distinction.

B. Two Irreconcilable Views of the Person

Some object that the Church's teaching reduces morality to the laws of biology. Faulty and impersonal interpretations of natural law may merit such an accusation. However, when the accusation of "biologism" is leveled outright against the Church's teaching on the proper regulation of births, it conceals within itself a pernicious vision of the human being which effectively divorces body and soul.

As John Paul wrote in *Familiaris Consortio*: "The difference, both anthropological and moral, between contraception and recourse to the rhythm of the cycle...is much wider and deeper than is usually thought, one which involves in the final analysis two irreconcilable concepts of the human person and of human sexuality."[62] In the one view, the body—including its fertility—is seen as integral to the person and, hence, as integral to self-giving love. In the other view, the body is seen as part of the realm of sub-human "nature" over which the person has dominion. From the latter perspective, man sees no moral problem in applying the same techniques of dominion to his body and fertility which he exerts over the forces of nature. In fact, doing so is necessary, they say, in order to "humanize" the processes of reproduction.[63] But such language betrays a radical divorce between the physical and the personal in man.

---

62. *Familiaris Consortio*, n. 32.

63. The "majority report" of what came to be dubbed the "papal birth control commission" used precisely such language. In seeking to justify contraception it spoke of "the duty to humanize...what is given in nature." For "it is natural to man to use his skill in order to put under human control what is given by physical nature." The processes of fertility do not need to be "humanized." They are *already* fully human!

We have previously quoted the Holy Father saying that the "whole development of modern science...is based on the separation, in man, of that which is corporeal in him, from that which is spiritual."[64] In his *Letter to Families* John Paul writes: "The separation of spirit and body in man has led to a growing tendency to consider the human body not in accordance with...its specific likeness to God, but rather on the basis of its similarity to all the other bodies present in the world of nature, bodies which man uses as raw material in his efforts to produce goods for consumption." (We engineer tomatoes and cattle to suit our preferences. Why not engineer our own bodies?) John Paul concludes: "When the human body...comes to be used as *raw material* in the same way that the bodies of animals are used...we will inevitably arrive at a dreadful ethical defeat."[65]

Humanae Vitae stands as a constant reminder that "biological laws... involve human personality."[66] When we tinker with the human body, we tinker not just with laws of biology, but with human persons in their body-soul integrity. Marital love and responsible parenthood require that spouses come to embrace the harmony of biology and personality. Dominion over the "forces of nature," when applied to the important question of regulating births, must never mean obliterating some integral aspect of human nature and personality. The only proper "dominion" to speak of in this case is that of self-mastery of one's drives and desires. Unfortunately, as John Paul observes, modern man shows a tendency to transfer the methods proper to the dominion of drives and desires to the domination of his physical constitution. Man looks to dominate his biology through medicine and technology in an attempt to dodge the ascetic effort required by spiritual and moral responsibility.

In fact, according to John Paul, the essence of the Church's teaching on contraception lies right here—in maintaining an adequate relationship between dominion of the forces of nature and mastery of self. Without self-mastery, man puts his intelligence at the service of manipulation rather than love. In turn, when intelligence is no longer informed by love, it exults in what it *can* do rather than in what it *should* do. Man comes to relate to himself and to all of creation not with loving care and respect, but with a selfish will to dominate and control. Man's proper dominion over creation, therefore, always begins with a proper understanding and experience of self-mastery in the male-female relationship. Man's freedom—or

---

64. 4/8/81, TB 215.

65. *Letter to Families,* n. 19.

66. *Humanae Vitae,* n. 10.

lack thereof—to choose the good in his sexual life will always reveal the manner in which he exercises dominion over creation. Our study of Genesis already revealed the profound interrelationship between the male-female communion and human dominion over the earth (see §11).

C. Self-Mastery and the Freedom of the Gift

Paul VI acknowledges that man "has made stupendous progress in the domination and rational organization of the forces of nature to the point that he is endeavoring to extend this control over every aspect of his own life—over his body, over his mind and emotions, over his social life, and even over the laws that regulate the transmission of life."[67] Yet John Paul asserts that dominating the natural processes of fertility through contraception "menaces the human person for whom the method of 'self-mastery' is and remains specific." Self-mastery corresponds to the fundamental constitution of the person as a subject. In this sense exercising self-mastery is a "natural" method of birth regulation because it is "natural" to man to be in control of his own drives and desires. Resorting to contraception, on the contrary, "destroys the constitutive dimension of the person; it deprives man of the subjectivity proper to him and makes him an object of manipulation" (397).

In other words, the only type of "birth control" in keeping with human dignity is self-control. Why do we spay or neuter our pets? Precisely because they cannot say no to the urge to mate. We can. If we say otherwise we deny our original solitude before God. We deny that which distinguishes us from the animals. We deny our dignity as subjects. We deny the essence of our humanity. As the Pope observes: "Man is precisely a person because he is master of himself and has self-control. Indeed, insofar as he is master of himself he can 'give himself' to the other. And it is this dimension—the dimension of the liberty of the gift—which becomes essential and decisive for that 'language of the body,' in which man and woman reciprocally express themselves in the conjugal union" (398).[68]

Without self-mastery, no true gift of self takes place, but only something akin to the mating of animals. In other words, if one cannot say "no" to sexual intercourse, his "yes" is emptied of its meaning. He is no different from the animals and he cannot express love. All he can do is indulge concupiscence (see §27). The man who fails to master himself—to master his own drives and desires—will inevitably seek to master others in order to satisfy those drives and desires. Manipulation replaces love.

---

67. *Humanae Vitae,* n. 2.
68. See *CCC,* n. 2339.

From this perspective, a little-recognized fact comes to light. In the final analysis, contraception was not invented to prevent pregnancy. We already had a perfectly safe, infallibly reliable way of doing that: abstinence. Certainly other motives came into play, but ultimately, if necessity is the mother of invention, the "necessity" that mothered contraception was the desire to indulge sexual instinct without restraint—without abstinence. This can only stem from concupiscence.

In these ways we see how John Paul's defense of *Humanae Vitae* plunges its roots deep into the soil of the garden of Eden—into the truth of man's original solitude, unity, and nakedness which empowered him to image God as a subject in the freedom of self-giving love. This is the "full truth" about man, the truth he must reclaim if he is ever to be himself. And contraception attacks this truth at its roots.

■ Magisterial statements on what constitutes responsible parenthood provide the appropriate balance sometimes lacking in various circles of those who accept the Church's teaching against contraception. In general, there seem to be two poles in a "mentality conflict" among such people. One pole seems to minimize the necessity of having just reasons to avoid pregnancy, while the other seems to think that couples are obligated to procreate unless avoiding pregnancy is a matter of life and death. The primary danger of the former mentality is that of selfishness in avoiding children.[69] Couples with the latter mentality, however, may end up practicing another less obvious form of selfishness. Large families are often the result of prudent consideration and selfless giving. Other times, however, large families may be a result of the couple's lack of freedom to abstain from intercourse. Self-mastery is an absolute prerequisite of authentic conjugal love. This is why the practice of periodic continence is such an aid to marital love. The freedom to say "no" demonstrates the authenticity of the couple's "yes." Thus, even if a couple has prudently concluded that they have no serious reason to avoid pregnancy, occasional periods of abstinence should be practiced (obviously these need not be during the fertile period) in order to foster authentic freedom in self-giving. The point is that parenthood can only be considered "responsible" when either the choice to avoid intercourse during the fertile time, or the choice to engage in it, is free of any selfish sting.

---

69. See *CCC,* n. 2368.

95. The Integral Vision of Natural Fertility Regulation
August 22, 28; September 5; October 3, 31, 1984 (397–405, 411–412)

If we are to understand how natural fertility regulation differs substantially from contraception, we must have an "integral vision of man" and of his vocation. We must understand who man is as a person made in God's image as male and female. We must understand who man is as a subject created "for his own sake," who can only find himself through "the sincere gift of himself."

Safeguarding these anthropological truths is the *raison d'être* of the encyclical *Humanae Vitae*. For contraception directly attacks the truth that man is created in God's image and likeness. It directly attacks man's subjectivity and his call to sincere self-giving. Yes, the very identity of man is at stake in the debate about contraception. Contraception is a betrayal of our humanity.

A. Naturalness at the Level of the Person

The Holy Father insists that the "whole question of the encyclical *Humanae Vitae*...goes back to the very subjectivity of man" (411). Anyone would certainly misinterpret the encyclical who would see in "responsible parenthood" merely a reduction to a "biological rhythm of fertility." John Paul insists that the "author of the encyclical energetically disapproves of and contradicts any form of reductive interpretation...and insistently reproposes the integral intention" (404–405).

When we view the issue of birth regulation with this "integral intention"—that is, with an understanding of man's incarnate subjectivity—we realize that this "question belongs not so much to biology as to psychology: from biology and psychology it then passes into the sphere of the spirituality of marriage and the family" (411–412). It passes into the sphere of religion and theology—a theology that seeks God's revelation in the body. John Paul observes that without this perspective, the method of natural birth regulation is frequently separated from its proper ethical dimensions and is, therefore, put into effect in a merely functional, even utilitarian, way. In this situation "one no longer sees the difference between it and the other 'methods'...and one comes to the point of speaking of it as if it were only a different form of contraception" (403).

Such is the case when the "naturalness" of natural birth regulation is viewed only at the level of biology. But the integral vision recognizes, as John Paul insists, that "this is 'naturalness' at the level of the person. Therefore there can be no thought of a mechanical application of biological laws. The knowledge itself of the 'rhythms of fertility'—even though indispensable—still does not create the interior freedom of the gift which is [needed] to make possible the giving of self to the other."[70] The call to regain this interior freedom is at the heart of *Humanae Vitae's* integral vision of natural birth regulation.

B. Personalist Interpretation of Natural Law

Being free with the interior freedom of the gift is man's natural state. It was man's state "in the beginning." The call to regain this freedom—inherent in the encyclical *Humanae Vitae*—is also inherent in John Paul's personalist understanding of the natural law.[71]

The natural law is often confused with the "laws of nature." The laws of nature pertain to those laws which govern irrational beings, whereas natural law pertains to man's rational participation in the divine law.[72] Thus, in speaking of the teaching of *Humanae Vitae* as a norm of the natural law, "we mean that 'order of nature' in the field of procreation insofar as it is understood by right reason" (401). Linking the objective truth of natural law with the modern "turn to the subject," John Paul stresses that the natural law refers to "man not only in the 'natural' aspect of his existence, but also in the integral truth of his personal subjectivity" (397). The order of the natural law "is the expression of the Creator's plan for man." Hence, the Holy Father states that the virtue expressed in natural fertility regulation is determined not so much by fidelity to an impersonal "natural law" but by fidelity "to the Creator-Person, the source and Lord of the order which is manifested in such a law" (401).

Although John Paul himself does not explicitly point this out, we see here a link between the natural law and the sacramentality of the body. The body reveals the mystery and plan of God for man. This plan, inscribed in our bodies, is only impersonal if our bodies are impersonal. But the body is the "sacrament" of the person. Furthermore, in Christ, the human body is the sacrament of the divine Person of the Word. Thus, from the perspective of the theology of the body, the natural law is anything but impersonal. It is the law of the gift. It is the law of the freedom of the gift of persons. In other words, it is the law of life-giving love written in our persons by a personal God who destines us for the communion of persons—human and divine. John Paul repeats that from this perspective, the reduction to a mere biological regularity, separated from the Creator's plan, deforms the authentic thought of the encyclical *Humanae Vitae*.

---

70. 11/7/84, TB 414.

71. See *CCC*, nn. 1954–1960.

72. See *CCC*, n. 1955.

So, in the case of conforming to the natural law in regulating fertility, the Pope emphasizes that it is not a question of "reducing ethics to biology," as some have mistakenly held. It "is a question of *the real good of human persons and of what corresponds to the true dignity of the person*" (402).

C. Having a Procreative Attitude

The integral intention of natural fertility regulation also presupposes of spouses "a definite family and procreative attitude: that is to say, it requires 'that they acquire and possess solid convictions about the true values of life and of the family' (*HV,* 21)" (399–400). In a contraceptive culture, children are often looked upon as a burden to be resisted rather than a blessing to be embraced. In such a milieu, couples often enter marriage with an attitude toward children that assumes they will not have them *unless* or *until* they "want" them. Without thinking much of it, couples who take this approach will simply look for the most expedient way to carry out their plan of avoiding "unwanted" children.

Suppose such a couple chose to use the natural method of avoiding pregnancy. This would not correspond to *Humanae Vitae's* integral vision of responsible parenthood. Although they would not objectively violate the value of the sign of conjugal intercourse, they would violate that sign subjectively. They would violate that sign "in their hearts." The Holy Father clarifies: "As regards the immediate motivation, the encyclical *Humanae Vitae* requires that 'there exist reasonable grounds for spacing births, arising from the physical or psychological condition of husband or wife, or from external circumstances...' (*HV,* 16)" (400). John Paul II concludes: "The use of the 'infertile periods' for conjugal union can be an abuse if the couple, for unworthy reasons, seeks in this way to avoid having children, thus lowering the number of births in their family below the morally correct level" (402).

"*Humanae Vitae* presents 'responsible parenthood' as a high ethical value. In no way is it exclusively directed to limiting, much less excluding children; it means also the willingness to accept a larger family" (402). The integral vision of natural fertility regulation, then, does not involve merely a "mode of behavior" in a certain field. It involves an attitude based on the integral moral maturity of the spouses. John Paul says that this morally mature attitude can be described in biblical terms as "living by the Spirit." He then adds that confusion arises about the difference between contraception and periodic abstinence precisely when this moral maturity is lacking. Herein lies the importance of the theology of the body understood as a pedagogy of the body. Instruction in the truth of the body and its language of divine-human love fosters just such moral maturity in men and women.

■ The following analogy may demonstrate not only the important moral distinction between contraception and natural fertility regulation, but also the necessary moral attitude that must accompany the integral intention of natural family planning. Our natural attitude toward others should be one that desires their life and good health. Circumstances, however, could lead us to have a righteous desire for God to call someone on to the next life. Suppose an elderly relative was suffering greatly with age and disease. You could have a noble desire for his passing. It is one thing in such a situation to suffer with your loved one while waiting patiently for his natural death. In such a situation there would be nothing blameworthy even to be grateful for his death when it occurred. This would be akin to having a righteous desire to avoid a pregnancy, waiting until the naturally infertile time to consummate your marriage, and even rejoicing that God has granted a time of infertility. But, returning to the elderly relative, it would be quite another thing to take the powers of life into your own hands and kill him because you cannot bear his sufferings. This would be akin to rendering yourself sterile because you cannot bear the suffering of abstinence. Taking this analogy a step further, it is also possible that your desire for your relative's death might be unrighteous. You may have some sort of hatred toward him that would lead you to wish him dead. You may not kill him yourself, indeed he may die of a natural cause, but nonetheless your rejoicing in his death would be blameworthy. This is akin to a couple who uses natural family planning with an unrighteous desire to avoid a pregnancy. Their rejoicing in the infertile time would also be blameworthy because it is motivated by a selfish, anti-child mentality.

"The concept of a morally correct regulation of fertility is nothing other than the rereading of the 'language of the body' in truth." And, as John Paul continues: "It is necessary to bear in mind that the 'body speaks' not merely with the whole external expression of masculinity and femininity, but also with the internal structures of the organism." Perhaps the most decisive "internal structure" of the human body-person is his and her fertility and the preparedness of the woman's womb to bear new life. "All this should find its appropriate place in that language in which husband and wife dialogue with each other, as persons called to the communion of 'the union of the body'" (402).

In this way the Pope observes that the theology of the body, understood as the pedagogy of the body, leads to the "theology of the family." In other words, when we understand the meaning of the body as a theology, we understand that its potential procreativity—its potential to establish or increase the family—is an integral part of the body's capacity to image and participate in the creative love of God. Hence, the theology of the family flows directly from the theology of the body.

96. Outline of an Authentic Marital Spirituality

October 3, 1984 (TB 404–406)

By demonstrating the evil of contraception and by outlining a responsible means of regulating fertility, *Humanae Vitae* outlines the Christian spirituality of marriage and family life. Conjugal spirituality consists first in understanding God's plan for the body, marriage, and sexual union. Secondly, it consists in opening one's flesh—and the "one flesh" spouses become—to the *in*-spiration of the Spirit who empowers spouses to live according to their great dignity and lofty vocation. John Paul reminds us that authentic marital spirituality can only be lived if spouses bear in mind the whole doctrine on chastity understood as the life of the Spirit (see Gal 5:25).[73]

John Paul has been developing precisely these themes in his catechesis on the body. Therefore, as he concludes, education in the theology of the body ("theology-pedagogy") "already constitutes *per se* the essential nucleus of conjugal spirituality" (404).

A. Christian Realism

According to John Paul, the feasibility of the norm confirmed by *Humanae Vitae* "constitutes one of the most essential questions (and currently also one of the most urgent ones) in the sphere of the spirituality of marriage."[74] Many people, in light of their own weaknesses, look at this teaching as hopelessly unrealistic. Paul VI, as a faithful witness to Christ, wants to reassure his readers that God's power is made perfect in weakness (see 2 Cor 12:9). He proclaims that through the Sacrament of Matrimony spouses "are strengthened and...consecrated to the faithful fulfillment of their duties; to realizing to the full their vocation." In this way spouses bear witness "to Christ before the world."[75]

This "strength" and "consecration," as John Paul emphasizes, is none other than *"the love planted in the heart* ('poured out into our hearts') *by the Holy Spirit"* (405). And the "sketch of conjugal spirituality" found in *Humanae Vitae* intends to place in relief precisely those "powers" which make the authentic Christian witness of married life a living possibility.

---

73. See 8/28/84, TB 400 (§§41, 81).

74. 10/31/84, TB 411.

75. *Humanae Vitae*, n. 25.

Humanae Vitae is certainly aware of man's weaknesses, but it does not base its conclusions on them. To do so would empty the cross of its power. To do so would drain Christianity of its life-blood. *Humanae Vitae* bases its conclusions on the *reality* of the power of God that has been poured into our hearts through Christ's death and resurrection. This is authentic *Christian* realism. As John Paul observes, *Humanae Vitae's* view of married life is marked at every step by such realism. *Humanae Vitae* preaches Christ crucified—a stumbling block to Jews and foolishness to Gentiles. But to those whom God has called, *Humanae Vitae* proclaims the wisdom and power of God (see 1 Cor 1:23–24). It calls Christ's followers to take up their crosses and travel on the narrow path of salvation (see Mt 7:14).

Can men and women live the teaching of *Humanae Vitae* relying on their own resources? A realistic assessment of human weaknesses says "no." But to whom is this teaching given? To men and women who remain slaves to their weaknesses, or to men and women who have been set free by Jesus Christ to love as he loves? As Christ says in the verses following his discourse on the "one flesh" union: "With men this is impossible, but with God all things are possible" (Mt 19:26). As both Paul VI and John Paul II remind us, the Church does not only lay down the demands of God's law and then leave men and women to their own resources in attempting to carry it out. The Church "'is also the herald of salvation and through the sacraments she flings wide open the channels of grace through which man is made a new creature.'" In his new creation man can respond "'in charity and true freedom to the design of his Creator and Savior, experiencing too the sweetness of the yoke of Christ'...(*HV,* 25)" (404).

Here our previous reflections on the ethos of redemption are most pertinent. Ultimately the teaching of *Humanae Vitae* is a question of faith. Do we believe in the gift of God? Do we believe that Christ died and rose again to free us from our sins and empower us to live according to God's original plan? Do we believe that the Holy Spirit—the very power and love of God—has been poured into our hearts? These could not be more crucial questions with which to confront men and women, husbands and wives, of today. To fault the Church for her teaching in *Humanae Vitae* is to fault the Church for calling men and women to holiness—to faith in the Gospel of Jesus Christ.

Let us recall John Paul II's definition of faith: *"faith,* in its deepest essence, is *the openness* of the human heart to the gift: *to God's self-communication in the Holy Spirit."*[76] Without such faith, it is impossible to live an authentic marital spirituality. And without an authentic marital spirituality

---

76. *Dominum et Vivificantem,* n. 51.

it's impossible to live the teaching of *Humanae Vitae*. But with such faith, men and women can move mountains (see Mt 17:20); men and women can walk on water (see Mt 14:29); men and women can live God's plan for marital love as it was established "in the beginning" (see Mt 19:8).

B. Infallible Means of Marital Spirituality

The encyclical also marks the road spouses must travel in living this spirituality. Paul VI admits that spouses must pass through the "narrow gate" and travel along the "hard way." But this, for all Christians, is the way that leads to eternal life.[77] John Paul adds that even if the gate is narrow, awareness of the future life opens up "a broad horizon of power" to guide spouses along their way. *Humanae Vitae* "points out how the married couple must implore the essential 'power' and every other 'divine help' through prayer; how they must draw grace and love from the ever living fountain of the Eucharist." Furthermore, spouses "must overcome 'with humble perseverance' their deficiencies and sins in the Sacrament of Penance" (405–406). Prayer and the sacraments—especially the Eucharist and Penance: These are the *"infallible and indispensable"* means, John Paul stresses, "for forming the Christian spirituality of married life and family life. With these, that essential and spiritual creative 'power' of love reaches human hearts and, at the same time, human bodies in their subjective masculinity and femininity" (406). As quoted previously: "The sacraments inject sanctity into the plan of man's humanity: they penetrate the soul and body, the femininity and masculinity of the personal subject, with the power of sanctity."[78]

The sacramental life is the place where we work out the restoration of God's original plan for our humanity. In the final analysis, men and women have two choices—holiness or the betrayal of their humanity. Spouses, too, must choose between holiness in their conjugal union or the betrayal of their marriage. God's love poured into the spouses' whole spiritual-sexual being—"allows the building of the whole life of the married couple according to that 'truth of the sign.'" In this way "marriage is built up in its sacramental dignity, as the central point of the encyclical reveals (see *HV,* 12)" (406). As John Paul writes in his *Letter to Families,* "When a man and a woman in marriage mutually give and receive each other in the unity of 'one flesh,' the logic of the sincere gift of self becomes a part of their life. Without this, marriage would be empty."[79] In

---

77. See *Humanae Vitae,* n. 25.

78. 7/4/84, TB 378.

79. *Letter to Families,* n. 11.

other words, when the consummate expression of the sign of married love is lived faithfully, it bears fruit in the whole life of the married couple. Conversely, when the whole of married life is lived faithfully, it bears fruit in the faithful expression of its consummate sign. The opposite is also true. If sexual union is lived as a counter-sign of authentic love, it undermines the whole reality of married life. And if the whole of married life is marked by a lack of commitment to the demands of love, sexual union will be marked by the same. In fact, it will be inherently dishonest.

Once again we see a parallel with the Eucharist. If we receive Christ's body worthily, our communion bears fruit in our whole life. Conversely, if we live a faithful Christian life it affords a worthy reception of Christ's Body in the Eucharist. However, if we receive Christ's Body unworthily, it affects our whole Christian life. In fact, we profane our union with Christ and eat and drink judgment upon ourselves (see 1 Cor 13:27–29). And if our life is marked by a lack of commitment to Christ, receiving his Body in the Eucharist can be nothing but a lie.

97. The Role of Conjugal Love in the Life of Spouses

October 10, 1984 (TB 406–408)

In his audience of October 10, 1984, John Paul again, even if very quietly, seems to offer a solution to an ongoing theological debate. This time it regards the role of conjugal love in the life of spouses. Some background information on the issue is needed if we are to realize the importance of the Holy Father's contribution.

According to John Paul, conjugal love—inspired by the Holy Spirit (by the Person-Love[80])—is the key element of the spirituality of spouses and parents. This may seem like an obvious observation. However, it actually represents a new emphasis in both Catholic theology and Magisterial teaching influenced by the personalistic turn of the twentieth century. Traditional theological and Magisterial treatments of marriage are marked by what, today, seems like a glaring underemphasis or even devaluing of the role of conjugal love in the life of spouses. The interpretation of suspicion may have played its role, but this deficiency can also be explained, at least in part, by the traditional way of "doing theology." Love as lived and experienced in marriage is primarily an interior reality. Traditional, objective analyses of marriage could not penetrate the subjective dimensions of love. Instead, traditional formulations—in keeping with their objective

---

80. See *Dominum et Vivificantem*, n. 10.

methodologies—focused on the specific and ordered *ends* of marriage: procreation being the primary end; mutual help and the remedy for concupiscence being secondary ends.

A. The Poles of the Debate

The modern shift in consciousness is much more attune to the need of incorporating the interior dimensions of love into a theology of marriage. Karol Wojtyla/John Paul II is not only one of the main proponents of this need, but he is also one of the main architects behind the construction of a modern theology of marriage that successfully develops this need. As we have already quoted him saying, without this interior perspective we ponder only "abstract considerations rather than man as a living subject."[81] Hence, both subjective consciousness and experience must "be taken into consideration and find their reflection in theology."[82] This is especially true in a theology of marriage and sexuality.

Even prior to the work of Karol Wojtyla, the twentieth century witnessed some bold theological developments in this regard.[83] But the sorely needed process of wedding traditional formulas of marriage with modern sensitivities has had its share of growing pains. Some, in their desire to read an affirmation of spousal love into the traditional schema of ends, have equated "mutual help" with conjugal love. Such a reading is not only erroneous, but results in an unnecessary "power struggle" of sorts between procreation as the "primary end" and conjugal love as the assumed "secondary end." Displeased with such a conclusion, some theologians have scrapped the traditional hierarchy of ends altogether in favor of placing all primacy on love. Such a move, however, can lead—and has led in many cases—to an interpretation of conjugal love divorced from the objective goods and purposes of marriage. Marriage then becomes relativized according to personal preferences.

In anticipation of (or in reaction to) this error, currents of thought on the other end of the spectrum have been reluctant to accept any incorporation of conjugal love into the Church's traditional schema on marriage. Such thinking is suspicious of emphasizing subjectivity because of the dangers of relativizing the objective meaning of marriage. Ultimately, er-

---

81. 9/26/79; second endnote, TB 94.

82. 4/15/81, TB 218.

83. For example, Dietrich von Hildebrand's book, *Marriage* (originally published in German in 1929 as *Die Ehe*), broke new ground with its bold emphasis on conjugal love as the primary *meaning* of marriage, distinguished from procreation as its primary *purpose*. This short, innovative volume is now published in English under the title *Marriage: The Mystery of Faithful Love* (Manchester, NH: Sophia Institute Press, 1991).

rors on both poles of the debate stem from a failure to link the objective and subjective dimensions of marriage. In comes the philosophical project of Karol Wojtyla/John Paul II. Once this problem is viewed through his new synthesis of metaphysics and phenomenology (objectivity and subjectivity), a simple and much needed solution emerges.

B. Authentic Love Rejoices with the Truth

Notice how the Pope, in the following definition of love, links subjectivity with objective truth. He states that *"love,* from the subjective viewpoint, is a *power*...given to man in order to participate in that love with which God himself loves in the mystery of creation and redemption" (406). In other words, love has an anchor. It has an objective reference point. That reference point is Ultimate Truth itself: for *God is love* (1 Jn 4:8).

The Pope continues by quoting St. Paul: Authentic love "is that love which 'rejoices with the truth' (1 Cor 13:6)." It is that love "in which there is expressed the spiritual joy...of every authentic value: a joy like that of the Creator himself, who in the beginning saw that everything 'was very good' (Gen 1:31)" (406). Prior to sin, subjectivity was completely objective. The relativizing of love only occurs with man's distancing from God. But a love cut off from God is not really love at all, only the counterfeit of concupiscence. Such a counterfeit is not "of the Father" but "of the world." Authentic love, however, is always "of the Father" (see 1 Jn 2:16). Thus, it is "actively oriented toward the fullness of good and for this very reason toward every true good" (406).

Is this authentic love possible? Or is man simply "stuck" in the reality of a counterfeit love because of sin? If he is stuck in an impure love, marriage can only be understood within two main schemas: the subjectivism of a "love" cut off from the objective good, or the objectivism of a sterile and loveless conformity to abstract principles. But John Paul repeatedly insists that man is not stuck in his impurities. The new ethos that flows from the redemption of the body is a reality in the name of which man must feel called, and called with power! This means "the subjective profile of love" can gradually become "objective to the depths."[84]

In other words, emphasizing authentic conjugal love does not mean abandoning the ends of marriage. It means fulfilling them! Nor does maintaining these ends mean de-emphasizing conjugal love. It means— and must mean—calling couples to the fullness of conjugal love. For only love can confer "adequate content and value to conjugal acts according to the truth" (407).

---

84. 2/20/80, TB 75 (see §21).

B. Conjugal Love Fulfills the Ends of Marriage

So, in assessing the proper role of conjugal love in the life of spouses, we come to realize that it is not an *end* of marriage at all. Instead, conjugal love is the inner form—the "soul"—of marriage. It coordinates the actions of the spouses in the sphere of the purposes of marriage. In other words, the ends of marriage are also the ends of conjugal love. The Council Fathers make this clear when they state: "Marriage *and conjugal love* are by their nature ordered toward the begetting and educating of children."[85]

While John Paul acknowledges that neither *Gaudium et Spes* nor *Humanae Vitae* use the language of the hierarchy of ends, he nonetheless maintains that they "deal with what the traditional expressions refer to." By linking the objective ends of marriage with the subjectivity of the spouses, these documents clarify "the same moral order," but they do so "in reference to love" (407). In this way they avoid the danger of an objectivized morality and a subjectivized love. Hence, the traditional teaching on the ends of marriage is not done away with, as some might think. As John Paul affirms: "In this renewed formulation the traditional teaching on the purposes of marriage (and their hierarchy) is reaffirmed and at the same time deepened from the viewpoint of the interior life of the spouses, that is, of conjugal and family spirituality" (407).

We see here a parallel with Christ's own words: "I have come not to abolish [the law and the prophets] but to fulfill them" (Mt 5:17). How is the law fulfilled? Precisely through love understood as life in the Holy Spirit (see §25). As St. Paul says, "Love is the fulfillment of the law" because "it does no wrong" (Rom 13:10). This is exactly what an authentic marital spirituality is—the fulfillment of the objective demands (or ends) of marriage through the subjective vivification of love understood as life in the Spirit. *This* is the role of conjugal love in the life of spouses.

98. Continence Is a Virtue Essential to Conjugal Love

October 10, 24, 31, 1984 (TB 406–412)

We have established that love is not rightly considered an end of marriage. Instead, as John Paul expresses it, love "is 'poured out into [the] hearts' (Rom 5:5) of the spouses as the fundamental spiritual power of

---

85. *Gaudium et Spes*, n. 50; emphasis added. See Ramon Garcia de Haro's *Marriage and the Family in the Documents of the Magisterium* (San Francisco, CA: Ignatius Press, 1993), pp. 200, 234, 244, etc., for a discussion of the role of conjugal love and the error of considering it an *end* of marriage. See also Rocco Buttiglione's *Karol Wojtyla: The Thought of the Man Who Became Pope John Paul II*, pp. 98–99.

their conjugal pact" (407). In turn, conjugal love orients spouses toward the fulfillment of the ends of marriage by protecting both the value of the true communion of the spouses and the value of truly responsible parenthood. Therefore, as the Holy Father concludes: "The power of love—authentic in the theological and ethical sense—is expressed in this, that love *correctly unites 'the two meanings of the conjugal act'*" (407).

This crucial statement takes us to the heart of the debate over *Humanae Vitae*. The real debate over this encyclical is a debate about the meaning of human love. It is a debate about the very meaning *of human life*—as the title of the encyclical itself indicates.

A. Love versus Concupiscence

As John Paul notes, the idea that the teaching of *Humanae Vitae* deprives spouses of the opportunity to express their love is the most frequent objection to the encyclical. But what kind of "love" are we speaking of here? Authentic love, the Pope maintains, excludes "not only in theory but above all in practice the 'contradiction' that might be evidenced in this field" (407). In other words, those who are vivified by the life and love of the Holy Spirit realize internally that there is no contradiction "between the divine laws pertaining to the transmission of life and those pertaining to the fostering of authentic conjugal love."[86] In fact, they realize that the teaching of *Humanae Vitae* provides them with the proper measure to ensure that what they express when they become "one flesh" is truly love and not merely a cheapened counterfeit.

If we are going to speak of a "contradiction" in this matter, the contradiction is contraception. It blatantly speaks *against* (contra-dicts) the very meaning of the marital embrace as a participation in the life-giving mystery of God's love. With regard to the Church's teaching, as John Paul says, there is no "contradiction" involved, only a "difficulty." This difficulty "arises from the fact that the power of love is implanted in man lured by concupiscence: in human subjects love does battle with threefold concupiscence (see 1 Jn 2:16), in particular with the concupiscence of the flesh which distorts the truth of the 'language of the body.' And therefore love too is not able to be realized...except through overcoming concupiscence" (407).

In effect John Paul is saying that those who seek to justify contraception in order to express their "love" for one another have actually (and perhaps unwittingly) confused love with concupiscence. Love does not seek

---

86. *Gaudium et Spes*, n. 51.

to justify what is wrong but "rejoices with the truth" (1 Cor 13:6)—whatever the cost. Concupiscence, on the other hand, is not concerned with maintaining the truth of sexual union as a sign of God's life-giving love. It is concerned with seeking its own satisfaction and is "afraid" of the cost of authentic love. As we observed previously, contraception was not invented to prevent pregnancy. Ultimately, it was invented to skirt the sacrifice required by self-control (see §94). Contraception can certainly seem like an attractive alternative to the difficulties inherent in attaining self-mastery. However, to the degree that one is not master of himself, it is impossible to be a true gift to another. To this degree it is impossible to express love in sexual union.

Precisely at this moment—in the moment of recognizing the "difficulty" involved in true love—man and woman must make a decision. They must activate their self-determination and decide what power will hold sway in their relationship: love or concupiscence; truth or counterfeits? Much is at stake in such a decision. As the story of Tobiah and Sarah illustrates so well, it is a test of life and death (see §89). Precisely in this decision, as stated previously, the choices and the actions of man and woman "take on all the weight of human existence." Precisely in this decision "husband and wife find themselves in the situation in which the powers of good and evil fight and compete against each other." But those who love are not afraid. For the "truth and the power of love are shown in the ability to place oneself between the forces of good and evil which are fighting in man and around him, because love is confident in the victory of good and is ready to do everything so that good may conquer."[87]

Authentic conjugal love prefers to suffer—even die—for the truth ("Husbands, love your wives *as Christ loved the Church*). "If the powers of concupiscence try to detach the 'language of the body' from the truth,...the power of love instead strengthens [the language of the body] ever anew in that truth, so that the mystery of the redemption of the body can bear fruit in it" (406). And the fruit that the redemption of the body bears is precisely an ongoing liberation from concupiscence through an ongoing strengthening of the virtue of continence. According to John Paul, the virtue of continence is so critical here that without a proper understanding of it we can never arrive "either at the heart of the moral truth, or at the heart of the anthropological truth of the problem" presented by *Humanae Vitae*.[88]

---

87. 6/27/84, TB 376.

88. 9/5/84, TB 403.

B. Continence Is a Permanent Moral Attitude

John Paul says that if the key element of the spirituality of spouses is *love*, this love is by its nature linked with the chastity that is manifested as self-mastery. Such self-mastery is also known as continence. As stated above, only one who is master of himself can make a gift of himself. In other words, only one who is continent can love.

In speaking of the natural regulation of births we speak of practicing "periodic continence." However, John Paul indicates that such continence should not be viewed merely as a temporary "technique." Properly understood, "continence itself is a definite and permanent moral attitude; it is a *virtue*, and therefore, the whole line of conduct guided by it acquires a virtuous character" (400). In other words, not only does exercising one's freedom to abstain from intercourse when there is sufficient reason to avoid a pregnancy constitute an act of virtue. Exercising continence in this way also fosters the freedom necessary to ensure that when spouses do become "one flesh" they act out of authentic love and do not merely indulge concupiscence. In this way we begin to see, as John Paul points out, that the role of continence lies not only in protecting the procreative meaning of intercourse, but also the unitive meaning. How so?

Continence, John Paul reminds us, is part of the more general virtue of temperance. Unfortunately, it seems both words tend to have a negative connotation, as if they were only a "saying no" to something. Continence certainly involves "saying no" to lust. As John Paul says, "The conviction that the virtue of continence 'is set against' the concupiscence of the flesh is correct, but it is not altogether complete" (409). The Pope observes that continence does not act in isolation, but always in connection with the other virtues such as prudence, justice, fortitude, and above all with charity. John Paul insists, then, that continence "is not only—and not even principally—the ability to 'abstain.' [This] role would be defined as 'negative.' But there is also another role (which we can call 'positive') of self mastery: it is the ability to direct the respective reactions [of emotion and desire], both as to their content and their character" (412). The virtuous person does not tyrannize his passions. The virtuous person orders his passions so that he "tends toward the good with all his sensory and spiritual powers."[89]

The mature virtue of continence, therefore, in connection with the other virtues, enables men and women gradually to experience sexual desire as God intended it to be—as the desire to make a free and sincere gift of self according to the true meaning of love and the nuptial meaning of

---

89. *CCC,* n. 1803.

the body. This is why the virtue of continence is so crucial in the relationship of the sexes. Without it, men and women are pulled to and fro by the tides of concupiscence. And for lack of knowledge of anything else, more often than not they will make the tragic mistake of calling that love. As stated previously, if a marriage were to be built upon such a foundation, it would be akin to building a house on sand (see §30).

99. Continence Authenticates and Intensifies Marital Affection

October 24, 1984 (TB 408–410)

As discussed in the second cycle of reflections, concupiscence tends to flare up in man like an unquenchable fire. It "invades his senses, excites his body, involves his feelings, and in a certain sense takes possession of his 'heart.'" Concupiscence also causes the "external man" to reduce the "internal man" to silence. In other words, because passion aims at satisfaction, "it blunts reflective activity and pays no attention to the voice of conscience."[90]

Those who continually indulge concupiscence remain blind to the Gospel of the body. If men and women wish ultimately to experience the transformation of the very "content and character" of sexual desire according to the truth of love—if they want to see and experience the body as an efficacious sign of the very mystery of God—they must progressively acquire mastery over concupiscent impulses and desires.

A. Acquiring Self-Mastery

John Paul observes that "conjugal chastity (and chastity in general) is manifested at first as the capacity to resist the concupiscence of the flesh." Then, the more such mastery is acquired, chastity "gradually reveals itself as a singular capacity to perceive, love, and practice those meanings of the 'language of the body' which remain altogether unknown to concupiscence itself" (409).

"Self-mastery is a *long and exacting work*. One can never consider it acquired once and for all. It presupposes renewed effort at all stages of life."[91] If men and women are to acquire self-mastery, they "must be committed to a progressive education in self-control of the will, of the feelings, of the emotions." And this "must develop beginning with the most simple acts in which it is relatively easy to put the interior decision into practice"

---

90. 9/10/80, TB 145, 146 (see §32).

91. *CCC,* n. 2342.

(408). Notice the Pope's wise pastoral counsel. In effect, he is saying, if you want to experience the mature virtue of continence, you must be patient with yourself and start small. It is similar to lifting weights. A beginner should not expect to bench-press 300 pounds. However, if he begins with a realistic appraisal of his own abilities and commits himself to a progressive program of training, he will increase his strength day by day. And what was once impossible will eventually become reality.

Of course, in this whole process of strengthening virtue, unlike a weightlifter, progress does not depend merely on our natural capacities. Recall that continence is not only a human virtue, but even more so a divine gift—a gift of the Spirit dwelling in our flesh (see §90). At every step of the way the supernatural gift of grace aids us, if we avail ourselves of it. As the following plea of St. Augustine illustrates, continence is not only something to work for, but something to pray for: "I thought continence arose from one's own powers, which I did not recognize in myself. I was foolish enough not to know...that no one can be continent unless you grant it. For you would surely have granted it if my inner groaning had reached your ears and I with firm faith had cast my cares on you."[92]

The Holy Father says that willingness to commit to ongoing growth in virtue also presupposes the clear perception of the values expressed in God's law. These are the values of the personal and sacramental meaning of the body and sex. The person who wishes to practice true virtue must set his will like flint on these values. He must put his hand to the plow and never look back (see Lk 9:62). He must prefer to die a martyr's death than to lust. Indeed, if some are willing to kill to indulge their lusts (this is what abortion, for example, amounts to), Christians, on the other hand, must be willing to die rather than give in to lust. If one does not prefer death to lust, he is not yet fully ready to overcome lust. As John Paul states, it is precisely such "firm convictions which, if accompanied by the respective disposition of the will, give rise to the virtue of continence (self-mastery)" (408).

Thus, the continent person exercises "control" precisely in order to uphold the incomparable *value* of sexuality—to protect it from the degradation of lust. This is an essential point. We cannot speak of continence as a virtue if one's "control" in sexual matters is based on a fear or *devaluation* of sexuality. That would imply acceptance of the Manichaean anti-value (see §§35, 44). Prudery and repressiveness may masquerade as virtue, but in reality they point to its lack.[93] In fact, at their root we often find the "inter-

---

92. Cited in *CCC*, n. 2520.

93. See *Love & Responsibility*, p. 188.

pretation of suspicion," which is the antithesis of the meaning of life (see §36). Such an interpretation leads either to the repression of all things sexual, or to the regular indulgence of concupiscence. People in either case remain under the dominion of concupiscence which makes man "in a certain sense blind and insensitive to the most profound values that spring from love" (408).

We expressed this previously when we stated that a person who gives place to lust, to suspicion, and/or to the Manichaean anti-value has no knowledge of the innermost layers of his own heart where that "echo" of the beatifying beginning resounds. True chastity, however, flows from the "ethos of redemption," and this ethos is based on a close alliance with those deepest layers of the heart (see §40). It is those layers of the heart that can recognize the value of the nuptial meaning of the body. Those layers can see in the body the value of a "transparent sign." This sign, in turn, reveals the gift of communion, that is, the mysterious reality of God's image and likeness.[94] Only when self-control is motivated by these values can we speak of continence as a virtue and as a participation in "life according to the Spirit."

B. The Fruits of Continence

We can recognize authentic continence versus a repressive continence based on the fruits each bears in man and woman's relationship. For example, does the exercise of self-control open a couple to those more profound and more mature values inherent in the nuptial meaning of the body? Does their exercise of self-control lead them to experience the authentic freedom of the gift? Or, does their exercise of "control" lead to an impoverishment of affection and an increase in tension and conflict?

If self-control leads to the latter, the solution is not to abandon self-control. This would only justify the unrestrained indulgence of concupiscence, leading to far worse conflict. The solution is to open to the conversion of heart that leads to authentic virtue. The asceticism necessary to practice continence as a virtue does not impoverish the relationship of the sexes. Quite the contrary! As the Holy Father expresses, it progressively enriches "the marital dialogue of the couple, purifying it, deepening it, and simplifying it." Thus, expressions of affection are not dampened. The virtue of continence actually "makes them spiritually more intense" (409).

Authentic continence does not repress sexual attraction. As the virtue matures, it enables men and women to live from that place of redeemed

---

94. See 12/3/80, TB 176.

sexual attraction (see §38). These pure, deep, simple, and spiritually intense experiences of which John Paul speaks flow directly from that mature sexual attraction that St. Paul writes about when he calls spouses to defer to one another "out of reverence for Christ" (Eph 5:21) (see §90). According to John Paul, this "deferring to one another" means the common concern for the truth of the language of the body. And deferring "out of reverence for Christ" indicates the Holy Spirit's gift of "fear of the Lord," which accompanies the virtue of continence. We have already described this reverent "fear" or "awe" as the gift of piety (see §44). Authentic conjugal love matures in a couple in measure with this piety, this "reverence for Christ." John Paul relates that such reverence seems to open that "interior space" in both man and woman that makes them ever more sensitive to the most profound and mature values of the nuptial meaning of the body and the true freedom of the gift.

When a husband and wife *see* each other's bodies as a sign of God's own mystery, when they *know* that their incarnate union is a sign of the "great mystery" of Christ's union with the Church—in other words, when the theology of the body is not just a concept but an *experience*—sexual attraction takes on its purest, simplest, deepest, and most intense character. It is precisely through "this interior maturing," John Paul says, that "the conjugal act itself acquires the importance and dignity proper to it in its potentially procreative meaning" (410).

Furthermore, not only does the marital embrace take on its full and glorious meaning. Conjugal chastity also reveals to the awareness and experience of the couple all the other possible "manifestations of affection" that can express the couple's deep life of communion. Although marital intercourse remains the consummate expression of spousal love, other expressions of affection are also revealed in their purest, simplest, deepest, and most intense character "in proportion to the subjective richness of femininity and masculinity" (410). Countless wives, for example, upon experiencing the maturation of continence in their marriage, can attest to the joy of being kissed, embraced, or tenderly touched by their husbands without the suspicion that he is out to "get" something. A virtuous husband is never out to "get" something. His manifestations of affection are truly that. He has no ulterior motive.

Harmony, peace, sincere affection, and spiritually intense communion—these are the fruits of the virtue of continence.[95] In this way we see

---

95. See *Humanae Vitae*, n. 21. There Paul VI outlines the "beneficent influence" of continence on marriage and family life. Those who practice continence as a virtue know precisely whereof he speaks.

"the essential character of conjugal chastity in its organic link with the 'power' to love, which is poured out into the hearts of the married couple along with the 'consecration' of the Sacrament of Marriage" (409). When spouses live from that "power to love" granted by God—when they live the "consecration" of their sacrament—marriage works! Using our former image, to the degree that we allow our tires to be inflated, we experience the car the way it is meant to be experienced. And it works!

100. The Church Is Convinced of the Truth of *Humanae Vitae*

October 31; November 7, 1984 (TB 411–415)

If John Paul extols the harmony of married life that flows from con-jugal chastity (understood also as the virtue of continence), some couples might look at their own experience and retort that continence is more often a cause of conflict—first within oneself and, in turn, within their common life as a married couple. But is such an experience of continence an expe-rience of the *virtue* in its integral sense? Has such a couple crossed the threshold from continence as a "constraint" to continence as the interior freedom of the gift?

John Paul observes: "It is often thought that continence causes inner tensions from which man must free himself." But he immediately empha-sizes: "In the light of the analyses we have done, continence, understood integrally, is rather the only *way to free man from such tensions*" (411).

A. Continence Affords Authentic Freedom

"Tensions" here would commonly be understood as pent-up sexual energy that seeks release. In this context John Paul speaks of sexual "ex-citement" as distinguished from "emotion." Excitement, he says, is aroused more directly by the body and seeks corporeal pleasure in the sexual act. Emotion, on the other hand, is aroused more by the whole real-ity of the person in his masculinity or femininity. It is not immediately aimed at the sexual act but more toward other "manifestations of affection."

■ It is easy to recognize that, according to these definitions, most men tend more toward "excitement" while most women tend more toward "emotion." Both excitement and emotion have their concupiscent expres-sions, which treat the opposite sex as a means toward selfish gratification. But both excitement and emotion also have their original and redemptive expressions, which open men and women to the possibility of an authentic communion of persons. In *Love & Responsibility,* Wojtyla describes such excitement and emotion as the "raw material" of love. But it is a mistake to consider the raw material as the "finished form." In our fallen state, mere excitement and emotion often stems from a utilitarian outlook contrary to the very nature of love as self-donation.[96]

If continence is understood only as a means of "containing" sexual excitement (and emotion) then, yes, such continence will lead to inner tensions from which man will seek to "free" himself. Freedom, in this sense, of course, would come—it is supposed—by releasing one's tensions without restraint. In this paradigm continence is viewed as the enemy of freedom. But does indulging one's desires without restraint lead to freedom or to slavery? If one cannot say no, is he free or is he in chains? And is such uncontrollable desire love or is it lust? The mere arousal of excitement and emotion is no guarantee of love. In fact, "if they are not held together by the correct gravitational pull," excitement and emotion "may add up not to love, but to its direct opposite."[97]

Recall the Pope's statement that the "antithesis and, in a way, the negation of...freedom takes place when it becomes for man 'a pretext to live according to the flesh.'"[98] In essence, those who want to be "free" from continence want to be free *from freedom* so they can embrace their bondage to concupiscence unhindered (see §43). Continence as an authentic virtue calls us to a radical paradigm shift. It calls us to the freedom for which Christ has set us free (see Gal 5). This is the freedom of the ethos of redemption. It is the freedom *from* the domination of concupiscence which frees us *for* the sincere gift of self. As John Paul repeatedly insists, the virtue of continence is "not only the capacity to 'contain' bodily and sensual reactions, but even more the capacity to control and guide man's whole sensual and emotive sphere." Therefore, continence is able "to direct the line of excitement toward its correct development and also the line of emotion itself, orienting it toward the deepening and interior intensification of its 'pure,' and in a certain sense, 'disinterested' character" (413).

Disinterested desire is interested in love, not its own satisfaction. Only to the degree that we experience this mature level of continence are we truly *free* from those inner "tensions." And only to the degree that we are free from those inner tensions can we become a real gift to another person. Precisely through such freedom we discover and experience that "mature spontaneity" and "noble gratification" spoken of previously (see §39).

---

96. See *Love & Responsibility,* p. 139.

97. *Love & Responsibility,* p. 146.

98. 1/14/81, TB 198.

B. Balance between Excitement and Emotion

The Holy Father clarifies that in distinguishing between excitement and emotion, he does not mean to imply that they are opposed to one another. The distinction only demonstrates the subjective richness of human persons in their sexual body-soul constitution. Furthermore, the virtue of continence affords a balance between excitement and emotion, enabling them to be lived as different elements in the same experience. Excitement informed by virtue is aroused not *merely* by the body, but by the body of one's spouse as the expression of his/her person. In turn, the virtuous conjugal act is not merely sensual but involves "a particular intensification of emotion." Virtuous intercourse, as an authentic communion of persons, is both physically and emotionally intense. And John Paul adds that "it should not be otherwise" (413).

We can observe that an *in*continent act of intercourse can also be a physically and emotionally intense experience. But such an experience is not anchored in the incarnate truth of persons and their call to communion. Such an act may hint at love, but it is not integrated with the truth of love and communion revealed by the spousal (or nuptial) meaning of the body. An incontinent act of intercourse, therefore, cannot *not* be an indulgence of concupiscence. As John Paul reminds us: "The very spousal meaning of the body has been distorted, almost at its very roots, by concupiscence." The mature virtue of continence, on the other hand, "gradually reveals the 'pure' aspect of the spousal meaning of the body. In this way, continence develops the personal communion of the man and the woman, a communion that cannot be formed and developed in the full truth of its possibilities only on the level of concupiscence." And the Pope adds: "This is precisely what the encyclical *Humanae Vitae* affirms" (414–415).

Thus, the Vicar of Christ firmly maintains that the Church is "totally convinced" of the correctness of the teaching of *Humanae Vitae*. It "teaches responsible fatherhood and motherhood 'as proof of a mature conjugal love'—and therefore it contains not only the answer to the concrete question that is asked in the sphere of the ethics of married life but, as already has been stated, it also indicates a plan of conjugal spirituality" (414).

101. Chastity Lies at the Center of Marital Spirituality

November 14, 1984 (TB 415–417)

In his audience of November 14, 1984, the Holy Father takes us for a final lap in his deepening circle of reflections by reviewing the key concepts of an authentic marital spirituality. By doing so it seems as if he is preparing us for what might be considered the summit of his commentary on *Humanae Vitae,* which he delivers in the following audience of November 21, 1984.

John Paul recalls that the fundamental element of the spirituality of married life as taught by *Humanae Vitae* is the love poured out into the hearts of the couple as a gift of the Holy Spirit (see Rom 5:5). Through their own sacrament, the couple receive this divine gift along with a special "consecration." An integral element of this love is "conjugal chastity, which, manifesting itself as continence, brings about the interior order of conjugal life" (415). What is the interior order of conjugal life? It is precisely that purity of heart to which Christ calls couples in the Sermon on the Mount. As a fruit of "life in the Spirit," this purity enables the interior reality of the heart to conform to the objective truth of the nuptial meaning of the body. In turn, this "interior order" enables man and woman to establish an authentic communion of persons in all of married life through the mutual gift of self.

A. Chastity Solves the Internal Problem of Every Marriage

In his book *Love & Responsibility*, Karol Wojtyla asserted that the realization of a true communion of persons in each particular sexual act presents "the internal problem of every marriage."[99] Thus, he affirms that chastity lies at "the center of the spirituality of marriage." For it is precisely the virtue of chastity that orders sexual excitement and emotion toward the truth of an authentic communion of persons.

"Chastity means to live in the order of the heart. This order permits the development of the 'manifestations of affection' in their proper proportion and meaning. In this way *conjugal chastity is also confirmed as 'life by the Spirit'* (see Gal 5:25)." In other words, Christian chastity, as we have affirmed previously, should be understood "not only as a moral virtue (formed by love), but likewise as a virtue connected with the gifts of the Holy Spirit—*above all, the gift of respect for what comes from God"* (415). John Paul defines this "respect" as the gift of *piety* and reminds us that the author of Ephesians has this gift in mind when he exhorts married couples to "defer to one another out of reverence for Christ" (Eph 5:21). Through this deference and reverence for the mystery of Christ, the one flesh union "finds its humanly mature form thanks to the life 'in the Spirit'" (417). In fact, as the Holy Father emphasizes, "Those 'two' who—according to the oldest expression in the Bible—'become one body' (Gen

---

99. *Love & Responsibility,* p. 225.

2:24) cannot bring about this union on the proper level of persons *(communio personarum) except through the powers coming...from the Holy Spirit* who purifies, enlivens, strengthens, and perfects the powers of the human spirit" (415–416).

This is a bold claim. According to John Paul, sexual union is only what it is meant to be as an authentic communion of persons when it is performed in union with God as an expression of his own Trinitarian life—the life of the Holy Spirit. There is no two-tiered distinction between nature and grace here. It is of sexual union's very "nature" to be full of grace—to be in some sense a sacramental expression of the mystery and inner life of the Trinity.

B. The Original Spirituality of Marriage

"It follows from this that the essential lines of the spirituality of marriage are inscribed 'from the beginning' in the biblical truth on marriage. This spirituality is also *open* 'from the beginning' to the *gifts of the Holy Spirit"* (416). Recall that we described the original gracing of creation as a special state of "spiritualization" in man (see §20). This enabled the first man and woman's created communion to participate in some way in God's Uncreated Communion. Loving one another as God loves—that is, loving according to the "breath" of the Spirit which *in*-spired their flesh (see Gen 2:7)—they experienced a beatifying immunity from shame (see Gen 2:25).

Through this experience of original nakedness, we discerned that man and woman understood and lived the body as an efficacious sign of the very mystery of creation (see §17). In turn, the entrance of shame marked the loss of this original gracing and, thus, the loss of this understanding of the body as a sign (see §26). However, the good news of the Gospel is that through the death and resurrection of Christ, the "new gracing" of redemption restores God's original plan for the body and for the "one flesh" communion of marriage. Through this new gracing the body (and the personal union of bodies) recovers its efficacy as a sign (see §77–78).

Thus, when a husband and wife open themselves to the gift of piety—the gift of respect and awe for what is sacred—the Holy Spirit instills in them "a sensitivity to everything that is a created reflection of God's wisdom and love." In turn, they regain "a particular *sensitivity to everything* in their vocation and life that bears *the sign of the mystery of creation and redemption.*" This sensitivity "seems to introduce the man and woman to a specially profound respect for the two inseparable meanings of the conjugal act." Such respect "can develop fully only on the basis of a profound reference to the *personal dignity* of what in the human person is intrinsic to *masculinity* and *femininity,* and inseparably in reference to the *personal dignity of the new life* which can result *from* the conjugal *union* of the man and the woman" (416).

C. Salvific Fear of Violating the Sign

Through the *in*-spiration of the Holy Spirit, this "specially profound respect" for the inseparability of the unitive and procreative meanings of intercourse wells up from within the couple. It is not imposed on them from "outside." They come to *see* the body and sexual union with something of the original good of God's vision and, as John Paul says, they are "filled with veneration for the *essential values of the conjugal union*" (416).

When a couple interiorizes the glorious plan of God for sexual union, it is no exaggeration to say they would prefer to die martyrs' deaths than to engage in contracepted intercourse. *Yes,* it is that serious. As John Paul says, such couples have a "salvific fear" of ever "violating or degrading what bears in itself the sign of the divine mystery of creation and redemption" (416).[100] But, of course, they do not *live* in fear. Instead, loving as Christ loves, they taste the eternal joy that Christ himself promised (see Jn 15:11). To the degree that they embrace the sacrifices involved in remaining faithful to the language of the body, they re-create something of that beatifying experience of the beginning. Indeed, through the sincere gift of their body-persons to each other they fulfill the very meaning of their being and existence (see §18).

At this point the sacramentality of marriage and the Gospel of the body are not only religious concepts, but also lived experiences. At this point spouses experience the marital embrace at a level that is mystical and even liturgical. At this point the apparent contradiction in this area "disappears" and the difficulty arising from concupiscence is gradually overcome. Is it possible to get to this point? Yes—not without a willingness to die with Christ and not based on one's own resources, but thanks to the power of the Holy Spirit's gift.

102. The Exceptional Significance of the Conjugal Act
November 21, 1984 (TB 417–419)

The audience of November 21, 1984 brings us to the pinnacle of John Paul's analysis of the marital spirituality implicit in the teaching of

---

100. See *CCC,* n. 1432.

Humanae Vitae. In these final reflections, one cannot help but be struck by the clarity of insight with which this celibate pontiff penetrates the inner life of spouses. He is able to enter their longings and aspirations and, in turn, point husbands and wives to the path that leads to their authentic fulfillment. In the process he demonstrates that—despite any surface interpretation to the contrary—contracepted intercourse is antithetical to the true love and affirmation for which men and women long.

A. The Deep Need for Affirmation

As John Paul stated in his catechesis on Genesis, the nuptial meaning of the body reveals both the call to become a gift, and the capacity and deep availability for the "affirmation of the person." This affirmation means "living the fact that the other—the woman for the man and the man for the woman—is...someone willed by the Creator for his (or her) own sake." This someone is "unique and unrepeatable: someone chosen by eternal Love."[101]

When we first read these words we asked: Is there any man or woman alive who does not ache in the depths of his or her being for such affirmation? Is this not what men and women are looking for in their mutual relationship—in all of their "manifestations of affection"? Are they not looking to be affirmed for *who they are* as God created them to be in their own uniqueness and unrepeatability? At the deepest level of the human heart, no one wants to be treated as an object for someone else's gratification. Men and women want to be loved sincerely, disinterestedly, for their own sake.

As John Paul says, such love "can happen only through a profound appreciation of the personal dignity of both the feminine 'I' and the masculine 'I' in their shared life. This spiritual appreciation is the fundamental fruit of the gift of the Spirit which urges the person to respect the work of God. From this appreciation," the Pope continues, "all the 'affectionate manifestations' which make up the fabric of remaining faithful to the union of marriage derive their true spousal meaning" (418). This true spousal meaning is the giving and receiving of the gift, which affords the love and affirmation for which men and women are longing in marriage. And it is precisely an uncompromising respect for the work of God (piety) that ensures this love and affirmation. As John Paul says, such respect "creates and enlarges, so to speak, the interior space for the mutual freedom of the gift in which there is fully manifested the spousal meaning of masculinity and femininity" (418).

---

101. 1/16/80, TB 65 (see §19).

The interior constriction of concupiscence presents the main obstacle to this freedom. Concupiscence does not bless the other "I" as a person created for his or her own sake. Instead, as the Pope observes, concupiscence is directed toward the other person as an object of pleasure. If the aim is merely to satisfy desire, one can do this in any number of ways. The person who is the object of concupiscence gradually realizes the sentiment of the other: "You don't need *me*. You don't desire *me* as the person I am. You desire only a means of gratification." Hence, far from feeling loved and affirmed as a unique and unrepeatable person, those objectified by concupiscence feel used and debased as an insignificant and repeatable commodity.

As John Paul indicates, herein lies the "enormous significance" of the attitude of respect for the work of God, which the Spirit stirs up in the couple. As men and women come to reclaim something of that original good of God's vision, they stand in "awe" of the mystery of God revealed in the other. In other words, when men and women come to see the body as a theology, they gain "the capacity for deep satisfaction, admiration, [and] disinterested attention to the 'visible' and at the same time the 'invisible' beauty of masculinity and femininity." They "gain a deep appreciation for the disinterested gift of the 'other'" (418).

It is precisely this "awe" and respect that frees men and women from the interior constriction of concupiscence. It frees them from all that reduces the other "I" to a mere object of pleasure and strengthens in them the freedom of the gift. When men and women live from this place of respect and interior freedom, all their manifestations of affection "protect in each of them that 'deep-rooted peace' which is in a certain sense the interior resonance of chastity" (419).

B. The Interior Harmony of Marriage

Chastity is not a "negative" virtue; it "is above all positive and creative."[102] As John Paul eloquently expresses, chastity resonates in the hearts of men and women as a deep peace reminiscent of that original "peace of the interior gaze" (see §17). One is at total peace when he knows he is loved. He can be himself without fear of rejection. He can be naked without shame. Such peace creates the fullness of the intimacy of persons.

This is what authentic chastity affords. It affords "the interior harmony of marriage" because "the couple live together in the interior truth of the 'language of the body'" (419). Far from eschewing the body, conjugal chastity "involves a profound and universal attention to the person in

---

102. *Love & Responsibility*, p. 171.

one's masculinity and femininity." Such attention brings with it the deep affirmation of the person, "thus creating the interior climate suitable for personal communion" (419). When spouses open themselves to "life in the Spirit," chastity becomes profoundly liberating. Spouses taste the freedom for which Christ set them free (see §§42, 43). And *all* of their manifestations of affection take on their true meaning in building their communion.

Even so, while all expressions of marital affection are certainly significant, according to John Paul, spouses who live "in the Spirit" come to realize "in the sum total of married life" the particular importance of "that act in which, at least potentially, the spousal meaning of the body is linked with the procreative meaning." The Holy Father expounds: "In the spiritual life of married couples there are at work the gifts of the Holy Spirit, especially the gift of piety.... This gift, together with love and chastity ...leads to understanding among the possible 'manifestations of affection,' the singular, or rather exceptional, significance of [the conjugal] act: its dignity and the consequent serious responsibility connected with it" (417).

In fact, John Paul concludes that recognizing and protecting the dignity of the sexual act is the specific goal of marital spirituality. As he states: "The virtue of conjugal chastity, and still more the gift of respect for what comes from God, mold the couple's spirituality to the purpose of protecting the particular dignity of this act, of this 'manifestation of affection' in which the truth of the 'language of the body' can be expressed only by safeguarding the procreative potential" (417).

C. Antithesis of Authentic Marital Spirituality

Now we approach John Paul's ultimate conclusion about the importance of the encyclical *Humanae Vitae* for an authentic marital spirituality. Keep in mind that without an authentic marital spirituality, we do not know *who man is* as male and female and *who he is meant to be*. Without an adequate understanding of marriage, we cannot have an adequate anthropology. For "man and woman were created for marriage."[103]

As we stated above, "life in the Spirit" leads to understanding "the singular, or rather exceptional, significance" of the conjugal act. "Therefore," the Pope concludes, "the antithesis of conjugal spirituality is constituted, in a certain sense, by the subjective lack of this understanding which is linked to the contraceptive practice and mentality" (417). One-hundred-twenty-eight Wednesday audience addresses have led us to this conclusion: Contracepted intercourse demonstrates in some way the "antithesis of marital spirituality."

---

103. 2/13/80, TB 74 (see §21).

From the beginning God created man as male and female and called them to "be fruitful and multiply" in order to reveal (make visible) his own invisible mystery of life-giving love and Communion. But this primordial sacrament not only imaged the mystery—it was also supernaturally efficacious. In other words, through their own life-affirming communion, man and woman actually *participated* in the eternal Communion of God right "from the beginning." This is the Word that the language of the body speaks. The anti-Word, however—that enemy of God and the enemy of man—wants to keep man from participating in God's life-giving Communion. Thus, Satan attacks "through the very heart of that unity which, from 'the beginning,' was formed by man and woman, created and called to become 'one flesh.'"[104] As John Paul says in his encyclical on the Holy Spirit, Satan "seeks to *'falsify'...creative love.*"[105] *"This is truly the key for interpreting reality.... Original sin attempts, then, to abolish fatherhood."*[106] Is this not the precise effect of contracepted intercourse?

Nuptial union is meant to bear witness to "creative love." As John Paul II says in *Mulieris Dignitatem*, every time a new life is conceived man and woman share in the "eternal mystery of generation, which is in God himself, the one and Triune God." In fact, he says, "All 'generating' in the created world is to be likened to this absolute and uncreated model" which "belongs to the inner life of God."[107]

An authentic marital spirituality calls spouses to open their bodies to the *in*-spiration of the Holy Spirit so that they might image and participate in the inner life of God. Insert contraception into this picture and we witness a specific and determined "closing off" of the spouse's flesh to the presence of the Holy Spirit—a closing off to "the Lord and Giver of Life." This is precisely why contraceptive practice and mentality manifests the antithesis of an authentic marital spirituality.

> ■ A woman at one of my presentations once asked a question that exemplified this "closing off." Recognizing the role of the Holy Spirit in the marital embrace and the conception of a child, she asked: "What if I want to have sex with my husband, but we don't want the Holy Spirit there?" This is exactly what the language of contracepted intercourse says. Conjugal life, and the marital embrace in particular, is meant to be liturgical. As the *Catechism* says, "In every liturgical action the Holy Spirit is sent in order to bring us into communion with Christ and so to form his Body. The

---

104. 3/5/80, TB 77 (see §24).

105. *Dominum et Vivificantem*, n. 37.

106. *Crossing the Threshold of Hope*, p. 228.

107. *Mulieris Dignitatem*, nn. 18 and 8.

Holy Spirit is...the Spirit of communion.... Communion with the Holy Trinity and fraternal communion [in this case, spousal communion] are inseparably the fruit of the Spirit in the liturgy."[108] By using contraception, spouses are performing an "anti-epiclesis" of sorts. The *epiclesis* refers to the invocation of the Holy Spirit which is at the heart of each sacramental and liturgical celebration, especially the Eucharist[109] "Let your Spirit come upon these gifts to make them holy, so that they may become for us the body and blood of our Lord, Jesus Christ." It would be an utter sacrilege for a priest to go through the motions of celebrating the Eucharist—*"the sacrament of the Bridegroom and of the Bride,"* as John Paul describes it[110]—and say, "Let your Spirit *not* come upon these gifts...." In some sense, this is what spouses are doing when they render their union sterile. They are profaning and thus negating communion with each other and with the Trinity. They are draining their union of the "'power that comes forth' from the Body of Christ, which is ever-living and life-giving."[111] But would spouses continue to make such a choice if they *knew* that this is what their actions implied? It seems apparent that in most cases spouses simply "know not what they do."

Someone might argue that couples who practice natural family planning are also closing themselves to the Holy Spirit. This *may* be the case, but not necessarily. Let us return to the priest and his celebration of the Eucharist. A priest may have legitimate reason to abstain from saying Mass on a given day. He does nothing wrong in this case. This is worlds apart from going through the motions of a Mass but profaning it through an "anti-epiclesis." However, a priest may also have an illegitimate reason for abstaining from Mass—perhaps out of contempt for the demands of being a priest, perhaps out of anger at God or his congregation. Such motives would indicate some sort of closure to the Holy Spirit. Similarly, if spouses have a contempt toward children, abstaining to avoid them could indicate a closure of some sort to the Spirit. Here is a test for determining whether or not a couple is open to the Holy Spirit in their acts of intercourse. Can they honestly pray every time they join in one flesh: "Come, Holy Spirit, if it is *your* will, let there be life"? Spouses who use natural family planning responsibly would have no problem praying this prayer every time they unite. They may, in fact, have a legitimate hope that it *not* be God's will to bring forth a child. They may also be virtually assured that it is a biological

---

108. *CCC,* n. 1108.

109. See *CCC,* nn. 1105, 1106, 1624.

110. *Mulieris Dignitatem,* n. 26.

111. *CCC,* n. 1116.

impossibility. But they are content to leave that entirely in the Holy Spirit's hands.

D. Ethical, Personal, and Religious Content of Sexual Union

"In addition to everything else," John Paul says that the contraceptive practice and mentality "does enormous harm from the point of view of man's interior culture" (417). Whether they know this or not, by using contraception men and women are cutting themselves off from the very source of married love. Since conjugal intercourse is meant to be a sign of and inspiration to their whole married life, spouses who sterilize their union inevitably weaken and cheapen their entire relationship. Every time they engage in contracepted intercourse, rather than consummating and strengthening their marriage bond, they are being unfaithful to the promises they made at the altar. How healthy would a marriage be if husband and wife were continually unfaithful to their wedding vows?

On the other hand, as the Pope observes, "Respect for the work of God contributes to seeing that the conjugal act does not become diminished and deprived of the interior meaning of married life as a whole—that it does not become a 'habit'—and that there is expressed in it a sufficient fullness of ethical and personal content." Furthermore, the gift of the Spirit fills the sexual life of spouses with a proper "religious content." Sexual union itself becomes an act of "veneration for the majesty of the Creator...and for the spousal love of the Redeemer" (418).

This veneration instills in the couple an unwavering conviction that God is "the only and the ultimate depositary of the source of life" (418). Spouses realize that to take this power into their own hands would be to make themselves "like God" (see Gen 3:5). It would be to commit the original sin all over again—*grasping* at the divine likeness rather than *receiving* it (see §26).

103. *Humanae Vitae* and the Authentic Progress of Civilization
November 28, 1984 (TB 419–422)

John Paul delivered the 129th and final address of his theology of the body on November 28, 1984. He concludes his catechesis with a brief sketch of the extensive project he just completed, outlining his goals and purposes and the structure and method of his analysis.

He says the entire catechesis can be summed up under the title: "Human love in the divine plan," or more precisely, "The redemption of the body and the sacramentality of marriage" (419). He describes the phrase "the theology of the body" as a "working term" which places the theme of the redemption of the body and the sacramentality of marriage on a wider base. However, he says that "we must immediately note that the term 'theology of the body' goes far beyond the content of the reflections that were made." Multiple problems (the Pope lists suffering and death as primary examples) not addressed specifically by this catechesis belong to a theology of the body.[112] And John Paul adds: "We must state this clearly" (420).

A. John Paul's Priority

The Pope's priority, of course, was to propose the biblical vision of embodiment in terms of erotic desire and man's call to communion. As he says, the words of Genesis 2:24 (the two become one flesh) "were originally and thematically at the base of our argument." These words confirm, among other ways, "the moment when the light of Revelation touches the reality of the human body" (420).

John Paul observes once again that he made his reflections in order to face the questions raised by the encyclical *Humanae Vitae*. The largely negative reaction that the encyclical aroused confirms both the importance and the difficulty of these questions. As the Pope's entire catechesis demonstrates, these questions do not concern only biology or medicine. To frame the discussion merely in such terms is to stop at the surface of the issue. These questions are "organically related to both the sacramentality of marriage and the whole biblical question of the theology of the body, centered on the key words of Christ" (420). Hence, the Pope's final cycle of reflections on *Humanae Vitae* "is not artificially added to the sum total" of his catechesis "but is organically and homogeneously united with it." In fact, the part "located at the end is at the same time found at the beginning" (422). John Paul adds that this last statement is important from the point of view of "structure and method," thus indicating how his deepening spiral of reflections returns to its origin by reaching its destiny.

John Paul is convinced that adequate answers to the questions raised by *Humanae Vitae* must be sought in "that sphere of anthropology and theology that we have called 'theology of the body'" (421). In other words, the Pope maintains that adequate answers to man's perennial questions and also to the difficult questions of our modern world concerning mar-

---

112. John Paul states that his Apostolic Exhortation *Familiaris Consortio* outlines the direction for the progressive completion and development of the theology of the body. We could also add that the entire library of John Paul II's teaching constitutes, in some sense, a building on the foundation of his "adequate anthropology" found in his first major catechetical project.

riage and procreation must focus on the "biblical and personalistic aspects" of these issues.

B. Biblical and Personalist Aspects

John Paul focuses on the *biblical aspects* in order to place the doctrine of today's Church on the foundation of Revelation. In light of some trends that tend to develop theology apart from the Scriptures, the Holy Father stresses that progress in theology takes place through a continual restudying of the deposit of Revelation.[113]

Countering the fears of others who are leery of his engagement with and incorporation of modern thought, John Paul states that the Church is "always open to questions posed by man and also makes use of the instruments most in keeping with modern science and today's culture" (421). In other words, if the Church is going to evangelize the modern world, she must enter into the mind of the modern world and appeal to that mind in presenting the unchanging truths of the Gospel (see §§8, 9). She must readily accept and thoughtfully respond to the questions men and women pose regarding Church teaching. (We might observe that 129 Wednesday audience addresses spanning five years is a thoughtful response indeed.)

Justifying his turn to the subject, the Holy Father states: "It seems that in this area the intense development of philosophical anthropology (especially the anthropology that rests on ethics) most closely faces the questions raised by the encyclical *Humanae Vitae*" (421). John Paul even says that examining the Church's teaching with a *personalistic* approach is essential for man's authentic development since modern civilization exhibits an "occult tendency" to measure progress on the basis of "things" rather than on the basis of the person. "The analysis of the *personalistic aspects* of the Church's doctrine...emphasizes a determined appeal to measure man's progress on the basis of the 'person,' that is, of what is good for man as man—what corresponds to his essential dignity." Thus, the encyclical *Humanae Vitae* "presents as a fundamental problem the viewpoint of man's authentic development...measured to the greatest extent on the basis of ethics and not only on 'technology'" (421–422).

C. Technology, Ethics, and Progress

Modern technology has provided incalculable benefits for humanity. But technology is only a good insofar as it is at the service of the true good

---

113. John Paul II has certainly made this point most emphatically by his own example. Virtually all his encyclicals, apostolic letters, and other magisterial statements begin with a reflection on the Word of God.

of man. In other words, technology is answerable to ethics. Regarding the issue at hand, the Catholic response to contraceptive technology is that it is *not* in keeping with the true good of man. This is precisely what the Pope's theology of the body has sought to demonstrate "from the beginning."

As John Paul II states: "Paul VI, in *Humanae Vitae,* expressed what elsewhere had been affirmed by many authoritative moralists and scientists, even non-Catholics—namely, that precisely in this field, so profoundly and essentially human and personal, it is necessary above all to refer to man as a person, the subject who decides for himself, and not to 'means' which make him the 'object' (of manipulations) and 'depersonalize' him." John Paul concludes that the teaching of *Humanae Vitae* is a question nothing short of the "authentically 'humanistic' meaning of the development and progress of human civilization."[114]

Precisely on this point we see the dramatic clash of two irreconcilable visions of the human person, of human sexuality, and of human progress. Some emphatically claim that contraception provides a key (if not *the* key) to solving many of the problems which hinder the progress of human civilization. In turn, such people accuse the Church of fostering such travesties as poverty, starvation, the abuse of women, and the spread of AIDS because of her insistence on the immorality of contraception.

What, however, is the root cause of poverty, starvation, the abuse of women, and sexually transmitted diseases? Do they not stem precisely from rejection of the "great mystery" of God's plan for human life inscribed in our bodies? Is not the proclamation of this plan and the universal invitation to participate in it precisely the road to authentic human flourishing? Of course this does not mean merely delivering a message. We must be willing to join in solidarity with those who suffer from poverty or those who are dying of AIDS. We must love them where they are and as they are precisely because of their great dignity as men and women made in the divine image. These are the issues at stake—the truth of love, the dignity of man, the very meaning of being created male and female in the divine image.

If what the Church proposes about the great dignity and meaning of our humanity is correct, contraception can *never* be the solution to our problems but only the beginning of a terrible setback for humanity. Whether the problem at hand is a pregnant woman living in a Brazilian favela struggling to feed the children she already has, or the pandemic of AIDS in Africa—the Church believes that a return to the "great mystery"

---

114. 10/31/84, TB 411.

of God's plan for man and woman is the *only real and lasting solution* to the problems we face.

D. Humanization and Evangelization

As we previously quoted John Paul saying, the relationship of the sexes "constitutes the pure and simple fabric of existence." Thus, the dignity and balance of human life "depend at every moment of history and at every point of geographical longitude and latitude on 'who' she will be for him and he for her."[115] Enslavement to concupiscence is the basic and fundamental force disrupting the relationship of the sexes and, in turn, the dignity and balance of human life. Give people contraceptives and we keep them in their chains. Give them the "great mystery" of God's plan for life and love as proclaimed in John Paul's theology of the body and we bring good news to the poor, we set captives free, we give sight to the blind (see Lk 4:18). We set men and women on the path to fulfilling the very meaning of their being and existence.

An authentically "humanistic" meaning of the development and progress of human civilization consists precisely in this. When we take John Paul II's anthem to heart—that Jesus Christ fully reveals man to himself—we realize why, for this Polish pontiff, humanization and evangelization are simply two sides of the same coin.[116] This is what the new evangelization *is* and must be—the universal proclamation of and invitation to participate in the "great mystery" of God's plan for human life. This great mystery is inscribed in our bodies "from the beginning." It is inscribed in masculinity and femininity and the call of the "two" to become "one flesh." And it is definitively revealed in the Word made flesh, in Christ's incarnate communion with his Bride, the Church.

This is what we learn in John Paul II's theology of the body—the *good news* of the Gospel is written in human flesh, in everyone's flesh, in every*body*. Our concluding reflections will seek to demonstrate how this theology of the body plays an indispensable role in the new evangelization. In some sense, the new evangelization is and must be a proclamation of the Gospel of the body.

---

115. 10/8/80, TB 159 (see §35).

116. See Phillip Egan, "Priesthood in the Teaching of John Paul II," in *The Wisdom of John Paul II* (London: CTS Publications, 2001), p. 37.

Love and Fruitfulness—In Review

1. John Paul's final cycle, premising some reflections on the Song of Songs and the book of Tobit, applies his "adequate anthropology" to the fiercely resisted teaching of Pope Paul VI's encyclical *Humanae Vitae*. Questions come from this encyclical which permeate the Pope's entire catechesis. Thus, this final cycle is homogeneously united with the preceding cycles.

2. John Paul examines the Song of Songs with the aim of better understanding the sacramental sign of marriage. He seems critical of those exegetes who are quick to disembody the Song, seeing nothing more than a "spiritual" allegory. Precisely in this profound affirmation of erotic love—not despite it—we are able to discern God's revelation. It is in the lovers' mutual fascination with the body that we see the divine mystery made visible.

3. The groom's fascination with the visible femininity of his beloved reveals an aspiration born of love on the basis of the language of the body. It is a search for integral beauty, the beauty of body and soul free of all stain. It is a love and appreciation not just for *a* body but for *some*body, for her entire feminine person.

4. The restlessness of their desire for a love that is "ever in search" but "never satisfied" speaks of their desire for integration of eros with "something more"—with agape. If love is "stern as death," this means that love goes to the furthest limits of the language of the body in order to exceed them. Ultimately even spouses must "break away" from the earthly reality of love which—when it is true—leads them into the heart of agape, the love of eternity.

5. In calling his beloved first his "sister" before his "bride," the groom speaks of their common humanity, reproducing in some way the whole history of the femininity of the person he loves. "Sister" demonstrates the disinterested tenderness of his desire toward her, demonstrating the sincerity of his self-gift. Unless lovers first recognize each other as brother and sister, they are unable to love one another properly as husband and wife.

6. The expression "you are a garden enclosed" reveals the lover's recognition of his beloved as a person created for "her own sake." Because she is "master of her own mystery," the lover knows that he cannot grasp or possess her. He must trust in the freedom of the gift. Spousal love—

which is simultaneously spiritual and sensual—enables an initiation into the mystery of the person without ever violating the mystery of the person.

7. In the union of the sexes, people's choices and actions take on "all the weight of human existence." We see very pointedly in the marriage of Tobiah and Sarah that in becoming one flesh, spouses find themselves at the center of the great contest between good and evil, life and death, love and all that is opposed to love. Yet the power of love is shown in the readiness of spouses to place themselves in the center of the battle. Love is ever confident in the victory of good and is ready to do everything so that good may conquer.

8. Tobiah's prayer shows that he desires not lust, but to be a sincere gift to Sarah according to God's original plan. Hence, in calling upon God's grace and mercy, Tobiah and Sarah face the test of life and death—and their love, supported by their prayer, is revealed as "more stern than death." In this way their "one flesh" union bears witness to God as the God of life.

9. Ephesians 5 brings us to the "mystical" and "liturgical" dimension of the language of the body. Conjugal life becomes liturgical (an act of prayer and worship) when, through the ethos of redemption, it enables men and women to reclaim God's original plan for their humanity. Above all, liturgical life involves the celebration of the sacraments. The sacraments penetrate both soul and body, the entire male and female personality, with the power of sanctity.

10. The ethos and spirituality of married life is formed by that "reverence for Christ" to which St. Paul exhorts spouses. This reverence is nothing but a mature form of sexual attraction. It is a gift of the Holy Spirit (piety) which frees men and women to experience the language of the body in a depth, simplicity, and beauty altogether unknown to spouses dominated by concupiscence. It enables spouses to be a true sign of God's eternal, creative love.

11. *Humanae Vitae* bases its teaching on "the inseparable connection" between "the unitive and procreative meanings" of sexual intercourse. This formulation appeals to modern philosophy's "subjective turn." Couples, however, are not free to assign their own meaning to the conjugal act. Its twofold meaning is already objectively pre-inscribed in "the fundamental structure" of the act and "the actual nature of man and of woman."

12. The immorality of contraception is revealed (theologically) in the integral truth of marriage as a sacramental sign. It is especially important

in the consummate sign of married love that the language of the body be reread in truth. Contraception negates this truth and falsifies the divine Word inscribed in the body. It turns the spouses into "false prophets." Rather than proclaiming the "great mystery" of God's life-giving love, they blaspheme with their bodies.

13. The moral norm of *Humanae Vitae* belongs not only to natural law, but also to the moral order revealed by God. It is based on a biblical theology of the body, which "is not merely a theory, but rather a specific, evangelical, Christian pedagogy of the body." The teaching of *Humanae Vitae* presents an integral aspect of the message of salvation for the purpose of modeling earthly life on the hope of life eternal.

14. Since the two meanings of intercourse are inseparable, by attacking the procreative meaning, contracepted intercourse also ceases to be a communion of persons and an act of love. Through the whole dynamism of tension and enjoyment, the bodies of husband and wife are meant to speak the mystery of God in all its truth. But contraception, by violating the interior order of conjugal union, turns the language of the body into a lie. This constitutes the essential evil of the act.

15. Pastoral concern means the search for man's true good and the proclamation of God's plan for human love. In turn, God calls every couple to be a witness and interpreter of his plan. In the exercise of parenthood, couples "interpret" this plan responsibly when they prudently and generously decide to have a large family, or when—for serious reasons and with total respect for the language of the body—they choose to space births or limit family size.

16. A couple who resorts to contraception may have an acceptable reason to avoid a pregnancy, but the end never justifies the means. Abstaining from that which causes pregnancy is the only means of avoiding pregnancy that does not objectively violate the language of the body. Through abstinence, couples show themselves capable of authentic freedom in self-giving.

17. Responsible parenthood requires that spouses embrace the harmony of biology and personality. When we suppress fertility, we tamper with the body-soul integrity of the human person. Thus, the essence of the Church's teaching on contraception lies in maintaining an adequate relationship between dominion of the forces of nature and mastery of self. Self-mastery corresponds to man's dignity as a subject with self-determination. Suppressing fertility deprives man of his subjectivity, making him an object of manipulation.

18. In the integral vision of natural family planning presented by *Humanae Vitae,* there can be no thought of a mechanical application of biological laws. Responsible parenthood requires a mature freedom in self-giving, and a positive family and procreative attitude. It requires that the language of the body—including its internal structures—be reread in truth. Thus, in no way is responsible parenthood exclusively directed to limiting, much less excluding children.

19. Natural law refers to the Creator's plan for man insofar as it is understood by right reason. Fidelity to the natural law is not a reduction of ethics to "impersonal" laws of biology, but is rightly understood as fidelity to the Creator-Person who inscribed his will for us in our own body-persons. It is therefore a question of what corresponds to the true dignity of persons.

20. *Humanae Vitae* outlines an authentic marital spirituality, and the theology of the body constitutes the essential nucleus of such spirituality. Spouses must pass through the "narrow gate" and travel the "hard way," yet they are strengthened and "consecrated" by the power of the Holy Spirit to bear authentic witness to Christ in their married life. Prayer and the sacraments—especially the Eucharist and Penance—are the "infallible and indispensable" means for forming an authentic conjugal spirituality.

21. The Church's renewed formulation, with its emphasis on the subjective dimension of love, reaffirms the traditional teaching on the objective purposes of marriage (and their hierarchy) and at the same time deepens this teaching from the viewpoint of the interior life of the spouses. Thus, conjugal love is not an "end" of marriage but the inner form of married life. Conjugal love directs spouses to the fulfillment of the ends of marriage.

22. Authentic love correctly unites the two meanings of the conjugal act. There is no contradiction involved here, only a "difficulty" since love must do battle in the heart with concupiscence. If the powers of concupiscence try to detach the language of the body from the truth, the power of love strengthens the language of the body ever anew in that truth. In this way spouses bear witness to the mystery of the redemption of the body.

23. Continence (self-mastery) certainly involves "saying no" to lust. But continence is not only—and not even principally—the ability to say no. This is the negative role of continence, but it also has a positive role. Mature self-mastery enables one to direct the very "content and character" of physical and emotional reactions toward sincere self-giving. If chastity

is first manifested as the capacity to resist concupiscence, it gradually reveals itself as the capacity to perceive, love, and live the true, sacramental meaning of the body and of sex.

24. To acquire self-mastery a person must be committed to a progressive education in self-control of the will, feelings, and emotions—beginning with the most simple acts in which it is fairly easy to practice control. The continent person exercises "control" precisely in order to uphold the incomparable *value* of sexuality—to protect it from the degradation of lust. We cannot speak of continence as a virtue if one's "control" in sexual matters is based on a fear or *devaluation* of sexuality. That would imply acceptance of the Manichaean anti-value.

25. The asceticism necessary to marital chastity does not impoverish the relationship of the sexes. It progressively enriches their dialogue purifying it, deepening it, and simplifying it. Expressions of affection are not dampened but become spiritually more intense. If marital intercourse remains the consummate expression of spousal communion, through conjugal chastity other expressions of affection are also revealed in their purest, simplest, deepest, and most intense character. Harmony reigns in married life as the fruit of a mature continence.

26. It is often thought that continence causes inner tensions from which man must free himself. Yet, when understood integrally, continence is the only way to free man from such tensions. Continence is not only the capacity to "contain" sensual reactions, but even more the capacity to control and guide the whole sphere of man's sensuality and emotions. Mature continence directs excitement and emotion toward the sincere gift of self.

27. Man and woman's personal communion cannot be formed in the full truth of its possibilities only on the level of concupiscence. In fact, the nuptial meaning of the body has been distorted by concupiscence almost at its very roots. The teaching of *Humanae Vitae* affirms the possibility of overcoming these distortions with God's grace and living conjugal love in its pure, integral truth. This is also love's most physically and emotionally intense form.

28. Chastity lies at the center of marital spirituality as a manifestation of "life in the Holy Spirit." In fact, spouses cannot experience conjugal intercourse on the proper level of persons *(communio personarum)* "except through the powers coming from the Holy Spirit who purifies, enlivens, strengthens, and perfects the powers of the human spirit." Through the Holy Spirit, man and woman are filled with veneration for the values of the conjugal union.

29. The gift of piety—of respect and awe for what is sacred—instills in the couple a profound respect for the twofold meaning of the conjugal act. When men and women interiorize God's glorious plan for sexual union, they have a "salvific fear" of ever violating or degrading "what bears in itself the sign of the divine mystery of creation and redemption." Thus, when spouses live by the Holy Spirit, contracepted intercourse becomes *unthinkable*.

30. Men and women who are the object of concupiscence gradually realize that they are not loved for their "own sake," but only insofar as they satisfy the other's selfish needs. Herein lies the enormous significance of respect for the work of God which the Spirit stirs up in those who are open to it. When men and women live from this place of respect, all their manifestations of affection protect and affirm in each of them a "deep-rooted peace." This peace is the "interior resonance" of chastity.

31. The gift of piety, together with love and chastity, leads the couple to understand "the singular, or rather exceptional, significance" of the conjugal act. Recognizing and protecting the dignity of this act is the specific goal of conjugal spirituality. Thus "the antithesis of conjugal spirituality" is constituted, in some sense, by a couple's lack of understanding of the exceptional significance of intercourse demonstrated by contraceptive practice and mentality.

32. Respect for what is sacred contributes to seeing that the conjugal act does not become an empty "habit"—and that there is expressed in it a sufficient fullness of ethical, personal, and religious content. Through the gift of the Spirit, the sexual union of spouses becomes an act of veneration for the majesty of the Creator and for the spousal love of the Redeemer.

33. Birth regulation is not only a biological problem, but is organically related to the whole question of the theology of the body. Thus, answers to man's pressing questions must focus on the biblical and personalistic aspects of the issue. The biblical emphasis demonstrates that the Church's teaching against contraception is rooted in divine revelation. The personalistic emphasis demonstrates that authentic human progress must be measured not merely on the basis of technology, but on the basis of the essential dignity of the human person.

34. Enslavement to concupiscence is the basic and fundamental force disrupting the dignity and balance of human life. Contraception only fosters this concupiscence. But the "great mystery" of God's plan for the sexes proclaimed by the theology of the body sets men and women on the path to fulfilling the very meaning of their being and existence. *Humanae Vitae*, therefore, is a question nothing short of the authentically "humanistic" meaning of the development and progress of civilization.

Epilogue

The Gospel of the Body and the New Evangelization

Having undertaken the mammoth task of studying John Paul II's theology of the body from start to finish, let us now conclude by looking briefly at its importance for the Church at this historical moment. Describing this moment in his Apostolic Letter at the close of the Great Jubilee, John Paul wrote: "A new millennium is opening before the Church like a vast ocean upon which we shall venture, relying on the help of Christ."[1] Though rough waters abound, John Paul beckons us to set sail without fear, and to "put out into the deep" for a catch: *"Duc in altum"* (Lk 5:4).[2] Two millennia ago, led by Peter's faith in Christ—"at your word I will let down the nets" (Lk 5:5)—the first disciples cast their nets and caught a multitude of fish.

Peter's 263rd successor has reflected with great faith on Christ's words in his theology of the body. He has sought—and found—in the Master's words the deepest answers to the most pressing questions of modern men and women concerning the meaning of our creation as male and female and the call of the two to communion in "one flesh." These are always questions about the meaning of life itself, the meaning of love, the meaning of existence. These are questions that take us to "the deepest substratum of ethics and culture." Our answers to these questions determine culture—whether men and women flourish in a culture of life or languish in a culture of death. If there is to be a great catch of fish in a "new evangelization," we sons and daughters of the Church must first recover the sense of having an urgently important message for the salvation of the world. The Gospel of the body proclaimed by John Paul II is that message. *How urgently it is needed!* We must follow Peter's example of faith and "put out into the deep" for a catch—*"Duc in altum!"*

---

1. *Novo Millennio Ineunte,* n. 58.

2. Ibid, n. 1.

As we reflected at the start of this book, the twentieth century, which began with the hope of unlimited progress, ended as the bloodiest century known to history. Modern man had placed his hopes for a messiah in his own genius—in science, technology, medicine. Whenever man loses sight of the "great mystery" and sets his sights on this world, he always meets disappointment, even despair: "The world is not capable of making man happy. It is not capable of saving him from evil, in all of its types and forms—illness, epidemics, cataclysms, catastrophes, and the like. This world, with its riches and its wants, needs to be saved, to be redeemed."[3]

We now stand in great need of a "passover" from death to life. Even after 2,000 years of Christianity, Christians themselves are still coming to terms with the fact that salvation comes only by way of the Cross. We are much like the disciples on the road to Emmaus—baffled by the tragic events of our own day, wondering what it all means and why it has all gone so sour. Yet, through his theology of the body, the Vicar of Christ has walked with us, opening up the Scriptures for us. Those who have heard his words can certainly say, "Were not our hearts burning within us as he unfolded the 'great mystery' of God's designs?" (see Lk 24:32) And just as the disciples on the road came to recognize Christ "in the breaking of the bread"—in his body given for them in the Eucharist—so, too, have we come, through our study of John Paul's catechesis, to see Christ revealed in his body: in our bodies because we, though many, are "one body" with him.

Inasmuch as John Paul's theology of the body takes us to the deepest roots of the modern crisis and outlines so clearly the path to the "redemption of the body"; inasmuch as John Paul's theology of the body appeals to the modern turn to the subject, incarnating the Gospel in the everyday experiences of men and women—it seems indispensable in the Church's efforts to reconnect the modern world with the "great mystery" of God's spousal love for humanity, Christ's spousal love for the Church. It seems an indispensable foundation for the "new evangelization" and for the building of a culture of life.

104. The Antidote to the Culture of Death

We are living in an age that Christians of the future will likely describe as the near-triumph of "the anti-life heresy." They will recount that this heresy threatened to destroy civilization at its roots with its resulting

---

3. *Crossing the Threshold of Hope*, p. 56.

culture of death. However, as has always been the case in the history of theological development, the Christians of the future will recognize that this attack against God's original plan for human life—commonly referred to in the future as his "marital plan"—will have been vanquished by a precise theological elaboration of the place of the nuptial meaning of the body and the marital covenant at the very heart and center of the economy of salvation.[4]

This is the gift of John Paul II's theology of the body to the Church and the world. It is the antidote to the culture of death and the theological foundation of the culture of life. Indeed, if the future of humanity passes by way of marriage and the family,[5] we could say that the future of marriage and the family passes by way of John Paul II's theology of the body. Put simply, there will be no renewal of the Church and of the world without a renewal of marriage and the family. And there will be no renewal of marriage and the family without a return to the full truth of God's plan for the body and sexuality. Yet that will not happen without a fresh theological proposal that compellingly demonstrates to the modern world how the Christian sexual ethic—far from the cramped, prudish list of prohibitions it is assumed to be—is a liberating, redeeming ethos that, even if it involves the element of the cross, corresponds perfectly with the most noble aspirations of the human heart. This is precisely what John Paul II's theology of the body is. But, as we have seen in our extensive study, it is also so much more.

A. Ramifications for All of Theology

As George Weigel writes, "John Paul's *Theology of the Body* has ramifications for all of theology. It challenges us to think of sexuality as a way to grasp the essence of the human—and through that, to discern something about the divine." Weigel continues, "Angelo Scola, rector of the Pontifical Lateran University in Rome, goes so far as to suggest that virtually every thesis in theology—God, Christ, the Trinity, grace, the Church, the sacraments—could be seen in a new light if theologians explored in depth the rich personalism implied in John Paul II's theology of the body."[6]

This is a striking proposal. Indeed, it is no exaggeration to say that the Pope's theology of the body will leave the Church reeling in self-discovery for centuries to come. Much like the thinking of Augustine or

4. These ideas expressed with gratitude to Sean Inherst.

5. See *Familiaris Consortio,* n. 86.

6. *Witness to Hope,* p. 343.

Aquinas, John Paul II's insights—in the whole corpus of his thought but particularly in his catechesis on the body—inaugurate a new era in the history of Christian thinking and set a new standard for theological inquiry. Yet theologians have hardly begun to unpack the great riches of the Pope's teaching. Recall Weigel's statement that "John Paul's portrait of sexual love as an icon of the interior life of God has barely begun to shape the Church's theology, preaching, and religious education. When it does it will compel a dramatic development of thinking about virtually every major theme in the Creed."[7]

Understanding the human body as a theology must not be relegated to the level of an obscure interest of a few specialized theologians. It must be the interest of every man and woman who desires to understand the meaning of human existence. Indeed ultimate reality itself is revealed through the human body—through the Word made *flesh*. If we stay the course, curiosity about the meaning of the body and of sexuality—so often considered innately prurient—actually leads us into the heart of the mystery hidden in God from time immemorial. Indeed, that biblical "one flesh" union "bears in itself the sign of the divine mystery of creation and redemption."[8] Hence, as we have learned, understanding Christ's revelation regarding the human body and its redemption "concerns the entire Bible."[9] It plunges us head first into "the perspective of the whole Gospel, of the whole teaching, in fact, of the whole mission of Christ."[10]

B. Mainstream Mysticism

Some might ask: "If this theology of the body is *so* important, where has it been for two thousand years?" This is a legitimate question. However, while recognizing that John Paul is presenting a clear development of thinking, we must also recognize that the fundamental message of the theology of the body is nothing new. It is the same Gospel which has been proclaimed since the descent of the Holy Spirit upon Mary and the Apostles in the upper room. John Paul II is penetrating that Gospel—which is the same yesterday, today, and forever—with new clarity, new insight, new depth. And he is rooting the revelation of that Gospel—as it always has been, even if it has not always been so well understood—in the biblical truth of the human body, of the incarnate person made, as male and female, in the image and likeness of God.

---

7. Ibid., p. 853.

8. 11/14/84, TB 416.

9. 1/13/82, TB 249.

10. 12/3/80, TB 175.

Mystics throughout history have plumbed the depths of the "great mystery" of the divine-human "nuptial union." But their ecstatic visions and the insights they afforded were not exactly mainstream. With the theology of the body, we might say that Pope John Paul II is bringing "nuptial mysticism" to the whole Church. It seems he is proposing it in some sense as the "normal" Christian view of the world.

Why has it taken two thousand years for such a liberating mysticism to be presented by a pope as food for the whole Church? We must recognize that the Church matures through time in some ways similar to a human person. The analogy is certainly imperfect, but we would not expect a child to understand himself the same way an adult does. We might even say that with John Paul II's theology of the body, the Church, as a corporate person, has reached puberty—a new "awakening" of sorts regarding the meaning of the body and the communion of the sexes. We might also observe that puberty is not full maturity, but only the beginning of the process that brings one into adulthood. Thus, if this comparison is at all accurate, the Church still has a good deal of maturing ahead of her, and a good deal of "growing pains."

Finally, if the Pope's insights are the fruit of two thousand years of "communal reflection" on the Word of God,[11] they have also been forged by the unprecedented triumphs and tragedies of this particular historical "moment." In the Easter Vigil liturgy we exult in the "happy fault of Adam which won for us so great a Redeemer." We might also exult in the "happy fault" of the sexual revolution in the twentieth century which won for us so great a theology of the body.

105. Incarnating the Gospel Message

In his encyclical *Redemptoris Missio,* John Paul wrote: "I sense that the moment has come to commit all of the Church's energies to a new evangelization and to the mission *ad gentes.* No believer in Christ, no institution of the Church can avoid this supreme duty: to proclaim Christ to all peoples."[12] He also wrote: "If we look at today's world, we are struck by many negative factors that can lead to pessimism. But this feeling is unjustified: we have faith in God our Father and Lord and in his mercy. ...God is preparing a great springtime for Christianity, and we can already see its first signs."[13]

---

11. See *Fides et Ratio,* n. 101.

12. *Redemptoris Missio,* n. 3.

13. Ibid., n. 86.

John Paul first used the expression "the new evangelization" in a pastoral visit to Latin America in 1983. Ever since he has "unstintingly recalled the pressing need for a *new evangelization.*"[14] This urgency stems not only from the fact that the number of those not yet reached by the Gospel is still immense,[15] but also because "entire groups of the baptized have lost a living sense of the faith, or even no longer consider themselves members of the Church, and live a life far removed from Christ and his Gospel."[16]

Therefore, one thing "new" about this evangelization is the fact that it entails not only the mission *ad gentes,* or "to the nations" who have not heard the Gospel, but also a mission towards men and women who are already baptized. The widespread phenomenon of the "baptized non-believer" has come to light as the social structures favoring Christianity have fallen in the West. Previous generations of men and women may have conformed in varying degrees to the Christian ethic, but as the social pressures to do so waned, the essential Christian ethos was found lacking. Men and women in large numbers were "culturally Christian," but had not experienced a conversion of heart to Jesus Christ and his teachings. The recovery of an authentic Christian "ethos," in fact, was one of the main goals of Vatican II. As the Council understood well, this can only happen through an authentic, compelling, evangelical proclamation of salvation through Jesus Christ.

A. Bringing Heavenly Mysteries Down to Earth

As John Paul clarified in his Apostolic Letter at the close of the Great Jubilee, the new evangelization is not "a matter of inventing a 'new program.' The program already exists: it is the plan found in the Gospel and in the living Tradition, it is the same as ever."[17] What is essential in order to meet the unprecedented needs of our day is a proclamation of the Gospel that is "new in ardor, methods, and expression."[18]

According to John Paul, *"the new evangelization* [involves] a vital effort to come to a deeper understanding of the mysteries of faith and to find meaningful language with which to convince our contemporaries that

---

14. *Fides et Ratio,* n. 103.

15. See *Redemptoris Missio,* n. 86.

16. Ibid., n. 33; see also Pope Paul VI, *Evangelii Nuntiandi,* n. 52; Pope John Paul II, *Catechesi Tradendae,* nn. 19, 42.

17. *Novo Millennio Ineunte,* n. 29.

18. Address to the Assembly of CELAM, March 9, 1983.

they are called to newness of life through God's love." It is the task of sharing with modern men and women "the 'unsearchable riches of Christ' and of making known 'the plan of the mystery hidden for ages in God who created all things' (Eph 3:8–9)."[19] This is *precisely* what John Paul II's theology of the body provides: a deeper understanding of the mysteries of faith and a meaningful way to share them with men and women of today.

Once the Pope's scholarship is actually comprehended (or presented in a way that people can understand), the theology of the body has a remarkable ability to bring the heavenly mysteries down to earth. These are not theological abstractions. They "ring true" in the human heart because the Pope's teaching is the fruit of a constant confrontation of doctrine with experience. As the Holy Father observes, "God comes to us in the things we know best and can verify most easily, the things of our everyday life, apart from which we cannot understand ourselves."[20] What do we know better, what can we verify more easily, what is more "everyday" than the experience of embodiment? This is where God meets us—in the flesh. And this is where the Church must meet the world in the new evangelization.

The *Catechism* teaches that the Church "in her whole being and in all her members...is sent to announce, bear witness, make present, and spread the mystery of the communion of the Holy Trinity."[21] This sums up well the essential goal of evangelization. And this eternal mystery of *communio* becomes a practical, incarnate reality through the lens of the theology of the body. It becomes close to us, we realize that it is part of us. The divine mystery of love and communion is stamped not only in our deepest spiritual reality, but also in our physical reality—in our whole personal experience of being "a body," and of being, as a body, male or female. This—our creation as male and female—is "the fundamental fact" of human existence.[22]

B. The Human Question and the Divine Answer

John Paul defines the basic task of evangelization as "the Church's effort to proclaim to [all men and women] that God loves them, that he has given himself for them in Christ Jesus, and that he invites them to an un-

---

19. *Springtime of Evangelization: The Complete Texts of the Holy Father's 1998 Ad Limina Addresses to the Bishops of the United States* (San Diego, CA: Basilica Press, 1999), pp. 53, 55.

20. *Fides et Ratio*, n. 12.

21. *CCC*, n. 738.

22. See 2/13/80, TB 74.

ending life of happiness."[23] This basic message is in itself "good news." But it needs to be *incarnated* if men and women are to find their link with it. Of course, this message was and *is* incarnated in Jesus Christ. However, someone might still respond, "What does some man who lived two thousand years ago have to do with me?"

As a professor of mine once said, we can proclaim that "Jesus is the *answer*" until we are blue in the face. But unless people are first in touch with the *question,* we remain on the level of theological abstraction. Herein lies the gift of grounding the Gospel in the body. It is the antidote to theological abstraction. It roots us in what is truly human and by so doing prepares us to receive what is truly divine. In other words, it puts us squarely in touch with the human question, thus opening our hearts to the divine answer.

Nothing puts us in touch with the enigma of human existence like the reality of our own embodiment. In some sense, embodiment *is* the human question. What does it mean to be a man? What does it mean to be a woman? There is no more important question for men and women to ask. And, as we observed early on, these are inherently sexual questions (see §6). Of course, the very ability to question and to wonder points to our deeper, metaphysical (beyond the physical, beyond the body) dimension. But the human anomaly is that the metaphysical dimension of man is manifested in his physical dimension. The body reveals the person. The body reveals man's solitude, and it is this solitude that *is* the human question.

As we have learned throughout our study, man's solitude is his own experience of being a person. This is the basic universal human experience. But what does it mean? This is the basic universal human question! Where do we find the answer? The same place we found the question—in our experience of embodiment. If solitude is the question, *communion* is the answer.

However, if the question (solitude) arises from within oneself as a person, the answer (communion) is discovered only by looking outside oneself towards the "other" person and in relation to that "other" person. By contemplating the "other" in the mystery of sexual difference, we realize that the body has a *nuptial* meaning. We realize that "man can only find himself through the sincere gift of himself."[24] This is the very mean-

---

23. *Springtime of Evangelization: The Complete Texts of the Holy Father's 1998 Ad Limina Addresses to the Bishops of the United States*, p. 55.

24. *Gaudium et Spes,* n. 24.

ing of "being a man" and "being a woman"—we are called to be a gift for one another, a gift that leads to a true communion of persons.

This is not abstract. Even if sin has distanced us from the beauty and purity of the original experience, everyone knows the "ache" of solitude and the longing for communion. Everyone knows the "magnetic pull" of erotic desire. This basic human longing for communion, in fact, is the most concrete link in every human heart with "that man who lived two thousand years ago." How so? Experience also attests that even in the most harmonious human communion, that "ache" of solitude is not entirely satisfied. The heart and body yearn for "something more." Indeed, the male-female communion (as the paradigm of all human communions) is only a preliminary answer to the enigma of our existence. It is only a glimmer, only a foreshadowing, only a sacrament of something far greater. And only the divine prototype, to which the biblical "one flesh" points, can ultimately satisfy the human longing for love and communion.

"For this reason...the two become one flesh." For what reason? To reveal, proclaim, and anticipate the union of Christ and the Church (see Eph 5:31–32). The eternal, ecstatic, "nuptial" communion with Christ and the entire communion of saints—so far superior to anything proper to earthly life that we cannot begin to fathom it—this alone can satisfy the human "ache" of solitude. This is the North Pole to which that magnetic pull of erotic desire is oriented. And *this* is why "Jesus is the answer." If the spirit of the Gospel is not *incarnated* as such, it will forever remain detached from what is essentially human. It will forever remain outside the scope of essentially human experiences (see §§11, 25). Yet, Christ took on flesh to wed himself indissolubly to that which is essentially human. Hence, if the Gospel is not incarnated with what is essentially human, it is essentially not the Gospel of Jesus Christ.

Notice how, in the following passage from *Evangelium Vitae,* John Paul II not only summarizes the call of the new evangelization, but roots it in the call to communion through the sincere gift of self which, as he also affirms, is rooted in the truth of the body and sexuality.

> We need to bring the *Gospel of life* to the heart of every man and woman and to make it penetrate every part of society. This involves above all proclaiming *the core* of this Gospel. It is the proclamation of a living God who is close to us, who calls us to profound communion with himself and awakens in us the certain hope of eternal life. It is the affirmation of the inseparable connection between the person, his life and his bodiliness. It is the presentation of human life as a life of relationship, a gift of God, the fruit and sign of his love. It is the proclamation that Jesus has a unique relationship with every person, which enables us to see in every human face the face of Christ. It is the call for a "sincere gift of self" as the fullest way to realize our personal freedom....

[As a consequence] the meaning of life is found in giving and receiving love, and in this light human sexuality and procreation reach their true and full significance.[25]

In light of all we have learned in the theology of the body, this passage takes on its full, incarnate meaning. The "God who is close to us" is so, in the most concrete sense, in and through the Incarnation, in and through human flesh. The call to an eternal life of "communion with himself" is stamped in our creation as male and female right from the beginning—in our interior spiritual reality and our exterior physical reality. Thus, there is an "inseparable connection between the person, his life and his bodiliness." The nuptial meaning of the body reveals human life "as a life of relationship." In the original human communion, we see the "gift of God" revealed through the primordial sacrament which is "the fruit and sign of his love." In the life of the first Adam, we already see a foreshadowing of the New Adam's "unique relationship with every person." And because the human body speaks of the great mystery of Christ, we "see in every human face the face of Christ." In light of all this, "personal freedom" can only be realized in the freedom of the gift—the sincere gift of self in imitation of Christ. This is the meaning of the Gospel—"giving and receiving love"—and it is all stamped in the meaning of the body, of human sexuality and the call to be fruitful and multiply.

106. The Church's Response to Modern Rationalism

John Paul asserts: "To make the Church *the home and school of communion:* that is the great challenge facing us in the millennium which is now beginning, if we wish to be faithful to God's plan and respond to the world's deepest yearnings."[26] The new evangelization, therefore, is not first an appeal to abstract, objective principles. It is an appeal to the deepest yearnings of the human heart for communion and a living witness to the truth that only Christ can fulfill this yearning. Furthermore, in the new evangelization, Christians must help men and women realize that their longing for Christ is written in the "great mystery" of the human body and its nuptial meaning.

But Christians can only pass this good news on to others if they are first infused with it and vivified by it themselves. As Pope Paul VI said in his great Apostolic Exhortation on evangelization, "The Church is an evangelizer, but

25. *Evangelium Vitae,* nn. 80–81.

26. *Novo Millennio Ineunte,* n. 43.

she begins by being evangelized herself."[27] There is no doubt that, in delivering his theology of the body, John Paul II's intended audience was, first and foremost, the Church herself. Very few Christians seem to understand that the "great mystery" hidden for ages in God is stamped in their own bodies and in their yearning for communion. Large numbers of Catholics have been caught up in the false humanism of the day and are hostile towards much of the Church's teaching. Hence, unless the tide is turned within the Church—unless the Church is first evangelized—she cannot evangelize others.

A. *The Spousal Analogy and the "Analogy of Faith"*

John Paul II's theology of the body provides great hope for the urgently needed renewal within the Church. When we view the Gospel message through the interpretive key of man and woman's call to incarnate communion, not only does the Gospel message take on flesh, but even the most controversial teachings of the Church (virtually all of which are related to the meaning of gender and sexuality) begin to make sense. Spousal theology demonstrates how all of the various puzzle pieces of the Christian mystery fit beautifully together. The truth of Catholicism "clicks" when viewed through the theology of the body. In other words, through the spousal analogy we become attentive to the "analogy of faith"—that is, to the coherence of the truths of faith among themselves and within the whole plan of Revelation centered on Christ.[28]

This is why the theology of the body will lead to a dramatic development of thinking about the Creed. This is why the *Catechism* speaks of the important connection between sexual rectitude, believing in the articles of the Creed, and *understanding* the mysteries we profess in the Creed. In other words, the *Catechism* points to the intimate connection between purity of heart, love of the truth, and orthodoxy of faith.[29] Conversely, Christianity unravels at the seams—its inner logic collapses and virtually everything it teaches becomes contested—as soon as we divorce ourselves from the "great mystery" of nuptial communion revealed through the body.

Modern rationalism, with its absolutizing of the conscious mind, effects just such a divorce. The body becomes divorced from the spirit and cannot be viewed as a theology. As John Paul wrote in his 1994 *Letter to Families*:

Saint Paul's magnificent synthesis concerning the "great mystery" ap-

---

27. *Evangelii Nuntiandi,* n. 15.

28. See *CCC,* nn. 90, 114, 158.

29. See *CCC,* n. 2518.

pears as the compendium or *summa,* in some sense, *of the teaching about God and man* which was brought to fulfillment by Christ. Unfortunately, Western thought, with the development of *modern rationalism,* has been gradually moving away from this teaching. The philosopher who formulated the principle *"Cogito, ergo sum"*—"I think, therefore I am"—also gave the modern concept of man its distinctive dualistic character. It is typical of rationalism to make a radical contrast in man between spirit and body, between body and spirit. The body can never be reduced to mere matter: it is a *spiritualized body,* just as man's spirit is so closely united to the body that he can be described as *an embodied spirit.* The richest source for knowledge of the body is the Word made flesh. *Christ reveals man to himself.* In a certain sense, this statement of the Second Vatican Council is the reply, so long awaited, which the Church has given to modern rationalism.[30]

We proposed *Gaudium et Spes* 22 as the Church's response to modern rationalism in the prologue, and said we would return to it after our study of the Pope's catechesis on the body. In what way is *Gaudium et Spes* 22—"Christ fully reveals man to himself"—a response to modern rationalism? And how does the Pope's theology of the body, as an extended commentary on *Gaudium et Spes* 22, shed light on this?

B. Man as "Absolute" or "Partner of the Absolute"

If modern rationalism makes of man an absolute, then man determines his own self by himself. He is answerable to nothing greater than himself and his own subjectivistic "reality." He is not ordered to anything or anyone else. He is not called to communion. He is a self-defined island. Fulfillment is attained by self-assertion and selfish gain. Other human beings become a utilitarian means to that gain or, if they are found to be an obstacle, they are crushed, discarded, even exterminated.

In such a world-view freedom means doing whatever one wants without any outside constraint. The Supreme Court of the United States, reaffirming the right of men and women to exterminate their own unborn children, concisely expressed this individualistic, rationalistic ideology when it asserted: "At the heart of liberty is the right to define one's own concept of existence, of meaning, of the universe, and of the mystery of human life."[31] It almost sounds like a religious statement. But it is the religion of the deceiver. The Supreme Court might simply have repeated his perennial lie: At the heart of liberty is the right to "make oneself like God" (see Gn 3:5).

Insert *Gaudium et Spes* 22 into the equation and it unmasks the sham

---

30. *Letter to Families,* n. 19.

31. Planned Parenthood v. Casey, 1992.

of modern rationalism: "The religion of the God who became man," said Paul VI in his closing speech at the Council, encounters "the religion (for such it is) of man who makes himself God."[32] Man does not define himself. Christ fully reveals man to himself. Man is not the absolute. The mystery of the Father and his love is the absolute. And how is this revealed? Through the gift and mystery of Christ's body—through the Word made flesh! Our humanity is not divine, but in Christ's humanity, we see our humanity wed indissolubly to divinity. In Christ we see that profound link between theology and anthropology that we spoke of in the prologue and unfolded throughout our study (see §3).

Asserting his own dignity as a free creature does not place man in a contest of wills with the Absolute. Such would be the case only if God were a tyrant, jealous of his own rule and leery of the freedom he bestowed upon his creature. This is the original anti-Word promulgated by the deceiver. The foundation of the universe is that God is love. Man is not the absolute, but he is called to open his heart to the greatest gift that the Absolute could possibly bestow upon a creature: Man is invited to be "partner of the Absolute." This, in fact, sums up the key distinction between secular and Christian humanisms. Either human freedom determines man as the absolute, or freedom is given to man so as to enter into "partnership" with the Absolute. If the former, man is not ordered in any fundamental way toward anything but himself, and freedom is fulfilled in his own egoistic, "masturbatory" gratification. If the latter, man is ordered towards communion with the Absolute, and freedom is fulfilled in the sincere gift of self to the "Other."

Furthermore, as we learn from John Paul's theology of the body, man determines himself in one direction or the other based on his understanding of his own body and sexuality. The body is either narcissistic or nuptial. It either throws man back on himself, or points him to relationship. As Stanislaw Grygiel, a professor at the John Paul II Institute in Rome, once stated, "If we don't live the sexual differences correctly that distinguish man and woman and call them to unite, we will not be capable of understanding the difference that distinguishes man and God and constitutes a primordial call to union. Thus, we may fall into the despair of a life separated from others and from the Other, that is, God."[33]

---

32. Cited in *Closing Speeches: Vatican Council II* (Boston: Pauline Books & Media), p. 10.

33. Quoted in "The Church Must Guide the Sexual Revolution" (Zenit International News Agency, August 31, 1999).

■ We can also recognize how man and woman's approach to regulating births pivots them either in the direction of a secular or Christian humanism. When a couple chooses to contracept, they take the powers of life into their own hands. They determine for themselves that this act of intercourse will be sterile. By doing so, they make themselves the "Absolute." However, when a couple chooses to cooperate with the way God designed human fertility, exercising the freedom to abstain from intercourse when serious reasons call for the avoidance of pregnancy, they show respect for God as the Absolute. They enter into "partnership" with the Absolute. Furthermore, if they choose to engage in intercourse during the infertile period, they *receive* infertility as a gift rather than *grasp* at it.

When we understand the body's nuptial meaning, we understand how *Gaudium et Spes* 22 leads us to *Gaudium et Spes* 24: If man is the only creature that God willed for "its own sake," man can only find himself through "the sincere gift of himself." This is how Christ fully reveals man to himself—by showing him that God is gift and empowering him to live a life of sincere self-giving. In other words, Christ reveals man to himself by making the sincere gift of his body on the cross ("this is my body, given for you") and filling our bodies with new life in the Holy Spirit. In turn, this "life in the Holy Spirit" restores in us the freedom of the gift.

Living in this freedom, we realize that other human beings are not means to my own selfish end. They are created for their own sake and the only proper response to them is love. In this view, at the heart of liberty is the freedom to choose the good, not to create it. True freedom is liberation not from the *external* "constraint" that calls me to good, but from the *internal* constraint that hinders my choice of the good. The truth sets us free. And the Truth is that the Son of God took on flesh and died and rose again to free us from all that hinders our capacity to love as he loves.

C. Turn to Christ

This is the message of salvation proclaimed with authority by Christ's body, the Church. Indeed, the Church herself, as the Bride of Christ, is the sign of this salvation. Furthermore, this message of God's love and salvation is written in human flesh right from the beginning—in the "great mystery" of our creation as male and female and our call to become "one flesh." As John Paul observes, "The Church cannot therefore be understood as the mystical body of Christ, as the sign of man's covenant with God in Christ, or as the universal sacrament of salvation, unless we keep in mind the 'great mystery' involved in the creation of man as male and female and the vocation of both to conjugal love, to fatherhood and to motherhood."[34]

With modern rationalism, however, man loses sight of the "great mystery" of his being—he loses sight of the ultimate Mystery that is Being. As John Paul writes:

> Modern rationalism *does not tolerate mystery*. It does not accept the mystery of man as male and female, nor is it willing to admit that the full truth about man has been revealed in Jesus Christ. In particular, it does not accept the "great mystery" proclaimed in the *Letter to the Ephesians* but radically opposes it. It may well acknowledge, in the context of a vague deism, the possibility or even the need for a supreme or divine Being. But it firmly rejects the idea of a God who became man in order to save man. For rationalism, it is unthinkable that God should be the Redeemer, much less that *he should be "the bridegroom,"* the primordial and unique source of the human love between spouses. Rationalism provides a radically different way of looking at creation and the meaning of human existence. But once man begins to lose sight of a God who loves him, a God who calls man through Christ to live in him and with him, and once the family no longer has the possibility of sharing in the "great mystery," what is left except the mere *temporal dimension of life?* Earthly life becomes nothing more than the scenario of a battle for existence, a desperate search for gain, and financial gain before all else.[35]

Rationalism does not tolerate mystery because "mystery," by definition, lies beyond rational categories. Those who subscribe to rationalism remain locked within the boundaries of their own finite ability to comprehend. Mystery, paradox, beauty—the transcendent meaning of birth, life, suffering, and death become lost. They make no "sense." The God-given dignity of every human being becomes lost. Love becomes lost. Even if man has made great progress in understanding his own biology and psychology, "with regard to his deepest, metaphysical dimension contemporary man remains a being unknown to himself."[36]

The Church responds to just such a man with the bold declaration: Christ reveals man to himself and makes his supreme calling clear. Man cannot live without love—and Christ is that love. Man cannot find himself except by making a sincere gift of himself—and Christ alone can inspire that gift. In other words, to you who think you are the measure of reality, turn to Christ who is the center of the universe and of history. To you who,

---

34. *Letter to Families,* n. 19.

35. Ibid, n. 19.

36. Ibid.

with Descartes, would say, "I think, therefore I am," turn to him who says, "I am because I am" (see Jn 8:58). To you who have lost the meaning of birth, life, suffering, and death, turn to him who was born, lived, suffered, died—and rose again! To you who think life is a battle to gain more and more, sell all you have and give the money to the poor (see Mt 19:21). To you who think freedom comes from rejecting any claim to truth, turn to him who is the Truth and he will set you free. To you who do not know love, turn to him who is love and receive the gift he gives—his own divine life. Abandon yourself entirely to him and you will find yourself.

This is the drama of human existence. This is the Gospel. And, we shall say it again, God stamped it right from the beginning in human flesh—in the "great mystery" of masculinity and femininity and the call to communion. But, as John Paul observes, the "deep-seated roots of the 'great mystery'...have been lost in the modern way of looking at things. The 'great mystery' is threatened in us and all around us."[37] From various points of view, we live in "a *society which is sick* [because it] has broken away from the full truth about man, from the truth about what man and woman really are as persons. Thus it cannot adequately comprehend the real meaning of the gift of persons in marriage, responsible love at the service of fatherhood and motherhood, and the true grandeur of procreation."[38] As a result we "are facing an immense threat to life: not only to the life of individuals but also to that of civilization itself."[39] This is why John Paul II's theology of the body will prove so pivotal in the new evangelization, because it reunites modern man with the "great mystery" of what and who man and woman really are as persons made in the divine image.

Knowing the true grandeur of God's plan for sexuality is, of course, one thing. Living it is another. In all truth, it is impossible to live the sublime vision of the body and sexuality that John Paul upholds...*unless* there is some way of subjecting our bodies and the deep impulses of our hearts to a profound and lasting transformation, to an efficacious redemption. I would propose that John Paul's proclamation of the *real power* of Christ's death and resurrection to effect just such a redemption is the greatest contribution of his theology of the body. *"Ne evacuetur Crux!"—Do not empty the cross of its power!* This, according to the Holy Father "is the cry of the new evangelization."[40] This also, I would add, is the cry of John Paul II's theology of the body.

---

37. Ibid.

38. Ibid., n. 20.

39. Ibid., n. 21.

40. *Orientale Lumen,* n. 3.

D. In Conclusion...

John Paul II does not mince words when he asserts that "the challenge facing us is an arduous one: only the concerted efforts of all those who believe in the value of life can prevent a setback of unforeseeable consequences for civilization."[41] In the concluding paragraphs of *Crossing the Threshold of Hope*, the Holy Father affirmed that "Andre Malraux was certainly right when he said that the twenty-first century would be the century of religion or it would not be at all."[42]

At the beginning of the third Christian millennium, it is time for the Church and the world to "cross the threshold of hope" into a new springtime. It is time to make our "passover" from a culture of death to a culture of life. "We are certainly not seduced," the Pope writes, "by the naive expectation that, faced with the great challenges of our time, we shall find some magic formula. No, we shall not be saved by a formula, but by a Person, and the assurance which he gives us: *I am with you!*"[43]

Christ the Bridegroom is with us! In the midst of the dramatic clash between good and evil which we are witnessing in our day, Christ makes a continual gift of himself to us—a gift of his body in the power of the Holy Spirit. With confidence in this gift, John Paul II seems to believe that with the celebration of the Great Jubilee "a new time of advent" is upon us, "at the end of which, like two thousand years ago, 'every man will see the salvation of God.'" In journeying to that end, a collision between the forces of good and evil "may in many cases be of a tragic nature and may perhaps lead to fresh defeats for humanity. But," John Paul continues, "the Church firmly believes that on God's part there is always a salvific self-giving."[44] Man and woman's call to life-giving communion is placed at the center of this great struggle between good and evil, between life and death, between love and all that is opposed to love.[45] John Paul asks, "Who will win?" He immediately responds: "The one who welcomes the gift."[46]

Mary, Mother of God...

Mary, bride without spot or wrinkle or any such thing...

Mary, one who welcomes the gift...

Pray for us that we might welcome the gift, now and at the hour of our death. Amen.

---

41. *Evangelium Vitae*, n. 91.

42. *Crossing the Threshold of Hope*, p. 229.

43. *Novo Millennio Ineunte*, n. 29.

44. *Dominum et Vivificantem*, n. 56.

45. See *Letter to Families*, n. 23.

46. *Dominum et Vivificantem*, n. 55.

Epilogue—In Review

1. If the future of humanity passes by way of marriage and the family, the future of marriage and the family passes by way of John Paul II's theology of the body. There will be no renewal of the Church and of the world without a renewal of marriage and the family. And there will be no renewal of marriage and the family without a fresh theological proposal that compellingly demonstrates to the modern world how the Christian sexual ethic is a liberating, redeeming ethos that corresponds perfectly with the most noble aspirations of the human heart.

2. Understanding the human body as a theology must not be relegated to the level of an obscure interest of a few specialized theologians. It has ramifications for all of theology and all of anthropology. Understanding the theology of the body must be the interest of everyone who desires to understand the meaning of human existence.

3. As the centuries pass, the Church is always advancing towards the fullness of divine truth. John Paul's theology of the body represents a crucial step in this advancement. While it is the fruit of 2,000 years of reflection on the Word of God, it has also been forged under the particular pressures and trials of this historical moment. In the Easter Vigil liturgy we exult in the "happy fault of Adam which won for us so great a Redeemer." We might also exult in the "happy fault" of the sexual revolution which won for us so great a theology of the body.

4. The urgency of the "new evangelization" stems not only from the fact that the number of those not yet reached by the Gospel is still immense, but also because entire groups of the baptized are without a living relationship with Christ and his Church. The new evangelization is not a matter of inventing a new program. The program is the same as ever. What is needed is a proclamation of the Gospel that is "new in ardor, methods, and expression."

5. In the new evangelization we must come to a deeper understanding of the mysteries of faith and find meaningful language with which to convey these mysteries to others. We must share with modern men and women the "unsearchable riches of Christ" and make known "the plan of the mystery hidden for ages in God." This is *precisely* what John Paul II's theology of the body provides: a deeper understanding of the mysteries of faith and a meaningful way to share them with men and women today.

6. "God comes to us in the things we know best and can verify most easily, the things of our everyday life, apart from which we cannot understand ourselves." What do we know better, what can we verify more easily, what is more "every day" than the experience of embodiment? This experience puts us directly in touch with the question of solitude. And if solitude is the human question, communion is the divine answer.

7. If the spirit of the Gospel is not incarnated with the basic human experiences—with the "ache" of solitude and the longing for communion—it will remain detached from what is essentially human. "To make the Church *the home and school of communion:* that is the great challenge facing us in the millennium which is now beginning, if we wish to be faithful to God's plan and respond to the world's deepest yearnings."

8. When we view the Gospel message through the interpretive key of man and woman's call to incarnate communion, not only does the Gospel take on flesh, but even the most controversial teachings of the Church begin to make sense. Through the spousal analogy we become attentive to the coherence of the truths of faith among themselves and within the whole plan of Revelation. Conversely, Christianity's "inner logic" collapses and virtually everything it teaches becomes contested as soon as we divorce ourselves from the nuptial mystery.

9. "Christ fully reveals man to himself." This serves in a certain sense as the Church's reply to modern rationalism. Here the religion of the God who became man meets the religion of man who makes himself God. There need not be a contest of wills between man and God. For God is not jealous of his own rule and leery of the freedom he has given his creature. Christ fully reveals that God is love. He fully reveals that man is destined to be a "partner of the Absolute." Christ thus fully reveals man to himself and makes his supreme calling clear.

10. With *Gaudium et Spes* 22 as a reply to rationalism, the Church says: To you who, with Descartes, would say "I think, therefore I am," turn to him who says, "I am because I am." To you who think life is a battle to gain more and more, sell all you have and give the money to the poor. To you who think freedom comes from rejecting any claim to truth, turn to him who is the Truth and he will set you free. Abandon yourself entirely to Christ and you will find yourself.

11. We are facing an immense threat to civilization because we cannot see the "great mystery" revealed through the body and the true grandeur of sexuality and procreation. How can we reclaim the true dignity of

man and woman's relationship and build a true culture of life? Only if there is the possibility of experiencing an efficacious redemption of our bodies and a transformation of the deep impulses of our hearts.

12. Faced with the great challenges of our time, it is naive to think we shall find some magic formula to save us. We shall not be saved by a formula, but by Christ and his cross. *Do not empty the cross of its power!* This "is the cry of the new evangelization." And this is the cry of John Paul II's theology of the body.

13. In the midst of the dramatic clash between good and evil which we are witnessing in our day, Christ makes a continual gift of himself to us. Man and woman's call to life-giving communion is placed at the center of this great struggle between good and evil, between life and death, between love and all that is opposed to love. Who will win? The one who welcomes the gift.

Bibliography

Works by Karol Wojtyla

The Acting Person. Translated by Andrzej Potocki. Edited by A. Tymieniecka. *Analecta Husserliana* 10, Dordrecht, Holland: Reidel, 1979.

The Collected Plays & Writings on Theater. Translated by Boleslaw Taborski. Berkeley, CA: University of California Press, 1987.

Faith According to St. John of the Cross. San Francisco, CA: Ignatius Press, 1981.

Fruitful & Responsible Love. New York, NY: Seabury Press, 1978.

Love & Responsibility. Translated by H. T. Willetts. San Francisco, CA: Ignatius Press, 1993.

Max Scheler y la etica cristiana. Madrid: Biblioteca de Autores Cristianos, 1982.

Person & Community: Selected Essays. Vol. 4, *Catholic Thought From Lublin.* Translated by Theresa Sandok. Edited by A. N. Woznicki. New York, NY: Peter Lang, 1993.

Sign of Contradiction. New York, NY: Seabury Press, 1979.

Sources of Renewal. San Francisco, CA: Harper & Row, 1979.

The Word Made Flesh: The Meaning of the Christmas Season. New York, NY: HarperCollins, 1994.

Works by Pope John Paul II

"Address to the Pontifical Biblical Commission," April 11, 1997

Blessed Are the Pure of Heart. Boston, MA: Pauline Books & Media, 1983.

Catechesi Tradendae. Boston, MA: Pauline Books & Media, 1979.

Centesimus Annus. Boston, MA: Pauline Books & Media, 1991.

Christifideles Laici. Boston, MA: Pauline Books & Media, 1988.

Crossing the Threshold of Hope. New York, NY: Knopf, 1994.

Dives in Misericordia. Boston, MA: Pauline Books & Media, 1980.

Dominum et Vivificantem. Boston, MA: Pauline Books & Media, 1986.

Ecclesia in America. Boston, MA: Pauline Books & Media, 1999.

Evangelium Vitae. Boston, MA: Pauline Books & Media, 1995.

Familiaris Consortio. Boston, MA: Pauline Books & Media, 1981.

Fides et Ratio. Boston, MA: Pauline Books & Media, 1998.

"Homily on the Mount of Beatitudes, Galilee," March 24, 2000.

"Homily at the Mass Celebrating the Restored Sistine Chapel," April 8, 1994.

Laborem Exercens. Boston, MA: Pauline Books & Media, 1981.

Letter to Families. Boston, MA: Pauline Books & Media, 1994.

Letter to Women. Boston, MA: Pauline Books & Media, 1995.

Mulieris Dignitatem. Boston, MA: Pauline Books & Media, 1988.

Novo Millennio Ineunte. Boston, MA: Pauline Books & Media, 2001.

Orientale Lumen. Boston, MA: Pauline Books & Media, 1995.

Original Unity of Man and Woman. Boston, MA: Pauline Books & Media, 1981.

Redemptoris Custos. Boston, MA: Pauline Books & Media, 1989.

Redemptor Hominis. Boston, MA: Pauline Books & Media, 1979.

Redemptoris Mater. Boston, MA: Pauline Books & Media, 1987.

Redemptoris Missio. Boston, MA: Pauline Books & Media, 1990.

Reflections on Humanae Vitae. Boston, MA: Pauline Books & Media, 1984.

Sollicitudo Rei Socialis. Boston, MA: Pauline Books & Media, 1987.

Springtime of Evangelization: The Complete Texts of the Holy Father's 1998 Ad Limina Addresses to the Bishops of the United States. San Diego, San Francisco, CA: Basilica, Ignatius, 1999.

Tertio Millennio Adveniente. Boston, MA: Pauline Books & Media, 1994.

The Theology of the Body: Human Love in the Divine Plan. Boston, MA: Pauline Books & Media, 1997.

The Theology of Marriage and Celibacy. Boston, MA: Pauline Books & Media, 1986.

"Truth Cannot Contradict Truth," Address to the Pontifical Academy of Sciences, October 22, 1996.

Ut Unum Sint. Boston, MA: Pauline Books & Media, 1995.

Veritatis Splendor. Boston, MA: Pauline Books & Media, 1993.

Other Magisterial Documents

Catechism of the Catholic Church, Second Edition. Washington, D.C.: Libreria Editrice Vaticana, 1997.

Code of Canon Law. Washington, D.C.: Canon Law Society of America, 1983.

Congregation for the Doctrine of the Faith. *Declaration on Certain Questions Concerning Sexual Ethics.* Boston, MA: Pauline Books & Media, 1975.

——*Donum Vitae.* Boston, MA: Pauline Books & Media, 1987.

Leo XIII. *Arcanum,* in *The Papal Encyclicals 1878–1903.* Edited by Claudia Carlen. Wilmington, NC: McGrath, 1986: 29–40.

Paul VI. *Evangelii Nuntiandi.* Boston, MA: Pauline Books & Media, 1975.

——*Humanae Vitae.* Boston, MA: Pauline Books & Media, 1968.

Pius XI. *Casti Connubii.* Boston, MA: Pauline Books & Media, 1930.

Pontifical Biblical Commission. *The Interpretation of the Bible in the Church.* Boston, MA: Pauline Books & Media, 1993.

——*The Jewish People and Their Sacred Scriptures in the Christian Bible.* Boston, MA: Pauline Books & Media, 2002.

Pontifical Council for the Family. *Preparation for the Sacrament of Marriage.* Boston, MA: Pauline Books & Media, 1996.

——*The Truth & Meaning of Human Sexuality.* Boston, MA: Pauline Books & Media, 1996.

——*Vademecum for Confessors Concerning Some Aspects of the Morality of Conjugal Life.* Boston, MA: Pauline Books & Media, 1997.

Sacred Congregation for Catholic Education. *Educational Guidance in Human Love.* Boston, MA: Pauline Books & Media, 1983.

Second Vatican Council. *Closing Speeches.* Boston, MA: Pauline Books & Media, 1965.

——*Dignitatis Humanae.* Boston, MA: Pauline Books & Media, 1965.

——*Gaudium et Spes.* Boston, MA: Pauline Books & Media, 1965.

——*Lumen Gentium.* Boston, MA: Pauline Books & Media, 1964.

Vatican Commission for Religious Relations with the Jews. *Notes on the Correct Way to Present the Jews and Judaism in Preaching and Catechesis in the Roman Catholic Church,* June 24, 1985.

Other Sources

Albacete, Lorenzo. *God at the Ritz: Attraction to Infinity. A Priest-Scientist Talks about Science, Sex, Politics, & Religion.* New York, NY: Crossroads, 2002.

Allen, Sr. Prudence. "Integral Sex Complementarity and the Theology of Communion," *Communio* (winter 1990): pp. 523–544.

———*The Concept of Woman: The Aristotelian Revolution 750 B.C.–1250 A.D.* Grand Rapids, MI: Eerdmans, 1997.

———*The Concept of Woman: The Humanist Reformation 1250–1500.* Grand Rapids, MI: Eerdmans, 2002.

Aquinas, Thomas. *Summa Theologica,* in *Basic Writings of St. Thomas Aquinas.* Edited by Anton C. Pegis. New York, NY: Random House, 1945.

Augustine. Sermon LXIX, c. 2, 3, *Patrologia Latina,* 38, 441.

Baptut, Jean-Pierre. "The Chastity of Jesus and the Refusal to Grasp," *Communio* 24 (spring 1997): pp. 5–13.

Beigel, Gerard. *Faith and Social Justice in the Teaching of Pope John Paul II.* New York, NY: Peter Lang, 1997.

Buttiglione, Rocco. *Karol Wojtyla: The Thought of the Man Who Became Pope John Paul II.* Grand Rapids, MI: Eerdman's Publishing, 1997.

Catholic Truth Society. *The Wisdom of John Paul II.* London: CTS Publications, 2001.

De Haro, Ramon Garcia. *Marriage and the Family in the Documents of the Magisterium.* Translated by William E. May. San Francisco, CA: Ignatius Press, 1993.

De la Potterie, Ignace. *Mary in the Mystery of the Covenant.* New York, NY: Alba House, 1992.

De Lubac, Henri. *The Drama of Atheistic Humanism.* San Francisco: Ignatius Press, 1995.

———*The Mystery of the Supernatural.* New York: Crossroad Herder, 1998.

Derrick, Christopher. *Sex & Sacredness.* San Francisco, CA: Ignatius Press, 1982.

Dooley, David, ed. *The Collected Works of G. K. Chesterton* Vol. I. San Francisco, CA: Ignatius, 1986.

Elliot, Peter J. *What God Has Joined.* Homebush, Australia: St. Paul/Alba House, 1990.

Fagan, Patrick. "A Culture of Inverted Sexuality," *Catholic World Report,* (November 1998): p. 57.

Freud, Sigmund. *Introductory Lectures in Psychoanalysis.* New York: W.W. Norton and Co., 1966.

Gneuhs, Geoffrey, ed. *The Legacy of Pope John Paul II: His Contribution to Catholic Thought.* New York, NY: Herder & Herder, 2000.

Giussani, Luigi. *The Religious Sense.* Montreal: McGill-Queen's University Press, 1997.

Hogan and LeVoir. *Covenant of Love: Pope John Paul II on Sexuality, Marriage, and Family in the Modern World.* San Francisco, CA: Ignatius Press, 1992.

Kreeft, Peter. *Everything You Ever Wanted to Know about Heaven.* San Francisco: Ignatius Press, 1990.

Kupczak, Jaroslaw. *Destined for Liberty.* Washington, D.C.: Catholic University of America Press, 2000.

Lawler, Boyle, and May. *Catholic Sexual Ethics,* second edition. Huntington, IN: Our Sunday Visitor, 1998.

Lawler, Philip. "The Price of Virtue," *Catholic World Report,* (July 1997): p. 58.

Mann, Judy. "A Lesson on Lust for the Vatican," *Washington Post,* (October 10, 1980): pp. B-1 and B-2.

May, William E.. *Marriage: The Rock on which the Family Is Built.* San Francisco, CA: Ignatius Press, 1995.

Newman, Cathy. "The Enigma of Beauty," *National Geographic* (January 2000): pp. 95–121.

Poupard, Cardinal Paul. "Galileo: Report on Papal Commission Findings," *Origins* (November 12, 1992).

Mary Rousseau. "Eucharist & Gender," *Catholic Dossier* (September/October, 1996): pp. 19–23.

Schmitz, Kenneth. *At the Center of the Human Drama: The Philosophical Anthropology of Karola Wojtyla/Pope John Paul II.* Washington, D.C.: Catholic University of America Press, 1993.

Shivanandan, Mary. *Crossing the Threshold of Love: A New Vision of Marriage in the Light of John Paul II's Anthropology.* Washington, D.C.: Catholic University of America Press, 1999.

Steinberg, Leo. *The Sexuality of Christ in Renaissance Art and in Modern Oblivion.* Chicago, IL: University of Chicago Press, 1996.

Von Balthasar, Hans Urs. *The Theology of Karl Barth.* San Francisco, CA: Ignatius Press/Communio Books, 1992.

Von Hildebrand, Dietrich. *Marriage: The Mystery of Faithful Love.* Manchester, NH; Sophia Institute Press, 1991.

Waddell, Helen. *The Desert Fathers*. Ann Arbor: University of Michigan Press, 1957.

Weigel, George. *Witness to Hope: The Biography of Pope John Paul II*. New York, NY: Harper Collins, 1999.

West, Christopher. *Crash Course in the Theology of the Body: A Study Guide*. Dundee, IL: The GIFT Foundation, 2002.

——*Good News About Sex & Marriage: Answers to Your Honest Questions About Catholic Teaching*. Ann Arbor, MI: Servant Publications, 2000.

INDEX

sexual attraction
  and choice, 87–88
  spiritual maturity in, 375, 412–413
sexual behavior, effect on society, 182
sexual communion, 79–81
  as sacrament, 80–81
sexual complementarity, 107
sexual counter-revolution and freedom,
  50
sexual desire. *See also* eros
  burning bush imagery, 201
  distortion of, 149–151, 155
  self-mastery of, 158–160
  and shame, 106–107
  spontaneity of, 200–201
sexual differentiation. *See also* gender
  difference
  complementarity of, 319
  importance of, 162
  relationality revealed by, 82–83
  and resurrection of the body, 247–248
sexual ethics, 49–51, 80
  anthropology and, 166–167
  of Church, 48–49
sexual intercourse. *See* conjugal union
sexual morality, 26–27, 365
  Church's teaching on, 229–230
  confusion about, 27
  and shame, 90
  and social justice, 146
sexual revolution, 1, 46–47, 50, 265
sexual union. *See also* communion of
  persons; conjugal union
  as affirmation of the person, 103
  ethical content of, 464
  as experience of being chosen by eternal love, 101–104
  as expression of original virginal value
  of man, 87
  as icon or idol, 264–265
  and knowledge, 117–119
  for love and procreation, 98
  in marriage, 166–167
  in original unity, 83–88
  personal content of, 464
  religious content of, 464

and sacramentality of creation, 116–117
sexual utilitarianism, 50
sexuality
  celibacy as fulfillment of, 286–288
  eternal sexuality, 175–176
  excitement versus emotion, 453–454,
  455
  gift of God in, 95–96
  harmony with spirituality, 22
  healing of, 149–150
  living the body, 155–160
  and Manichaeism, 183–184
  and meaning of life, 99
  meaning of masculinity and femininity,
  25–26
  reconciliation offered by Christ, 59–60
  sacredness of, 418–419
  and sensuality, 404
  separated from communion of persons,
  152–153
  and shame, 148
  as temporal fulfillment of communion,
  83
  viewed as "dirty," 185–186
shame. *See also* lust
  beginning of, 143–144
  dimensions of, 144–151
  double meaning of, 149–151
  effect on nuptial meaning of the body,
  150
  elimination of, 104
  experience of, 218
  and fear, 145–147
  and gender difference, 143–144
  immanent and relative shame, 147–149
  lack of in original nakedness, 89–90
  as loss of purity of heart, 112
  and love, 90, 104
  and lust, 149
  and naked body in art, 233
  and nakedness, 143–144
  phenomenon of, 91–93
  and sexual morality, 90
  and sexuality, 106–107, 148
shamelessness, 89, 148
  in marriage, 151
Sign of Contradiction (Wojtyla), 38–39

For more information:

About Christopher West's—

- speaking schedule
- audio and video resources

visit:

christopherwest.com

or

theologyofthebody.com

Pauline
BOOKS & MEDIA

The Daughters of St. Paul operate book and media centers at the following addresses. Visit, call or write the one nearest you today, or find us on the World Wide Web, www.pauline.org

CALIFORNIA

3908 Sepulveda Blvd, Culver City, CA 90230	310-397-8676
5945 Balboa Avenue, San Diego, CA 92111	858-565-9181
46 Geary Street, San Francisco, CA 94108	415-781-5180

FLORIDA

145 S.W. 107th Avenue, Miami, FL 33174	305-559-6715

HAWAII

1143 Bishop Street, Honolulu, HI 96813	808-521-2731
Neighbor Islands call:	866-521-2731

ILLINOIS

172 North Michigan Avenue, Chicago, IL 60601	312-346-4228

LOUISIANA

4403 Veterans Memorial Blvd, Metairie, LA 70006	504-887-7631

MASSACHUSETTS

885 Providence Hwy, Dedham, MA 02026	781-326-5385

MISSOURI

9804 Watson Road, St. Louis, MO 63126	314-965-3512

NEW JERSEY

561 U.S. Route 1, Wick Plaza, Edison, NJ 08817	732-572-1200

NEW YORK

150 East 52nd Street, New York, NY 10022	212-754-1110
78 Fort Place, Staten Island, NY 10301	718-447-5071

PENNSYLVANIA

9171-A Roosevelt Blvd, Philadelphia, PA 19114	215-676-9494

SOUTH CAROLINA

243 King Street, Charleston, SC 29401	843-577-0175

TENNESSEE

4811 Poplar Avenue, Memphis, TN 38117	901-761-2987

TEXAS

114 Main Plaza, San Antonio, TX 78205	210-224-8101

VIRGINIA

1025 King Street, Alexandria, VA 22314	703-549-3806

CANADA

3022 Dufferin Street, Toronto, ON M6B 3T5	416-781-9131

¡También somos su fuente para libros, videos y música en español!